By
Dr. R. Read

ISBN 1-56459-004-6

Request our FREE CATALOG of over 1,000
Rare Esoteric Books
Unavailable Elsewhere

Alchemy, Ancient Wisdom, Astronomy, Baconian, Eastern-Thought, Egyptology, Esoteric, Freemasonry, Gnosticism, Hermetic, Magic, Metaphysics, Mysticism, Mystery Schools, Mythology, Occult, Philosophy, Psychology, Pyramids, Qabalah, Religions, Rosicrucian, Science, Spiritual, Symbolism, Tarot, Theosophy, *and many more!*

Kessinger Publishing Company
Montana, U.S.A.

Eighteen Books
Of the
SECRETS
OF
Art & Nature,

BEING

The Summe and Substance of

Naturall Philosophy,

Methodically Digested.

First designed by *John VVecker* Dr in Physick, and now much Augmented and Inlarged by Dr *R. Read.*

A like work never before in the English Tongue.

LONDON

Printed for *Simon Miller* at the Starre in St Pauls Church-yard, 1660.

TO THE
READER.

*S*ince *that there is nothing that addeth more to the delight and satisfaction of* Ingenious *persons then the increase of* knowledg, *I have here endeavoured to Publish somewhat that may be a* companion *for* solitude, *and yield* entertainment *to* vacant hours, *This work being an* Encyclipædia *of* Arts *and* Sciences, *interwoven with facetious Conceits to recreate the fancy. There are different sorts of knowledg: Some there are that being prickt forward with an (imaginary) happy fruition of their ambitious desires, study* Politicks; *Others more moderate and less ambitius, desire only to acquaint themselves with pristine Learning, these regard* Antiquity. *A third sort of a duller capacity neglecting both these, only study the encrease of their* fortunes, *impoverishing their* soul *to enrich their* body. *A fourth and last sort there are, whom a better* Genius *will no way suffer me to discommend, that delight themselves to compleat the* vacuum *of* nature, *(if any such thing there be) and their own intent in searching and easily producing the effects of what they formerly stigmatized with the brand of* impossibility, *since* admired, *and at length* understood, *being only hood-winked with a seeming contradiction. These I say find and perceive those*

a

To the Reader.

those Secrets which former Ages have been unworthy of: they *with admiration at length understood the bare connexion of a few exteriour parts, which now we have here discovered, not only to receive* connexion *but* nutrition; *and not nutrition only but* sympathy; *and then* sympathy *to receive a mutuall concurrency with the soul animal, which have run into such a Secret that would have stretcht their admiration beyond the bound of humane conception. This now appears plain to us, and indeed so it is with other things natural. The hand of time hath since wiped away that oblination which concealed those Characters that (as you may plainly understand) we have here discovered; so that I may here safely use* Horace *his words*

Omne tulit punctum qui miscuit utile dulci.
That is esteem'd without *exception* true,
That yieldeth *profit* both and *pleasure too.*

and that this is so, I shall refer my self to the ingenuous application of my serious Reader.

One thing more I have to impart unto thee, and that is, the great pains, cost and charges that have been expended in Publishing this Book: and thus far I think my self obliged modestly to say, that he had regard to the world and his credit, more then his peculiar profit.

Lastly, I shall humbly intreat, that if there be any thing that through the Publisher or Printers fault hath been omitted, to pass a gentle censure, and herein you will oblige

Your reall Friend

R. R.

A Summary view of the whole Work.

Book I.
Secrets of God, Nature, Man in Generall.

Book II.
Secrets of Angels, good and bad.

Book III.
Secrets of the Sun, Moon, and Stars; Fire, Ayr, Water, and Earth.

Book IV.
Secrets of the Internal parts of Man, the Passions, Reason, and Memory.

Book V.
Secrets of Life and Death; Remedies for all Diseases in the body of Man, both Internall and Externall; old Age, Eating, Drinking, Venery, Sleep, Exercise, and beautifying the body.

Book VI.
Secrets of Earthly Creatures, tame; of the whole, greater, as Horses, Asses, Oxen, Bulls; lesser, as Sheep, Bucks, Goats, Hogs, Dogs; of the parts, as Bones, Horns and haire: of wild Creatures; greater, as Bucks, Bores, Hares, Foxes, Wolves; lesser, as Mice, Moles, Weesils, Ants, Scorpions, Wiglice, Fleas, Lice; creeping things, as Snails, Caterpillars and Serpents.

Book

The Contents.

Book VII.
Secrets of Fishes.

Book VIII.
Secrets of Birds; as Hens, Pigeons, Peacocks, Swallows, Bats, Pheasants, Partridg, Turtles, Quails, Blackbirds, Choughs, Geese, Ducks; Insects, as Bees, Drones, Wasps, Flyes, Wevils, Locusts.

Book IX.
Secrets of Plants, of Trees in generall; more particularly, of Fruits, Leaves, Flowers, Seeds, Roots, Woods, Shrubs, and Plants.

Book X.
Secrets of Metals, liquid, as Quicksilver; hard, as Gold, Silver, Brass, Iron; soft, as Lead, Tin, Antimony; pertaining to Metals, as Brimstone, Vermillion, Orpiment; not burning, as Chrisocolla and Salt.

Book XI.
Secrets of Glass.

Book XII.
Secrets of Jewels, and how to counterfeit all sorts whether white, black, red, green, blew; fit or unfit to Engrave.

Book XIII.
Secrets Artificall; as Houses, Gardens, Fountains, Cloath and Cloathing.

Book XIV.
Secrets of Meteors; as Hail, Rain, Snow, Thunder,

The Contents.

der, Lightning, Tempests, and the like.

Book XV.

Secrets Organicall; as Grammer, Logick, Rhetorick, Poetry, Speaking or Writing.

Book XVI.

Secrets of Sciences; as naturall Magick, Metaphisicks, lawfull and unlawfull, Mathematicks, Geometry, Arithmetick, Musick, and Astrology; politique as Peace and War.

Book XVII.

Secrets Mechanicall, performed by Millers, Smiths, Bakers, Cooks, Painters and Apothecaries.

Book XVIII.

Secrets of Sports, Delights and Recreations.

Authors made use of in this Treatise.

Albertus Magnus.
Alexis.
Dr. Anthony.
Absirtus.
Ælianus.
Andreas Cordubensis.
Andreas Albius.
Ærtius.
Andernacus.
Apuleius.
Anatolius.
Avicena.
Aristotle.
Archimedes.
Antonius Mizaldus.
Aratus.
Arnaldus Villanovanus.
Atheneus.
Ambrose Parrey.
Augustinus Stenchus.
Andernacus.

Bayrus.
Lord Bacon.
Dr. Brown.
Beritius.
Mr. Browne Chyrurg.
Blessius.
Brasanolus.
Mr. Bates.
Dr. Butler.

Cardanus.
Caravanus Hispanus.
Cato.
Cleopatra.
Cassianus.
Cornelius Agrippa.
Constantinus Cæsar.
Costabenluze.
Countesse of Kent.
Dr. Clarke.
Nicholas Culpepper.

David Wezelius.
Democritus.
Didymus.
Damageron.
Dyonissius.
Diascorides.
Diophanes.
Sr. Kenelm Digby.

ENonimus.
Epedocles.
Egidius Bouxellensis.

Fallopius.
Dr. French.
Favorinus.
Felix Platerus.
Fioravantus.
Fronton.
Florentinus.

Gallenus.
Pet. Gassendus.
Gabriel Arater.
Gesnerus.
Gargilius Martialus.
Gregorius Valla.
Gemma Frisius.
Galileus.

HErmes.
Dr. Harvey.
Hierocles.
Hippocrates.
Hollerius.
Henricus Rantzovius.
Mr. Holliard.
Henricus Wolsius.
Tho. Hobbs.

JO. Bapt. Porta.
Dr. Johnson.
Jacobus Carpensis.
Jarcas.
Joan Langius.
Joan Weierus.
Mr. Jones.
Joan Baubinus.
Joan de Rupescissa.
Kircherus.

LEmnius.
Ludolphus Rolevincus.
Linius.
Lady Howard.
Leporinus Dalmata.
Lucas Rhor.

MAgia Veterum.
Mercurius Tresmeg.
Magister Odomarus.
Marcellus Palerius.
Manuscripts above three hundred.
Dr. Mathias.
Mr. Moulins.

NIcolaus.
Nostradamus.
Nicolaus Taurellus.

OLaus Magnus.
Ovidius.

Octavius Landus.
Oppianus.
Orpheus.
Oribasius.
Orus Apollo.

PAracelsus.
Paxamus.
Palladius.
Pamphilius.
Pet. Galatinus.
Palagonius.
Philostratus.
Plinius.
Pictorius.
Plutarchus.
Polibius.
Phillip Melancthon.
Prescianus de Corduba.
Ptollomeus.
Publius Vegetius.
Pet. Crescentius.
Sir. Hugh Platt.

R. Amundus Lullius.
Randoletius.
Dr. Read.
Rhasis.
Roscellus.
Ruverius.
Ld. Ruthin.
Rhenodeus.

SCaliger.
Seneca.
Servius.
Sextus Platonicus.
Simeo Sethi.
Sylvius.
Sotion.
Straton.
Semoneta Cardinall.
Scribonius Largus.
Sebastion Sherly.

THeophrastus.
Tarentinus.
Theomnestus.

VArro.
Virgisius.
Varignana.
Vicentius Luureus.
Vindanionius.
Vitruvius.
Vanderhaiden.
Tho. White.
Zoroaster.

OF SECRETS.

BOOK I.

What GOD is. Chap. 1.

IT is manifest that in the order of causes we must admit of one to be the first, and that shews that the propriety of that cause is to be the cause of all the rest: (for in this series of causes all things are contained; and that there is but one order of causes and no more, it shall appear afterwards) and that is the production of no other cause. The Antients called this first cause GOD. When therefore they were to define GOD, they thought they could not do it better, than by saying that he was the first cause of all things. I cannot deny but this definition agreed onely to GOD, that the definition and the thing defined may be convertible: yet I would enquire of our modern Writers, who have exactly apprehended the decrees of the Antients, whether this definition agrees onely and alwaies unto GOD? The Antients did affirm this, but the Moderns do not at all; they confess that was from eternity, when there was nothing besides himself. When therefore there was nothing in being, how can he be said to be the first cause of all things? But the Antients are to be confuted another way: for they do not grant that GOD alone was from eternity. Logicians number the predicament of Relatives amongst accidents, and that is true; for whatsoever subsists by it self in the which it is, it hath an existency peculiar to it self and not to other things. Since therefore to be a cause is contained in the predicament of Relation, it must needs follow, that the name Cause is an accident amongst things that it is ascribed to. How then appears the acuteness of the Antients, who defined GOD onely by an Accident? They might be plainly confuted in many words, but I will clear the point where the error lies. In this description of the Antients, where they say that GOD is the prime cause of all things, there are two considerations: for the word first shewes, that GOD hath his existence from himself, and not from any other. This part of the description shewes onely what GOD is of himself; but the other, wherein they say he is the cause of things, shewes what he is by accident: for this is not said in respect of himself onely, but in respect to other things. Wherefore if GOD be to be defined truly and simply, the latter part of the description of the Antients must be taken away, that the description may contain nothing but what is essentiall to GOD, who hath his existence from himself, and not in respect to other things: wherefore we should define GOD to be *an essence having existence from himself.* Divines call GOD Αὐτόνον, *a being from himself.* If the word may be drawn in the abstract, we shall excellently define GOD in one word, saying that he is αὐτουσία, *self-being:* for nothing that is generated hath an existence, to which this name may be given, and it is proper onely to GOD, and that alwayes; and this comprehends all and onely those things that GOD is of himself, and is said to be in respect of himself. *Nicol. Taurellus.*

Of Nature.
That Nature is not the prime cause of all things. Chap. 2.

Perhaps some man may think that Nature is the first cause of all things; which notwithstanding is a most absurd thing, as may be shewed by many arguments: I shall lay down one or two. The first cause that hath no cause before it whence it arose, is the cause of it self: But Nature is not from it self, but from a principle above it. For since it is finite (as appears by the motion of the Heavens) it is defined by another, for nothing can define it self. Again if Nature made it self (which is the property of the first cause) she made her self naturally. But what things are made naturally, are made of a preexistent matter, and so must Nature be made, if she be naturally made: which if we grant to have been when Nature was not, it will follow, that something was made naturally before there was any Nature, and that Nature made things before she had a being her self. Therefore Nature is not the first cause of things. *The same.*

Of Man. Chap. 3.

It is evident enough by a mans actions, that he consists of two parts, namely a soul and a body. This is no Secret, for it is known to all men by sense: but such things as are secret are found out by signs. The efficient cause of a Man is Father and Mother, Nature being the means; for the seed of both the Parents must be so disposed, that they may produce, for substance, quantity, quality, place, and other circumstances, a humane, that is an animall and naturall effect. Whereupon the first question is, Whether besides these causes, namely the soul and the seed of both the Parents, there be no other cause to which the ofspring of man may be ascribed? Here I shall examin the opinions of the old Philosophers. As men are now begotten so they were alwaies, as the old Philosophers say; but it is contrary to our faith. But do you seek for a secret of Reason, not of Faith? Take this. If there were alwaies the same way of mans production, then there is no other efficient cause of mans being, besides the Father and Mother; why then did the Philosophers think of the first cause of all things? For if vicissitude and propagation was the same alwaies as now it is, we can admit no other efficient cause, but mankind and nature, because the propagation of things is either humane or naturall. Again, If mankind had alwaies the same beginning it hath now, when a Sonne is begotten by his Father, the Generation of Mankind must be extended to eternity, which is most absurd, as I shall prove by these reasons. It is cleare by Metaphysicall Axiome, *Nothing that hath something first, and something that follows after, and receives more and less, can be infinite.* But propagation hath first and latter, for the Fathers is before the Sonne. Moreover we all know that mankind consists in individuals, and that kind cannot be eternall whose individuals are not eternall; since therefore no man was from eternity, how can mankind be from eternity? and if mankind be not from eternity, then mans propagation cannot be carried up so farre as eternity, or to that which is infinite. Now that no man was from eternity it appears by this, because they are all dead, and not one alive, that hath lived two hundred years since. Therefore if they all dye, it follows that all had a beginning, so that no man was from eternity. For had any man been from eternity, he must needs have continued to eternity, for mortality cannot befall eternity. Moreover that mans generation had a beginning, it appears, because it is performed in time, and whatsoever is performed in time, must needs have a beginning; now no man that hath reason will say; but that the production of man is done in time, and that it was alwaies done in time is proved, because as man is now begotten, so was he alwaies begotten, as the old Philosophers confess. Adde to this, That all men are so made, that they have no existence before they are begotten; since therefore all men did sometimes begin, it must follow, that mankind by propagation had a beginning. *Nic. Taurellus.*

The world is not in making, but is made. Chap. 4.

Effects are of two sorts: For some are separated from the cause, as a house from the Builder of it: Some again remaine in their cause and cannot subsist without it, as heat from fire. To what effects then shall we referre the world? If you say that the world is from God, (and all men confess that it is an effect of his) it is in substance seperated from him; and it will follow that God is in time before the world, for this is the property of such effects; now that which is after another thing cannot be from eternity. But if you judge that the world doth subsist in its cause, as heat in fire; you must know that these effects are not substances, but accidents to those things they are in. So that the world can by no meanes be reckoned amongst the Catalogue of those effects. But that this may be better understood, I shall briefly lay it more open.

pen. The world hath its being from God, which we express by the word *fieri*. Now effects are then said to be in *fieri*; when they receive their being that they have from their cause; Namely, at that very time that causes are joyned with their effects. This conjunction that is in the first order of effects, lasteth so long, untill the work be compleat: Wherefore we say that the world (because we must needs confess, that it must be referred to those effects) not to be in *fieri*, but to be made already, for it is a perfect substance, and it hath long since obtained the end it was made for, by its operations. Since therefore the world is no longer a making, it doth not receive its being from any other: wherefore if the world was from eternity, as it is now, it could never receive its being from any other thing. Let now *Aristotles* followers shew how God can be the cause of the world; if the world never received its being from him: and if they confess it did receive its being from him, that could not be from eternity, for things that are from eternity, must needs continue to eternity, and things that have an end must needs have a beginning. Since therefore the world ceaseth to be made by God, it had a beginning when God undertook the making of it; and so it was made by him, not from eternity, but in time. *The same.*

BOOK. II.

Concerning the Secrets of Angels; of the substance, difference, and power of the Devils. Chap. 1.

The witty industry of men hath found out many things by reason and experience, which because they are known to very few, are deservedly reckoned amongst secret and wonderfull things; these are either humane or naturall. But the unsatiable desire of men was neither content with art nor experience; But the power of the Devils must be called upon to assist him. By their aid many things are wont to be done, which amaze both wise and ignorant men. Now that we may shew this part of secrets that are accomplished by reason, and which may well stand with our Faith and Religion; I shall first declare what the Devils are, and how they may be distinguished by their differences, and what power they have over humane affaires.

What the Devils are. Chap. 2.

The Devill hath his name from knowledg, by which name we comprehend the simple intelligences (as the Philosophers call them) namely the incorporeall substances that are entangled with no clog of the body, and were created by God. They were the first work of all things, that they might be happy in a due contemplation of God, and of his Works. Now a due contemplation is this, which produceth no envy or desire to the thing contemplated, but only the praise of the work Master, as the thing that is contemplated requires. But that some suppose that the Devils were made for mans cause, it is beside the truths of Philosophy, as I shall shew else where. For though God ofttimes use the Ministery of good or bad Angels to protect or to punish men: yet this is not the principall end for which those spirits were created, since every intellectuall substance first subsists by it self, and not for another. Mens souls indeed when they are separated from their bodies, are free from the contagion of matter; yet they cannot properly be called Angels, because the end they were made to, was to informe the body. For this cause Divines hold rightly, that souls separated from their bodies, are at rest untill the last day that their bodies shall be raised again, because their actions are limited by the ministration of the body. But the nature of Angels is otherwise, for they attain their end and perfection without any body to clog them with. Nor need we be moved at all with that which *Cornelius Agrippa* recites out of *Augustine, Basill, Gregory, Apuleius,* and *Psellus.* For though Devils appear ofttimes in divers bodily shapes; yet they are but apparitions or bodies assumed, whereby the substance of these Angels is no wise to be defined. For Angels, that they may fit themselves, to comfort or to deceive men, assume such forms as are most proper for our senses, and shortly after lay them aside again,

gain, without any corruption of themselves. Moreover to understand the substance and nature of the Angels, this also must be considered, that the Angels are not infinite in substance or quantity; as elsewhere we said that God hath an infinite existence. Wherefore though Philosophers count all things infinite that have no bodies, yet Angels and all things, God excepted, are finite: which I demonstrated in its proper place, where I shewed that God is infinite both for Substance and Unity. In Unity because he only hath this way of existence. Now it is clear from hence, that the Angels are finite: for nothing is infinite in quantity that is many, nor doth infinite agree to any thing, that hath parts one without the other. And that there are many Angels, besides experience, reason will prove it sufficiently. For the good for which the Angels were made, requires not to consist in one, but is better they should be many; and it is more convenient that multitudes of Angels, then one alone should attain felicity to the due praise of God. *Nic. Taurellus.*

Of the differences of the Angels. Chap. 3.

Agrippa reports that *Magicians* make a threefold distinction of the Angels: for they make some to be supercelestiall; namely, *mindes* totally separated from bodies, which are addicted only to contemplate and adore God; wherefore they call such Gods, by reason of some participation they have of the divine nature; because they are alwaies full of God, and are inbriated with divine Nectar. These Angels are alwaies attending upon God, nor are they president over the bodies of the world; nor are they appointed to minister unto things here below, but the light they receive from God, they infuse into the inferior orders, and they distribute to them severally to all their offices. In the second place, Next to these they ranke the celestiall Intelligences, which they call Angels of this world, namely, such as besides the Worship of God, are appointed to govern the Heavenly Orbs, and are set over each Sphere, and Starre: wherefore they distribute them into so many orders, as there are Spheres in the Heavens, and Starres in those Spheres. Thirdly, They place those Angels that are as it were Ministeriall to dispose of things here below: which *Origen* calls invisible virtues, to whose charge are committed such things as are to be done upon the Earth. For ofttimes seen by no man, they direct our journey and business; ofttimes also they are present in Battels, and by secret aid they affoard to their friends the success they wish for: for they are said to be able to do good, or hurt at their pleasure. Those likewise men divide into severall orders, some to be for the fire, some for the water, some for Aire, some for the Earth; which four sorts of Angels are reckoned according to the four faculties, of heavenly souls, mind, reason, imagination; namely, the vivificating and moving faculty. This is but a meer invention concerning Angels (as *Wierus* saith clearly) for it cannot be proved by reason or experience, nor by divine or true humane authority. Indeed the first order of Angels is consonant to truth. For God as he is infinite in wisdome, and goodness, created all most infinite intellectuall substances, to contemplate love and adore him: some whereof he united to bodies, to propagate their kind, but some he defined by no materiall substance. Of these may be made the first order of spirits, but that they will have this to be the end for which they were made, that they might infuse to each order of the Heavenly spirits the light they receive from God; this is contrary to true Philosophy, and contains in it horrible Idolatry: for by this means they obtrude upon us the Gods of the Gentiles. Also if we shall deal but Philosophycally, we easily descry the absurdity of this opinion. For what rationall man will say that the more Noble Creatures were made for the use of the more Ignoble? But the Heavenly intelligences are more Ignoble than this first order of Angels: wherefore then should we maintain that the supercelestiall spirits were made for the use of the celestiall intelligences? The same reason will confute the celestiall intelligences. For since they are more Noble then we, and we then the Celestiall Spheres, it cannot appear that the Celestiall Intelligences were made for our sake, and much less for the Heavenly Spheres. But I elsewhere treated of the Celestiall Spirits, where I shewed that the opinions of the Philosophers are most absurd, who for this cause invented Celestiall Spirits, that they might restrain the power of the first matter, by

reason

reason whereof all corporall things are corruptible, and that they might regulate the motions of the Spheres with a most swift course. For these operations are exceeding farre from the nature of a Spirit, and the work is imperfect that wants externall help; like a house ready to fall wanting a good foundation. But the other end for which Magicians say, the Heavenly Intelligences were made, namely, That they may by their influences (as they term it) supply the Interior Angels; and so with their divers virtues, they may govern humane affairs, is no less contrary to sound reason, then what I refuted before. For if we admit Celestiall influences, they are but naturall, nor are our souls moved by them, but only so farre as they are obnoxious to bodies. But who will say that the effects of incorporeall Spirits are naturall? The lowest order of Spirits comprehends gardian Spirits, such as are alotted to our birth, and such as are the Rulers of humane actions according to the different position of the Stars, shall we think any thing of this. Truly if the opinion of Astrologers be true, that we are obnoxious to good or bad fortune, to vices or virtues, as we are under the dominion of this at that Starre? yet I should never grant, that this is effected by the intermediation of the mundane Spirits, since there is no Angell at all that is made subject to the actions of the Heavenly bodies: therefore since the differences ought to be taken from the substances of the things to be divided, that they may constitute true species; we cannot search out the true differences of Angels, for that their substances are more subtile, then to be comprehended by our understanding. But if that be true that some Philosophers hold, that some Angels are immortall and others mortall: From hence we may well make a difference, for what is mortall, cannot be of the same nature with what is immortall. But this is but a fained opinion of some that were ignorant of Philosophy, though voluminous *Cardanus* should press it. For all Angels in themselves are incorruptible as our souls are, nor can they perish, unless by the same way they were made by the first cause they should be annihilated. But that the prime Cause will not have that to be, is proved by that very end for which the Angels were first created. For it is that which continually grows more and more perfect. But the condition of corruptible things is, that they have their end alwaies without them, which in its set time attains its perfection, which when it hath obtained the actions cease. The world of it self might last unto eterniternity, but God will not have it so, because it was made only for this end, that a certain number of men might be born in it. The world will attain this end not by continuing to eternity, but in a set time, as I shewed elsewhere at large: and then shall the actions of the world cease, and another world shall be substituted in the place of this, whose end shall be farre different from this. But the end of men and Angels is so that it is defined by no time, but is perfect by it self and shall never end; but may perpetually be more perfect. Moreover though the substance of Angels be unknown to us, yet we may draw forth their differences by their divers actions. For if the actions of Angels be different, their differences also may well appear to us. This is manifest by many mens experience, and by the Authority of Sacred Scripture, that some Angels do good, and some do harme. Wherefore from hence we shall raise the differences, that Angels are distinguished by goodness and wickedness. But that this is a difference of Accident and not of Substance is evident from hence · because the evill that is in the wicked Angels, is no effect proceeding from God, but from the evill Angels themselves. Now that the Angels did not make themselves, I shall shew elsewhere, where I have demonstrated by many reasons, that this is the sole work of God. Yet because we can find out no difference more manifest, it may be tolerated. *Wierus* reports, that Divines have reckoned many orders of wicked Angels, that are opposite to nine degrees of good Angels. The first are called *false Gods*; who taking upon them the Name of Divine Majesty, will be adored for Gods, and honoured with Sacrifices and Adoration: as the the Devill did who tempted Christ, *Mat.* 4. *Mark* 1. *Luke* 4. The second are lying spirits, As that was which entered into the Prophets of *Ahab*, 2 *Kings* 11. This sort of Devils deal in Oracles, and delude men by divinations and predictions of *Apollos* Prophets. The third are the vessels of iniquity, which Devils are the Inventers of all mischievous and wicked Arts; as that

C Divels

Devill *Plato* speaks of called *Theutus*, who taught Men Cards and Dice, &c. called vessels of fury, *Esai.* 13. vessels of anger, *Jerem.* 50. vessels of death, *Psal.* 7. The fourth are Revengers of Evill. The first are Juggling Devils, who imitate Miracles and do service most to all such kind delusions, to deceive the people, *Eccl.* 39. The sixt Order are the powers of the Ayre, that intermingle with Thunders, Lightnings, and Tempests, corrupting the Aire, and producing plagues and other mischiefs, *Rev.* 13. The seaventh Mansion is supplyed by Furies that sow all mischiefs, Wars, discords, *Rev.* 7. The eighth are Accusers, and such as search men out. The last Tempters, and such as lay snares for men, who are supposed to be present to every man in particular, and are therefore called their evill *Genius*, *Rev.* 9. It is no doubt but the Devill attempts to destroy Mankind all the waies he can. Wherefore that he may enlarge his Kingdome, alluring many Millions of Men to him; it is very probable, that for this purpose certain Devils are appointed to certain Offices: otherwise one Devill can performe divers waies of deceptions. But because these things cannot be demonstrated by certain reasons, we need not speake any more of it. The same.

Of the Power of Angels. Chap. 4.

Our Souls are confined to our Bodies, whence it is that by our understanding only that is free, we can surpass this huge Mass of Celestiall and Elementary Bodies; nor can we operate more then our parts will admit: but the Angels are free from all bonds of Bodies, nor are they hindred by any Body be it never so thick, but they can move which way they please: since therefore Angels are substances no way subject to this world, when they do any thing they are not tied to naturall meanes: for they have nothing contrary to nature, that they may be naturally affected by it, nor are there any substances by Nature that are their Superiours, that naturall things may work upon them, though they suffer nothing by them, as the power is of Heavenly things over things here below. But that the power of Angels is limited, we may collect from hence, that doubtless the malignity of wicked Angels is so great, that if they could they would overthrow all Men and all the World. But I shall briefly shew that they are confined, though this be exceeding difficult, because in this point Men are of sundry opinions. For by infinite Histories almost of many Authours, so many and so great forces of Magicians are recorded, as also daily experience evinceth, that the Devils may seem to be able to do what they list. But others think the contrary, and that such things are meere delusions, which are ascribed to Magicians and Witches. I will not gainsay, but the Devils do many miraculous things by Witchcraft, yet we cannot deny but that what they do is reall oft-times, as the examples after alledged concerning Incantation will make manifest. Wherefore though the Devils by reason of their sin committed were driven out from the society of good Angels, yet their forces were not taken from them, whilst their substance remains. They are then most mighty Spirits as they were at first: yet are they hindred two waies, so that they cannot do what they would. First as they are finite substances, again that which they can do, they cannot do if God hinder them. For though we grant that the Devils can do any thing whatsoever, this must not be understood without bounds: for God can do what pleases, because none can hinder him. Logicians define that to be a propriety that belongs to a thing only and that alwaies, and to all of that kind. When therefore I cannot laugh because I am over sad, yet I have not lost my property to laugh: who doubts but the Devill can kill a Man, or steale from him the most Secret Treasures? who also doubts but that he would do it? Yet he doth it not because his power is restrained by One that is more powerfull. Now we must enquire what the Devils can do if God permit. A finite substance must needs have a finite power: since therefore the Devils are finite substances, they must needs have a finite and determinate power. But it is determinated, not as ours is by naturall things, but by things not naturall; namely, by Negation and Privation. Which is thus to be understood; for by reason of Negation they cannot make any thing of nothing, and by reason of Privation they cannot alwaies make any thing of something, since to make any thing of any thing is proper to an Infinite power, as it is to make

any

any of nothing. For a matter that confers nothing to produce such an effect is all one as nothing. Hence it is that many well deny that Devils can turn any Men into Wolves, of which matter I shall speake very soon after this. This therefore we may aver concerning the limited power of the Devils; namely, that they cannot make substances : neither without nor with meanes; for this is proper to nature, the first to God only. That Women may conceive by the Copulation of Devils, and Men be born thereof is a most absurd thing. For God hath granted this to Men alone. Although perhaps the Devill may Secretly steal from Man his seed, when he copulates with Women, yet that will not profit for generation, because the force of it vanisheth suddenly, so soon as it comes to the outward Ayre. Moreover the Devils cannot corrupt any substances without naturall meanes; for this is proper only to God. For this cause it may appear that the Devils have no power in Celestiall matters, because they can naturally do nothing upon them, unless they can change the position of the Stars : yet that they cannot do that, it is evident by this generall Maxime, *God hath given to every substance what sufficeth to attain its end.* But this makes nothing to prove that Devils can change Heavenly things. Of subcelestiall matters the reason is otherwise, upon which God would have naturall operations to prevaile, to cause a vicissitude in things. *The same.*

Of the Miracles done by the Devils. Chap. 5.

Now though the Devils power be limited that they cannot do what they will; yet by many Histories and experience it is proved, that ill spirits do work many strange things, which because we cannot finde out by any reason, they may very well be reckoned amongst miracles. It is true that by ignorance some things are called miracles, which are not so indeed, but in respect of other things, because they are done naturally. Yet we cannot say that all things the Devils doe, are done naturally : for since they are, as we said before, incorporeal substances, they perform their actions without naturall means. Hence it is that they can see in the dark, and are moved exceeding swiftly, whether they please, and are retarded by no density of bodies. They need no organs to speak with, as we do : as is clear by answers given by Oracles, and by those Magicians that speak in their bellies, called *ventriloqui*. Truly these things exceed our capacity, because they are not performed by naturall means. But there is another kind of miracles which the Devils practise by Conjurers and Witches: Of this sort are their works and predictions. These comprehend things past, present, and to come, which are said to be foretold to ignorant people who know them not. And though the Devils are ignorant of many things, (for Divines say that onely God knowes our hearts) nor do the Angels know when the Sonne of man comes to put an end to this life : yet Magicians use to foretell many things, which the very business, and future event makes good, to the great astonishment of many. The operations of Magicians are various, that may be reckoned amongst miracles, though many men by a too curious presumption, endeavour, I know not by what reason, to ascribe all the power of the Devils, to the force of nature. Wherefore I shall relate some things which I rather judg to be performed by miracle, than by any natural means. First, it is evident that Magicians are carried through the Ayre most swiftly, and so are Witches, and they will walk upon the water, as the Pirate *Odde*, who without any Ship went over the deep seas : also they produce hurtfull tempests. Some deny this stoutly, saying that the Devill is a perfect Astronomer, and observes tempests that are coming, and at that time he perswades the poor women, that by this or that means they shall beleeve they can produce rain or hail : yet the Devil is called Prince of the Ayre : nor doth it seem contrary to truth, if we should think that he can cause tempests. For since he can do many other things that are beyond our capacity, wherefore can he not do those things that are often done naturally? He cannot indeed make substances, as I said before : which yet must not be understood but with a condition; for he can make substances if he have naturall means. For the Devill can break the clouds, or carry them to some other place by great winds : also he can raise the waters, even where they may be turned into hail. By this and other means that we know not, Witches can raise tempests by the Devils aide : yet God suffering this to punish Nations. Further, Magicians (under which title we comprehend all that use the Devils help) by jugling fascination, incantation and witchcraft, perform very many things. By fascination to delude the spectators eye, either to seem invisible, or else to resemble other strange bodies: hence your Necromancers are thought to call back Soules of dead Men from death into their Bodies again, such was the Witche of *Endor,* that at despairing *Souls* request called up *Samuell*: but by Witchcraft they cause many diseases, and they cure them sometimes by meanes unknown to us, or by meanes that is above our naturall capacity, and the Methodicall Art of Physick. Thus Witches kill Children and divers Cattell, which we find by various experience, and by relation of others that are worthy to be believed. But if you will say they are meere delusions of the Devill, whereby he makes foolish Women mad that are entangled by him, that they believe they do those things that neither they, nor the Devill can do: if we can so avoid it, we may as well deny any thing else be it never so evident. But as for diseases brought upon us, and the cure of them, it may be justly doubted whether they proceed naturally or not: because I said before that the Devils cannot corrupt any substances, but they must use naturall meanes for it: for this belongs only to an infinite being, to do any thing without meanes. Now God hath appointed no meanes for generation and corruption of substances but what are naturall. *Boetius* in his History of *Scotland,* l. 11. relates a History of King *Duffus,* which *Cardan* hath confuted foolishly enough. *Cardan* and *Wierus,* will have that to be a lye, which they judge to be impossible: as that by Wax melted at the fire by Witches, King *Duffus* should fall into a Consumption, and so be killed. Who is so sottish as to thinke that this can be imputed to Wax melted at the fire? I shall speak afterwards what may be thought of the meanes used, in Magicall Arts. But here the question is whether the Devill could kill King *Duffus* with a Consumption by a preternatural meanes, namely by causes and Symptomes, which are preternaturall in respect of a Comsumption? King *Duffus* without any sign of Choler, Flegm, or any other noxious humour, or of his temperament hurt, was tormented in the night with perpetuall watchings, sweatings, and pains. The motion of his Pulses were good, the operations of his *Senses* were perfect, and his Appetite was frequent; by which signs we are taught that it was no naturall disease. Yet for all this I do not believe it was a lye that is here written of *Duffus*: for the Devill can cause many diseases of the reasons whereof we are ignorant. Also he can do this or that being subtile, he can easily pass through all parts of the body, which he can bind, pull back, or torment otherwise: also he can hinder the operations of the naturall parts that are ordained to sustaine life necessarily, as I shall presently shew concerning the incantations of Magicians. Moreover by filthy stenches and other secret Poysons unknown to us, he can infect our Lungs and other parts of our bodies, whence diseases arise preternaturally; yet he cannot corrupt the body but by naturall meanes. For when a man is killed with a Sword, this death is properly corruption; but that is only then, when the dead Body is converted into another substance, or doth rot. Again some question whether the Devils can cure diseases they never made? some deny this; but their reasons are very weake or none at all. To confirme this, This Argument may have some weight, because the remedies of diseases must be contrary to the causes of them: nor can they be cured naturally, which have preternaturall causes: for by this reason it may seem to be proved, that diseases that arise from naturall causes, can only be dissolved by naturall meanes. But however we argue daily experience teacheth, that there are some Physicians, who by Magicall Arts, to Mens great astonishment, will cure such diseases, that the Devils were never the cause of. But you will reply, they use naturall meanes for it? I cannot indeed deny that: yet sometimes they cure them without meanes; and sometimes they use meanes, which by the Devils influence, rather then by any naturall virtues in them, drive away the diseases. And though diseases that come naturally must be cured by naturall meanes, yet the manner of Application, whereby naturall diseases are cured by Devils, may be such as passeth our power. As for example, We know that a Gravell stone, that is greater then the urinary passage, must be broken, or else great force must be used to drive it

out.

out. If neither of these can be done by reason of its greatness, hardness, or weakness of the Patient, by ordinary Remedies, Methodicall Physicians hold the disease incurable: yet Magicians will easily cure it by the Devils help : for being that he can pass through all parts of the body without hindrance, what can hinder, but that he may break the hardest stone? Thinke so of all the rest. But as I said the Devils power is limited, and that we shall now observe : for the Devils cannot cure all diseases alike, as I shall shew in few words. The cure of diseases is either naturall by alteration, or by generation : or violent, by taking away those things, that are preternaturall in the Body ; or by restoring things dislocated ; or divine, which changeth substances a supernaturall way. The Devill indeed by using naturall meanes, that we know not of, and by violent cure, heales many diseases, that are incurable to us. But there is another way of cure that is proper to God alone, and to such as he is pleased to grant the gift of it, of his especiall favour : as if any part were corrupt, dead, or cut off, the Devill can by no meanes cure that. There is a Magician in *Helvetia*, who boasts that he can as easily cure limbs broken in pieces, as if they were but lightly bruised; but I believe it is but in a vain brag. Moreover those things are exceeding strange that Magicians do by Incantations, when they hinder the actions of naturall or animall bodies. As *Faustus* who would so fasten the wide mouths of Country Clowns that were roaring when they were Drunk, that they would be as Mute as Fishes. So sometimes is the Act of venery hindred, and the fire is stopt that it cannot burn, blood is staid when one bleeds much. Animals as Moles, Serpents, Birds, are compelled : and the force of things, that wound, is hindred, that they can do no hurt. After the same manner are Merchants bound, and those that play for gaine, also Thieves, Robbers, Thunderbolts, &c. for mens security ; and many more like these, which *Wierus* holds to be partly Fictions, partly but sports, that they must rather be referred to delusions, or wicked cruelty, then to reall miracles. But I fear least that whilst we will not be credulous, we shall not escape the fault of incredulity. *The same.*

BOOK. III.

In the precedent Books I have briefly spoken concerning God, Man, Nature, and Angels; and after such a manner that I have expounded Secrets in them all, which our understanding may reach to by contemplation, but not by externall operation. But now since reason requires in order, that we should treat of those things also, which are performed not by knowing, but by working, namely by cunning Art, that most men being ignorant of them, they may deservedly be accounted for Secrets. Therefore in this Book I shall speake of the principall parts of the world, the Heaven and the Elements; but in the following Books we shall handle things contained in them.

Of the Stars.
Of the Sun and Moon. Chap. 1.

THe Sun by the driness of his own fire draws up moist substance. But the Moon moysteneth of it self, and so doth cause a convenient mixture and temperament about Her. *Sotion* cals the daies Moonless from the twenty ninth day of the Moon unto the second; others call them Interlunary and silent ; at which time the Moon is hid under the Sun-Beames, and Shee doth not appear to men. *Ptolomy.*

How the fortune of every year may be conjectured.

It is easie to guess at the fortune of of every year by the Stars, if a man consider XII. XIX. VIII. IV. and XXX. that went before, and compare them with the condition of the precedent year. For *example.* I would know what shall be the condition of the year 1554. beginning *September* 24. untill the year 1555. to the same day. First I consider the year 1542. and that year I took a Journey for no reason, I had a Son, I was unhappy in my gain, and it was my own fault. Not that many did not seek after me: I put forth some things: wherefore now that I have no Wife all the rest will answer in proportion. Likewise I consider the year 1535. wherein I was most unhappy as ever I was

in

in my life : sorrowfull, pensive, fearfull, and my gain's small, and so I will compare this year to the year 1553. as I do the year 1535. to the year 1534. in which I was happy enough. I will do the same with the year 1546. wherein I gain'd well, but I had very much grief and oppression : likewise I will referre my self to the year 1550. wherein also I had great woe : and so that the year 1524. wherein at the end of the year I had honour with contention, without profit, and with great grief. Now the cause of these things is XII. because *Jupiter* returns to the same place on the day of my Nativity, and the order of the twelve signes is compleated in the progress : and *Ptolomy* ascribes very much to this return; nor is it probable that he would have ascribed so much to this revolution of the principall places, unless he had approved it by many experiments; wherefore this circumvolution is the most potent, and it signifies for life, honours, and riches, and of the Magistrates. Principally XIX. is, because the Moon returns almost to the same place, and sometime also *Mars*, and therefore it signifies the state of the body, journies, and fortune, and the qualities of the mind and senses. In the eighth year *Venus* returns to her place, therefore it signifies Joys, Gifts, Sons, conversation amongst Women almost like to that I said, comparing it still to the condition of the precedent year : for nor shall a blind man see, nor a poor man grow rich ; but all things must be measured by proportion. In the fourth year places past return to their trigonall, which also fals out in the eighth year : and therefore the fourth is the weaker; and in this progress also by reason of the Suns motion, the ascendent and the cupss return to the same place; therefore such years have very great similitude with their correspondents in all things : yet not so exquisite as the eight, and much less as the twelf. But in the XXX. year *Saturn* returns to his place, wherefore it signifies the same actions in labour, and adorning things constant : but this similitude is very small by reason of the change of Ages. Yet these things are not alwaies true, but as all other rules are concerning naturall things, and so much the rather, because *directions* disturb all those orders. But *directions* signifie but only one thing, nor do they break it off, unless it be the order of two years, but not of the rest. *Cardanus*.

How we may see the Stars in the day.

It is clear to all men, that a small light being neare to a greater and more excellent, doth vanish. If you hold a Torch or great flame against the bright Sunne, it will go out and fade away. The Stars are hid in the day time by the Suns over great shining brightness, though they shine equally day and night; wherefore they that would see them do not want a means. At noon day when the Sun is eclipsed, and the earth is very dark, and the light doth not offend our eyes, the Stars may be seen all over the Heavens. *Thucidides* saith it fell out so in his time, and so it hath often been in our times. And our eyes are not only cleared by a great darkness, but are also hurt ; as we read of *Xenophons* Souldiers, and of *Dionysius* King of *Sicily*, who blinded men in dark prisons by a most clear light. For since that our eye-sight cannot stand against the Sun nor endure it, it is presently over-aw'd : So that they who would look any way, presently reach forth their hands to their clothes or some other defence. Here we begin. He that desires to see the Stars, as we are taught by *Galen* and *Philoponus*, must go down into some very deep pit, or some such place, that by reason of the darkness of it, and the great space therein, he may look upon the clear Heavens, and not clouded, without any dammage to his eyes, and without winking he may secretly see the clear shining Stars. For the great darkness in such places do congregate the visive spirits as in the night, and will not let them be dispersed with too great light : yet you shall not adventure this when the Sun is in the Meridian, for the great light will hinder you ; and the lower you descend, the clearer and sooner shall you see them, otherwise nor see clear nor so soon.

If any man be let down into a deep den and dark, he shall see a Candle burning in the Sun, yet that will not be presently seen, because the greater light of the Sun keeps it off, though the Candle be never so bright. So I have found men of great Authority, and have heard and read of many that have been deceived. If they cannot see the Stars in the day, they go about to find them thus ; They put a Looking-glass in the

the water, and when the Sun is in the meridian, they think they behold the fixed Stars in the Heavens, and they shew them unto others. For the perpendicular beams of the Sun falling upon the superficies of the water, strike upon the glass obliquely, and are reverberated from each superficies to the eyes of the beholder, if he be rightly placed, and they represent the figure of the Sun: but the beams striking the water aslant, and therefore being refracted, strike upon the glass and the sight: It will appear of the same figure and smaller, by reason of the refraction of the thicker medium, and you will think you see a Star that followes the body of the Sun; which appears in dark places: wherefore many suppose that is *Mhrcury*, because it departs a little from the body of the Sun, and they alwaies see it follow him. Some make haste to see the Dog-Star in Summer, but if you give little credit to demonstration, but you beleeve sense and experience more; seek for the true place of it in the equinoctiall, and you shall not find alwaies the same distance, so that sometimes the Stars seem to be farther off, and sometimes nearer; but in the glass it alwaies shewes the same distance if you set it equally: yet I deny not but by such a help, the Sun rising or setting, but also at noon, may be seen more freely: I say nothing of Eclipses: For since our weak eyes cannot, being neer, see the Sun that is so bright; by this means you may see it clearly, without any offence, as in a cave, and so you may do with a black cloth or paper, with a hole in it. *Porta of Natural Magick.*

Of Fire. Chap. 11.

A Candle not to be extinguished.

You shall make a Candle not to be put out thus: Fill a Candle with powder of Brimstone and linnen clouts broken very small; then cover all over with wax, and set it on fire, it will not be put out with much wind or blowing. Moreover if you make a Candle of cotton with wax one pound, and two ounces of quick brimstone, and as much quick lime, adding thereto an ounce of oyl of Nuts, and you put this into the water so soon as the lime begins to fire, it will set on fire the other ingredients even in the midst of the water. *Anton. Mizaldus Lib. arcan. Mirabil.*

A Candle burning under water.

Provide a long vessell and pretty large, put a piece of wood to the mouth for the Candle to stand upon unmoved when it is lighted, and turning the bottom upwards the light may strike to the bottom; so you may dip it totally into the water, nor will the water come into it, being it is full of ayre, and it will burn under water much according as the vessell is large.

A wonderfull Candle.

Men say that if you take one part of Saltpeter, and add to it Frankincense, common Oyl and Milk of Spurge, a fift part of each, a tenth of Brimstone, of Wax half, and shall make a Candle, it will be wonderfull for heat, smell, noyse and motion. Others there be that fill half an egge shell of Marigold flowers, and they put one part of Gunpowder upon it, and close it in wax, and they put this into most cold water, for ofttimes the fire kindles and the flame shines forth. *Cardanus de Varietate.*

Torches not to be blown out with wind.

Men boyl their wicks in Saltpeter and water, and drying them, they wet them in Brimstone and Strongwater, and with this mixture they make Candles: for it consists of Brimstone, Camphire, and Rosin of Turpentine one half, Colophonia two parts, Wax three parts, so they make four Candles: they put them together, and in the middle they cast in live brimstone, and it will the more forcibly resist all things. If you cover a Candle over with Snow, and set it in fire, the Candle will seem to burn in the Snow. *Alexius.*

A Candle that cannot be put out.

There are many wonderfull things, but yet when you know the cause you admire no more: As if Brimstone be equally dissolved with Wax it becomes unextinguishable; but the Brimstone must be very pure. Likewise if a Candle be smeared over with powder of Brimstone and Charcoal, and dipt all into the water in winter, and the upper part of it be covered with Paper, and be hanged where a drop falls with Ice,

it

it will be compassed round with a thicker Ice; if you light it it will burn, and to the great wonder of many the Ice will seem to burn. *Card. de Subtilitat.*

Artificiall Fires not to be extinguished by Water.

Water is wont to inflame vehement Fires, because the moisture that exhales is made more fat, nor is it extinguished by the smoke that surrounds it, but the fire feeds on it all; whereby being made more pure, and recollected, it burns the brighter for the cold water: hence it is that some fires are kindled and enflamed by water. The matter of them is Ship and Greek Pitch, Brimstone, Lees of Wine, called Tartar, Sarcocolla, Saltpeter, Oyle of Peter. This was attributed to *Marcus Gracchus*. Wherefore quick Lime is added, a twofold part, and they are all mingled equally with yelks of Eggs, and are buried in Horse dung.

Another.

Take Oyle of Brimstone, of Peter, of Juniper, and of Saltpeter, equall parts, black Pitch, Goose and Ducks Grease, Doves Dung, liquid Vernice, of each alike as before, of Asphaltum five parts, mingle them all with Strongwater and bury them in Horse Dung.

Another.

Take liquid Vernice, Oyle of Brimstome, of Juniper, of Lineseed, of Peter, Gumme of the Larch tree, of each equall parts, of Strongwater three parts and a half, of Saltpeter, dry Bay wood powdred as much as shall suffice, that being all mingled together, they may be as thick as Clay; put all these in a glass Vessell, and bury them three Moneths in Horse Dung, if therefore balls of these stick to Wood, they will take fire of themselves when it Rains: yet this doth not alwaies fall out so. But this is certain, that once being lighted, no water will put them out. But a powder that easily takes fire, and the flame of it doth burn most vehemently, is made of Gunpowder, and third part of Brimstone and Greek-Pitch. *Card. de Subtil.*

That nothing may be burnt in Fire.

If you take like parts of Isinglass and Alum and mingle them together, and powre Vinegar upon them, whatever you smeere with that mixture and cast it into the fire it will not burn: and if you annoint your hands with marsh-Mallows pownded with whites of Eggs, and strew Allum upon it, you may handle fire without being hurt. *Albert. Mag.*

A fiery mixture which may be kindled by the Sun.

But especially when it is in the Meridian, and in those Countries where the Sun is very hot or about the rising of the Dog-star, nor doth it proceed but by a composition of things that are easie to take fire: and you must be very carefull in making of it, and it is after this manner: provide Camphry, then Oyle of live Brimstone, of Rosin, of Turpentine, of Juniper, and yelks of Eggs, liquid Pitch, Colophonia powdred, Saltpeter, and twice as much of Strongwater as all the rest, a little Arsenick, and Tartar; pound and mingle all these together, and put them close up in a glass Vessell; and this must remain two Moneths covered close in Horsedung, alwaies renewing the Dung, and mingling them together, and water must be drawn forth of the same Vessell as I shall shew you: this must be thickned either with our Powder or with Pigeons Dung, and besmeer Wood finely sifted, that it may be like to Pap, or some other combustible matters, and use it in the heat of Summer. All these things are imputed to *Marcus Gracchus*. Pigeons Dung retains a mighty force to burn. *Galenus* reports, that in *Mysia*, which is a part of *Asia*, a House was thus set on fire. Pigeons Dung was cast forth where it touched a Window that was neare it, and touched the Wood of it that was newly annoynted with Rosin, this being corrupted, and hot, and sending forth vapours at Midsummer when the Sun was at the highest and shined much upon it, it set on fire the Rosin and the Window, and so other Doors annoynted with Rosin took fire, and began to send up the flame to the House: and so soon as the fire took hold of the Roof, the whole House was quickly burnt down, because it had a mighty force to set things on fire. *The same.*

Torches that cannot be put out with winds.

Torches are made for Journies, that cannot be put out by winds; which proceeds from

from the Brimstone, for it is hardly put out when it takes flame: Hence it is that Torches smeered with Wax and Brimstone are carried in Winds and Tempests, and will not be extinguished. But for Souldiers to March with, or to carry other things needfull they use such a one: They boyle their Weeks in Saltpeter and water, and drying them, they wet them in Brimstone and strong Water, then they make Candles with this mixture: It consists of Brimstone, of Camphrie, and Turpentine, Rosin one half, Colophonia two parts, Wax three parts: they make foure Candles and put them together, or they put live Brimstone between them, and so it will resist the more stoutly. *The same.*

That one may not be burnt with fire.

Belbinnus saith, when you take the white of an Egge and Allum, and besmeere a Cloth with it, and you wash it with Salt-water, and dry it, no fire will burn it. Another saith, Take red Arsnick and Allum, and grind them, and mingle them with the juyce of Howsleek and Buls Gall, and annoint your hands with it, if you take up a red hot Iron it will not burn you. Also if you take of the Loadestone, Itching powder, the Huckle Bone of a Ram, strong Vinegar, Marsh-Mallows, beate them well together, and annoint your hands with it, no fire will burn them. *Albertus Magnus.*

A wonderfull Lamp, wherein appear things terrible, in quantity, having a Rod in the hand, it will fright a Man.

Take a green Frog, and cut the head off upon a Cloath of green for Funerals, wet it with Oyle of Elder, and put in some Touch wood, light this in a green Lamp, and you shall see a black Statue in whose hands there shall be a Lamp, it is wonderfull. *Albertus.*

A mixture of fire that will burn under water.

First provide Gunpowder that is used for Warre, from whence as it were from a burning noise, these Guns are called *Bombards*; this powder is an ingredient of all these compositions, and is the Basis and ground work of them all: Adde to this a third part of Colophonia, a fourth part of common Oyle of Olives, a sixt part of Brimstone, mingle them well: when they are all dried, try them. If it burn more violently then you would have it, adde a little more Colophonia and Brimstone, but if too weakly, adde a little more Gunpowder, wrap this mixture in Straw and Linnen Cloaths, or in Coffins made of them as hard as you can, then bound about with Cords and Bands, dip all in boyling Pitch, and dry it well, then cover it again with Straw, smeer it with Pitch to keep it from wet, that it may not break out by force of the fire: when they are well dried in the Sun, leaving a little hole through, put fire to it, and when it begins to burn stay a little while, then cast it into the Water and it will not be put out by it: but sometimes it will go to the bottome, sometime is mounting to the top, and turns up and down in it. Nor is it amiss to put some Oyle of Peter to them: for it is a most violent fire, and being seen afar off, it will make it leap up and down, as the Loadestone doth Iron, and it burns, and will along time hold fire in the Water; for Artists have borrowed this from nature; nor can any other reason be given for Baths that boyle continually, but because they are bituminous and burnt inwardly, and are fed with Water that causeth them to boyl alwaies. Warlike Engines are often fild with these compositions, whence it is that they will cast fire Balls afar off and break; which they prepare thus. They wrap this powder in hards, and they smeer it over with the foresaid mixture, and fold them in, and they fill hollow Engines with the Powder and Bullets, the composition strewd in by turns, and putting fire to it, they cast fire Balls amongst their Enemies companies, which is instead of Oyle, and burns more seriously. Some put in Hogs Grease, Goose Grease, Brimstone that never came at the fire, which the Greeks call *ἄπυρον*. Oyle of Brimstone, and bituminous Saltpeter oftimes purged, burning-Water, Turpentine, liquid Pitch, which all men call *Kitra*, commonly called liquid Vernice, Oyle of yelks of Eggs, and sometimes to adde weight to these and to thicken all the moist ingredients, they mingle some powder of Bay Tree with them, all being shut up in a glazed Vessell, hide them all under Dung for two or three

three Moneths, every other ten daies renewing the Dung, and mingling all again, taking out the composition, if it begins to burn when you put fire to it, it will never go out, till it be all consumed : no Water will extinguish it, but will make it burn the more : but it will be choaked with Clay, Earth, Dust, and with all dry things: if you cast it on a Helmet, Buckler, or Armed Men, it will make them red hot that they must be burnt if they do not forthwith put them off. I shall shew you another that is more violent : Take Turpentine, liquid Pitch, and Vernice, adde Pitch, Frankinsence and Camphrie the most parts, live Brimstone a third part and half, Saltpeter purged two parts, burning Water three parts, and as much of Oyle of Peter, but adde some powder of Willow, and a little Charcoale; mingle these together, and make round Balls, or fill earthen Pots with them. It will burn, so that it is in vain to go about to extinguish it. *The same.*

Food for fire.

Food that upon the smallest cause will take fire, (they commonly call it fire food,) is made thus. Let the greatest Spongs of Trees be exactly cleansed from the wooddy part, and boyling them a long time in Lye, let them be well dryed, to every pound of them, adde Brimstone two ounces, Saltpeter half an ounce; and so boyle them in the Lye untill the Lye be consumed, then dry them in the Sun, sprinkle them with *Aqua vitæ*, (some call it burning Water) then dry them again : the oftner you do it, the better they will be, they are kept either in Frankinsence or common Sandarach. Another that is far easier to make, but it will not take so soon, thought it will do much. Burn lightly Cotton, Linnen, especially black, and whilst they burn, extinguish the fire, and keep them. *Cardan de varietate.*

Things that attract fire.

Heraclitus said that all things were performed by discord and concord, so Naphtha attracts fire, and it leaps forth to it wheresoever it feeles it : so the root of the Herb Aproxis attracts fire as Naphtha doth. *Cornel. Agrippa de Occult. Philosoph.*

To light a fire by the Sun.

Fire may be easily kindled by a round Viol of Glass full of water set unmoved against the Sun. For when it is directly set against the Sun, lay behind the Viol some combustible matter in the line that passeth through the Viol, it will greatly take fire from the beames of the Sun, multiplied and condensed, to the admiration of the beholders, to see fire raised by water. *The same.*

A mixture that takes fire by water.

If you will make the Image of a Man or any other, that shall fire being put into the water, and if it be extinguished shall be less; Take quick Lime, mingle it with some Wax and Oyle of Sesamum and Naphtha, that is with white Earth and Brimstone, and make an Image of it : for when you shall put water to it, the fire will kindle. *Albertus.*

Fire that is kindled with Spittle, that is of great use for Thieves and Pilferers.

Take Oyl of Brimstone, of the Larch-tree, of Cedar, liquid Pitch; of each sixteen Ounces : Saltpeter sixteen Ounces : Salt-Armoniac, Vitriol, Tartar calcined : of each eight Drams : Quick-Lime made of River-Pebbles : Loadstone calcined; of each five Ounces : Sheeps-Suet, Ducks-Grease; of each six Ounces. Cover all these with Aqua-vitæ, and for three Moneths bury them in Horse-dung. Every fourth day shake them ; then boyl them at the fire, untill the Liquor be gone, and the Feces remain. Break that Vessel, take it forth and powder it. If this Powder be strewed on any thing, and water be powred upon it, it takes fire and burns. *Scaliger.*

To provide a Wick shall not consume.

Cut Allum de Plume, like to a Wick; put that into Oyl, and it will never be consumed. *Nostradame.*

A Stone that yeelds fire by rubbing it.

Take Styrax Calamita, Brimstone, Quick-Lime, Pitch ; of each three Drams : Camphire one Dram : Asphaltum three Drams : powder them and put them into an earthen Veſſel well cloſed, ſet them by the fire, untill they turn to a ſtone; which being rubbed with any Cloth, will kindle, and it will be extinguiſhed with Spittle. *Ruſcellus.*

A Candle which the wind cannot blow out.

Take a Wick, wrap it in Quick-Brimſtone powdred in a linnen Cloth: Then with Wax make a Candle, once lighted it will never go out, ſo long as any of it remains. *Noſtradame.*

A fire that draws Iron, an Invention of the Sonne of Amram.

Take liquid Pitch, Juniper-Gum, Oyl of Turpentine, Oyl of Bitumen, Oyl of Brimſtone, Oyl of Saltpeter, Oyl of Yelks of Egges, Oyl of Bays, of each ſix parts: Powder of dry Laurel, Camphire; of each ſoked in Aqua vitæ fourteen parts: Saltpeter the weight of them all. Put them into a glaſed Veſſel with a narrow mouth, well luted, and ſtop it well: Hide them in Horſe dung ſix Moneths; every fourth day ſhake them, then diſtill them in a Seraphine. *Scaliger.*

Another.

Take the Dregs of the Larch-tree-gum, Turpentine, which remains after the Oyl is diſtilled, of Oyl of the ſame liquid Pitch, Pitch of the Cedar, Camphire, Bitumen, Mummy, new Wax, Ducks Greaſe, Pidgeons dung, Oyl of live Brimſtone, Oyl of Juniper, Oyl of Bays, of Lin-ſeed, of Hemp-ſeed; of each five pound: Oyl of Peter, of Bricks, of Yelks of Egges; of each three pound: Saltpeter, ten pound; Salt-Armoniac, ſeven Ounces. Let all theſe be ſo wet with Aqua vitæ, that they may be covered with it; then bury them in Horſe-dung, and every third day renew the heap. After this draw out the ſpirit in a Seraphine, you ſhall thicken this with the fineſt Powder of Oxe-dung. The tawny Moore ſings miracles of this, that it will fire even by the Sunne-beames, and yet the Veſſel it is in will not burn; but onely putting Piſs or Vinegar upon it, you may put it out, or choak it caſting earth upon it. It will burn conſtantly in water and not be extinguiſhed; for it will not yeeld at all to it. Now a dayes, they put theſe fires into Veſſels, and caſt them amongſt the Enemies. The Antients called that kind of Veſſel, Απόκ&c. *Scaliger.*

A fire that cannot be extinguiſhed.

Take Verniſh wherewith Hides are guilded, ten pound: Quick-Brimſtone, four pound: Oyl of Roſin, two pound: Saltpeter, one pound and an half: Frankincenſe, one pound: Camphire, ſix Ounces: of the beſt Aqua vitæ, fourteen Ounces. Mingle them all well at a gentle fire, and make a mixture, wherewith hards being wet, and put into earthen pots, and fired, will make a fire not to be put out, whitherſoever they are caſt. *Fiorovantus.*

A fire not to be extinguiſhed.

Take of the Verniſh aforeſaid twelve pound: Oyl of Roſin, Oyl of Wax, of each one pound: Oyl of Turpentine, eight Ounces: Quick-Brimſtone, two pound: Salt peter, four pound, Camphire, one pound: Aqua vitæ, two pound: Greek Pitch powdred, three pound. Mingle them all at a gentle fire, and make a mixture. *Fioravantus.*

To ſee a fire out of a Cup full of water.

Take a Hen Egg, take forth both the White and the Yelk, and fill it with the powder following. Take Quick-Brimſtone, Quick-Lime, of each what is ſufficient; powder them, and put them into the ſaid Egg-ſhell, ſtop the hole with Wax; when you would ſee fire in it, put it into a cup full of water. *Fallopius.*

To ſee fire under Water.

Take Quick-Lime, Quick-Brimſtone, of each what may ſuffice: Oyl of Peter, of Wax, of each a little. Mingle them, and put them into the Water. *Fallopius.*

To take fire in your hand.

Take Marſh-mallows what is ſufficient, mingle it with the white of an Egg; annoynt your hands with it, when they are dry you may handle fire. *Fallopius.*

A Stone that will fire with any moyſture

Put a Loadſtone into an earthen Pot, or ſome ſuch Veſſel covered with Quick-Lime, and it will be the better if you put in Colophonia with the like quantity of Lime: When the Vessel is full, lute it with fullers earth with a hole for vent, and so put it into the furnace untill it be baked: then take it out and cast it into an earthen pot, lute it again with clay and put it into the furnace, doing so by turns untill it be white as snow, and put a dew upon it: when you have occasion, with Spittle or Water it will raise a flame: when that is out, hide it in a hot place for your use. *The same.*

Another way to do it.

If you adde of Quick-Brimstone and Saltpeter, purged the like weight, Camphire twice as much to Quick-Lime, and beat all in a Morter till they be very fine, that they may fly into the air, then bind them all fast in a linnen cloth, and put them into an earthen Vessel that is luted with Potters earth, and dry them in the Sunne, and put them into a furnace: when they are well baked in the Potters Vessel, wherein lies the greatest diligence to be used they will become hard as a stone, you may take them out for your use. *The same.*

Otherwise.

Take the Calx of the foresaid Loadstone, Saltpeter often purged four times as much, Camphire the like quantity, Quick-Brimstone that never came at the fire; and Oyl of Turpentine, and the congeled dregs of Wine, which we shall alwayes hereafter call Tartar: Pound or grinde all these with a Mill or Pestle, and sift them, what remains unbroken, pound again and sift it. Moreover you must have *Aquavitæ* ready, and you must pour that in, that it rise higher then the rest: Put all into a glased Vessel, and cover it that it breath not out: Put it under Horse-dung for two or three Moneths, renewing it every tenth day, untill it become as thick as honey, and you see no difference in it; then let it heat at a strong coal fire, untill all the moysture evaporate, and it be dried throughly to a stone: When you know this, break the Vessel, and take it out and powder it again; if a little water or moysture be poured upon it, it will presently flame: And of all the rest, this is the principal way. *The same.*

How to make Composition for Rockets for the Air.

Of one Ounce. Take of Charcoal, Saltpeter, and Gunpowder, of each an Ounce and a half, being well mingled together.

Of two Ounces. Gunpowder, four Ounces and a half, Saltpeter, one Ounce, mixt well together.

Of four Ounces. Gunpowder, four pounds, Saltpeter, one pound, Charcoal, four Ounces, all mixt together.

Of four Ounces. Take of Gunpowder, four pounds; Saltpeter, one pound, Charcoal, four Ounces; Brimstone, half an Ounce, all well mixt together.

Of five or six Ounces. Of Gunpowder, two pound, five Ounces; of Saltpeter, half a pound; of Charcoal, six Ounces, of Brimstone and Iron scales, two Ounces, of each all well mixt.

Of ten or twelve Ounces. Gunpowder, one pound one Ounce; Saltpeter, four Ounces; of Brimstone, three Ounces and a half; Charcoal, one Ounce, mingle them well.

Of a pound or two. Of Gunpowder, twenty Ounces; Saltpeter or Charcoal three Ounces, of scales of Iron and Quick-Brimstone, each one Ounce, mingled all together.

How to make your Coffins for Rockets.

You must provide a mould of well seasoned Wood, or Brasse almost seven Inches, in length equal, turned and exactly hollow; as also a Stopple or Former to roal the Paper upon, very smooth, not exceeding three quarters of an Inch, diameter: Make your Coffin, of Paper, Parchment, or strong Canvas: Roal it very hard upon your Roaler so often, till it will go very stiff into the body of the Former, and with a piece of fine Packthread tie it within half an Inch, and chalk the Coffin first, dipping it into fair Water, so that it may be throughly wet when it is chok't: Thrust it into the body of the Former, with the Roaler in it.

To make Composition for your Stars.

Take one pound of Saltpeter, of Gunpowder and Brimstone each half an ounce, which being mixt together with a quantity of Oyle of Peter, roule it into little Balls, and use it as occasion serves.

Another way.

Dissolve one ounce and a half of Camphrie in a quarter of a Pint of *Aqua vita*, dip in Bumbaste Cotton into it, role it up in small Balls and use it.

To make strange Apparitions in the Ayre.

Provide Gum Dragon and put it into an Iron Pan and rost it in the Embers, beate it into powder, and dissolve it into *Aqua vita*, till it becomes a Jelly, then straine it, as also dissolve Camphire in other *Aqua vita*, mix these together, and sprinkle it with this following Composition. Take of Brimstone half a Pound, Saltpeter one pound, Charcole half a pound; after they are well stird together, mingle them with the foresaid, make all up into little Balls and roul them in Gunpowder dust.

To make Serpents.

Roule strong Paper nine or ten times about a Goose Quill or a Roaler about four Inches long, Chalke it almost in the midst, fill it with the Composition for Rockets, the shorter end fill with whole Gunpowder.

How to know good Gunpowder.

All Gunpowder is made of these Ingredients Saltpeter is the soul of it, Sulphur the life: it is incorporated with Vinegar and *Aqua vita*: if you would choose the best, you shall know it, 1. if it be brought and incline to a blewish colour, 2. if when you handle it is dry and leaves little moisture behind, 3. if it being fired flash quickly and leave no dregs behind it.

A flying fire.

Take one pound of Brimstone, eleaven pounds of Coales of Willow Tree, six pounds of Salt-Peter, these three must be most finely powdred in a stone Morter, afterwards at your pleasure put some of it in a Coffin of Paper to flye, or to make Crackers. *Alb.*

That fire may be kindled with a round Cryftall.

If a little Globe perfectly round, or a plain Glass be provided, as a small Looking-glass, and be set a little opposite to the Sun, it will burn behind it, uniting the Beames together on the contrary side: for you must so long remove the matter that must take fire, either nearer to it, or further off, untill you find the Cone of the Beames reflexed; then stay awhile and the fire will shine. And thence we shall wonder more if there appear a small part of a great circle. Physicians say that a Fontanell cannot be better made upon any part of the body, then by a Cryftall Ball set against the Sun Beames. *The same.*

To light many Candles with one Wick.

You shall light many Candles with one Wick, if you first wet in water, and smeer them over with Brimstone and Orpiment dissolved in Oyle; but they must be both purified, for nothing takes fire from a small or very little fire unless it be first wet in Water. *Cardan. de varietat. rerum.*

Woods that take fire by rubbing.

The woods that take fire by rubbing, are those that are most hot, as the Laurell, purging Thorn, the Holm, the Teil tree. *Menefter* adds the Mulberry, and this is conjectured because it presently blunts and takes off the edge of a Hatchet: of all these they make Augres, that in penetrating they may the better hold out, and may more forcibly performe the work; but the receiver is made of soft wood, as Ivye, Canes, Briony, and such like being dried, and free from all moisture. But these are the worst for fire to be produced, and are rejected, that grow in shady and secret places. And this is the best way to do it, nor do I thinke it materiall whether you rub Bay Boughs against Bay Boughs, or else with Ivye pilled, or a Cane against a Cane, and which is better to do it, with a Cord to move it quickly and strongly, and when it begins to smoake, to cast a little Brimstone upon it to feed it, or some dry Spunge or Touch-wood, of the Blades that spring forth, found about the roots of Coltsfoot: for they will the sooner take fire and hold it. Of things that procure fire, Oyls are rejected as unfit, because the matter is too fat and moist. *The same.*

How to get fire from Amber.

Some say that Amber when you rub it much, and blow on it with a paire of Bellows toward a Lamp, a great fire flames from it, and it will be burnt up with it, and yet not touched. *Albert Magnus.*

To take fire in your hand.

If you carry fire in your hand, that it shall not hurt you, take Quick-lime dissolved in hot Bean water, and a little Madrumlis, and a little Marsh-Mallows, and mingle that with it well, then annoint your hands in the Palme with that and dry them, put fire into them, and it will not hurt you. *Albert. Magnus.*

That one may seem to be all on fire.

When that you would have one seem to be all on fire from head to foot, and yet not be hurt; take white Marsh-Mallows, mingle them with the white of an Egge, annoint your body therewith, and let it dry on: then annoint you with the white of an Egge, powder it all over with fine powder of Brimstone: the fire will burn upon it and do no hurt, and if you do it on the Palme of your hand, you may hold fire safely. *Albertus.*

To seem all on fire.

When you have smeered your self with the foresaid mixture, let it dry, and strew on fine powdred Brimstone, put a flame to it, when it begins to burn you will seem to be all on fire. If Brimstone do not please you, sprinkle you with *Aqua vitæ* that I speak of, put fire to it, and you shall be pretty safe under it. *The same.*

To preserve any thing from fire that it shall not burn.

Consider of things that being extremely cold, are stupefactive and subtile, and by reason of the connexion of their substance are not conquered by fire, as are the stone *Amiantus,* which some call stone Allum, Lime quenched, whites of Eggs, juyce of Marsh-Mallows, Henbane, flea Seed: these are mingled with juyces untill they are like an Unguent, then smeer your hands with them, and you may hold fire and receive no hurt: yet not so that you may handle them safely without fear, or walk through the fire. Of the stone *Amiantus,* Napkins are Weaved, when they are foule cast them into the fire, so they are made clean again. *The same.*

That things may not burn in the fire.

If you will have any thing cast into the fire and not be burnt, Take Isinglass one part, and as much Allum; let them be well mingled, power on this wine Vinegar, and mingle with it what you please: cast it into the fire, annoint with this mixture, and it will not burn. *Albertus Magnus.*

A Candle to fright a Man.

Take Linnen Cloath, white and new, and make a Garment of it, and put into it an Adders skin, and Bay-Salt, and bless the Oyle of Olives, and give it to whom you please, when it is lighted, he will be frighted at it, and tremble exceedingly. *The same.*

That Men may not burn in the Fire.

A wonderfull experiment that will make men pass through the fire without hurt, or to carry fire or red hot Iron not hurting their hands. Take the Juyce of Marsh-Mallows, and the white of an Egge, and Flea-seed, and Quick-Lime, and powder and mingle it with the white of an Egge, and the Juyce of a Reddish; with this mixture annoint your hands or body, and let it dry, after this you may boldly handle fire and not be hurt. *The same.*

That Thred may not burn in the Fire.

Why a Thred tied about an Egge will not burn in burning Coales nor yet in the flame? because there is no fire unless the heat come to the heighth: but it is alwaies kept back by the Egge that it cannot proceeding so farre: because the Egge cannot be burnt: but what doth not burn, doth alwaies coole in some manner, that which is exceeding hot. *Card. de Subtilitate.*

Fire that is extinguished by Oyle, and is kindled by Water.

Here we must consider those things that more easily kindled in the water, or burn there

there of their own accord, as Camphire and Quick-Lime. Therefore if you make a mixture of Wax, and Oyl of Peter and Brimstone, and it take fire; when you cast in Oyl or Mud, it will quench it, for it revives and makes the fire greater if you cast in Water. Torches are made of this composition, that will not be extinguished, if you pass over Rivers, or through great Rain. *Livy* reports, that some old Women in their sports, passed over *Tyber* with lighted Torches made of these things, that it was wonderfull to the beholders of it. *The same.*

Burning Water.

You must have old, strong, and black Wine, put into it Quick-Lime, Tartar, Salt, Quick-Brimstone, and draw forth water in the glased chymical Vessels, this will burn wonderfully, nor will it leave burning till all be burnt, or but a very little left; if you put it into a dish, or some Vessel with a large mouth, and put flame to it, it will presently take fire. If you cast it against a Wall, or out of a Window by night, you shall see the Air full of innumerable sparks, and all of a light fire. It will burn held in your hand, nor will it burn much: yet observe this, that if you distill it often, it will burn the less, for that *Aqua-Vitæ* hath contrary to Vineger. If you will have it to abound less with Flegm, when you distill it, put a spunge wet in water, to the mouth of the Vessel, and this will not let the Flegm pass through. *The same.*

To cast Flame afarre off.

That is done well by Colophonia, Frankincense, and Amber chiefly: for if it takes fire, it riseth high, casting the flame far from it: If you will hold a Candle between your fingers, and in the palme of your hand powder finely beaten, when you cast it, the powder will fly through the flame of the fire. *The same.*

Greek Fire.

You shall make Greek Fire thus. Take Quick-Brimstone, Tartar, Sarcocolla, Oyl of Pitch, boyled Salt, Oyl of Peter, and common Oyl, make them boyl well, if you put any thing into it, it takes fire, be it Wood or Iron, and it will not be extinguished, unless by Piss, Vineger, or Sand, *Albertus.*

Sleeves of Mettall to melt the hardest things with Fire.

Vessels are made four Cubits long, or at least three, nine Inches broad, three fingers thick, bending at the lower part, and framed also after the fashion of a Couch, without any bottom, of black Marble spotted with white spots: In the middle of the length there is a hole, and in that a pipe exactly placed, through which the wind of Bellows may be carried in: At the lower part there is a hole, by which the melted matter may descend: The neather part of the Vessel is stopt, leaving only (as I said) that little hole, with clay and coals pounded together, and made like plaister, and more clammy. These things thus ordered, from the forme are called metallick sleeves. They are filled within with the matter we would melt, and this fire shut in by turns with coals, hath a mighty force, and all things that melt not, must needs burn. There is no small convenience of the blast that the Bellows send in through the pipe. This first, as it is clear, kindles the fire, and raiseth the flame, and makes the fire penetrate the more vehemently. Moreover being cold, it constrains the heat that comes from the mettal, and driveth it inwardly, and so it dissolves the matter wherein it is. Moreover if any thing be melted, it keeps it from burning, and moderates the heat. *Cardan. de subtilitate.*

How you may make a Fountain that shall shine in the dark.

You that came with greediness to read these things, which bountifull and almost prodigal Nature liberally bestows upon mankind for use, which lye hid and close, and by this meanes provides to make a man innocent, (which truly is not to be despised) who shall out of her dark corners ingeniously search out of things, what their vertues are: For you have many things, that in dark nights will be seen and perceived. *Aristotle* hath shewed us many, and experience more, whether they be small creatures, of the kind of Insects, called Glow-worms; or sponges, heads and scales of Fishes: as of the Fish called *Trichia*, commonly Harenagus; so the Sea-Kite, called the candle, because the eyes of it shine in the night. The Scallops fins shine in the dark, and in the mouthes of those that eat them; so do the eyes of Wolves and Cats. Also in a Forrest in *Germany*, called *Hercynia*, there is a Bird to be seen, whose feathers

thers shine like fire, and by the light thereof, Travellers pass through those innumerable deserts, and govern their uncertain Journeys by means of them. And so it is with some kinds of Oysters, and most kinds of shel-Fish, or the Moss that grows upon them. *Ælian* speaks of the sea, and land *Pianie*, it had that name from its bright shining ; and so are many Sea-Fishes called in Greek, *Aglaophotides*. I have often seen Sea-Water tossed with the hand, to glitter like to sparks of fire. *Josephus* reports, that there is a Valley, wherein is a place called *Baraas*, called so from a root of the same name, that shines like fire. So is *Nyctigretum*, which *Democritus* so much wondred at. So the stock of very dry Oke, and rotten with mouldiness, will in the night shine like silver, and affect our sight. The Carbuncle shines in the dark, illustrating the Air about it, according to the bigness of it. And there are many more things that shine in the night, as is proved by the authority of the most sound Authors. But I must in order shew how a moysture may be extracted from thence, from which the light shall be spread more wide, and at greater distance, and that may be seen in the night. The example is this following. Glow-worms that shine with a fiery colour, are the chief of all : I cut off their tails from their bodies, and taking care that nothing else be mingled with the clear parts, bruising and grinding them as a Saphire stone, for fifteen dayes or more I bury it in a Dunghill, put all into a glass, and it is best that they touch not the sides, but may hang in it : When those days are over, I put the Vessel into a furnace, or a bath of hot water ; and having fitted it, I receive by degrees the clean liquour that drops from it, into a dish underneath, and I put this into a clear cryftall round ball. Let this shining water be hanged thus in the middle of a chamber, and it will lighten the Air about it, that you may read great letters in the night, but the light of it is so small that you cannot see it in the day. Like to this almost is the water that is diligently distilled from the scales of the foresaid Fishes, which I have often seen done, and it will not be known from the former almost, and the same way is evident to provide the rest, and we use them for such purposes. *The same.*

Burning water.

You shall make burning water thus. Take Dragonwort which distill through a Limbeck, and water that will burn will come forth: Also mingle it with Wine, or what liquor you please, and it will burn if you put a light Candle near it. *Albertus.*

Burning Glasses.

But since there seem to be two ways to kindle fire by a Glass. The first is, that all beams falling upon the Center of the Glass, may be united in one point by reflection, this is performed by a round Concave Glass. The other way is, that all the beams equi-distant may be united, which proceed from the Sun into one point, which also is parabolical. There are extant concerning this, Books of *Archimedes*, where he shews burning Glasses that are made with a conical Section, and I find in *Conrad. Gesner.* that *Franscifcus Maurolycius Messansensis*, hath written of it. The business is thus, When a Superficies cuts a right Cone, and the dimetient of the Superficies is equi-distant to the side of the Triangle, that is described within the Superficies, that cuts the Cone through the Axis from the top. That Superficies is called a Parabole. Let it be A B C. whose right line falling from the top B. dividing A C. the right line under it into equal parts, and the crooked lines B A. and B C. likewise, B D. shall be called the dimetient, and A C. the diameter, the basis of the Cone is K. the middle between B D. I say that H K L. hath always the same proportion, to any perpendicular that comes from the side falling upon the dimetient, as is the proportion of the perpendicular to the part of the dimetient, intercepted between the top and the perpendicular. As let F G. be the perpendicular, therefore H L. shall have the same proportion to F G. as G F. hath to G B. and H L. shall be called then the right side, and all the equi-distant lines from B D. or beams shall reflect upon K. now H L. is alwayes four times as long as B K. But if you would make a Glass that shall burn at a great distance, as *Galen* saith *Archimedes* made one that burnt the Galleys of the enemies. It is evident, that Glasses, whether they be taken from the Parabole, or from the Circle and Sphere, they must be very

very great, that is they must be portions of the largest Spheres, or largest Cones, equall to Paraboles, yet not the largest of all. As for example, If I will burn a thousand Paces off, I must make a Circle whose Dimetient must be two Miles long, and of this I must take such a portion that the roundness may not be concealed, namely, a sixth part, to which I must adde a Dimetient for the depth at one end, and the Dimetient being fixed, I must carry about part of the Circle which shall describe to me part of the Sphere : and when I have polished this, it will being opposed against the Sun, kindle fire a great way, and that most violently for a thousand paces. But it is now not so needfull because of Warlike Ordinance and Guns : but of old it was the safest way. But the burning that proceeds from a Parabole is more forcible. And that is done thus. Let there be a place to be burnt a Mile off, I make B.K. of a thousand paces, to this I draw a right Line that is equall to it, K.D. but to B.D. I make from the Perpendicular a Line equall which is B.A. and on the other side B.C. equall to B.A. and drawing D.A. and D.C. I make D. the Center of the Cones Base, and A.D. the Axis, for the Angle A.D.C. is a right Angle, and I turn about A.C. that a Cone may be made, and a Circle may be described from the Line D.C. as the Semidiameter for the Cones Base, this I divide with two Lines, cutting themselves with the Diameter at right Angles, C.E. and F.G. in the Center D. Also it shall be that the point B. may describe the circumference of a Circle about the Cone, which shall be K.B. Wherefore I draw a right Line from the top of the Cone to the end of one Diameter of the Base, let it be C. where it cuts the circumference of the Circle, as in B. from that point I draw straight Lines to the ends of the other Diameter, B.F. and B.G. wherefore the Superficies wherein is the Triangle B.F.G. where it cuts the Superficies of the Cone, it makes two oblique Lines, B.F. and B.G. which must be made of the best Steel that they may not bend, taking but a part, as B.L. and B.M. being equall, which are the sides of the Parabole. Then take a great lump of Plaister of Gyp N. greater in breadth then L.B.M. which you shall gently rub on the top with a whetstone, untill the Parabole L.B.M. put into it, and turned about may touch in all parts, and may be turned without any impediment ; which when you have accomplished, you shall fit a bright Glass to this lump, and shall make it Parabolicall, which being foiled with Lead on the backside, which may reflect all Beames from the Sun equi-distant, which are the most forcible upon the point K. that is at a Mile distance, and will presently burn. These things are plainly demonstrated by *Archimedes,* as also *Antonius Gonzaga* hath brought it to us. *Card. de Subtil.*

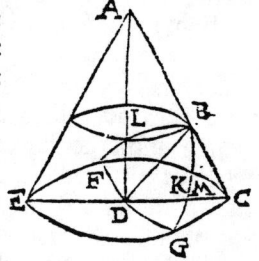

Fire out of Water.

That Fire may come forth of Water, Take an Egge-shell and put live Brimstone into it, and Quick-lime and shut the hole, and put it into water and it stirs and moves, and if Camphire be put upon the water it kindles and burns in the water. *Albertus Magnus.*

That all things may be revealed in Sleep.

A fume to see when one sleep what good or evill shall befall. Take the congealed blood of an Ass, and the fat of a Wolf and Storax, mingle all these in equall weight, and make them up, and forme them into Pellets, and perfume a house with them, and then you shall see in your sleep one that shall tell you all things. *The same.*

A Candle when it is lighted, is stirred here and there.

If you will make a Candle, or Wick, that being fired shall shake and go up and down Take the skin of a Wolf and of a Dog, and make a Wick of them both, and burn them with Oyle of Olives, and it will presently move. *The same.*

A light to make one Fart.

The Operation of this Lamp is wonderfull, which so long as a man holds it, he shall not leave Farting untill he let it go : Take the blood of a Snaile and dry it in Linnen Cloath,

Cloath, and make a Candle with it, and light it, and give it to whom he please, and say, be thou lighted: so shall he not leave Farting till he let it go, which is wonderfull. *Albertus.*

To make a whole Company fall a Sneezing altogether.

Take Guiny Pepper a greater or lesser quantity according to the Company, wrap it in brown Paper and put it into the Fire, and it shall make all that are near fall a Sneezing. Ld. *Bacon.*

A Candle which being lighted where Frogs are, they shall make no noise, but all be quiet.

Take the fat of a Crocodile, and make it up with Wax, white it in the Sun, and make a Candle of it, and light it in the place where Frogs are, and when they see that they will presently cease crying. *The same.*

A Candle that shews all manner of Colours.

A Glass Lamp very clear, and transparent, whatsoever it shines upon with its light, it will make them appear yellow, if Oyle next the Wick be sprinkled with powder of Saffron; of all other colours the same experiments holds, if there be no other light in the Chamber. *Mizaldus.*

A coloured Chamber.

You shall see the Chamber green thus: Let there be a green transparent Glass Lamp, that the beames passing through may be coloured with the Mediums colour, and (which most conduceth to this purpose, let Verdigrease be mingled with the Oyle, or all moist substance it feedeth on, let them be well ground together, that the Liquor may be green; let the Wick be of Linnen or Cotten of the same colour, or else provide it of Cotten smeered with it; Let it be burnt in that Lamp, the light that strikes upon what is against it, will shew all things green, as also the faces of the standers by. But if you desire to see all things black, mingle Inke or Sut therewithall or some such matter: but the best is the Inke that comes forth of the Cuttle, for put to Candles if they be lighted the flame is black. So some say *Anaxilaus* made sport; for oft-times with Cuttles Inke he made the standers by like Blackmoors, and extream black. If you grind all yellow things, as Orpiment, Saffron, Lupins Rinds, and mingle them with Oyle, and light a Candle's Wick in it, with a yellow Lamp, all will appear yellow. If you desire to have it partly green, partly black, partly yellow, mingle all these together, as *Simeon Sethi* saith, if a man dip a Wick in Cuttles Inke, and Verdigrease, Men that stand about it will appear partly green, partly black, by reason of the mixture of things. But I thinke the greatest care must be to take all other lights away that they hinder not by their light, and the colour that comes from the Lamp be overcome by them, and so the delusion should be frustrated: If it be in the day, shut the Windows, least any light coming in should make void the deceit. *The same.*

That in a Palace all things may appear black.

When you would have all things seem to be black in a Palace, Take froth of the Sea and Vitrioll, and mingle that with the Wicks, and wet the Candle with it, and light the Lamp therewith. *Albertus.*

That Frogs may not Croke in the night by a Lamp.

Albertus reports that if a Candle be made of the fat of a Dolphin, and Wax made white in the Sun, and then lighted and set on the banks of Lakes, that all the Frogs will leave Croking. But *Africanus* speaks more naturally and certainly in his *Geoponicks* in Greek, that all that will be performed by a Candle: for if you light it and set it there, all the Frogs will presently be silent. Impostors use to put a Frog in a hole boared in a Wall, and then they cover it with a Paper, and they paint a Crow upon it, lighting a Torch on the out side, or putting fire by it. The Frog Waxing hot will Croke, that you will thinke it is a Crow, so they shew you a Crow that cries. *The same.*

That one lighting a Lamp may be afraid of it.

Make Linnen Cloath of the Selvages, and in the middle let there be the cast Skin of a Snake, and let it be easily thrust into the skin, and put Salt to it, let some body be commanded to light this in Oyle: for when the Salt toucheth the fire, it will leap away

away, the Snakes skin winds it self strangely when it boyls, that it will make Children afraid; so if you light the skin of a Dog and a Wolf, or of a Woolf and a Sheep twisted together with Oyle, they will stirre, even then flying one from the other by an imbred antipathy. *The same.*

That Men may seem to be without Heads.

When you would have Men in the house seem to be without Heads: Take yellow Brimstone with Oyle, and put it in a Lamp, and light it and set it in the midst amongst men and you shall see a wonder. *Albertus.*

That Men may seem to want Heads.

Take a Snakes skin, Orpiment and Greek Pitch, Rhapontic, and Wax of young Bees, and the blood of an Ass, grind all together, and put all into a new earthen Pot full of water, and let it boyle at a gentle fire, afterwards let it cool, and make a Wax Candle, and every one that is in the light of it will seem to want a Head. *Albertus.*

That Standers by may seem to want Heads.

Let Orpiment finely powdred boyle in Oyle in a new earthen Pot: and it will not be amiss to put Brimstone to it, laying a cover upon it, that the yellow vapour may not flye away; light this in a new Lamp, and all that stand by will seem to want heads and hands: hold your eye close with your fingers, whilst you light the Candle, and you shall perceive by degrees how it is done. *The same.*

That the Standers by may seem to have Heads like to Horses or Asses.

You go about a very hard work: yet diligence in working will overcome the difficulty. Cut off a Horses or an Asses head, not when they are dead, least the virtue faile, and make an earthen Pot big enough to receive it, full of Oyle, and the fat of it, that it may swim above it; shut the mouth of it, and stop it fast with clay: put a gentle fire under, that the Oyle may boyle for three daies compleat, and the flesh sod may run to Oyle, and the bare Bones be seen. Beat it with a Pestle, and mingle dust with the Oyle, and with these annoint the heads of the standers by, likewise put in the middle of the Lamp some Wicks made of Hards, and let it stand not too neare, nor too far off, but as it is convenient for it, and you will seem to have a monstrous countenance. By these you may learn to make many more, for I have seemed to say enough, if you be diligent in them. Oyle drawn from a mans head newly cut off, will make Beasts seem with Mens faces. So with divers heads of Creatures you may make Monstrous bodies, if you make Lamps of them and light them to give light in the house; pray keep this for a Secret: for the Ancients keep these things close enough: nor can it easily be pickt out of their writings. Yet *Anaxilaus* teacheth you otherwise, and not amiss; you must take the venome that comes from Horses in copulation, and in new Lamps light the Candles made of it, and this will make Men seem Monsters with Horses heads, and the same is reported of Asses. So the matter that comes from Bores when they grunt after Sows, being preserved and put into a Lamp, when it is lighted will do the same. So will the filth pickt out of the Ears or secret parts of other Creatures do the like. If you shall burn that which we call Sperm, and annoint the Spectators faces with it, they will seem to have the head of those Creatures: keep this for a Secret. *The same.*

That Men may seem to have Dogs Heads.

Take the fat out of the Ear of a Dog, then put a little of it with new Cotton into a new Lamp of green Glass and set this Candle amongst Men, and they will all seem to have Dogs heads. *Albert. Mag.*

That Men may seem to have the Heads of any other Creatures.

Take Quick-Brimstone and Lithargyre, and these being powdered together, strew them into a Lamp that is full of Oyle, and a Candle must be made with Virgin-Wax which must be mingled with the fat of that Creature, whose head you would have one to appear to have; he holding this Candle lighted at the light of that Lamp; and give him some Wine to drink with a good farewell, and they that drinke of it will seem to have the head of that Creature. *Albertus.*

Secrets of seeming Transformation. Book III.

That Men may seem to have three Heads.

Take the haires of a dead Ass, and make a little Cord and dry it, take the Marrow of the principall bone of the right shoulder and mingle it with Virgin Wax, and annoint the cord, and put it upon the Threshold of the house: they that come into the house shall have three heads, and they that are in the house will appear to be Asses to them that come in. *Albert.*

That a Mans Head may appear like an Asses Head.

Take a piece of an Asses fat and annoint a Mans Head with it. *Albertus.*

A Candle that will make Men seem to have Horses Heads or any other Creatures Heads.

I have a long time thought much upon it, whether such Secrets as these were unknown to the Ancients: or where those things are true which are spoken of them, and are promised by Impostors; and I did not a little rejoyce when I found amongst the Ancients those that took great care of these things; especially *Anaxilaus*, giving credit to *Pliny* affirming them: and I have not laboured a little to find out these matters to fill up our History; and it is not in vain to remember them, and to bring them to light, and to make experiment of them; let him that tries them first be well experienced in these, and so by degrees pass on to other things: and first let men be taught how all things may be seen. *The same.*

That a Mans Face may appear very leane and pale.

You shall easily do it thus: Powre into a large Cup of Glass, Greek wine, cast Salt into it, a great handfull, set it on burning coales that do not flame, lest the Glass break, it will presently begin to boile, put a Candle to it and it will take fire; then put out all other lights, and all that stand there will have such Faces that they will be afraid one of another. The same thing falls out in places under ground where Bells are cast, and things made of Mettall, then all things that are in secret will look with a hideous complexion, that you will wonder at the wanness of mens Lips, they that looked red will appear black and blew. Also kindle Brimstone in the middle of those that are standers by, and it will work the more powerfully. So I find that *Anaxilaus* the Philosopher was wont to make sport. For he that shall carry about Brimstone put into a new Cup, with the fire put under it, will make all that are at a Feast look strangely by the repercussion of the Brimstone that burns. The same thing hath oft-times befell me by accident, when in the night I walked at *Naples* in the fields about the Hills called *Lucogæi*: for the Brimstone that burns of it self there gives such apparitions. *The same.*

That Men may seem to be Elephants.

Take winter Cherries and bruise them, mingle them with a little Dolphins fat, and make Balls of them as big as the Kernels of Pome-Citrons, then make a smoke of them over a fire of Cowdung, which Cow must be Milked, and stop all holes in the house that the smoke cannot get forth, except only at the doors, and let the Larch-tree be under ground within side. For all that are in the house will appear to be great Men in the fashion of Horses and Elephants, and this is wonderfull strange. *Albertus.*

That Men may seem to be in a various form.

Take the eyes of an Owle, and of a Fish called *Libinitie*, and the Gall of a Woolf, pound them together and mingle them with your hands, and put them into a glased Vessell, when therefore you would work with it, take the fat of any Beast, that this may become of the same forme; melt the fat and mingle it with that Medicament, and annoint with Oyle what Candle wick you please, then set it in the middle of the house, and all the people in the house will seem to be like that Beast whose fat you took. *Albertus.*

That Men may look like Angels.

Take the eyes of a Fish, and the eyes of an Osprey, and bruise them and work them with your hands, and put them into a glased Vessell seaven daies, then powre some Oyle to them, and make a light of it in a green Lamp, and set it before men that are in the house, for they shall appear in the forme of Angels by reason of the light that is lighted. *Albert.*

That Men may appear black.

Take a black Lamp, and powre upon it Oyle of Elder of Quick-silver, powre into that Oyle of Quick-silver blood that is reserved after blood letting, and put into that blood Oyle of Elder or Quick-silver. *Albert.*

Another Lamp that will make Men appeare in a filthy fashion.

Men will be afraid one of another, and they will look like Devils. Take the haires of the taile of a black Dog, amongst which there must be no white haire, and take some of his fat, melt the fat, then take a Funerall Cloth and make a wick of it, then annoint it with that, and light it in a green Lamp with Oyle of Elder, and let it burn in the house, and let there be no other light there, and thou shalt see wonders. *Albertus.*

A Lamp that a Man holding in his hand, shall see no body that is there present.

But he shall only see him that stands behind him. Take a Fish called a Dolphin: then take Linnen Cloath or Funerall Cloth, and sprinkle upon it something besides Azimat, powre upon it some of that melted fat: then take it in your hand and wrap it up into a wick, light it in a Lamp, and you shall be green, and it shall come to pass as I said. *Albertus.*

To make a house look Silver colour'd, and very light.

If you desire it you shall do it thus. Cut off the tailes of black Lizards, what drops cleare from it keep for use: and you must take what you can get from many of them and put it together, you must wet a wick of Paper or of Broome, and if you can mingle some Oyle with it; and so you shall see all things look of a Silver colour, you shall do the like in all other things. Now to proceed in the order intended, I shall set down the other Experiments, following the same method, that I may not withhold those any longer that are very desirous to read them.

That all things may seem white and Silver coloured.

Take a Lizard and cut off his tail, and receive what drops from it, because it is like to Quicksilver: then take a wick, wet it with Oyle, and put it into a new Lamp, and light it in a house, and it will appear bright, white and like Silver. *Albert.*

That the whole house may appear green and full of Serpents, and fearfull sights.

Take the skin of a Snake and the blood of another Snake that is a Hee, and the fat of another Snake, put all these three together, and put them into a Funerall Cloth, light them in a new Lamp. *Albert.*

That the whole house may seem full of Serpents.

Take the fat of a Snake, and put a little Salt to it, and take a Hearse Cloath, and cut it into four pieces: then take the fat and put it into any Cloath, light this and set it in four corners of the house with Oyle of Elders in a new Lamp, and you shall find what I said to be true. *Albert.*

A faire light that the house may seem all full of Serpents, so long as the wick doth burn.

Take the fat of a black Snake, and the skin of a black Snake and a Hearse Cloath, and make a Candle of that Cloath: then annoint the wick with that fat, and put the Snakes skin into the hollow part within it, and light it with Oyle of Elders in a green or black Lamp. *Albert.*

To see a house full of Grapes; and all Men shall be deceived with the delusion of the Grapes.

When the Grape begins to bud, set a Vessell full of pure Oyle underneath, into this dip the bough with the leaves: make it fast that the wind drive it not here and there, nor let the Sun shine upon it, covering it with Plaister and Leather, yet leaving a hole whereby the stalke may be put in, and so let it remain; when the Grape comes to its full ripeness, let it be crushed forth through a Linnen Cloath, and keep the juyce pressed forth, in Oyle, a few daies in the Sun, at least lighting Candles made with this you shall see all places full of Grapes, and to be compassed about with leaves and trees, when perhaps other trees want leaves: do the same with other fruits, for I think it will hold in others also. *The same.*

To see green things look flying.

Take a new Hearse Cloth, and put the brain of a Bird into it, and the feathers of his taile, and wrap them up, and make a wick of them, and put it into a new green Lamp; light this in a house with Oyl of Olives, and all things in the house shall become very green, and they shall appear flying, green and black. *Albertus.*

A light wherein the Stars will seem to wander.

Some burn a Snaile or Centaury, and by the smoke of that flame they see the Stars wandering so, and they will seem to move from their places all the Heavens over: and this comes not to pass from this only, but from the smoake of any thing. For he that stands in the place where a thing diaphanous is thickest, the forme of any thing movable will seem to him to wander from the place where it is: for his sight is deluded and he will think it moves. Now if you desire to do this to greater wonder, hide the fire that the beholder may not perceive there is any, and the beames passing through may be refracted: thus an ingenuous man may do many rare things to delude the sight, which he may learn out of Books concerning Opticks. *The same.*

A Lamp that when it is lighted, the standers by shall seem one to another, like Images and Stanes.

Take Zimat and pound it well, and take a Hearse Cloath and wet it in Fish fat, or with pure Oyle of Sesama, put it into a green Lamp, and put a little of this Medicament upon any thing, and you shall see a wonderfull thing. When this Candle is lighted they will all laugh and dance, and be mad for joy, and especially women. And take the blood of a Hare and the blood of a certain Bird called Solon, and it is like a Turtle, and take half as much of the blood of a male Turtle. Powre this into a Lamp and light it in the middle of the house wherein Maids and Women are singing; and it is wonderfull and proved. *Albertus.*

A light that will burn, if you press it hard with your hand; but if easily, you will put it out.

Draw water from Camphire in glass Chymicall Vessels, and make the vent holes right with Clay, that the spirits may not flye out forcibly, with this annoint your hands within and upon the flame if you hold it fast it will much burn your fist, but if you open your hand you weaken the force of it. *The same.*

Another Caudle, which when it is lighted, and water is powred upon it, it groweth stronger, but if you poure on Oyle, you put it out.

Take Quick-lime that was never quenched in water, and mingle it with an equall weight of Wax, and half so much of Balsam, of yellow Naptha, with as much Brimstone, make a light of this, and sprinkle water upon it, and it will burn the more; but Oyle sprinkled on it will put it out. *Albertus.*

Of many experiments of Lamps.

I see there are many experiments of Lamps yet behind, which though they are not so pleasant and wonderfull as the matter requires, yet that I may not seem to omit any thing, I thought fit to set them down, it will not be needless or useless to set them in the first rank following.

To make Women rejoyce mightily.

Make Candles of the fat of Hares and light them, and let them stand awhile in the middle where Women are: they will not be so merry as to dance; yet sometimes that falls out also. *The same.*

To make a Carbunkle or any thing to shine in the night.

Take Glow-worms that shine in the night a great number, and stamp them and put them into a Glass Viol and stop it; bury it in hot Horse-dung, and let it stay there fifteen daies, then distill water from them with a Limbeck: lay this up in a Crystall or Glass Vessel, for it will give so great light, that in a dark place any man may read or write: some make this water of Glow-worms, the gall of a Snaile, the gall of a Weasil, the gall of a Wolf, and of a water Dog; they bury them in dung, and distill water out of them. *Albertus.*

Take Wax, Brimstone, Vinegar, of each a part, boyle them together untill the Vinegar be consumed, afterwards make Candles of them, which being lighted cannot be put out. *Roscellus.*

To make Fire with Raine.

Take Oyle of Peter, Quick-Brimstone, yellow Brimstone, fresh Quick-lime, Greek Pitch, Ship Pitch : mingle these, and this mixture will take fire in any moisture. *Falloptus.*

Of the Earth. Chap. 3.
A vessell that shall send forth Wind.

This may be done, if you make a wind ball of Brass, or some other mettall, it must be round and hollow, and in the Belly of it must have a very narrow hole to poure water into it, and if it be difficult outwardly, use the former experiment: when it waxeth hot by the fire, having but a small vent it will blow strongly, but it will be a moist vapour and of an ill sent if it be thick. *The same.*

To correct pestilent Aire.

Without any danger many things of a very ill sent will correct it, as Castoreum, Galbanum, Sagapenum, Brimstone, the smell of Horns and Leather burnt, and Gunpowder; which is a most present remedy to drive away the Plague, was put in practice (saith *Lemnius*) in former ages, when at *Tornay* in *France*, a violent Pestilence was amongst them; for the guardian Souldiers that kept watch in the Tower fil'd their great Guns with Powder, without Bullets, and shot them off toward the City, and this they did in the morning light, and at twilight late in the evening: hence it came to pass, that by the huge noise and the filthy smoake of the powder, the contagion of the Ayre was discussed and drove it to some other place. *Mizaldus.*

Of Water. Chap. 5.
To make Sea-water fit for use.

Take Salt-water a good quantity out of the deep Sea where no fresh water comes, parch a pound and half of Salt, and mingle it with a stick together, untill such time as a Hen Egge boyld will swim upon it, then leave stirring it, and poure to it two gallons of old Wine, or white Wine, and mingle all well together: after this mingle them in a Vessell Pitched within, and smeer it all over. If you desire to prepare more Salt-water, observe the quantity by the same proportion, and you may do it. *Cato de re rustica.*

To part water from Wine.

If you put a Linnen Rag into Wine mingled with water, and let it hang without the Vessell, the water will all come forth of the Vessell by the rag, and will leave all the wine behind in the Vessell. By this experiment you may discover what is mixt from what is pure wine, nor could this be done if the wine did mingle with the water. *Card. de Subtilitat.*

Burning Ice.

If a Candle be smeered over with powder of Brimstone and Charcole put into water in Winter time, being covered on the upper part with Paper, and be hanged where Ice drops, it will be compassed round with a thick Ice, then if you light the Candle it will burn, and it will be a great wonder to those that are present to see the Ice burne. *Card. de Subtilitat.*

How one may safely go over Rivers.

Rivers are best past over with a thick Leathern Gut, and when need is, blow it up as well as you can, and tying both ends, bind it under your Arme pits: Thus both Horsemen and Footmen may safely go into Rivers in great necessity, and sometimes by this help only they may venture to pass. Also it is more safe to be done with Drums of Leather put under their feet, and with a staffe with a Leather Drum at the end of it, for so they may not only wade over, but also walk upon the water, and it will seem almost miraculous. *Card. de Subtilitat.*

That a Vessell turned downwards may draw up water.

You shall do it thus: prepare a Vessell with a very long neck, the longer it is, so much the greater wonder: It must be glass and transparent that you may see the water ascend; fill this with boyling water, whereby it may be very hot all over, or else set the bottom of it to the fire, and presently that it grow not cold, turn the mouth down that it may touch the water, and may only suck it in: so those that search into natures Secrets, saying, that water is drawn up and suckt away by the Sun-beams, from the hollow places of the earth in Mountains, whence Fountains have their originall: nor are they small experiments that arise from hence in Mechanicall Engines; as *Hieron* saith, but being not proper to this place I shall place them where they are more convenient to be handled. *Vitruvius* hath the like relation concerning the originall of carriages for burdens, but now they are usuall with most men. *The same.*

Aqua Fortis.

Take Allum, and Vitriol, or Saltpeter, or all three calcined, of each one part, powder them, mingle them, and put them into a gr oud Vessell, well luted, then into the Vessell that receives them, put two ounces of water for every pound of the powder: which being done, place it so without any cover, but let the mouth of the Retort be joyned with the receiver with flower and white of Eggs, that no respiration of it may be possible. Let the Vessell receiving be set in cold water, and continually wet it over with wet Linnen Cloaths. For so it will come to pass that the spirits will unite better with the water of them, and they shall not stick to the receiver. When you have done this kindle the fire, first very gently, and under the report only untill the matters be dissolved; then annoint it, and put also above the Retort Charcole well fired, and augment the fire for five or six hours, then let it cool: afterwards take out the water, and keep it for use in some vessell well stopt. But the fire must be so made, that the receiver may not be any way broken by it, but if you desire to make any stronger *Aqua Fortis,* adde of Saltpeter two parts unto it. *Alexius.*

How to make Saltwater Potable.

If you make a Vessell of Wax hollow and empty, and dip it into the Sea, the water that gets in by the pores of the Wax will be potable: so an earthen pot not baked if the mouth be close stopt, will purifie the water, for that which strains through it, is made fresh, which was salt before. It is done otherwise more plentifully and speedily, put fresh water Sand into salt water, and stay awhile, putting a Linnen Cloath before the mouth of the Vessell under that must receive it, it will be strained through, and will be fresh, having lost all its saltness. *The same.*

Water against Locusts.

Chuerch is a City of the *Scythians* of *Cataonia,* in which there is a Lake that drives away Locusts: of old for that very cause the King of *Cyprus* sent for Water from thence, a vessel full whereof being hanged upon a Tower made of Pewter, it came to pass that at that time the Island was not troubled with Locusts. *Scaliger.*

To heat Water without Fire.

If a brass vessel that is large and round, and hath but one hole open in it, be filled with Quick-lime and Brimstone, of each a like quantity equally and perfectly mingled, and the hole be diligently stopped that there be no vent, and it be presently let down into a well or pit that runs not forth, it will keep that water hot many dayes, and will make this good, as many men have tried it. *Mizaldus.*

Of the Earth. Chap. 5.
Burning Earth.

There is between *Lazige Metanaste,* black earth that partakes of bitumen and petroleum, nor unlike to wax for the calmness and use thereof: For it will burn like to a Candle, I saw of it with the Arch-Bishop, who was Embassadour for the King of *Pannonia.* But hereafter I shall say that these things are wonderfull, and so may others now say who never saw what I shall write concerning Earth in *Scotland*: But when we see the stone burn like a Candle we cease admiring. *Cardan. de varietate rerum.*

The way to make Lutum sapientiæ.

Take the best Potters earth, wherewith Earthen Vessels are made, be it white or ash colour, four parts, common Ashes half a part, Horse or Asses dung dried one part, and

and if you will have it more perfect, adde Bricks powdred, or some small quantity of the Filings of Iron, make very fine powder of them, sift, and mingle them: then put them into the Earth, sprinkling upon them by degrees some shearings of Wollen Cloath, which is called Flocks, one part, common water what is sufficient, then mingle them. Then put them orderly into the Earth, sprinkling by little and little upon them, first the Flocks that they may be strewed equally over it; then the water, then mingle all well together; first with some Staff, afterwards with a Shovell, and make a Mass. This when it is well mingled, must be laid upon a Planke or a Wall, and there trod, and with a shovell well beaten, untill it seem to be enough: for the longer it is beaten and mingled, the better it will be. This lute is good to lute Glasses, to make grosser kinds of forms or molds, to make Furnaces, and many other things. But if you will not spend so much labour to make Lute, Take only Potters Earth, Flocks, Ashes a little, and dung. Some make it without dung, others without Flocks, each following his own design. But to lute the mouths of Glass Vessels, that they may not breath through, the foresaid lute is good; especially if you adde Quicklime two parts, and whites of Eggs, what shall seem sufficient: for so it is safer, and grows hard like to Glass; whence it is, that the Glass cannot easily breath through it. Moreover such lute must be kept in some moist place, yet so, that it become neither too moist nor too dry; for if it once grow hard, it is of no use. For if you would soften it with water, it will be wet a little on the out side, but within it will keep its hardness. Wherefore when it it is too hard, let it dry exceedingly, then powder it, and do with it as you did before. *Alex.*

Why Bricks burnt are more heavy.

But that is a wonder, that some say Bricks burnt are more heavy then they were before they were put into the Furnace. The reason may be because when they are made, they are dried in the Sun, and they receive a great quantity of Ayre, which lying within makes the stone much lighter, then it is when it is baked in the fire: wherefore when the Brick is burnt, it grows more heavy though the moysture be spent. Also Bricks burnt more then enough look like Iron colour: whence the same thing may be the cause both of their weight and colour: It is small in respect of the matter, but that smallness is made by force, and by melting the earth that hath some what of mettall in it, wherefore almost continually, when Bricks are bakt more then they should be, they are bent and wrested crooked. But that is a great Question, why if the fire be stopt in the Furnace, but never so little, the Bricks should break? yet that is not alwaies, but when immoderate heat is contracted by the fire ceasing, then it will break the Bricks. Also the same, when it is kindled again will break them: for the things that are now dry, when they wax hot with new heat, they breake: as we see in Glass. The reason is, because before that which is hard, melt and can be softned, the wind distending it, it breaks. Wherefore by reason of that inequality Potters suffer great loss. *Cardan. de Subtilitate.*

BOOK. IV.

I have dispatched those parts of the work called Integrals, in the former Book: but now since I must treat of those things that are contained in those parts; first of all I shall speak of Man, namely because he is the most noble workmanship of all Gods works, and for whose sake not onely the world, but all things contained in it were created. But since the Secrets are many that are referred to Man, and they are comprehended under divers heads, they must not be comprehended in one, but in two Books. The first whereof shall contain Remedies for the Minde, and the next for the Body. To the Minde we refer the Affections, which men call Passions of the Soul, namely Love, Hatred, and the like. Also the Internall faculties of the Soul, as Memory, Phantasie, Reasoning, that produce no work without themselves, are the governesses of outward actions.

Of the Minde.
How to strengthen the Memory.

It is a wonder that some report, how that the Tooth of a Badger, or his left Foot bound to a Mans right Arm, will strengthen the Memory. But perchance that is more likely which *Simeon Sethi* saith, namely that the gall of a Partridge smeered upon the temples arteries once in a moneth that it may penetrate, doth profit much to confirm the Memory. Also Balme confirms it and sharpneth the wit; for eaten it will make a man industrious, which also Cresses may do. Also the brains of a Hen do help the wit and memory, so that it hath recovered some who began to dote. But Balme besides this doth make the minde quiet, and merry, exceedingly driving away cares; so eaten after supper it makes pleasant sleep, as Cabbage makes sad sleep, and French Beans troubled sleep, and Onions or Garlick make fearfull sleep. Hence from these grew the opinion of Hags, who feeding upon Smallage, Chesnuts, Beans, Onyons, Cabbage and French Beans, seem in their sleep to fly into divers Countries, and to be diversly affected, as their temperaments are severall. *Cardan de Subtil.*

To procure Love.

You must know that the power of natural things is so great, that not onely they affect all things that come near to them with their vertue, but besides this they infuse the like power into them whereby they by the same vertue affect other things; as we see in the Loadstone, which stone not onely draweth iron Rings, but infuseth its force into the Rings, that they can do the same, as *August.* and *Albertus* report they saw it. Likewise Rings for a certain time are put into a Sparows nest, or Swallows nest, which we use afterwards to procure Love or good will. *Cornel. Agrip.*

To dissolve Witchcraft.

If any woman hath bound thee by Witchcraft to love her, and thou wouldest fain dissolve it, take her smock and piss through the neck of it, and through the right sleeve of the smock, and you need not fear what she can do. *Albertus.*

Another to dissolve Witchcraft.

If you would dissolve the chains of Love, go into a wood, and finde where the Woodpecker builds her nest with her young ones; and when you come there climbe up the tree, and binde up the hole as well as you can; for when she sees you, she will flie for an herb, which she layes upon the band, and it breaks presently, and then the herb falls down to the ground upon a cloth that you must lay under the tree to catch it; be sure you watch and take it. *Albertus.*

To increase Memory.

The whitest Frankincense beaten into fine powder, and drank with Wine if it be cold, or water of decoction of Raysins; but in Summer drank in the increase of the Moon, when the Sun riseth, and also at noon, and Sun setting, will wonderfully increase the memory, and profit the brain and stomach. *Rhasis.*

To make the Husband and Wife to agree alwayes.

Orpheus in his Book of Stones, bids the Man to carry with him a Harts horn, for so he

Book IV. *Secrets of the Internall parts of Man.* 31

he promiseth that the Man shall alwaies have peace with his Wife. *Mizal. Memor.*
The heart of a male Quale carried by the Man, and the heart of a female Quale by the Woman, will cause that no quarrels can ever arise between them. *Mizal. Memor.*

How to provoke Love.

It was my purpose at first to do all things onely by naturall meanes, and especially those things that are done by the wicked Magicians arts, utterly to confute their Science, for they ensnare the minds of men with these gives and fetters of errors, for many men follow this, and I see that many men are much tormented by these deceitfull pleasant Baits, and that they admire exceedingly, and that those wits that are the most sublime, fall to ruine; such indeed as are most desirous to learn. I shall not be troubled to rehearse those things out of them that procure love, not at all deviating from nature, who recovers what was alienated from her: Let the Readers take all in good part. Wherefore to begin; it is worth knowing, That I have no other intention, than kindle the sparks of love in the minds of Men or Women, to make them more mild, and obedient to our will; and since this comes to pass by such things, whose power of working lyeth secretly in them: I shall make use of those, whereof some I have had experience of from our forefathers, and many more are found out by the industry of men of later times. And in the first place *Hippomanes* was by the Antients commended to the Skies, however there were some that have added many old Wives Fables, that Women are delighted with, who perhaps are addicted to demonstrations, and give no credit to miracles, that are wonderfull in nature, or to their hidden causes: But evident experience is against them; that appoint poyson of two sorts, one distilling from the obscæne parts of Mares, when they are overstrongly stimulated with fury of lust, is thus spoken of by *Virgil*;

> *Then Hippomanes (for Shepheards call it so)*
> *Distils as Venome from their parts below.*
> *Hippomanes, that wicked Stepdames pluck*
> *Mingling with Herbs bad words, that bring bad luck.*

Hence *Tibullus* sings;
> *Hippomanes drops from Mares that would be Horsed.*

This is not unfit for the purpose, for I have shewed how to use it in another place, and shall shew the forces when it shall be convenient: The other is as great as a Fig, and is round and broad, almost black, and it grows to the forehead of a new foaled Colt, and the Mare so soon as she hath foaled, devoureth her after burden, and forgetting labour, by licking and wipeing it, she pulls up that which is called *Hippomanes*; now if any man take this away before, the Mare will not let her Colt suck; She hates it, and beats it away, as if it were none of her own, and will never love it. Which *Virgil* in his Æneiads well describes.

> *From the young Colts forehead that pluckt off,*
> *Takes from the Dame her love.*

Wherefore it was no absurd opinion to thinke flesh did procure love, and to be a great inticement to it, and that something to help lovers was bred in it: And *Pausanias* delivers this, *Ælian* doth not omit it, that *Phormis Areus* knew that there was so great virtue in it, that with this being mingled with Brass, and powred forth, he made a Mare, cutting of the Taile, wherein he had included *Hippomanes*, that by that Mare of Brass, Horses might be so much deceived, that only at the sight of it, they should grow furious: for it did so allure them, and made them so mad, that breaking their Halters, they would run with more fury upon this, then upon a living Mare. For though their Hoofs slipt from this statue of Brass, they would not forbear it, but thereby they would be more hot, and Neigh more exceedingly over it. Nor would they be beaten off, but with Whips, and the great violence used by their Grooms that guided them. Hence was this name given to it *Hippomanes*,

F 2

nes, that after the similitude of the desire of Horses, it will make Men mad with Love, and run violently after it: and Men of great authority say, they know this to be true: and if a Snakes skin be cast from them, when they are bent upon the course of nature, it will so twist it self when it is cast into the fire, that it will afright Children: If you twist a Wolf and Dogs skin together, or a Wolf and a Lambskin, and light them with Oyle, they will move here and there, shewing how they shun one the other by an imbred hatred. *Albertus* saith the same.

To make a Man bold and confident.

Take the heart of an Ape, and tye it about your neck, letting it hang just over your heart, and it will increase Audacity. Lord *Bacon*.

To prosure love.

All men will love thee, if thou carry with thee a Swallows heart: and a Woman will love him exceedingly, from whom she shall receive the powder of a Pigeons heart in meat or drinke. Moreover if any one put but some Hares gall under his head, he shall sleep perpetually, but you shall raise him well enough, if you give him Vinegar to drink. Out of the fabulous Tales of *Albertus*. *Mizaldus Memor*.

Of Inchantment, and how one may be ensnared by it.

Now I shall speak of Charms, and I shall not neglect to set down some that were Charmers. For if you please to see the Monuments of the Ancients, you shall see that many things of this kind are delivered by them to posterity, and the new inventions of this latter Age, do agree with the Ancient form that was not absolutely in vain. Nor do I think I need detract from the credit of Histories, it cannot fit true causes to things, by strong reasons. Moreover many things are not to be searched out: But what I think of other operations, I thought fit to publish: you shall find very much in *Theocritus* and *Virgil*;

I know not who with eyes hath charm'd my tender Lambs.

Isigonus and *Memphrodorus* say, That in *Africa* there are some Families that have power to Charme Men with their voices and tongues, and if perhaps they praise very much, or admire more then it is fit, faire Trees, rank Corn Fields, fine Children, brave Horses, or fat and well fed Cattle, they will presently wax lean, and dye suddenly: and there is no other reason to be given for it; which also *Solinus* writes. The same *Isigonus* saith, That the *Triballi* and people of *Sclavonia*, are many of this kind, who have two Pupills in their eye, and bewitch desperately those they behold; so that they will kill those they look long upon, especially if they be angry, so dangerous is their sight; young Striplings feel the most hurt by them. *Apollonides Philarchus* saith, That in *Scythia* there are such Women called *Bithia*, and another sort called *Tibii*, and many more of this kind: in one of whose eyes you may see two Apples; and in the other eye the likeness of a Horse: *Didymus* makes mention also of them. *Dæmon* speaks of some such Charme in *Æthiopia*, whose sweat if but touched, would make a body fall into a Consumption, and it is evident that all Women will Charme, that have two Apples in their eye. *Tully* also writes of them: So *Plutarch* and *Philarchus* speaks of Nations living about *Pontus*, that can enchant others, not only young people who are of a weak temper, but strong, well grown people, and by their venemous looks, they will make them languish, and fall into consumptions, and to dye thereof: and not only such as alwaies keep company with them, but such as are strangers to them, and very far from holding any commerce with them, are inchanted by them: and though the witchcraft be performed often by touching, and mingling of meats and drinks, yet is it frequently performed by sight, such force is in their eyes as it were a destroying spirit, passeth from their eyes to the heart of him that is bewitched, that totally infects him. So it falls out that a young Man that hath clear subtile, hot fresh blood yields such spirits, because they arise from the heat of his heart, and more pure blood, because the lightest spirits ascend to the upper part of the body, and are cast forth by the eyes, which are full of parts and veins, and the brightest of all the parts: and with the spirit it self at once, there is cast forth with the rayes a fiery force; that those that look upon red and blear eyes,

use

use to fall into the same disease; and such a mischance had I: for this infects the Ayre, and that being infected, infects another: so the Ayre next the eyes carrying with it the vapour of the blood, corrupted with whose contagion the beholders catch the same redness in their eyes. So a Wolf takes a Mans voice away, and a Basilisk, kils a man, which by sight raiseth poyson, and with the very raises darts forth deadly wounds. But as it is with a Looking-glass, by reflection the beams are cast back, again upon the Authour of them. So Women that are not clean, as *Aristotle* saith, are afraid to behold a clear Looking-glass, and the Glass will be dull by such a one looking upon it: and this comes to pass, because a bloody vapour, by reason of the brightness of the Glass, unites into one, and makes a kind of foulness upon it, which is clearly seen; and you shall very hardly wash this spot from a new Glass, which doth not fall out alike in a Cloath, or a stone, because in that it goes on and comes down to the depth of it, but upon a stone it is dissipated, because of the unevenness of the parts; But the Glass being hard, stands against it, and being smooth keeps it unbroken, and being cold by congealing the Ayre it makes drops; after the same manner, if you breath upon a clear Glass, the superficies of it will be moist with your moysture of your mouth, and the thinner part will run down: So from the eyes the beams are sent forth, which carry the spirits, and these coming to the eyes of the beholder, strike through them, and affect the inward parts of him that is thus stricken, and runs to the heart of him, as the proper place from whence the spirits first grow: so are they congealed into blood about the lapse of the heart, and this inchanted blood, differing from the naturall blood of him that receives it, corrupts all the rest of his blood, and so he falls sick, the contagion remaining as long as the force of that venemous blood is in his body, and since it is an affection of blood, he ever sees with an un intermitting Feaver, and if it proceed from Choler or Flegm, perhaps it might remit sometimes. But to make all more clear, we must first know, that in Authors we shall read of two kinds of Fascination: one of love, another of hate and envy: and if it proceed from love or desire, of one that is beautifull, though the beams be cast at a great distance; yet the venome is taken in by the eyes, and the Image of the faire Object, sits close to the lovers heart and kindleth; whence he is wont to be alwaies tormented; and because the blood of the beloved is so deare to him, it wanders in him, often represents the party, and shines in his blood, and is never quiet, and it is so drawn by him, that the blood of him that wounds, falls upon him that makes the wound. *Lucretius* doth describe it after his fashion;

> Love doth the body touch that wounds the mind,
> For commonly all wounded are; we find
> The Blood will there appear, where is the blow,
> If it be neare, the face blood-red will showe.

But if envy or ill will bewitch any one, that is very dangerous, and commonly this venome proceeds most from old Women. Nor can any man deny, but if the mind be wounded, the body must needs be ill; and the mind affected, fortifies the body, and makes it more vigorous; and it not only changeth a mans own body, but it will change another mans; and so much the more, as the desire of revenge is greater in the heart: will not covetousness, sorrow, love, change a mans colour and complexion? doth not envy make one exceeding pale and lean? will not a Teeming Woman make a marke upon the Child in the Womb when She longs, like the thing shee desires? So when envy bends her cruell sight with desire of revenge, and the mischievous beams shine more forcibly from her eyes, and the heat flies from her, she doth much harm to the fairest bodies of those that are neare her; and like a dart it strikes into their eyes, and burns their hearts, and makes them lean, especially if they be Cholerick or Sanguine: for by the opening of the pores, and subtilty of the humours, the disease easily feeds upon them. And not only is the body made so by passion, but *Avicenna* proves, that venome may be easily found in a mans body: Many are venemous by nature, and therefore it is no wonder if some be made

such

such by Art. The Queen of the *Indies* sent to *Alexander* a very beautifull Virgin, that was fed with the Poyson of Adders, as *Aristotle* writes : and *Avicenna* upon the authority of *Rufus* reports it ; and *Galen* saith there was another that would eat Henbane safely, and a third that would devoure Wolfs-bane, that no Hen would come near to it, and by the frequent use thereof as I find in the old Writers, *Mithridates* King of *Pontus* made venome so naturall to him, that when he would have poysoned himself, that he might not yield himself to the *Romans*, he could find no hurt by taking poyson. If you give Hens that are fatted with Adders and Lizards flesh, or them boyl'd with wheate in Broth, to Hawks to feed on, they will sooner cast their Feathers, and many more things will be done, which are too long to record here : So there are many men that naturally have power by touching to cure diseases. Many men by eating Spiders and Oleander, fear no biting of Serpents, nor do they regard any venome if it be agreeing to their nature : but their very sight or breath that proceeds from them, will not only consume men, but Plants and other things, that they will wither away, and ofttimes where such venemous Creatures lurk, the Corn will decay and participate of their venome, only by their eyes and the venemous breath proceeds from them. Do not Women that have their tearms on them, infect Cucumbers, and Pompions, by touching and looking upon them that they will consume by it ? Are not Children handled more safely by Men, than by Women? and you shall find more Women that are Witches than you shall Men, by reason of their Complexion : for they are further from a wholesome temperament, and they will feed on things more hurtfull, so that every Moneth they are filled with more superfluities, and melancholy blood boyls forth whence vapours arise up to their sight, and they send forth venemous fumes to those that stand by them, and fill the body therewith. But if you be in Love with a young Maid, and would Charme her to love you, (or if a Woman would do the like to a Man,) how it may be done : *See the same.*

The manner how to make one in Love with you.

They must be of complexion sanguin, and some also are partly cholerick; they must have large eyes, shining and fiery, and it is much to the purpose that they live chastly, lest by frequent copulation the juyce of the humours be exhausted ; then by frequent looking on, and by very long imagination, at a convenient distance, let them set their eyes right against the eyes of another, beams against beams, and sight against sight, so by looking on of both parties love is kindled, and taken in. But why the party looked upon should be taken with your enchantment, and not with any other, may be understood by this and the former reason : It proceeds from the intention of the party that enchants, for the spirits or vapours are sent away to the party to be allured, and the party being thereby affected is made like to the person affecting : for that passion or imagination being very much fixed, and being a continuing habit, about the thing desired, hath a command of the spirits and blood : then the thing being wished for, the other person may be taken with the goodness of it, and so be inflamed with the love of it. Although the minde (as *Avicenna* sayes) by onely desiring, and by the power it hath, may produce such affections. *Musaeus* saith, that the eye layes the foundation of love, and are the chiefest allurements, and *Diogenianus* writes, that affection comes by sight, for a thing unknown cannot be said to be beloved ; and *Juvenal* makes it monstrous

That one should love a Maid he never saw.

For the clear cast of the eyes makes one mad after her he sees, and the ground-work of love is laid by it. The other parts do not truly give the cause ; but they move so far, that when a man sees one he likes, he will stay to behold her beauty, and staying he is taken by the sight of the eyes, and there men report that *Cupid* lies and shoots his darts, which being sent from the eyes, hit the others eyes, and so wound her heart. *Apuleius.* For those eyes of thine coming through my eyes into my breast, kindle a most fierce fire in my marrow. I have shewed to you that seek for it, no small ground, unless you want reason to understand, and you may be confirmed with many more arguments. If perhaps any shall wonder, considering disenses that come

by

by contagion, as itch, scabs, blear eyes, plague; if a man may be infected by touching, seeing, speaking, and catch these diseases; why the contagion of love, which is the greatest plague of all diseases, should not presently take hold of a man and totally consume him? Nor doth it take in others only, but it falls back into themselves, and they themselves draw the Inchantment to themselves that thus enchant others. Also in old Authors we read of *Eutelida*, who by reflexion from waters or looking glasses that represented the Image of himself, he became in love with it to his own destruction: He seemed so fair in his own eyes, that he was destroyed by the same enchantment he had destroyed others with: so he lost his former shape of his body, and was punished for a peculiar desire. So children do hurt themselves by their own enchantments; and their parents ascribe the cause to Witches. *The same.*

To continue Love once obtained.

Procure such a quantity of Hair of the party beloved as will make a Ring or a Bracelet, and wear it either on your finger or wrist, and it shall by secret exciting the Imagination produce its certain effect. *Lady* Danoegh's *manuscript*.

For those that are enchanted and bewitched by Women.

Put of the excrements of the womans belly in the morning, some part into the right sock of him that is bewitched, and so soon as he smels the stink of it, the witchcraft is ended. *Alexius.*

Another.

Put Quicksilver into a quill or an empty small-nut shell, and stop it in with wax, and lay it under the pillow of one that is bewitched; or lay it under the threshold of the door that he goes into the house by, or in his chamber, and it is a certain cure. *The same.*

Another.

Let him that is bewitched annoint his body over with Oyl of Crows, and Oyl of Sesamine.

Another.

The smoak of a dead mans tooth is a remedy that will perfectly do it. If a man carry with him the heart of a male Rook, and the woman the heart of a female Rook, they shall alway agree. *Alexius.*

A Love Charm.

These are Charms of themselves; the brain of Murilegus, and of a she Lizard; the menstrual blood of a whore, a Lizard called *Stincus*; so is *Hippomanes*. All these things rather change the minde, than compell one to love them from whom they take them. But they are commonly made of excrements, or of creatures bred of putrefaction, or of the seed of Man; as is that made of it, and the matrix of a Bitch that is salt; if a Dog be kept long by her and not admitted to her, then he runs almost mad for lust. There are other Love-Charms which are not to be eaten, that are taken from dead mens cloaths, Candles, Measures, needles, and generally such things as are provided for Funerals. *Card. de Subtilitat.*

The cure of Love from Enchantment.

There are many things which our wise Ancestors ordered for this purpose. If you would remove a Love-Charm, you shall do it thus: Turn away your sight, that the party may not look upon your eyes, nor set his eye-sight against yours; for whence love useth to proceed, from thence remove the cause: avoid the company continually, fly from idleness, employ your mind about weighty matters; let blood, sweat and void all excrements abundantly, that also ill air may be cast forth; also there are other things contrary to the first. If it be an Enchantment of envious people, you shall know it thus; the person shall lose his colour, shall hardly lift up his eyes, alwaies stoops downwards, sighs often, is pent up, and yet there is no sign to be seen of any hurt he hath; he weeps abundantly salt and bitter tears. To cure him from his Enchantment, you must make sweet perfumes, because the air is contagious and polluted, to correct the air, and also by sprinkling of Water, Cinnamon, Cloves, Galinga, Lignum Aloes, Musk, Ambergreese. Wherefore it was an old custome continuing even to our age, and women use it if they see that their Children are bewitched; to purge them

from

from it, they perfume them with Frankincense, and wrap them about : they must be kept in clear air, and pretious Stones must be hanged about their necks, as the Carbuncle, Jacinth, Saphyre. *Dioscorides* thinks that *Alysson* hung up in the house, purging Thorn, and Valerian are a sufficient Amulet. Let them smell of *Hipopus*, and Lillies, let them weare a ring of the Hoof of a wild or tame Ass, Satyrium, called also Dogstone is good. *Aristotle* commends Rue. All these things do abate the forces of Enchantments. But I have set down in this Book such things as are proved by experience, and most likely to be true of different kinds. *The same.*

To make Men mad, that they may be easily out of their senses.

It is done easily with Wine. Thus, Take the roots of Mandragora, and put them into Wine that is hot, and yet working up with Bubbles, put a cover on, and set it in a convenient place for three Moneths, when you want it, give it one to drink, he that drinks it, when he fals into a deep sleep, grows mad, that he will rave much for a whole day, but when he sleeps again, his madness is gone; nor will it do him much mischief, and it is pleasant for to make triall of. The same is reported of the froth of a Camell dranke, by one that is drunk, yet as I shall shew, they will be more cruelly mad : and some take Womens terms, but the most dangerous are the terms of Cholerick and barren Women, but they are more powerfull, mingled with the brains of a wild Cat, so they must remain a night and a day, then distill water from them in Glass Stils, and mingle this with their drink, and the party will be mad so long as this pernicious venome remains, untill he can overcome it, which will be in a Moneths time : and if some please, they can receive this rage when it abates. Or thus, Take the brains of a Mouse, of a Cat, of a Beare, and the froth of a Dogs mouth, and of a flitter Mouse, very well mingled with Myrrh, and put them into a vessell, and set them into Horse dung, let them stand there eight daies, then distill Water from them, who drinks of this looseth his memory by the venemous quality of it, and is deprived of his understanding, *The same.*

BOOK V.

This Book is properly for Physick, for it contains the Symptomes of Mans Body, as it is subject to Diseases, and the most Secret Remedies thereof. In this Book therefore I Treat of Diseases; the division whereof I shall presently after give you in a Table. This is a most large Subject, because there are so many sorts of Diseases; And also because for one and the same Disease many Men propound many Remedies, out of which I have chosen only the chief. But because Death and Life belong to Mans body, to health and the reason of Diseases, before I Treat of Diseases, I thought fit to say something of Life, Health and Death.

Of the Body.
Of Life. Chap. 1.
How to prolong Life.

Many affirme that *Ambrosia* will prolong ones life to the longest date; also Italy produceth this Herb, though it be rare : but if it be sow'd it will not grow. It is easily known, because the seed alone, as it produceth plenty of Wine, smels very sweet, it hath leaves like to Rue, with a very long and slender stalk, and it never flowers ; wherefore the use of this Herb is supposed to prolong life, nor is it without reason, which it performs by its property. *Card. de variet.*

Of Death. Chap. 2.

Aristotle saith, That Death is not so troublesome that comes by old Age, only for this it is the worse : because a very old Man endures many miseries before it comes. Like that which befals one from the biting of a certaine Viper, which *Plutarc* speaks of : Next to that is Death, coming by drinking of Poppy : for they dye sleeping : The fourth is by drinking Hemlock, of which elsewhere, as *Theophrastus* writes : But this often torments one, as also Poppy doth; and as for biting with Vipers that is
not

not so common to every man. The fifth manner of death comes by new plaistered Wals of Chambers, and Charcoale burning when one sleeps. I have asked some taken thus almost dead, and they said they felt no pain: the last befals them that are drowned, for what death comes by drawing blood, is painfull about the end, as *Tacitus* saith. *Card. de variet.*

That one may dye Laughing.

Frogs, Toads, Serpents, and all venemous creeping things delight in a Plant called, *Apium risus*, Physicians say, if any one eat of this, he dieth laughing. *Cornel. Agrippa.*

That one may dye without pain.

Pliny reckoneth the juyce of raw Leeks amongst deadly things. For the report is, That *Mela* a *Roman* Knight, being guilty and called to an account by *Tiberius*, being in desperation, drank the juyce of Leeks about three penny weight of *Roman* silver, and he presently died without pain. *Mizald. Secret. Sort.*

An Oyle that kils Men with the ill sent of it.

Take Turpentine two Pound, yellow Brimstone one Pound, *Assifetida* eight Ounces, Serapinum six Ounces, Mans dung eighteen Ounces, Mans blood ten Ounces; mingle them and put them into a Retort, very well stopt, and Distill them at a very vehement fire, untill all the spirits be come forth. *Fioravantus.*

To make a Wound with a small touch.

Take a Toade that lives amongst hedges, and hath a sharp back, as it were with little bunches upon it: some call him Bufo. This is the more hurtfull and so much the more deadly, the more shadowie and cold places he lives in, in Woods and rushy grounds: for he sucks up much poyson there. Men put this Toad into a long bag, and as much Salt as the bignes of an *Indian* Nut; then taking the bag into their hands, they shake it violently a long time untill he die: then they keep the Salt which retains the deadly poyson of the Toade. Or else they bury the Toade in Salt, and for fifteen daies they bury it in Horse dung, they keep this Salt and dissolve it with meats; he that eats it, it will run through his inward parts and hurt him, and infect his blood: and he will soon dye: or else they put it in moist places to dissolve, and a Napkin wet with such water, or any of it but touching a mans bare flesh, will make a most cruell wound, but this comes from the venome.

An Antidote.

Take the fairest leaves of S*t John*s wort before it flower, as much as you can take in both hands, and set them in old Oyle in the Sun a Week, then let them stay in a Bath of hot water one day, and press forth the juyce with a Press, and keep what is pressed forth in the same Vessell, and take continuall pains, and when the flowers and seed come forth and are ready, mingle these together; and when it grows hot at the fire, cast in a hundred Scorpions, a Viper, and a Toade, cutting away their heads and legs; Take this from the fire in the heat of the Dog-daies, and covering the vessel, and making it fast with a skin, set it fifteen daies in the Sun: then adde to it the roots of Gentian, white Dittany, both Birth-worts, Turmentill, and Rheubarb, of each equall parts: put in likewise of Bolearmenick, prepared and Emrald in pouder a little, cover the Vessell three Moneths in Horse dung, putting in a double proportion of the best Theriac; then sttaine it, and keep it in a Vessell well glased with Tin: with this annoint the region of the heart, and under the short Ribs, all the Pulses and the Back, and it presently cures all venemous bites; wherefore for this and what I shall write afterwards, you can have no better remedy. *The same.*

Of Health. Chap. 3.

To increase the strength of the body.

All Creatures that are long lived, are good to lengthen Mans life, and all that are restorative, serve to renew our lives, and restore youth: which Physicians have often proved, as it is manifest concerning Vipers and Serpents. And it is known that Stags renew their age by eating Serpents; so the Phænix is restored by the nest of Spices shee makes to burn in: the Pellican hath the same virtue, whose right foot, if it be put under hot dung, after three Moneths a Pellican will be bred from it. Wherefore some Physicians with some confections made of a Viper and Hellebore, and of some of the flesh of those Creatures, do promise to restore youth, and sometimes they do it as *Medea* did to old *Pelias*. Also it is believed, that a Bears blood suckt with ones mouth from a fresh wound made, will make a man very strong, because that Creature is so mighty strong. *Corn. Agrip.*

Of Diseases. Chap. 4.

Some are of the Body
- Either of the whole Body, or Universall.
  - Internall.
  - Externall.
- Or of the parts, or Particular, and either
  - Of the Trunk
    - Of the Head.
    - Of the Chest.
    - Of the Belly.
  - Of the Limbs
    - To lay hold of any thing.
    - Or to Walke.

Of infectious Diseases in generall.

There are some diseases known to be infectious, and others are not; the infectious are those contained in the spirits, and not in the humours; and therefore by Sympathy pass from body to body, of which kind are Pestilences, Laptitudes, and the like. 2. Such as taint the breath, which evidently passeth from man to man; such are Consumptions of the Lungs, &c. 3. Such as come out of the skin, that taint the Ayre and bodies next it, which consists in Scabs or Leaprousie. 4. Others meerly in the humours, that do not infect neither by the spirits, breath, or exhalations, but by touch, as nome of the *French-Pox*, the biting of a Mad-Dog, or the like. Lord *Bacon.*

Of Universall Internall Diseases.

Take Opium one dram, live Brimstone one dram, Myrrh, Agarick, Rue, *Cassia fistula*, of each one dram; with juyce of Wormwood make Pils, as great as Pease, The dose is one dram before the fit. *Roscell.*

For a Quartan Feaver.

Take Treacle-water, water of Gentian, of each one Ounce, Liquor of Tartar one Ounce, Oyle of Pepper three drops, mingle them; give it three houres before the fit, the body being first purged. *Anonymus.*

Pils approved for a Quartan.

Take Rue, Myrrh, Opium, of each five drams, Saffron two drams, *Cassia fistula*, live Brimstone, of each two drams, Henbane five drams, make Pils, the dose is one dram with water. *Roscell.*

Ague Quotidian, or Tertian.

Take two heads of Garlick, peel them clean, and a handfull of Nephoes, Neymaydens, pownd it with the Garlick, and put therein a pretty handfull of Bay-salt, this being altogether mingled, bind it to both the hand-wrists before the fit cometh, and keep it on 24 hours. *My Lady Veare.*

For a Quartan Ague.

Take of red Sage new, Shepheards Purse, of each alike, of Glass, Salt, Frankincense of each alike, let the Glass be beaten very small in a Morter, there adding the rest, beat them well together, and put them in a faire linnen Cloath, and bind it on both the hand-wrists half an houre before the coming of the Ague, and in two or three dressings it will drive it away. *Dr. Matthias.*

Ague in Womens Breasts.

Take Hemlock leaves and fry them in sweet-Butter, as hot as the Patient may endure,

dure, lay it to the Breast, and lay white Cotton warmed upon the same. Dr. *Mathias*.

An excellent remedy for a Quartan.

Take of the best Theriac three Ounces, Oyle of Juniper foure Ounces, old Oyle two Ounces, of Cloves one Ounce, otherwise foure Ounces, of Spicknard one dram, the best Wine one Ounce. Let them boyle untill the Wine be consumed, then adde a little Wax if you please, and make Annointment, wherewith annoint the Back bone, for one or two houres, before the fit compass. *Out of a Manuscript.*

Another.

Take black Pepper foure grains, with the juyce of Gentian make one Pill, and guild it over, give it with Wine or Treacle-water three houres before the fit. *Anonymus.*

For Tertians and Quartans.

Pliny reports, That if you pare the Nails of the Hands and Toes of the sick Party, and mingle the paring with Wax, and it will be a remedy for a *Tertian, Quartan,* or *Quotidian* Ague; and if you make this fast to any other Mans doore before the Sun arise, it will cure these Diseases. Likewise all parings of Nails if they be cast into Ant hills, the first Ant that begins to draw them away, must be bound about the parties neck, and that will cure the Disease. Some say that wood thunder strucken, if you hold your hands behind you, will drive away the Disease: and for *Quartan* Agues, some bind about the sick Parties neck a piece of a naile that belongs to the Cross, wrapt up in Wooll, or a piece of the Cross, and when the Disease is cured, they hide this in a cave, that the Sun never shines into. *Corn. Agrip.*

For a Quartan.

Hermes writes, that if both the eyes of a Bear be bound up in a linnen cloth above the left shoulder, it will cure a quartan. *Albertus.*

Another.

It is reported that one little piece of Ox dung drank with half a scruple of Masterwort, is a remedy for all Quartans. *Mizald.*

Another.

I have cured many of Quartan Agues, but amongst the rest the Sonne of *Bartholmew Cressey* a Citizen of *Pistorium*, when he had been afflicted with it seven moneths, and that with a double Quartan, returning still with incredible swiftness; as also his Wife and his Mother, both sick of Quartan Agues, and of a scowring so many moneths, for they both kept their beds. I cured them with vomits, and abstaining from meat on their fit dayes, purging them with *Confectio Hamech*, annoynting their back bones in their cold fit, with Oyl of Scorpions, Goose grease and juyce of Gentian: and others I cured with the juyce of the roots of *Mulleus* given in drink. *Cardan.*

Another.

Some report that the bone of a dead Man who never had an Ague, hung over the sick party will free him from it. *Cornel. Agrip.*

Another.

Cantharides covered up in cobwebs, and hanged over one that hath a Quartan, will perfectly cure it. *Mizald.*

Another.

If you take the heart of a living creature newly drawn forth, whilest it is yet hot and living, and hang it over the sick, it helps him. *Cornel. Agrip.*

Another.

Worms found in the middle covering of a fullers Teasel, are said to be excellent against Quartans, if you tye them wrapt in parchment about your arm or about your neck. *Mizald.*

Another.

Seven Wiglice of the bed wrapt in a great Grape husk, or of a Prune, and swallowed down alive before the fit, will not only cure Quartans, but also those that are bit by Vipers. *Dioscorid:*

Another.

Juyce of knot-grass with seven grains of Pepper drank before the Quartan comes, drives it away: but some say, the Plant must be gathered, and the juyce pressed forth on a Thursday, the Moon decreasing. *Mizald.*

Another.

There are some secret medicinal qualities of the Marigold, which many have long desired to know, and now I will discover them to you. I writ this property of the Marigold, when one that began to addict himself to the practise of Physick came to visit me as he used to do: who after that he had read this History of the Marigold, assured me, that he knew a Monk that cured Quartan Agues, giving before the fit in White-wine seven Marigold seeds in pouder to drink, doing this for some daies together: this I was willing to let you know. *Mizald.*

Another.

The juyce of Plantane given with Honey and water two hours before the fit, helps it, and by taking it ofter cures it, as I have understood it hath being used by many. *The same.*

Another.

When a dead Mans bone is hanged about a Man it cures a Quartan; and if it be used so for the griping of the belly, it cures that also. *Albertus.*

For Agues.

And some say, that if you take the dog-tooth of a Crocodile from the left side of his upper jaw, and hang it over one that hath an Ague, it cures him, and it will never come again. *Albertus.*

For Tertians.

Likewise the eyes of a Frog bound about the sick patient before the Sun rise, if you let the blinde Frogs leap into the water, it will cure Tertians; upon the promise of him that hath tried it. *Cornel. Agrip.*

For Agues.

Now to shew what vertues there are in Nature in numbers, appears in the herb Five leave grass; for by this number of five, it resists poysons, drives away Devils, is good against witchcraft; and one leaf of it taken twice in a day in Wine cures one dayes Ague: three leaves cure a Tertian: four a Quartan: Likewise four grains Tarnsel seed drank cures Quartans, and three grains cures Tertians; so Verven drank with Wine cures Agues, it in Tertians you cut it up at the third knot of the stalk, and in Quartans at the fourth. *Corn. Agrip.*

For Agues.

Serenus Samuonicus reports in his Precepts of Physick that if you write this word *Abracadabra*, diminishing one letter after another, by order of running backward, from the first letter to the last, as I shew you here, if any patient be sick of a Semitertian or any other Ague, this Paper bound about him, and hanged about his neck, will recover his health, and the Disease will by degrees depart from him. *Cornelius Agrippa.*

For Childrens Agues.

If you lay upon a Child that sucks and is troubled with an Ague, a Cucumber as long as the Child, and let it lye upon him so long as he sleeps, he shall be presently cured: for all the Feaverish heat goes into the Cucumber. *Mizald.*

Another.

It is a memorable story that I have read in the Greek Georgicks of the Quintily; and it hath been procured with good success by many, as I have heard; What is that you will say? if you lay on a sucking Child or one that is weaned, a Cucumber as long as the Child when it sleeps, that they may lye together; this cures the Ague, all the Feaverish heat being drawn forth and extinguished and repressed. *Mizaldus.*

To cause a Feaver.

A Feaver is raised if you boyl in Oyle horned Beetles, and annoint the Pulses therewith. And sometimes a Feaver will do much good, as where there is a Convulsion or Gout, a Feaver caused helps them, that proceed of a cold cause, and sometimes also when they are troubled with a Palsey. *Card. de varier.*

For Tertian Agues.

Buglofs growing with three stalks, beaten with the feed and root, and dranke against the cold fit of a Tertian is very profitable; but that which grows with foure stalks boyled in Wine and drank, is good against Quartan Agues. *Dioscorid.*

For Putrid Feavers.

I would not have it omitted, that he who fills an earthen pot with Peach flowers, and stopping the pot lets it stand some dayes to ferment under ground, or to putrifie in horse-dung, may prefs forth Oyle, with which if he annoint his pulses, temples and back bone, before the putrid Feavers come, he shall certainly cure them. I confefs ingenuously I had this of a German Physician. *Mizald.*

A precious Medicine for the Green-ficknefs.

Take of Centaury, Rew, broad Time, Mayden-haire, of each one handfull; of Origan half an handfull; make all this into pouder, then put this pouder into a quart of Ale, and let it boyl to a pint; then put into it a quantity of Honey, and let the patient drink it. Dr. *Anthony.*

Against the Plague.

I will add out of *Anton. Ludovicus* a Physician of *Lisbon*, who had excellent skill, that Lampreys eaten frequently in the plague time, by an imbred vertue, are very effectual against so cruell a difease. *Mizald.*

A Cake against the Plague.

Take white Arsenick two ounces, red Arsenic one ounce, make a round Cake as thick as your finger with the white of an Egge, or mucilage of Gum dragant, sew this up in a linnen rag, and lay it to your heart: you need not put your shirt between: (for though Arsenick taken inwardly be mortall, it is not by any secret venome, but onely by corroding, so that you cannot call it poyson) for if you apply it outwardly, it is certain that it resifts poyson. *Jacobus Carpensis.*

Another for the Plague.

Take a pint of ould Sack, a pint of Sallet-oyl, and a quarter of a pound of english Madder, mingle them together, and drink a good draught thereof morning and evening; and if you be not infected, it will keep you from infection; and if you be infected it shall bring out the fore. *Probatum est.* Dr. *Matheas.*

Another for the fame.

Take morning-milk, and boyl therein a handfull of *Cotula fatida*, otherwife called Margerum, then strain it out, and drink the milk so sodden every morning, and it preferveth from infection; likewife Sheep pend in the Hall and lower rooms where the houshold lieth, preferveth from the plague those that are not infected, and cleanseth the infected house, so that they be not let abroad in the morning untill they both pifs and dung; for by the sent thereof the plague is either preferved, or the house cleansed from it. Dr. *Matheas.*

For the Plague a perfume.

Take black Pitch, white Frankincense, of each six ounces, of Mirrhe four ounces, of the wood Aloes half a dram, of Beniamin and Storax of each one dram, of Juniper berries and the leaves of Rosemary of each two drams; make a grofs of pouder of these, and caft it in a chafing dish of coals and perfume the house. Dr. *Matheas.*

Another for the Plague.

Take of Aloes one ounce, of Myrrha and Saffron of each three drams, of Bole armenick, Terra sigillata, Zedoary, white Dictamnus, the roots of Tormentill of each one dram, make Pills of these being all well poudred and mixed with the juyce of Marigolds or red Coleworts, of which every day take one, and once every moneth take a dram. *The fame.*

Another for the fame.

Put four or five leaves of pure beaten Gold into juyce of Lemmons, let it lye therein for 24 hour space, then take the same juyce and put to it a little pouder of Angelica, and then mingle them with White wine; and let the patient if he be never so sick,

sick, drink a good draught thereof, it is a most pretious drink, and it is greatly to be wondred, what help and remedy some have enjoyed thereby which have used this drink, although it hath been supposed by many Learned Physitians, that the sick persons were past all hope of remedy, yet by Gods help they have recovered again. *Dr. Jones.*

A little bag against the Plague.

Take of Saphyre, Emerald, Jacinth, Ruby, red and white Corall, of each one dram; Saffron one scruple, Pearls half a dram, white Arsenick two drams, Amber greece six grains, Annis root sweet and dry half an ounce, Harts horn burnt one dram, Orpiment half an ounce, pound them all and make a little bag with purple silk, and lay it to the region of the heart. Some use their own Urine for an Antidote. Others use to smell to the root of Elecompane steept in Vineger, or of Angelica, Juniper or Bay berries. Many will not go into publick company untill they have eaten something: yet if any one be infected with the plague, drive it forth so soon as you can, from the stomach and ordinary passages with a sweating powder, yet not before you know that nature is enclined to sweat, and let the Patient take a Clyster: Then give him Theriac, Mithridate, and such remedies that are good against pestilent diseases: not that these remedies are to be taken only once as some do use them, or else continually, but three or four times the same day, alwayes allowing six hours between. If a Bubo or Carbuncle appear, set on Leeches not far from it, if it be in an ignoble part: but first it were best to apply large Cupping glasses, and with great flame, or a Cocle, or a Whelp, or the Lungs of some Creatures. But at the beginning of a pestilent disease, before he take an Antidote let not the Patient sleep, lest the venome of the disease with the blood, lay hold upon the principall parts and presently kill him: apply to the heart and other parts corroboratives, and as much as he may, let him refresh himself with meats that agree with his stomach most, and let him commit his life and all other things to God with earnest prayers, and take advice for the rest of a Learned Physician, that God by his mercy and favour, and the Physitian by his art and industry may help him. *Rautzovius.*

An Electuary to preserve a man against the Plague and other Diseases.

Take choice Cinnamon half a dram, Zedoary one dram, Bole armenic prepared three drams, Camphire seaven graines, Citron seed unhusk'd. Sorrell seed, Citron pills, of each one dram and half, roots of Dictami, Tormentill, Pimpinell, half a dram; shavings of Ivory, bone of a Stags heart, of each one dram; gold and silver prepared of each one scruple: fragments of Saphyre, Ruby, Emerald, Granate, of each one scruple: mingle them, beat them into pouder, to which add conserve of Roses, of Sorrell, Buglofs, of each two drams, white Sugar one pound dissolved in water of Buglofs and Endive, make an Electuary. The way to use this preservative against the Plague is thus: Take upon a knife as much as two Beans and eat it; but when the Plague is begun, take half an ounce of it every day in Wine and Sorrel water. Take against a Pleuresie half a ounce with some convenient broth, or mingled with some juyce or water in a sufficient quantity. I use to add sometimes to this Electuary Elks claw, and Unicorns horn and Amber, of each one dram. *Priscian de Corduba, Medic. Leonis decimi Pontif.*

Another remedy against dangerous and pestilent Diseases of Children.

Our Matrons use to give to Children when they grow ill, a little of the bone of the heart of a Stag, and of Unicorns horn, red Corall, white Amber, Pearls, pouder of Gold, Elks claw, of each alike: All these beaten in a mortar they mingle together for hot Diseases, with Rose water; but in cold Diseases with Lavender water, and they give about a spoonfull. *Rantzo.*

Sweet balls against the Plague.

Take red Roses two ounces, root of Annis, Cyperus, of each half an ounce; root of Angelica six drams, Bay leaves, Rosemary leaves of each six drams, Bay berries three drams, Cloves, Lignum Aloes, Nutmegs, of each half an ounce; Pearls one ounce, Styrax calamita, Ladanum, of each one ounce, Musk dissolved in Rosewater twelve grains, Amber greece two scruples, with Gum dragant dissolved in Rose water make a mass. *Out of a Manuscript.*

Book V.   *Secrets in Physick and Surgery.*   43

To prevent the Plague.

Take conserve of Roses, Violets, Bugloss, white water Lillies, of each half an ounce, confectio Alkermes, two ounces and half, roots of Angelica two drams, Zedoary two scruples, Electuary de Ovo one dram and half, Venice Treacle four scruples, syrup of Lemmons what is sufficient; make an Opiat: use this once or twice a day. *Out of a Manuscript.*

A Remedy for the Plague.

Take a great white Onyon, make it hollow within, and fill the hole with the best Treacle and Aqua vitæ, cover it well with its cover, and roast it in the embers, then press out the juyce and give it the sick to drink; what is left pound and lay it upon the plague sore. *Roscellius.*

Why Sicknesses and Infections raign more in Summer than in Winter.

It is because Diseases are chiefly bred by heat, and the Sun exhaling the heat outward, the spirits and inwards are more faint and weak, and the pores being opened are most subject to Infection.   *Lord Bacon.*

The best thing against the Plague.

In the morning before you go far from your habitation, wash your mouth with water and vineger mingled together; then drink a quarter of a spoonfull of the foresaid liquor, and so press your nose, that your brain being freed from all externall ayre infected, may with less difficulty by the vapour and steem held in your mouth, be moistned: also it will be a great help to wash by turns the principal emunctories of your body, as your temples, arm-pits, and groins, the parts more rare and loose above the rest, that by this means they may be defended from the dangers of the ayre infected; and that they may be more safe from all pestilentiall ayre, it will be good to use a silver ball full of holes, in the hollow part whereof a piece of a sponge is kept moistned in the former liquour. For by this means the ayre being altered, I have often preserved my self from the plague (to God be praise) unto this present day. *Egidius Bruxel. D.*

To keep one from the Plague.

Take Sugar infused in Treacle water, and dissolved perfectly, three ounces, tincture of Brimstone one dram; make tables according to Art; by this used I have known many men preserved from the plague.

An approved Remedy against the Plague.

Take the sharpest vineger, juyce of Garlick of each two drams, Theriac of *Alexandria* one dram; mingle them, and give it to the patient presently, and having taken it, let him sweat well upon it. *A Manuscript.*

The so much famed Countess of Kents *Pouder, good against all pestilentiall Diseases, French Pox, Small Pox, malignant Feavers, melancholly. The dose for a Man is twenty or thirty Grains, according to his constitution; half the quantity for a Child dissolved in a little Sack warmed.*

Take of Magestracy of Pearls, Crabs eyes prepared, white Amber prepared, Harts-horn, Magestracy of white Corall, of *Lapis contra yarvum*, of each a like quantity; to these add a proportionable quantity of the black tips of the great claws of Crabs; beat all these to a fine pouder, and sift them through a very fine sive; to every ounce of this pouder adde a drachme of oriental Bezoar: Make all up in a ball with the jelly of Harts-horn; colour it with Saffron, adding thereto a little Musk and Ambergreece; draw them out into small Troches in the cleer ayre. *Countess of* Kents *Manuscript.*

An Antidote against Poison.

One saith, that in the closets of the great King *Mithridates* conquered, *Cneus Pompey* found in a Manuscript written with his own hand, a composition of an Antidote of two dried Nuts, as many Figgs, and twenty leaves of Rue beaten together with one grain of Salt; he that takes this fasting, needs fear no poison that day: the same Antidote is admirable against the Plague raging, if it be taken upon an empty stomach. Plagues are many both known, and unknown: with this Antidote I have preserved many against desperate pestilences, by my advice, and giving it my self. *Mizald.*

Against Poysons.

That there is an effectual Stone against Poysons, there are many witnesses of great authority, and Physicians very antient and many. *Julius Scaliger* and *Amatus Lusitanus* boast, that they have seen such a Stone; and they say that they have seen it given in a little Wine to many that were infected: for by the vertue of it, it will provoke so much sweat, that you would think all the body to be melted by it: by this only the pestilent venome is driven forth: The Arabian Physicians call this Stone *Bezoard*, and from this, medicaments to drive forth venome, are called *Bezoardica*. *Mizald.*

That no Man may be infected with venome.

To this add the opinion of *Didymus*, that if any man eat millet bread first, he shall never be hurt by venome. *Mizald. mem.*

An Experiment of an antient Physician of the King of England; and it is a wonderfull Pouder against venome, and against all poyson.

Take Pimpernel, root of Tormentil, Cinamon, of each half an ounce; Lignum Aloes, Juniper berries, Ginger, of each one dram; sometimes there is added Carduus Benedictus, root of Angelica, of each half a dram: make a fine pouder of all these, and keep it close in a box for use. *Rantzo.*

An Antidote of King Nicomedes against Poyson.

Take Juniper berries two drams, earth of *Lemnos* two drams and six carrats; pouder all these, and mingle them with Oyl or Honey, and lay them up for use; and when need is, with two cups of Honey and water, give the quantity of a Walnut. *The same.*

To procure Appetite.

Take a preserved or roasted Quince, Pear or Warden with Sugar, or a preserved or roasted Pippin, and so eat it; also damask Prunes well stewed with white Wine and odoriferous Rosewater, adding thereto a little Sugar, and three or four Cloves, and three or four tops of Rosemary, are very good to eat, and the Syrup thereof souced is good to nourish, loose, cool and comfort. *Mr Hunniades.*

That no man may fall into a Hectick Feaver.

They give water of these Ingredients; they make Lead into fine pouder, or calcine it, and they mingle sharp Vineger and Salt together, they distill water from it by the fire, and of this they give one small cup once in a moneth, and they continue it six times when a dangerous Hectick falls upon any person. But if they undertake a deadly Disease to cure in a long time, they do thus; they take Ceruse, Verdigreece, Litharge and Red lead, of each equall quantities; the juyce of Squills what may suffice to mingle them together, they put them into a glass, and set them forty dayes in Horse dung; then they take it forth, and after that they mingle mans sweat with it, and they give of it to eat to one that is dying, thus with continuall languishing for a large time they preserve life. But for such a Disease this is the Remedy.

An Antidote.

So soon as the Disease is found out; if in the decoction of Liquorish a little of the pouder of Scammony be taken, it presently recovers the patient. If any venome were first taken, do thus; distill water in Chymical vessels of glass, from Pigeons dung, and egge shels, with a fourth part of Pepper, and a little Frankincense, and twice as much of a lee made of the ashes of Vine branches mingled with them; and for the first moneth, for seaven dayes give one small cup; for the second moneth, eleven; and fourteen for the third; untill six moneths be expired, and this will extinguish the force of the poyson: but the Consumption you must cure it thus; Drink water from the herb Perionaria, with the mixture of Pine kernels, every day before dinner untill you be recovered. *The same.*

For a Consumption.

But I have cured multitudes of a simple Consumption; and amongst the rest two sons of a Carpenter that dwelt at Barbed gate; I used (besides a moderate diet) of bread baked with Pompion seeds bruised and strained, or a ptisan of Oysters, Crabs and Snails, and drinking white Wine, this remedy alone: Hogs blood, and Snails purged, and Frogs with the buds of Brambles I distilled in Balneo; and I gave a quantity of this water according to the patients age, untill he grew fat: so I cured the son of Jacob and Mary Adolphus, a Carrier of great note and fidelity, and my very good friend. *Card. de curat. admirand.*

Whether the sick be in danger.

A Disease that begins when the Moon is in that Sign, that had some malignancy when the party was born, either in the quartil, or opposition of it, is like to be most dangerous; but if it respects the malignancy, it is dangerous: but if the Moon be in a place that was beneficiall when the party was born, there will be no danger. *Ptolomy, Galen* from the *Egyptians,* and especially *Mercurius Trismegistus.*

A sign of Death or Life.

Men say that a green Nettle steeped twenty four hours in the urine of the sick patient, will foreshew his recovery if it remain green; but otherwise death or very great danger. *Mizald.*

Whether the sick shall recover.

If you will try whether the sick party shall live or not, sprinkle the patient with the infusion of white Chamelion root for three dayes, three times a day; he that can endure this, they say he will not die. *Theophrast.*

Certain presages of Death.

By the face: 1. The Nostrils are extenuated very sharp: 2. The Eyes hollow: 3. The skin of the Eyebrows hard, dry and loose, as though it were tand: 3. The Ears cold, shrunk and almost doubled: 5. The Face black, swarthy and illfavoured.

By the Eyes and Lips: 1. If they be deprived of sight, or overflowing with moisture: 2. If they stare or start out of the head: 3. When one Eye seems less than the other, or drawn unto one side: 4. When they are moveable, gastly, staring, stiring quick up and down; when the patient sleeps with his Eyes open; when the Lips are thin, cold, pale and hanging down, and the Nose very sharp, it is a certain sign of death approaching.

By the Patients lying in bed: When the Neck, Hands, and Feet are stiff and not to be moved; sodain starting; sleeping with their mouthes open; tossing, tumbling from one end of the bed to the other: gnashing of the Teeth, by frequent plucking the bed-cloathes, peeling straws, &c.

By the Breath: If in a hot distemper a long cold breath, if his sweatings be cold, it is infallible that death is near at hand. *Nicholas Culpepper.*

Presage of Death.

I find in the books of Soothsaying, *Servius* being the Author, that if a Fir-tree be stricken with thunder, it presageth the death of the man or his wife that oweth the Tree.

Whether the sick man shall live.

That is not against reason, that the sick that make a representation of your image in the pupil of their eyes may be cured: yet many of those die that may be recovered, because the force of death is not yet come so far: yet hardly one doth recover that might be cured: for so long as vitall heat remains, the apple of the eye shews the representation of him that looks upon it. *Cardan.*

Of universal outward Diseases
Cure of the Leprosie.

Some say, that Leprous persons washed in a Bath wherein a dead carcass is washed, are cured by it. But we know not concerning what Leprosie they speak: for one is a kind of Scab, another is called Elephantiasis: Likewise it is not observed, whether that happen alwayes, or perhaps sometimes by chance: yet it is not without reason in the thing it self: for the matter which was wont to be driven outwardly to the skin, by antipathy to the carcass, is no more sent forth by nature: For this reason of contrariety is naturally even in Insects, and much more in perfect Creatures, especially in Doggs and Horses, that they hate the sent of dead creatures of their own kind: how much more Mans nature which is so accurate in apprehending. Therefore Nature in her secret way dares not any more send out the peccant humour, and much more if this be done when the Patient is sensible of it. *Cardan de varietat.*

H

To know a true Leprosie.

You shall discern by urin such as are Leprous, for it is full of lead coloured ashes that are sprinkled in it: if they sink there is no contagion in it, but if they flote and stick to the superficies of the urine, it is a most certain sign that it is contagious. *Lemnius.*

For an Elephantiasis.

Some that have had the Leprosie have been cured by frequent eating of Frogs in Lakes; namely the heat of their blood being abated, and the burnt melancholy being corrected. This you must understand of Frogs that leap, and not of those that creep or go slowly, for they are venemous. *Mizald.*

A safe Remedy for an Elephantiasis.

Hens fed with Vipers, and sod are wholesome food for Leprous persons, as some have proved. *Mizald.*

An Ungnent for a Leprosie.

Take Turpentine washed, oyl of Bayes, of each four Ounces, Vineger eight Ounces, White lead, Lytharg, Aloes hepatica, of each eight Ounces, whites of Eggs two mingle them, make an Unquent. *Roseellus.*

Cure of the Leprosie.

Also the bath of the first born Son, wherein there remains some of his blood will cure Leprous persons, as I have seen the experience. I beleeve that the cause is sympathy. For the more corrupt blood entring by the veins and arteries draws to it that which is corrupted. Now the blood that is poured forth at ones birth, and is in potentia like to our blood, and more corrupt, and yet more hot by the bringing forth of a Son: this will vehemently urge, purge and extinguish, as the Sun beams put out the flame of fire, and cause it to vanish. But what Leprosie this is, and how it differs from an Elephantiasis, Scabs and Itch, I have spoken elsewhere. *Cardan to subtilitat.*

To cure Piles or Hemoroides.

Take Frankincense small beaten, Sheeps dung, of each a pretty quantity, throw it upon a chafing dish of coales, and let the diseased take the fume thereof into the fundament by a close stool. *Dr Johnson.*

To cure Hemoroides or Piles.

Take a handfull of Elder leaves, boyl them in water till they be very tender, then take a piece of Scarlet as much as a mans hand, or broader, and wet it well in the decoction, and lay it to the place as warm as well may be suffered, and when it is cold, revive it again, being wet in the same decoction as before. *Mr Rogers.*

To make a man Leprous.

Either the blood of the Leprous person is taken, in which Wheat stands long sokeing, and this be given to Hens or Pigeons to fat them, and so the Leprosie is taken, which is observed in all other contagious diseases. Or otherwise, some take Cantharides, the stone Amiantos and a fift part of Orpiment, these are made up with the juyce of the roots of Thapsia or Squills to make a liniment: and with this they annoint hose or shirts, and they will cause an inflation, ulceration and an inevitable Leprosie, wherefore take great heed of them: and if they will have it worse, and to work more strongly, they add mans sweat, especially of a red and cholerick man, the juyce of Wolfsbane, Toads poyson, or some such like things, and in a short time they will make a mortall wound. If a Dart be wet in this juyce it will wound and it cannot be cured. But this is the best

Antidote

Against a Leprosie: Let Bread hot from the oven be steeped in the juyce of Endive, Hops and Wormwood, of Vineger and Brimstone infused in it as much, and then let it be dried; cast into this a sixt part and half of the juyce of Maudlin galanga, that is of Goats Rue, and flesh of Vipers equall parts, round Brithwort a twelfth part, a sixt part of Citron pills, and half as much of the seed of it, and of Theriale an equall weight, a little Hellebore and Scammony; mingle them all, and set them to the fire untill the moisture evaporate, lay it up for use, take of it every third day; If any thing yet remain upon the skin use this Liniment; Take Vipers fat, Goats suet

half

half as much, Bears greafe a fourth part, as much oyl of Capers, of live Brimftone a fixt part, Liverwort four times as much, then pour in Vinegar, and boyl it untill it be fomething dry, then with wax make a liniment and annoint with it every other day, untill the fcales fall off. *The fame.*

For creeping Tetters.

Againft Tetters of the face, and other parts of the body, (the French call them *Dertas*) take the root of fowr Dock, and cut it in fmall pieces, then fteep it a whole day in fharp Whitewine Vinegar: then take it out, and three or four times a day rub the place where the Tetter is, very well with it, and put it as often again into the Vineger: or which is better, put in new roots: This is often proved. Some promife that the fame will be performed by Borrage roots, that are firft chewed by a labouring man that is fafting, and often rubbed on the place. This is eafie to try. *Mizald.*

An approved cure for Scabs or Itch of the body.

Take *Unguentum Album Camphoratum*, of *Populeum*, of *Diapompholigos*, of each half an Ounce; of Quickfilver quencht in fafting fpittle, ftrong Vinegar, or the juyce of Lemmons three Drams, make all thefe into an Oyntment according to Art: let the grieved party three times together, at night anoint the palms of his hands, wrifts, and all the joynts of his body, and the foals of his feet, chafe it well that it may foak in: if he be not well in the three dayes, after eight dayes ufe it again, other three dayes as before. *Probatum* by Dr. *Mathias.*

For Scabs.

Take Pomatum two ounces, liquid Styrax half an ounce, Lytharg of filver half an ounce, common Salt two drams, juyce of Lemmons what is fufficient; make an Unguent. *Rofcellus.*

An excellent Oyntment for all kind of Scabs, wherewith I have feen Scabs like Leprofie cured.

In *May* take bafil Mints the heard with the root, purge them clean from filth and wafh them, then bruife them, prefs forth the juyce, and keep it in a narrow glafs well ftopped for a year. And when you would prepare an Unguent, take as much in quantity of Wax and Oyl of each as of the juyce to make your Oyntment; when you have done this, fet them together upon the coles and boyl them, and temper them to an Unguent. *Hieron. Tragus.*

For a Cancer.

Take Rofewater, Allum, Verdigreece, of each what is fufficient, mingle and wafh them every day thrice with cloth woven from thread. *Out of a Manufcript.*

An Antidote againft the Cramp.

Take a dew Snail when he is creeping on the ground, and you fhall fee on the fore part of his body near the head, the proportion of a Scollop fhell, and at that place with a flender knife you muft cut it clean away, and put it into a little bag and let it dry therein, and then hang it about the parties neck, and it will cure him both of Cramp and Convulfions. Mr. *Harvey.*

Cramp or Ache.

Take half a pound of Butter unfalted, and put into a new earthen pot; fet it over a foft fire, let it boyl till it be as clear as water, fkiming it as occafion ferves; fhred a good handfull of Danewort or ground Elder, and put therein; fo let it remain a good while, then ftrain it out and wring it hard, that you may have the juyce of the herbs, then anoint the grieved place by the fire. Mr. *Jackson.*

For the Cramp.

It is a Difeafe which cometh by the contraction of Sinews, as is evidently feen by chafing near to the place grieved: to prevent it Rings made of Sea-horfe teeth are very effectuall, as likewife bands of green Periwinkles tied about the calf of the leg. Lord *Bacon.*

An Unguent for the French Pox.

Take Unguent Aragon, Agrippa, Marciolum, Dialthæas, of each one ounce, Frankincenfe, Maftick, of each two ounces: Oyl of Bays, of Willows, of Lillies, of each

two ounces

ounces: Litharge, Quicksilver, of each half an ounce: Theriac half an ounce, Saxifrage two drams, Unguent of Sanders half an ounce, old Hogs grease without salt fourteen ounces, Vine ashes one ounce; mingle them and make an unguent. *Roscellus.*

A Bath for Consumptions and Palsies.

Take six new Calfs heads, together with their mesenteries and feet, as many Sheeps heads, all well cleansed, as you would do to eat them: boyl them in water in a great vessel or two, and make a bath. Let the sick use this every other day, in the morning for an hour or two, and as many in the evening. This bath must be repeated nine times, and must alwaies be prepared fresh. *Out of a Manuscript.*

Of Particular Diseases.

Of Diseases of the Head.
A Charm for the Headach.

✠

Miland vah vitalet

To cure the pain of the Headach, I saw a handwriting hang over one, as you see it written on the side, after that the Patient who could finde no help by Physick had thrice said over the Lords Prayer. *Cardan.*

For distillation and Rheume.

Take Nigella, and Cummin, let them be pared, and put into a linnen cloth, and tie it close and smell to it. Also take Nutmeg and Mace, and chew it in your mouth, or make into pouder, snuff it up into your nose, and it will cure you. *Mr Brown.*

For the Megrum.

Dissolve Euphorbium in Vinegar, dip a cloth therein and lay it to the contrary side of the head of him that hath the Megrom. It cureth Gouts also being dissolved in Vinegar: lay it to the forehead and temples, it cureth the Megrum presently. *Dr. Jones.*

For sounding in the Ears.

Take of Euphorbium half a dram, Aniseed, Siler mountain, let them be brought into fine pouder and serced, and with juyce of Rew, Wormwood and Fennell let them be mingled a day and a night; then strain it into a glass, and at night going to bed let seuen drops be warmed, and put into both the ears. *The same.*

For pain of the Head.

It is wonderfull of an Olive tree, that some have found help by it, and been freed from Headach, when no other thing would do them good: they did write this name (*Athena*) upon the leaf of it, and bound the leaf about their heads, as *Zoroastres* writes in his Commentaries concerning Husbandry: which one thing because it smells of superstition, I leave it to your own discretion. *Mizald*

For Headach.

The Loadstone laid upon the Head takes away all pain. *Hollerus* saith he had this Receipt out of the Commentaries of the Ancients.

Headach, a remedy by Vomit.

Take twelve grains of Stibium, made into very fine pouder, put it into four ounces of Claret wine and so let it stand thirty hours, shake it every six or seven hours: at the thirty hours end, pour the wine from the pouder so long as it runneth cleer; let the grieved drink it with a little Sugar, or Sirup of Violets: it mightily purgeth superfluous humours from the head. *Dr Matheas.*

Another for the same.

Take Aloes hepatick four drams, Briony, Mattick asarabacca, of each one dram, mix these made into pouder with the juyce of Fennell and a little clarified Honey to preserve them, take eleven drams thereof and make it into five Pils, which you must take early in the morning, and fast three or four hours after; this must be given nine dayes together; to the weak give a less quantity: pouder of Nutmegs snuft up is good. *The same.*

Swelling of the Tongue.

Take White wine vineger, and make therewith Mustard as strong as you can, let the grieved put the same into his mouth with a spoon, and gargle it up and down, this

Book V.   *Secrets in Physick and Surgery.*   49

this you must do often, for there is no other way to save life: when the mouth is much blistered and raw with the Mustard, you must take three parts of Plantane water if you can get it, for want thereof Rosewater will serve, and a part of Vinegar, and with this often gargled in your mouth it will cool the heat quickly, and heal the tongue or blisters; beware of letting blood, for it is present death, and if he have gargling, let him keep a piece of Nutmeg upon the tongue. *Dr Mathius.*

For pains of the Head.

Take the tops of Willows what is sufficient, a little Rosemary: boyl them in Vinegar untill a third part be wasted, with this wash your Head. *Roscellus.*

Against forgetfullness and crudities of the stomach, for old men.

Take the three Peppers, Galanga, Cassia lignea, Calamus aromaticus, Saffron, Spicnard of *India*, Cardomom, Carpobalsamum, Asarum, Ginger, Seeds of dry Myrtils, of each two drams: pound them and sift them, make them up with the best Honey purified, and make an Electuary: The dose is one dram when you go to sleep. *A Manuscript.*

To stop bleeding at Nose.

Take a Spider the biggest you can get, put him in a fine linnen cloth, bruise him a little, and hold the same up to the nose of him that bleedeth, but touch not his nose therewith, but let him smell to it and it will work the effect. *Mr. King.*

Pills excellent for a weak brain, especially for old men, and such as are cold of constitution.

Take the best Ambergreece and Amber, of each one dram, Lignum Aloes half a scruple, Cubebs two scruples, with the best Wine make 25 Pills, take two before supper. *Guil. Gratar.*

Pills excellent for Memory.

Take Cubebs, sweet Cane, Nutmegs, Cloves, of each one dram and half, best Frankincense, choice Myrrh, oriental Ambergreece, of each one dram and half; Musk five grains, with Marjoram water make Pills, take one when you go to sleep, two when the Sun riseth, or about five hours before meat. *The same.*

For Memory.

Simeon Sethi saith, that a Partridg gall annointed on the temples, once a moneth that it may penetrate, is very good to help the memory.

The brain of a Hen helps both wit and memory, so that it hath recovered some who began to dote. *Guil. grat.*

An Antidote that wonderfully helps the Memory, against Lethargy and Forgetfullness: comforts the stomach, and adds force to all parts against flegm and cold.

Take Ginger, Galanga, Mastick, Cummin, Origanum, of each six drams; Nutmegs, sweet Calamus, Asarum, Cubebs, Lignum Aloes, Mace, Smallage seed, Ammi, of each two drams: white Frankincense, Cloves, Cardammus, Zedoary, Pellitory of the wall, Castoreum, long and black Pepper, Costus, Cyperus, of each three drams; dry Mints five ounces: Pouder them fine, and with Sugar penid and a quantity of clarified Honey make a Lohoch. *Guil. Gratarol.*

For Memory.

If you have a Lapwings heart, or eye, or brain about your neck, it is good for the Memory, and quickens the understanding. *Cornel. Agrip.*

To increase Memory.

If any man swallow a Lapwings heart, or a Swallows, or Wesils, or Moles, whilst it yet pants and lives, this will make one have a good memory, and to remember things past, to have a good understanding, and to divine well. *Cornel. Agrip.*

For the Falling sickness.

Some say that he who drinks in a pitched cup, shall be cured of the Falling sickness. *Mizald.*

Another for the Falling sickness.

If the Herb Crowfoot be bound about the neck of one that is Lunatick or hath the Falling sickness, with a red thread, the *Lune* decreasing in the first part of *Taurus* or *Scorpio*,

Scorpio, the patient shall finde great help by it: Some steep the root of it in Wine, and give it those that have the Plague to drink, to make them sweat: which I beleeve is very dangerous if they have a feaver; otherwise convenient if their forces will endure it. *The same.*

For the Falling sickness.

The distilled water of the flowers of Tile tree, is wonderfull to cure Children of the Falling sickness, what way soever you give it them: Some joyn with it Misseltoe of the Oke, with very good success. *The same.*

Another for the Falling sickness.

Dividing before the full Moon young Swallows of the first breed, two stones are found in their maws, whereof one is of one colour, the other of divers colours; these before they touch the earth, if they be wrapt in a Calf, or Stags skin, and bound about the neck and arm, they will both ease and cure the patient. An *Italian* told me this, and said he had tried it. *Mizald.*

Another.

So soon as Children are born, if before they tast any thing, you give them half a scruple of Corall finely poudred in the Nurses milk, they shall never have the Falling sickness. *Arnoldus de Villa nova.*

Another.

Burning either or both horns of a Stag, the scent of them will drive away Serpents, and discover the Falling sickness. The Jet stone doth the like, when it burns, by the fume of it. Yet that the fume may not be dispersed, the party must be covered with blankets, for then if he be subject to the Falling sickness he will fall. *Dioscor. Galen, Apuleius and others.*

For the Epilepsie.

Little balls of Misseltoe of the Oak stringed through with a thread, do the same thing to drive away the Falling sickness; and to prevent it, that the root of the male Piony doth, and the Emerald hanging about ones neck. *Mizald.*

For the Falling sickness.

The professors of natural Magick say, that Verven gathered when the Sun is in *Aries*, and joyned with the seeds of male Piony bruised, and drank in White wine strained from them, doth wonderfully cure the Epilepsie: many have tried this by my advice, which I learned out of a book written by *Hermes* anciently concerning the seven Planets. *Mizald.*

Another.

Conradus Gesner adds, that he gave that bone that describes the coronal suture, to some that had the Falling sickness, and they were cured by it. *Mizald.*

Another.

The gall of a Tortois smeered upon the nostrils of one that is in the fit of the Falling sickness, will presently raise him up. Some to drive away this cruel disease, fasten three nails made on St *John Baptists* eve, in the place where the Patient fell, and they knock them in so deep that they cannot be seen, and whilst they do this they name the sick mans name. This was told me for certain. *The same,*

Another.

An Elks claw hath great force against the Falling sickness; for a piece of it set into a Ring, and worn on the finger next the little finger, so that the claw may be turned next the palm of the hand, will much refresh those that are fallen in the very fit, and presently raiseth them up. The same will a piece of it unset, put into the hand and held there perform; for this strait drives away the disease and makes the sick stand up. *Lemnius* saith he tried it once or twice. I put a piece of it into ones left ear, and I did rub and scratch the ear with it a good while, and I found it a certain cure for one that had the true Falling sickness, and it seemed miraculous. *Joh. Agric. Ammozius* saith, the same is done if one hang or carry about him a small piece of the same hoof, so it do but touch his skin. And I am certain this Amulet will perform it to prevent the disease. I hear also that in *Poland* they drink the pouder of it for the same malady, But you must choose the claw of the hinder right foot, and take heed of Impostors who sell Ox hoofs for Elks claws. *Mizald.*

An excellent Pouder for the Falling sickness.

Take Gentian, Piony, Antimony prepared with urine, of each three ounces: Mans skull, Musk, of each three grains: make a Pouder: take one dram every day. *Roscellus.*

For the Falling sickness.

Some say also, that if a Piony root with Castoreum and some of a menstruous cloth be given to the Patient, it will cure him. *Cornel. Agrip.*

Another.

Likewise a stone taken out of a Swallowes nest, is said to refresh such as fall immediately: and bound about them will always preserve them: especially if it be wrapt up in Swallows blood, or the Swallows heart. *The same.*

Another.

The distilled water of Cherries newly gathered and drawn by a gentle fire, if it be put into the mouth of the Patient so soon as the fit comes, the force of the disease will abate, be it never so violent. A pretious thing and often tried by *Joh. Monardus* an excellent Physician of *Ferrara. Mizald.*

A Remedy for the Falling sickness.

After the same way we hang the root of male Piony new gathered, and Pimpernel with a red flower about those that have the fit of the Epilepsie.

The King of Denmarks Receipt against the Falling sickness.

Take the skull of a Man, especially of a thief that is hangd, and that died of no disease, (for they ascribe more vertue to this than to any other) dry this skull upon a gridiron, and pouder it: Then take three Piony seeds, and one dram of the pouder in a spoonfull of Lavender water in the morning, do so for three days together. This pouder must be taken fasting, and the patient must stay at home three days, drinking but little, and eating meats of light digestion, as Eggs, &c. It will not be amiss also, that the Patient every day take a spoonfull of Lavender water: Also Unicorns horn is good against this disease. *Rantzovius.*

For a fit of the Epilepsie.

Orpheus and *Archelaus* say out of *Pliny*, that those that are fallen into a fit of this disease, will be presently freed from it, if you rub their lips at that time with mans blood, or do pull and prick lustily their great toes. *Mizald.*

For the Falling sickness.

For the Falling sickness *Alexander* hath written, (and to none are we more endebted for Physicall Remedies) that the fat of a Chameleon boyld in Oyl, annointed upon the belly and back bone of the sick, will do so much good, that he will presently rise up, and will be cured in seven times annointing him. *Nicolaus* saith, that one must whisper into the sick mans right ear. Let us pray admonished by wholesome precepts: adding the Lords Prayer, and before the prayers be ended the patient will stand up: may be it may sometimes fall out so, or else the whispering into his ear may do him good: or being it is done by blowing, as many Physicians think, the disease may in the mean time leave him. *Rinaldus* speaks more to the purpose: When the Moon and *Jupiter* are in conjunction, give unto the Patient for three days, of Mace, seed of Piony and of the root, half a dram; leavs of Avens and Primrose (which is the Dasie) one dram: pouder it and divide it. *Cardan. de varietate.*

Against the Falling sickness.

Some report if a Ring be made of the white hoof of an Ass, the Patient that wears it shall not have the Falling sickness. *Albertus.*

A Charm for the Falling sickness.

If you make a Ring (as some say, and I have seen one so made) of silver, having this written within it, + *Dabi*, + *Habi*, + *Haber*, + *Hebr.* +, that the Patient shall not fall if he wear it upon his finger. *Cardan.*

A Remedy for a Convulsion from wind.

They say that the knots of Misseltoe wood that grows upon the Oak, will cure that kind of Convulsion that proceeds from Wind, our Countrymen call it *Grampus.* It must be laid the part where the grief is to drive it presently away: that wood is full of fat thin juyce, or else it is from the secret property it hath. *Cardan.*

To bring forth the Small Pox.

If any complain of heaviness in the head, and you fear it is the small Pox, give the sick a little English Saffron, in warm Milk; keep the sick warm, and it will bring them out, and being come forth, take raw Cream and Saffron, beat it together and annoint the sores with a feather, and it will heal them without sign or spots. Dr *Mathias*.

For Melancholy.

It is no small Remedy to cure Melancholy, to rub your body all over with Nettles. *Cardan*.

Against Fear and strange Apparitions.

He that holds in his hand a Nettle and five leaved grass, shall be safe from all fear and frightfull apparitions. *Mizald*.

Against the bitings of mad Dogs.

Those that are bit by mad Dogs and desire water, and yet are afraid of it, if they be suddenly cast into the water when they think not of it, one fear drives out another, and they are cured by it. *Lemnius*.

Another for the biting of a mad Dog.

Take the Liver of the same mad Dog, boyl it well, and let the Patient eat thereof, not knowing what it is, and it helpeth. Dr *Mathias*.

Against the fear of Water.

Ætius reports, that if those that are afraid of water, eat but once the Runnet of a young beast with vinegar, they will presently desire to drink water: this remedy is highly commended. *Mizald*.

For Drunkenness.

For Drunkenness, Wormwood and the stalks of Almonds are good to chew beforehand, to keep us sober. *Cardan*.

For an Inflammation of the Eye.

There is a certain Fish or great Serpent called *Myrus*, whose eye if you take it forth and binde it to the patients forehead, they say it will cure an Ophthalmy, and that the Fishes eye will grow again: but he will be blind of one eye that doth not let the Fish go whilst he is alive. *Corn. Agrip*.

For a stroak in the Eye.

Take a handfull of Carduus Benedictus, stamp it small and temper it well, with half the white of the Egge, and therewith make a plaister, laying it on flaxen hards, and binde it hard upon the eye, and there let it remain untill it be somewhat dry, and then apply another, and so use it every day till your Patient be whole. Mr *Harvy*.

Eye and Sana to unite.

Take twelve streyns of new laid eggs of white Hens, labour them in a morter together with a pestle untill they be united in manner of an oyntment, and so reserve it in a glass, and twice a day and once a night put a little of it into the eye, and it will knit the tincle together again if it be hurt. Mr *Huighes*.

For a Pin and Web or Pearl in the Eye.

Take May dew taken from green Barley, a little Bay salt, and a small quantity of Honey, of each alike; put all into an egge shell, boyl it therein and skim it with a feather, and when it is boyled strain it with a fine cloth, keep it in a glass, and therewith annoint the eye; but withall take of Hemlock and Bay salt a pretty quantity, pound it together and apply it to the hand wrists. Dr *Johnson*.

For Eyes blood-shot.

Take of red Rosewater four spoonfuls, of Smyrene three spoonfulls, the runnings of two Eggs, the quantity of a small Bean of Honey, put all these in an egge shell, set it upon some embers in a chafing dish untill it boyl, skim it with a feather and reserve it for use, dropping three or four drops into the Eye morning, noon, and night. *Probatum*. Dr. *Clarke*.

For the Pin and Web in the Eye.

Take of Dasie leavs and roots, red Fennell and ground Ivie, of each alike, stamp them well together, and mingle therewithall Womans milk; for a Woman you must

must take the milk that a man child sucketh, and for a man the milk that a woman child sucketh, this being mingled together with the Herbs strain it out, and put it in a glass for your use, and morning and evening put a drop or two in the parties eye, Dr. *Mayern*.

For diseases of the Eyes.

For diseases of the Eyes, as the Haw, Clowds, white spots and the rest, One told me that this following remedy is the best in the world. Burn the head of a Cat all black in a new earthen pot, till it become to Ashes; make it as fine as any flower, and with a hollow clean Quill, blow some of this powder daily into the eye that is sore. But if any heat, especially in the night offend the eye, put two or three Oken leaves wet in water upon the eye, and then turn them again sundry times. He that invented this Secret, said that the sight may be recovered by this remedy after one year, that the party hath been blind only: and you may try it if you please. *Mizald*.

A most excellent Eye Salve against all Diseases of the Eyes.

Take Fennell, Wormwood, Smallage, Rue, Stonewort with the roots, eye bright, Sage, Bettony, Orpiment, Pimpernell, *Carduus Benedictus* of each equall parts. Bruise all these in a Mortar, and mingle them, and powre in Boys urine, then take Corns of Pepper beaten fourteen, Honey two Spoonfuls, Camphir one dram. Beat all these together in a Mortar, and press them through a Linnen Cloath, and keep the juyce strain'd forth in a Glass, and every day morning and evening drop one drop into the Patients eye. Take notice that this water must be set nine daies in the Sun, and distilled before it be used. *Hen. Rantzovius*.

Bloody Flux to stop.

Take a Pottle of Fountain Water, of Cinamon half an Ounce, of Rice husked half a pound, boyl these together till it come to pulse, and when it is cold, warme so much upon a Chafing Dish of coales, as you will eate: green Medlers from the Tree, work the same effect. Dr. *Mathias*.

For stinking of the Nostrils.

Take crud lignum Aloes, Roses, Cloves, of each two Ounces, Spicknard, sweet Calamus, Myrrh, Calamint, of each one dram; make them up with good old Aromaticall Wine, adding Musk six grains, make Pils as great as Pease, and dissolve one at a time with oyle of Spike, and drop it into the Nostrils, or put it in with a Tent, first washing the part with pleasant sented Wine. *Alex*.

For stopping of the Nose.

Take juyce of Beets, of Marioram, of each one Ounce; Oyle of bitter Almonds one dram; Mingle them and draw them up into your Nostrils. *Fioravantus*.

To stench Blood.

Bloud running immoderately out of any part of the body, will be presently stopt, if Hogs dung yet hot, be wrapt up in fine thin Cotten linnen and put into the Nostrils, Womens privities, or any other place that runs with bloud. I write this for Countrey people rather then for Courtiers, being a remedy fit for their turne. *Mizaldus*.

To stentch Blood.

If bloud run out of the Nose it will be often stopped by pressing the Nostrill that bleeds, close with your finger; Some write upon the Patients forehead with his own bloud, *Consummatum est. Card*.

A Charme to stop Bloud.

It happened once to me, that my lip being cut off, the bloud could be stopt by no art, especially because I did eat. I laid Salt on it, and I bound it up, but all in vain. Wherefore I used that charm, is taken from our Lords Passion; and the bloud stopt presently, that I wondred at it; and let me eat or speak no bloud more appeared, though I felt great pain of it, and the wound was open. You will admire, and I cannot tell whether it were my faith or the words that cured me. *Sanguis mane in te, sicut fecit Christus in se. Sanguis mane in tua vena, sicut Christus in suâ pœna. Sanguis mane fixus, sicut Christus quando fuit Crucifixus*. Repeat this thrice. *Card*.

For Deafneß.

Take Cats grease, juyce of Wormwood, old Oyle, of each what may suffice equall parts. Mingle them, and drop thereof into the ear. *Sextus Empiricus.*

The best thing for Deafneß.

Take Sage, Marjoram, Rosemary flowers, Hysop, Mugwort, Horsemint, Calamint, Camomile, Yarrow, St. *Johns* Wort, Southern wood, Savory, of each one handfull. Boyle them in water in a Glased earthen pot, and hold your ears over it, that the smoak may enter, chewing something, as Beans, continually, that the holes may open the better, and do this so long untill the decoction grow cold: when this is done, take oyle of Coloquintida, and drop in one or two drops; then wet Cotten in the same Oyle, and stop your ears. Lastly, Lay some of the same Herbs upon it, when you go to sleep, use this every day, and it perfectly cureth. *Roscellus.*

For the Tooth ach, and when they are on edge.

The benumming of the Teeth, called in Greek αἰμωδία, is cured by chewing of Purcelane, in your mouth, as *Aphrodisæus* saith. Also rubbing the Teeth with Salt will do it, or chewing some cheese made of Sheeps milk. And you shall find no remedy better for your Teeth astonished, than a small Plaister made of Pitch, or melted Rosin, with powder of Allum, and Galls, so you lay it upon the temporall artery a little above the tooth that is paind, and let it lye so all night, or for some daies together. But that is best to scarifie the grinding teeth of the uppermost Jaw. Believe (as the Proverb is) *Robin* that hath proved it. *Miz.*

Pain of the Teeth wonderfully cured.

Of late I had a great pain upon my upper Teeth, the two last of the left Jaw; and by consent with them, all the other Teeth were afflicted on the upper Jaw of the same side, and the whole Jaw indeed, that I thought the bone would be torn in pieces: it also tormented my eye, ear, and part of my nose, and nothing would do me good, but it still came again, with my right hand I pulled my Teeth but found no ease. At last by chance I perceived that when I gently moved the pained Tooth with my left hand, and laid hold of it with my thumb on the out side of it, and my forefinger on the inside, presently not only the pain of that tooth but of the whole Jaw left me. But that seemed more strange to me that the more gently I touched it, the better it was for me, and the pain left me the sooner, and it was presently well: and still as the pain returned I tried this often above twenty times, untill it quite left me, and so I was cured. *Cardan.*

For numneß of the Teeth.

When Teeth are astonished by eating sower things sharp or cold, Purcelane chewed is wont to be the remedy, and it cures all hot fiery itching, and heat of lust and venereous dreams, &c. *Mizaldus in Horto medico.*

For the Toothach.

Take a Moles tooth out, and let the Mole go, this will cure the Toothache, saith *Cornelius Agrippa.*

Another for the Toothache.

It ofttimes cures the Toothach, if you touch the Teeth with the hip boanes of a Toad, for there is Antipathy between them. *Card.*

Another.

Take wood of Guaicum one handful, *Aqua vitæ*, what may be sufficient: mingle them and hold them in your mouth. *Out of a Manuscript.*

Another.

Take Aloes Succatrince, of Myrrh, of each alike, fine Wax, as much as shall suffice, make here of a ball, and steep it in *Aqua vitæ* four or five hours, then with a cloath wash the Teeth that ake. Note that the Glass must be stopt when the Ball is put in. *Mr. Clarke.*

Another.

Take long Pepper, Mastick, Origanum, Savory, Wood of Balsamum, Pellitory of Spain, of each half an Ounce, bruise them, and infuse them in one Ounce of
Aqua

Aqua vitæ, drop a little of this water into your Tooth. *Roscellus*.

For the Squinsey.

Mans bloud is so soveraign a remedy, that those that have the Leprosie have been cured with that only in a Bath; and *Orpheus* and *Archelaus* write that the Squinsey will be cured by it.

Another.

Take the dung of a Hog newly made, and as hot as you can get it, apply it to the place, and it cureth. Dr. *Matthias*.

Another.

Take of young Swallowes and their nests, of Strawberry strings one handfull, one handfull of Costmary, the Herbs being small shred and fryed in a Pan, then press out the Oyle, and keep it in a glass, annoint the sore throate of him that hath the Squinsey, and wrap a warm red cloath about it. Note, the Swallowes and their Nests, and the Herbs small shred, must be pounded together, before you frye them. Dr. *Mathias*.

Another.

A Cataplasme made of the powder of burnt Swallows and of their Nests, is singular to dissolve swelling of the Throat, and to cure the Squinsey. *Miz.*

Another.

A hedg Toad boyled and laid on for a Plaister to them that have the Squinsey, is so good a remedy, that I cured one with it that was dying, and the Candles were lighted for his Funerall, as the custome is. I believe that a thred can do the like, which a Toad hangs by untill he dieth. *Car.*

For Scrophulous Tumours.

All the feet of a great hedg Toad cut off whilst he is alive, whilst the Moon is in her void course, and hasteneth to her conjunction, hanged about the neck of one that hath the Kings Evill, will be so effectuall, that they often times cure the Patient. *Cardan.*

For the Palate of the mouth fallen down, ready to choake a man.

If the uvula grow lose by a distillation from the head, the juyce of raw Coleworts laid upon the crown of the Head, will draw up the uvula again into its proper place: This is a Secret in Nature. *Mizald. in Horto medico.*

Roughness of the Tongue.

To mollifie or coole the roughness of the Toung, and to temper and moysten the heat and dryness of the Tongue or Throate, take as often as you shall need, a spoonfull of Syrup of Violets, Mr. *Young*.

For the uvula inflamed.

The dry excrement of a Boy mingled with honey of *Athens*, is an excellent remedy for the inflamation of the uvula, that is dangerous to choake a man. But that Boy must be fed two daies with Lupins, wth the finest Bread well leavened and salted: and he must drink old wine moderately, that he may digest it well. The third day the excrement must be taken and dried, and used as I said before. The flesh of Hens and Partridges boyled in broth is good to eat for him, but that his excrement will stink the more. This was *Galens* Secret, as he saith, which he obtained from a Friend, with much intreaty, as he writes himself.

For extream heat in Children, proceeding from inflammation of their brains.

Nettles beat in a Mortar with a little Populeon added to them, and applyed to the Arteries of their Temples and Wrists, is an admirable remedy to extinguish the heat of young Children, in two daies at least, if it be renewed every four houres. *Langius.*

That a Child may not sneez.

Ætius saith, That a Child will not sneez in that house where there are Storks feathers.

For swounding.

Those that fall into a swound are raised again if you pull the joynt of the Ring, or of their middle finger; or rubbing of it with gold, and a little Saffron: for from this a reviving spirit runs to the heart, the fountain of life. *Lemnius*.

Stitch of Wind or Collick.

Take Fenugreek, Linseed, Cumminseed, Anniseed, Bay-berries, Fennellseed, Corianderseed, of each a pretty quantity; seeth all those very well in water, and put both the water, and the seeds very hot into the bladder, knit it fast, and apply it to the place, as hot as you can suffer it, and when it is cold, warme it again in the skillet, and apply it still untill you be well, which will be in a short time. Mr. *King*.

Collick.

Take of *Carduus Benedictus* seeds, stamp them, and drinke them with white wine: it doth help the Collick and pain in the lower bowels; the seed of the great Lote used so, worketh the like effect. Dr. *Ruwrig*.

For the Cough.

Take three, or four spoonfuls of clear running water, or more if you please, if it be in the Summer, if it be in the Winter take the like of *Aqua vitæ*, put thereto a spoonfull or more of Sugar, or Sugar-candy beat into fine powder, let the Patient drink thereof morning and evening for three daies together. Dr. *Johnson*.

Another.

Take Elicampane root, mixed with the powder of Licorish, and white Sugar-candy, whereof you must take a spoonfull at one time. *The same*.

Another.

Take foure peny worth of Ginger, eight peny weight of Elecampane roots, half an Ounce of Licorish, all made into powder, one Ounce of powder of Anyseeds, one Ounce and half of Sugar-candy; mix these together and eate often every day. Dr. *Jones*.

Of Diseases of the Brest.

For Childrens Coughs.

Tabariensis saith that if you hang a stone of a sponge about the Childs neck who Coughs exceedingly, his Cough will leave him; and when this is put into an Asses head, or the hinder part of a Beetle, he is in a swound, and will not turn himself untill it be taken forth from him. *Albert*.

For difficulty of Breathing.

Jacobus Clarenzanus a young youth, who for seaven years was troubled with shortness of Breath, with frequent, long, and cruell fits, and was left by other Physicians, was cured by me in two Moneths time, and grew fat: but I used another way, for I applied the depilatory of *Paulus* to his coronall suture, which he used for pains of the hips, adding some honey of Anacardus to it, for in one day I drew forth two pound of water: I did the same the day following, but there came not forth so much water: and thus he was cured. I think *Spanish* flies will do the same, that honey of Anacardi will, and also Euphorbium; Also I mingled one grain of Elaterium with three Ounces of Milk, and I bad him snift it up into his Nose: and this did much good; but before all this, I purged his body with Pils, and dried it with thin diet, but yet moist, and of little nourishment, then I gave him the decoction of Guaiacum to drink. *Card. de curationibus admirandis*.

Stomach to purge.

Take the weight of a French Crown of Aloes Succotrina in the pape of an Apple, and it will purge the Stomach. Dr. *Mathias*.

Liver to purge.

Take a dram and half Ruburbe sliced, put into it three or foure spoonfuls of endive or succory water, and let it infuse all night on warme Embers, and in the morning let it warm alittle, then drink it. Dr. *Mathias*.

Blood Purge.

Take Guiacum sliced, and steeped all night in water, and sodden to the half, make broth with that liquor, with a little Mutton and fruite and eat it, it purgeth the bloud, and drinketh up its humours. Dr. *Clarke*.

Another.

Another.

If you make purging diet drink, and boyle therein Scurvy Grass, it purgeth and clenseth the bloud exceedingly. *Dr. Read.*

Brest stopt.

Take five or six sticks of Licorish clean scraped and bruised, a good stick of Cinamon bruised, a race of Ginger sliced, maiden haire a handfull, two Croppes of Hysop, of Coltsfoot two or three leaves, of spring Water a quart, infuse all these in a Jugge close stopt, set it by the fire upon some Embers, for the space of six houres, then take six spoonfull of the liquor, and a spoonfull of Sugar Candy, and mix them well together, and so drink it in Summer cold, and in Winter warme. *Dr. Mathias.*

For a Plurisie.

The powder or shavings of a Bores tooth half an Ounce made very fine, and mingled with Barly Water, or of red Ciches, or some pectorall decoction, and drank by one that hath the Plurisie, is an approvd remedy to free the Patient from danger. *Mizald.*

Another.

Take a ball of stoned Horse dung, throughly dryed, beat it into powder, and let the sick drink thereof, and it will cure him. *Dr. Clarke.*

The best and most easie remedy for a Pluresie, wherewith to speak nothing of others, I cured a Smith almost dead, wonderfully in two daies time.

Take a sweet yellow Apple, cleansed from the kernells within it, fill this with Frankinsence; then cover it with a cover of its own, and rost it under hot embers, untill it be well rosted, and not burnt; cut this Apple into four parts, and give it the sick to eate; when this is done as it must be done, the Impostume will presently open, and the matter of it will come forth, and the sick Patient will be cured. So was this Smith cured when his Teeth were shut together, that we were fain to open them with an Instrument: but when he had taken down the Apple and lain still half an houre, he presently cast up a great quantity of matter, then he fell asleep, when he awaked he called for meat, and was recovered by Gods assistance. *Alex. Pedamont.*

Another.

The filing or pouder of the greatest Teeth of a Bore must be given in a spoon with Lineseed Oyle. *Octavius Landas.*

An Unguent for a Pluresie.

Take Oyle of Roses six Ounces, Turpentine one Ounce, Brimstone finely powdred one Ounce, Hoglice pounded one Ounce. Boyle all together for one houre, then straine forth the Oyle and annoint the part affected with it. *Roscellus.*

Sore Brests.

Take of March Sand a small handfull, put the same into grounds of Ale, put thereto a pretty piece of Butter unsalted, and break it into pieces as big as Beanes, with the yelks of two new laid Egges, stirre it well together, then thicken it with flower, put as much of this in a frying Pan as will cover the Brest, and when it is well fryed, spread it on a Cloath, and lay it to the Brest as hot as the grieved may suffer it; this will draw, break, and heal the Breast without the help of any thing. *Dr. Mathias.*

For an Impostume within the Chest.

If any one have a Pluresie or Impostume in the Brest, let him take a scruple of Nettle seeds in powder with Syrup of Violets, or some other pectorall Syrup, and swallow it down by licking it up by degrees; he shall cast up the clammy matter without pain. *This was a Secret of one who was no ordinary Physician at Paris.*

An excellent water for a Consumption.

Take Coltsfoot, Snailes cleansed, Hysop, Maidenhaire, greater Comfrey, of each what is sufficient; put them into a leaden still, and distill them in balneo, let the Patient drink thereof every morning one cup full, upon an empty stomach. *Roscellus.*

Another.

Another.

Take flowers of Brimstone ground fine upon a Porphyrstone with Rose water, what is sufficient, conserve of Roses what will serve to make an Electuary. The dose is half an Ounce, when he is fasting that is your Patient. *Anonymus.*

An excellent Electuary for a Consumption.

Take Lungwort, Rosemary, Betony, Maydenhaire, of each two drams, clarified Honey one pound, lesser Comfrey eight Ounces, Coltsfoot one Ounce, Violets one dram; mingle them and make an Electuary according to art. *Roscellus.*

An approved and easie remedy for a Consumption.

Take Coltsfoot, Hogs Lard well beaten of each what is sufficient, one fresh egge. Mingle them and make a Cake on the fire, when the sick hath used this nine mornings, he shall find an admirable help by it. This will also fat lean People. *Alexis.*

Another.

I cured a young Maid of *Franciscus Alciat*, who was belonging to the Canon Law, her name was *Dataria*, after I had left her past recovery in likelihood, of a dangerous Consumption. Shee had a vehement Feaver, short breath, a great Cough, and shee spit up much corrupt matter: wherefore when other remedies were to no purpose, I commanded that she should have no meat besides a Ptisan, and water mingled with Sugar: but that every morning she should drink four Ounces of the Decoction of the Tailes and Claws of Crabs, in Barly water with two drams of Sugar, and she recovered perfectly and was cured. With this very remedy I have cured very many who are well; and one of them I gave remedies to, was a Maid that was daughter to a Man, that died of a true Consumption. *Card.*

For an Imposthume in the Chest, and a Consumption.

I cured *Adrian Belga* of a dangerous Imposthume, a young Man that was forsaken of very able Physitians, a very mannerly Youth: for I never found any more gratefull than himself. He was a Clark belonging to *Don Alphonsus Peson*, the Kings Treasurer. I tried diverse waies to cure him, for he had a feaver, and a continuall Cough, he spit up filthy matter, and was of short breath, four years since this began; and I was forced to let him blood, because I feared more danger, as I did the disease he had; at last by the use of Snails, and a Syrup made of them, and by a slender exact diet: Wherein other Physicians had failed, not observing it, alowing him egges and flesh, at last I cured him that he married a Wife, and he is yet well and mindfull of me. But I used also distilled waters that I spake of before: and also the Decoction of Guaiacum, with moistening and expectorating meanes: Namely, the Honey of Marsh Mallows, and Comfrey roots, Scabious, and Licorish, with the Leaves also of long Birthwort. *Card.*

To stop Vomiting.

Take a Toste of houshould Bread made of Wheat; toste it at the fire till it be brown, then moysten it well with stong Vinegar that is made of Wine, and lay it on the Stomach as hot as the sick can well endure. Dr. *Manby.*

Another.

Take a handfull of Garden Mints, boyle them in Ale, and skim them as often as need is, give the sick a draught thereof warm. *The same.*

A good remedy for short Breath.

The Juyce of Basil drank half an Ounce with half a scruple of Saffron, doth wonderfully help those that are short winded. *The same.*

For inward wounds.

If any one be wounded inwardly, let him drink the Decoction of Avens roots, and that will cure him. And if wounds outwardly be washt with the same Decoction, it will do much good; it avails also for pains of the brest and sides, and to dispell internall crudities.

For a Bruise.

Take a Pint of pure Sallet Oyle, bruise a good quantity of Camomile and put there in, set it in a Glass in the Sun five daies, straine it through a fine linnen Cloath,

Cloath, and let it stand in the Sun as before five daies more, then strain it again, and set it in the same the third time, and so let it stand till it be clean purified from any dregs, and then put it into a clean Glass, and keep it close stopt till you have occasion to use it, annoint the bruised place two or three times a day, chafing it before the fire, and it will help: this Oyntment will last twelve years. *Mr. Clarke.*

Another.

Take Brooklime, Smallage and browesworr, fry them together in Sheep suit, then take it and straine it through a fine linnen cloath, and it will be ample, then take a pretty quantity of *Sperma Ceti*, and mix it well with the same Oyl, and then often annoint the grieved place therewith, and it will help. *The same.*

Yellow Jaundice.

Take Alloes Hepatick, the Gall of a Bull, of each alike, mingle it with Syrup of Violets, and take thereof every third day, use this Medicine so long as you see need, *Probatum est. Mr. Moulins.*

Another.

Take an old piece of rusty Iron, be it Horse-shoe, or any thing else, lay it in the fire till it be red hot, then take it out of the fire, and let the Patient make water upon it, and take in the fume thereof at his Nose and Mouth, using this three daies together morning and evening, and it shall perfectly cure him. *Dr. Clarke.*

Of Diseases of the Belly.

For pains of the Stomach, and to procure an Appetite.

A spoonfull of the powder of Amber must be taken in white Wine, or in broth. *I had this from the most Reverend Legat Pronotary Biglia of Millan.*

For pains of the Collick, and inward Impostumes.

Scrape the skull bone of the Patient, or file away some part of it in that place where the suture is in the forepart of the head, in the upper part like a Cross; of that powder, with broth or water, or wine if there be no Feaver, give the Patient one dram, or half a dram at one time to drink; it will make him vomit and purge exceedingly: wherefore you must give it before the Patients forces are spent. *The same.*

To strengthen and bind up the mouth of the stomach.

Take powder of Coriander prepared one Ounce, of Anniseed half an Ounce; of red Corall, Cinamon of each half a dram, powder of conserve of red Roses dried five Ounces; Let the Patient take a spoonfull after meat. *Out of a Manuscript.*

Bloody Flux to stop.

Take a quarte of red Wine, and set to the fire untill it boyle, roast two or three Egges hard, and take out their yelks, and with some of the Wine put into a Vessell untill it be cold, bruise the yelks of the Egges, straine it and put it into the Wine over the fire in manner of a Caudle, adde there unto two or three penyworth of Cinnamon finely beaten and searced, and put the same into the Wine over the fire, let the diseased drink of this morning and evening very warm. *Dr. Martin.*

Another.

Take fine flower, the yelk of an Egge, and so much Pepper reasonably beaten, as you can well endure, knead all these together and make it into paste, then make it up into Cakes a little broader then a Shilling, bake them upon the backside of a frying pan, turn them that they burn not, and so eat them. *Dr Mathias.*

Belly lose to help.

Scrape a handfull of Polypody clean, boyle it over the fire, then put the root and the water into a cloose stoole, let the sick sit thereon, use this two or three times in a day, and this used three daies will cure the same. *Dr Mathias.*

Liver to open, and Stomach to comfort.

Fill a runlet of four Gallons, and a quarte of ordinary Beere when they tunne, and when it hath almost done working; put therein three ounces and a half of Wormvood, an ounce and three quarters of Reddish-roots, stir them both with a stick to the bottome of the Runlet, and when it hath done working stop it, and after it is a

fortnight

fortnight or three weeks old, drink a good draught of it every morning fasting for four or five daies together, and then for ever after take it as you see cause. It openeth the Liver, and comforteth the Stomach above all things. Gather the Wormwood in *May* before it is seeded, and lay it in a clean Room upon a Shelf, turning it every second day till it be through dry; gather the Reddish-roots between *Michalmas* and *Alhallowside*, and lay them on a clean Board to dry; wash the Wormwood that the water may run from it when make your drink; scrape your roots clean and pick them, and slice them into slices before you put them in. D*r* *Mathias*.

An approved drink for the Tisick.

Take a pottle of clean water, put it in a skillet to the fire, put therein of Barly husked four handfuls, let them boyle a while, then prepare two Fennell roots, two Parsely roots, two or three branches of Hysop, and the roots aforesaid must be clean scraped and slit; of Fennellseeds, and Anniseeds of each two drams, Licorish clean scraped, a little bruised half an ounce, Figs in number twelve sliced in flakes, two Dates purged from the white Rind next to the stone, put all these together, and let it boyl till the consumption of half the water be consumed, drink of this morning and evening three daies together. D*r* *Johnson*.

For a Stomach cold and moist.

Take five leaves of Sage, three crops of Rosemary, seaven crops of Camomile, stamp all well together, adde thereto a reasonable draught of drink, use it three or four mornings.

To corroborate the stomach.

Take *species diarrhodon Abbatis* three drams, powder of the three sanders two drams, *Aromaticum rosatum* one dram and half. Of the four great coldseeds, each half an ounce, Syrup of Apples one ounce, whitest Sugar what is sufficient. Make little Tables of two drams weight a piece, let the Patient take one every day two houres, before dinner, adding conserve of Rosemary flowers half an ounce, Myrobolans Chebuls two ounces. *Vincent Laur.*

A Medicament against heat of the Stomach, which the Germans call Den God.

Take old Sugar of Roses and Crabs stones, which being powdred sprinkle into your Sugar of Roses, adde a little Bolearmoniack: Mingle all these together; yet observe that the Crabs stones must be half as much in quantity as the Sugar of Roses. *Rantzovius*.

Another.

Take one ounce and half of chalk, three Nutmegs, one ounce and half of the finest Sugar that is brought from the Canarie Islands, make a powder. *Rantzovius*.

To dissolve Fleghm in the Stomach.

Take the pulp of fat figs, pulped through a sive six ounces, the inward part of wild Saffron seeds one ounce and half, the best Rheubarb three drams and half, Cloves, Cinnamon, Nutmegs, of each one dram. Mingle all together, and with Syrup of Citron Pils, make an Electuary pretty solid: let the Patient take half an ounce twice in a week three houres before dinner. *D. Lepor. Dal.*

For Looseness in the Belly.

Take of Crocus metallorum, or Stibium ten or twelve grains, made into very fine powder, put it into four or five spoonfull of Muskadine, and let it stand two daies, shaking it thrice aday, the third day power it out cleare from the dregs as you can, and so exhibite it. *The same.*

For vomiting at Sea.

Bruise Wormwood and Peneroyall with Oyle and Venegar, and rub the Patients Nostrils with inside often: Smallage seed drank doth as much: for it hinders loathing of the stomach, that it will not move, and if it do move it will stop it, and so will Wormwood. *Alex. Pedemont.*

For the Collick.

The root of white Henbane hanged over one that hath the Collick, it helps him. *Aristotle.*

Book V.   *Secrets in Physick and Surgery.*   61

Another.
Alexander saith that if you take some of a Childs navell string, that comes forth when it is cut, and put this under a stone of a ring of Silver or Gold, he that knows not of it shall never be troubled with the Collick. *Albert.*

Another.
The Hoofs of living Creatures burnt are a singular remedy against the Collick. *Rhasis.*

Another.
Moist and new Spermaceti helps pains of the Collick, and all inward pains, given with other things that disperse wind. Yet let men take heed they use it not when it is old, or deal too much with it, for it is exceeding dangerous. *Out of a Germane Physician.*

Another.
I know one who drank dry Ox dung ignorantly in broth, and it presently cured him of the Collick. I have heard also by sufficient men, that many countrey people have been cured by drinking it. Some do not drink the dung but the juyce pressed from it, which is far better. *Gesner.*

Another.
The heart of a Larke bound to the thigh is excellent against the Collick, and some have eaten it raw, with very good success. *A certain Spaniard reports it.*

Another.
If the tender horns of young Bucks be cut into small cakes, whilst they are yet covered with a hary thin skin, and put into a new earthen pot, well covered, and so set into the Oven to torrefie, powder made of them, with Pepper and Myrrh added thereto, drank with the best Wine, will help pains of the Gut Colon. *Scribon Largus.*

Another.
Any Bone of a Man hanged so that it may touch the flesh, is thought to cure pains of the Belly that come at certain times. *Miz.*

Another.
This is certain that Wolfs dung, guts or skin eaten, will cure the Collick; or if you do but carry them about you, for they strengthen the Colon. *Card.*

Another.
The Navell string of a Child cut off when it is born, carried in a silver Ring that it may touch the flesh, hath cured many of the Collick, as I have seen it: that by this means they lived healthfull many years: It may be they had a good faith to believe, for I cannot think this will help all. *The same.*

For torments of the Belly.
They report, that when the Belly is pained, if you apply a living Duck to your Belly, the disease will pass into the Duck, and she will dye, but you shall be cured. *Cornel. Agrippa.*

For Collick and Nephritick pains.
Take of the most biting Raddish one ounce, stones of Medlars two drams, break them gently, and steep them eight houres in four ounces of the best white Wine, then strain it, and it being moderately hot, give it the Patient to drink when he goeth to bed, and when he is in bed, renew the same dose and give him, if need be, a greater quantity, or a less, as age and constitution will admit. Some there are that will give me great thanks for so wholesome a remedy. *Miz.*

An Electuary against Wormes.
Take seed of Hartichoke one Ounce, white Dittany two Ounces and a half, Saffron half a dram, Honey clarified two pound, or what is sufficient, make an Electuary. The dose is half an Ounce. *Roscellus.*

Venemous Wormes Biting.
Take an Adle Egge, which is found in a Hens nest, which is hatched, take the Egge and break into a dish, and beate the same well with a wooden spatter, then wet Tow therein, and lay it to the Wormes biting. *Dr. Mathias.*

For Worms.

There is nothing better to drive out Belly Worms, and the rest, than Worms dried on a Tile at the fire red hot, and to give the powder of them to Children troubled with the Wormes, for this presently drives them all out of the Body. *Lemnius.*

Another.

Take a handfull of Water-cresses, fry them in a Pan, till they be somewhat hard, but not burned, put them between two linnen cloathes and apply it very warm unto the Navill. Dr. *Mathias.*

Another.

Take *Unguentum de Arthenita*, half an Ounce of Alloesepatick a dram, a dram and a half of the Leaves of Centry and Wormwood brought into powder, as much of the Oyle of Savin as shall suffice to make it into a Plaister and apply it to the Belly. Dr. *Clarke.*

Another.

I have proved by experience that Raysins eaten will drive forth Wormes from Children, if you give them to eate alone fasting; for as bitter things do it, so sweet things taken plentifully do the same, and are an enemy to Worms, for they will stretch and break with plenty of sweet things. *Lemnius.*

For a Dysentery.

Take Hares runnet, Hares blood what is sufficient, of each a like quantity; Mingle them and give them the Patient. This cures all Belly Fluxes. *Alexius. Mizaldus.*

Another.

Many have cured bloody Fluxes that were infectious, with the decoction of the tops Althæa in Wine, if there were no Feaver: or of Plantaine or Barly if there were a Feaver. *I was assured it was a Secret of a Spanish Physician.*

Another.

Mens bones made into fine powder and drank in sharp red Wine, cure all raging Fluxes of the Belly. *Miz.*

For an hepatick Flux.

Rhasis saith, That Ducks livers have a property to stay all Fluxes that proceed from the weakness of the Liver.

For the Jaundies.

Broth made of Strawberry Leaves and Roots, eaten for some daies together of one that hath the Jaundaies, cureth him perfectly. *This was a Secret of a certain Monk, whereby he gained a vast summe of Money.*

For the water of people that have the Dropsie.

The powder of the Loadstone three half peny weight drank in juyce of Fennell, draws away the water. *Mizald.*

Another.

It is a wonder that some say, how that a River Snake if he be tide by the taile with a cord, and a Vessell set under him full of water, that which he casts out of his mouth in a few hours or daies will be a stone, that falling into the Bason, will drink up all the water. Bind this stone to the Belly of any man that hath the Dropsy, and it draws out all the water. *Hollerius.*

Another.

Clysters of the Decoction of *Carduus Benedictus* in urine, being often given cure all Dropsies. *A Manuscript.*

Take *Indian* Spicknard, Woolfs-Liver, of each half a dram, powder them, and mingle them with Syrup of Wormwood, make eighteen Pils, let the Patient take three every day upon empty stomach. *Anonymus.*

Another.

Take liquor of Tartar, water of Gentian, of each one Ounce, spirit of Vitriol three drops, oyle of Brimstone four drops, Treacle water what may be sufficient. Mingle them, let him that hath the Dropsy drink this before he goeth into a stove to sweate. *Anonymus.*

Another.

Another.

Take of Polipodium two handfuls, with the roots clean pickt, four or five Parsely roots, with a little Marsh mallows, boyle them in a Pottle of faire running water, till half be consumed, adde thereto an Ounce of Sene, two or three Licquorish sticks, take in a morning a quarter of a pint, with as much Diaphænicon as a Hazell Nut, also a spoonfull of Syrup of Roses, the same at night. Dr. *Mathias.*

A Sere-cloth to draw forth water in Dropicall Bodies.

Take of Sallet Oyle half a Pint, if the Humour be hot Oyle of Roses, when the Humour is so hot that it scaldeth, a quantity of red Leade, and a like quantity of Wax, all which boyle together till they look black, then dip your cloathes into it, and being throughly soaked, take them out, let them lye while they are cold, then role them up, it will remain good four or five years. Dr. *Mathias.*

For the Stone, of the Emperour Maximilian the second.

Take the best Rheubard two drams, Galanga, grains of Paradise, Anniseed, Fennelseed, Agarick, Mastick, Cinnamon, of each one dram, Licorish half an Ounce, Jews stone three drams, Mithridate five drams, Mace four drams, Cloves half a dram, *Aqua vitæ* one part, Malligoe two parts. Put all these into a Glass excellent well stopt for fourteen daies; then distill them, let the Patient take a spoonfull twice aweek upon an empty Stomach. *Out of a Manuscript.*

A pouder for the Stone.

Take Cherry tree Gumme, Grommel seed, of each two drams, Parsely seed, Melons seed, Mallows seed, Licorish scraped, of each three drams, Sugar candy ten drams, make a very fine pouder. *Out of a Manuscript.*

For the Stone, and foulness of the Bladder.

Take Fennell root, rest harrow, Germander, Betony, Pellitory of the Wall, Wall-Flowers, Rosemary Flowers, Sage, Bay berries, Juniper berries of each half a dram, Broom seed one scruple, of Violets and Marsh Mallows, Anniseed, of each one scruple, four great Cole seeds, Cinnamon, Nutmegs, of each one dram, Licorish scraped two drams, make a fine pouder. The dose is one scruple with the Decoction of red ciches. *D. Blesius.*

A pouder for the Stone.

Take Melon seeds one dram and half, Cherry tree gum, half an ounce, Grommell seeds two drams, Licorish scraped one dram and half, Sugar candy two ounces and a half. Mingle all and make a pouder. The dose is half an ounce, with broth of red ciches. *Isabella Cortesa.*

A Syrup for the Stone.

Take Saxifrage, Grommel seed, Kernels of Cherries, Kernels of Winter Cherries, Gentian, red ciches, of each what is sufficient. Boyl them all in water of Quinces, untill a third part be consumed; then strain it, and take of the strained liquor a pint, the best Honey one pound, Vinegar one ounce, skim it, and make a Syrup; let the Patient take of it every morning one spoonfull fasting. *A Manuscript.*

An excellent Bath for the Stone.

Take Hysop, Mallows, Parsely, Pellitory of the Wall, of each one handfull, Linseed half an ounce, Saxifrage one handfull; Put them all into a small Bag, and boyle them in a sufficient quantity of water, and make a Bath. *A Manuscript.*

A pouder for the Stone.

Take Goats blood prepared half an ounce, Jews stone, Crabs stones, Peach Kernels, of each one dram, Parsely seed two drams, Smallage seed two drams; Make a very fine pouder. *A Manuscript.*

Another.

Take Rheubarb three drams, Juniper berries five drams, bark of Cassia half an ounce, Anniseed one dram, Fennellseed one dram, Jews stone half an ounce, Agarick, Ginger, Cinamon, Galanga, of each one dram, Mace two scruples, Mithridate two drams, Licorish scraped six drams, best Wine two parts, *Aqua vitæ* one part. Put all into a Glass, let the Patient take one spoonfull twice in a Moneth. *A Manuscript.*

Another.

Take Aniseed four ounces, *Roman* Cumminseed steeped in Vinegar one day, and dried again four ounces, seeds of Smallage, Parsely, whitest Sugar, of each four ounces. Make a most fine pouder, let the Patient every morning fasting, take half a spoonfull with bread tosted, or red ciches broth, for one Moneth together. *A Manuscript.*

Another.

Take roots of Elecampane, roots of Pimpernell, Aniseed, Fennell, Parsely seed, Juniper berries, white Saxifrage seed, of each half an ounce. Make a very fine pouder, let the Patient use of this every last day of the full Moon, that is one day before the new Moon, in the morning fasting, and take it in Wine. *A Manuscript.*

Another.

Brasavolus ascribes an incredible virtue to the pouder of Medlars, to drive the stone forth of the kidnies, and to provoke urine.

Another.

Some say that the berries of white thorn taken in Wine, are very effectuall to drive out the stone. *The same.*

Another.

If the picture of a Lion be engraven upon a most pure plate of gold when the Sun is in *Leo*; and the Moon not respecting the sixt House, nor the Lord of the ascendent *Saturn* or *Mars*, and the Moon departing from them; this Seal bound about the Reins will cure the most cruell pains of the Kidnies. And if Troches be made of the pouder of the most choice Frankinsence, with Goates bloud; and take a pint from the foresaid plate of Gold, and when they are dry, if they be disolved in white Wine, and drank by the Patient, they have wonderfull force against stones in the kidnies, and of the bladder. *Andreas Cordubensis, ad summum Pontificem Gregorium, & Albertus Magnus.*

Another.

All kind of stones that are found in fishes heads, poudred and drank in Wine, cureth the Collick, and stone of the Kidneys, breaking it into pieces. *Galenus*, and *Avicenna.*

Another.

Against the stone, many magnifie from their own experience the pouder of the Pikes skin drank in water, of Pelitary of the Wall and white Wine. Others promise the same success from the skin of a Fish called a Mullet, with the distilled water of wild Tansey. *Mizald.*

Another.

Pouder of Glass is made by *Abenzoar* thus. A piece of clear *Venice* Glass that is thick and transparent, is smeared over with Turpentine, and put into burning coales untill it be red hot. Then he quencheth it in water, and smeers it over again, put it into the fire, and quencheth it; when you have done this seaven times, you must grind it into most fine pouder, the weight of one dram of this, or four scruples drank with white wine, forcibly drives out the stone. *Galen* and *Avicenna.*

Another.

A Sparrow called Troglodytes, which is the least of all Birds except the Wren, and it is a Sparrow that lives about hedges and Walls, and flies but a very little way, this Bird hath a wonderfull naturall force. For being pickled in Salt, and eaten raw for meat, he drives forth hard stone by urine, and hinders them from breeding again, and cures the disease. The best way to pickle him is to pull away his Feathers, and to cover him all over with abundance of Salt, and to eat him when he is dried. If you have many of them, you may rost them as Men do other small Birds; Also you may burn them Feathers and all in an open earthen pot, and give the Ashes of one that is burnt with a little Pepper and Cinamon. Some do pickle them alive in Salt, first pulling off their Feathers, which is the better way. Some eat them whole being roasted, so that they cast away nothing but their Feathers. *Ætius* and *Paulus Ægineta.*

Another.

Another.

Cherry tree gum dissolved in white wine, did help the stone, as was proved by *Mizald*.

Another.

Take the best *Aqua vitæ*, Oyl of sweet Almonds, of each two Ounces; drink this upon an empty stomach. *From a sure Friend.*

Another.

Rest harrow is said to be excellent against the stone, for it soon frees the Patient from pain, and quickly expels the stone; the pouder of the bark of the roots being drank with white wine. *Mizald.*

Another.

In this place very luckily came into my mind a Secret of a very learned Physician, which is easie and familiar to drive stones of the kidnies forth. It is only Syrup of Hysop, with twice or thrice as much water of Pellitory of the Wall. Which remedy being used for ten or twelve daies by a young Man in Winter, and others have used also fasting, he told me that he had driven forth many stones out of his body. *Mizald.*

For a weak Back.

Take four or five cap Dates, peel them, and stamp them in a Mortar, and put them to a yelk of an Egge, with a quarter of a pint of Muskadine, let the patient drink thereof morning and evening. Dr. *Rawlins.*

Another.

Take Amber, Nutmegs, and Corrall, of each of them alike, beat them into very fine pouder, put thereto a little grated Cinamon, and mingle them all well together; and straine the same pouder upon a fine toast of Manchet, being first sprinkled over with very good Muskadine, being toasted brown on both sides: let the Patient eat the same fasting, and use it five or six daies together, and doubtless by Gods help this will cure him. *The same.*

A Charme for such as have the Stone and the Gout.

It is without superstition: The root of Male Piony gathered in *May*, the Moon increasing, and hanged about one for an Amulet, helps the gout and the stone. *Cardan.*

For pains of the Kidnies, and the Tenasmus.

Young Pigeons by a secret property help the stone of the Kidnies, and cure corrupt blood: but you must kill them by cutting off their heads. Their flesh hath a power to cure the Tenasmus, and gourds frequently eaten are wont to breed it. *Rhasis.*

For the stone in the Bladder.

A water may be thus made, which being injected with a Catheter, will break the stone of the Bladder. For two things being necessary that it break the stone and may not hurt the Bladder; the first is performed by the manner and matter; for we must preserve the last vapours of Scorpious Ashes, Parsely of *Macedonia*, Tecolithas or Crabs stone; for a water will be made so that will dissolve a Porphyr stone. *Cardan.*

To purge the Kidnies.

If seed found in the lesser Burdock be made into fine pouder, and drank with a little of the best white wine; it will purge the Kidnies effectually from stones, but something sooner if it be drank with *Aqua vitæ*. *Mizaldus from an experienced Man.*

To provoke Urine.

A Hedg Toad cut in twaine and applyed to the Reins will vehemently provoke Urine, that sometime people that have the Dropsie Ascites have been cured by it. *Cardan.*

Another.

The stalke of Hartichoke boyled in Wine and dranke, will drive forth plenty of stinking Urine; and so will help a Virulent and Venerious Gonorrhæa.

norrhæa. *Dioscorid. Oribasius, Paulus*, and *Langius*.

For difficulty of making water.

Worms called hundred feet that are found in Wine Cellars, will mightily provoke Urine stopt, if they be bruised and drank with white Wine, or dried into pouder, and so drank with wine. It is a Secret a friend freely imparted to me, and so do I as frely give it to you. *Mizald*.

For the strangury.

Stones taken forth of the heads of Snails and greatest house Snails, will make those that are troubled with the strangary make water, making the passages slippery, if they be beaten to pouder and drank with wine. They help also women in labour by relaxing and dilating the parts. *Mizald*.

Another.

A Goose tongue is admirable against the strangury. *Cardan*.

For Diseases of the Bladder.

Some things do by similitude affoard great ease, as three Ox Bladders boyled in water, the water must be drank, and the Bladders dried, and drank with water, some say this will cure all diseases of the bladder, but especially voiding too much Urine, when they cannot hold their water. *Cardan*.

For Scabs of the Bladder.

The Decoction of the hearb called Horsetail, will cure the Scab of the Bladder, an intolerable disease, as many have proved it. *Mizald*.

For a Gonorrhæa.

The root of Hartichoke boyld in wine and drank, is a present remedy for a veneriall Gonorrhæa: as was proved by *Joan. Langius*.

A remedy for heat of the Urine.

Take roots of Mallows, Marsh Mallows, Parsely, of each one handfull, boyle them in River water, untill a third part be wasted, strain it; then put in fresh Butter the quantity of a Nut, and drink it off two houres before Dinner upon an empty stomach. *A Knight of Ferrara*.

For piss a Beds.

Take the juyce of Cyprus leaves, Oyl of Sesama, of each two Ounces, mingle them, and drink them in the morning, and when you go to bed, for three daies, and in the mean time eat no Sallets nor Pot hearbs. This is best for Women. *Bayrus*, as I remember.

For the running out of the Urine.

The bladder of a Sheep or Goat burnt, and drank with water and Vinegar, or a Hares testicles boyled in sweet wine and drank, helps such as make their water against their will. *Miz*.

To coole the hotness of the Urine.

Take Purselaine seeds, Lettice seeds, Endive seeds, white Poppy seeds, of each two Ounces, Henbane seed half a dram, Sebestine two Ounces, Saffron one dram, Licorish five drams, Pine Apple Kernels ten drams, Fountain or Spring water six pounds; mix them all together, and let them be sodden till the third part be boyled away, then let the water be strained, whereof take one Ounce in the morning mixed with Julep of Violets, and the fourth day you shall have certain ease. *Dr. Webster*.

Urine stopt.

Take a pint of good white wine, two roots of Pellitory of *Spain*, two roots of Parsely clean scraped, shred small, and boyled in the wine a pretty while, then take a handfull of Bees, pound them, and put them into the liquor aforesaid, then strain them into another Vessell, sweeten it with Sugar, *Probatum est*, Mr. *Williams*.

Urine like blood to cure.

Take of good Muskadine half a pinte, into which put the yelks of two or three eggs new laid, being first well beaten, and mingled together, drink the same in a morning fasting, and the like at night when you go to bed; this must be used two or three daies together. *Dr. Whistler*.

For pains of the Piles.

Take leaves of Mallows, Violets, Marsh Mallows, of each one handfull and half, Melilote, Fenigreek, flowers of Camomile, Linseed, of each one handfull, Mullets two handfuls; make a decoction in an equall quantity of water and red Wine. *A Manuscript.*

Another.

Take crums of Bread of Barly if you can get it, and wet it in Womans or Goats milk, adding the yelk of an egg and Saffron. *A Manuscript.*

For the Whites an Unguent.

Take red Corall, Myrrh, bark of Frankinsence, juyce of Roses, Cyprus Nuts, leaves of wild Pomegranates, Mastick, Frankinsence, Amber, Spicknard, Galla Moschata, Coriander prepared, of each one scruple, Oyl of Roses, Mastick, Spicke, Rue, of each half an Ounce, with a little Wax, make an Unguent. *Rosselius.*

To remove the Matrix from its place.

The greater Burr leaf, applied to the crown of the head draws the Matrix upwards, but applied to the soles of the feet draws it downward. This remedy is held to be the best against suffocations, precipitations and dislocations of the Matrix. Cato writes of a Colewort leaf, that laid on the crown of the head, it will draw the Matrix that is fallen downward, or ill affected otherwise, up again. *Mizaldus.*

For Women troubled with strangling of the womb.

It is proved most certainly, that the smell of Bitumen, be it raw or burnt, will presently recover women that are strangled with the Mother; wherefore some that are subject to this disease, use to wrap some of it in Wool, and hang it about their necks; for by often smelling to it, it will drive away fits of the Mother. *Langius.*

That Women may become barren.

If Childrens teeth when they fall, be hanged up before they come to touch the ground, and be set in a plate of silver, and hanged over women, this will hinder them to conceive, and to bring forth. *Albertus.*

Another for the same.

If Sorrel seed be bound up in a cloth and hanged over her left brest, she will never conceive so long as it hangs over it. *Albertus.*

Another for the same.

When a Woman drink Rams piss, or Hares blood; or if Hares dung be hanged over a Woman, she will never conceive. *Albertus.*

Another way that Women may be barren.

If any one take out the heil bone of a female Weesil, she remaining still alive, and hang this over a woman, she will not conceive so long as it hangs over her; but when you remove it she will be with childe. Or if you take the two testicles of a Weesil and bind them, and ty them cross over the woman, and if she carrieth them with her, she will not conceive. *Albertus.*

That a Man may be an Eunuch alwaies.

That a Man may alwaies be an Eunuch, take of that worm that shines in Summer, and give it him to drink. *Albertus.*

Birth to make easie.

Take a little Castle-sope, temper it in the hand, untill it be soft, then make it into little Pills, whereof the party may swallow down five, being a little rowled in sugar, then let there be in a readiness a good draught of posset drink, wherein some Succory hath been boyled, let the party drink it as hot as she can suffer it and it will work the effect. *N. Culpepper.*

Another way.

Take Polypodium and stamp it very well, and make a plaister thereof and apply it to the feet of the woman that travaileth with child, and this will cause a speedy delivery of the child whether it be alive or dead. *Probatum est.* Dr *Chamberlain.*

Another way.

Take of new Cow-dung, Cinamon two drams, of Mirrh, and Cassia Lignea, of each a scruple, of white Amber one dram and half; beat them together into fine pouder, whereof

whereof in odoriferous Wine the weight of one dram. Dr. *Chamb.*

To draw back Rheume.

Take a Figge and slice it in the middle, and dip it in English Honey, and lay it to the nape of the neck, and it will draw the Rheume back. Mr. *Loftis.*

Against barrenness in women.

The seed of sowr Dock or of Monks Rheubarb bound to the left arm, cures barrenness in women. *Africanus.*

That a woman may conceive.

If a woman cannot conceive, take Harts horn and pouder it, and mingle it with Cows gall; let the woman hold this over her, let her use copulation and she shall conceive presently. Or give to the woman that knows not of it Mares milk, let her copulate that hour, and she shall conceive presently. *Albertus.*

Things that help conception.

Nature is helpt by things of like nature. Mares milk drank after the terms, a Hares matrix, a Goats stones, help conception. And some things for their property, as Valerian, pouder of Cyprus wood, bark of Mulberry tree, and Mugwort. *Cardan.*

Things that hinder Abortion.

Some think the woman will not miscarry, if a Worm that is found living in the grass, before it touch the bare ground be hanged about her neck. *Cardan.*

Mother a Remedy.

Take of Fennell seed, Caraway seed, Parsly seed, Anniseed, Gromell seed, Galingale seed, of each two ounces, of Senu leaves two cods, one ounce of Spikenard, a quarter of an ounce of Time; make all these into pouder, and searce them thorow a fine searce, and put them into a box; let the diseased drink of this pouder in White wine the weight of six pence, and eat of the same with Meat instead of Salt as he findeth himself grieved. Dr. *Murford.*

Mother to cure.

Take of Anniseeds, Fennell seeds, Coriander seeds, of each one spoonfull, dry them well by the fire, beat them into a very fine pouder, put all into half a pint of very strong Ale without any hops in it, put thereto a spoonfull of Sallad oyl; let the patient drink it blood warm in a morning fasting, and at night: In the day time, drink this drink hereafter mentioned; take five branches of Motherwort, three leaves of Setwell, one Parsley root, one Vervain root, one Dill root, pound all these together and infuse it in half a pint of milk of a Cow of one hare; take both those drinks for four days together, and afterward for a week together, drink every morning a draught of Claret wine. Dr. *Anthony.* The same.

Codds swollen.

Take new horse-dung, mix the same with vineger and fresh butter, fry it in a pan, and as hot as the patient may endure, lay it to the grieved place. Mr. *Clows.*

Another for swollen Codds.

Take of the blades of green Wheat, and of Parsley, of each a handfull, boyl it in fresh butter with a little milk, and a little oatmeal, and lay it to the grief, as hot as the party may suffer it. Mr. *Lark Ch.*

Whether a woman be with child.

If you would try whether a woman be with child, let her piss in a brass bason, and for one night let a clean fine steel needle be laid in it: if she be with child, it will be full of red spots; if not, it will be black, or rusty, or cancred. *Mizaldus saith it was proved.*

To know how many Sonnes the woman shall have.

It hath no reason for it which they say the knots of the navell string will shew, how many sonnes will be born of one mother: for either they speak simply, and that according to the superstitious predictions of Astrologers; for it may be the woman may die, or live chastly, which may have otherwise many sonnes; or if they do not speak simply, it may be that they may have many knots that are married to one man, and fewer that are married to another: and this cannot be, that the same thing can be known by divers numbers of knots, or else the woman must have the greatest number

ber of knots to what man soever she is married. Since therefore it seldome falls out that this possibility should not faile: for either the Woman will not be married to that man that shall produce this, or if she be never so happily married, she may be hindered by diseases or some other accidents: how then can that be known which almost never happens? Wherefore we must conclude, that fruitfull Women commonly have more knots upon the Navel string in bearing, and barren women but few, and not exactly distinguished, that so the event may be foretold, and thus is the truth of this problem found out. *Cardan.*

To make a Woman retain her Child, an excellent meanes.

Take Oyle of Myrtills, Mastick, Turpentine, of each one dram, red and yellow Sanders, Hypocistis, Acacia, of each five drams, burnt Ivory, red Roses, of each five drams, Bolearmoniack, Terra sigillata, shavings of Ivory, of each two scruples, Mastick, Myrrh, Vernice, Dragons blood, Storax liquid, Greek pitch, Mummy, of each one dram, Ship pitch, Greek pitch, of each what is sufficient; make a Plaister which lay part upon the Reins, part upon the Matrix, or upon the Region of the Bladder. *Roscellus.*

That a Woman may be quickly delivered, and without pain, an approved way.

Take Clary a sufficient quantity, pound it well, and press forth the juyce: take half a cup full, mingle it with wine, and give it the woman to drink, when she is in labour, then bind the herb that is pressed hot to her Navell. *Alex.*

To hasten the birth.

The skin cast from a Snake when it is bound upon the hip of a woman it hasteneth her delivery, but so soon as she is delivered take it away. *Albert.*

For delivery.

The seaventh Daughter is reported to hasten the birth exceedingly. *Corn.*

To make easie delivery.

If a woman in hard labour hold a little piece of Basil in her hand with a Swallows Feather, she shall presently be delivered without pain: which *Mizaldus* learned of a friend that had tryed it.

Another.

The weapon of a Fish called a Ray bound to the Navill, is said to make easie delivery, if the forke be taken from the Fish being alive, and the Fish be cast again into the Sea. *Corn.*

And *Democritus* saith, That if the tongue of a Chamelion be taken from it whilst it is alive, that it is effectuall to foreshew future things, and it is good for labouring women to keep it about their houses; but they must be carefull that they bring it not within, for it is a most dangerous thing.

To bring forth the afterbirth.

Some say that the water of Marigolds is good for all sore eyes: and that it cures all pains of the head: and that a fume made of the flowers of it, received by a tunnell into the privities of a woman, or any way taken in, will easily bring forth the after burden that staies behind, and will bring back those things that are gone astray. I got this Secret from an old Midwife with much craft, when she stood in need of my help, when a great Matron was in Travail. *Mizald.*

A Purging Oyntment.

Take Oyl of Roses, Violets, sweet Almonds, Rue, Elder, Spurge, gall of a Wether, gall of a Bull, and of a Hog one Ounce, Wax what is sufficient; mingle them and make an Unguent, annoint the stomach and Navell with it. *Roscellus.*

Of Diseases of the Hands.

From trembling of the Hands.

Mugwort steeped in Rosewater, cures trembling hands, if you wash them with it. *Mizald.*

To draw thorns out of your fingers.

Take Southernwood a sufficient quantity, bruise it, and mingle it with Vinegar, and apply it. *Out of a Manuscript.*

Of Diseases of the Feet.

A remedy for the Gout, which was used by the King of Dacia.

Take Turbeth, Hermodactils, of each two drams, Ginger, Sal gemmæ, Cinamon, of each five drams, Diagridium, Anniseeds, Fennell seeds, of each one dram, Sugar-candy one Ounce: Make a pouder, take one dram of it and a half, to two drams, if the first quantity be too little; and in Summer you must take it with Endive water; in Winter, with the Broth of a Pullet, some five or six houres before dinner, sleeping one houre after it, or resting your self, and you may take it twice in a moneth, or onely once, and that on the last day but one of the Moon; yet for three daies before you take it, take every morning six Ounces of Honey, and water like to a Syrup, for this makes way for the pouder: but in the mean time every evening when you go to sleep, take two or three Pils of ground Pine, which are made of ground Pine pouder and Turpentine what may suffice. But the Patient must live as sober as he can, that he may find the benefit of such a remedy. *Out of a written Book.*

For the Gout.

Take Ship pitch two pound, Colophonia, Wax, of each five pound, Cresses seed, Bay berries, live Brimstone, Cummin, Saffron, Wormwood, Anniseed, Penniroyall, Mastick, of each two Ounces, Cinnamon one dram, Ginger two drams, Cloves five drams; make a Plaister according to Art. *Out of a Manuscript.*

Pils for the Gout.

Take Aloes, choice Myrrh, of each one dram, choice Rhubarb, Agarick in Troches, of each five drams, make a Mass with Syrup of Rose Solutive; of one dram make five Pils, let the Patient take of them two houres before meat, every fifteen daies. *Out of a written Book.*

Pains of the Gout beginning.

Take Oyle of Poppies two pound, of Spicknard two Ounces, mingle them, and set them eight daies together in the Sun, then press them forth, and keep them for your use. When you need them, add a little water distilled from Opium. The Oyle of Henbane will do the same. *Henr. Wolffius.*

Pils for the Gout.

Take the juyces of black Hellebore, Fumitary, Coloquintida, Gentian, Butterbur, Rheubarb, of Agarick, Rheubarb in pouder, Mastick, of each one dram; mingle them all well together, make a Mass, and make Pils of it; The dose is one dram, of which make Pils. *Henr. Wolffius.*

A remedy for the Gout.

Take Oyle of Cinnamon, Oyle of Wax, Oyle of Salt, of each one part, mingle them. *Andernacus.*

Another.

Take Frankinsence the weight of an Egge, the juyce of Singreen, a little strong Vinegar, mix all these together, and warme it, and annoint the place. *Dr Manley.*

Another.

Take of Goats milk for want of Cows milk five Ounces, the yelks of two Eggs, of Oyle of Roses one Ounce, Saffron half a dram, crums of Bread, as much as will suffice, to bring it to the forme of a Cataplasme, being stamped till they be well mixed together, and then apply thereof to the member or part grieved. *The same.*

Another.

Take a new earthen pan with a flat bottome, with upright brims like a Cheese-fat, but somewhat deeper well glazed, or some stone vessell after that fashion, which hath never been occupied, then take a Goat of four years old, for a Man a Male Goat, for a Woman a Female Goat; let this Goat be beheaded in the new of the Moon, you must not save the first nor the last bloud, but let the middle bloud run into your pan, and let it stand in the same pan untill it be thick and cold, then cut it out into gobbets like Trochiskes, and in a faire Sunny day, lay them abroad upon a net the better to turn them to dry on both sides, let them be very well dried before you lay them

them up; When you would use it, take a spoonfull of the pouder of the same blood, with Vinegar and Wine, or with the distilled water of Parsely, at such time as the Patient doth find himself least grieved, and you shall see a wonderfull effect. *Probatum.*

Another way to preserve your Goats blood.

Take the Goats bladder, and cast out the water that is in it, whilst it is warme, and put therein presently the bloud as before preserved in your pan, then hang this bladder with the bloud in it in the Chimney, where it may have the aire of the fire that it may be thorow dry, then use it as before prescribed. Add unto this the laudable remedies. Dress a hedg Sparrow in salt, and take him raw in meat, this doth heal the diseased presently, for it expelleth the stone, which is already ingendered by the Urine, and hindereth the same from further ingendering any more. *The same*

For the Gout when it first falls down.

Take Barly meal three Ounces, meal of Lentils two Ounces, Terra sigillata, Dragons bloud, of each two drams; let the meals be boyled at a gentle fire with Water and Vinegar, then put in the pouders, to which add Oyl of Roses two Ounces, new Wax one Ounce, make a Plaister, and when the defluxion is stopt, add pouder of Cammomile flowers half an Ounce, Saffron one dram, yelks of Eggs two in number. *Out of a Manuscript.*

Another.

An experiment of a Kings Chirurgion, against the Gout of hands and feet: Take a handfull of Mugwort, let it boyle in sweet Oyle of Olives, untill a third part only remain, annoint the pained part with it, you shall soon find the pain abated. *Miz.*

Another.

Burn the head of a Kite, the Feathers being pluckt off, and take as much of that as you can hold in three fingers, it helps the Gout. *Miz.*

Another.

If you take the right foot of a Tortois, and hang that over the right foot of him that hath the Gout in his feet, it will help him, and so it will, if you hang the left claw over the left foot; so the forefoot helps the hand, and the toe helps the toes. *Albert.*

Another.

It must not seem strange that the skin of the right heel of a Vulture laid on the right foot, and the left on the left foot, will cure the pains of the Gout. *Card.*

For the hip Gout.

The decoction of the rind of the white Poplar will extreamly ease the Sciatica, and the juyce of Broom boughs steeped in Vinegar will do the like. *Mizald.*

For diseases of the joynts.

The Oyl wherein Frogs are boyled untill the flesh part from their bones, is excellent against all pains of the joynts and nerves, and benummed limbs if they be annointed with it. *Miz.*

For the joynt Gout.

I first cured *Joan. Antonius Scazosus, Joan. Baptista Mareschalus,* one of the Secretaries of the Senate, and the Daughter of *Joan. Angelus Linatus,* and innumerable more of pains in their joynts. But I shall relate the cure of those three as most notable, *Joan. Antonius Scazosus* was sick of the joynt Gout two years, and no Physicians could help him, but I cured him with the decoction of Guaiacum with Betony, and Pils of Hermodactils. But *Joan. Baptista Mareschalus* was sick of it four Moneths, and I took him to cure in *December*; moreover he had two Feavers, one intermitting, another continuall, and what was worst of all, he loathed meat, and being hardly able to move, his Physician had good reason to leave him for incurable: or else he said he must wait for the spring time to cure him: and for that cause we disagreed; for I thought that was no good counsell, because the parts affected grew dayly weaker, for in mans body nothing stands still; and if they mend not, they must necessarily grow worse. Wherefore I boyled Coloquintida in clarified Honey, and I gave him the Honey mingled with Aromaticks to swallow down in bolus: and he drank the decoction of the wood in water, and so I cured him perfectly before Winter

ter was ended, that he never fell into a relapse for that Disease, and he is yet living. But the Daughter of *Angelus Linatus* had made triall, not only of all the Physicians for two years, but all Mountebanks, she had taken Wine, Water, Unctions, Fumes, of Artificiall Cinnaber, and she could not be cured. Her legs paind her, and she was so vexed with trembling, that sometimes she could not sleep all night, and was now hopeless as she had reason, having tried so many mighty Remedies. Wherefore giving he Wine with the best bark, I undertook the cure of that part, and bethinking my self of a remedy that was contrary to the cause of the disease, and the disease it self, and would strengthen the part, I commanded to take great quantity of the gum of the wood; which I mingled with Frankincense, Lignum Aloes, Seed of Balsam, sweet Storax, and Citron pills, (also I used great quantity of Jet stone with it) and I cured her perfectly, that she was well. Also I healed *Pet. Ant. Bezutius*, near to the Church of *Brera*, not far from the gate *Beatrix*, who had the Joynt-gowt, almost with the same remedies that I cured *Scazosus*, when he was left by his Physitian, all things growing worse continually.

That hands and feet may not be hurt by cold.

If one would not have his hands or feet hurt by cold, let him annoint them with Fox grease. *Mizaldus*.

To cure parts that are asleep.

When the limbs are straightned, the spirits cannot pass, whence they are so benummed, that a man cannot safely stand upon them, and they seem to be asleep: and besides that, one feels a kind of biting as if there were Ants; that comes because the parts are unequally affected; for the parts astonisht are joynd to the sound parts; therefore this infirmity both for weakness and pain is sometimes troublesome to a man: there is no more present remedy than to stretch forth the part and to rub it, or with the hand of the other side to lay hold of the great toe, and to rayse the foot of the leg that is benummed. *Cardan*.

Of particular Diseases external.

For wounds of the Head.

Take Aqua vitæ two pound and a half, Mastick in pouder, Myrrh in pouder, and Aloe poudred of each one ounce. Let them boyl one boyling at the fire, then strain forth the water, when the wounds are washt, strew in the following pouder. Take Frankinsence, Myrrh, Aloes, of each one ounce, mingle them, make a pouder very fine. *Rosselius*.

Another for the same.

Take Frankinsence, Myrrh, Aloes, Rosin, of each one ounce, make a pouder, strew it on the wound, but first wash it with Aqua vitæ.

Ears sounding.

Take of Almonds and the kernels of Peaches, and let them be clean pilled in hot water, then stamp them and press oyl out of them, put the oyl with wool in the same into the ears that are grieved, which Tents must be made of fine linnen cloth, do this with new Tents every day once for the space of nine or ten days. *M. Clarke*.

Ears watering.

Mingle Turpentine with Oyl and Honey, and drop it into the ears, it cureth the watering of the ears. *Mr. Baley*.

An Oyl against Wounds, Cramps and Pains.

Take pure Turpentine one pound, common Oyl one ounce, Frankinsence, Myrrh, Sarcocolla, Mastick, Saffron, of each one ounce, Sow bread, Horstail, madder, of each one ounce, Earth worms three ounces: Put them all in a Retort, and distill them according to Art. *Fallopius*.

A wonderfull Oyl for all sorts of Wounds.

Take Turpentine one pound, Frankinsence, Mastick, Myrrh, Sarcocolla, of each one ounce, Aqua vitæ eight ounces; mingle them and distill them in a Retort, after that separate the Oyl from the water and keep them. *Fallopius*.

Another especially for wounds of the Nerves.

Take pure Turpentine one pound and half, yellow Wax one pound, Nutmegs, Cloves,

Book V. Secrets in Physick and Surgery. 73

Cloves, of each one ounce, wood ashes six ounces, beaten bricks what may be sufficient, mingle them and distill them in a Retort. *Fallopius.*

Another for the same.

Take oyl of Firr, whites of Eggs boyled, of each one pound, Rosin six ounces, Ivy gum two ounces: mingle them and distill them in a Retort according to Art.

A Balsam for Wounds: of the same Mans.

Take pure Turpentine one pound and half, oyl of Bays, Galbanum, gum Arabick, gum Ivy, of each one ounce; Frankinsence, lignum Aloes, Galanga, Cloves, Nutmegs, middle Comfrey, Cinamon, Zedoary, Ginger, white Dittany, of each six drams, Storax liquid two ounces, Musk, Amber, of each one dram: pouder what must be poudred and mingle them: add to them Aqua vitæ seven pound, put them into a glazed vessel well stopt for eight days, then distill them first with a gentle fire, untill the Oyl begins to drop, then increase it untill you have distilled it all; then part the Oyl from the water and keep it.

Oyl for Wounds.

Take Turpentine two pound, Linseed oyl one pound, Rosin of the Pine tree six ounces, Frankinsence, Mastick, Myrrh, Sarcocolla, Mace, Saffron, lignum Aloes, of each two ounces : put them into a Retort, and distill them, first with a gentle fire, afterward with a stronger. *Fallopius.*

Oyl to cure Wounds in 24 hours, and for a Rupture.

Take common Oyl six pound, Oyl of Firr tree one pound, choice Myrrh six ounces, washt Aloes, Frankincense, of each six ounces, Mummy two ounces, common Glew six ounces, Cochineal four ounces, Ship-pitch six ounces, Gum of the Sycomore tree two ounces, Lees of Oyl two pound, of Marsh mallowes seven ounces; put all these into a strong glass Retort, and boyl them twelve hours in Balneo : then strayn them, and add to the strained liquour Dragons four handfulls, flowers of wild Pomegranates, four handfulls; great Comfrey, with the flowers, hearb and root four handfulls, Betany, Tobacco, of each four handfulls ; Balsam, herb and fruit, four handfulls, Cyprus leaves four handfulls ; Elm bladders forty, Yarrow, Seacole, of each four handfulls ; ripe Dates twenty five : St Johns wort, Thorow wax, small Century, Shepherds purse, of each four handfulls: boyl them again in Balneo eighteen hours, then set them in the Sun a whole Summer in a glass very well stopt. After this take all out, strain it, pressing it very hard, and to the Oyl add at last beaten Saffron three ounces, and boyl all together for three hours, and keep this Oyl for your use. If you would use this Oyl for a Rupture, you must first shave off the hayre, then for fifteen days you must annoint the Rupture twice every day : then bind it over with a Hogs bladder and firm ligature : and you must be carefull that the Patient keep his bed for fifteen days. *Roscellus.*

For Wounds.

For all Wounds the Remedy that follows is the best, and the most easie to provide: You must take Greek pitch, Brimstone and white Frankinsence, of each equall parts, then pouder them, and mingle them with whites of Eggs, and the lips of the wound being rightly ordered and drawn together, and the blood being wiped away, this is put upon a linnen cloth, and must be laid to the wound, and bound on with a band and must so continue some days. *A wonderfull and an approved thing.* Mizaldus.

Sores and Cuts old or new to heal.

Put fair and cleer water into an earthen vessel that hath not been used, and when the water is reasonably hot, pour it into quick unslenched lime, the lime being before in another new earthen vessell : let it remain and rest so long therein untill it be setled, which will be in six hours, then skim off the froth with a feather, keep the same water in a glass, or some other vessel close stopt for your use ; it is good for all Ulcers, new wounds or Cuts, biting of a mad dogg or others ; you must bathe the Sore with this water warmed ; and when you have so done, take of this water clean, and when it is blood warm, wet a fine cloth in the water and lay it eight or ten times double upon the sore, do this untill it be whole : Note that to every quart of water, you must use a quarter of a pound of good new stone lime, the pan that goes to the fire,

must

must always go to the fire, and the other pan always go for the Lime. Dr. *Sadler*.

Blood to stop in a green wound.

Take a Puff which groweth in the field like a bell, slit him asunder, and lay a slice as thick as your two fingers upon the Cuts; then bind up the wound, but not very hard, and at three days end bind up the same; and if the Puff do cling so that you cannot get it off, take Oyl of Roses warmed, or instead thereof a little warm Milk, and bathe the place therewith, untill the Puff fall away of himself; you may keep those puffs two or three years. M. *Moulins*.

For malignant Ulcers.

A wonderfull water soon made, which no gold can value, is made thus. Clear spring water is put into a vessel never used before; when it boyls it must be poured into another vessell that was never used, that hath new quick Lime in it, and there it must remain so long untill all the froth be taken off, and the water is clear, the Lime sinking to the bottom of the water, like to Pap. Then the water that swims above it is to be poured off neatly by inclining the vessell, and not stirring the Lime; this water must be kept in a clean viol or some other pure vessell, for use. It can hardly be believed what power and force it hath for all wounds, especially such as proceed from the French Pox; for by bathing the part with a rag suddenly wet in it, and afterward laid on instead of a Plaister, and being sometimes removed, it cleanseth away the filth, easeth the pain, fills the ulcer with good flesh, and in short time extinguisheth all Inflammations; and this is a strange miracle: for quick lime will inflame by its heat. Enjoy this Secret, which I have refused to discover to many for a great reward. *Mizald*.

A precious Oyl or Balsam that may be dropt into Wounds that are upon any part of the body except the Head.

Take Oyl of Roses nine ounces, Rheubarb cut small six ounces; let all these close stopt for three days, stand in a great viol or flagon of Tin: then let the flagon with the Ingredients aforesaid be set in Balneo, and let it boyl well half an hour: then cast into the flagon, Mastick finely poudred, six drams; also of Frankinsence, Bdellium, Opoponax, Camphir, of each half an ounce, or parts equall; after that strain that Oyl through a clean woollen cloth, that all the vertue of the Ingredients may be pressed forth, and you have an Oyl ready for your use that is excellent. *Rantzovius*.

A notable vulnerary Cataplasme against any Wound or stroke, which was used by the King of Denmarke, Christian the second.

Take Wax three ounces and half, Colophonia or Greek Pitch, Smalt, Mummy, of each one ounce and half; Myrrh one ounce, Redlead half an ounce, white Corall three drams, Loadstone one ounce. First dissolve the Wax with the Colophonia; then add the Mummy, after that the Smalt; place these over a gentle fire, and stirre them well; then putting in the foresaid Ingredients that are left, let all stand by an easie fire, for a little time, and stirre them well and often; also try often whether it be sufficiently boyld, and setleth toward the bottom. Drop a few drops from above from the hot spatula into cold water: and if you find it begins to be thick, and to stick to the spatula, take it from the fire, and stirre it long, untill it grow cold of it self, and become a solid mass, lest the three following Gums be burnt in it. Add then Frankinsence and Mastick of each one Ounce, Camphire one ounce and half, and stirre it so long in the earthen pot untill it become cold and hard, and may be handled and made up with the foresaid fatty substance: Thus have you a Plaister rightly made. If then the wound be new, spread it on a linnen cloth, and lay it on the part hurt. This Plaister is good for all wounds, be they cut with the edg, or thrust with the point.

A Vulnerary Potion of the same Man.

Take wild Wintergreen, and Betony, of each one dram, Sanicle, Lionsfoot, of each half a dram, with two measures of Wine close stopt in a glased earthen pot; which must be close stopt with wheat dough; yet leave a hole in the middle of the cover, that the vapour may come forth: Boyl this Potion two hours, give of this Potion to the wounded

wounded Patient one spoonfull every morning and evening to drink, and lay upon the wound a Cabbage leaf, or the former Plaister.

Another Vulnerary Potion whereby Wounds are strangely cured.

Take two quarts of old Ale, cast into it one handfull of Doricknium, and the stalks of red Mugwort, and a little of the hearb called in high-Dutch *Rodichew*, or for want of that, take the hearb Perwinkle, boyl it to half in an earthen vessell, covering it well with a cover: then strain it forth into an earthen pot or stone bottle, so that the mouth of it may be well stopt, that the ayre come not in, and keep it for your use. You shall give of this potion to a man fasting in a morning, that is wounded, and at noon after dinner, and at night when he goes to bed, every time three spoonfulls; and you must command the Patient to fast three hours after it; and as oft as he drinks of it, let him put a little of it into a Sawcer and wash his wounds: also let him lay a red Colewort leaf, or one that is dark coloured, dipt into this liquor, upon the wound, so that the rougher side of the leaf be next the wound; and it must be firmly wrapt about with linnen, and if the wound can be drawn together, it must be stitcht with a needle, that the scarr be not great, yet this potion will heal the wounds however.

For a sodain Swelling.

Take one part of Wine vineger, and two parts of fair water, put to this as much fine Flower as will make it thick, and lay it warm to the grief, it will heal any sodain swelling that looks red. Mr. *Boon*.

Another.

Take a good quantity of water, put thereto a good quantity of Salt, and steep it well together; then wet a cloth five or six times double therein, and lay it thereto; and it helps any sodain swelling. *The same.*

White Scurf to cure.

Take Elecampane roots, scrape them very clean, pound them in a morter, put thereunto a quantity of Sallad Oyl, and double as much Vinegar as Oyl; work these together till they be very thick, then cut off the hair close and annoint the forehead with this Oyntment, and when the sore is fallen off, wash the head with Cow piss warmed. *The same.*

That a Wound may be made without pain.

There is a white Loadstone, not unlike to the Loadstone with which I saw such an experiment done. *Laureatius Guascus Cherascius*, a Physitian and Emperick of the Province of *Piemont*, brought this stone lately hither, and he promised to do strange things with it, that if it did but touch a bodkin or needle, it would enter into the flesh without pain; and when I thought, as I had reason, that it was a foolish thing, he made experience of it, by one of my Chamberfellows. I to make triall of such an incredible thing, rubbed the point of a needle upon the same my self, and thrust it into my arm, and I first felt a very small pain: but afterwards when it ran almost directly through the whole muscle, I felt the needle indeed enter as it went deeper and deeper, but I felt no pain, and then I told my familiar friends what I had found by it. *Cardan.*

A most excellent Plaister, which the Chirurgion of John Frederick formerly Elector of Saxony, when he lived in the County of Tyrol with Charls the fift, at Oenopontum, taught the most Illustrious Duke of Holsatia, against any blow and wound of gunshot, and it hath a wonderfull vertue to cure them.

Take Galbanum, Ammoniacum, Opoponax, Bdellium, Wax, common Oyl, of each two pound; prepared Lytharge of Silver one pound, Oyl of Bays half an ounce, Myrrh, Frankinsence, Mastick, Arstolochia, Cadmia, or Lapis Calaminaris prepared, Gelamy one ounce, Camphire half an ounce, Turpentine one dram; reduce it into pouder and make it red hot in the fire, and whatever must be dissolved dissolve, and make a Plaister thus: Steep the four Gums a whole night in the sharpest wine Vinegar, in a vessell made of Alchimy, or an earthen pot that is leaded, so that the Vinegar may swim above the gums in greater quantity, then boyl the Gums untill they melt, and all sticks, filth, and the like may be separated from them; then press them out

out through a linnen cloth into a pot or pipkin, and boyl the Gums again untill all the Vinegar be consumed, and till the Gums will part from the pipkin; melt the Oyl and Wax in a bason of Alchimy, put in the Lytharge, and stir it with a stick that the Lytharge may settle to the bottom, and when it begins to be of a brownish colour, make triall with a broad knife, or spatula, and if it do not cleave fast to the knife but runs of, it is a sign that it is well boyled: wherefore remove it presently from the fire, and let it cool a little, yet not too soon. After this of the four Gums steeped in Vinegar, at each time cast in the quantity of a Bean or small Nut, by degrees into the Plaister, untill the Gums be entred well: for should you throw them all in at once, the Plaister would boyl over, and perhaps all run forth. But to be more provided, have always a bason of water ready, that if it boyl too much it may be held over the water to keep it cool: and again put that into the Plaister that is poured forth into the water. And as soon as the Gums are entred into the Plaister, boyl it again a little while, then add Myrrh, Mastick, Frankincense, Lapis Calaminaris, Aristolochia; bring these again into very fine pouder by degrees over the fire, yet not with too much heat, lest thereby the pouders burn and consume away. Last of all cast in the Turpentine and Oyl of Bays, and when it is totally removed from the fire, and waxeth cold, cast in the Camphire: After this cast it into hot water, untill such time as it be made fit to be handled and worked by your hands. After this macerate it with Oyl of Mugwort that it may be bright and pure, then wrap it in a Does skin well prepared; thus you may keep it for use forty or fifty years. This Plaister is good against all wounds made with gunshot, all blows, and inflammations of wounds. *Henr. Rantzovius.*

To keep open an Issue.

Take of white Wax half a pound, of Verdegreece three ounces, Mercury sublimate one ounce, mingle them well together. *Dr. Matthias.*

A way to provide a Pouder good for any Nerve cut asunder, which the Chirurgion hath to cure.

Take Crabs eys beaten into very fine pouder in a little linnen cloth, strew this pouder upon the Nerves, and bind up the place with dry bands of linnen, that no moysture may come at the Nerves. Let this Ligature ly on for 24 hours unremoved: After this is past let the Chirurgeon look upon the wound, and try how it is glewed together, and then let him bind it up again with hot bands, as he would do any green wound, and after one day or two let him unlose the bands. *The same.*

A certain way how to stop Blood running forth of any Wound.

At the entring of the Spring when Frogs lay their Spawn, then take three ells of thick woollen cloth, or four, more or less, as you need; wash this cloth well with this Spawn, and then dry it in the Sunne; then do it again the second and third time, washing and drying it in the Sunne; and then lay it up carefully for your use: when you will use this, cut off a piece twice as big as the wound, and lay it over the wound for a Plaister, and this will presently stop the bleeding, as is certainly proved in many. *The same.*

To assuage Swelling.

Take of new dung and fresh Butter and fry it in a frying pan, then spread it upon a cloth like a Poultis, and lay it on as hot as the Patient can suffer it. *Probatum est.* Dr. *Johnston.*

A Cautery to make without pain.

An Escharotick is easily made without pain, that shall penetrate the skin in twenty four hours: If the skin be whole, it is laid upon it, onely compassed about with leather, but if there be corruption under the skin, as in Impostumes, it must be washt with the sharpest Vinegar. The Medicament is made of quick Lime and thin Sope mingled together finely, that it may be like to an Unguent. *Cardan.*

A strange cure of a malignant Ulcer.

The youngest Brother of the King of *France* had a most filthy Ulcer, and extreme foul: he was cured by the continuall breathing on it, of a Boy of twelve years old. And there is reason for it; for the breath that proceeds from the Heart of a Youth that is healthfull, is sincere, and may correct corrupt humours. *Cardan.*

For Ulcers.

I know some who gathered the Dew before Sun rising in *May*, with linnen clothes spread upon the grass, this they would press out, boyl and skim, and then they would wet clothes in the decoction and lay upon eating Ulcers to very good purpose, for they would thus cure the Ulcers by the acrimony of the dew, adding onely a little Alum and Frankinsence to the decoction. *Mizald.*

For Burning and Scalding.

Take four ounces of the juyce of Onions, common Salt half an ounce, mingle them well together annoint the soar. *Lord Bacon.*

Another.

Take of Sheeps suet half a pound, of Sheeps dung, and Violet leaves, of each two handfulls; stamp them well together, then heat it in a frying pan or some other thing, and strain out the juyce; and when you dress the sick Patient, warm it and annoint the sore places with a feather, untill it be whole. *Dr. Johnson.*

A Caustick that will suddenly eat through the skin.

Sometimes we are desirous to eat through the skin suddenly, not trusting to section: I have elsewhere described a most easie Medicament, but now a most effectuall: for it is made of Sope-water, or of a strong lee of ashes. It is made thus; pour on twelve pounds of strong lee upon quick Lime and Oke ashes, and let them drain through, then poure it again upon new Lime and Ashes, and do this so often, untill that the water will beare an Egg. Then adde to every pound of Lee one ounce or half, an ounce of Vitrioll, and by degrees boyl it thick in a brass Posnet, untill you can take it forth and make little Cakes of it: for it is taken forth by degrees with a spoon, if this be well made, it will penetrate the skin in half a quarter of an houre. *Cardan.*

For pricking of a Sinew.

Take oyl of Camomile, and Earth wormes, of each half an ounce, of oyle of Saffron one ounce and a half, of oyl of whites of Eggs two drams, of *Aqua vitæ* as much as shall suffice, mingle them together, and so apply it to the prick. Mr *Jones.*

Another.

Take oyl of Turpentine, oyl of Roses, oyl of Earth-wormes, oyle of whites of Eggs, of each three drams, mingle them all together, apply either of these actually hot, both will mitigate paine; and for more security and speedy help, to ease the pains apply there with all this remedy following.

Another.

Take of crums of Bread, of Cow milk, mingled with oyle of Roses, and Camomile, with white of Eggs, and Saffron, of each as much as shall suffice, boyle these together to the thicknes of a Plaister, and apply it warm.

To know if any part be Sphacelated.

If you would know whether any part be to be cut off, and is quite dead, take the green of Leeks, and bruise them, and lay them one night over the part; if the day following the part be not so wan or black, it signifies that there is some life in it, otherwise that it is dead and to be cut off, that all the sound parts perish not by it. A certain *Spaniard* saith to me, that this was often proved, who was a diligent searcher of nature, and I am willing to communicate it to posterity. *Mizald.*

To draw darts out of wounds.

You shall draw the heads of Arrows or any Iron out of a wound, if you wet a tent in the juyce of Valerian, and put it into the wound, and lay the bruised Herb upon it. For so not only will the Iron be driven forth, but the wound will be cured; unless an *Italian* do ly notably, who protested he had tried it; the leaves of Garden Clary will do as much; for bruised and laid on, it draweth forth Splints. *Miz.*

For Members that have the Palsey.

Take of the best Weathers fat two cups, boyl them to half, then add oyl of Roses one cup, and boyl them again untill half be consumed, and annoint the parts that have the Palsey with it. *Roscellus.*

Another.

Another for the same.

Take Rosemary, Marjoram, Mints, Savin, Horf-mints, Sage, what is sufficient, bruise them very well, and with marrow of Ox feet make an Unguent. *Roscellus*.

For the Palsie of the Nervs.

Take Mans blood what is sufficient, distill it seven times according to art, untill all the water be come forth, annoint the Nervs that have the Palsey with it. *Fallopius*.

For a Rupture.

Take Rosemary leaves and flowers, Myrtill leaves, of each half an ounce, Rosin, Plaister of Betony, of each two ounces, clear Turpentine what may suffice, make a Plaister. *Out of a Manuscript*.

For a prick with a Dagger, Thorne, or any other thing, that cannot be tainted.

Take clean boulted Wheat flower, temper it with Wine or Vinegar, and a little Bolearmoniack, beate them at the fire untill they be as thick as Pappe, and make a Plaister, and lay it upon the sore, and before your Plaister be laid on, annoint it with oyle of Roses, and bowlster it on both sides, and Rowle it up. Mr. *Goddard Chir*.

For Lice of the privy parts.

Take Hogs grease, Quicksilver, Sage, of each a sufficient quantity; mingle them all well together, and make an Unguent, annoint the parts that are lowsy with it. *Fallopius*.

Another.

Take Venice Sope, what is sufficient, add to it Quicksilver killed; mingle them and stir them well, that they may be like an oyntment, and annoint the parts that are Lowsy with it, and the Lice will dye presently. *Casparius Schwenkfeldius*.

Lice to kill, a Shipboard, bed or body.

Take May Butter, or unscalded Cream one ounce, three peny worth of Quicksilver, warme them in a luted Pot of Loame, and so stir them till they be incorporated together, then take a small linen cloath of three Inches, and steep it therein, then take a piece of silke, and sow into it, and hang it about your neck: often found certaine by Dr. *Thomson*.

Another for Lice of the Head.

Take flowers of flower gentle boyled in Lye, if you wash your head with it, it kils the Lice, and it cures the bran and scurf also. *Hieron Tragus*.

That any part may swell much without pain.

If any one wash the part with the distilled, or decoction of Wasps and Hornets, it will swell like to a great Dropsye, or a part that is poisoned, but without pain. The remedy is Theriac drank, or smeered on the part. By this cheat some Women use to counterfeit a great belly, and deceive some that are very cautious, they do it so cunningly; and they make the people think they are in great misery, and so beg from street to street. This was a Secret of *Rogatus*, the chief Physician of *Paris*, who was School-Master of the poor people that belong to the Church, an excellent man, and this Art I had from one of his contemporaries, a familiar Friend of his. *Miz*.

A Restorative.

Take a pound of Cup dates, pick them very clean, and take forth all the stones, then seeth them in a pint of Muscadine, that is pure and not mingled, and let it seeth till a good part be consumed, then put it into a glass, and as you have occasion to use it, put three or four spoonfuls thereof at a time, into your pottage or broth, and if you think good, you may use it as aforesaid, every male in broth, and it will be better, and do you exceeding much good. Dr. *Mathias*.

Another.

Take a pint of Muskadine, divide it into equall parts, put into one half part a quarter of a pound of Rasins of the sunne stewed and bruised in it, and unto the other half part, two yelks of new laid Eggs beaten and bruised in it, then put the Wine altogether with the yelks and Rasins, strain them, and drink a good draught of the Wine so put up morning and evening as long as it lasteth. *The same*.

Another.

Take a pound of Dates and wash them clean in Ale or Beer, then cut them, take out

out the stones and the white skins, then bray them very small and fine in a marble morter, till they be as tough as wax; then take a quart of clarified Honey, and put the Dates before poured into it, let them remain untill the be dissolved; take also of long Pepper half an ounce, and as much of Mace, Cloves and Nutmegs beaten into fine pouder; then seeth the Dates and Honey over a soft fire, and cast in the pouder by little and little, stirring it very fast, let it seeth untill it grow thick, then let it to cool, and put it up into a close box or gally pot, and thereof eat first and last, and it shall restore a man be he never so weak or low brought: use this sometimes upon a full stomack and you shall not surfit therewith. Dr *Samwayes*.

For the biting of a mad Dog.

Colewort leaves and also the seed bruised with Vinegar and maserwort, do perfectly cure the biting of any dog, be he mad or not. It will not be amiss to add here what was shewed by an Oracle, That the root of Eglantine Rose, or Sweet-briar, is the principall and onely remedy against the biting of a mad dog, unless you will forswear *Pliny* and *Galen*. *The same*.

For the biting of a mad Dog, and stinging of Scorpions.

For a Man stung by Scorpions, the remedy is the ashes of Scorpions drank in Wine: and they say that the biting of a mad Dog is to be cured, if much hair of the same creature be burnt to ashes and drank in Wine. *Plin. Lemnius*.

Another for the biting of a mad Dog.

For the biting of a mad Dog, Crabs are burnt upon a fireshovell that they may be poudred. A spoonfull of this pouder must be given with the pouder of the root of Gentian and a little Frankincense. But this Antidote must be given oft times, and be taken continually for six weeks, whereby the madness and fear of water may be cured. *Mizaldus*.

Against the madness of Dogs.

An Herb called Alyssum is excellent against the madness of Dogs, and therefore as *Galen* and *Aetius* say it is called Alyssum, from madness. *Mizaldus*.

Another against the biting of a mad Dog.

River Crabs are excellent for those that are bit by mad Dogs, but they must be burnt in a posnet after the rising of the Dog-Star, when the Moon is XIV days old, and the Sun is entred into Leo. A spoonfull thereof is to be drank in a small cup of water, whilst the biting is yet fresh, and if it come to grow old the quantity must be augmented. *Galen* saith, the force is so great, that none die to whom it is given in time.

Canker to kill.

Take Doves-foot, Archangell, Ivye with the berries young, Red bryer tops and leaves, White rose leaves and buds, Red sage, Celandine, and Woodbine, of each a like quantity, chop it and put it in white Wine and clarified Honey; then break into it Allome, and put into it a little pouder of Alloes hepatick, and distill these together softly in a Limbeck of pure Tinne: keep this water close, it will not onely kill the Canker, if it be daily washed therewith, but also two drops put inth the eyes will sharpen the sight, break Pearl and spot, especially if it be dropped in with a little Fennel water, and close the eye after. M. *Moulins*.

For a Canker or swelling of the Mouth and Yard.

Take of white Wine and fountain Water of each half a pound, of Smiths water one pound; mingle these together, put therein Bramble leaves, and Woodbine leavs, red Sage, and Plantaine, (if you have not the water distilled) of each a handfull. The inner Rind of an Oake shred small a handfull, boyl it all together, then strain it, and put therein as much Sugar-candy as will take away the sharpness of it, the quantity of a Beane, of white Copperas, wash the Mouth, likewise spout it into the yard with a syringe, it hath been very often experimented. Dr. *Mathias*.

Potion to purge.

Set a pinte of White wine to the fire till it be blood warm, then put thereto of Anniseed, Coriander seed, and of Sene Alexandrina of each a spoonfull, a Licorish stick the length of a finger, scraped and bruised; half a spoonfull of Vinegar or better cut in small flakes: steep these all night in warm embers, the pot being close stopt, the next day let it seethe a little over the fire; then strain it out, and put thereunto three or four spoonfulls of Syrup of Roses solutive, so drink it. Mr. *Calton*.

A Potion to purge.

Take of Syrup of Roses solutive two spoonfulls, Whey five or six spoonfulls; mingle them together, and drink it fasting, it purgeth Choller and Schirhous humours. M. *Horsman*.

For the biting of a Viper.

Trifoly is wonderfull, that is like to the herb Hyacinth, when it flowers in the Spring, and it hath seed like to the wild Hyacinth. For this sod is a principall remedy against the biting of the Spider Phalangium, or the Viper, if it be fomented with water, and it easeth the pains. But with the same fomentation upon a part that is not bit, you shall raise a pain like to those that are bitten, or upon any other man that is well. For it cures the bitings, and afflicts the part not bitten as those bitings do. *Jacobus Sylvius Medic.*

For the stings of Scorpions.

The seed of wild Saffron bruised in your hand, or hanged about the neck, is very powerfull against the bitings of Scorpions; some say the roots of Laurel and Iris are good for the same purpose. *Mizaldus*.

Another against the stings of Scorpions.

Sometimes poysons are so great puissant to poyson, that Wolfsbane given in warm Wine is approved to be a most wholesome medicament for those that are stung by a Viper or a Scorpion, as some most experienced Physicians affirm. *The same*.

Another for the same.

This is wonderfull amongst the rest, that he who eateth Radishes before, if he be stung of a Scorpion, the Scorpion loseth his sting; and if you strew Radishes upon Scorpions you will kill them. *The same*.

An approved healing Salve for Sores old or new.

Take Wax, Rosin, Turpentine, Barrows flick clarified, of each a little quantity, but least of the Turpentine; first melt your Wax over a soft fire of embers, then put in your Rosin, and last your Turpentine and Barrows flick, let all these boyl, stirring them well together; then take it off the fire, and when it is thorow cold, take it out of the skillet, and scrape clean the bottom that there may no skum hang there, and keep it to your use: it will draw and heal, and if you spread a little Diacalsachos thin when you lay it on, it will skinn the sore place without any other thing. Mr. *Brown* Chyrurg.

Against venereous Bubos.

Some maintain that water distilled from Mans dung will burn, for it is very fat and thin enough, yet not so much as *Aqua vitæ*: It is approved that it is contrary to swellings, especially of the throat. *Cardan*.

To take away pestilentiall swellings.

Live Oysters remove pestilentiall bubos, and draw all the venome to themselves; but they must be fastned to the arm, where the vein axillaris runs, for a bubo that is under the arm-pits; but if it be in the groin, they must be laid to thigh where the vein of the leg runs. *Hollerius*.

For pestilentiall Bubos.

Henbane applied to pestilentiall bubos, will, as it is reported, dispers them; and if one have this hearb by him before they come forth, he shall never have any such bubos. *Mizaldus*.

For Carbuncles.

Coriander seed in pouder mingled with Honey, and laid upon a Carbuncle, destroys it. *Arnoldus de villa nova*.

For a Fellon.

Take of black Sope, Salt and Sothernwood, of each a pretty quantity; pound all these together, and apply it often times. Mr. *King*.

For pestilentiall Carbuncles.

Galbanum softned and spread upon linnen, and laid upon a Carbuncle, if it be curable, it will stick so fast to it that it cannot be pluckt off, but it will pull it forth by the roots, but if it be incurable, it will not stick at all. *The same.*

To provoke sweat.

Take bricks very hot, wrap them in cloathes and lay them to the feet and sides, or stone bottles put into boyling water and fild therewith, being well stopt with corcks, and fast bound at the head; use them as the bricks. *M. Rouland.*

For venomous stings.

If any man be bit or stung of any venemous creature, let him presently drop in two or three drops of the milk of a Fig-tree into the wound, and he shall find wonderfull help: He may also lay upon it some mustard seed brayed with Vinegar. *Mizald.*

For scrophulous Tumours.

If you cut off the feet of a great hedg-Toad whilest he is alive, when the Moon is neer her conjunction with the Sun, and bind them about the Patients neck, they are so profitable that they ofttimes cure him. *Cardan.*

Proud or dead flesh to remove.

Take of Mercury sublimate one dram, boyl it in a pottle of water till half be consumed, wash the sore therewith and it will keep down proud flesh, take away dead flesh, and preserve the sore clean; after you have washed the sore therewith, lay on it a cloth well wet in the same water eight or ten days, *Probatum.* Dr. Read.

For scrophulous Tumours.

It is a wonderfull experiment of a seventh Sonne, that every seventh Sonne, where there is no Daughters born between them, will cure the Kings evill, onely touching it, or speaking the word. *Corn. Agrip.*

To cure the knots of the Joynt-Gowt.

If rotten wormeaten Cheese be moulded with broth wherein a gammon of Bacon hath been long boyld, it will take away the knots of the Joynt-gowt without any Instrument, if it be laid on for a Plaister, as *Galen* saith; and *Coccus Gnidius* will wonderfully do the same beaten with Myrrh and Vinegar.

For all Impostumes.

Keep an old Gander fasting three days; then give him pieces of an Eeel new killed, and preserve his dung; you have a present remedy for all Impostumes. *Out of a most experienced Chyrurgion.*

Fellon to kill.

Take new rusty Bacon, Snails with Shells, and Leaven, of each alike; pound these together, apply it to the place, and it will draw and break it. *Lady Camden.*

For Warts.

If you would cure Corns or Warts, cut off the head of a live Eel, and whilest the blood runs, rub them with it: then bury the head of the Eel deep in the ground; and as that decays they will all fall away. *The same.*

Another for Warts.

It is a tradition, that Warts rubd with Fig leaves will all decay, if they be buried under the earth: Some ascribe the same to a Pigeons heart. *Mizaldus.*

A good experiment against Warts.

Put Hens feet under hot coles untill they be scaled of the skin, and rub the Warts with the skin that is parted from the bones, three or four times whilest it is hot, and they will be gone. *Alexius.*

Against Corns.

Hermodactils, and the seed poudred and mingled with Oxymel of Squils, or juyce of Marigolds, will drive away Warts and hard knots, though it be in the secret parts, and gotten by foul copulation. *The same.*

Chilblanes to cure.

Take Lime water and warm it over the fire blood warm, then take a fine cloth and bathe the chilblanes therewith when you go to bed, and wet a cloth in the same six or seven double, lay it upon them, and in two or three nights they will be cured. *Probatum.* Mr Delawne.

For Warts.

Physick is in nothing more superstitious than in driving away Warts: *Serapio* saith, that if you touch them severally with severall chiche peason in the Calends of the Moneth, and cast these chiches behind you, that will cure them.

Another for Warts.

Take a red Onyon, bruise it well, and mingle it with Salt, annoint the Warts with it. *Roscellas*.

A Water for Corns and Warts.

Take Saltpeter, Vitriol, Verdigreece, of each two ounces, Allom zuccharinum one ounce, quick Lime half an ounce: Distill them in a retort, the first water is nothing worth, but the second is good against Corns and Warts. *Fallopius*.

An approved Remedy for Corns on the feet.

Beat a head of Garlick and bind it on, and renew it every day: But you must every other day wash the feet that have Corns with Lee; and when they are dried, bind on the Garlick, untill they fall. The holes must be cured afterwards with some abstergent and healing Unguent.

Against Scars.

It is known that Scars are hid and concealed by that which was the cause of them. *Cardan*.

Of the Form of the Body. Chap. 5.

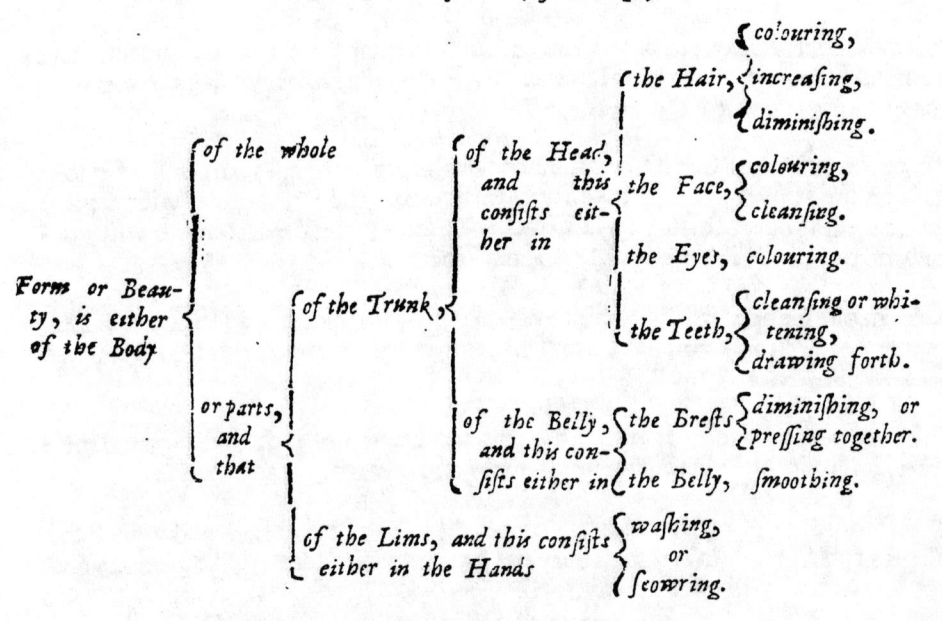

Form or Beauty, is either of the Body
- of the whole
- or parts, and that
  - of the Trunk
    - of the Head, and this consists either in
      - the Hair, { colouring, increasing, diminishing.
      - the Face, { colouring, cleansing.
      - the Eyes, colouring.
      - the Teeth, { cleansing or whitening, drawing forth.
    - of the Belly, and this consists either in
      - the Brests { diminishing, or pressing together.
      - the Belly, smoothing.
  - of the Lims, and this consists either in the Hands { washing, or scowring.

Of the Form or Beauty of the whole Body. Chap. 6.

To make men fat.

If you mingle with the fat of a Lizard Salt Peter, and Cummin, wheat meal, Hens fatted with this meat, will be so fat, that men that eat of them, will eat untill they burst. *Cardan*.

Of the Form or Beauty of the Parts of the Body, and first of Colouring the Hair.

To make the Hair of the Colour of Gold.

You shall make your Hair and Beard of the Colour of gold thus: Take the pieces of Rheubarb, which the Apothecaries pare off, and cast away as good for nothing; and steep them in a Lee made of Misletow of any Tree, the leaves and boughes of it, untill they grow soft; then pressing them forth after you have boyled them a while gently, wet a spunge in the Lee, and wet your hair with it, or your Beard if you please: Then dry them both with hot linen cloathes, which is safer then to dry them

them at the Sun or fire. When you have done this often, then you shall have your desire without any hurt. *From an Italian.*

To make your Hair as white as silver.

Take River water twenty five pound, roots and leaves of Centory three ounces, boyl them together untill a third part be consumed; then when they have stood fifteen dayes in the Sun, adde Gum Arabick, Dragant, Alum, of each two ounces; Venice Sope, Tartar of White wine, of each one pound: mingle them, and boyl them so long, untill they be a water, which the *Italians* commonly call *Blonds*; that is, yellow *Venetian*: And when you will use it, in the morning wet your hair well with it, and wrap them in a linen cloath; then in the evening wash your hair in Lee wherein the Herb called *Vitriola* is boyled, and dry them at the sunne or the fire; which when you have done twice or thrice a week, your hair will be white, clear, and silver coloured. *Alex.*

To make your Hair yellow.

To make your hair yellow as gold, take red Allum, six ounces, Vitriol four ounces, Salt Peter two ounces; distill a water from them, and wet your hair or beard with a spunge dipt in it, and pressed forth again: And do this several times, it will be performed. *Mizald.*

To make your Hair red.

Take one handfull of Nut-tree leaves, distill them in a glass Retort, and with that only wet your hoary hairs fifteen daies, and they will be red: This colour will last one moneth. But wet not your face with that water, for it will grow black. *Alex.*

To dye your Hair yellow.

You shall make them very yellow with oyl of Honey, and yelk of Egges. Also with a Lee made of Vine-tree, Barly straw, scraping of liquorish, and leaves of box, Safforn and Cummin: If you wash your hair often, they will be very yellow, and like to gold. *The same.*

To make your Hair seem green.

The distilled water of Capers will make your hair green. *Cardan.*

To make your Hair black.

You shall make your hair or beard black thus: Take common Lee what you please, infuse therein the leaves of Beets, Sage, and Bayes, Myrrh, and the shells of Walnuts; then boyl them all, and wash your beard or head therewith, or wet them with a spunge dipt therein, and a little pressed forth. You will wonder at the event. *Mizaldus.*

To dye Hair black.

Hair will grow exceeding black by a Lee made of the rind of fig-tree, galls, dates, bramble, cyprus, and the like. But this way you shall dye a hoary beard, or hairs black very well: Lythargy of silver, and burnt brass, mingled to four times so much strong Lee, and when it riseth up in bubles over a gentle fire, wash your hair with it, and dry them, and wash them again with hot water. *The same.*

To dye the Eye-brows black.

The Eye-brows are thus coloured black: Break galls in oyl, then bruise them with a little salt Armoniach, then mingle them with Vinegar, wherein the rind of brambles and mulberries have been boyled, annoint your Eye-brows therewith, and let them remain so all night, then wash them with water. *The same.*

To make haire black.

Take lee five parts, Lytharge six ounces, Sage, leaves of a black fig tree, of each one handfull; mingle them, and boyl them untill a fourth part be consumed, and make a lee. With this wash the head twice a week, and then dried, must be annointed with this oyntment. Take the juyce of Sage what is sufficient, black Tartar one ounce, Lytharge half an ounce. Mingle them and make an oyntment, wet a leaden combe often in this, and kemb your haire, and they will soon grow black. *Alex.*

Another.

Take the juyce of the pils of green Walnuts three ounces, red Wine a quart; boyl them togther untill a third part be consumed, then adde common oyl five pound, mingle

mingle them well and annoint your hair. *Marinellus.*

Another.

Take Myrobolans Indi, Gals, of each one ounce, Lytharg one dram, salt peter, roch Allum, burnt brass, of each eight ounces, *sal gemma, traganth*, of each one ounce, pouder them all, and mingle them with water, wherein the kernels of dates are boyld, annoint your hair with it.

Another.

Take red Poppy juyce, and juyce of green Walnut shels, oyl of Myrtils, oyl of Costus, of each what is sufficient. Boyl them awhile together, and keep them in some vessell for your use.

Another.

Take Cyprus nuts, and boyl them in Wine and red Wine Vinegar, make a lee, wash your head with it. *Marinellus.*

Another.

Take Gals boyld in common oyl two ounces, roch allum two drams, *sal gemma* one dram, oyl of Costus what is sufficient, mingle them, make an oyntment to annoint the hair. *The same.*

Another.

Take Litharge of silver, Vinegar, of juyce of Citrons what is sufficient, boyl them half an houre, make a lee to wash the hair. *The same.*

Another.

Take leaves of Capers what is needfull, boyl them in milk untill a third part be consumed, and annoint your hair therewith. *The same.*

Another.

Take flowers of Wallnut tree, beat them well, mingle them with common oyl, make an oyntment for your hair.

Another that a Matron of Venice used.

Take oyl of Tartar being hot, what may suffice, annoint a Spunge or Comb, to kemb the hair in the Sun, your head being first washt. Having done this thrice every day, it cannot be but in seven daies, your hair will be black: but if you would have them sweet sented, last of all, annoint your hair with oyl of Ben, because it will make your hair not only sweet but black, which is rare. *Alex.*

To prevent hoary hairs.

Annoint your head and hair with Bitches milk, it is *Probatum. Nostrad.*

To Augment your hair.

That hair may grow again quickly.

The ashes of burnt Bees, with Mice dung, if you annoint this with oyl of Roses, it will make hair grow in the palme of your hand; to these you may adde the ashes of small Nuts, Chestnuts, Dates, and the rest of that sort, for of all these the force of growing again is destroyed, or they will come forth much softer. *The same.*

To make haire and beard grow, that shall not fall away again.

Take Bees burnt to ashes so many as you please, Linseed burnt and poudred as much, oyl of green Lizards, (and it is made thus, the green Lizards being alive, must be put into a glass Viol, full of common oyl, and set by the fire untill they be dissolved, then they must be set in the Sun for fiften or twenty daies,) what is sufficient, mingle them, and make an unguent, and with this annoint the parts bald of hair, morning and evening, and thus they will suddenly grow again and not fall off. But the head must be first washt in the following lee. Take lee made of ashes, what you need, Maidenhaire, Agrimony, tree Ivye, of each five handfuls. Mingle them, and boyl them: then strain it, and keep it covered for your use: when you have washt your head twice or thrice a week with this, and then dried it, and after that, gently annointed it with this unguent, it cannot be but your hair will grow thick and long, and will stick fast. *Alex.*

Another.

Let Bees be dried in a Basket at the fire, untill they may be poudred: mingle this powder with oyl, and annoint the place where you would have hair to grow, and you shall see wonders. *Nostradamus.*

Secrets in beautifying the Body.

To diminish the hair.
To make any part bald.

That hairs may fall from any part, and may grow no more: a Cats dung dried and powdered, and mingled with strong Vinegar, to a pap will do it: with this you must rub the hairy place often in a day, and in a short time it will grow bald and without hair. *An experiment of a Countrey Man.*

Another.

The piss of Mice or Rats will make a hairy part bald, but it is restored and cured with the blood of Moles, or the skin of them rubbed upon it. *Mizald.*

A dipilatory whereby a hairy place is made bald.

If you annoint it with the common decoction of Quick-lime, and a third part of Orpiment, and strong Lee, and try with a feather when it is ready. But *Columella* bids to boyl a black frog in water, untill the water be boyl'd away one third part, and to annoint the body with this where you would have it bald. There are other certain things, as the Gum of Ivy and Vines, that will make a part bald. But the former is more commodious. But if you would have them grow again, you shall make the place bald by this way, and pull the hairs out by the roots: Annoint it with Ants egges, juyce of henbane, hemlock, fleawort seed, Batts, and Swallows blood. *The same.*

That Children may never have Beards.

That Boys and Girls may never have hair grow on their secrets or beards, annoint the privities with the blood of a Fish called a Tunie: for it is cold and thick, and it will do the same if you annoint it on any part. Also the meal of beanes will do the like, if you daily wash the part with water, for they scowre, and hinder the hair untill the skin is stopt with a glutinous humour, but such remedies as almost all the rest of this nature are not for continuance.

To drive away hair.

Take fresh Quicklime two ounces, Orpiment poudred one ounce, the strongest lee two quarts. Mingle them, and boyl them in a pot untill they grow thick, or a Ducks feather put into it, will burn, stirring it continually, then keep it in a Glass, or some glazed vessell. When you will use this, first annoint the parts with oyl of sweet Almonds (that you may not feel the heat so much,) and afterwards annoint them gently with this oyntment. But if any may have so thin skin that he cannot long endure the heat, let him annoint the part with the following water, and the heat will presently cease. Take Rosewater two ounces, Plantane water one ounce, whitest Sugar half an ounce, mingle them, you may use this water and unguent but only every other day: but if you will not use this, then take this that is next. Take salt Armoniack, Goats gall what shall suffice, mingle them well, and make an oyntment to annoint hairy parts. *Alex. Piedmont.*

Another.

Take juyce of roots of Celandine, Orpiment, Ivy, of each what is sufficient, Ants eggs, of Vinegar, of each one part. Mingle them very well, and make an oyntment, and if hairy parts be often annointed with this, the hairs will fall without doubt; But if you feel any pain afterwards, wash the part with the foresaid water.

That hairs may fall, and none may grow again.

Take Cats dung and pouder it fine, and sift it, and mingle it with Vinegar to an oyntment, annoint the hair with it. *Out of a Manuscript.*

To colour the face.

To make the face red like a Rose.

Distill water from grains of Paradice, Cubebs, Cloves, shaving of Brasil, and strong-water, often distilled, (and after it hath stood awhile at a soft fire, or corrupt Horse dung,) with this wet your face often when it begins to work. *The same.*

Another.

The root of *Solomons* seal, by only rubbing, makes Maids pale Cheeks look red. *Mizaldus.*

To deface the great redness of the countenance.

Take four ounces of Peach Kernels, and gourdseed blanched two ounces, bruise them and press them strongly to draw forth an oily liquor; with this morning and evening touch the Carbuncles and redness of your face, and they will depart, or be much better. *The same.*

For a red face full of Pimples.

Boyle Elecampane roote in white wine, till the wine be almost consumed, then bray him in a Morter with Quicksilver, Brimstone, and Barows grease, quench the Quicksilver first with fasting spittle, and then annoint the place. *Dr. Davison.*

Another of the same Author.

The Onyon heads of Lillies sod in water, take away the redness of the face, if you annoint with them morning and evening. This I had from a Matron that was excellent for painting faces.

A water to colour the face, that it shall shine with smoothness.

Let the whites of Eggs be boyled untill they be hard, distill water from them, it will be fit for use, so is Rosemary water, bean flower, water and juyce of Lemmons. But this is the best water invented with great cunning. Bring Talcum into the finest pouder, and put it into an earthen pot, and put into it a great quantity of live Snails, and cover them that they creep not forth. When they want meat, they will devoure the Talcum, and concoct; it when you know they have eaten it all, bruise them with their Shels, and put them into a glass still, distill water from them, and keep it for your use. *The same.*

Water that makes the skin shine.

Take fountain water, distilled as much as you please; put into every Viol of water, Myrrh one ounce, egge shels not boyled foure ounces, Juniper Gum half a spoonfull, crums of Bread softned in Goats milk one handfull. Mingle them, and distill them untill all the water be drawn forth: this being done, Take Lard, which some call Pomatum, if you can get that; if not, Goats or Hens fat, or Lambs fat or Calfs, yet they must be once or twice strain'd with pure water: then they must be set in an earthen pot at a gentle fire to melt, adding by degrees as much of the former distilled water, that it may be like cold oyl or oyntment: but the fat cannot be mingled with the water, but that the fat will rather swim on the top like to oyl, you must adde some Tartar burnt, but not much, or Pot-ashes, or Borax dissolved in the water, that they may mingle perfectly. When this is done, keep the oyntment in glass Vessels. To make it sweet sented, add some Camphir, white Ben, Musk or Amber, which are dissolved in Rose water, and strain'd, or oyl of Gesamin, which will do the same. *Alexius.*

Oyl that makes the skin fair and shining.

Take white Tartar two pound, Talcum, Salt, of each half a pound. Mingle them and set them into a Potters Furnace, or Lime kill, untill it be burnt; when this is done, grind the matter upon a Marble, then put it for fifteen or twenty daies into some bag with a sharp end, and set it in some moist place, free from the Ayr, setting some Vessell under to receive the oyl that runs from it, and keep this as a precious thing. When you will use it, you must first wash the skin with lee, and dry it: then you must annoint it with the foresaid oyl upon some linen cloath, and rub it softly; this defaceeth all kind of spots, and makes the skin soft and supple. *The same.*

To make the face red.

To make a pale face red, and one that hath an ill colour beautifull: take red Sanders, and the sharpest Vinegar twice distilled what you please, mingle them, and boyl them at a gentle fire, and add to it a little Allum, so you have a most perfect red to colour the face, and if you would have it sweet sented, put in a little Musk, or some other sent as you please. *Mizaldus from an Italian.*

To adorne the face.

Allum bruised and shaked with whites of Eggs that are new, being heated and moved continually, will grow thick to an oyntment; If you annoint your face with this two or three daies morning and evening, it will not only take forth spots and wrinkles,

wrinkles, but it will grow very clear and faire. *The same.*

Another.

Take juyce of Lemmons two ounces, Rose water two ounces, Mercury sublimate two drams, white lead two drams. Mingle them like to an oyntment, annoint the part in the evening, and in the morning do it with butter. *Cardan.*

Womens fucusses.

Womens paintings that make the face cleare and smooth: are crums of Bread steeped in Goats milk or whey, distill water from it, and with this adorne your face. It is excellent to make the face white, and to make the skin clear. Asses milk is as good, for it makes the skin smooth, fine and soft; wherefore *Pompeia Sabina Nero's* wife did not keep 500. Asses for nothing, for she bathed her whole body over with Asses milk. *The same.*

Water that makes a face look young.

Take live Brimstone one ounce, Frankinscence two ounces, Myrrh two ounces, Ambergreece six drams; pouder them severall, then mingle them, adding one pint of Rosewater, distill them in a double Vessell, or *Balneum Maria,* as they call it. The water distilled from it, must be kept in a vessell exactly stopped. When you will use it, dip a fine white rag in it, and wash your face before you go to sleep, and in the morning wash it off with Barly or fountain water. The face will be so clear and beautifull, that all will wonder and desire to kiss it. *Out of a certain Book of Womens adorning.*

That the skin may be exceeding white.

Take distilled Vinegar one pound, Litharg of silver one ounce, mingle them, and set them in a glass Viol upon a Brick by the fire for one hour, and then in the Sun for eight daies, and preserve it. Then take water of gourds one pint, salt Gemmæ one ounce, mingle them, and set them in another glass by the fire also, for one houre, and keep them as before. But when you will use this water, take it with the salt of the foresaid Vinegar, with the silver Litharg, of each one part, mingle them, and make water like to milk, and if you wash your face with this with a wet sponge very finely; it will grow white soft and fair. *Alex.*

That a painted face may wax pale.

Chew Saffron in your mouth, and when you talk with the party, come near to her and breath upon her face, and it will make it wan: but if she be not painted, it can do her no disgrace. *The same.*

A water that makes the face black.

From the green shels of Walnuts, the Chymists in *France* draw a pure water; if you wash your hands and face with this, you will be black as a Gyptie by degrees. But if you would make them white as they were, distill Vinegar, juyce of Lemmons, and Colophonia, wash with this, and it will deface the black of the other. *The same.*

To find whether women be painted.

If Women be painted with red, it will be discovered if you chew some Cummin seed, or a Clove of Garlick: for if it be naturall it will abide, but if painted with white lead, Quicksilver or Oyntment Citrium, it will presently vanish. *Langius.*

To make the face clean and to take out the spots.

For all spots and freckles in the face.

Take Myrrh powdred what you need; whites of Eggs five, *Aqua vitæ* a little; mingle them and beat them very well, then distill them untill all the water be dropt forth: then add to it as much of *lac Virginis,* as the foresaid water weigheth, and keep it in a Glass: *Lac Virginis* is made when Lytharg is boyld in Vinegar and strained, then add some oyl of Tartar to it, and it will be like to milk when you will use it, wash your face first with a linnen rag dipt in water, wherein Bran hath been soked awhile, or with a red cloath rub it well, which is better, then with a fine clean rag of linnen dry it, and annoint your face with the foresaid unguent morning and evening, and let it dry of it self. It is admirable to see it. *Alex.*

Another.

If Gold made red hot be often quenched in the best wine, and a little Tartar be put to it, it drives away all spots be they never so foule, upon any part of the body; also it helps a leprous red nose, and that hath many warts. *Lemnius.*

A water for Tetters of the face, Warts, and other spots.

Take Salt peter, whole Tartar, of each one pound, bruise them all severally; then mingle them and sift them, make a very fine powder. When you have done this, put the pouder in some dish, and make a Mass like to a Sugar loaf; then put a light Charcole upon the top of it, and so let it burn. For because Salt peter is of thin and moist parts, and Tartar of thick parts they must needs run to a lump. When this is done, put that lump into some dish, powring upon it hot water, and break it with your fingers, untill it be very well dissolved, then when it is filtred and set in a new earthen pot by the fire, that it may be hardly hot untill it be dry, you must keep the powder that settleth in the bottome, wherein all the virtue lyeth. This being done, take a glass Bottle, in which you must have of distilled Vinegar four ounces, *Aqua vitæ* thrice distilled one ounce, then poure in the foresaid pouder, mingle it, and set them three daies in the Sun, very well stopt, and so keep it. And when you will use it, wash the Tetters with it morning and evening, and all such kind of spots, and in a few daies they will be perfectly cured, and the skin will be very fair. *Alex.*

Another.

Take the dregs of white wine, and dry them, and when they are dried, make them into powder in an iron Vessell. This being done, let them remain in a bag, in a moist place, twenty or thirty daies : setting some glass vessell under, untill all the pouder be turned into oyl, keep this in a Glass. With this annoint any spots or Tetters, and they will be soon gone, and the skin will be soft. If you would have this sweet sented, add thirty Cloves. *The same.*

For all spots, Clothes, Morpheus, Tetter, and Leprosies beginning.

Take Vitriol four ounces, Salt peter three ounces, filings of Steel one ounce, Camphir half an ounce, distill them. *Cardan.*

For Spots and Pimples.

You shall thus deface all spots of the face, infuse fifteen new laid eggs shels, and all in the sharpest Vinegar : then bruise them in the Vinegar, with one ounce of Mustard seed, and distill them in a glass Vessell; wet some Cotton in the water, and lay it on when you go to bed. This takes away all Pimples. *The same.*

Another.

The blood of a white Hen smeered over a Pimpeld face, and so left to dry, and then rub off, blots out all the spots. *From an Italian.*

To scowre off all Scales from the face.

Cows or Goats milk mingled with poudred glass, and wet your face with it, this scowrs off all scurf, and makes the face clear. Also the juyce of Dragons cures all spots, especially those that deforme the countenance. *The same.*

For swellings of the face.

Conradus Gesner, saith he saw a woman that was freed from small swellings in her face, only by washing them with water of Strawberries distilled : but they were first set in a glass Vessell under Horse dung to ferment.

To scowre the face, and to blot out all spots there.

Take *Venice* Turpentine two pound, new whites of Eggs twelve; mingle them, and distill them in a glass Retort, take the water, and add to it Camphir poudred ten Scruples, let it be well melted and keep it. When you will use it, take of this water one ounce, water of Snails one ounce, mingle them, and wash your face often therewith. *Alex. Piedmont.*

To take off black and blew spots from the face.

You may thus take off black and blew spots from the Cheeks, especially from Women when they have their terms. Annoynt the place with white Lead, and Bean meal, mingled with Vinegar, or with yelks of Eggs mingled with honey. *The same.*

For

Secrets in beautifying the Body.

For Pushes of the face arising from heat of the Liver.

Take Hogs grease refined, Quickbrimstone, of each one part, water of the Peach tree and Fern distilled, of each what may suffice. Mingle them at a gentle fire, and make an Unguent, annoint the Pushes therewith and it will cure them. But you must abstaine from wine and other hot things. *The same.*

A sweet sented mixture.

Take Musk three drams, Ambergreece two drams, Zibet one dram: grind them upon a Porphyr stone with oyl of sweet Almonds, and make a sweet oyntment, very pretious. *Isabella Cortesa.*

To colour the eyes.

To change the colour of the eyes.

If you would change the colour of Childrens eyes, you shall do it thus; with the ashes of the small nut shels, with oyl you must annoint the fore part of their head: it will make the whites of Childrens eyes black; do it often. There are many experiments to make white and grey eyes black, and of divers colours; but I let them pass because those that have need of their eyes, will not so easily try them, nor do they all performe what they promise. *The same.*

To cleanse and whiten the Teeth.

A pouder to whiten the Teeth.

Take red Corall, flowers of wild Pomegranates, Pumex stone, burnt Allum, Gals, Acacia, Galla Moschata, of each three drams, Cyperus, Froth of the Sea, Cardamomus, salt Armoniack, Mineral salt, sal Gemmæ, of each two drams, Spicknard, wood of Olives, Cyprus nuts, Costus, Spodium or Myrrill seed, Mastick, of each one dram, Cloves half an ounce, make a pouder. *Out of a Manuscript.*

A pouder to keep the teeth white.

Take the shels of three eggs, red Corall three drams, threds of white Silk burnt in a new pot to ashes, two drams, Cinnamon two drams, Cloves one dram, Pellitory of *Spain* two drams: beat all these into very fine pouder, and rub your Teeth with it every morning and evening. *Rantz.*

Another.

Take Harts horn burnt in a new pot to ashes one ounce and half, Mastick of Chios half an ounce, salt Armoniac six drams, mingle them.

Another pouder to rub the teeth.

Take Corall white and red of each one ounce, Pellitory of *Spain*, Mace, Mastick, of each one ounce, Pumex stone, Bolearmoniac, of each one ounce, make a fine pouder. *Henr. Rantzovius.*

Another.

The best pouder was anciently provided to rub the teeth of the shels of Fish, whereof Purple was made, and other shels burnt to ashes: but now you may quickly use and safely crusts of Bread burnt, pouder of Pumex stone, red Corals, cuttle fish shels, Harts horn, and the like, each of these will cleanse and polish, so will Cochineal, if you will rub them with red. But the oyl of Brimstone is best, for it polisheth, smootheth, and takes off all spots, also you may do it with Alum and Salt distilled. *The same.*

To draw out teeth.

To draw out teeth without pain.

Some say that roots of Sparagus dried, and stuck into the teeth, will pull them forth without pain. *Mizal.*

Another.

Boyl wild Cucumber, first bruised and infused in Vinegar, untill it be as thick as Vinegar, then scarifie the Gums about the teeth, and wet the tooth round with this Medicament, then bid the Patient shut his mouth awhile, then take the tooth in your fingers, and it will come forth without pain. *Alexius.*

A water that draweth out teeth without pain.

Take salt Armoniac, and distill it in a Limbeck, touch the tooth with that water, and it will fall out and no pain be felt. *The same.*

A powder for the same.

Powder of red Corall put into the hollow tooth makes it fall out. Dissolve salt Armoniac with juyce of Henbane, touch the tooth and it will fall. *The same.*

That the teeth shall seem to heare.

It is a great wonder, yet every man may try it; put a stick to a harp, that one end may touch the mouth of the party, if any other take the head of the stick or Javelin in his mouth, he shall hear the sound of the Harp, voices and words spoken as if he heard with his teeth afar off. Whereas otherwise he could hear no noise at all. *Cardanus.*

To make the Brests less.

That the Brests may not grow.

Balme beaten to a Cataphlasme, and laid on womens brests, hinders the growing of them. *Fallopius.*

To hinder the Brests from increasing.

Bruise Hemlock, and lay a mixture of it with Vinegar upon Maids Brests, and it will not suffer them to grow; this is chiefly for maids, yet it will keep milk back at the time it should breed. But soft and lose brests you shall keep down thus, White earth, whites of eggs, sowre Gals, Mastick, Frankincence, all beaten, must be mingled with Vinegar hot, and annointed upon the brests, and so it must remain all night; if this do it not, renew it again. Also stones of Medlars are good for this purpose, unripe Services, wild Plums, Acacia, Pomegranate Pils, wild Pomegranate flowers, unripe Nuts, pine kernels, wild Pears, Plantane, if they all boyl in Vinegar and be applied to the brests. *The same.*

That Womens Brests may be made like to Virgins Breasts.

Rondeletius after *Pliny* saith, that it is proved by experience, that a scale Fish laid to Womens brests, will so bind them together, that they will look like Virgins brests. The same may be done to the Secrets. Let those that are given to pleasure and ornament prick up their ears.

To take away the wrinkles of the belly after Child birth.

Let unripe services be long boyled in water, mingle the white of an Egge, and gum Arabick dissolved in water, wet a linnen cloth in this water, and lay it over the belly; or Harts horn burnt, Lapis amiantus, salt Armoniac, Myrrh, Frankincense, Mastick, all in powder, mingle them with Honey, this takes away all wrinkles. But if you seek to close again natures passage, for it useth to be relaxed in child birth, if your Husband be not pleased with it, you shall fasten it thus. Beat sowre Gals very fine, mingle a little of the pouder of Cloves therewith, boyl them in Wine, wet a cloath in it and lay it on. Or thus you shall straighten a Whores common open dore; with Gals, Gum, Alum, bole Armoniac, dragons blood, Acacia, Plantain, Hippocystis, Balaustia, Mastick tree great and less, Comfrey, Cyprus nuts, Grape stones, Acorn cups, out of which the Acorn first shews it self, Mastick, and *terra lemnia.* Boyl all these in red wine or Vinegar, wet the passage often therewith, this will close it exceedingly. Or else pouder them all, and cast them in with a quill, or make a fume of them. But if you would make a woman deflowred a Maid again, make little pellets thus: burnt Allum, Mastick made into fine pouder, adding a little Orpiment to them, that they will almost not be felt, make these with water into pils and press them hard, and let them dry very thin, and put one into the place of the Hymen, where it was first broken, changing it every six houres, alwaies wetting it with Rain or Cystern water, and that for four and twenty houres this will cause blisters, which touched will bleed, that it can hardly be discovered. Some set a Leech to the place, and so they make hard crusts, which being rubbed will bleed, when they have made the passage straight, before with what I mentioned. *The same.*

To make white hands.

To white the hands.

Take juyce of Lemmons what is sufficient, common Salt a little, mingle them, wash your hands therewith, let them dry of themselves; then wash them with common water. *Out of a Manuscript.*

To black the hands.

Pouder of gals put into water, if you wash your hands therewith will make them exceeding black, it is so far from making them white : the remedy is an Orange pill. *Mizald.*

Against the ill smell of the arm-pits.

The root of Hartichoke boyld and laid on for a Plaister, cures the ill sent of the arm-pits, and of all other parts of the body. It doth the same boyld, and drank with wine. For it makes a man make such abundance of ill sented Urine, that it will cure the virulent gonorrhæa. *Dioscord. Oribasius, Paulus, Langius.*

Of Meat. Chap. 6.

To keep meal a long time.

Wheat meal ground in *August*, is wont to last long in *Italy*. *Card.*

To keep ripe Grapes.

When the Grape is ripe, and when it is gathered, take care to provide for your Family, and be sure it be ripe and dry before you gather it, least the wine be not the best : pick forth continually all green Grapes, and skins cast them away on heaps upon hurdles, sift them, and put them into pitched Wine vessels, or places seasoned with Pitch to keep them in; cover them close, and smeer the outside well, give this to your Oxen in Winter, you may if you will wash them through a little for your Family to drink. *Cato.*

That flesh may seem full of wormes.

Harp strings cut small and cast upon flesh newly boyled, will seem like to Worms. *The same.*

That flesh may seem bloody.

The congealed blood of a Hare baked and poudred, and strewd upon flesh, it will make it look bloody, that you will vomit up what you have eaten by loathing it, and many things more which I leave to gluttons. *The same.*

To endure hunger easily.

Avicenna reports, That one who was to travell drank a pound of oyl of Violets mingled with fat, and he was never hungry afterwards in ten daies, and he saith that oyl of Almonds and Cows fat will do the like by the unctuousnesse thereof. *Avicenna.*

Against Hunger.

Travels and Wars ofttimes make a man fall into want of all things, that he must endure grievous famine. It will be good to set down some remedies against it. When famine is great, the Liver of any Creature rosted, will fill more instead of bread. Also Bread baked of sweet Almonds and Sugar, doth nourish much. Also Bisquet or Sea bread must be carried with us, because it doth not by its drinesse cause thirst, and will keep long uncorrupted. We read also of one who was overwhelmed by the fall of an house, when he had no hopes of life, he kept himself alive seaven daies and nights by drinking his own water. *Rantzo.*

Little Pellets against hunger.

Avicenna made little balls against hunger, which must be kept that the Sun melt them not. Take sweet Almonds blancht one pound, Cows fat melted one pound, oyl of Violets two ounces, Mucilage of Marsh mallow roots one ounce : bruise them all together in a Mortar, and make bals, like bals of *Italian* nuts.

Of Drink. Chap. 7.

To cure corrupted Wine.

Some use to poure forth corrupted Wine into a clean Vessell, and to add by degrees, to it a tenth part of milk, and then after eight daies they broach the vessell, and sell it out by retaile, and it will seem clear and good, but if it stand long in the cup, it will corrupt again. Also that which is poured forth, leaves a fat, like butter upon the brims of the cup, whereby the fraud is discovered, yet it is a gainfull way; But if you would prevent this corruption before the wine be troubled, a tenth part of *Aqua vitæ* mingled with it, will do it: Brimstone is farre better, but the sent betraies it. *Cardanus.*

To amend corrupt Wine.

But here comes into my mnid a Secret that Vintners have cause to buy at dear rates, yet I will impart it freely. If you cut a Raddish in pieces and put it into a Wine Vessel, it will draw to it self all the ill sent (if there be any in it) and all the sowrness. But that it may not corrupt there and do hurt, it must be presently taken forth again, and if need be, a fresh one must be put in. Mizald. *de Secret. hort.*

That Wine may not corrupt.

That Wine may not corrupt, the bark of the Vine will do it by Sympathy, and because it drieth: also Allum whilst it is new, and before it works, mingled with it will do it. *Cardan.*

To correct corrupted Wine.

I must not conceale it, that as by a Colewort leaf in a Wine Vessel, the Wine will easily corrupt, so by the sent of Beet leaves infused in it, it will be easily recovered. Mizald. *in horto medico.*

How Wine that is stopped may be made fresh.

It is performed thus, Take Virgins Wax one pound, or what is sufficient, cut it small, and put it into the Wine, and it will in short space recover it self. *Out of a Manuscript.*

To correct Wine, and renew its force.

You shall repaire Wine corrupted if you rack it off into another Vessell that is first scraped and made very sweet, with the hot decoction of Bay leaves, Myrtils, garden Clary, Walnut tree leaves, or Orris root, Juniper berries, and so washt well when you will use it, it will tast very pleasantly. *Mizald.*

Another.

Corrupt stinking Wine is cured, if according to the bigness of the Vessel, you hang a bag in it of clean wheat, and then take it forth again. For this will draw all the corruption to it, and so the Wine will be made clear and sweet. *Pictorius.*

Another.

You shall thus help naughty troubled Wine: Take some whites of Eggs, which when you have a long time beaten them well, and taken away the froth, cast them into the wine vessel, and stir the wine. The same is done if you string twelve Walnut kernels that are old, and rost them under the Embers, and whilst they are yet hot, you let them hang down into the wine, untill the wines colour pleaseth you. Then you must pull them forth. *This was a Secret of a Vintner.*

To take away the sowreness and corruption of Wine.

You shall do it perfectly thus, Take a good quantity of Ciche Peason, and annoint them with oyl, rost them, bruise them, that they may grow thick like paste or pudding, cast half a pound of this into the wine that begins to grow sour, and that tast will be amended within a naturall day. *Mizald.*

For the sourness of Wine.

Wine that is soure will be made sweet with a good quantity of sweet water, as *Tarentinus* saith, so it be close covered, and let them down into a Hogshead of wine, for after three daies if the water stink, the wine will grow sweet and good.

To cure soure Wine.

If wine be very soure, let wheat be boyld so long in water untill it crack, then when it is cold, put it into the wine, and shut the Vessel, the way is to take the hundred part of wheat. *Card.*

A charme that Wine may not corrupt.

If you write these words in the Vessel; *Gustate, & videte, quam bonus est Dominus,*

Book V. *Secrets in ordering and making Artificiall Wines.* 93

the wine put into the Vessel shall never grow bad that year, *Aphricanus*.

That Wine may not grow sour.

Leek seed cast into wine, will make that it shall never grow soure, and it will make Vinegar return to be wine, that is, to leave off all its sournels. *Petrus Crescentius*.

To make sharp Wine mild.

If you will make sharp wine mild and sweet, do thus : Take meal of Vetches four pound, and Wine four cups, sprinkle it over with new sweet wine boyld : then make little cakes, let them drink it in twenty four houres, then mingle them with that wine in the Vessel, and stop it up forty daies, and the wine will be pleasant and sweet, and well coloured and sented. *Cato*.

Against ill sented Wine.

Cooks are wont to cure Vinegar with Smallage, amongst their meats, and so do those that belong to wine Cellars cure ill sented wine, putting the Smallage in bags. *Pliny*.

How the ill sent of Wine may be corrected.

Thick and pure tyleshards must be heated at the fire and dried, then hung to a With must be tied in the Vessel, and shutting the Vessel, you must try after two daies whether the wine be amended : if not, do it again so long as need is. It is no wonder if it do amend by the smell, and by a double heat. *Cato*.

If you would try whether Wine will keep.

To try whether wine will keep long, Take half a Sawcer full of Barly-meal Cake, and poure into a new cup a pint of that wine you would make tryal of, set it on the coales, let it boyl twice or thrice, then strain it, and add the barly meal to it, set the wine in the open aire ; the next day tast of it in the morning, if it tast as that doth in the Hogshead it will last ; if it be sourish, it will not last. *Cato*.

That Wine may not soure.

Hang fat Pork from the cover of the Vessel ; by its fatnefs, and salt it will hinder it from separation and attenuation, for those are the causes that make Vinegar.

For corrupt Wine.

Corrupt clammy wine is restored with Cows milk moderately salted. Some attempt to do it with Brimstone, quick Lime and Allum ; and that these may not hurt him that drinks it, you must put in Orris roots, and Juniper berries by my advice. *Lemnius*.

To make Wine last all the year.

If you will have new wine all the year, put your new wine into a wine Vessel, and pitch over all the outside : Let it down into a Fish pond, take it out after thirty daies, and you shall have new wine all the year. *Cato*.

That white wine may be made red.

You shall presently convert white wine into red without any hurt, if you cast into it the pouder of Honey baked and dried, and mingle them by pouring from Vessel to Vessel. The root of all the docks will do it with more ease, if the root be put in green or dry. *Miz*.

How you shall make Wine have divers sents and tasts.

Herbs, Seeds, or Spices, are to be infused in *Aqua vitæ* four and twenty houres, so is their force to be drawn forth. Then mingle a little of this water with the wine you will drink. *Anonymus*.

That Wine may please your palate, both for tast and sent.

Let an Orange, or Lemmon stuck with Cloves hang in the wine Vessel, that it touch not the wine; it will never tast flat nor musty. *Alexius*.

To make new troubled Wine soone become clear.

Small, broad, thin, light, shavings of the Beech tree that are chopt off with the Ax, or with the plainer to make the wood smooth, must be put into the Vessel, and the wine will be clear in two daies. *The same*.

That neither thunder nor lightning may hurt Wine.

A plate of Iron with salt, or flints laid upon the covering of the Vessel, will keep off hurt of thunder and lightning. *The same*.

O   *That*

That new Wine shall not boyl over.

Make a circle of Penniroyall or Origanum, and put it about the neck of the Vessell: or annoint the inward lips of the Vessel with Cows milk, this will keep in the new wine that boyls. *The same.*

To make new Wine old.

Take Melilot one ounce, Licorish, Celticknard, of each three ounces, Aloes Hepatica two ounces, bruise them, and mingle them with wine. *Euonymus.*

That Wine may have no flower.

Strew into wine Oenanth dried, or meal of Vetches, mingled with the wine; and when the flower and meal are sunk to the bottome, pour off the wine into another Vessel. *Alexius.*

How to part water from Wine.

Make a Vessel of Ivy, pour in wine, and if there be any water in it, it will soon drop through. *The same.*

How to part wine from water.

Put liquid Alum into a wine Vessel, then stop the mouth of the Vessel with a Spunge anointed with oyl, and inclining the Vessel let it run forth, and only the water will come forth. *The same.*

Otherwise.

Take the Selvage of the Loom, or a Cotton rag, and dip it into a wine Vessel, that it may hang out of the Vessel: that will seperate the water.

Whether Wine have any water mingled with it.

Put wild Apples or Pears into the Vessel, if they swim a top, it is a sign the wine is pure, if they sink, that it is mingled with water: or a Greek cane, or straw, or some such thing annointed with oyl, if it be put down into the wine, and taken forth again, if any drops stick to it, there is water in it. *Democritus Florentinus,* and *Sotio.*

Whether Wine be sophisticated with water.

If you would try whether there be water mingled with new wine; put in an Egg; if it presently sinks down there is water, if not, it is pure wine. Moreover if you would break the force of wine boyling in the Vessel, cast a little piece of Cheese into it, and you shall see a wonder: But how this comes to pass, *Georgius Valla Placentinus* will shew you.

That water mingled with wine may swim upon the top of it.

The blood of a Dunghill Cock dried and poudred, and mingled with wine mixed with water, will make the water swim above. *From the relation of a certain* Monk.

To part Wine and water.

A bullrush dried and put into wine mingled with water, will draw all the water to it, and leave the wine: this is very handsome and profitable to try wines mingled with water. *Mizald.*

To make Wine exceeding pleasant.

Wine will please the palate, and have both a good sent and colour, if an Orange or Pomecitron be stuck full with Cloves and hanged in the Cask, that it may not touch the wine, for so it will never tast flat nor musty.

That Wine may have no ill tast.

Oyl poured upon wine or any liquor, will keep it from an ill savour, and that it shall not corrupt, for all aire that makes putrefaction and ill vapours are kept out by this covering that swims above it. *Pliny.*

Another.

If you want the convenience of the Sun in Summer time, you shall not set your wines in Caves under ground, that it grow not unsavoury, unless you put into it some fat salt Hogs flesh wrapt in linen, or something that is larger, as your Vessell is great or small. But still as you draw forth the wine, let the Hogs flesh be put down lower to it, untill the Vessel be quite drawn out, so will the wine never lose its virtue, nor have any ill tast. *Lemnius.*

To quench the heat of the Wine quickly.

Theophrastus writes, that if you put a Pumex stone into a Vessel of boyling wine,

wine, the heat of it will be presently alaid.

To coole Wine.

That wine in Summer may not grow soon unsavoury in the Cask, but may be well relished and keep cold; place your wine Vessels in an other Vessel that is full of cold water, then strew in some Saltpeter to the water; for this will keep the wine so cold, that it will hardly be endured by your teeth. *Lemnius*, and *Langius*.

To make Greek wine.

Where the feild is far from the Sea, you shall make Greek wine thus: Poure nine score gallons of new wine into a brass Caldron, and put fire under, when the wine boyleth, take away the fire, and when that wine is cold, pour it into a Vessel large enough, and a part put into another Vessel big enough, one handfull of Salt into fair water, and make brine of it. When the brine is made, beat sweet Calamus in a mortar and pour it into it, one pint of it will make it sweet sented. After thirty daies make fast the Vessel. When the spring comes, pour it forth into lesser Vessels that hold nine Gallons apiece: let it stand two years in the Sun, then bring it into the house. This wine will be as good as Greek wine. *M. Cato.*

Another.

If you will make Greek wine, take Sea water out of the deep Sea, when the wind is still, and the Sea calm, where no fresh water comes, seaventy daies before the vintage, pour this Sea water into a Vessel, but do not fill it, let it be forty five gallons less then full: put on a cover, yet leave a vent hole: when thirty daies are past, poure it off gently and cleanly into another Vessel: leave the grounds to settle in the bottome; after twenty daies, poure it off again into another Vessel; and let it stand so untill the Vintage. When you would make Greek wine, leave the Grapes upon the Vine, let them be full ripe, and when it rains and they grow dry again, gather them, and lay them in the Sun two daies, or three in the open Aire, if it rain not. If it do raine, lay them upon Hurdles safely within dores, and if there be any rotten Grapes, take them away. Then take Sea water what may suffice, and into a Quinquagenary Vessel, pour Sea water, Q. X. then take away the husks from the Grapes that are mingled, and sweep them into the same Vessel, untill the Vessel be full, pressing them in with your hand, that they may drink in the Sea water, when the Vessel is full, cover it with a cover, and leave a vent hole: when three daies are over, take them out of the Vessel and press them with a wine Press, and keep that wine in good, dry, clean Cask. To make it well sented do thus, Take a Vessel well pitched, put a small fire into it, and perfume it with a Posie of flowers, sweet Calamus and oyl of Dates, that the perfumers use, put them into the Vessel and cover it, that the smell be not gone before the wine be put in. Do this the day before you put in your wine; then quickly put the wine out of the press into Vessels; let it remain fifteen daies open before you stop it up, that it may take ayr, then stop it. After forty daies pour it into nine gallon Vessels, and put into every Vessel pint of new wine boyled thick. Do not fill the Vessels with wine above the lowest handles of the Vessel; set the Vessels in the Sun where there is no grass, and cover them, that no rain come to them, and let them not stand above four daies in the Sun, after four daies, put it into a leather bag and stop it close in.

That wine may tast like Malmsey.

The flower and seed of garden Clary, put into a Vessel of wine whilst it works, will make it tast so pleasant as Greek or Malmsey wine. Prick up your ears Vintners, but I beseech you defraud no man with your wicked Sophistications and cheating mixtures. *Mizald. de horto medico.*

Borage wine good for melancholy people, and pains of the heart, making men merry and curing madness, &c.

Take Borrage flowers as many as you please, put them into new wine untill it be fully purified, when it is setled, pour it off into another Vessel gently, and keep it for your use. *Arnoldus villanovan.*

Wine of winter-Cherries doth manifestly drive forth the stone of the kidnies, and the bladder, and opens the Urine that is stopt.

Take winter-Cherries bruised as many as may serve turn; strain wine hot or cold upon them sometimes, untill it have gaind the tast and virtue of them, season it with Sugar or Honey. *Arnoldus* and *Dioscorides*.

Wine of Quinces, good for the stomach, fluxes of the Belly, and Liver, for diseases of the Kidnies, and difficulty of making water, It binds, &c.

Take Quinces made clean and cut twelve pounds, put them into a pipe of new wine for thirty daies, then set it up for use. *Alexius*.

Hippocras wine.

Take inward rind of Cinnamon six drams, Ginger half an ounce, Nutmegs two drams, Cloves, Grains of Paradice, of each one dram, Cardamus one scruple, Pepper, sweet Calamus, Coriander prepared, of each one scruple, the best wine eight pound, white Sugar what may serve turn. Pouder what must be poudred, then mingle them, and strain them according to art. This wine may be clarified with Almond milk. *Euonymus*.

Another for weakness of the stomach.

Take choice Cinnamon half an ounce, white Ginger two drams, Cloves, long Pepper, Nutmegs, of each two scruples, white Sugar half a pound. Bruise all these well, and mingle them with three measures of the best white wine, and strain them. *The same*.

Another.

Take choice Cinnamon one ounce and half, Ginger half an ounce, Cloves two drams, Galanga one dram, Grains of Paradise one dram, red wine two measures; mingle and strain them according to art, with Almond milk. *Alexius*.

To make Hippocras an easie way.

Take choice Cinnamon two ounces, Ginger one ounce, Cubebs half an ounce, white Sugar one pound and half. Beat all these, and put them into a frail, Grapes are pressed with, and with that put in two measures of the best wine, leave them some time, and the wine will receive the virtues of them. *The same*.

Hippocras wine that is purgative against a quartan Ague, a Quotidian and a Bastard Tertian, it concocts and prepares the Humours, and afterwards purgeth them by stool.

Take choice Cinnamon, Raysins of each half an ounce, Ginger, Zedoary, Cloves, Mastick of each one ounce, Polypod four drams, Epithymum six drams, Esula one pound, Sugar what is sufficient: mingle them, and make it according to Art a drink to be kept for use. *Euonymus*.

Hippocras wine with Aqua vitæ.

Take choice Cinnamon two ounces, Ginger half an ounce, Grains of Paradise, long Pepper of each one dram and half, Cloves one dram, Nutmeg half a dram. Bruise them all, and put them into a full Vessel of *Aqua vitæ*, three or four times distilled, kept close for four daies, and stir them twice or thrice every day, then strain it, and keep it. Put a little spoonfull of this into a measure of the best red wine, and add thereto one pound of Sugar: but if the wine be sweet, there needs no Sugar. *Euonymus*.

To make Malmsey.

Take the best Galanga, Cloves, Ginger, Mace, of each one dram, leave all these well bruised grossely, in a woodden Vessell well stopt, infused in *Aqua vitæ* twenty four hours; Then hang them in a linnen bag by a thred, into a Vessel that will hold a *somme* as they call it, or half a *somme* of clear wine for three daies, and you shall have wine so good and so strong as naturall Malmsey. *The same*.

Malmsey.

Take Musk, Lignum Aloes, Cinnamon, Cardamus, Cloves, two drams of each, Sugar candy, half an ounce, bruise them a little, and hang them in a bag into the wine. *The same*.

Roman

Romane wine.

Take choice Cinnamon, Juyce of Licorish two drams, Anniseed one dram, Mace half a dram, Sugar three drams, bruise all these grossely, and hang them in the wine in a bag.

Greek wine.

Take Ginger, Galanga, of each half a pound, grains of Paradise, Cloves, of each three ounces, make them into gross pouder, then hang them in a bag in a middle size Vessel of Wine. *Euonymus.*

Muscadel.

Take Licorish, Polypod, Anniseeds, of each two drams, Nutmegs three drams, Calamus one dram, bruise them lightly, and hang them in a bag in wine. *The same.*

Rhenish wine.

Take Cinnamon, Ginger, Cloves, of each half a dram, beat them a little and mingle them, then put them up into a linnen bag, and hang them in a glass Vessell of *Aquavitæ*, very well stopt for twelve houres, when you would use this, crush the bag into some great glass, that you will poure wine into, so that the sides of the cup be sprinkled with that Aromaticall liquor made with *Aquavitæ*, that the liquor pressed out into the bottome, may wet the sides of the glass only, then pour in your wine, and it will tast like Rhenish wine.

Zedoary wine.

Take Cinnamon three ounces, Cloves, Nutmegs, grains of Paradise, Cardamus, of each half an ounce, Zedoary six drams, Cubebs, long Pepper, of each two ounces: bruise them grossely, and hang them in a bag in a measure of wine called commonly *Oma. The same.*

Claret.

Take Cinnamon two ounces, Galanga, Ginger, of each one ounce, grains of Paradise, long Pepper, of each one dram, Cloves two drams, Honey one pound and half, Sugar two pound, white wine four measures: pouder what must be poudered, mingle them, and often strain them, clarifie it with whites of Eggs. *The same.*

Another.

Take Cinnamon one ounce, Ginger, grains of Paradice, of each one dram and half, Cloves two drams, Coriander prepared three drams, white Sugar four ounces; bruise and strain them all, and keep them in a Vessel of Pewter. *The same.*

Another.

Take Cinnamon half an ounce, Cloves one dram, Ginger two ounces, white Sugar half a pound, Honey one ounce, white wine three measures: mingle them, and make Claret according to Art. *The same.*

Another.

Take choice Cinnamon one ounce, Ginger half an ounce, Galanga, Cloves, grains of Paradice of each two drams, Saffron one dram, best Honey clarified two pound, the best wine two measures. Bruise them all, and strain them through a bag, whose upper part must be linnen, and the under part wollen; If a woman must drink this wine or some dainty person, put in Sugar for Honey. *The same.*

Claret laxative.

Take Cinnamon one ounce, Galanga six drams, Esula, Turbith, pils of Hermodactils, of each half a dram, make pouder of them, and make Claret according to Art with Honey, Sugar and Wine. *The same.*

Sugard Wine is good for old, cold, weak persons, and for those whose naturall heat and moysture is decayed: for it nourisheth and breeds good blood, and fils the principal parts with spirits.

Take Mallagowe Wine, whitest Sugar, of each four pound, boyl them at a gentle fire to a Syrup, then keep it for use; you must use it with two parts of water. *The same.*

Wine to keep the Belly loose.

If you would make wine to keep your belly in good order, at the time of dressing the Vines, when earth is taken from their roots, as much as you think you shall need of that Wine, so many Vines you must rid away earth from their roots, and mark them, cut their roots about, and cleanse them; Beat black Hellebour roots in a Mortar, lay those roots about the Vines and old dung and old ashes, and two parts of earth must be cast about that, and the roots of the Vines must be cast upon the earth. Make this wine by it self; If you would keep it untill it be old, keep it to move your belly, and do not mingle it with other wine. If you drink a cup of it mixed with water before Supper, it will purge without danger. *M. Cato.*

Another.

To make purging wine, when you dress the roots of your Vines, mark them with red marking stone, that you may not mix it with other wine. Lay three handfuls of black Helebour about the roots, and cast earth upon them. When in the Vintage time you gather those Grapes, keep them by themselves, put a cup of it into a potion; it will move the belly, and purge the next day without danger. *The same.*

Another.

Cast a handfull of black Hellebour into nine gallons of new Wine, when it hath workt enough, take the Hellebour out of the wine, keep this to purge by stool. *Cato.*

Diuretick wine.

If you cannot make water well, beat Juniper berries in a mortar, put one pound into two gallons of old wine; let it work in a brass or leaded Vessel, when it is cold, put it up into an earthen Vessel. Take a cup of it fasting in a morning and it will help. *The same.*

Wine against gripings, with a looseness of the belly.

If your belly gripe and be loose, and worms trouble you, take thirty sour Pomegranates and bruise them, put them into an earthen pot, with three gallons of sharp black wine, stop the Vessel, after thirty daies tap it and drink of it, drink fasting an *Hemina* of it. *M. Cato.*

For ill concoction and the strangury.

A Pomegranate gathered when it is ripe, is good for bad concoction and strangury; put three pound weight into nine gallons of old wine, and a clean Fennell root bruised one pound, stop the Vessel, and after thirty daies broch it, and drink of it. *Cato.*

To make wine.

Floure gentle steeped in water, will drink like wine, a pleasant deceit for those that have a Feaver. Mizaldus *in horto medico.*

To make Artificiall Respas Wine.

Take three ounces of Oras Roots, slice it into small slices, and put it into a gallon of white Wine, and let it stand close covered twenty four hours, when you serve it at the table, colour it with a little Red wine, and it shall not be known from reall respas Wine. *My Lord of* Pembrokes *Manuscript.*

To Make Mead.

Take of well Coulord and new Honey, which hath a good tast soon mixt, and sharpe, which never came to the fire, being thick in substance; also Fountain water clear eight parts as much as the Honey: mingle well together over night, untill it be strong enough to bear an Egge, as you try brine; the next day, boyl it till it bear a scum, then skim it, and to make it purge the better, put in the whites of three or four Eggs beaten with Rose water, then skim so long as any scum ariseth, then put in those Spices, Lignum Aloes two ounces, Nutmegs, Cinnamon, Cloves and Mase, of each half an ounce, let it boyl with those a pretty space, (some use to hang it in a Vessel when it it Tund,) then take it of, and let it stand till it be cold, the next day take a Canvas sheet, fold it double, and strain it into a Cowle, it will be a day before it all run out, when it is all run out, tun it, and let it stand a day to purge, then bury it, leaving a little vent hole. Be carefull in the boyling, for being slack boyld, it nourisheth but little, and doth much move and stir the belly, and breedeth wind, but being well boyld, it disperseth wind, nourisheth more, and will keep the longer.

To

To make Metheglin.

Take nine gallons of fair running water, put it over the fire in a clean Vessel provide these Herbs following, of wild Carrets with his flower and root six handfuls, of Bettony four handfuls, Harts tongue, Penyroyall, Rosemary, Cinkfoyle, Scabious, Polipodium of the Oake, leaves and root; Century of each one handfull; Fennell seed, Anniseed, of each four ounces; Cinnamon, Ginger, Nutmegs, Cloves, Mace, of each two ounces; Elecampane roots one ounce, Raysins of the Sun, stond four pounds, Mugwort one pound, Licorish half a pound; bruise the Herbs, and beat the Spices to pouder, put all into the nine gallons of water, and boyl it till it come to six gallons, then draw out your Herbs and strain them into the six gallons of water, put four gallons of Honey, and boyl it again to eight or nine gallons; then take it of, and let it stand till it be luke warme; with a little Barm of new Ale set it a working, and so let it continue for three daies space, and when it is well setled, take off the skim with a Skimmer. Tun it in a sweet Vessel sutable to the proportion of your Liquor, and let it stand close stopt seaven years, and the last year of the seaven it shall be the most wholesome.

That one that hath drank wine may not smell of it.

Chew Arris root that comes from *Africa*, and the wine you drink shall not be smelt. *Alexius.*

That one may be soon made drunk and take no hurt.

Infuse *Indian* Lignum Aloes in wine, or boyl Mandrake pils in water untill it wax red, mingle that with wine. *Alexius.*

That a man may not be drunk with much wine.

Take the juyce of white Coleworts, juyce of soure Pomegranates, of each two ounces, Vinegar one ounce; let them boyl awhile at the fire, and make a Syrup: take one ounce of it before you drink, or eat five or seaven bitter Almonds fasting. The lungs of a Goat or Sheep rosted and eaten, also Colewort seed, and Wormwood and naturall Salt, and the Amethyst carried about one, all these preserve a man from drunkness. *The same.*

That one may drink much at a sitting and not be drunk.

He that drinks wine shall not be drunk if he be crowned with boughs of ground Pine or Ivy tree; or if before Supper he eats four or five raw Colewort leaves. The ashes of a Swallows beck, or the ashes of burnt Swallows drank in wine with Myrrh, will not suffer a man to be drunk for ever. The juyce of Peach leaves pressed forth, will do the same, if you drink a small cup of it fasting. *The same.*

That drunkards may grow sober.

Vinegar drank in good quantity, recovers one that is drunk, and Coleworts eaten and Cakes and Junkets made with Honey. *The same.*

That one may not perceive his drunkneß.

He that shall eat a Goats lungs rosted, shall never find that he is drunk, let him drink for a wager. *Africanus.*

To make drunkards out of love with wine.

There are many, that when they have drank too much wine are dangerously hurt by it, and fall into diseases and dye. Now if you would have them loath and abhor wine, and the fountain called *Clitorius* is far off: let three or four Eels be put into wine untill they dye, let a drunkard drink of this wine, and he will loath and hate wine ever after, nor will he ever drink of it again, but live soberly. Also *Athenæus* saith, that a Mullet strangled in Wine, if it be presently drank by any man, it will emasculate him: if by a woman, she will never conceive. *The same.*

Otherwise to make Drunkards loath Wine.

Observe where the night-Owl makes her nest, take away her eggs, seeth them and give them a Child to eat, he will never love Wine. *Farcas.*

Whether there shall be plenty of Wine.

If an Houp sing before the Vine buds, it signifies plenty of wine that year. *Mizaldus.*

That

That Ale may keep good all the year.

Ale made in *Germany* in *March*, will last good all the year. *Cardan.*

For Beere decayed.

When Beer hath lost its naturall taft, or begins to decay, we ufe to recover it, and make it tafte well, with well fented Ingredients, as Arris root, Vinegar, Nutmegs, Cloves, Bay berries, and dry Bay leaves, fweet Calamus, Origanum, Beets. *Lemnius.*

Whey or Milk, like rock water.

It is made thus, Heat your milk and pour in at night white wine Vinegar, or juyce of Oranges, or Verjuyce, but let it not boyl, then fowing a linnen cloth like a bag, and preffing forth that which is thick, it will at firft come forth troubled, but ftraining it often, at laft it will be clear like Fountain water. *Cardan.*

To make Vinegar sharp.

Let a fourth or fift part of the Vinegar be made boyling hot by the fire, pour that into the reft, fet it eight daies in the Sun, and it will be very fharp and good. Moreover old grafs roots, Rayfins, wild Pear tree leaves ftamped, Madder root, Whey, burnt Acorns, burning Coles, the decoction of Ciche Peafon, and burning Potfheards, all thefe caft into Vinegar, will make it fharp. *Alexius.*

To make Vinegar strong presently

You fhall make Vinegar ftrong forthwith, if you caft into it pieces of new barley bread, for in two daies it will be very ftrong. *Mizald.*

To make Vinegar of Wine presently.

If you would prefently turn Wine into Vinegar, caft into it Salt and Pepper, with four leaven, mingle it, and it will do it prefently. If you would do it fooner, quench a piece of Steel or Brick red hot once or twice in it, or Raddifh roots, or unripe Services, Mulberries, Prunes, Medlars; the fame is done by the fair flower of the Gilleflower. *The fame.*

To make Vinegar presently.

If you would make Vinegar by and by, caft a bruifed Beet root on the Wine, and it will be Vinegar after three houres. *Mizald.*

That Vinegar may be made Wine.

That four Wine or Vinegar may be made Wine, you make do it with Leekfeed, or with Vine leaves and tendrels caft into it. *Lemnius.*

To make Vinegar by Art.

Vinegar may be made with Salt put in, or any four thing which will corrupt (I have tried Pepper) with huge gain, if you keep Pepper wort. It is done alfo by fire, for when it is fcalding hot, it is fet in the Sun, Vinegar being minged with it, and it will all grow four. *Cardan.*

To make Vinegar of water.

Wild Pears are kept three daies on an heap, then they pour on a little water, and fo for thirty daies together. It may be fo done afrefh; for the fweet part being taken away, and by help of putrefaction, Water thus turns into Vinegar. For Dates and old Figs, and Grapes, their fweeter juyce being preffed forth, and water poured unto them, the firft and fecond pouring on makes wine, but the third makes moft fharp Vinegar. *Cardan.*

Against thirst from heat.

Againft thirft that comes of heat, hold in your mouth Cryftall, Corall, Silver, Sugarcandy, or a flint ftone that hath lain long in cold water. Alfo Licorifh root new taken out of the earth and chewed, or drank with water, will foon quench your thirft. As watching quencheth thirft that comes of heat; fo will fleep that thirft which comes from drought. Alfo it is good to rince your mouth with cold water. New Figs eafe thirft, and cool heat, Pine kernels, Purcelane leaves put under the tongue, Strawberries, Pears, Prunes, Cherries, Quince kernels, Cucumber and Lettice feed, are excellent to quench thirft; bread wet with cold water, and taken with wine is very good for it. Wine is cooled by putting the Veffel and the Wine into cold water, and if tofted bread be fteeped in cold Fountain water, and after this is taken

ken out let the wine be poured in, and so drank, the water being often changed.

The Physicall virtues of distilled waters.

Distilled waters are either cold or hot, they either coole Blood, or Choler, or heat, fleagm, or mellancholly.

To coole the blood overheated: Lettice, Purslane, Water-lillies, Violets, Sorrel, Succory, Fumitary, Endive.

To coole Choler in the Head: Nightshade, Lettice, Water-lillies, Poppies.

To coole the Brest: Violets, Poppies, Coltsroot.

To coole Choler in the Heart: Sorrel, Quinces, Water-lillies, Roses, Violets, bark of Walnuts.

To coole the Stomach: Quinces, flowers of Roses, Violets, Purslane, Nightshade, Sengreen or Housleek.

To coole the Liver: Endive, Succory, Nightshade, Purslane, Water-lillies.

To coole the Reins and Bladder: Endive, Water-cherries, Plantane, Water-lillies, Melons, Gourds, Citrouls, Strawberries, Sengreen, Grass, Black-cherries.

To coole the Matrix: Endive, Lettice, Water-lillies, Purslane, Roses.

Waters that heat.

To heat fleagm in the head: Betony, Sage, Marjerom, Cammomile, Fennell, Calaminth, Lillies of the Valley, Rosemary Flowers, Primroses, Eyebright.

To heat fleagm in the Brest: Maidenhair, Bettony, Hysop, Horehound, Carduus, Ortis, Scabions, Balme, Tobacco, Self-heal, Comfrey.

To heat fleagm in the Stomach: Wormwood, Fennell, Mints, Cinnamon, Mother of time, Marigolds.

To heat fleagm in the Heart: Cinnamon, Balme, Rosemary.

To heat fleagm in the Liver: Century the less, Wormwood, Origanum, Agrimony, Fennell.

To heat fleagm in the Spleen: Birthwort, Watercresses, Wormwood, Calaminth, Gentian.

To heat fleagm in the Reins and Bladder: Rocket, Nettles, Saxifrage, Raddish, Pellitory of the wall, Cinkfoyl, Burnet, Elecampane.

To heat fleagm in the Matrix: Mugwort, Savin, Peniroyall, Calaminth, Lovage.

To heat Mellancholly in the Head: Hops and Fumitary.

In the Brest: Balme, Carduus.

In the Heart: Burrage, Bugloss, Balme, Rosemary.

In the Liver: Cichory, Fumitory, Hops, Asarabacco.

In the Spleen: Doddar, Harts tongues, Tamer is Time. *Nicholas Culpep.*

Of the matter of Generation.

Every man that is naturally engenderd is engendred of the Seed of the Father, and the Menstrue of the Mother, according to the opinion of all the *Philosophers* and *Physicians*, who all joyntly agree that all the Seed as well of the Father, which is cal'd the Sperme, as that of the Mother, which is cal'd the Menstrue, goes into the substance of the Child. This being resolved, we are next to consider how these Seeds are received into the Woman. How the Woman when she is in the Act of Generation, yields her Menstrue at the very time when the Man doth his Sperme, so that these two Seeds concurring and meeting together in the Womans Matrix, begin both at once to mingle together, she is then said to conceive, when these two Seeds are received into the Matrix, in such a place as is appointed by nature for such an Act; after the Seed so received, the Matrix of the Woman is closed as a Purse on every side, so that none of the Seed received can be shed or lost. *Dr Harvey.*

How to know whether a Woman hath Conceived.

The signs of Conception are many: For first, If presently after the Act she feels her self cold, and have pain in her Thighs, it is most certain she is conceived. Secondly, If she cast forth little or no Seed. Thirdly, If the Man in the Act feel his Yard suckt with a kind of closure in the Womans Matrix. Fourthly, If the Woman still covet and desire to couple, or if she find a tickling in the mouth of the Matrix, or if

P her

her complexion be altered, and she become more ruddy, if she hath strange longings, all which are infallible signs that she is with Child. *Ambrose Parey.*

A Woman being with Child, to know whether it be a Male or a Female.

To be resolved in this if it be a male Child, the colour of her face is red, and she is very nimble; if her Belly swell and wax round on the right side, if her milk be thick and well digested, lay Salt one the Nipple of her Brest, if it melt not, it is a sign of a male Child, and on the contrary a Female, if she feel a paine on her left side it is a Female, if she be heavy and pale, her milk black, her belly is long, her left side round, it is a female; take a drop of her milk and drop it into her own water, if it sink it is a male, if it swim aloft it is a female. *Nich. Culpepper.*

Certain signs of Chastity.

The first is shamefastness, blushing, fear, a chast and modest gate and speech, with small regard to apply themselves to man or mans affections; but some are so subtill as to performe all this. Secondly, Observe her Urine if it be clear and bright like Gold colour. Those that have been defloured have their Urine troubled, as also the Sperm of the Man will be seen in the Urine, as also the call or fell which is within the Matrix, by coupling with a man is broken.

Of Venery. Chap. 8.

To make one valiant in Venus Camp.

If any man desire to be a strong Souldier in the Camp of *Venus*; let him be armed with such meat; chiefly with Bulbas roots, for they all provoke Venery. So Rocket taken plentifully, Onyons, Ciche Peason, Parsnips, Anniseed, Coriander, Pine kernels; amongst these *Satyrion* moves exceedingly, and stands most forcible in this business, and provokes Womens desire. Nettles are belonging to *Venus*. If we had that Herb *Theophrastus* mentioneth, which an *Indian* brought, that not only they that eate of it, but those that touched it were very strong for Venery, that they could Act as often as they pleased, commonly they would performe twelve times that used it, but he said he had performed seaventy times, that at last his Seed came forth by drops of blood. Wherefore if you will provoke *Venus* with them all, or with some of them only, use this Receipt. Take Satyrion roots, Pine Kernels, Anniseed, and Rocket seed, of each alike quantity, half so much of the land Crocodile, a little Musk, make them up with the choicest clarified Honey. Nor must I omit Sparrows brains, Birds tongue, wild Rocket, and the like; but if any man would provoke a woman let him sprinkle well upon his Glans with oyl, Musk or Civet, Castoreum or Cubebs, or any one of these, for these do quickly provoke. But that both of the Parties shall be thus delighted: beat long Pepper, Pellitory of *Spain*, Galanga, mingle a little of the pouder with honey and use that. *The same.*

To provoke Venery.

It is wonderfull that the great toe of the right foot annointed with the ashes of a Weesil with Honey or Oyl, will suffice abundantly for those that by reason of age or otherwise are almost dead in this matter, and are very unfit to serve *Venus* in her Wars any longer. *The Authors of this were those old searchers into Natures Secrets, and many modern Writers confirm it.*

To make women lusty.

If weomen do presently eat Ganders stones, so soon as their terms are past, these will not only make them prone to Venery, but also to conceive; I have read the same of the Matrix of a Hare. *Rhasis, Albert.*

That a woman may admit of her Husband.

When a woman will not lye with her Husband, then let her Husband take some of the Suet of a middle Goat, that is between the great and small Goats, and let him annoint his Yard with it, and then lye with her; she will love him and not ly afterwards with any other. *Albertus.*

That a woman may take delight with her Husband.

If a woman can find no pleasure with her Husband, let him take the marrow of a Wolfs left foot, and carry that with him, and she will love no man besides himself. *The same.*

To increase Venery.

Take Chestnuts steeped in Muskadel, then boyl them, being twenty in number, Satyrions ten, land Crocodils two, Pine Kernels, Pistaches, of each four ounces, Rocket seed two ounces, Cubebs one ounce, Cinnamon half an ounce, Sugar twelve ounces, make an Electuary. *Out of a written Book.*

Another.

Take twenty Chestnuts boyld in the best wine, Pistaches, Pine Kernels cleansed, of each four ounces, Land Crocodiles two, Satyrions ten, choice Cinnamon half an ounce, Colewort seed seaven drams, Cubebs one ounce, whitest Sugar what is sufficient, make an Electuary, let the sick take the quantity of a Chestnut before or after Supper. *Roscellus.*

Another.

Take the whitest Sugar four ounces, Pistaches one ounce, Ginger two drams, long Pepper, Land Crocodiles, of each two drams, Pine Kernels cleansed five ounces, beat them very well, and mingle them to an Electuary.

Tables for the same.

Take Cinnamon, Ginger, Pepper, Cresses seed, Rocket seed, Mustard seed, of each half a dram, Birds tongue, Onyon seed, Land Crocodile, of each one scruple, whitest Sugar dissolved in Rose water, four ounces, make Tables. *Roscellus.*

To beget Boys or Girls.

The decoction of the male *Mercury*, (for the Herb is distinguished into male and female; for the juyce of it drank four daies from the first day after her purgations, makes the womb fit to conceive Boyes; but the female *Mercury*, the juyce of it drank after the same manner for so many daies gives her force to conceive Girls: if when the terms are past and the womb setled, the man and woman lye together as they should, and embrace one the other. *Diosco, Pliny.*

That women may bring forth handsome Sons.

Hence it was cunningly invented, how women may bear beautifull Sons. *Empedocles* saith, That when a woman conceivs, sight will confirm the Birth. For ofttimes women have fallen in love with Pictures and Images, and they have brought forth Children like unto them, and it is recorded that women have been delivered of black and hairy Children. And men searching for the cause, when they had much troubled their brains, they found pictures on the walls, that stood over against them; upon which the women cast their eyes when they were in the Act, and so the imagination begat Children like to them. Wherefore I think this ought to be kept in memory, being so usuall, and which I suppose the best means, and which I have advised many to, that the Pictures of *Cupid*, *Adonis*, and *Ganymede*, should hang before them, or some solid forme of their Antecessours; then women in their Venery may imagine, that their mind may be carryed away with the strength of imagination, and being with Child may still contemplate of it, and the Child when it is born, will be like that they conceived in their minds when they were in the Act of Venery. I know it doth not profit very little. When I had often prescribed this, a woman heard me, and she presently caused a handsome Boy carved in Marble to be set before her eyes: she desired at her lying with her Husband to have such a Boy, and when she was great with child, she often thought of it; and after that she shewd me her Son like to that, and very fat, so pale, that it lookt white as Marble. The truth was tried, and some such practices are lawfull and successfull. But let no inordinate copulation be, or wicked postures; for by such practises odious to God and good men, strange monsters have been brought forth. *The same.*

How well coloured and fair Children may be begotten.

Great is the affection of the mind, or force of imagination, but greatest of all when it exceeds: what is it you may not do almost by it? Women when they are with Child, when they desire most eagerly, think of it vehemently, they change the spirits within, and in them are painted the forms of the things they thought of; those move the blood, whereupon in the softest matter of the Child they imprint the form: thus do they print upon Children perpetuall severall marks not to be blotted out, unless

unless they go out when their desire is begun otherwise; wherefore the Searchers out of things have found out with great pains, that Children are so marked as the mind is affected, and chiefly in principall actions, as in copulation, with Man when the Seed is ejected, and such like. Therefore there being in man a swiftness of thoughts, and nimbleness of mind, and variety of desire, this makes the marks different: therefore there are more differences in Men then in other living Creatures; for the rest having minds unmoveable, they have every one in its own kind a faculty given them to beget their like. *Jacob* knew this force of the mind, and imagination as the Sacred Scriptures testify.

How to know whither a woman be chast, and whether she ever lay with a Man or be with Child.

Antiquity affords us some experiments of this thing; and so doth this latter age, with things that are to be admired, and easie to be procured; that men seeing them, will sooner deny their sense, and confess themselves to be fools, than they will approve the truth; and those that are delighted with the desire of such a thing, go about to search for it, and greedily thirst to find it out. The Jet stone, (which is very frequent with us, wherewith we make Beads withall to pray, and to number and summe up our Prayers,) some scrapings of it, or the stone beaten in a Mortar, and sifted, so being brought into very fine pouder, and then drank with wine or water; if the woman do make water presently and cannot hold it, that is a sign she hath lost her Maiden-head; If she were never defloured, she will hold her water, and her retentive faculty is strengthned by it. White Amber is as good as the former (or Crystall,) which they call Electrum, if being poudred, it be drank with wine fasting, and so taken inwardly: for if she be polluted, this will make her make water. We may try it sooner by the fume of Purslane seed, or leaves of the great Burdock strewed upon burning coals, and put under her for a fume, and if that flye upward, it will discover the truth of the matter: let it be carried by a tunnel or some small instrument into the mouth of the Matrix, it will cause her to Urine presently, nor can she forbear if she have made use of a man. But if she be chast, the smoke will do nothing, but she will hold her water, which signifies that she is a Maid. But if any man will make sport to make a Woman Urine, Agallochum called Xyloaloes cut into pieces and laid thick upon the live coles, or the pouder of it, untill it burn, and the woman do receive this smoke at her Secrets, it will performe this and much more, that it will be sport enought to behold. *The same.*

For those that are bewitched.

The Pye eaten will recover those that are bewitched, as some think: also the fume of a dead mans tooth, and if the whole body be annointed with a Crows gall, and oyl of Sesama, that will do it also. *Ex Cleopatra.* Or if Quicksilver put into a Hazelnut shell, or quill, be stopt in with wax, and laid under the Pillow of one that is bewitched, or under the threshold of the dore that the man enters in by into his house or chamber. *Wierus.*

To cure such as are bewitched.

If the man (saith *Varignata, Nicolaus,* and *Arnoldus,*) piss through his wedding Ring, he shall be freed from any Witchcraft that hinders him from the Act of Venery. And if the excrement of the beloved be put into his shoe that is in love with her, when he smels the stink, the love is broken off: for this is an odious thing. *Taken out of Ovids first book of the Remedy of Love.*

> Phineus those drugs do like thy Table smell;
> My stomach loaths them as it would do Hell.

Cure for debility in Venery.

Some that blush or fear, are hindred from Venery, and suppose they are bewitched; many things are thought to cure this disease: flying Ants mixed with oyle of Elders, and the Mans Yard annointed therewith, and many other things spoken of before: *Cardanus.*

That the Woman shall abhorre Copulation, and the man shall desire it.

If a red Buls pisle be poudred and a crown weight be given the woman to drink in wine or broth, she will abhorre to lye with a man. *Rhasis.* But the same pouder mingled with fit Ingredients will provoke men that are dull and impotent, to Venerous Acts. *Marcellus Empiricus.*

To charm both Men and Women, and to make them impotent for Copulation.

If you bind the prick of a Wolf in the name of the man or woman, this will make them so unfit for Venery, that they will almost seem to be Eunuchs, untill the knot be untied. *Albertus.*

That a woman shall admit of no man but her Husband.

Take the gall of a Goat, and the fat, and dry it, then pound them both, and warm them with pure oyl, and annoint the mans Yard with it by turns, as he lyeth with the woman, and she will never admit of any man but him. *Albertus.*

To take off the edge of the desire of Venery.

You may thus blunt the desire of Venery, eat Rue and Camphir, for this will destroy erection, and makes a man an Eunuch, it so stops and hinders *Venus*, and if you lay but the seed under you, or drink or eat it, it will dry. Wherefore the Matrons of *Athens* were wont to lay Rue leaves under them when they went to bed : so Lettice eaten often takes away the power of copulation ; wherefore *Pythagoras* called it εὐνεχον, which also the Poets intimate in words very dark. *Callimachus* writes, that *Adonis* when he had eaten Lettice was kild by a Bore, and *Venus* buried him under a Lettice ; because *Atheneus* saith *Venus* grows faint by such a Potherab, and men are made impotent for her service by it. *The same.*

That no man may affect unlawfull Venery.

The heart of a male Quail carryed about by a man, and of a female by a woman, causeth that no quarrels nor wranglings shall ever be betwixt them. And if a Turtles heart be carried in a Wolfs skin, he that carrieth it shall never be tempted to be in love. *Mizald.*

Whether a woman be chast.

To try whether a woman be chast, you shall do thus. The Loadstone will try it, and discover it. I have a long time made diligent search, and I find that some experiments are true of stones, which I have often wondred and laught at. If the Loadstone be put under the head of a wife whilst she sleeps, if she be chast she will embrace her Husband, if not, she will as it were with her hand thrust him out of the Chamber. *Albert.*

That a woman cannot commit Adultery with any man.

That a woman shall not be able to commit Adultery, cut off some of her hair, and cast the pouder of them upon thy coffin ; but first annoint the coffin with honey , and then ly with the woman, and when you would let her lose, do the same with your own hair. *Albertus.*

That whores may hardly be known from maids.

The distilled water of Sharewort, drank or put into the Matrix, wonderfully stops the whites in Women, that by long injecting it, the corrupted can scarse be discerned from the chast ; this will be done sooner and more effectuall, if they sit over the decoction, as one told me that tried it. *Mizaldus.*

Of Sleep. Chap. 9.

Tables to provoke one to sleep.

Take the rinds of Mandrake roots one handfull, Henbane seed one ounce, white and red Poppy seed, of each one ounce. Bruise all these and boyl them in two pound of Fountain water, untill a third part be consumed, then strain it, and adde the whitest Sugar one pound, and when they are again boyl'd almost to the perfect consistence of Sugar, adde Nutmegs, Galla Moschata, Lignum Aloes of each two drams, barks of Mandrake, seed of Henbane, seeds of red and white Poppy, of each three drams, Opium two drams, make tables according to Art. *Roseellus.*

Another.

Another.

Another more violent to make one sleep, is made thus. Take the best Opium with equall weight of *nux Metella*, seed of black Henbane, dissolve them in the juyce of Lettice, but it will be better to set them in the water covered with Horse dung: then put them into Stils, and when they begin to grow hot, draw forth the water, keep the feces and dry them under hot embers, that you may beat them into fine pouder, and sift them; after this, with fresh water make a strong lee, when all the vapour is fled by force of the fire, mingle this with the water kept before, and fit it for to be eaten or drank; not in the same, but a smaller quantity; than was spoken for that is too much to take, and give it to no body, unless there be great need. Or else mingle Mandrake water, Opium, and Poppy seed, with Garlick and things that work upon the head; the quantity of a bean is enough to take.

Sleep to provoke.

Take Rose water a spoonfull, and as much Vinegar, oyl of Roses two spoonfuls, half a handfull of Rose leaves made into pouder, mix all together, and take crumbs of leavened bread made of wheat, and make a Plaister thereof, and lay it upon the forehead and Temples, *Probatum*. Dr. *Mathias*.

A sleeping Apple.

An Apple to make one sleep, is made of all these; Opium, Mandrake, juyce of Hemlock, Henbane seed, Wine lees, to which must be added Musk, that by the sent it may provoke him that smels unto it. Make a Ball as big as a man may grasp in his hand, by often smelling to this, it will cause him to shut his eyes and fall asleep: but it is but in vain to try to do this at certain hours; for mens temperaments vary: but he that shall go about it, may try it by such means, and all in vain. To hinder the danger of these things there is help enough: if you annoint their Temples, Nose, and Testicles with distilled Vinegar, or other things dissolved in Vinegar, that may drive away sleep and awaken the parties. *The same*.

To see strange things in your sleep.

It is said that if one going to sleep annoint his Temples with the blood of the Houp, he shall see wonders in his sleep, which is not contrary to reason. *Card*.

To make one sleep.

To cause sleep by Physicall meanes, green Henbane, put under ones Pillow will do it. The juyce of the greater Bul-rush drank; Oyl, wherein the left eye of a Creature called Eritrus boyled, is dropt into ones ear; or setting a Leech to the corners of the Eyes, and taking it off again, and dropping in of Opium, it is very potent. But it is more potent if you make a Suppository of it, but take it out when the party begins to sleep. Or annoint the soles of the feet with the fat of a Dormouse, or with an Unguent made with water and Vinegar and Potters earth. It is reported also, which is hardly to be believed, that if the Teeth be annointed with the filth comes out of a Dogs ear, it will make a man sleep profoundly. *Card*.

A means to make a man sleep sweetly.

That we may have as great joy sleeping as waking, when we sup before we sleep, if we eat moderately horse tongue, Balme and the like, when we sleep we shall have many fine conceits in Dreams, that a man could not desire to be more merry, and to see more pleasing things, as fields, gardens, trees, flowers, we shall see shady dark places covered with green grass, and casting our eyes about, the whole world springs up, and looks very pleasantly. Or if we annoint our Temples with the juyce of Smallage, or of young Poplar buds, or of common Acorus, or of garden nightshade, or of Stramonium, or of wolfs bane, and chiefly when that they are green; or else the neck and throat through which the sleepy veins ascend; and the places where the veins are most apparent in our hand and feet. It is good also to annoint the Liver; for the blood evaporating upward, comes to the Liver from the Stomach, from the Liver to the Heart, so are these spirits that burn here and there died, and represent Images to us in our sleep of the same colour. *The same*.

To cause troublesome Dreams by a fume.

Make pouder of the heil bone of a man newly killed, and adde a little Loadstone to it. Being thus mingled, if you cast this pouder on the burning coales, that in many places the smoke may fly up to the roof of the house, those that are asleep, will think they see many strange sights of spirits and fearfull and terrible apparitions. Likewise if you lay upon the head of one that sleeps the heart of an Ape that was newly taken from him whilst he lived, he shall see nothing but wild Beasts in his sleep, and think that he is torn by them, that he will be exceedingly frighted and tormented; the Onyx stone will do as much, bound about ones neck. *The same.*

To prevent sleep.

There is a Berry brought out of *Ægypt* cald Coffe, which being dried and beaten to pouder, and boyled in fair water, is much used among the *Turks* to make them lively and prevent sleep, which of late is become of great use in *England*.

To drive away ill Dreams.

They say that the teeth of a stoned-horse hanged about ones neck, or his left arm, will cure such as use to be frighted with ill dreams. *Cardan.*

That one may not sleep.

Psellus the Platonist saith, that Dogs, Crows, and Cocks, will keep a man waking, so will the Nightingale and the Reremouse, and the Owl; and of these, especially the head, heart and eyes; wherefore some report, that if any man carry a Crows heart or a Bats about him, he shall not sleep untill he lay it aside. The same doth the dry head of a Reremouse bound upon the right arm of one that is waking, for this is to be laid upon one that is asleep, they say he will not awake unless you take it from him. *Alb.*

That one may not sleep.

The eye of a Swallow laid in a mans bed, will not suffer him to sleep if you let it lye there. *Albertus.*

Of Exercise. Chap. 10.

That men may be tormented with long Dancing.

If you will torment men with long leaping here and there, or make them cry, laugh, sing, and fall into such passions, you may easily do it, and the causes are most naturall. But to pass by the reason of it, I shall say a few things. First, There is a kind of Spider called Phalangium, which from *Tarentum* about *Apulia*, is called *Tarentula*, the whole Countrey is so full of them, that very few escape them: their biting is more fierce than that of Wasps sting, and those that are wounded by them, are diversly affected: for some sing continually, cry, rave: but they all dance well. The Mowers whilst they are at their labour, suspecting nothing, are ofttimes cruelly wounded, and by musicall tunes they are refreshed and recovered. For these Spiders lye in some holes, and hide themselves in the Corn, and so men may easily catch them: with the leaves of reeds in your mouth counterfeit a hissing, that you may imitate the sound of a Fly; when the Spider hears that, he comes presently forth, for he often feeds on flyes, as our Spiders do, that in the largest houses spin webs, and spread them to catch flyes. Take this Spider and make pouder of him, mingle as much of this pouder as you can take with two fingers, with other things, that it may not hurt the Patient: for it is poyson, when he hath taken it, he will fall to leaping and dancing, especially if he have any musick. *The same.*

That men may not tire upon a Journey.

They that Travel, if they carry Mugwort with them, will never tire: and Mugwort beaten with Hogs-grease and laid on, cures the pains and wearinels of the feet. *Petrus Bayrus.*

BOOK VI.

BOOK. VI.

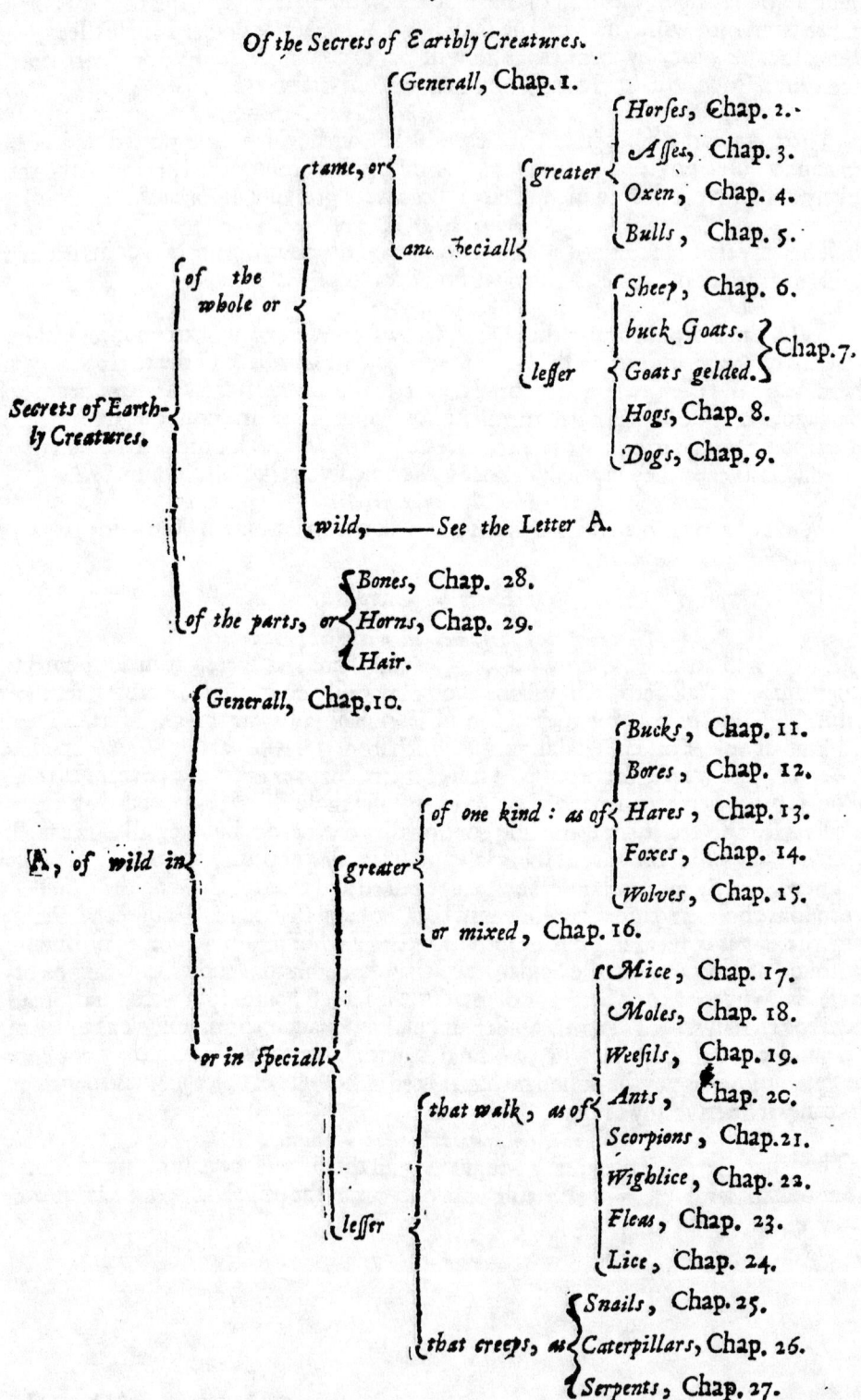

Of the Secrets of Earthly Creatures.

Secrets of Earthly Creatures
- of the whole or
  - Generall, Chap. 1.
  - and Speciall
    - tame, or
      - greater
        - Horses, Chap. 2.
        - Asses, Chap. 3.
        - Oxen, Chap. 4.
        - Bulls, Chap. 5.
      - lesser
        - Sheep, Chap. 6.
        - buck Goats. } Chap. 7.
        - Goats gelded.
        - Hogs, Chap. 8.
        - Dogs, Chap. 9.
    - wild, ——— See the Letter A.
- of the parts, or
  - Bones, Chap. 28.
  - Horns, Chap. 29.
  - Hair.

A, of wild in
- Generall, Chap. 10.
- or in Speciall
  - greater
    - of one kind: as of
      - Bucks, Chap. 11.
      - Bores, Chap. 12.
      - Hares, Chap. 13.
      - Foxes, Chap. 14.
      - Wolves, Chap. 15.
    - or mixed, Chap. 16.
  - lesser
    - that walk, as of
      - Mice, Chap. 17.
      - Moles, Chap. 18.
      - Weesils, Chap. 19.
      - Ants, Chap. 20.
      - Scorpions, Chap. 21.
      - Wighlice, Chap. 22.
      - Fleas, Chap. 23.
      - Lice, Chap. 24.
    - that creeps, as
      - Snails, Chap. 25.
      - Caterpillars, Chap. 26.
      - Serpents, Chap. 27.

Book VI.   *Secrets of Horses and other Cattle.*

Of tame Creatures that live upon the Earth in Generall. Chap. 1.

That Beasts may return home.

If you will have Beasts return to the house, annoint the Beasts forehead with Tallow and Sea Onyon, and he will go home. *Albert.*

To make Beasts follow a Man.

Aristotle in his Book of living Creatures, faith that if one put common Wax upon the horns of the Cow that hath a Calf, she will follow him whethersoever he will, without any labour.

That Beasts may eat no more.

If you annoint the tongue of a Beast with any Tallow, that Beast cannot taste; nor will it eat any meat, but will first starve and dry, unless you rub it off with Salt and Vinegar. Also if a Wolfs tail, skin, or head, be hanged over the manger, Beasts will not feed.

To fat Cattle.

Not only four footed Beasts, but all living Creatures are soon made very fat after three daies fasting, with meat that they like best; some judg that Henbane and Tortois flesh is best agreeing to Horses, as also Barley and the like grain. For Sheep, salt with their meat, for that will make them drink, whereby they will be most fatted. The cause is, that hunger in these Creatures consumes all their superfluous moysture, and increaseth their heat, and makes them feed stoutly for many daies. Moreover Beasts do not eat naturally but when they are hungry. *Card.*

That Cattle may be more greedy after meat.

Such vertue there is in the Lees of oyle and such profit, that it will preserve Oxen from diseases, and make them more hungry after meat, being mingled by degrees with their meat and drink every fourth and fifth day, so outwardly with Wine Lees and Creme of Lupius mingled and laid on upon Cattle and Sheep; it will preserve both their hair and their wooll, and their skin from Scabs and Ticks; also it augmenteth the wooll, but it is best to wash the Sheep before hand with Salt-water. *Card.*

Against all sorts of diseases of Cattel.

An excellent remedy against all Diseases of Cattle is made thus : Take Myrrh, male Frankinsence, Pomegranate shels beaten, of each one pound; Pepper three ounces, Saffron three ounces, Acacia, *May* Butter, burnt Rosin, *Roman* Wormwood, wild Betony in pouder, ordinary Betony, Century, Sagapenum, Saxifrage, Dog-fennell, of each half a pound. Pouder all these well, and sift them, and mingle them with three pints of the best Honey, and boyl them gently a little upon a cole fire. Afterwards keep it in a tin or glass Vessel, then when you have occasion, give to your Cattle that have a Feaver or are diseased, every day a great spoonfull of this confection with an hemina of warm water, and Oyl-lees three ounces; But if they be sick without a Feaver, or also begin to recover, give this confection with Wine and Oyl, for many daies, untill the Beast be well. This is an approved and most forcible Potion. *Publius Vegetius.*

To make Cattle stale.

If you touch the privities of Cattle with bruised Garlick, they will presently stale; though they could not before, and will not be troubled at all. *Mizald.*

If Cattle piss Blood.

If a Beast piss blood he shall be cured thus. Draw blood from the upper vein, also bruise the root of the Herb Daffodil, and pour it down his throat with two small cups of sweet white wine which will seem clammy. It is good also to boyl wheat meal with Hogsgrease, and the pouder of the Pomegranate shell, and to pour down his throat, not thick, but thin drinks; and you must not only not run a Horse, but you must also abstain from walking him; that the vein that is broken may joyn again: For it happens that by running or leaping, veins may be broken; wherefore they must be cured with astringent things, and such as glew together; you may lay this healing Plaister upon his rains. Take Onyons, live Snails beaten, five heads of Garlick, one pound of Pimpernell, bruise them all together, and lay it upon the reins of his back. This is good also for them that are sway-backt. But for those that bleed at their Nostrils, you shall foment their heads with the coldest water and Vinegar mingled together, adding a little salt thereto, after this lay the strengthening Plaister on, upon the head and temples, and by this Medicament the Veins being bound up, the flux of blood will be stopt. *Publius Vegetius.*

For a scouring of Blood in Cattle.

If a Beast be troubled with a Dysentery, the Arsgut is reversed, to cure this, it must be cut round about very prudently, least the gut that is before it should break. The Intestine falls out if it be touched thereby, and so the Beast will lose its life; for it will never return back again but will remain so, and the Arsegut will be above it. *The same.*

If a Beast vomit Blood.

If a Beast vomit blood, you must poure down its throat the juyce of Broom, with wine, and the juyce of Leeks mingled with Ice and oyl. Sometimes Beasts vomit blood, and they are helped with this potion. Boyl in a new pot with water, *Romane* Wormwood, and Spicknard of each alike quantity, and give it them to drink. *The same.*

For a Cough of Cattle.

Also you may cure any dangerous cough in Cattle, with an hemina of sweet Wine, and three ounces of oyl and a raw Egge, if for three daies together you pour it down the Beasts throat, with bean flower, and two spoonfuls of Fenegrick added to it. Therefore a pint and half of Beans parched, is excellent good for Cattle that cough, if you boyl those beans without Salt, Goats suet three ounces, Butter three ounces, three heads of Garlick cleansed, and all boyled with barley and water made to a Ptisan, you must give this three daies together. *The same.*

For Warts upon Cattle, a remedy of the same Authors.

Sometimes Warts breed on many parts of the body of Cattle, and deforme them; you shall cure them thus. The Warts must be tied with a fine thred, then a Potentiall Caustick must be laid upon, and they will fall away of themselves. Some cut them off with a knife, and cure them with a burning iron lightly touching them.

For Convulsions of Cattle.

It is certain that Cattle will have Convulsion fits, and these are the tokens of it. They will fall suddenly, and their joynts are extended, they pant all the body over, and sometimes they fome at mouth. You shall give them meat strew'd over with water, Vinegar, and Saltpeter, also the pouder of wild Cucumber, and poudred Saltpeter must be given them to purge them for seaven daies together. Also you must mingle half a small cup of bloud of the Sea Tortois, with as much Vinegar, and as much Wine, with a little Masterwort, and this you must pour into their Nostrils. It is held to be good to rub their backs very often with Oyle and Vinegar and Saltpeter. *The same,*

For the Gout in Cattle.

The Gowt also sometimes troubleth Cattle, and Mens diseases befall Beasts. These are the tokens of it. The Beast can neither stand nor go, but if you force it, it will go lame, and ofttimes fall down: The excrements are indigested, Barley comes forth whole, for the Beast is in such pain he cannot digest his meat, and therefore looks pitifully, and his whole body is hot, and the Veins stick forth; Nature will fall down, dung will cleave to his feet, because they are so hot, as it happens with those that are surbated: It is best for him not to let him lye down, but to walk him gently, and to rub him in a dry place untill he sweat, with rubbing of many hands to make him to sweat the more: let him bloud on the upper Veins of his head, but not much, the next day draw bloud from his hinder legs above the Ankles or Pastern bone; on the third day from the upper part of his legs, or from those parts that are next under the places where the pain lyeth. Remember that you must alwaies draw but a little bloud. Give him hot water to drink, into which cast the pouder of Saltpeter and Wheat meal, also fine pouder of Frankinsence; you shall pour in a whole Sawcerfull steeped in Wine, and on the third day pour in small cups of this into his Nostrils: you shall

shall also boyl Beets and pour in three small cups of the water of them, you shall exercise him every day. and shall purge his belly also with the same, that the naughty humour may be purged forth that would descend into his Veins. You shall give him this Potion. You shall infuse a Sawcerfull of Thime in old sweet wine, and pour into his Nostrils a small cup of that, you shall give him green Hay, and if you cannot get that, then give him dry Hay besprinkled with Saltpeter. If nothing will do him good, then geld him, and that will cure him. For geldings are seldome troubled with the Gowt. *The same.*

For Scrophulous swellings of Cattle.

Ofttimes hard kernels, or swellings under the ears, or scrophulous humours trouble Cattle in their throats, and make all their Jaws swell: For they are under the head, and they are choaked thereby, as it were with the strangullian of the part. You must first cure this with hot Fomentation, and Poultesses of Barly meal, and three ounces of Rosin boyled in strong Wine: and when the swelling is ripe, you must open it with a sharp knife, and let out all the matter contained in it, and you must put in Tents dipt in Vinegar, Oyl, and Salt: and the daies following you must wisely cure the part, with Vulnerary means, and fit medicaments; the wound must be kept open untill it be well; for in these parts if you heal it up too fast, it will soon turn to a Fistula, and if it should do so, it may be healed with paper, and a Tent or an injection and purgation. *The same.*

For Cattle bewitched, the same Author.

A Beast bewitched is sad, goeth slowly, waxeth lean, and if you help him not, he will fall into some disease. Wherefore you shall pour into his Nostrils some Bitumen with a little Brimstone, with Bay-berries and water. Moreover you shall take Coriander herb or seed, with Brimstone, Rosin, and Wax, and make a fume upon the coles about him, and shall sprinkle him all over with hot water. That fumigation cures all four footed Beast.

For maggots, worms, or the like Vermine.

You shall cure all worms of the belly and such Vermine, thus. If you give with a horn for three daies together an hemina of the ashes of the dry wood of the Olive tree, with an hemina of new Oyl. There as also another confection, but it is that which ofttimes frees a deadly passion. Take Wormseed, *Roman* Wormwood, raw Lupius, Herb Century, fine meal of Vetches, and Raddish seed two ounces, adde to these Hartshorn half an ounce, of Smallage one ounce, *Pontic Sinoper* three pieces; *Opoponax* half an ounce, Tent Wine or some other sharp Wine two Sextarii, green Oyl one Sextary; warm these bloud warm, and pour them with a horn down the Horses throat, sloping the horn that it may the more easily run down. The next day set the same Beast sloping, and give him a Clyster of the former Potion a full Sextarius; that an injection being given both waies each other day, may infuse that which is said to coagulate, whereby those noxious Vermine are restrained, and the cavity being peirced through, those venemous Creatures dye with torments.

Of Scabs and Tetters of living Creatures.

Sometimes also Scabs and Tetters breed upon the joynts or knees, between the Nerves in places where the joyning is, and there is a wound made like to Chaps called Ragades, and it is not easily cured, but by vitriolick and astringent things, not without ligature, and sometimes by cauterizing. Also there must be laid on convenient Plaisters. *The same.*

To make Cattles hair grow again.

If their hair grow slowly, you shall burn a live Snaile upon Vine branches, and shall put the Ashes of it into a new pot, adding three ounces of raw Alum, Stags marrow what may suffice, and infusing this in Wine, you shall boyl them, and lay it on for many daies, this is supposed to call forth hair suddenly. Ashes of burnt Beans, or raw Lupius, or of burnt Fig leaves mingled with fat, is to be applyed daily. But if the hairs fail, for no cause precedent, you shall bruise them together, Raysins and Spicknard, and boyl them in Vinegar, and you shall lay this remedy hot upon the body that wants hair. *Pub: Vegetius.*

To make white hairs black.

If you would make white hairs black : Take Vitriol seaven scruples, Rose Laurel juyce four scruples, Goats Suet, what is sufficient to temper with it, use this. *The same.*

To make black hairs white, a Receipt of the same Author.

Again if you would make black hairs white : Take one pound of wild Cucumber roots, Nitre twelve scruples, pouder them, add an hemina of Honey, mingle them and use them. *The same.*

Of Secrets of living Creatures in speciall.

Of Secrets of Horses. Chap. 2.

That a fierce Horse may grow tame.

A restive Horse, or any other Creature, will be easily made gentle in the Stable and iron shooes made by the Smith, if you put a small round Pibble stone into each of his Ears, and then take the Ear in your hand, and bind it, and hold it so : for thus he will stand and not stir, and will be quiet, were he never so fierce before. If you thrust into each Eare one stone, he will stand as quiet as a sheep. I had this Secret from a Horse-courser, who was Groom to the King of *Navarre*. *Miz.*

That Horses may not tire in running.

The great teeth of Wolves bound about Horses, are thought to make them so nimble, that they will never be weary with running. *Pliny.*

For a Horse that Neighs too much.

If a Horse Neigh too much, bind upon his head a stone with a hole in it, so he will leave off. I add, that a Horse that casts his ears backwards, is often times deaf foaled, and he will never Neigh in the company of other Horses. *Simoneta Cardinall is the Author.*

Whether a Horse will learn to Amble.

The *French* men know well how to make a Horse to Amble : for being that a Horse moveth three severall wayes, either by bending the last joynt of his foot or his knee : The *Italians* binding the two right side feet together, and the two left, cause the Horse to move them both together, the shoulder blade being moved also, but especially the knee is bended and moved. The *French* bind the last joynt of every foot with a straight band; whereby the Horse is constrained to move his knees. Hence you see, that to make a Horse to Amble, you must cause him to bend his knees. For if he move his lowest joynts only, though he do move both the right joynts together, and both the left, yet this is no Ambling. Wherefore there are two kinds of Ambling of Horses. The *Italian* and the *French* way. The easier way of Ambling is that which is performed by the higher joynt; for by the mean distance there, much ground is past over. Mules then go easily, moving their lower pastorn, and that kind of motion is called *Traina*. But when an Ambler moves his knee, the knee bends more than the foot, because it fals higher when he sets it down. *Card.*

That Horses may be foled with divers colours.

Horses will be bred of divers colours, if only when the Horse backs the Mare, you cover the Mare with a cloth of divers colours : for what colours the Horse them beholds, such colours will the Colt certainly have. *Absyrtus*, you may try the same in Dogs and other Creatures.

To breed Horses and Cattle of sundry colours.

He that would breed Horses or Cattle of divers colours, must do that, which I desire all to follow who desire to do the same. *Jacob* took twigs, and Poplar and Almond boughs, and such as would easily be pilled from their Rinds, and he pilled them here and there, leaving some bark between, and he cut them round, and winding like Snakes with white and black colour distinguished, and these rods he laid in the fields, and watring troughs, where the sheep folds were; and when they coupled and looked about, they saw these rods, and so the young Lambs were of divers colours, and their white fleeces were spotted with black spots here and there, which was not displeasing to be seen, so it fell out with all Cattle that brings Wooll, and perhaps with all the rest.. This will prevaile for Horses, and those that keep them do most observe this way, when they are admitted to back the Mares, and when they have backed them, they hang the Stables where the Mares were backed with cloathes that are of diverse colours, and from hence it comes, that Horses are made of so many colours, as dapple grays, bright bays, and many other colours. *The same.*

That Horses may have a small head, and fair Mane.

The head of a Colt often washed with cold water will grow small and fine; but if you wash his neck with hot water, that will make it gross, and the hairs will grow, and the main will be much fairer. *Cardan.*

For stubborne Horses.

If a Horse will not be back't, or will not go into a Ship, or is afraid of wheels, or any thing else, and this happens most to Geldings, and fearfull Horses, and such as have ill Eyes; wherefore hang a little stone by a thred, and let it down into the Horses Ear. If this do no good, because it troubles their senses, bind up their eyes with a fillet; this hath often done good, also beat his legs with a wand, if the Horse run backwards or riseth. Also fire put under his tail, or an iron goad, that when he runs back may prick and hurt him; This is excellent: also if he lye down upon the ground let there be thorns under his belly, but if he be but stubborn a little and not restive, he must be whipt a little, and brought near to the thing he fears, but if you force him too much, he will often grow worse, supposing greater danger. *The same.*

That Horses may fall down as if they were dead, and then rise more chearfull.

A Serpents tongue inclosed in Virgins wax and put into the left ear of any Horse, will make him fall to the ground as though he were dead; and being taken out again, will not only make him rise, but it makes him far more lively. *An English man related this Story.*

That Horses may grow fierce.

It is certain that Benjamin being put into a Horses nose will make him furious, so also it will do a man: but our Benjamin is too weak, or any other; for Benjamin was formerly an herb. *Card.*

That Horses or Sheep may not pass over.

If you make a cord of a Wolfs gut, and bury that under the sand or ground, no Sheep will go over that place, though you drive them with a cudgell. *Alb.*

That Horses may not be troubled with Flies.

If any one annoint the hair of his Horse with the juyce of Gourd leaves, or of any other Creature, in the heat of Summer; it is a wonder, that no Flys will trouble them. *Cardan.*

For pricking of Horses with a Nail.

Since that Horses are so usefull, it fals out ofttimes to great loss upon a Mans journey, that a Horse casts his shoe, or is prickt with a nail in his foot. Some carry with them shoes and Hammer, which serveth also for Pincers. But if the Horse do halt by reason of a nail, that must be pulled forth, and the Hoof being moderately pared hollow that the Cornet be not hurt, nor yet any filth lye hid in it, cleanse the Ulcer, and poure in melted Brimstone: make the shoe hollow to the outside, that it may not press upon the part that was hurt; annoint all the rest of the Hoof with fat and wax, and the holes of the Hoof that are not filled with nails. Thus did I quickly cure an Ambling Horse of the Arch-Bishop of *Amulthon*, which he gave to me freely, when he was exceeding lame. *Card.*

For Horses that are prickt, a sure Remedy.

Let the iron shoe be presently pulled off, and the place pricked be presently washed with wine. When you have done this, take the middle skin of Elder, and lay this upon the part affected, then drop upon the skin some drops of Tallow, with a hot iron, and set on the iron shoe handsomely, and ride whether you please. *Out of a Manuscript.*

For a Horses blindness.

Take *Roman* Vitriol half an ounce, Salt Armoniac two drams, Ginger beaten half an ounce, Camphir two drams, Cloves half an ounce, Rose water half an ounce, Fennel water half an ounce, best wine two drams, mingle them, and set them in a glass in the Sun for thirty dayes. When you will use this, take a fine feather and dip it in this water, and drop it into the Horses eyes, and take care that the Horse do not rub his eyes. *Out of a written Book.*

For a Horses Cough.

Steep five Eggs at night in the sharpest Vinegar that is strongest, and in the morning when you find the outward shell consumed, take out the Horses tongue out of his mouth, and thrust this Egg down his throat, and this will cure his cold. *Out of the Secrets of a Horse Farrier.*

For Scabs of Horses, a certain Remedy.

Take Hogs grease half a pound, Oyl of Bays one ounce and half, Quicksilver two ounces, white Hellebour one ounce, mingle all well. *Out of a written Book.*

For the Haw in the Eye, a Remedy fit for Men and Horses.

Take a Hen Egge, and poure forth all the white, and add to the yelk so much Salt as the white of the Egge to fill up the place, mingle them well, then take a piece of Elder wood that is green, and as big as a Mans arm, and half an Ell long, and make a hole in it long waies, of a sufficient length, that the yelk with the Salt may be put into it. When the yelk is put in, stop very well the said hole, with a pin made of the same wood, that it may not exhale in any case. Put it into the fire, and burn it to a cole; or untill the mixture put into it, fall away from the cole: take this and keep it. When you use it, make very fine pouder of it, and through a quill, blow it into the eye as much as a Pease at a time. *Out of a Manuscript.*

For Horses that can hardly stale.

If Horses can hardly piss, beat their bodies gently all over with Boughs of Elder with their leaves, and then apply the leaves to their neck, head, and whole body. For this small tree is best for impediments in Cattle. *Simoneta Cardinal.*

Another.

Some apply about the Horses bladder an Onyon, with the pill taken off: others take Smallage seed beaten, with two heminas of Wine, or Onyon seed; the same way with Wine, or Pigeons dung, or Poly leaves or Lovage bark dried, or a dram of Saltpeter, with a Garlick head bruised and infused with Wine. Some use nothing but black Wine. *Absyrt.*

For pissing of Blood.

If Horses piss bloud, Bean meal cleansed and baked, must be mingled with Stags grease, and with a little wine must for three daies together be poured down their throat. Or give the Horse with a horn an hemina of Goats milk, fine Wheat meal half an hemina, ten Eggs, and three small cups of oyl, all well mingled together. *The same.*

For diseases of the Lungs.

Diseases that consist in the Lungs, are cured by sharp Vinegar warm'd and pour'd down, or Mans Urine, with fifteen drams of Hogs grease melted: but take heed you give them not Womens Urine that hath her courses upon her. *The same.*

For a Horses Cough.

When the Cough first comes, you must give him Barley and Bean meal mingled together in his drink: and if the Cough groweth stronger, give him two small cups of Honey, as much liquid Pitch, as much Oyl, Butter twenty four drams; warm all and mix old Hogs grease a pretty quantity with it, and so pour it down his throat. If this will not do it, pound Horehound with Oyl and Salt: mingle them with wine and give it down. Others use the juyce of Horehound, Oyle, and the root of the wild Rue. Others put in Frankinsence, or use it with Oyl. *The same.*

For shortwinded Horses.

Agarick and Fenegrick are excellent for the most short winded Horses. So I cured my own Horse. The Ancients commend the bloud of a Puppy that is not above ten daies old given in drink. Also a strong remedy is made of bitter Nuts, water and Honey, and the roots of wild Cucumber, made into small Cakes, and exhibited with Honey. Also the root of the herb Cotton weed thrust into the brest, or into the roots of the Ears or Nostrils, or an Errhin made of the root of the Mulberry tree; and the head rubbed with Wine, adding a little Oyl to it. Moreover ordinary means must be sharp and strong, as Brimstone, Salt peter, Pepper, Castoreum. So Rue is good in most diseases, commonly Horses abstaine from meat themselves. All things must be given with milk or Wine. Also the root of Gentian is most profitable. *Cardan.*

For the running Worm or wildfire of Horses.

The running fire which some call the worm, Horse Leeches; take the little worm that breeds upon the top of the Fullers Teasil, and do not hurt it, but shut it up within a Goose quill, and cutting the skin of the Horses forehead, they put the worm into it, and sowe up the cut skin, in twenty daies this worm will dye, and in so many daies the Horse is cured. Others put in the fruit of Helebour. The stinking Nettle given in meat and drink, (some call it Scrophularia,) is a good remedy for this disease. Others cure it by fire, others with cutting a vein, and purging: and these two almost belong to all diseases of Horses. For being that they sleep but little and eat much, and travell much, and keep no order, they stand in need of both remedies. For purges, that Medicament is best, which consists of Myrrh, Gentian, long Birthwort, dwarf Elder roots, Bay berries: They use to run Horses after purging, and to have them to water after burning, but they are fed after both in open Pasture-fields. Generally if the Horses be not kept in the fields, they must be kept in warm Stables, and have good meat given them to eat. Geldings need not so much letting of blood, for they have not such abundance; also they are hurt by it, and the more as it aboundeth. *Cardan.*

That Horses or Oxen may not fall into diseases.

Horses and Oxen will have no disease, if you hang Harts horn about them. *Absyrt.*

A Remedy against all Diseases of Horses.

Against all infirmities of Horses or Oxen, so soon as they begin to be sick, this potion will help them: The root of the Sea Onyon, the roots of Poplar, (which in Greek is called ῥάμνος, for it is more dark and cloudy,) and common Salt what is sufficient, must be put in water together, and that water must be given Cattle to drink untill they be well. But if you would prevent desperate diseases, that your Cattle may never be troubled with them, when the Spring begins, provide this potion for them, and for one and forty daies together give it them to drink. *Publius Vegetius.*

For an Inflamation of the eyes.

For the inflamation of the eyes, you must mingle together and annoint the Eye with male Frankinsence (or as others have it) Lambs marrow also, of each one dram, Saffron, Cuttle bone, of each one dram, Oyl of Roses ten drams, ten whites of Eggs. Another remedy for the eyes inflamed, is made of Frankinsence, white Starch, and Honey of *Athens*. *Absyrt.*

For white spots in Horses Eyes.

Let salt Armoniac very fine poudred be mingled with Honey of *Athens*, or some other good Honey, and smeered upon it, or put as much Butter to it. Or blow in through a quill some pouder of Cuttle bone, or annoint it with root of Masterwort and Oyl beat together, twice in a day. Or blow into the Eye Rocket seed whole as it is, and let it stay there untill the smaller seeds by their sharpness extenuate the Eye, and wipe away the white spots. *The same.*

For scouring of Horses.

If Horses scour, draw bloud from the head Veins; let the Horse drink warm water mingled with Barley meal. If that do no good, pour Oyl into his Nostrils. Also Pomegranate shels stop the scouring of the Belly, given in pouder with Sumach of *Syria*, by the mouth. *The same.*

Of the pain of the Colick in Horses.

Wash a Horse is that griped in his belly with hot water and cover him, then pour in

Myrrh

Myrrh five drams, old wine six heminas, Oyl three heminas mingled together, and divided into three parts. Also heat the Belly with hot Sea water, or Myrtill berries boyled in water. Moreover Poley leaves, Southernwood, or bitter Almonds, must be mingled with sharp black wine, or else Pomegranate pils with water. Also Smallage seed is good, with as much Cucumber seed, both given to drink with an equall quantity of Wine and Honey, or seed of Cardamous poudred and given with water. Also Claver grease is cast moist to the Horse to eat, and Barley. Further a Clyster is given to a Horse tormented in the belly, which is made of Beets boyld in water, with forty drams of Salt peter, and thirty drams of Oyl. Moreover you may give him a Clyster made with Wine and Salt peter. If you pils upon the ground, and take the Clay from that place, and rub it under his belly, this will ease his pains. *The same.*

For a Feaverish Horse.

A Horse that hath an Ague must be cured with a hot bath; but in Winter you must so bath him that he take not cold. Let most of his meat be Vetches or Wheat meal, give him warm water to drink: annoint all his body over with warm Wine and Oyl, purge his belly, draw bloud from the neck Veins, or Veins about his throat, breft, or feet; Rub his knees with it hot: when he seems to be well, wash him in hot water. But if he be feaverish from weariness, and grow lean, give him an hemina of Goats milk, a measure of white Starch, or Oyl, half an hemina, four Egges, mingling therewith the juyce of Purslane bruised, for three daies or more, untill he be well. But if he be feaverish by reason of the humours fallen upon his Jaws or parts about his head, he must be fomented, and his palate must be annointed with Oyl straind with Salt and Origanum bruised. Warm his feet and knees with hot water. Rub the parts about the mouth with juyce of night shade and wine Lees, feed him with Sea weeds, green Grass or Hay, without any Barley. But if he bleed at nose, pour into his nostrils juyce of Coriander or Masterwort with water. *The same.*

To fat lean Horses.

If a Horse grow lean, give him parcht Wheat, or Barly baked, a double quantity: let him be led to water thrice a day. If his leanness continue, mingle bran with the wheat, and ride him gently. If he will not eat, pour into his nostrils water that is good to drink, wherein were bruised leaves of Night-shade and Poley. Barley and Vetches steeped in water are to be set before him; some grind two small cups of Gith, and with this they mingle three small cups of Oyl, and with an hemina of Wine, they pour it down his throat. You shall cure a Horse that loaths his meat with bruised Garlick, infused in an hemina of Wine and pour'd down his throat. If he cannot make water, mingle the whites of ten Eggs with the rest, and give it him with a horn down his throat. *Constantinus Cæsar ex Absyrto.*

A soft Plaister for lame nerves of Horses.

Take Goats suet one pound, Mollicidina half a pound, Rosin one pound, Verdigrease half a pound, mingle them. *Publius Vegetius.*

The composition of Carters pouder.

They call it Carriers pouder, which being mingled of many kinds of ingredients, cureth Horses and other Creatures by it self, and is also mingled with other potions as the cure requireth. *Chiron* thinks this composition to be most soveraign.

Take Gum tragants three pounds, Aloes six ounces, Myrrh six ounces one scruple, Costus one ounce one scruple, Ammoniacum one ounce one scruple, Cassia one one scruple, Gentian, long Birthwort, Centory, Betony, Saxifrage, Elder, Opium, Southern-wood, of each one pound, Maudlin six ounces, Cardamous six ounces, Mace three ounces, Spicknard three ounces, Celtick spike six ounces, Asarum one pound, Daucus seed three ounces, Castoreum, Opopanax, Galbanum, Strutius, of each six ounces, root of Panax one ounce, Licorish six ounces, three handfuls of Wormwood, the juyce of Vervain dried and sifted five ounces. Bruise all these together, and keep them diligently in a glass Vessel or of tin; when need is, give each Horse one spoonfull or more as his strength is, or to other Cattle, adding Wine and
Oyl

Book VI.   *Secrets in the cure of all Diseases in Cattle.*   117

Oyl thereto.   Sometimes you may mingle it with other potions, if Art and the disease require it. *Pub. Vegetius.*

To make Mares cast their Foles.

Aristotle saith, That when Mares smell the stink of a Candle put out they will cast their Foles, they loath this so much: so do many Women great with Child.

Secrets of Asses. Chap. 3.

That an Ass may not bray.

If an Ass have a stone bound to his tail, he cannot bray. *Simoneta Card.*

Asses that swound.

I will not conceal that which *Plutarch* would not: If you ask me what it is? that Horses and Asses will fall in a swound, if they carry Figs upon their backs. But the Remedy is more wonderfull that cures them, and men also. When Beasts are in a swound, and Men faint away for want of forces, a piece of Bread will recover them; for if they swallow but a little bit of Bread, they presently are refreshed and recovered, and go merrily upon their Journey. *Plutarch* saith, It will do as much in Men: for saith he, when *Brutus* passed through deep Snows into *Apollonia*, and fainted by the way, Bread being cast to him from the Enemy that defended the wals of the City, he was brought again presently to himself.

How to cure Asses that halt.

Moreover you shall cure Asses that halt, if you rub the whole foot round with hot water, and pick it clean with a Knife: having done that, you shall pour in old Piss, wherein Goats suet is melted especially, but if you cannot get that, then take Ox suet, do this untill the Ass be well. *Constantinus Cæsar ex Ablyrto.*

Of the Secrets of Oxen. Chap. 4.

To tame Oxen.

When you buy young Steers, if you put their necks into Forks that may hold them in, give them meat so for a few daies, they will be tame and ready to be commanded. *Varro.*

That Oxen may not surbait their feet.

That Oxen may not wear their feet away underneath, before you drive them upon any way, annoint the soles of their feet with liquid Pitch. *M. Cato.*

To keep Oxen in health.

That Oxen may be well, and drink well; and that such as refuse their meat may be more greedy after it, sprinkle their meat you give them with Lees of Oyl, but little at first untill they be used to it, afterwards more, and give it them seldome to drink mingled with water equally every fourth or fift day. Do but this and Oxen will be sound in body and free from diseases. *The same.*

That Oxen be not weak.

Give Vetches steeped and bruised every moneth in their drink, you shall cure Murrain of Oxen with wild Mallows bruised. *Democritus.*

That labouring Oxen may not be wearied.

Annoint their hoofs with Oyl and Turpentine boyled. *The same.*

That Oxen may not be troubled with flies.

Bruise Bay berries very fine, and boyl them in Oyl and annoint Oxen with it, or annoint the Oxen with their own drivle that fomes at their mouth. If you annoint a Buls Nostrils with Oyl of Roses, he will grow blind, and be troubled with a vertigo. *Africanus.*

To make Oxen fat.

You shall fat Oxen, if the first day they come from Pasture, you cut Coleworts small and steep them in Vinegar, and give them that to eat: then give them Chaff, and Wheat bran mingled together for five daies. On the sixt day give them four heminas of ground Barley, and for six daies following augment their food by little and little. And in Winter feed them about Cock-crowing; then again at break of day, and when you water them, give them food again in the evening: but in Summer

R   fodder

fodder them first about day light; and secondly about noon day, then let them drink: and about nine of the clock at night, give them fodder again : in Winter give them hot water to drink, and in Summer lukewarme. But wash their mouths with Urine, taking forth the drivle that sticks there, and cleanse their tongue from Worms, pulling them forth with pullers, for Worms breed in their tongues; afterwards they rub them with Salt. Also there must be care taken for their Litter. *Sotio.*

If an Ox begin to grow sick.

If an Ox begin to grow sick, give him continually one raw Hen egge, and make him swallow it whole. The next day after bruise a head of Garlick, with an hemina of wine, and give it him to drink, let him hold up his head and chew it, give it in a wodden Vessel, and he that gives it must stand high, and must be fasting when he gives it to the Ox that must be fasting also. *M. Cato.*

A medicament for Oxen.

If you fear a disease, give to them that are well, Salt three corns, Bay leaves three, Scallion stalks three, African and common Garlick of each three cloves, Frankinsence three grains, Savin three branches, three Rue leaves, white Briony three stalks, three small white Beans, three live Coles, Wine one ounce and half : All these must be choicely gathered, beaten, and given by one that is fasting; give to every Ox for three daies of that drink. Divide it so, that when you have given it to each of them thrice, you may have spent it all, give it in a wodden dish, and let the Ox stand high that takes it, and so must he that gives it. *The same.*

That Oxen may be fat, and how they must lye.

Lay under Oxen Oaken planks that come from Horses Stables, and straw with them, for this will be soft for them to lye upon, and hard for them to stand upon. Oxen will grow fat with sweet leaves of the Elm tree, standing in the Sun, and going into the water. *Card.*

Of headach of Oxen.

First you must know if Oxens heads do ake : when therefore he lets fall his ears, and will not eat, then his head akes. Wherefore rub his tongue with bruised Thyme, Wine, Garlick, and beaten Salt. Also Barly Ptisan mingled with Wine is good. You may likewise cure him by putting a handfull of Bay leaves into his mouth, or with Pomegranate pils. So with Myrrh, as much as a bean mingled with two heminas of Wine, and poured into his Nostrils. *Democritus.*

Of the scouring of the Belly in Oxen.

The leaves of purging thorn bruised and given with Bitumen to eat, cures them. Others give Pomegranate leaves bruised, covered with Barley meal dried. Some give two heminas of torrefied Wheat flower to drink, with half a measure of water mingled together. *The same.*

Of the griping of Oxens Bellies.

An Ox that is troubled with griping of the belly will not stay in one place, and will eat no meat, but sighs and mourns. Wherefore you must cast a little fodder to him, and you must prick the flesh about the hoofs, that they may bleed. Some open about the tail, to bleed him there; and they bind it up with a cloath. Others bind Onyons and Salt together, and being wrapt hard, they thrust this farre into his tuel, and make him run. Some pound Salt peter and give him at the mouth. *The same.*

Of a Feaverish Ox.

An Ox that hath an Ague will eat no meat, he stoops downwards, weeps, and hath filth sticking in his eyes, is hollow eyd. He is cured thus : Take grass from shady places, and wash it, and give it him to eat, or else Vine leaves. Give him the coldest water to drink, but not in the open air, but in some very shady place; wipe his Nostrils and Ears with a Sponge wet in water. Some burn his face with a Caustick, and the places also under his eyes, and they rub them twice a day with a Sponge wet in old piss, untill the crusts fall off, and the wounds come to Cicatrize. Also his ears must be cut, that the bloud may run forth. Some mingle dried flower of Barley, with Wine, and give him that to eat. Others dissolve it with Brine, and

keep

Book VI. *Secrets in the cure of all Diseases of Cattle.*

keep him hot with cloaths: Others give him Cytisus with wine, which is not only good for Oxen, but for other Cattle also. *Dydimus.*

For Oxen that Cough.

Give the Ox Barley ground and steeped, and the finest Chaff cleansed, and three heminas of Vetches, divided into three parts, for three times. Some bruise Mugwort and mingle water to it, and then they press it forth, and this they infuse for seaven daies together to give him before his fodder. *Constant. Cæsar.*

Of Oxen that have Impostumes.

If an Ox have an Ulcer, that is impostumated, you must wash it with old Urine of the Ox, being hot, and wipe it with wool, and then lay on a plaister of fine Salt mingled with liquid Pitch. *The same.*

For lame Oxen.

If an Ox grow lame of cold, you must wash the foot, and open the part affected with a Lancet, and wash it with old Urine: and then strew Salt on it, and wipe it with a Cloath or Sponge: after this you must drop in Goats suet rubbed against a red hot iron. If the Ox be lame by treading on a thorn or some sharp thing; you must do likewise. But Wax with old Oyl, Honey, and Vetch meal mingled together, and cooled must be applied to the Ulcer, then a thin potsheard being sifted and melted with Figs or Pomegranates bruised must be laid on; and it must be covered over with a cloath, and carefully bound up, that nothing may easily enter in untill the Ox can stand, so he will be cured: but you must unbind it the third day, and dress it again with the same things. But if he halt by reason of the flux of the matter, heat the part with Oyl and boyld Wine, then lay on raw Barley meal hot. But when it is ripe, and breaks being soft, and runs forth, wash the part, and opening it wide enough lay on Lilly leaves, or Sea Onyon with Salt, or Knotgrass, or Horehound bruised. *Florentinus.*

For scabs in Oxen.

Some annoint all scabs and eruptions of Oxen, with old Ox piss and Butter: Others lay on Rosin and liquid Pitch for a Plaister, and so cure them. *Constantinus Cæsar.*

Of Worms of Oxen.

Some sprinkle the Ulcers with cold water and so kill the Worms. *The same.*

For Lice of Oxen.

You must cast down the Ox upon his belly, and his head looking upward, you must see his tongue whether there be any bladders upon it: these you must burn with sharp hot irons, and then annoint the Ulcers with the leaves of the wild Olive tree beaten with Salt, or with fine Salt and Butter, or Oyl, or the wild Cucumber root bruised, and mingled with Figs, must be given the Ox to eat; or else give him two heminas of Barley meal parched and torrefied, Wheat meal as much wet with water. *The same.*

If an Adder bite an Ox.

If an Adder have bit an Ox, beat a Sawcerfull of Gith, which some call *Macedonian* Parsley with an hemina of old Wine. Put that into his Nostrils, and lay to the place bitten Hogs dung. And do the same if need require for a Man. *M. Cato.*

Of Secrets of Buls. Chap. 5.

To make Buls tame.

Untamed fierce Buls bound to a Fig tree wax tame, and stand still. *Pliny* saith, I think that if a wild Fig tree be tied about their necks, it will do the same.

Another.

Ælian saith, That a wild Bull will grow tame, if you bind his right knee with a band. I add here what *Seneca* saith, That as red colour will make Buls angry, so a white colour will make Bears Lions mad.

Of Secrets of Sheep. Chap. 6.

To make Sheep follow a Man.

Didymus saith, That Sheep are wont to run after him, who stops their Ears with a skin.

That a Ram may not run at one.

Bore his horns through close by his ears. *Const. Cæsar.*

That when the Sheep is with Lamb, you may know what colour the Lamb will be of.

Open the Sheeps mouth, and if her Tongue be black, the Lamb will be black, if white, the Lamb will be white, if divers coloured, so will the Lamb be. *Didym.*

That Lambs may not be sick.

Give them Ivy to eat for eight daies, and they will never be sick. *The same.*

That Sheep may not be rugged.

That Sheep may not look rugged and filthy, take Lees of Oyl, and cleanse them well, water wherein Lupins have been boyled, and good Wine Lees, mingle all these together equally. Next day when you would turn them forth, annoint them all over, and let them stay two or three daies to sweet together, then wash them in the Sea, if you have no Sea water, wash them with Salt and water. If you do this, they will not be rugged, and they will bring more and finer wooll, nor will they be troubled with Scabs: use the same, for all four footed Beasts that are rugged. *M. Cato.*

To fright Sheep from their meat.

Wolfs dung hid in Sheepfolds, will not only fright the Sheep from their ordinary meat, but will make them run here and there as if they were driven by some evill charm, and they will bleat and shake as if the Wolf were present, or as if the great and utter enemy of the Sheep were broke in amongst them; and they suppose only by the sent of his dung that he lyeth in wait for them: nor will they eat untill the said dung be taken away. By this Art I have found some Leeches that pass through the Countries, and boast themselves to be great Farriers, and expert to cure Cattle, and so have cheated simple Countrey Men of great sums of money; or instead of money, have carried away a fat Sheep with them. *Rhasis* and *Albertus* say, that a Wolfs tail will do as much, and there is nothing of that Creature from head to tail, but hath the same effect, such is the naturall Antipathy between the Wolf and the Sheep. *Mizald.*

A wonderfull Remedy for the diseases of Sheep.

The stomach of a Ram boyled in water and wine cureth all diseases almost of Sheep, if it be given to them in drink, and there is some ground for this, for here is Sympathy. *Card.*

How and when Sheep must be sheard.

You must not shear your Sheep in Summer nor Winter, but in the Spring time. The wounds they receive by being shorn must be annointed with Tarr: and the rest of their body with Wine and Oyl, or with the juyce of bitter Lupins boyld. But Wine mingled with an equall quantity of Lees of Oyl is better, or Oyl and white Wine, mixed with wax and fat to annoint them with: For this hurts not the wooll, and keeps off Scabs, and Ulcerations. But you must observe, that when they are well rubbed, after the first hour of the day that the dew that fell into their fleece in the night is dried up, they must be sheared, best in the Sun. For the Sheep sweating whilst he is shorn, the sweat comes away in the wooll, and so the wooll is made better coloured and softer. *Didym.*

That Sheep and Goats may not dye of the Murrain.

If the stomach of a Stork mingled with water, be given to each a spoonfull, they will never have the Murrain. *Const. Cæsar.*

That Cattle may give much Milk.

All Cattle will give abundance of Milk, and feed their young fat, if they eat of tree Trifoyle, or you bind Dittany to their bellies. *Aphricanus.*

A cure for the Plague of Sheep.

You must take care first that Sheep do not take the Plague. Wherefore when the Spring begins, take Mountain Sage and Horehound, bruise them, and give them in drink for fourteen daies: do the same again in Autumne for as many daies. If the disease catch them, use the same remedies, also the Hay of tree Trifoyle is good to be eaten by them, and the most tender roots of reeds steeped in drink. When they are sick they must be removed to some other place, that the sound may not mingle with the sick, and they having fresh Ayre and water may recover. *Leontius.*

For Scabbed Sheep.

The Scabs will not come at first if one smeer the Sheep with what I mentioned after they are shorn: but if it come by your negligence, you shall cure them thus. Unsalted Oyl Lees must be strained, and water in which bitter Lupins are steeped, and white Wine Lees, of each an equall quantity must be heated in a vessel, and let the Sheep be annointed with this for two daies and stay within. On the third day wash him with hot Sea water, and after that with fresh water. Some put Cypress Nuts into the water. Some annoint with Brimstone, and Cyprus pounded with Ceruse and Butter. Some, where an Ass pisseth in the way, take up the Clay mingled with it, and smeer that on; Some are more diligent and do better, they use none of the foresaid remedies, untill the part affected be shorn and rubbed with old Piss. Also you shall cure Scaboed Sheep, washing them with Urine, and annointing them with Oyl and Brimstone.

Remedies for divers Diseases in Sheep.

If the heat of the Sun hurt Sheep and they fall down continually, and will not eat: press out the juyce of wild Beetes, and pour down that, and make them eat the Beetes afterwards.

If they be short winded: Cut their ears with a Knife, and remove them to other Pasture.

If they be troubled with a Cough: Almonds must be purged and pounded, and mingled with three cyathi of Wine, and poured into their nostrils.

If their belly swell by hurtfull Pasture: You shall cure them by letting them bloud, launcing, and opening the Veins above their lips, and the Veins under their Tailes, near to the Tuel; also you must pour in an hemina and half of Mans Urine.

If they eat Worms with the grass, you must do the same.

If they swallow a Leech: pour down their throats sharp hot Vinegar or Oyl.

If they have Impostumes upon the skin: Cut the skin, and put into the wound fine pouder of clarrified Salt with Tarr.

If any creeping Vermine have bitten or stung them, give them Nigella with Wine, and do and give to them what I said before concerning Oxen.

Wolves will not run upon Sheep, if you bind a Sea Onyon about the Bell-weather. *Anatolius.*

Of Secrets of he-Goats and she-Goats. Chap. 7.

That Goats may not run away.

Goats will not straggle up and down, if you cut off their Beards. *Florentinus*, and *Zoroaster.*

That she-Goats may give much Milk.

Give them the Herb Cinkfoyl for five daies together, to eat before they drink. Goats will give a great deal of milk if you bind Dittany to their bellies. *Florentinus.*

Of Secrets of Hogs. Chap. 8.

To fat Hogs.

Hogs will be fatted with wheat Bran, and the sweepings of the Barn floore, and all sorts of grain. But Barley besides that it fats them, will make them inclined to Generation. *Florentinus.*

A Cure for Murrain of Hogs.

Hogs will never have the Murrain, or if they have, they will be cured, if you put into

into their Wash roots of Daffodils, or else where they often wash themselves and wallow in. *The same.*

That Hogs may not be sick.

Hogs will not be sick, if you give them nine River Crabs to eat. You shall know when they are ill by pulling some Bristles out of their necks: for if the hair be clean, they are well; but if they be bloudy, or have any filth about the root, that is gross matter, they are not found. Wherefore *Democritus* the Physician commands to give three pounds of the roots of Daffodils a little bruised to every Hog with his meat: and he testifieth that before seaven daies be over that will recover them. If they be Feaverish, draw bloud out of their tail, if their throats be swoln, let them blood in the shoulders; But if the disease they have be unknown, shut them up twenty four hours, and give them no meat at all; but put the roots of wild Cucumbers to soake a day and a night in water, and the next day after give them the water to drink: for when they have drank largely thereof, they will shortly after vomit up the cause of the disease. But because it is a greedy Creature, and is most sick of the Spleen, quench the burning coals of Tamariske in water, and give them the water to drink. This will cure Men also if you pour Wine into the coales instead of water, and Men drink the Wine. *Democritus* gives a plain testimony of it. The same *Democritus* promiseth a Remedy for a Mans Spleen, if you quench a red hot Iron in water, and then mingle that water with Vinegar, and give it a man to drink who is troubled with the Spleen. But when Hogs are bitten by creeping things, the same cures are good for them that we shewd before for other Cattle. *Didym.*

Of the Secrets of Dogs. Chap. 9.

To make a Dog follow any Man.

Take the fat of the Matrix of a Bitch, and mingle it with bread, and cast it to a Dog to eat: and he will follow thee: annoint your shoes with the same fat, and that will make any Dogs follow you. *Fallopius.*

That a Dog shall never forsake you.

Give to a Dog a boyld Frog, and he will never part from you: yet I believe that I have sometimes given many boyled Frogs to Dogs, that yet did not obey me. But when they are beaten by others, if they run from you, if they take meat only from you, they will not forsake you. Some think that if you give a Dog bread that is kept under your Armpits, that it may be wet with your sweat, that will make Dogs more obedient and loving to you. *Card.*

That Dogs shall not Bark.

If you will not have Dogs to bark, take forth the eye of a black Dog whilst the Dog is yet alive, and carry that about you, other Dogs will never open nor bark at you, nor at any Dog that goes with you, though he run by them: perhaps this proceeds from smelling the Dogs eye. They will work more violent, and you shall be softer if you carry Wolves eyes or a Wolfs heart with you. Some say as much of the tongue of an Hyæna, carried in your hand, for that will not only make Dogs quiet from barking, but it will keep them that carry it safe from all Dogs. *The same.*

To make Dogs silent.

The like virtue is in the eyes of an Hyæna, for what Creature soever the Hyæna looks upon, it presently stops, grows dumb, and cannot stir. The same virtue is in the eyes of some Wolves, for if they see any Creature first, he is stricken mute, and grows so hoarse, that if he would cry out he hath no benefit of his voice. *Agrip.*

That Dogs may not run from you.

He that carryeth a Dogs heart with him, all Dogs will run away from him. *The same.*

That Dogs may very quickly give themselves to hunting.

First you must resolve to what kind of hunting you would breed up your Dogs, and then give unto them presently after they are taken away from sucking the Bitch, the bloud of that Creature in Gobbets to eat, that you would have them learn to hunt, as for Harts, Harts blood; for Hares, Hares blood: do the like for Bores, Foxes, and

Wolves,

Wolves. If it be for Partridges, give them the heart, head, and guts of the Partridg. By this means they will quickly hunt after these Creatures, nor will they follow small Birds or other Creatures they meet with in the way, and turn off from the game, they are in pursuit of. *Out of a written Book.*

That Dogs may not be mad.

There is a Nerve under the tongues of Whelps, that is like to a Worm, very round and long. Take this out, and they will be kept from running mad, and this makes them bark very little, nor will they bite any man dangerously. *Colum.* and *Plin.*

To kill any Dog.

Take Henbane seed, Nettle seed, of each a little quantity, mix it with Oyl of Turpentine and Verdigrease, and give it to any Dog, in four and twenty houres it will certainly kill him. *W. Moseley.*

For Dogs madness.

Shut up mad Dogs and give them no meat for one day, then give them some black Hellebour with their drink, and being purged, feed them with Barley bread. Thus you may cure those that are bitten by mad Dogs. *Theomnestus.*

To cure Dogs diseases.

Sponges fryed with fat are poyson to Dogs, when they swallow them down: for they cannot vomit them up again, they swell so much, nor can they digest them, for they are too hard for concoction. By the same reason, though not so much, the skins of living Creatures will kill them: *Nux vomica* doth the same, so will beaten glass; Other poysons they can vomit up again: the way to cure them is to give them plenty of Oyl to drink, also this is ofttimes profitable against diseases that breed of themselves. *Cardan.*

For Dogs Fleas and Scabs.

You shall kill Dogs fleas with Sea water and pickle, and then to annoint them with Oyl of Cypress, and black Hellebour, water and Cummin, and sour Grapes. But it is best to annoint their bodies with Lees of Oyl; for that will cure their Scabs. *Theomnestus.*

Of the Secrets of wild Creatures in Generall. Chap. 10.

To tame wild Creatures.

Cratevas Hippocrates his Herbarist saith, That by the sprinkling of Wine wherein the Plant *Oenothera* hath been steeped, all Creatures fierceness will be taken off, and not only of Men. *Theophrastus* understood this of the root. So *Ælian* writes that *Ænutta* will make Stags and Dogs drunk.

To drive away wild Beasts.

To be safe from wild Beasts, besides weapons these are remedies. Fire; For they fear that: but Serpents do not, for some will come of themselves, either by reason of the light or heat. A cord drawn like a gin, or if you want that, a stick cleft in the middle; for where they see Snares, they are afraid. If a Man go backward towards them and hide his head, Cattle especially are frighted with this. Also a horn if one blow it very lowd. It is plain that Engins of fire will drive them off four waies, by sight of the fire, by the lowd noise, by the filthy smell, and lastly if you hurt them. Also a noysome smell would make them flye most of all, if the force of the sent could be augmented as well as a sound or light. *Cardan.*

To be free from wild Beasts.

If any man be annointed with the fat of a Lion, he is free from wild Beasts; for they fear the smell of him, alive or dead. But you must go toward them undauntedly, for if you run away they will scarce smell the sent. *Card.*

Of the Secrets of wild Beasts in speciall.

Of the Secrets of Deer. Chap. 11.

How Deer renew their youth when they are old.

It is known that Deer renew their age by eating of Serpents. So the Phænix is renewed by her ashes, in the fire of spices that she makes for her Tombe. *Corn. Agrippa.*

To chase away Deer.

Deer are afraid of a cord that hath Feathers tied hanging about it here and there, for they see the Feathers move. But they despise such scare Crows, when they see men standing by them. *Democritus.*

To allure Deer.

Deer hearing the noise of Pipes and Musicall sounds, will not run away, but stay to hear the Musick, and so are taken. *The same.*

Of the Secrets of wild Bores. Chap. 12.

That one may be safe from wild Hogs.

If you would be safe from wild Hogs running upon you, you must carry bound about you Crabs claws and feet, for an Amulet. *Democritus.*

Of the Secrets of Hares. Chap. 13.

To know the age of Hares.

If any man would know how many years old Hares are, you must search into the cavities of nature, for doubtless one Hare hath more cavities then another. *Archelaus.*

How to fat Hares.

It is a late invention to make them fat, for being taken out of the Hare Warrens, they are shut up in hollow places, and being thus shut up, they will be sooner fatted. *M. Varro.*

To make Hares come together.

The juyce of Henbane mingled with the blood of a young Hare, and sowed up in a Hares skin, is said to call all the Hares together that are in that part of the Countrey where it lyeth buried, no less then the Matrix of a Bitch draws Dogs to it. *Out of an old Book;* some say it is true.

Of the Secrets of Foxes. Chap. 14.

That Foxes may not eat Hens.

Foxes will eat no Hens that have eaten a Foxes liver. *Cornelius Agrippa.*

Of the Secrets of Wolves. Chap. 15.

To drive away Wolves.

If the tail of a Wolf be buried in a Farme, that will keep off all Wolves from coming thither. *Rhasis* and *Albertus.*

That Wolves shall not hurt Cattle.

If a Wolfs tail be hanged over the racks where Cows feed or other Cattle, the Wolf will never come there untill that be taken away. *Albertus.*

To catch Wolves.

You shall hunt Wolves thus. *Blemmi* are small Sea Fish, some call them Wolves: these help to catch Wolves on the land this way. You shall fish for these Fish, and take as many as you can get alive, pound them in a Mortar, and make a great fire in the Mountain where Wolves are, when the wind blows; then take and cast some of these Fish into the fire, mingle well therewith Lambs flesh cut very small with the blood and put that to the pounded fishs, then retire from the place; for so soon as the fire begins to smell very strong, all the Wolves in those Coasts will resort thither. And so soon as they have eaten of that flesh, or but smelt of it, they will grow blind and giddy, and fall fast asleep: then come upon them and kill them being in a trance. *Diophanes.*

Of the Secrets of living Creatures. Chap. 16.

A living Creature by the mixture of divers kinds.

You may produce a living Creature by the mixture of divers kinds, if you do thus; Seek for living Creatures that bring forth many young ones at once, such as are most salacious, and are most prone to copulation, and the Males are alwaies alluring the Females, let these ingender together, being of equall magnitude of bodies;

choose

choose such as go with their young very near, or just the same time, or not much longer: so by the copulation of divers kinds you shall have Monsters, half one kind, and half another, according as nature varieth many wayes. Of a Dog and a Wolf, will a wild Beast be bred, which is wont to be called *Crocuta*, and *Aristotle* shews the way how to produce this. The Lyoness copulates with the *Pardus*, from whence are ingendered bastard Lions, that have no Maines, and are all spotted as *Philostratus* saith. Wolves also copulate with Panthers, so is a Creature produced of double kind, which is called *Thoes*, by its spotted skin it is like a Panther; but the face is like the he-Wolfs., as *Oppianus* relates; so with a Fox, Wolf, Tyger, an Ape, a Lion and such like it may be done; that as the Greeks commonly say, *Africa* continually affords some new Creatures: for by reason of want of water in these dry parts and thirsty Regions, the Beasts come from far to one place to drink; and there, by force or willingly, they copulate one with another, and so by divers mixtures divers Creatures are made; and in *Africa* they do not much wonder at it, because they are so common; wherefore take these examples to produce new Creatures. I have read in *Ælian*, that with *Sybaris* a Shepheard, there was one called *Crathis*, who falling in love with the fairest she-Goat, was mad for lust after her, he would kiss this Goat, and embrace her as his dearest Mistris: and this lover of a Goat would give her the choicest meat that she might please him better. Thus he reports a Child was born of this Goat, like the dam on the legs and lower parts, but like the sire on the upper part of the body. *The same.*

Of the Secrets of Mice. Chap. 17.

To kill Mice.

You may kill Mice if you lay in their way Hellebour mingled with Barley meal dried, or seeds of wild Cucumber with black Hellebour and Coloquintida, and Barley meal. But if you make a fume with Vitriol, Origanum, Smallage seed and Nigella, you will drive them away. If you put Oake ashes in their holes, the ashes falling upon them will make them scabbed, and so kill them. If you mingle filings of Iron with leven, when they taste of it they will dye. *Paxamus.*

To blind Mice.

If you would make Mice blind, mix Sithymal bruised with Barley meal dried and sweet Wine, and when they eat of it, that will make them blind. *The same.*

To drive away Mice.

Take one live Mouse, and pull off the skin from his head, and let him go, and that will drive away all the rest. Also the fume of Lupins hæmatites, will with green Tamarix burnt, make them leave that place. *Paxamus.*

To make Mice come together.

Anatolius bids you poure Lees of Oyl into a brass Bason, and set it all night in the middle of the house, and by this means he reports, all Mice of other neighbours houses also will come thither.

To cause Mice to meet in a place.

Take two living Mice or more, put them both into a large earthen pot, and make a fire of Ash wood about them. When the pot grows hot, you will laugh to see how at the cry of those imprisoned Mice, and piping they make, all the Mice that are in hearing will run thither, and go straight forward into the fire, as if they came to help the besieged. I should think the fume of the Ash wood is the cause of it. *Mizaldus* from *Albertus.*

Remedies against field Mice, and houshold Mice also.

Apulejus saith, That Mice will never hunt after seed sown, if the seed be steeped in Buls Gall before it be sown. If you stop Mice holes with Rose-Laurel leaves that will kill them. Some of the Greeks mingle wild Cucumber, or Henbane, or bitter Almonds, and black Hellebour beaten together in equall quantities with dryed Barley meal, and with Oyl they make it to a Paste, and this they put into the holes of Mice in houses and fields. *Pliny* saith, that the Ashes of a Weesil will drive them away, or of a Cat put into water and sprinkled upon the seed sowed.

To drive Mice from root of Hartichoaks.

Hartichoake roots are exceedingly desired by Mice, and they are so allured by them, that they will come in Troops to them from far distant places; as *Varro* a Greek Author tels us in his choice precepts of Husbandry: but there is a remedy for this. For he saith that wooll wrapt about the roots, will take off the edg of their appetite, or Hogs dung or Figtree ashes will make them be gone.

That a Shrew may not bite any one.

That the Shrew may bite no Man, this Shrew must be taken alive and compassed in with Potters earth: when this grows hard, you may hang it about your neck, and be sure the Shrew cannot bite you. *Vegetius.*

That Mice may not eat your Cheese.

If you put the brain of a Weesil to the Runnet, they report that Mice will not so much as nibble at that Cheese, nor will the Cheese ever be rotten. So great discord there is between Mice and Weesils. *Corn. Agrippa.*

That Mice may not eat Books.

Mingle Printers Ink with the infusion of Wormwood, and the Mice will never eat the Letters. *Dioscorid.*

Of Secrets of Moles. Chap. 18.

How to catch Moles.

If you will catch Moles, put Leeks or Onyons in their holes, for so they will presently come forth as if they were amazed. *Albertus.*

How to make Wolves come together.

Put a Mole in an Earthen pot with Brimstone set on fire, and the Mole will call the other Moles to her, as if she cried for help. *Albertus as I remember.*

How to drive away Moles.

Paxamus bids us make a hole through in some narrow sound Vessel, and put into it chaff, and Rosin of the Cedar tree. (*Palladius* reads it Wax,) as much as is sufficient with Brimstone: and with this to stop diligently all the holes and passages where the Moles lye, that the smoke may not penetrate through them; yet so that one large hole must be left open, in the mouth whereof the said Vessel must be placed, the matter of it being set on fire, that may send the smoak of the Rosin and Brimstone into the Mole hils. By this trick all their walks under ground being filled with smoke, you may kill them, or drive them all away. Some make white Hellebour, or the bark of Dogs-cole poudred and sifted with dried Barley meal, and Eggs strewd upon it, and temper'd with Milk and Wine, into Cakes, and these they put into the Mole holes. Many to drive Moles away, breed up Cats in Gardens, and keep tame Weesils to drive away this plague by hunting after them. Others fill the holes with marking stones, and the juyce of wild Cucumber, or else catching one Mole, they cast him into an earthen pot with Brimstone set on fire, supposing that will bring all the rest thither. Some agin at the mouths of their holes set traps with hair. Countrey Men are content to set a twig, or an Elder bough fast down. *Pliny* kils them with Oyl Lees only.

Of the Secrets of Weesils. Chap. 19.

That Weesils and Squirrels may be made tame.

Here is a wonderfull thing which I will not conceale now; It is strange that Weesils and Squirrels having once bitten Garlick with their teeth, they will hardly ever dare to bite again, and thereby grow tame. *Mizald.*

How to kill Weesils.

You shall either kill or drive away Weesils, if you mingle salt Armoniac and leven (others read Wheat) together, and cast that in the place where they often come. Some catch one and cut off his tail and testicles, and let him run away alive, that will make all the rest run away. *African.*

That Weesils shall do no hurt.

All Weesils are put to flight by the stinking smell of a burnt Cat, as all Insects are by any of their own kind. *Card.*

To call Weesils to one place.

The gall of a Beast called Stellio, mingled with water, will make all Weesils come thither. *Corn. Agrip.*

To drive Cats from Bird Cages.

Cats are driven from Bird-Pens, if you sprinkle Chickens and young Birds with the juyce of Rue: or as many say, if Rue be stuck round about them. *Miz.*

That a Cat may conceive without a he-Cat.

Living Creatures are not only friends one with another, but they agree with many other things, as mettals, stones, and vegetables. So a Cat loves Nip, and it is reported that she will be great with Kitten by rubbing against that, for that serves instead of a he-Cat. *Agrip.*

Of Secrets of Ants. Chap. 20.

To drive Pismires away.

If you burn some Ants that you find, this will fright away all the rest, as it is proved by true experience. *Diophanes.*

How to drive out Ants.

You shall drive Ants out of their holes, if you burn Snails shels with Styrax, and bruising them, you strew them among their Hillocks. Also you may drive forth Ants with Origanum and Brimstone poudred, and scatter upon his Hils. But Ants will dye all, if you dissolve juyce of Ben with Oyl, and poure that upon them. *The same.*

That Ants may not eat Herbs and Plants.

Ants will not touch trees, if you annoint the bodies of them with Oyl Lees mingled and boyled with bitter Lupins. *The same.*

That Ants shall not come to a Beehive of Honey.

Ants will not come near a Hive of Honey, though it have no covering, if you put white wooll about it, or inclose it in Potters earth, or red marking stone. Some annoint the stocks of trees with benjoin mingled with Vinegar, and pour it also into their holes. *The same.*

To kill Ants.

Ants will all dye, if you make a smoke with the roots of wild Cucumber, or with the smoke of the sheath Fish, especially that of *Alexandria* upon a slow fire.

To drive away Ants.

You shall drive away Emmets with Buls gall and Pitch, mixed with Lees of Oyl, red stone and Pitch do the same; if you mingle them to an unguent. Some hang a Fish called *Coracinus* upon the tree, and so they destroy Ants; If Pismires be burnt the rest will flye away by reason of their smell. *The same.*

Another.

Against multitudes of Ants *Palladius* gives this remedy; If saith he, Ants have Hils in your Garden, put the heart of an Owle there; if they come forth of their holes, then stop all open places of your Garden with Ashes, Chalk, or Oyl. And a little after that he adds, you shall force them to leave the place, if you sprinkle Brimstone and Origanum in pouder upon their holes. But *Pliny* saith the best remedy against Ants is, to stop their holes with Sea Mud, or Ashes that are not moist. But above all they are killed with the herb Turnsoil; some think that water mingled with Bricks unburnt, is a great enemy to them.

Otherwise.

Take Brimstone half a pound, melt it at the fire in an earthen pot, add salt of Tartar or salt of Ashes three or four ounces, mingle them, and stir them well, untill the colour be reddish, take it from the fire, and pour it forth upon a board, first wet with water: and when it is grown hard, pouder it small, and pour upon it as much Fountain water as shall suffice, and leave this in a glass, untill the water be coloured, sprinkle this Tincture upon their Hils, or upon stocks of Trees, and this will kill them or drive them away. It is certain. *Alexius.*

That Ants may lose their place.

Take dry Origanum, and pouder it finely, and strew it upon the place where Ants are, and they will quit their fortress. *Albert.*

That Ants may not creep up the Trees.

That Ants may not creep up trees, Lupins, are poudred and mingled with Fish pickle, and with this the lower part of the stock of the tree is annointed round about. *Columella, Pliny,* and *Palladius.* Likewise Ants run away by reason of the heart of a Houp, but his head, feet, or eyes will not do it. *Agrip.*

Otherwise.

Green Lupins with Oyl, and annoint the roots or stocks of Trees with this: Some kill them with Lees of Oyl only.

Against Ants.

Some mantain that the heart of a Bat will hinder Ants from coming forth. But Brimstone will hinder them; I think by its ill sent and fume. I never found any thing for Trees better then water; Make a circle of Wax about the Trees, and fill up the place void with water. *Cardanus.*

Of the Secrets of Scorpions. Chap. 21.

Against Scorpions.

Catch one Scorpion and burn him, for that will drive away all the rest. But if any man do diligently annoint his hands with juyce of Raddishes, he may without fear or danger handle Scorpions and other creeping things. Also Raddishes laid upon Scorpions will presently kill them. You shall cure the the sting of a Scorpion, if you touch the part with a Seal-Ring of Silver. Sandaracha burnt with Butter and Galbanum, or with Goats Suet, will drive away Scorpions and all other creeping things. If any Man boyl Scorpions in water, and annoint the place that is stung by a Scorpion, he shall cure the part, and take away the pain. *Diophanes.*

That Scorpions shall not creep into houses.

Scorpions will not creep into houses, when a small Nut shall be fastned to the roof of the house. *Plutarch.*

To chase away, and to kill Scorpions.

If you compass in the place where Scorpions are with a twig or branch of the true Turnsoil, *Pliny* saith that they will never stirre, for they cannot if they would; but if the Herb touch them, or be strewed upon them, he saith they will dye presently. Some report that the same is performed by the touch of the root of the Herb which is called Scorpion Grass; and that he shall not be hurt by a Scorpion that carrieth the Herb about with him. The *Africans* promise, that if you mingle and bruise a handfull of Basil with ten Sea Crabs, or River Crabs, all Scorpions that are near will come together to it. The same Authors report, that if any man be stung with a Scorpion, let him ride upon an Ass with his face turned toward the Asses tail, and all the venome of the Rider will go from him to the Ass. This you may know when it is done, if the Ass blow and fart. *Miz.*

How you may handle Scorpions without danger.

If a man hold the Herb stone Sage, or Scorpion Grass in his hand, he may safely handle Scorpions. *Tarent.*

For stingings of Scorpions.

The Stellio is so contrary to Scorpions, that it frights them if it do but see them, and makes them astonisht with a cold sweat. Wherefore they kill the Stellio in Oyl, and let him corrupt there, with which they cure the stingings of Scorpions by annointing the part. *Corn. Agrip. de Philos. occultâ.*

To make a Crocodile not able to move.

If any Man touch a Crocodile with the birds feather of the Ibis, he is presently made that he cannot stir. *The same. Agrippa.*

Of the Secrets of Wiglice. Chap. 22.

To kill Wall-lice.

Tar and juyce of wild Cucumbers smeered upon the bed-steds, or put into the beds will kill Wall-lice. So will Sea Onyons cut and brayed with Vinegar, if the bed-stead be wet with that by a Sponge. Likewise boyl Citron leaves with Oyl, and smeer the joynts of your bed-sted. Or mingle Buls or Goats gall with sharp Vinegar, and with that wet the wals and the bed-sted. You may do the same with old Oyl and live Brimstone in pouder mingled and smeering them with that. There will be no wiglice if you boyl fish glew, and smeer it on the beds. And you shall kill all that are, if you mingle Buls gall with Lees of Oyl boyled, and sprinkle that and the Oyl where they are. Or if you put Ivy or Caper leaves in Oyl, and annoint the places with that; by this medicament even those that are in the wals will be destroyed. But an effectuall remedy is prepared thus. Take a Sawcerfull of wild Stavesacre, or Sea Onyons cut into small pieces as much, sharp Vinegar one spoonfull; these are bruised together, then they are made hot, and so the places are smeered with it. Also mingle one part of Tar with four parts of sweet Wine, and smeer the place with that. The same is done by the gall of a Goat or Calf, with as much sweet Wine and Vinegar. *Dydim.*

Another.

Wiglice are killed by the fume of bloud-suckers, if the bed be kept close covered that the smoke cannot come forth; and likewise bloud-suckers are killed by the smoke of bloud-suckers. So Harts tongue dried and burnt to a smoke performes the same, and so do Ivy leaves bruised and mingled with ten Horse-Leeches. *Floren.*

Another.

The feet of a Hare or Deer bound upon the feet of the bed, that support it, about the part that is behind your back when you lye down, will suffer no Wall-lice to breed there: But when they come forth, if you put under the bed a Vessell full of cold water, the Wall-lice will never bite you whilst you sleep. Also scalding water will burn and scald them all, if you cast it upon them: but that hinders not, but they will breed again as fast as they did. *Democritus.*

Another.

Take Wormwood, Rue, common Oyl, and water, of each what may suffice, boyl them all well untill the water be consumed, then strain the Oyl, and mingle as much Hogs grease with it as needs, make an unguent and annoint the joynts of your beds with it. *Alexius.*

Another.

Take Hogs grease, Quicksilver, of each what is sufficient, mingle them very well, and make an oyntment, and smeer the chinks and joynts of your beds with it: The Tincture of Brimstone will do as much, whereof I made mention before in the Chapter concerning Ants. *The same.*

For Wiglice.

Make a smoke with Ox dung, and it will drive away Wall-lice. *Anonymus.*

Another.

Take Wormwood two handfuls, white Hellebour one ounce, boyl them in Lee untill a third part be consumed, wash the joynts of your beds with it. *Miscellus.*

Of the Secrets of Fleas. Chap. 23.

Make a pit, and bruise Rose Laurel, and put it into that pit, and all the Fleas will come thither. Wormwood or the root of wild Cucumber laid in Sea water, and the water sprinkled about the house kils them all. So doth Nigella infused in water, and the water besprinkled over the place. Or the decoction of Flea bane sprinkled. So doth Mustard seed and Rose-Laurel seed, both heated at the fire and sprinkled about the house. Sift Quick-Lime, and when you have swept the house, strew this there and it will kill them. The same is done by Lees of Oyl, daily sprinkled upon the Pavement. Also wild Cummin bruised and mingled with water, and ten drams of wild Cucumber seeds poudred and put into the water, and the water sprinkled about the house will burn up the Fleas. The same is done by the root of *Chamelaa*, and the leaves of black Poplar bruised, and infused in water, and Thistles boyld in water. Likewise pickle that is strong besprinkled, and Sea water will kill fleas. And if any one set a Bason in the middle of the house, and make a circle about it with an Iron Sword (but the best Sword for this purpose is that that hath first killed a man,) and besprinkle with the decoction of wild Stavesacre, or Bay leaves bruised, all the place besides that which is within the circle, or else with Brine or Sea water boyled, he shall make all the fleas gather into the Bason. Also an earthen Vessel set into the ground, that the brims of it may lye even with the Pavement, and smeered with Buls fat, will gather all the fleas into it, even those also that are yet hidden in your Cloathes. Make a little hole under the bed, and put Goats bloud into it, and it will gather together all the fleas, and will draw all the rest out of your Cloathes and Garments. Also out of rags and thickest Tapestry, wherein the greatest store of fleas lye, they may be called forth, if Goats bloud be so set in a Pot or Vessel. *Pamphilus*.

To kill Fleas and Wall-lice.

Wormwood, Rue, Southernwood, wild Mints, Savory, Wallnut leaves, Fern, bastard Spike, which we call Lavender, Nigella, green Coriander, Flea seed, Bean Trifoly; lay all these or some of them under the Blankets, or boyl them in Vinegar of Sea Onyons, and with that besprinkle the beds. *Alexius*.

Another of the same Author for Fleas and Wall-lice.

The decoction of Thistles or Arsmart, or Coloquintida, or Brambles, or Colewort leaves, sprinkled about the house, drives them away.

To make all the Fleas gather to one place.

Annoint a small staff with the fat of a Hedghog, and stick it up in the middle of the Chamber, and all the fleas will stick to the staff. *The same.*

Another.

If the bloud or fat of a Bear be put under the bed in a hole or vessel, all the fleas will gather and dye there. *Arnoldus de villa nova*.

Another.

Besprinkle the rooms with Lee and Goats milk mingled together.

How Fleas must be driven away.

Take Lupins and Wormwood, boyl them both in water, and sprinkle the Chambers therewith. Wormwood and Coloquintida in water, do the same boyl'd with Peach leaves, Vervin, and Coriander. *Fallopius.*

Against Garden Fleas.

Fleas will never spoil Herbs in Gardens, if you use naturall meanes, to mingle Rocket in many places of the Garden. So sharp Vinegar tempered with juyce of Henbane sprinkled upon these Creatures, will help you much. *Anatolius.*

Of the Secrets of Lice. Chap. 24.

For Lice of the eye lids.

Rub your eye lids with Sea water, salt water, or Brimstone and water, and apply them, or with Vinegar of squills Allum, and Aloes, annoint the hairs of your eyelids. *The same.*

For Crab-lice of the Secrets.

Take an Apple boyld soft, and cleansed from its core and skin, a little Quicksilver, mingle them together to an unguent, annoint the parts that are lowsy with it, and the Lice will dye. *An Italian.*

For Lice and Nits of the Head.

This unguent will kill them: Take common Oyl three ounces, Wax one ounce, Stavesacre, Quicksilver killed with a Mans fasting spittle, of each three drams, make an Oyntment, wash with this instead of Sope, when you wash your head. *Bayrus.*

Another.

Take Sandaracha, Saltpeter, of each one dram, Stavesacre two drams, make them
up

up with Vinegar and Oyl, and annoint you with them. White Hellebour and Salt-peter, Stavesacre, and Oyl of Tar, are good both severally and altogether; so is Sumach, root of sour Dock, and Oyl.

Of the Secrets of Snails. Chap. 25.

Of Snails.

What concerns Snails, If you sprinkle new Lees of Oyl or Sut of the Chimnies upon them, you shall do as much to Pot-hearbs, as if you sowed Ciche Peason amongst them, that is good for many things wonderfull in Gardning. *Mizald.*

Of the Secrets of Caterpillars. Chap. 26.

Against Caterpillars.

What concerns Caterpillars, Some strew Fig ashes to drive them away, others sow Squils in the Gardens in beds, or hang them up here and there. Some stick up in many places the claws of River Crabs. If the Caterpillars will come for all these things, then use this device. Set Ox Piss and Oyl Lees mingled equally upon the fire to boyl, when they are cold besprinkle the Pot-herbs and trees with this. *Anatolius.* But *Pliny* would have them touched with bloudy rods which they stand in danger of. *Palladius* burns handfuls of Garlick stalks without the heads, all over the Garden. To these take Bats dung, and make a stinking smoke with it in many places of the ground, for this is excellent. *Pliny* saith, They will be driven from Pot-herbs if you sow Chiche Peason with them; and mingle them one with another, or Crabs be hung by the horns, upon boughs of trees in divers places. But the Greeks observe that they will not breed, and also those that are bred are destroyed, if you take some of them out of a Garden that is next, and boyl them in water with Dill, and when the water is cold, besprinkle the herbs and trees with them, where you see the Caterpillars breed and fostering their egs. But take great heed that the water touch not your hands or face. Moreover it is a sure remedy and easie to be provided, to burn Bitumen and Brimstone about the roots and arms of trees: Or to make a smoke with Mushroms that grow under Nut trees; or else burn Galbanum or Goats claws, or Harts horn, turning your back toward the wind. Some put Ashes of Nettles three daies into water, and after that they wet abundantly the Pot-herbs and Trees with it. Many steep the seeds to be sown in Lee made of the Fig tree. Our Gardners by an easie Art do at this day so drive them away: Where the Caterpillars creep in open Sunny places after Rain, in the morning they use to shake the leaves of Pot-herbs, and boughs of Trees: for so whilst they are yet stiff with the cold of the night, they easily fall down, nor do they ever creep up again; for thus are they presently and easily to be killed. Moreover if you would destroy all sorts of such Creatures as hurt Trees and Herbs, *Diophanes* the Greek will shew you the way how. Get saith he, The Paunch of a Weather new killed, with all the Excrements in it, and bury this under ground a little, but not very deep, in the Garden where these small Creatures use to frequent; at two daies end you shall find Beetles, and abundance of such Creatures in heaps about it: you may carry them from thence, or bury them deep enough in the same place, that they never rise up again: having done thus two or three times, you may destroy them all. Our Countrey People wind wisps of straw about the bodies of Trees, and about the roots: and the Caterpillars are taken in these when they come to creep up the Trees, and thus are they either driven away or catched in these gins and snares laid for them. *Mizald. de Secretis hortorum.*

Another.

Hurtfull Creatures are driven away from Pot herbs, by water wherein Crabs have been set in the Sun, or Craw fish for ten daies. *Card. de Subtilit.*

Against little Creatures that do mischief in Gardens.

Dung that is the best for Pot-herbs and Plants, is the finest Ashes, that is naturally hot, for Garden fleas, Worms, Caterpillars, Snails, and the rest that hurt the Plants and devour them, are either killed or forced away thereby. *Mizald.*

Of the Secrets of Serpents. Chap. 27.

Against Serpents, remedies and Secrets.

Florentinus, that for Husbandry amongst the Greeks was the chief, writeth that Serpents will not lodg in Gardens or other places, if you plant round the borders, Wormwood, Southernwood or Mugwort, or else place them handsomely about the corners of the Garden : and if the Adders be used to any place, the smoke of a Lilly root, Harts horn, or Goats hooff will scare them away. *Palladius* saith, That they, and all evill spirits may be chased away by some stinking smoke. *Democritus* saith, They will dye if you cast Oake leaves upon them ; or if one that is fasting spit into their mouths. *Apulejus* writes, that strike them only with a Reed, and that will destroy them ; but they will often revive again. *Tarentinus* well skilled in Husbandry amongst the Greeks, saith, that he cannot be stung with an Adder, who is annointed with the juyce of Raddish, or hath but tasted of a Raddish. This *Athenæus* and *Galen* ascribeth to an Orange or Pomecitron, and they confirm it by a very handsome story : but it will not be amiss to hear again *Florentinus* the Adder killer. Adders saith he will never come where the Deers suet lyeth, or the root of Centory, or the Jet stone, or the dung of an Eagle, or of a Kite ; And every creeping thing will be driven away if you mingle Nigella, Pellitory of *Spain*, Galbanum, Harts horn, Hysop, Brimstone, Dog Fennel, and Goats hoofs ; and then pouder them, and pour the sharpest Vinegar upon them : and make little Bals of that mixture, and so raise a smoake with them : for the ill sent of those things being scattered in the Ayr, will make all creeping things to shift away, as if they were beaten with a Whip. Some say that the boughs of the Pomegranate Tree will drive away all venemous Creatures and Adders : Wherefore of purpose it is laid under the Blankets and Furniture in those houses where Adders use to haunt, and other Creatures that are venemous, whole Troops whereof *Florentinus* brought together as one would catch Fish in a Net ; by setting a Hogshead where salt Fish had been formerly in, into the ground, Garden, or other places about, where these Adders and hurtfull Creatures frequent. For to that presently all creeping things resorted, and quickly fell into it. *Pliny* speaking of the Osier saith, Adders will not come at this shrub, and therefore Countrey Men alwayes carry a stick of this in ther hands. Moreover it is a most certain experiment and approved, that Coblers shoos being burnt, will effectually drive away Serpents ; and not only those that wander in Gardens, Fields, or Houses, but those also that are crept into Mens mouths and bodies whilst they slept with open mouths in the fields in Summer. This is spoken of by *Marcus Gatinaria*, a Physician very famous, that in his time the like accident befell a Man, who, when abundance of Remedies had been used to him in vain, which were otherwise very good, found help beyond all the rest, by the smoke of old shoos burnt, receiving the stinking smell at his mouth by a Tunnel : For so soon as the cruel Beast (for it was a huge Viper) smelt the filthy savour of the fume, those that stood by saw her go forth at his Fundament, to the great wonder and amazement of them all. This I writ, And do you note it for a great Secret easie to be procured, and which may do many Men good. But here I must not omit to tell you that Serpents hate fire exceedingly : not only because it duls their sight, but because fire naturally is an enemy to venome. They hate also all strong sents, as Onyons, Garlick, and the like ; but they love Savin, Ivy, and Fennel ; as Buffs love Sage, and Vipers Rockets. Above all they hate an Ash tree mortally, that they will not lye so near it, as to be under the morning or evening shade of it, when the shadow casts very long, but they will remove far from it. *Pliny* saith that he had tried it, That if you put a Serpent and fire both within a circle made of Ash tree boughs, the Serpent will run into the fire before he will adventure to pass over the circle made with the boughs of the Ash : this is a great bounty of Nature, that the Ash tree buds before Serpents do come abroad, nor doth that Tree cast her leaves untill the Serpents begin to hide themselves, and are not any more to be seen. *Virgil* the Father of all Learning, chaseth them away with Cedar Tree, or Galbanum set on fire to smoke them with.

Smoke

Smoke of Galbanum 'gainst Adders good,
As is the smoke of the sweet Cedar wood.

Mizaldus writes this out of the Ancients above mentioned.

To stupifie Serpents.

Round Birthwort diligently beaten with a field Frog, adding a little writing Ink thereto, will make Serpents stand still as if they were dead, and stick fast, if you do but write with that mixture, and cast the writing before them. *Alb.*

How you may handle Serpents without danger.

Annoint your hands well with juyce of Raddish, and you may safely take Serpents in your hands. *Card.* from *Tarent.*

For biting or stinging of Serpents.

If any one be stung with a Serpent, unless he be in a Feaver, let him drink the juyce of Ash leaves with white Wine: and with the leaves let him cover the part that was stung: this is very strange, but it is appproved to be true, nor is the reason concealed: for there is a strong Antipathy between the Ash tree and all Serpents. *Mizald.*

Of the Secrets of Bones. Chap. 28.

To soften Bones.

It is reported that Bones will be made soft with juyce of Smallage, Yarrow, Raddishes, Horehound, with Vinegar, if you lay them in these juyces, and bury them in Horse dung. *Card.*

To make Bones white.

Bones are strangely made white, being boyled with water and Lime, if you alwayes skim it. *The same.*

To make bones soft.

Take *Roman* Vitriol, common Salt, of each as much as is sufficient: Pouder them and distill them, and keep the water for your use, and when you have occasion, steep the Bones in it and they will be soft. *Isabella Cortese.*

To dye Bones green.

Take one measure of the sharpest Vinegar, Verdigrease, filings of Copper, of each three ounces, Rue one handfull, bruise what must be bruised, and beat what must be beaten, and mingle them: steep Bones in this fifteen daies. *Isabella Cortese.*

To dye white bones black.

Take Litharge, Quick lime of each six ounces, Fountain water what is needfull, mingle them, boyl the Bones in this water, and they will be black. *Isabella Cortese.*

To dye all Bones and Wood, a certain way.

Take the strongest Vinegar, put it into a glased Vessel, put filings of Brass to it, *Roman* Vitriol, Allum, flour of Brass or Verdigrease, of each what is sufficient, mingle them, leave them so for seaven daies. Then boyl them at the fire with the Bones or Wood, putting a little more Allum to them, and you may dye them what colour you please. *Alexius.*

To soften Ivory.

If you will make Ivory soft to take any impression, boyl it in the water with root of Mandragora, six houres at the least, and it will be soft as Wax. *The same.*

To polish Ivory.

I will not let pass, that Ivory is said to be polished very neatly, and that heaps of Salt will be made into salt water, if they be covered with Raddishes. *Mizald.*

Of the Secrets of Horns. Chap. 29.

To soften Hornes.

It is the Art of Chymistry that will soften horns by long boyling, if you put a little ashes into the water; this will not be done under eight houres time. With these you make hafts for Hilts of Swords, Combs, Chess men, boxes for Oyntments, Cases, and other Vessels, but all must be made by the same Art; but the *French* have a far better way. *Card.*

How to make horns black.

It is plain that Vinegar and *Aqua vita*, and Vitriol will make black horns that are cold, or but a little warm. Some things also are to be added, that will make them hold the colour. *Card.*

Of the Secrets for hair, see before concerning the Secrets of Horses.

BOOK. VII.

Thus far I have spoken of Man, so much as needfull was for Secrets. Since therefore I had to speak of other Creatures, in this Book I shall lay down the Secrets of other Creatures that live in the Waters; and in the next I shall treat of Birds and such as live in the Aire.

Of the Secrets of Fish in Generall. Chap. 1.

Take Origanum, Savory, Elder of each three drams, bark of Frankinsence, Myrrh, Sinoper, of each eight drams, half a pound of dried Barley meal dissolved in pleasant well sented Wine, of the Liver of a Hog broyled three ounces, as much Goats suet, and the like quantity of Garlick. These must be all beaten severally, then mingle thin Sand with them, and put them all about an houre or two before into the place where fish are, and compass the place with nets. Others put in the Herb Delphinium, the Masculine, and they first beat it small and pouder it and sift it; this will allure the fish to it, that you may take them up with your hands. Some take half a pound of Garlick, and as much Sesama seed torrefied, Penniroyall, Origanum, Thyme, Elder Savory, wild Stavesacre, of each thirty two drams, Barley meal dryed half a pound, Spelt as much, bark of Frankinsence sixteen drams, they mingle this with Earth and Bran and cast it into the water. *Florentinus.*

How all sorts of Fish may be called to one place

Take bloud of an Ox, a Goat, a Sheep, dung of Oxen from the small guts, and of Goats from their small guts, the like from Sheep, Thyme, Origanum, Penniroyall, Savory, Elder, Garlick, Lees of sweet Wine, of each one part, the fat or marrow of the same Creatures what may suffice: beat all these severally, or all together, and make lumps of it, and cast them into fish Ponds, or places where fish are one houre before, then pitch your Nets round about. *Democritus.*

To take River Fish.

Take Sheep suet, Sesema seed torrefied, Garlick, sweet Wine, Origanum, Thyme, dryed Elder, of each a fit quantity, bruise them, mingle them with Bread and cast them in. *Dydimus.*

To take all sorts of Fish.

Take the bloud of a black Goat, Lees of sweet Wine, a quantity of dryed Barley meal, mix them with the Lungs of a Goat cut into very small pieces, make them in lumps, and cast them in. *Democritus.*

That no man may catch Fish.

If you strew Salt about the Fishing Line, no Fish will bite. *The same.*

A Bait to catch Fish.

Take one ounce of a Whale, and the yellow Down of Thistles that flye away with the wind, Anniseeds, Goat-smilk Chees, of each four drams, Opoponax two drams, Hogs bloud four drams, beat them all well, and mingle them, pouring upon them sharp Wine, and make little Bals of them, as you do for perfumes, and dry them in the shade. *Tareminus.*

A Bait to catch River Fish.

Take Calfs bloud, and Calfs flesh cut very small, put them into an earthen pot, let them lye there ten daies, then use this for your Baits. *The same.*

A Bait of the same Authors, how to catch Fish presently.

You must make up Bals with dried Barley meal, and cast them to the Fish.

To allure Fish.

Rose seeds with Mustard seed, and the foot of a Weesil bound to your Nets, or cast near unto them, will invite the fish thither. *Albertus.*

To catch Fish.

Distill in a Glass retort Glowormes that shine in the Night, you must do it at a gentle fire, untill you have drawn forth all their moysture. Mingle this water with four ounces of Quicksilver in a Viol, or some round Glass vessel very well stopt, that the water run not forth. Then place this Glass in some Net handsomely, that it break not; when you let this down into the Rivers, it will shine so bright, that the Fishes allured by the light will come thither in troops. *Alexius.*

To invite Fish.

If you bruise Nettles with five leaved Grass, with the juyce of Housleek, and annoint your hands therewith, and cast this also into the water, where fish are in lumps, put but your hands into that fish-pond, and fishes will resort to you by sholes. You may do the same, if you put this mixture into a Net or into a Weil, or Dragnet for fishes. *Hermes.*

Another.

Fishes will come abundantly in a calme River, or by the Sea shore, if you strew into it Lime mingled with the decoction of round Birthwort. And if they taste of this pouder, they will lye as if they were dead, and swim above water. *Pliny.*

Another.

If you take *Cocculus Indicus* and make Bals of it, with Cummin, old Chees, Wheat meal, and Wine, (let the Pellets be no bigger then Peason) and cast these into standing waters, or very calme places, all the fish that taste of it will be presently stupified, and swim to the shore as if they were drunk, so that you may take them with your hands, many have tried this. *Mizald.*

How to catch Fish with ease.

Fishes are taken with Baits: Now the Baits must have four properties; they must smell well, for this will make them come from remote places, such things are Aniseeds, juyce of Panace, and Cummin is best of them all: they must taste well, that they may more desire it, and they may be thereby deceived; such are bloud, especially Hogs bloud; Chees, but chiefly made of Goats milk; Bread; principally of Wheat; Butterflyes, the best are golden coloured. The Bait must fume to the head, that it may make them drunk by its violent quality, as *Aqua vitæ*, Lees of Wine. Last of all, It must be stupefactive, to make them senseless: such are Marygold flowers, that are to be had new every Moneth: for this Herb whose flowers are yellow, cut in pieces, will make great fish astonished in one houres time. So is Lime, for though it correct water, yet it will kill fishes. So is the juyce of all the Tithymals, and both the *Nux vomicas*, called *Nux metelli*, or the sleepy Nut. But nothing is better than that fruit which is brought from the East, and is called *Cocculus Indicus*. It is a black berry, like unto a Bay berry, but smaller and rounder. Our composition to take fish is tried to be certain. Take a quarter of an ounce of Orientall berries, Cummin seed, and *Aqua vitæ*, of each a sixt part of an ounce, Chees one ounce, Wheat meal three ounces, make little Pellets, beating all together. *Card. de Subtilit.*

Of Nets.

The rubbish that remains when Myrobalans are pressed, Mans dung, white Bread, must be all beaten severally, and then mingled together, and put into a Net, use this and it will take effect. *Tarentinus.*

Another for Purse Nets.

A Bait that I found in writing, of those that live only by eating Fish. Take the shels and fish together that breed upon Rocks, and let these be your Bait. *The same.*

To catch all sort of Fish at any time.

Take Celtick Spike, four leaves, Cyperus one leaf, Parsley of *Macedonia*, as much as an *Ægyptian* Bean, Cummin as much as you can hold in three fingers, Dill seed a little. Pouder them and sift them, and put them into a Cane, and when you are minded, wash Earth Worms, and put them into a Vessel, and mingle with them of your former Bait what is sufficient, making the Lump up in your hands with the Earth Worms, and then put them into an old shooe, and carry this for to Bait fish with. *The same.*

To make Fishes come to one place in the Sea.

Take three shell Fish that breed upon the Rocks of the Sea; and pulling forth their substance, write these words in their shels, and you will wonder to see how all the fish will come together: The words are, *Jao, Sabaoth*, fish eaters use this device. *The same.*

Of the Secrets of Fish. Chap. 2.

To catch great Sea Fish, as Glauci, and Orphi, and like.

A Cocks stones must be beaten with torrefied Pine Kernels and mingled, you must take Cocks stones eight drams, Pine Kernels sixteen drams, they must be beaten like to Wheat meal, and little Baits made with them, fishes are allured with this. *Tarent.*

To catch Barbels and great Giltheads.

Take of the Fish Phlænus that breeds in fresh Rivers eight drams, torrefied whole Lentils eight drams, River shrimps four drams, Malabathrum one dram, beat all these and mingle them with the white of an Egg, make Pellets and use them. *The same.*

To catch Lampreys.

Take of the sheath Fish six drams, wild Rue seed eight drams, Calfs fat eight drams, Sesamum sixteen ounces, beat them, and make Pellets for your use. *The same.*

To catch the Polypus, and Cuttle-Fish.

Take Salt Armoniac sixteen drams, Goats Butter eight drams, beat them and make moist Baits, and wet seeds herewith, or linnen cloaths that have no welts upon them, and these fish will feed about it, and never go from it. But you must pull your Net suddenly, and you shall draw up Lobsters and Burrets and many more fish to be cast into your ship. *The same.*

How to catch shell-Crabs, and other shell-Fish.

Take Salt Armoniac six drams, Onyons one dram, Calfs fat six drams, make your Iron Hook in the fashion of a Bean, and annoint it with this mixture, and they will come presently to the Hook and catch themselves, when they have once smelt to it. *The same.*

To catch Mullets.

Take the Liver of a Tuney Fish four drams, Sea shrimps eight drams, Sesamum four drams, Beans broken eight drams, of the flesh of raw Tuneys two drams. Bruise these and mingle them with sodden sweet Wine, make Baits thereof to Bait fish with it. *The same.*

Another.

Take a Rams Pisle, put it into an earthen pot not yet baked, put this into another pot and stop it fast, that there be no vent for it, put this into a glass Furnace, that it may be baked, from morning untill night, and you shall find it grow soft like Chees: make Baits with it. *The same.*

Another of the same Author to catch Sea Mullets, Giltheads, Barbels.

Take the shell of the Cuttle-Fish, with green water Mints, which is Moss, mingle these with water, dry Barley meal, and Chees made with Cows milk, use this.

To catch Sea Mullets.

Take Leaves of Malabathrum, as much as one little Ball, Pepper ten grains, Nigella three grains, flowers of sweet Rush, the inward part of Garlick, of each a little; bruise and mingle them all, then wet the crums of white Bread in an hemina of Mareotick Wine, and make a Past therewith, being all well worked together, this is a good Bait. *The same.*

For Mullets and Codfish.

Take fine white Bread, Goats Chees, Quicklime, beat them, and mix them together, pouring on of Sea water, and make Baits therewith. *The same.*

To catch the Sea Pagri.

Take the decoction of Nigella, with Locusts and Earth Worms, bruise them, and

adding

adding fine wheat flower with water, make a mixture as thick as Honey, for your use. *The same.*

How Tuneys must be catcht, out of the same Author.

Burn Wallnuts to ashes, and bruise Marjoram with them, and with fine white Bread wet with water, and Goats milk Chees make your Baits.

To catch Fish called Cerri.

Beat Garlick, Bread, and Cows milk Chees together, with Goats milk Chees and fine wheat flower, make Pellets and cast them into the place. *The same.*

How to take a Ray-Fish.

Take the dung of a Swallow, and wet it, and make a Paste with meal of Barley.

Another.

Boyl Lettice seed, and with Butter and Barley meal, beat them into a body.

For Stock-fish.

Take green Moss from the Rocks, boyl that in Oyl, and make up your Baits. *The same.*

To catch Fish called Glauci.

Rost fair Tunyes and Aeosæ together, take out their bones, and adding Moss, and course Barley meal thereto, make lumps for Baits. *The same.*

To catch Fishes called Trachuri, and Melanuri.

Wet Asses dung in the juyce of Coriander, and with Barley meal make lumps for your use. *The same.*

To catch a Polypus, the same Author.

Bind about *Vocaris, Mormyri,* and *Arada,* let these serve for your Bait.

To catch the Cuttle-fish.

Grind the Lees of Wine without water, with Oyl, go to the place, and cast this into the Sea, where you perceive the Cuttle, hath cast forth her Ink, so will the Cuttle come where the Oyl appears, and there you may catch her. *The same.*

To catch Lobsters.

Bind a Mormyrus to some strong thing, and bruise ten puræ, and mingling therewith a little Moss, lay it upon the Rock, and so take them. *The same.*

To catch Ruffs, Out of the same Author.

Take a Goats Liver, and put Baits of it upon your Hooks. If you will catch many sorts of fish that the Sea affords, you may do it with a Bait of Goats or Asses Hoof.

To catch a River Fish called Grytes.

Take two pound of Barley bran, of whole Lentils a quarter of a Peck, mingle them and with pure fish pickle a sufficient quantity infuse them. Add thereto Sesama seed a quarter of a Peck, strew a little of this, and cast it about for the Fish; so soon as you have done this every small gryte will come to it, and though they be five furlongs off they will all resort thither: but great Fishes will flye from the sent of it; wherefore use it thus and you shall speed. *The same.*

To catch Sea-Hogs, Porpusses.

Take Sesamum four drams, Garlick heads two drams, salt Quails flesh two drams, Opopanax one dram, mingle these with the scrapings of old Colledg wals, make Caks thereof for Baits. *The same.*

To catch Eels.

Take eight drams of the Sea Scolopendra, River shrimps eight drams, Sesamum one dram, make Pellets for use. *The same.*

To make Eels alive again.

Eels that dye for want of water will live again, if whilst the body is whole, you bury it in Horse dung with Vinegar, and if you add some Vultures bloud to it, any Eel will revive again. *Corn. Agrippa.*

How to catch Crabs.

Crabs are catched with Rods slit at the ends, in which slits you must put some guts of Frogs, setting them in order, ten or twelve in rank, near to the Gulfs where the Crabs lye: then the fisher Man comes with his Net, taking up the Rods one by one, and puts the Net under, and when the Crab that is faſt cannot ſo ſoon get loſe, he fals into the Net. Thus the Fiſherman with great delight carryeth home a hundred or two very ſtrong and great Crabs, for the ſmall ones will not eaſily come ſo high for meat, but others put them from it. *Cardan.*

Another.

Take Frogs cut in the middle, put theſe into many Nets, put them where the Crabs uſe to come, and they will go into the Nets. *I had this of a Fiſherman.*

To make Frogs come together.

They ſay that where a Goats gall is buryed, there will Frogs reſort. *Agrip.*

Againſt the troubleſome croking of Frogs.

Frogs will not croke in the night (which noiſe is then very unpleaſing to moſt people) if you light a Candle and ſet it on the banks of lakes and Rivers where they be, or two, or more, as the place is great, and the Frogs many: *Aphricanus* ſaith, This is his Geoponicks, and I told it to a Preſident at *Paris* who complained of the filthy noiſe the Frogs made near him in the night, and he tried it, and found it true to his great content. *Mizaldus.*

BOOK VIII.

Of the Secrets of Aëreal Creatures or Birds.

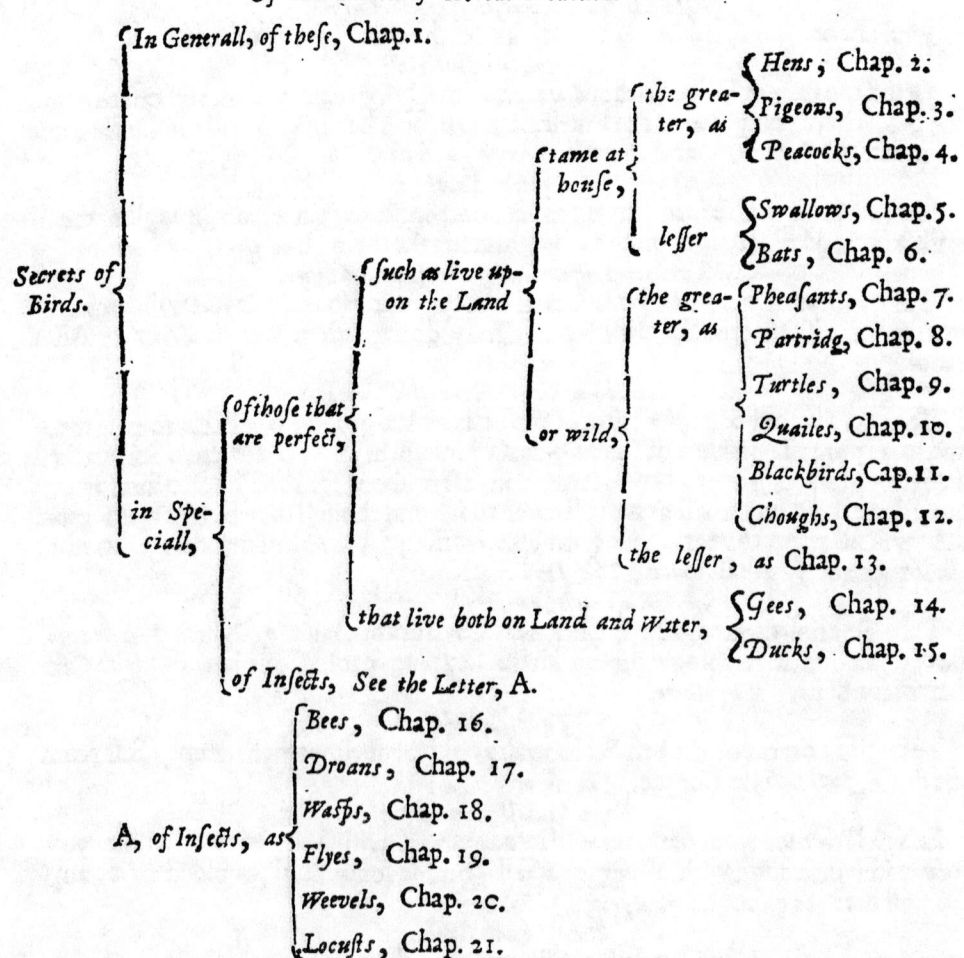

Secrets of Birds:
- In Generall, of theſe, Chap. 1.
- in Speciall,
  - of thoſe that are perfect,
    - ſuch as live upon the Land
      - tame at houſe,
        - the greater, as
          - Hens, Chap. 2.
          - Pigeons, Chap. 3.
          - Peacocks, Chap. 4.
        - leſſer
          - Swallows, Chap. 5.
          - Bats, Chap. 6.
      - or wild,
        - the greater, as
          - Pheaſants, Chap. 7.
          - Partridg, Chap. 8.
          - Turtles, Chap. 9.
          - Quailes, Chap. 10.
          - Blackbirds, Cap. 11.
          - Choughs, Chap. 12.
        - the leſſer, as Chap. 13.
    - that live both on Land and Water,
      - Gees, Chap. 14.
      - Ducks, Chap. 15.
  - of Inſects, See the Letter, A.

A, of Inſects, as:
- Bees, Chap. 16.
- Droans, Chap. 17.
- Waſps, Chap. 18.
- Flyes, Chap. 19.
- Weevels, Chap. 20.
- Locuſts, Chap. 21.

Of the Secrets of Birds and flying Creatures in Generall. Chap. 1.

To make Birds come together.

Misletoe of the Oake tied to Sylphium, and bound to any tree with the feather of a Swallow, will make all Birds come thither. *Alb.*

To catch Birds with your hand.

Put any Corn in Wine Lees, and juyce of Hemlock, and cast it to Birds, every Bird that tasts of it, will be drunk and lose its force. *The same.*

To breed up Birds to sing.

Birds are taught to sing finely, especially Linnets, and such as live upon Thistles. The foot must be tied with a thread, and the Bird must be fastned to a half circle of wood, the semicircle must be thrust into the frame of a looking glass, there must be another of greater compass below, that it may go up and down : the Bird playes with his own shadow, thinking he sees another in the glass; on the sides of the upper circle, there must be set two small pots, the one full with Millet or Panick seed, or Nut Kernels, the other with water, and so artificially made, that when one goes away, the other may come : you will wonder at the industry of this small Bird, which never had the like care before to live. *Cardan.*

How to catch Birds.

White Hellebour mingled with ordinary Birds meat, if Birds feed of it they dye, and are catched, and yet a man may safely eat them. But it is more certain, that if Millet or Panick be sod with white Orpiment, that Birds will dye with this presently, and then they are safe to be eaten, for the force of the Poyson is twice rebated.

To drive Birds from fruit.

Garlick hanged upon Trees, will make Birds that come to eat the fruit flye away far enough, as *Democritus* observes from the Husbandry of the Greeks.

To drive Birds from Seed and Corn.

Magicians suppose a hedg Toad shut up in a new Earthen Pot, and buried in the middle of a Corn field, will drive Birds away from the Corn : but they say you must dig it up again about the time that you Reap the Corn, and cast it out of the fields, least your Corn be smutty and bitter. *Pliny.*

How to catch Birds.

Nux vomica will stupyfie Birds if you mingle it with their meat. I remember I took Crows in my hand, when I had poudred that Nut, and mingled it with flesh. If small birds eat corn steeped in Wine Lees, and the juyce of Hemlock, or *Aqua vita*, or only in the Lees of the stronger Wine, or in the decoction of white Hellebour with an old Ox gall, this will astonish them. Those birds that flye in flocks to it, are catched in flocks: as Partridg, but Gees more then they, but chiefly Ducks. When you would make some tame of the wild kind, you must cut their wings, and you must make a Trench about the waters, and feed them there with plenty of pleasant food : for Ducks amongst other things, that is the best which we call *Sargum*. In the Night when the tame ones cry, the wild ones will come thither to the meat, (for all Creatures agree in four things) they all seek for meat, they all seek after their pleasure; they will all fight, and all are in fear, and here they understand one the other. Wherefore drawing your Nets (which are called coverings) for they are fastned to posts, you shall sometimes catch a thousand Ducks at once. This may seem strange, yet it is true, and there is no better way of Fowling; you must chuse tame Ducks that are most like the wild Ducks in their colour. *Cardan.*

How to teach Birds to speak.

Birds are taught to speak in dark places, by candle light, by hunger and Wine, and you must chuse such birds as are young, and have the broadest tongues; of Parrets chose those that have five claws upon a foot, for these are more apt to speak. Moreover hunger is the principall means to force them to it, as *Persius* writes.

Who taught Parrots for to give the day?
And Pies to speak the words that we do say;

*The Master of all such Arts and Wit,
Hunger before all things will do it.*

Dark places make Birds more carefull, and to recollect their senses and memory, and so men will remember better in the dark, and muse and deliberate. But a Candle is set, because if it be perfectly dark, birds will sleep, and are afraid that they rather lose their sense than increase it. Wherefore a small Candle is necessary. *The same.*

For Lice of Birds.

If Birds be lowsy, annoint them with Linseed Oyl, and that will cure them. *The same.*

To understand Birds Notes.

If you would understand Birds Notes, take two Companions with you on the fift of the Calends of *November*; and go into some Wood with Dogs, as if you went to hunt, and the first Beast you find, carry home with you, and make it ready with a Foxes heart, and you shall presently understand the Notes of Birds or Beasts: and if you would have another to understand them also, do but kiss him, and he shall understand them also. *Albert.*

To make Birds of prey change their Feathers.

If you would have them change their Quils and Feathers, give them Mice to eat with pouder of small Fishes, or else Hens flesh, that were fed with Serpents. *Cardan.*

Of the Secrets of flying Creatures in speciall. Chap. 2.

Of the Secrets of Hens.

Cram Hens thus, shut up Hens that are the first that will Lay, make gobbets with water and Barley meal, dip them in water, and then thrust them down their throats, consider by their crops when they have enough; cram them twice a day, and let them drink at noon, and let them not drink afterwards in one hour. *Cato.*

To fat Hens.

In your Kitchin make you a Pen that hath many places distinct one from another, with holes where the Hens may put forth their heads to eat their meat; in these Pens shut up Pullets or young Hens severally by themselves, and give them meat every hour, a little at a time, but no water to drink, let their meat be Wheat boyled moderately in water. The Pens must have holes underneath for their dung to fall forth, which every day must be clean taken away. Moreover Hens must not be cooped up above three Weeks, for they would dye with too much fat. *Out of a* Hollander.

Another.

Hens will fat best and be most corpulent fed in a dark house and hot, having their first Feathers pulled out, and by giving them meat of Barley meal mingled and made up with water. Others use Barley and Darnel meal together, or Barly and raw Linseed meal, some again mingle dry Barly flower, and others pour Wine to it. Some give them fine white Bread soked. Most fat them with Millet seed. *Florent.*

That Hens may not eat their eggs.

Pour forth the white of the Egge, and pour to the yelk of it liquid Gyp, that it may grow as hard as the shell. For Hens being greedy will attempt to eat it, and when they find nothing there to eat, they will soon forbear to spoil their Eggs. *Florent.*

To make Hens lay great Eggs.

If you desire that your Hens shall Lay great Eggs, mingle red earth dissolved with their meat, and they will Lay bigger Eggs. Also they will Lay great Eggs, if you beat a burnt Tileshard and mingle it with Wine and Bran, and making Paste of it, cast it to your Hens. *Leont.*

How to catch Hens and they shall not Cackle.

There are some that go for *Gypsies* that will catch Hens, Ducks, Geese, Conies, with a hook, and pull them presently to them: for they cannot make a noise, nor hardly move to betray the Thief, when they pull them by degrees suddenly to them. *Cardanus.*

Book VIII.   *Secrets of Poultry.*   141

To defend Hens from Fleas.

In the Hen-Roosts when Hens have Hatched, you must take the straw away that was under them, and lay on fresh straw that fleas and such Vermine may not breed, which will not suffer the Hen to rest. *Varro.*

To keep Hens safe from Foxes.

Some say that a Fox boyled and cut into pieces, and given to Hens for meat, will defend the Hens from all Foxes for two Moneths: for the same Remedy holds for Ducks and Geese. This was tried in the Valley of *Angus* called *Glemores*, in *Scotland*, where there are great store of Foxes. *Cardan.*

That Hens may not have the squach.

Wet Origanum, and give the water to drink, or else wash it with Urine, or smeer their Nostrils with Garlick, or else put Garlick into water, and let the Hens drink of that. *Leontius.*

That Hens may not cast their Eggs before their time.

Hens will keep their Eggs to their full time, if you rost the white of an Egge, and rost as much Raysins and pound these together, and give that to the Hen before any other meat. *Pamphil.*

To make Hens giddy.

Mingle Honey and Benjoin together, and steep Wheat in that and cast it to the Hens. *Berythius.*

That a Cat shall not hurt a Hen.

A Cat will never come near a Hen, if you hang under the Hens Wing wild Rue; nor will a Fox or any other Creature hurt them; and it will do it much more if you mingle the gall of a Cat or a Fox with their meat. *Afriean.* and *Democrit.*

For the Diseases of Hens eyes.

You shall cure a Hens eyes with Womans Milk, or with the juyce of Purslane, annointing their eyes on the outside. Or else annoint them with Ammoniacum and Cummin, and Honey mingled in equall parts together, but bring your Hens into shady places. *Paxamus.*

For the squirt in Hens.

You shall cure the scowring of Hens if you mingle a measure of fine Barley meal with as much Wax, and make it up with Wine into gobbets, and give the Hens this before other meat, or if you give them the decoction of Quinces to drink; also rosted Quinces are good. *The same.*

For lice in Hens, the same Author.

You shall free Hens from the lowsy disease, with rosted Cummin, and Stavesacre beaten, of each a like quantity, annoint the Hens with these mingled with Wine: also you may wash them with the decoction of wild Lupins.

For the pose of Hens.

Filthy water to drink makes Hens have the pose or squach in their heads, wherefore give them Porus. You shall cure this snottynefs of their Nose with Garlick cut into pieces, and cast into scalding hot Oyl, and when the Oyl is cold, wash their mouths with this. If they eat the Garlick also, they will be the better cured. Stavesacre is good alone, and also mingled with Vetches, and given to Hens. So is Sea Onyon cleansed and steeped in water, and then cast to Hens with dry Barley meal. If this pose trouble them more, Lance the parts under the joynts of their Legs with a Knife, and press out the parts that are about their eyes, and rub the small Ulcers with Salt. Some make a smoke with Origanum, Hysop, and Thyme, and they hold the Hens head over the smoke, and they rub her beake with Garlick. Other boyl Garlick in Mans Urine, and rub the Hens bill hard with it, taking care not to touch her eyes. *Paxamus.*

That a Cock shall not tread a Hen.

If you annoint the fundament of the Cock with Oyl, the Cock will not, nor can he tread the Hen. *The same.*

That a Cocks shall not Crow.

If you would not have a Cock to crow, annoint his head and forehead with Oyl. *The same.*

To hatch Eggs without a Hen.

Fill two Pillows with Hens dung beaten very small, then put in Hens Feathers, and sow them both together, that they may be thick and soft; place the Eggs with the smaller end upward upon one Pillow, then place the other upon it in a hot place; move them not for two daies, after this untill the twenty daies turn the Eggs constantly, so that they may hatch alike; then on the set day, which is about the twenty first day, take the Chickens that are apip out of the Eggs by degrees. This is no wonder, for *Aristotle* shews that the Syracusians hatched them under ground, and in *Ægypt* they are hatched almost with no help at all. We in our Age have found it true, that with a gentle fire and dung Chickens may be hatched, yet of many Eggs but a very few Chickens. They put fire under, that the dung may not cool. *Cardan. ex Democrito.*

Another.

Bury the Eggs in warm dung, and every six daies put new dung to them, that it may not grow cold, but may foster them in a set time, retaining the same heat that the Hen useth to sit upon Eggs, hath; you must alwaies turn them untill the Chickens you desire be hatched, you may do it in a warm Oven. *The same.*

To know whether the Eggs will bring Cocks or Hen Chickens.

If any one would know whether an Egg will bring a Cock or a Hen, he shall know it thus. *Aristotle* saith it, and *Avicenna* proveth it, That of a round short Egg will come a Cock Chicken, but of a long sharp Egg a Hen: and it stands with reason. For the perfection in Cock Eggs derives it self equally to all parts, and contains the ends of it, but in a long Egg, the matter goeth farther from the Center, wherein there lyeth vitall heat.

That the Chickens may be very comely.

If you cause a Male ring Dove to tread a Hen, or else a Partridg or Pheasant, the Chicken will be very pleasant to behold. Peacocks, Pheasants, Partridges, and such like, will have white Chicken, if you cover and hang about their Hen houses or places where you keep them, and where they feed, couple, sit, and hatch their Eggs, with white clothes. I am indebted for this Secret to one that bred up Fowles for a Prince. Many have described it, but I know not whether they ever made triall of it. *Miz.*

That a Chicken may be hatcht with four feet, and four wings.

How a Chicken may come forth with four feet and wings: *Aristotle* saith, you must chuse those Eggs that you find to have two Yelks, with a thick skin running between them, but the whites are kept back, which the more fruitfull Hens are wont to Lay. You shall know these by their largness, and you may discerne it if you hold them against the Sun; for it is produced of abundance of matter, and by the treading of many Cocks mingled, that will serve for two Chickens. When the Hen begins to cluck, let her sit upon these Eggs, and the time appointed by nature, for hatching being over, the Chickens will have four legs and four wings, your care must be to see them brought up well. But if they should be parted by the thick membrane, then would there be two different Chickens hatcht, and no part would be superfluous. So may a Serpent be bread with two heads, and all other Creatures that come of Eggs: If such a thing should happen, it were no small wonder: Ofttimes Monsters are bred in fruitfull Creatures that bring many young ones, and but seldome in more barren and imperfect Creatures, but in others the facility of generation prevails: and thence it is that the baser Creatures produce more monstrous Births than the more Noble do. *The same.*

A Creature that will infect both by seeing and touching.

I deny not but a living Creature may be generated that shall poyson one by seeing and touching, as if it were a Basilick; but take heed you that try to produce this Creature, that you do not endanger your self, which I think may easily come to pass, if so soon as the Creature is brought forth, it should infect the Ayr round about it. Infuse fruitfull Eggs where you have a liquid moysture of Arsenick, or Serpents poyson, and other deadly things, and let the Eggs lye therein for some daies: it will work the stronger inwardly if you place them right: set them under Hens that cluck, but shake them

Book VIII.   *Secrets of tame Foul.*   143

them not in your hands, least you destroy what is the mischief sought for. There is no greater cause to be found to produce divers Monsters than by Eggs: and ofttimes Hens do hatch these, and also they come of themselves. Wherefore *Leontius* commanded to bring a flat plate of Iron, Nails heads, and Bay boughs where Hens sit, that they might not bring forth prodigious and monstrous Births. We may commodiously use dung, for it is most like to naturall heat, and it hath a great putrefying force in it, which is the parent of Monsters: and as many kinds come forth by the putrefaction of living Creatures, as there are things that do putrefie: If a man understand this well, and considers of it, he may hence draw no small Principles to find out Secrets. *The same.*

That Capons may change their qualities diversly, and how to make them fat.

Men say that Cocks and Capons if they feed on Garlick boyled, they will be more fierce to fight. Also Capons with their Feathers pulled off their bellies, and rubbed with a Nettle, will sit upon Eggs and foster Chickens: also sowe up their eyes, and they will grow wonderfull fat. *Card.*

That a Chicken having its throat cut shall not bleed.

Some report that the Ashes of a Toad hanged about a Chickens neck, will keep her from bleeding though her throat be cut. *The same.*

To make a Chicken dance at Table.

If you will have a Pullet dance in the dish; Take Quicksilver, and pouder of Calamint, and put that into a Glass Viol close stopped, put that again into the hot Pullets belly. When the Quicksilver groweth hot, it will stir up and down, and make the Pullet dance. *Albert. Mag.*

To keep Eggs.

You shall keep Eggs all Winter in Chaff, in Summer in Bran. Others wash the Eggs and cover them with thin Salt; some steep them three or four hours in warm pickle, and then they take them forth and cover them with Chaff or Bran. *Leontius.*

To know whether Eggs be full or empty.

You shall know whether an Egg be full or empty by putting it into the water, the hollow will swim, the full will sink. *The same.*

To hatch Eggs without a Hen.

If you want a Hen, you may hatch your Eggs without a Hen as *Democritus* shews. Pouder Hens or Pigeons dung, and sift it fine, and cover your Eggs all over with this; but not alone, least they break one against another, but lay Hens Feathers under and about them, and make nests: let the copped end of the Egg turn upwards, and every twenty four hours by courses, renew it and turn your eyes about, that they may heat equally: so Hens that are hatching use to do: keep them in a warm and hot place: when twenty daies are past, and the Chickens are compleat, and the Chickens beak begins to break the Egg; hearken whether they Peep or not: (for ofttimes the shels are so thick, that the Chicken cannot break through;) when the Eggs are A-pip, take off the shels, and bring a Hen; or if you will you may do it otherwise. Bury the Eggs in Warm dung, and in six daies put fresh dung under them, that it may not grow cold, but may hatch the Eggs at the set time; and be like the heat of the Hen; alwaies turning the Eggs untill the Chickens be hatcht. *The same.*

To make Eggs soft that you may put them into Glass Viols.

Infuse Eggs so long in sharp Vinegar untill their shels grow soft, then thrust them into a narrow mouthed Glass, and pour cold water to them, and they will grow as hard as they were before; for Vinegar softens the Egg-shels, and water hardeneth them. *Cardan.*

To write in Eggs.

Bruise Gals and Allum with Vinegar, untill it be as thick as Ink, and with this write what you please upon an Egg, and when the writing is dried in the Sun; put the Egg into Salt pickle, and when it is dried, boyl it, and take away the shell; and you shall find the writing within the Egg. But if you cover the Egg with Wax and write upon it with a point of any sharp Iron, making your Letters as deep as the shell; and then steep the Egg in Vinegar all night; and the next day take off the Wax, you shall

shall see the Letters made by the Vinegar in the Egg very transparent. *African.*

To make an Egg bigger then a Mans head.

You shall separate ten or more Yelks and Whites of Eggs, and mingle the Yelks together, and put them into a Bladder, and bind them round like an Egg, put this into a Pot full of water, and when you see it bubble, or when the Egg is grown hard take it out, and put in the Whites fitting it, as it ought to be, that the Yelks may be in the middle, then boyl it again. If you would have it covered with a shell, make your shell thus. Grind white Egg shels washt clean, to very fine pouder, steep this in strong Vinegar untill it grow soft, or in distilled Vinegar; for if an Egg be left long in Vinegar, the shell will dissolve, and grows exceeding tender, that it may easily be thrust into a narrow mouth'd Glass, as I said; when it is thrust in, fair water put to it, will make it hard as it was before, that you will wonder at it. When the shels are dissolved like to an oyntment, with a Pencill lay it on upon your Artificiall Egg, and let it grow hard in cold water, thus shall you make a true and naturall Egg. *The same.*

To make an Egg flye up into the Ayre.

In *May* fill an Egg shell with *May* dew, and set it in the hot Sun at noon day, and the Sun will draw it up: and if sometimes it will hardly ascend, it will be raised by help of a staff or Board to run up by. *The same*

Of the Secrets of Pigeons. Chap. 3.

That Pigeons may not flye away but stay with their young ones.

Annoint the Doves Windows and corners of the Pigeon house with Oyl of Balsam, and they will stay at home. Pigeons will not flye away if you throw unto them Cummin seed, and Lentils soked in Water and Honey. And if you set them Honey and Water to drink, or if you give them Lentils boyled in sweet Wine to eat, this will make them to love their young ones. *Didym.*

A Charme to keep Pigeons in the Dove Coat.

This love charm is prepared for Pigeons at home, Tiles poudred and sifted, and Costus, with sweet pleasant Wine mingled, must be given to Pigeons that rove abroad for to feed. Some mingle Barley meal boyled with dry Figs, and putting some Honey thereto, they set that before them. Some again give them Cummin seed when they would be gone. Pigeons will stay if you set a Bats head upon the top of the Pigeon house; or if you, according to the season of the year, lay the boughs and flowers of the wild Vine within the house. *The same.*

A Bait to allure Pigeons that they shall bring other Pigeons with them to the Dove house.

Take the oldest Potters clay burnt in a Bakers Oven untill it be red, or old Lome out of the Furnace one ounce, female Vervin four drams, Wheat steeped in *Aqua vitæ* and bruised four drams, Cardopata six drams, Camphir half a dram, Cummin three drams, distilled Wine, one ounce and half, Honey what is sufficient to make Pellets as big as Peason, put these amongst the Pigeons meat. Some add Urine and Mans bloud; Then take Vervin as much as you will, and hang it in the Dovecoat. *David Vezelius an Apothecary of Colmaria.*

To make Pigeons increase.

If you hang a mans Skull in the Pigeon house, the Pigeons will increase there, and live quietly. The same thing is performed by a Womans milk, that hath nursed a Girl two years, if you hang that milk in a Glass in the Pigeons house. *Albert.*

To allure Pigeons to a Dove house.

Pigeons are invited by this paste; Take Maizum, Marchpane, or Sorgum four pound, Cummin six pound, Honey ten pound, Costus one pound, Agnus castus seed five pound; Boyl all these in water, untill the water be consumed, then add pleasant Wine what is sufficient, with fifteen pound of old Cement or Mortar, and make a heap in the middle of the Dove coat. When other Pigeons smell this sent, they will flye thither, and this they will smell when they are mingled with the Pigeons of that place: and when they are once come thither, they will never forsake that place.

That Pigeons may stay and bring other strang Pigeons along with them.

If you annoint Pigeons with an Unguent, they will bring other strange Pigeons home with them. But if you cast Cummin seed to them when they would flye abroad for meat, they will stay within, and bring others home also, invited by the perfume of the Unguent. But if you take Agnus castus seed and steep it three daies in old Wine, and then sprinkle Tares with that Wine, and cast them to the Pigeons, and then let them presently flye abroad, strange Pigeons smelling their sweet breath will come all home with them. But they will come in sooner if you perfume the Dove house with Sage and Frankinsence. *Didym.*

That Cats may not disquiet Pigeons.

Hang branches of Rue, and lay them in the Windows, and passages of the Pigeon house, for Rue hath a naturall virtue against Beasts. *The same.*

That an Adder may not come to the Dove coat.

Adders will never trouble a Pigeon house, if you write at the four corners of the house, *Adam*. If the house have any Windows, write the same word in them also. Serpents will be driven away also with the fume made with Dog Fennel. *Democrit.*

That Cats may not hurt Pigeons.

Nor Cats, nor any other Creatures will do the Pigeons any hurt, when there are no houses near, where they may lye in wait for them. *Quintiliorum.*

That creeping things may not creep into a Pigeon house.

It is not possible for creeping things to crawl up into Pigeon houses, when they are carefully plaster'd, and kept very smooth with pargetting. *Quintil.*

To preserve Pigeons against hurtfull Creatures.

The head of a Wolf is supposed, whether by the sent or sight of it, hanged in a Dove coat, to drive away Weesils and Firrets. *Card. & Agrip.*

To fat a young ring-Dove.

As soon as you have taken a young stock Dove, first give him parched Beans, boyled, and out of your mouth blow water into his mouth, do this for seaven daies: After this, make hulled Beans clean and Barley meal, let there be a third part of Beans set to soke with the Barley meal, do this handsomely and boyl them well: having done this, work them well in your hands, annointing your hands with Oyl. First work a little of it, then more, touch it with Oyl, and knead it, untill you can make Gobbets; give this meat with water moderately. *Cato.*

Of the Secrets of Peacocks. Chap. 4.

That Peacocks and other Pullets may be bred white.

Peacocks and other Birds will be white, if their places where they are shut up be plaister'd white, or covered with white coverings or Hangings of Linnen, and they be hindred by small Lattices, that they may not get forth of those places. The flowers must be kept clean that they see nothing but white. When they couple, Lay Eggs, Hatch their Yong, so will their Broods be all white; do so with other Creatures. *The same.* But when Peacocks are Hatched first, you must give them no meat for two daies. On the third day give them Barley meal worked up with Wine, and well beaten together: Spelt beaten and steeped in clean water, these things they must eat. *Didymus.*

Of the Secrets of Swallows. Chap. 5.

To have young Swallows white.

If when the Swallow sits you annoint her Eggs with Oyl, in fifteen daies the young ones will be white, but in time they will change colour and grow black as other Swallows are. *Cardanus.*

Of the Secrets of Reremice. Chap. 6.

For Flittermice.

In common entrances hang up the leaves of the Plane tree, and Bats will never come there. A smoke of Ivy will kill them. *African.*

Of the Secrets of Pheasants. Chap. 7.

To fat Pheasants.

Shut them up, and give them meat the first day, and the next day Honey and water, or sweet strong Wine must be set before them, this is the way to fat them. Their meat must be raw Barley meal worked up with water, this must be set alone, and by degrees a little. Then set them beaten hulled Beans, Barly, Water, whole Millet seed, Linseed boyld and dry mingled with Barly meal. You may add Oyl to these, and make Gobbets, and give them their fill of these to eat. Some cast Fenegrick to them for five or six daies to purge Choler from these Birds that desire it. They will be fat at longest in sixty daies. These Birds are cured with the same remedies we prescribed for tame Hens. *Varro.*

Of the Secrets of Partridges. Chap. 8.

To catch Partridges.

Partridges are most hot by nature, and most eager for copulation; and hence the Males grow jealous, and fight one with another. Whensoever therefore two cock Partridges are found where hen Partridges are, the cocks will fight immediately, nor will they ever leave off fighting untill one yields and is conquered. He that is Master, all the Hens follow him ever after, and he grows so proud, that he will tread the conquer'd cock as if he were a Hen; and from that time he attends upon the conquerour as the hens do, and is ranged amongst them. You shall easily catch Partridges, if you cast forth Wheat meal kneaded up with Wine. *Berytius.*

Of the Secrets of Turtles. Chap. 9.

To fat Turtles.

Millet seed and Panick, will fat Turtles, and by drinking plentifully. They love also Wheat and clean water. *Didym.*

Of the Secrets of Quails. Chap. 10.

To fat Quails

Quailes will be fatted with Millet seed, Wheat, Darnel and fair water. But because Quails feeding on black Hellebour cannot be so safely eaten, because eating of them will cause convulsions and Vertigos, therefore it is best to boyl Millet seed with them. But if any man by eating of them be overtaken with these diseases, let him drink the decoction of Millet seed: Myrtill berries have the same virtue. These also are excellent where any one hath eaten poysonous Mushrooms. But Millet seed hath also another naturall force; for he that eats Millet bread cannot after that be hurt by any poyson. *The same.*

Of the Secrets of Black-birds. Chap. 11.

How to fat Black-birds and Thrushes.

Black-birds must be fed in a hot house, in a place where Partridges use to be kept, and Partridg-Feathers set there, sticking upon the wals and corners of the house Bay boughs with their Berries. But the meat they eat, must be cast to them upon a clean pavement; that is dry Figs steeped in water and pressed again, and bruised, and mingled with Wheat or Barley meal. Also Myrtle berries and fruit of the Mastick and Ivy tree must be given to them, and also of the Bay tree and Olive tree, and such like things. But Millet and Panick and fair water will fat them more. *The same.*

Of the Secrets of Choughs. Chap. 12.

To drive away Choughs.

You shall fright away Choughs if you catch one and hang him up: for the rest that see him will flye away thinking some snare to be set in that place. You shall keep Jayes and all other Birds from coming, if you cast forth Black Hellebour infused together with Barly. You shall do well to fright Choughs and Jays away from your fields by some noise before they settle down there. The cracking of a Rattle in severall places, Clappers and Drums will serve to drive such Birds away. *Leont.*

How to catch Hawks.

Those that keep Pigeons are wont to kill Hawks by sticking two twigs into the ground smeered with Birdlime, and laid across, there they bind some Creature between these sticks that Hawks will prey upon, and so they are catched, being bedawbed with Birdlime. *Varro.*

Of the Secrets of small Birds. Chap. 13.

How small Birds are fatted.

Small Birds delight in Millet and Panick seed, and this is the meat and medicament of Nightingales and Blackheads, called in *Italian*, *Paston*. Take Chiche Peason the huls taken off, and not too finely poudred two pounds, Butter five ounces, Honey three ounces, Almonds six ounces, Saffron half a quarter of an ounce; Some make this up with the yelks of Eggs. If they be sick, you must cut the small white Wheal that lyeth upon her tail; if it swell, and the filthy blood runs forth, they will fall to their meat. They must be kept in a place where they have freedome enough, and hot: I have tried this often, for heat is very friendly to all small living Creatures that have blood, and chiefly for Birds. *Card.*

Of the Secrets of Geese. Chap. 14.

How to fat Geese.

Geese will fat themselves in hot houses, with two parts of dried Barley meal, and four parts of Bran made substantiall with hot water, and set to them that they may eat as much as they please. They eat thrice a day, and about midnight, they drink very much. But when they are grown great, cut dry Figs in pieces, and steep them in water, and let them drink of that water for twenty daies; Thus men feed them to make them have a great Liver, and that the Gees may be fat. They shut them up, and give them steeped Wheat or Barley the same way. Wheat soon makes them fat, and Barly makes their flesh white. Feed them with the foresaid things, either severally, or with both for twenty five daies, twice aday casting gobbets to them, made of that, so that for the first five daies a Goose may have seaven great pieces every day, and after that by degrees, increase the number of the gobbets for twenty five daies, that the number of the daies may be thirty in the whole. When these daies are ended boyle Mallows, and in that decoction being yet hot, steep leaven and give the Geese, do the same thing four daies together. Also the same daies give them water and Honey, changing it thrice every day, and not using the same again, do this continually untill sixty daies be over, and use dry Figs bruised with the said leaven to feed them with, and thus after sixty daies you may kill your Geese, that will be white and they and their Liver tender and white. The Liver must be taken forth and put into a large Vessel into hot water, which must be twice changed. But the bodies of Geese and their Livers are better than those of Ganders. Your Geese must not be of but one year old, but between two and four years old. Moreover as soon as the Goslings come forth of the Eggs, you must cast to them dry Barly meal, and Wheat made wet, for them to eat, and green Cresses. *Quintil.*

Another.

Cram a Goose as you do a Capon, but that you must first give him something to drink, and that twice a day, and meat as often. *Cato.*

Some chuse Goslings about six weeks old to fat, they shut them up in a Coop, and there

there they set for them fine dry Barly meal, and Wheat flower wet for to feed on themselves as long as they list. Then they give them water enough to drink in proportion to their meat. Thus in about two moneths they will grow fat. Men are wont to cleanse their Rooms as often as they dung in it, because these Creatures love a clean place, but they will never leave any place clean. *Varro.*

To rost a Goose alive.

A Goose, or Duck, or some lively Creature, (but the Goose is best) must be pulled all clean off her Feathers, only the head and neck must be spared. Then make a fire round about her, not too close to her, that the smoke do not choke her, and that the fire may not burn her too soon: nor too far off, that she may not escape free: within the circle of the fire let there be set small cups and pots full of water, wherein Salt and Honey are mingled, and let there be set also Chargers full of sodden Apples, cut into small pieces in the dish. The Goose must be all Larded and basted over, to make her the more fit to be eaten, and may rost the better, put then fire about her, do not make too much haste, when as you see her begin to Rost; for by walking about, and flying here and there being cooped in by the fire that stops her way out, the unwearied Goose is kept in by drinking of the water, which cools her heart and all her body, and the Apples make her dung, cleanse and empty her. When she grows scalding hot, her inward parts rost also, then wet with a Sponge her head and heart continually; and when you see her giddy with running, and begin to stumble, her heart wants moisture: she is Rosted, take her up, and set her upon the Table to your Guests, and as you cut her up she will cry continually, that she will be almost all eaten before she be dead *The same.*

Of the Secrets of Ducks. Chap. 15.

To fat Ducks.

Ducks will be fat with great store of meat, as most kind of Birds will, with Wheat, Millet seed, or Barley. But some desiring to have their Ducks more tame, search out the wild Ducks Eggs about Lakes and Ponds, and set them under Hens, and when they are hatched, they bring them up tame. *Didymus.*

To catch Ducks with your hands, an easie way.

If a man note the place where Ducks use to drink, and pouring forth the water, pour in strong Muskadell; when they drink that they will be drunk and fall down, and so you may catch them. Wine Lees will do the same. *The same Author.*

Of the Secrets of Bees. Chap. 16.

Of Bees, and the remedies of their Diseases.

The place where Bees must be set must be turned toward the Winter or Spring-time Sun-rising, that they may be hot Winter and and Summer, and the fresh Ayr that comes in may refresh them. The best water near Bee hives is that which runs through stones and Pibbles, and is very clean and not muddy at all. This makes the Bees healthfull, and to provide good Honey. But you must lay in great stones and pieces of wood above the water, that the Bees may stand upon them to drink with ease. If there be no running water there, you must draw it forth of a Well, or from some Fountain, and bring it along with Pipes. But these must be near to the Bees, least they fall sick with carrying water. They most delight to feed upon Thyme, and so they will make very much Honey, and breed young Bees. Also Sage, Savory, and Cytisus, are most pleasant meats for Bees; and the fresh swarms will light most upon the shrub Cytisus, and they take less pains for it. But their Hives they live in must be excellent good, made of Oake or Fig tree, Pine or Beech tree, thin Boards a cubit in breadth, and two cubits long. They must be smeered on the outside with Ox dung and Lime; for they will be longer before they will be rotten. They must have holes made slant waies, that the winds blowing in gently, may dry up Spiders Webs and other corruptions, and may cool them. This Creature delights exceedingly in rest, and doth not well like that Men should come to the Hive. Wherefore he that keeps Bees must about them build up a Wall of hollow stones; that the Bees may

may fly in there into holes, and so escape birds that lye in wait for them, and be preserved from Dew. They love their wonted places to feed in, and if they change their Habitations, they are not willing to fly abroad for meat, wherefore it is best to keep them in the same Countrey. If they feed on Tithymal, and taste the juyce of it, they fall into a scowring, and therefore if any grow thereabouts, it must be pulled up by the roots, and the bees must be cured with the shell of a Pomegranate pouned, sifted, and mingled with their Honey, and sharp Wine. You shall cure their Lice with the boughs of an Apple tree, and of the wild Fig tree burnt to make a smoke: but their dark sight must be cured with the fume of Origanum. *Florent.*

The way to get Bees.

When Bees are about to swarm, (which is wont to be when there are many young ones, and the old bees will send them forth to live of themselves : as the *Sabins* often did when their Children became very many,) There are two signs that alwaies use to appear before. One is, that some daies before, especially in the evening, many bees will hang about the hole of the Hive, like Grapes, hanging in heaps one upon another. The other is, That when they are now about to flye forth or have attempted it, they make a vehement noise, as Souldiers do when they are about to March; Those that come forth first, flye in sight, waiting for the rest that are to follow and are not yet ready. When the bee-keeper observes them do this, he casts some dust amongst them, and tinkling with a Kettle, he astonisheth them, and makes them stay. Not far from thence he rubs a bough with balme or Erithace, or some things the bees love : when they settle, he brings a Hive rubbed within with almost the same delights for bees, and setting it near to them, he makes a little smoke round about them, and so forceth them to enter into their new Colony, being once gon in, they stay there, and are so well pleased with it, that should you set the Hive next to them, they last come forth of, they will choose to remain in their new habitation. *M. Varro.*

How Bees may be carried to other places.

If you sell your Bees, or for any other cause have occasion to carry them to some other place, you must do it gently in the night, binding up your Hives in skins, to be at the place you go to, before day. For thus you shall neither disturb these Creatures, nor spoil their Combs. *Florent.*

That Bees may not flye away.

Bees will not flye away if you smeer the holes of their Hives with the dung of a Calf newly Calfed. When the swarm is settled, and dwels in the Hive, take the King or Queen (call him which you please,) gently by the Wings, and crop off the ends of his Wings, for whilst the King stays within, the bees will never depart. Bees will not flye away, if you bruise the leaves of the wild and Garden Olive tree together, and about the evening annoint their Hives with the juyce, or else with water and Honey, both the Wals and the Hives. When the bees are young, you must set them meat in Basons, Honey, Wine, wherein is Thyme and Savory, full of flowers, that they may not be suffocated. Others bruise Raysins, and mingle a little Thyme to it, and make Lumps, and with these they feed the Swarms very well, when they stay at home, and are hungry by reason of heat in Summer or cold in Winter; but when ten daies of the Spring time are past, you shall drive them forth to seek their meat with the smoke of dried Ox dung; and you shall cleanse and purge their Hives, turning them up and down : for the smell of their filth makes them sluggish, and Spiders Webs hinder them. If there be many Combs in the Hives, you must take forth the worst, least the bees grow sick for want of room. But you must not take above two combs from one Hive, for that would make them lean and weak. *Didym.*

What time is best to take the fruits of your Bees.

The best time to take the Honey and Combs is, when the Pleiades rise, that is according to the *Roman* account about the beginning of *May.* The second time to take them, is at the beginning of Autumn. The third time is, when the Pleiades set, that is about *October;* But there is no set daies for this, but as the Combs are in perfection. For if you take the Honey forth before the Combs be compleated, the bees will

X

not

not endure it, and they leave working for thirst. The same thing they do also if you be too covetous and take all they laboured for, away from them, and leave the Hives quite empty. For you must leave them a tenth part, both in Summer and Winter: but in Winter you must take from them but one third part, and leave them two thirds to live on. So they will have plenty to subsist on, and they will not grow careless for want. But you must drive them forth with the smoke of Ox dung, or else with the fume of the male wilde Mallows, and he that takes the Honey must smeer himself with the juyce of them, to prevent the Bees stinging him. Balme also rubbed on is good, and so is the flower of the Mastick tree. *The same.*

That he that takes the Honey may not be stung by the Bees.

Torrefie Fenegric meal, and pour upon it the juyce of wild Mallows with Oyl, and make all as thick as Honey; annoint your face, and all the naked parts of your body very well with it, then sup your mouth full of it, and spirt it three or four times into the Hive. Also set on fire dried Cow dung in a pot, and let the smoke of it enter into the small dore of the Hive about half an hour, then take away the pot, and hold it higher on the outside, that the smoke may flye about the Hive, and so you have done your work for that busines; Likewise you shall root out the nests and cells of the Droanes, if you mingle Barley meal with your Ox dung. *Paxamus.*

To know whether Honey be sophisticated.

You shall know whether Honey be mingled by casting it into the fire, for that which is falsified will not burn clear. *Diophanes.*

Of the Secrets of Drones. Chap. 17.

To destroy Drones.

If you will take away the Drones, when the evening begins, besprinkle the inside of the coverings of Vessels with water, and about day break, open the Vessels, and you shall find the Drones cleaving to the drops of water. For they being alwaies filled with Honey are thirsty, and having an insatiable desire after water, they will not depart from the moysture. And therefore it were easy to destroy them all, that not one should escape. They are great, lazy, and without a sting. *Democrit.*

Of the Secrets of Wasps. Chap. 18.

That Wasps may not sting you.

Annoint your self with the juyce of wild Mallows against the stinging of Wasps. *Paxamus.*

Another.

If a man annoint himself with Oyl and the juyce of wild Mallows, or have the Plant it self in his hand, the Wasps will not touch him; and if he be newly stung that the sting is left behind, the juyce or Oyl only will help it. *Mizald.*

Of the Secrets of Flies. Chap. 19.

For Flies.

Berytius the *Grecian* taught Men to drive Flies away with this whip. If saith he you steep Hellebour and Orpiment in milk, and sprinkle the place where flies come, with that, you will either kill or drive them all away. Allum poudred with Origanum, and mingled with milk, will do the same; what things soever are annointed with this mixture, are secured from flies. Also Bays bruised with black Hellebour, and infused in Milk or Honey, and water is good for this use. For with the sprinkling of this, they are killed as with venome, or else they will flye away and never come again.

A generall way to drive far off all Insects.

All Insects are driven away generally by five means. Either hindering the breeding of them; so we use to destroy Locusts Eggs: Or we hinder their coming, by shutting all windows and places close, because flies cannot well endure dark, close places. Some things do plainly drive away and kill Insects, as those two extreams do; namely fire, and especiall the flame, and extream cold. Hence any sharp favour, and

Book VIII.   *Secrets of all kind of Insects.*   151

and extream bitter, as Vinegar, or decoction of Bays, wild Cucumber, white Hellebour, Coloquintida or Lupins will do it. Some things do it by a propriety of their sent, as Brimstone, Vitriol, flowers and leaves of Elders, both Corianders, Horns and Hoofs. Some things do offend them many waies, as Rue, Verdigrease. The Ancients used two things very commodiously against them all, which are now forgotten by Men of our times, that is Pitch and Lees of Oyl. Pitch defends from the Ayr, and Lees of Oyl from living Creatures. I observe that amongst sweet sents, Storax by its smoke will drive away almost all Insects. *Cardan.*

To congregate Flies.

If you would make flies come together into one place, make a pit, and bruise Rose Laurels and put into it, and the flies will all come to it. *Anatolius.*

To drive out of your houses Flies, Spiders, Scorpions, and such like.

Burn a Houps Feathers in the room, so many as you please to make a smoke, all those Insects that smell the sent will be gone and never come again. *Alexius.*

Against Flies.

If you will not have Flies come near to your house, put Sizing and Opium, and Lime together, and white your house therewith, and the flies will not come in. *Albertus.*

That Flies may not trouble Oxen.

Flies will not disturb Oxen, if you boyl Bay berries in Oyl, and annoint them with it, and they will never sit upon any Cattle, if you smeer them with Lions fat. *Anatolius.*

That Flies shall not trouble Horses nor Mules.

If a man wet the hair of Horses and Mules with the juyce of the leaves of Gourds at Midsummer, it is a great wonder flies will never molest them. *Cardan.*

To kill Flies.

Hellebour with Milk or sweet Wine, and a little Orpiment infused together and sprinkled, will kill flies; and if you beat Allum and Origanum with milk, and smeer the place with that, they will not sit upon it. *The same.*

For Fleas.

Cummin well chewed in your mouth will make a juyce, that if you annoint your face, hands, and whole body well with it, if you can, they will never trouble you; for this sent is a great enemy unto them. And if you sprinkle the Windows with Wine, wherein beaten Cummin seed is infused, dores, wals, and pavement, fleas will never come into that Chamber, avoiding the sent thereof. And if you would also drive flies away from the house, take Savory, Elder leaves, and Cummin, of each what is sufficient, mingle them, and boyl them with water, and besprinkle this well about the house and wals, and the flies will never come there. But you must leave no meat there; for then they will come to the meat and not care for the sent. *Alexius.*

For Gnats.

If you hold a green moist Hemp bough near unto you, when you sleep, Gnats will not trouble you. *Democrit.*

Another.

A Horse hair stretched out near the Gate, and over the middle of the house, will destroy Gnats, and never suffer them to come in. Vitriol and Nigella expell them by their smoke. If you bind a Sponge, wet in sharp Vinegar near your head and feet, Gnats will not touch you. Rue soked, and the house besprinkled with the water, will drive them away, so will Fleabane, boyled and the house made wet with it. The smoke of Galbanum, Brimstone or Cummin will do the like. Ox dung burnt about the wals keeps out Gnats. The same may be done with a sixt part of Inula, and Purple shell fish two drams burnt, and the Blankets smoked therewith. A Sponge wet with Vinegar hanged near the dore, will gather all the Gnats thither. Gnats will never trouble him that layeth Hemp under his bed. Steep Rue in water, or boyl Fleabane, and sprinkle the house with the water, and the Gnats will not enter. So will the smoke of Bdellium keep them off. *Democrit.*

X 2   To

To make Flies and Bees, that are drowned, come to life again.

If drownd Flies be put under warm ashes, they will revive, and Bees drownd will revive in juyce of Nip. *Corn. Agrippa.*

Of the Secrets of Weevils. Chap. 20.

To kill Weesils.

Take Brine, Garlick, of each what is needfull, boyl them, and with this Brine besprinkle your wals and pavement. *Alexius.*

Another of the same Author.

Take Sagapenum, Lees of Oyl, Castoreum, Savin, Brimstone, Harts horn, Ivy, Galbanum, of each what is needfull, and make a smoke with them.

That Mites may not hurt wheat, and that Mice may not come to it.

Make a Paste with Lees of Oyl, add a little Chaff to it; you must mingle them well together, daub your whole Granary thick with this Clay, after that besprinkle well with Lees of Oyl, all the place that is dawbed before, when it is dry, lay in your Corn cold into it. *Cato.*

Of the Secrets of Locusts. Chap. 21.

Against Locusts.

If Locusts come in clowds, let all men keep close within doores, and not be seen, and they will flye away beyond you. But if before you see them they come suddenly, they will touch nothing if you sprinkle things with bitter Lupins or wild Cucumbers boyld in Oyl. For they will presently die. Also they will pass over any Countrey where they come, if you catch Bats and hang them up upon the highest Trees. But if you catch some Locusts and burn them, they will be giddy with the sent, and some will die, others will fall down and may be killed, or will be destroyed by the Sun. You may drive away Locusts if you make pickle with them, and dig pits and sprinkle that pickle there. For before the day be past, if you come, you shall find them in the pits fast asleep, and I leave them to your wit how to kill them then. Locusts will touch nothing that is wet with Wormwood, Leeks, or Centory steeped in water. *Democritus.*

BOOK. IX.

Of the Secrets of Plants.

Secrets of Plants both in *Generall*, of these is spoken, Chap. 1.

and *Speciall*,
- of the whole,
  - of Trees, in
    - *Generall*, Chap. 2.
    - in *Speciall*,
      - of the Garden, Chap. 3.
      - of the Woods, Chap. 4.
  - of Shrubs, Chap. 5.
- of the parts, See the Mark, A.

A, of the parts,
- of Roots, Chap. 6.
- of Leaves, in
  - *Generall*, Chap. 7.
  - *Speciall*, Chap. 8.
- of Flowers, in
  - *Generall*, Chap. 9.
  - *Speciall*, Chap. 10.

A, of the parts,
- of fruits, in
  - Generall, Chap. 11.
  - Speciall, Chap. 12.
    - Trees, Chap. 13.
    - Shrubs, Chap. 14.
    - Plants, Chap. 15.
- of Seeds, in
  - Generall, Chap. 16.
  - Speciall, Chap. 17.
- of Wood, Chap. 18.

Of the Secrets of Plants in Generall. Chap. 1.

To make Plants grow greater.

Generally seeds sown when the Moon increaseth will make Plants greater and with less taste, as on the contrary when the Moon decreaseth, that is from the full of the Moon, the Plants will be smaller and sharper tasted: hence I think it proceeds that great fruit are seldome so well relished and sented as smaller use to be. *Card. de varietat. Rerum.*

How to make barren Plants fruitfull.

If a Plant be wholly barren, *Aristotle* adviseth, that the root should be divided and a stone put into it: for if the bark be thick, a temperate heat will make it fruitfull.

To preserve Plants from blasting.

Hartshorn and Ox dung burnt, will, as some say, keep Plants from blasting. *Card. de Subtilit.*

To keep Plants from Worms.

If Plants be molested with Wormes, they must be purged with a Brass Nail. Brass leaves a constant bitterness in the Plant, so doth Ox gall sprinkled upon the roots: for Wormes are fed with sweet things, and that gall is most bitter. *The same.*

What things kill Plants.

Men say that the bough of a Nut tree gnawed with ones teeth, who first chewed Lentils, will kill the tree if it blossome. There is no other reason for it, than as if at these times the Plant should suffer violence, or the pith of it should be hurt within the bark: and the reason is plain, if Quick lime should be stuck into the principall part of the root; some likewise think, that if Bean Pods be laid about the roots, that they will hinder many Trees from growing. Moreover you will kill Plants or Trees if about the Dog daies you bore them through with an Auger as far as the Pith, and cast in Oyl of Peter and Brimstone: for being hurt in the Summer they dye the sooner: Likewise if you cut the bark round at that time, they will wither away. It is most certain that the life of the Tree lyeth either in the bark or the pith: and both these are to be found in the root, body, and boughs, if therefore you cut unprofitable Plants at these times, and strew Brimstone and Ashes upon them, they will dye. *The same.*

To make Plants like a Dragon.

Linseed put into Raddish roots, and presently set into good earth well dunged, will produce a Plant like unto a Dragon. The taste thereof will be like Salt and Vinegar, and therefore it is much desired in Sallets, for if you have that, you need neither Salt nor Vinegar, as I was told by one of the chief of the Kings Gardeners. *Mizaldus.*

Of the Secrets of Trees in Generall. Chap. 2.

That Trees may grow quickly.

You must dig about the Trees you set every Moneth untill they are three years old if you will have them grow suddenly. *Cato.*

To make Trees fruitfull.

Rose seeds with Mustard seed, and the foot of a Weesil hanged amongst the boughs of a barren Tree, will make it exceeding fruitfull as some say. *Mizald.*

That all Trees may bring fruit much bigger then ordinary.

Take an old plate of rusty Iron, and make it like to an Ox horn, that at the sharp end it may have a hole. Which being washed on the inside with pickle, put into it the Kernell of an Apple, Pear, or Peach stone, or of any other fruit, so that the part of the Kernell which begins to bud, may be toward the hole; then in the bottome fasten another plate very close, that it may bud no other way than through that hole. This being done, moysten all outwardly also with the same pickle: Then in *September* or *October* plant it, that the earth may alittle exceed the Iron: for when the Kernels inclosed begin to feel the moisture, and by degrees are moystned sufficiently: they will shoot forth their roots and sprouts, creeping here and there, and bending so long in the plate, untill they pass quite through; because the roots being by nature hard and sharp, creeping here and there, will prick, untill by help of the Earth that eats through, and makes the plate thin) they make holes that the roots may come forth. But the plant by growing and wandring about, will draw into it self the taste of the Brine, and the colour of the Iron; And when the sprouts are forced to come out, they joyn together, and must necessarily glew into one, that of many sprouts one great branch is made, and by consequence must needs bear greater fruit than ordinary, which will be pleasant to behold. *Alexius.*

That fruitfull Trees may be made better.

The Lees of Oyl mingled with water, cast about fruitfull Trees will make them better. *Cato.*

Of Engraffing of Trees which is done under the bark, and into the stock.

There are three waies of Engraffing, and one of them properly is called Sciencing, the second is called Insoliating, and the third Inoculating. Therefore Trees that have thick Rinds, and are full of juyce, as the Fig-Tree, Cherry-Tree, and Olive, that draw much moysture from the Earth, are to be Engraffed near the Bark. But you must before you Engraff them, have a Pin provided of strong wood, that you may by little and little let it in between the Rind and the Tree, that the Bark may remain unbroken. For this is chiefly to be observed: then by degrees drawing forth the Pin, put in the Twig. This way is called Insoliation; But in Trees that have thin Rinds, and are dry, namely, such as have their moysture, not in the Bark, but within the Pith, as the Citron-Tree and the Vine, and all Trees of this sort that divide the moyst middle part, and send forth shouts; this way is called Engraffing. But in both the foresaid waies you must make a compendious Engraffing, that the Twig that is to be Engraffed may not dry up with too long delay. You must take your Graffs from the best and most vigorous and fruitfull Trees, cutting them off with sharp crooked Knives, from those parts that respect the North side; and they must be tender, and light, and full of Buds, having two or three tops: but at the bottom all united, they must be as thick as your little finger, and of two years growth: for Graffs of one year soon shoot forth, but they are unfruitfull; you must sharpen your Graffs at the but end with your Knife, as we use to cut a Pen to write withall, yet heed must be had that the pith be not dissolved, or diminished. The Graff must be set in after that posture, that the Woddy part may joyn to the Wood, and the Bark to the Bark, and the Graff must be scraped and sharpned of equall magnitude to the cut made, and the hollow part it must be thrust into; wherefore it must be pared two fingers breadth. After the Engraffing you must take nothing from the Graff but leave it so, only you must cover the place with Clay and Lome, close stopped in; Yellow Earth is unfit for this purpose; for it burns the bodies of the Trees. Engraffing is so needfull, that if a man shall Engraff shoots of Trees into the Trees themselves, they will be more lasting and better. Moreover the Graffs must be taken at the end of the Moon, about ten or more daies before you Engraff them, and laid in a Vessel well closed and stopped, that they may not evaporate and breath through. The Graffs must be shut up close, but that which is Engraffed must be ready to sprout; Wherefore

Wherefore you must take your Graffs ten or more daies before. I must tell you the reason why we do not presently Engraff the Graffs. For if the Graff being yet hot and moyst, should presently be set into the Tree, the Graff must needs shrink a little before it unites, and so there will be some void space between the Graff and the cleft of the Tree whereinto it is set, so the Air will enter at the hollow places, and will not suffer them to grow together. But if the Graffs some daies before be shut up in into a Vessel, they will shrink in the Vessel, as they would do after they are Engraffed, and after that when they are Engraffed, the bands will not relax, nor the Air enter, but they soon unite. Moreover the Graffs must not be set in when the North wind blows, but when the South wind; for it is plain that Rainy weather is good for Graffing, but ill for Infoliation: you must further know, that after the Autumnall Equinoctiall, untill the Winter Equinoctiall is a fit time to Engraff; also after the blowing of the West wind, that is from the seventh day of *February*, untill the Spring Solstice. Some say the best time for Engraffing is, presently after the rising of the Dog star, and again in Summer under the heat of the Dog daies. But if the Graffs be brought from a very far distance, they must be carried in some Vessel, and stuck into Clay, and the Vessel must be close stopped, that the wind come not at them, and they shall evaporate in carrying. *Florent.*

Of Engraffing that is done by Inoculation or Emplaſtring.

Inoculation is fitly and well performed before the Summer Solstice. And I have Inoculated about the Vernall Equinoctiall, upon a clear day, when the Trees first began to bud, and it hit excellent well. The Tree must be cleansed, into which the Science must be inoculated, that is from its superfluous sprouts, and Moss, leaving the best and most hopefull boughs, into which you mean to Inoculate. Then you must take a Sprout of the most fruitfull Tree, that is of that Year, and of that, the Bud must be Inoculated in an exact place of the Stock prepared: but you must perfectly scrape off the Rind: but the Wooddy part must be left untouched and perfect; For this is held to be very needfull. The best way is, to Inoculate the Bud that comes from the Twig, into the Bud of that Tree which is to be Inoculated, for that being cut upon the Stock, and the other set into that, they will soon grow together. Also you may without a Bud make Infoliation upon some other part of the Stock, upon some smooth place. The Barks of both Stocks, must be of equall thickness. So soon as they joyn, I presently cut away what is above the place, where the joyn, that it may send no nourishment but into that only, that is joyned with it. But when the Twigs Infoliated have gotten three leaves, let the bands be dissolved and taken away. And I oftentimes have not only Infoliated the Bud it self, of one years Twig alone by it self, but I left the Bud unhurt upon the Twig, and I have scraped away the Bark that was behind the Bud, and when the wood was made to appear, as we use to do with a writing Quill, and cut as it ought to be, I Infoliated the Bud with that part of the Wood which remained, and I obtained a more fruitfull Tree by this Infoliation. Moreover if the wild Part of the boughs be Engraffed into, they will bring twice as much fruit. *Didym.*

To remove and transplant Trees.

What concerneth planting of Trees, they must be set at a handsome distance one from the other, that when they grow, they may have room to extend their boughs. For if you set them thick, you can neither sowe under them what you might, nor will they be fruitfull, unlest you pull up some between. When you will transplant them, before you attempt that, you must diligently mark what winds they lye open to, that you may Plant and set them in the same posture. When you do that, you must at the bottome of the Trench cast in bundles of Vine Branches as thick as your Arm, so that they may lye a little above the Earth. For in Summer, with little labour, you may water the roots by those boughs. But the best way will be, the Year before you will Plant, to dig your Pit, that the Earth may be well soked and prepared by the Rain and Sun, and so it will soon take hold of what is set. And if you would make your Pits, and set your Trees the same Year, you shall dig your Pits at least two Moneths before; and afterwards you shall heat them with burning of Straw; and the

the larger and opener you make the Trenches, the better fruit will your Trees bear. You shall open your Trenches like to a Furnace, that the bottome may be larger than the top, so the roots will have more room to spread : and cold in Winter, and heat in Summer will enter in at a narrow hole. But generally you shall so dispose your small and great Trees, that the weaker be not pressed by the stronger : for the weaker cannot be equall for strength or bigness, and it grows great in an unequall time. Moreover great care must be had, that after great Tempests and cold injurious times of the Year, you do not Prune or cut your Trees, especially those that bring fruit : and further that one Tree may not drip upon another, when the wind doth blow, especially if they be of different kinds : and that you do not open the roots in Summer against the Sun, or that the Sun may beat upon them, or any man take the tops of your Trees, pulling them down too hard with his hands, and that Cattle eat them not, for they will not grow afterwards, chiefly if they be young. All Shrubs before they be Transplanted must be marked with Sinoper; that when you set them, may look the same way, as they did where they first stood. Otherwise they will suffer wrong by cold or heat in those parts where they are set contrary to the places they stood in before in other ground. Wherefore the same Coast of the Heaven must be kept in the Transplantation, that the Northern parts may not be cleft; standing opposite to the South Sun; or the Southern parts of the Trees chil, being turned toward the North. Most men command not to Transplant any Tree under two Years, nor yet over three Years growth, and they think you must take heed that the roots wither not by too long delay : and that Trees ought not to be taken up from the North parts, or from that Climat of the Heavens as far as the Sun rising in Winter, whilst the winds blow; or that their roots should be exposed to those winds, for that will kill them, and the Husbandmen will not know the reason of it. It is good also to bring a great deal of that Earth where the Trees grew, sticking to their roots : and bind them all about with Turff. They must be watered so oft as it Rains not, and great heat continues, for so they will increase better, and be more fruitfull, and yield more pleasant fruit. *Mizaldus* from *Columella*, *Cato* and *Pliny*.

For Blastings and Frosts ready to fall upon Trees.

If you would prevent Blasting and Milldews ready to fall upon Trees; You shall burn much straw if you have it, or else pull up the Grass of Orchards, Gardens, or Fields, with Shrubs and Bryars, and burn them in many places; chiefly on that side the wind will blow : for so *Diophanes* writes, the mischief at hand may be diverted. *Berytius* in his famous School of Greeks Geoponicks, when he saw these gather in the Air, he would he saith, presently burn the left horn of an Ox, with Oxes dung, and so he made much smoke round about the Orchard or Field, and laid this against the wind. *Apulejus* writes, that the smoke of three Crabs burnt with Ox or Goats dung and Chaff, is a present remedy. But if the Blasting prevents you; *Berytius* saith, you may repaire the loss thus. Bruise and infuse in water the roots or leaves of wild Gourds, or Coloquintida: and before the Sun rise besprinkle those plants that are Blasted. Fig tree or Oke ashes will do the same, infused in water, and besprinkled as before. *Apulejus* saith it will be good to stick some Bay boughs in great quantity, and to plant them about your Orchard or Field : for as I oft observed, all Blasting and danger will overpass them, and be gone ; which is very frequent in dewy places and Valleys where the winds come not very much. *Mizald.*

Against the corruption and Frost that hurts Trees.

Against corruption that especially befals Vines, *Pliny* bids us burn three live Crabs hung to the Trees or Vines. The Greeks against Frosts in Orchards, set Beans within and without. *The same.*

For sick Trees.

If any Tree be sick, you must pour to the roots of it Lees of Oyl, equally mingled with water; Also some say the chief help is, to pour about the Tree Dregs of Wine, or water of the decoction of Lupins, or to sow Lupins about the roots. *Didymus* and *Pliny.*

For decayed fainting Trees.

If a Tree be starved and faint, it will become more juycefull, if you dig about the roots and stock, and pour in stale Urine of a Man, or Beasts Piss. *Pixm.*

That a Tree may stand unhurt.

You shall preserve any Tree sound and free from diseases incident to Trees, if you sprinkle Ox or Bulls gall about the roots, or laying the stalks of Beans or Pulse about them, or the Stubble of Wheat to cover them, and so cast the Earth over them again. *Mizald.*

Against the heat of the Dog-daies, and mortification, or rottenness.

If a Tree be tired with the heat of the Dog-daies and so be endangered to mortifie; you must bid them that serve you pour to the roots three measures of water of three Fountains: yet so that the Moon hinder not the remedy. Or wreath about the stock of the Tree round, the Herb Symphoniaca, which *Apuleius* calleth Henbane, or *Apollos* Herb. Or make of that about the bottom of the stump a bed. If the Tree be mortified, and astonished as if it languished of a Consumption, annoint it with an Unguent, and you shall see it revive as it were. *Democrit.* and *Mizald.*

That Birds may not sit upon a Tree.

That Tree will never be touched by Birds which hath a bundle of Garlick hanged upon the boughs: or is Pruned with a Pruning Knife that is smeered with Garlick. *Democrit.*

For barren Trees.

If a Tree blossome abundantly but brings no fruit, if you drive a post of Oake or Beech into a hole in the root, and cover it over with Earth, it will grow fruitfull again. *Zoroaster* writes that Bean stalks cast about the roots will help it. *Columella* bids to bore a hole through the Tree, and to put into the hole a green stick of the wild Olive Tree, for so the Tree will grow more fertil, as if it had taken in more fruitfull seed. *M. Cato* thinks that you should mingle Oyl Lees with an equall quantity of water; and to pour that round about the Tree. If it be a very great Tree one Amphora of the mixture will be sufficient; if the Tree be smaller, you must pour according to this proportion in reason. If the Trees be fruitfull, this mixture will make them better. *Africanus* bruised well Purslane and Tithymale, and annointed the stocks of Trees with this juyce, that they might thrive and bear more fruit, and sometimes he added Pigeons dung unto these. *Mizald.*

For Trees that let fall their fruit.

If Trees drop their fruit as if they were sick, and cannot hold them to maturity. *Sotion* a diligent Garden of *Greece*, and skillfull, pulled up Darnel which is called wild Tares, by the roots, and made a wreath of them, and wound them about the stock of the Tree: or else he bound Sea Crabs about it with the same Tares: or compassed it in with a Hoop of Lead. Moreover he rid the Earth from the roots, and bored a hole in it, and beat in a Wedg into it made of the Dog-tree, and cast Earth upon it. Some lay the roots open, and cleave some of the thickest of them, and into the clefts they put a piece of a Flint, then they bind it, and cast in the earth upon it. *Palladius* smeers the Tree with red Earth or fresh Lees of Oyl mingled with water, or else he hanged a River Crab, with a sprig of Rue, or a bundle of Lupins upon it. *The same.*

For Trees that let fall their blossoms or leaves.

If blossoms or leaves fall from Trees, you shall help them thus, as you may find in the Greek Husbandry of the *Quintilii*; dig about the roots, and lay the stalks of Beans steeped in water about them, a great measure about a great Tree, and a small measure about a small, and so shall you cure the falling of their blossomes and leaves. *The same.*

Against Wormes of Trees.

If Wormes hurt Trees, *Florentius* teacheth to defend them thus: Gring *Terra Lemnia*, called Sigillata, and Origanum with water, and with that mixture annoint the roots; or plant Squils round about. But if you drive in Pitch-Tree stakes about a Tree, the Wormes will dye or fall away. Hogs dung mixed with Wine will preserve

serve a Tree from Worms, as *Didymus* writes in his Husbandry; if you often cast it about a Tree, Pigeons dung may do the like laid about the naked roots. So will Buls Gall often cast upon the same: for thus a Tree will not soon grow old, nor will it easily breed Worms. *Palladius* pours on for three daies the Lees of old Wine. *Mizaldus*. You shall see more helps against the diseases of Trees, Book the sixt.

That Cattle may not hurt Trees.

It is certainly reported that Crabs, and also Sea Crevice bound about Willows, and hanged also upon other Trees, will keep Cattle from hurting them: that proceeds partly from their ill form, and partly from their filthy smell: for all Cattle abhor the ill smell of a dead Creature, and sometimes of a living, if it be of the same kind. *Cardan.*

To destroy Trees.

To destroy a Tree, cut the Bark away round, for every Tree dyeth that is spoiled of its Bark: but some sooner, some later, as the Oak soon, and the Tyle tree, but the weaker Trees dye later. It is also to be considered, what times we do it, for in *February* and *March* they will dye presently: but in Winter strong Trees are longer dying. But the Cork must have the Bark pulled off that it grow not worse. So the weapon of the Sea Ray stuck into any stock of a Tree will kill it, and a menstruous Cloath laid to the roots, especially of a Wallnut Tree as *Democritus* writes. *The same.*

To root out Trees.

You must bore a hole in the Tree, and pour in Boys Urine, or an Onyon, or thrust in a Myrtill Wedg, especially when it blossoms; or ridding the Earth from the root, you must lay on Ditttany, Beanes, or a menstrous Cloath; for so the Tree will consume and dye. Some bore into the Pitch, and put in Quicksilver. *Democritus* shews how to root up a Wood; by Lupin meal one day steeped in the juyce of Hemlock, and sprinkled about the bare roots.

To kill Trees.

Pour common Oyl upon the roots, and the Trees will soon perish, or make a hole as far as the Pitch, and pour in Quicksilver and Oyl, stop the hole with Wax and Chalk, and the Tree will soon wither. *Fallopius.*

That Trees may not be hurt by Cattle.

Cast at least ten River or Sea Crabs into water for eight daies, shut them in, and let them stand in the Sun in in the open Ayr for ten daies, sprinkle of this water upon those Trees you would have preserved for eight daies, and you will wonder at the virtue. Dogs dung mingled with most stinking Urine, and sprinkled on round, will do the same. *Democritus.*

Of the Secrets of Trees of Gardens. Chap. 3.

Against Wormes of an Apple Tree.

An Apple Tree of all Trees is most subject to Wormes, that is, to be eaten by them. A Sea Onyon laid about it, will preserve the Tree from them. If they come by nature, Buls Gall, or Hogs dung mingled with Mans Urine, and poured to the roots will destroy them. But if they be hard to destroy, the Bark must be digged into with a Brass Pin, or scraping Tool, and rended, untill the point of it take upon the Wormes, and drive them from the place: but where there is a place ulcerated, you must stop that up with Ox dung. Moreover if the best Apple Tree Plants be set into the ground, their roots being annointed with Buls gall, that only their Tops may be extant above the ground, they and their fruit will be free from Wormes. *Mizald.* out of *Pallad.* and *Anatol.*

That a Tree may bear abundance of Apples.

If you would have an Apple Tree bring many Apples, bring about the Trunk of the Tree, a foot above ground an open Pipe of Lead cut; and when the Apples begin to blossome, and the Trees to flourish, take away that Circle of Lead, do this yearly that the Tree may be fruitfull. *Mizald.*

That

That an Apple Tree may not break with the weight of the Apples.

Because Apple Trees and many others use to be so full with fruit, that they are in danger to break, and some boughs are torn off, you must prop them up with forks strong enough to support them. *The same.*

For Apples that fall.

If Apples drop down, cleave the root, and thrust in a stone and that will hold them fast.

For barren Pear Trees.

If a Pear Tree be barren and languishing, you may cure it, as I said before for other Trees. Many when the Tree grows great, use to rid the earth from it very deep, and to cleave the root near to the Trunk of the Tree, and to drive in a wedg into the cleft, made of the Pine Tree, Beech or Oake, and then to cast in the Earth upon it. *The same.*

That the Pear Tree may not bring hard stony Pears.

If the Pear Tree bring forth stoney Pears, the Husbandry of the Quintilii bids us to uncover the lower roots of the Tree, and to remove from it what hard earth we find there, and sifting fresh Earth, to lay it in the place of the former, adding dung to it; this will help exceedingly if you do not cease from watering of it. *The same.*

That a Pear Tree may bring abundance, and pleasant fruit.

If you would have your Tree bear more and more pleasant Pears, bore a hole in the stock next the root, and knock in a wedg of Beech or Oak; as *Diophanes* bids us: or else pour Wine Lees upon the naked roots.

A remedy for a sick Pear Tree when it blossoms, or that is troubled with Wormes.

If a Pear Tree be sick when it blossoms, you shall help it by ridding the Earth from the roots, and pouring on old Wine Lees for three daies; and then cast the Earth on again. If a Tree and its fruit be tainted with Wormes, if you annoint the roots with Buls Gall, or Ox Gall often, they will all dye, and will never breed again. *Mizald.*

A remedy for a sick or barren Quince Tree, or any way amiss.

If a Quince Tree be sick, pour on Oyl Lees equally mingled with water, upon the roots: or temper Quicklime with Chalk and water, and smeer it about the stock of the Tree. If it be barren, Worm eaten or otherwise ill, turn to those things I have already set down for it in Generall and Speciall.

A remedy for a Plum Tree, that faints, and is not fruitfull.

If a Plum Tree faint, and be not fruitfull, Oyl Lees equally mingled with water must be poured upon the roots, or Ox Piss, or Mans Piss only, that is stale, and equally mingled with water or Ashes of the Furnace, especially made of Vine branches. *Palladius.*

Against Worms that eat a Plum Tree.

If a Plum Tree be hurt by Wormes or Ants, it must be annointed with red Earth and Tarre.

A remedy for a Cherry Tree corrupting.

If you find that it begins to corrupt by reason of too much moysture, you must make a hole in the body of the Tree, to let that moysture forth; if there be Ants, pour upon it the juyce of Purslane, mingled with half as much Vinegar: or annoint the stock of the Tree when it blossoms with Wine Lees. *Palladius.*

That Cherries may come rare and betimes.

It will bring Cherries rathe, if before it blossoms, you lay Quicklime to the roots, or hot water be often poured upon them; but the Tree will soon wither after it.

That a Cherry Tree may bear Grapes.

If a Man Engraff a Vine upon a black Cherry tree, it will bring Grapes in the Spring time. *Florentinus.*

That a Mullberry may be more fruitfull and bring white berries.

Some write that the Mullberry Tree will be more fruitfull and Taller, if you make a hole quite through the body, and put in two wedges, here of the Turpentine Tree, there of the Mastick Tree. If the Mulberry be Engraffed upon a white Poplar or Inoculated, it will bring white berries. *Berytius.*

To make a Peach tree flourish.

It will grow more pleasantly, if as soon as we have eaten the Peaches, we set the stone of them, leaving some part of the fruit upon them. *Florent.*

A remedy for a Peach tree that languisheth away.

If a Peach Tree seem to waste, you must mingle old Wine Lees with water, and pour that upon the roots, and often throw on fresh water, and water it in the evening, and making shades before it, defend it from the Sun that dryeth it too much, and it will be good also to hang upon it a cast skin of a Snake. If Worms trouble it, you shall kill them by mingling Ashes with Lees of Oyl, or Ox Piss with a third part of Vinegar. If hoar Frosts offend it, lay dung to it, or Wine Lees mingled with water; or which is better water wherein Beans are boyled. Broom bound to it is profitable against all Inconveniences, or else Broom hanged upon the Boughs. *Mizald.*

That Peaches may not fall.

If Peaches drop off, uncover the roots and drive in Pins of Turpentine or Mastick wood, or make an Auger hole in the middle of the Tree, and drive in some pins of Willow. *The same.*

To make one fruit of a Peach tree, and a Nut Peach.

You shall compound a Peach and a Nut Peach by insition, which Husbandmen call Engraffing, as when you take new fruitfull shoots from the Peach Tree and the Nut Peach, and such as foreshew great hopes of prospering well, marking them round about two fingers breadth, that the Buds may be placed in the middle, so you shall with a sharp Knife take off the bark from the wood, cleave these in the middle, that being joyned close, they may grow together, and the place where the cleft was, may not be seen, but that it may appear one bud; Engraff one of these on that part of the Tree that seemeth fairest, and most likely, cutting away the rest, that they may not draw away the nourishment, that it may be sufficient for every Graff: open the bark that the Knife may not hurt the wood; and cut round such proportions as the bud requires, and fit it in so exactly, that it may equall the part cut away: bind it about so that you hurt it not: you must defend the cleft with Clay and Lome, laying something upon it that the Rain do not fall into it, so it will grow, and the fruit will be of a middle kind retaining the nature of the Peach, and the stone Peach, for it will be like to them both, which the Trees severally did never afford. So Pomegranates may be sweet upon one side, and sour on the other. And *Diophanes* bids us Engraft Apples upon pleasant Pear Trees, and such he calls *Mirapidia.* And Apples are Graffed with Quinces, and they produce most gallant Apples called by the *Athenians Melimella,* as *Diophanes* also writes. Likewise severall kinds being mingled, as Citrons with Lemmons, and sweet Oranges with sour, will produce half sweet and half sour; a Peach compounded of a red bloud colour and white; so are your Honey Apples, and the rest brought forth by a various way of increasing. *The same.*

An Almond Peach.

Also with great diligence a fruit is produced, that outwardly is like a Peach, but it tasts inwardly like a sweet Almond, which we may well call an Almond Peach. Take a twig from the Peach Tree, and if you Engraff this into a sweet Almond Tree, and the bud that springs from thence be Inoculated into another, and you do this three or four times, you shall have a Peach that inwardly hath a sweet Kernell. An ingenious Artizan may compound many such things; it sufficeth me to have shewed you the way. *The same.*

How a Medlar must be purged from wormes.

The Medlar Tree being old is often troubled with Worms, which are greater and different from Wormes of other Trees: they must be cleansed with a point of

Brass,

Brass, and Oyl Lees, or Mans Urine that is stale, or else you must pour on Quicklime, but sparingly, that you hurt not the Tree. The water of the decoction of Lupins can do much to this purpose. *Mizald. ex Pallad.*

That Medlars may not drop, nor Ants be troublesome.

If Medlars drop down, cut a piece from the root of the Tree, and fasten it into the body of it. If Ants trouble it, you shall kill them with Synoper temper'd with ashes and Vinegar. *The same.*

How to help an old Nut tree.

If you would help an old Nut Tree, water it thrice a Moneth for a whole year with Lee. *The same.*

How to make bitter Almonds sweet.

Theophrastus saith, and *Pliny* from him, that of bitter may be made sweet Almonds, if you dig about the stock, and make a hole about the bottome of it, and wipe away all the foul matter that fals down. *Africanus* seem to warn us of it in his Georgicks writing thus; of bitter you shall make sweet Almonds, if you dig about the Trunk, four fingers from the root, and make a hole, by which the juyce may yearly pass forth, untill such time as the Almonds grow sweet.

That the Almond tree may bring abundance of fruit.

If an Almond Tree continueth to bear leaves and no fruit, bore a hole in the body near the ground or rather near the root, and stick a Pin of a fat Pine Tree into it, and pour on mans Urine, and then cover it with Earth, or so stick in a Flint, that the bark may cover it close. Also it will yield more fruit, if an Iron pin be knocked into the Tree, and when a hole is made, an Oken pin be forced into it. *Mizald. ex Pallad. & Theophrast.*

Against hore frosts of the Almond tree.

Where there is fear of frosts, before the Almond Tree flourish, dig round about the roots, and lay them open, mingle very small white stones with Sand, lay them there, and when the time comes that it should bud, dig them again, and remove them thence. *The same.*

That the Fig tree may not lose her fruit.

Stop Rams horns about the roots of it, or scarify the body of the Tree where it swels most, that the moysture may run forth. *The same.*

Against Wormes of Fig trees.

If the Fig Tree be troubled with Wormes, we must set a bough of the Turpentine Tree, or stalk of the Mastick Tree, with the Fig Tree, the top being turned upside down. Quicklime strewed at the roots or put into hollow parts of the body will destroy them. Some pull them forth with Brazen Crooks. Others rid the roots of earth, and they pour on Lees of Oyl or old Urine: Bitumen and Oyl are good also. *The same.*

That the Fig trees may hold their green Figs.

That Fig Trees may hold their green Figs, do all things as I shall say concerning the Olive Tree; and this besides: When the Spring comes, ram in the Earth well and the green Figs will never fall; the green Fig Trees will not be rugged, and will be more fruitfull. *Cato.*

That the Olive tree may bear her fruit.

If the Olive Tree bear not fruit, rid away the Earth from the roots, then lay straw about them; Also add as much water as Oyl Lees together, then dig about the Olive Tree; for the greatest Tree four gallons and a half are sufficient of that mixture; lesser Tees must have a reasonable proportion. If you do this to Trees that are fruitfull, they will never be the better, add therefore no straw to them. *M. Cato.*

Of the Secrets of Trees that are wild. Chap. 4.

To root out wild trees.

Steep Lupin meal one day in the juyce of Hemlock, open the roots, and pour this in. Or about the Dog daies bore them into the Pith, and cast in Oyl of Peter with brimstone. *Democrit. and Plin.*

Of the Secrets of Shrubs. Chap. 5.
Of Engraffing of Vines.

He that will Engraff a Vine, must chuse a thick stock, that can receive one or two branches; some Engraff within the ground descending about half a foot deep, and they make their Engraffing almost in the lowest part of the Vine; Some Engraff upon the ground which is best; but what is Engraffed above the ground seldome knits, being still shaken with the wind. But if we must needs Engraff above, by reason of too much smoothness below; you must have a stake prepared, and bind that to it which is set above, to provide against the winds. Some Engraff near the top of the stock. If you Engraff a Vine into a Cherry Tree, you shall have very early Grapes; for at what time the Cherry Tree useth to produce her own fruit, she will bring Grapes also, that is in the Spring. The time of Engraffing is the Spring, when the Ice is past, that when the Vine is cut, it may yield neither much liquor nor very watry, but that which is thick and clammy. The twigs that must be chosen to Engraff, must be round, solid with thick buds, chiefly from the Arms of the Tree. Two or three buds are sufficient for a branch : but if it be to be covered with Earth, then three or four. Moreover it is not convenient to cut above two twigs from one branch to Engraff withall; for whatsoever is left after the first seaven buds, is unprofitable and barren. But new twigs will grow together faster that have some part of the twig that was of the year before. Nor do we presently Engraff twigs taken from the Vine, but after they are cut, we cover the Wound, and lay them in a Vessel, that they may not evaporate, yet before they begin to bud, and whilst they are yet shut, we must Engraff them. Those that are Engraffed into the Earth, at the bottome of the Vine, will be set in faster, lifting up the Earth withall for their nutriment, but they will be longer before they bear, as other Twigs planted into the Earth. But those that are Engraffed higher will hardly fasten, being alwaies shaken with the winds : yet they will sooner bear fruit where they do grow. Those twigs that are set high above must be smooth and plain, as thick as ones Thumb, but you must make the roughness of it smooth with a sharp Pruning Knife. Moreover the Graff that must be set in, must be taken away two fingers and half in length upon one side as we see Men cut Writing Quils, so that on one part the Pith may appear unhurt, and on the other side the bark. The whole Graff must be set in as far as it is pared, that there may be no space void between the Stock and the Graff, and if it gape, it must be filled up with Lime and Potters earth, which will hinder the keeping of the moysture that is in it. Moreover the part of the Stock which concerns the cut, must be bound about with a band : it must be single, and no knots in it, and then it must be smeered over with clammy Earth. Some mingle Ox dung with the Clay. Those that are thus bound we water their band with a Sponge about twilight in the Evening, in the greatest heat of Summer. But when it begins to bud, and is about four fingers long, you must fasten a Vine prop near it, and bind it to keep it safe from the wind. When the twig is encreased, you must cut away the band with your Pruning Knife, to free it from being kept too streight, and the moysture may pass from the body to the branch. But when the Moon is in the Waine, you must cut your Grafts to Engraff: for so they will be stronger. Some Engraff not only in the Spring, but after the Vintage. For then the Vine hath more force. *Florent.*

Of Engraffing by boring a hole.

I think the best way of Engraffing is by boring a hole : for the Vine wherein the Engraffing is made, will then not remain idle, but will also bring fruit, and the Graff that it nourisheth increaseth also, the Vine being nothing endamaged by the boring of it; nor is it pressed by binding. Engraffing by boring is made thus. Bore a hole in the Stock of the Vine with an Auger called *Gallica*, and cut off a branch of the best Vine that groweth near, and put it into the hole, it must not be cut off from an old Vine, for so the twig will live, nourished by its old parent, and will also joyn into one with the stock, that receiveth it, but will not perfectly unite untill two years. Then therefore after that the scar is made, you must cut away the Twig that

was

was taken from an old Vine, as far as it holds of its former Parent, and cut away with a Saw, the stock of the Vine into which the Engraffing was made, so far as it sticks forth above the place boared. And for the future the Engraffed twig shall remain to be a part of the principall Vine.

That the same Bough may have divers Grapes, that is, severall, some white, some black, some yellow.

You must take two different Twigs of diverse kinds, and cut them through the middle, observing this that the cleft come not into the buds, and that no part of the pith fall out; and you must so joyn one unto another, that the buds may fall into one, and touch as near as can be, that two buds may become to be as one. Then you must bind the twigs fast together with Paper, and wrap it over with a Sea Onyon, or the most glutinous earth, and so plant it, and after three or five daies past, water it, untill it begins to bud and grow. *Didym.*

That a Vine may bring late Grapes.

You must take away the boughs that first spring forth, and others will breed in their places. Take great care of the Plant, and it will bring forth new sprigs, these coming to maturity, will be late to bear Grapes. Wherefore put those boughs into Earthen vessels with holes at the bottome bored through, and cover the upper part diligently, and bind the vessels to the Vine, that the winds may not shake them. *Florentinus.*

That a Grape may grow without stones.

Some make Grapes without stones thus: They cut lightly and equally that part of the twig that they mean to set into the ground, and with an ear picker they take forth all the pitch: then they set the twig bound about with moyst Paper. But it were better if all the part of the twig that is to be set under the earth, were set into a Sea Onyon and then Planted. For the Sea Onyon is good both for the Birth and uniting of it. Some cut the Vines that are already fruitfull, and they pick forth the pith of the boughs with an ear picker, as much as they can, taking it forth very deep, not cleaving the twigs as I shewed, but leaving them entire, and they pour in the juyce of Cyrenian Laser dissolved in water, or new wine boyled thick, and they bind the twigs round to the roots, that the juyce may not run forth. Every eight daies after they pour in the same juyce into the branches, untill they bud, you may do the same with the Pomegranate, and Cherry, if you would have them both grow without stones. *Democrit.*

Of the Theriacall and purging Vine.

It is manifest that the Theriacall Vine is good for many things, and especially for the bites of Serpents. I shall shew you the way to make it. The boughs of the Vine that we would plant, we cut the lower part of them three or four fingers, and taking forth the pitch, we put into the twigs the confection called *Theriaca*, then we wrap up the cleft parts in Paper, and plant them. They that would be more diligent in this matter, put the antidote into the roots also; we may make a purging Vine the same way, if we'll put Hellebour into the cleft twig. But you must know that a branch taken from a Theriacall Vine to be planted, hath not the same force: for it faints; being transplanted and removed or Engraffed, namely, the antidote with time being evaporated and gone. Wherefore the antidote must be seasonably smeered about the roots. *Florentinus in his Georgicks.*

That a Vine may not breed Lice, nor Catterpillars, nor be endangered by Lice.

Annoint the bark with Bears fat, and the Vine will breed no Lice: or annoint the pruning Knives, with Bears grease, and let no man know it, namely those, you will prune the Vine with, and neither Lice nor Ice will trouble the Vine. But annoint the Knives with Oyl, wherein there is Garlick bruised. But if you boyl in Oyl those Caterpillars you find upon Roses, and annoint your Knives with that, the Vine will suffer no hurt by any other living Creatures, nor yet by hore Frosts. Or annoint your Pruning hooks with Bears grease, or the bloud of Frogs. Or whet your hooks on a Whetstone that is first smeered with Oyl and Ashes. Vine branches burnt and mingled with Vine drops and Wine, and set in the middle of a Vineyard, will suffer no Wormes to breed there. *Aphricanus.*

That Vines may not be hurt by Frosts nor Blasting.

Lay dry dung in divers places of the Vineyard, according as the wind sits toward the Vineyard, and where you see Frost lying upon it, burn your dry dung. The smoke that ariseth thence will disperse the Frost. But those Vines that are most easie to be scortched by Frosts, must be pruned latest, (because pruning moves them to bud) and so they will put forth later; As therefore Horsetail, so the Vine will little fear Frosts, because as I suppose, it springs up late, when the Sun is of some heat. Some set Beans in Vineyards, and they think that will preserve their Vines from Frosts. *Diophanes.*

Against Frosts of Vines, a remedy of the same Author

If it fall out that Vines are hurt by frosts, and it is plain that the Grapes are spoiled, they must be cut, and that very short, that their force may continue. So the next year they will make amends for the fruit of the former year. Some by experience in *Bithynia* affirm, that when frost is suspected, it is good to cast about with the wind the Ashes of the Tamarish tree, and if that cannot be had, of any tree whatsoever, for the Ashes falling into the buds of the Vines, drives away the frost that is ready to fall down.

Against Blasting of Vines.

Whenas you see blasting gather in the Ayr, burn immediately an Oxes left horn with Cow dung, and make much smoke round about the field as the wind sits, that the wind may drive all the smoke toward the blasting; for the smoke will disperse all ill Ayrs. *Apuleius* saith, That three burnt Sea Crabs with Ox dung or straw, or Goats dung, will sufficiently help by their smoke. *Berytius.*

For barren Vines.

Cleave the stock with a paring Knife, Saw, or Oaken Wedg, which is best, and put a stone into the cleft, to keep the parts of the stock asunder, and pour into it old Urine of a Man, about four heminas, so that by degrees it may run through all the stock, that the roots so watered may be recovered. Then cast in dung mingled with Earth; But they that put the stone into the stock must dig and turn away what is about the roots. The time to do this business is in Autumn. *Democritus.*

For Vines that are astonished.

You shall know Vines that are astonished, because their leaves are very dark and red. You shall help them if you make a hole in the stock with an Auger, and put in an Oaken pin into the hole, or if you break away a little of the root, and thrust in a stick and cast Earth about it. So shall you help your Vine. Others water such Vines with Sea Water; Some annoint these and all others however they are affected, with Oyl and Bitumen mingled together. Others as they found by experience in *Bithynia*, how they ought to help Trees that are mortified, penetrate into the stocks with pins. Some pour Mans Urine upon the stock and roots. *Cassianus.*

For Vines that weep.

You shall cure a Vine that is sick with Ashes of Vine boughs, or Oak, mingled with Vinegar, and spread about the body of the tree. Mans Urine is exceeding good also powred upon the roots. But some cut up sick Vines hard by the ground, then they lightly cover them with the Earth that lies about them, mingling a little dung therewith, and when the tendrels bud forth, they root out the weak ones, and maintain the strong ones, and also the next year chusing the most fit shoot of those that that are left, they take away the rest. *Demogeron.*

For sick Vines.

Vines that weep much, so much as one can hardly believe, cast out that which is not distributed into the whole body of the Vine. We must therefore cut the stock with a pruning hook, and make an Ulcer or hollow hole in it. If this do no good; we must also cut holes in the thickness of the roots, and we must seeth Oyl Lees to half, and annoint those wounds therewith. And we must annoint the hole that is under the cut, without also, for this is approved to be much the better. *Sotion.*

For

For weeping Vines.

For weeping Vines, which you shall know by their whitish and dryish leaves; also they have large broad branches that are tractable as Thongs. You shall cure these with Ashes made up with Vinegar to annoint them about the bodies, and sprinkling it round about the stock of the Vine. Also the Vines themselves must be smeered with Vinegar and Ashes made up to an Unguent. Some pour on Sea water upon the roots. Some take care to cut off the tops of the boughs, and to hinder it that way. these Vines are called by the Greeks *Rhyades*, because by reason of their weeping they contain no fruit. *The same*

For Vines that corrupt their Grapes.

Some Vines there are that will corrupt their fruit so soon as it is new come forth, before the Clusters can be fed together, and come to maturity. Such are to be cured with leaves of Purslane. Others mingle Barley flower with the juyce of Purslane, and smeer that about the stock. Others annoint last the Cluster with Purslance. Some cast four heminas of old Ashes upon the roots, or else Sand. *Varro.*

To foresee whether a Vine will be good and fruitfull, or bad.

Take one single Grape between your fingers from the Cluster gently. If any thing leap forth, it shews fruitfullness. Some promise that if there be much Corn, then that all moist fruit shall abound. Moreover we conjecture that Wine will be good and strong, if there be many showers in the Spring-time. The same is foreseen when showers are constant, Grapes being at that time about the bigness of Tares, and are yet sower. But Rain that comes about the time of the Vintage, will not only make watry Wine, but ill and unsavory Wine. *Democrit.*

Of the Secrets of Roots. Chap. 6.

To make Rape-roots exceeding great.

Rape-roots will be very great, if the Plant be taken forth of the earth a finger deep, and then the Rapes be more gently covered in their furrows, only casting the earth upon them. *Cardan.*

To make a Raddish sweet.

If you desire sweet Raddishes, you must for two daies before, steep the Seeds in Honey and water, or juyce of pressed Grapes, or water and Sugar, and when they are dry sow them. *Florentinus.*

To make Raddishes greater.

If you desire to have greater Raddishes, take away all the leaves, and leaving only the tender stalk, cover it often with earth. *Pallad.*

For field fleas that hurt Raddishes.

Because Raddishes are often hurt by field fleas, the way to keep them safe from them is to sow Tares amongst them. *Theophrast.*

That Garlick may grow sweet.

Garlick will be more sweet, if in planting of it, Olive stone Kernels be mingled with them, or if the Cloves of Garlick be gently bruised, when they are set in the ground, or Lees of Oyl be added to them when they are planted. *Sotion.*

To make Garlick leave his stinking smell.

If Garlick be set in the ground and dug up again, when the Moon is under the horizon, it will quit its bad sent, and they that eat it shall never spoil their sweet breath. *Sotion and Pallad.*

How to take away the ill sent that comes by eating of Garlick.

The ill sent by eating of Garlick is abolished if you eat raw Beans after it; Others eat a Beet root rosted in the embers after the Garlick. *Didym.*

To make a Leek grow monstrous great.

If you prick the head of a Leek with a sharp quill or reed, and hid a rape or Cucumber seed in that hold, the head of the Leek will swell so great, that it will seem a wonder. *Mizald.*

Against the ill sent of Leeks.

He that eats Cumminseed first, shall never breath forth the stinking ill smell of Leeks, though he eat Leeks in abundance, for the eating of that takes away the ill sent of this. *Sotion.*

To counterfeit a Mandrake.

You must have a great Bryony root, which is often sold by Impostors to foolish Women, and by Juglers; upon this with a sharp edge of a Penknife carve the form of a Man or Woman, adding the privy parts. When you know it is perfect, prick with a Bodkin the groins or places of hair, and put in Millet seed or some other small seed into it, which shooting forth may be like unto hair, and then digging a pit, leave it there so long, untill it hath gotten a certain skin over it, and sent forth its small roots like hairs. *The same.*

Of the Secrets of Herbs in Generall. Chap. 7.

That fleas may not gnaw Herbs.

Pot Herbs will not be bitten by fleas, if you mingle a few Tares with them when you sow them. But this is chiefly convenient for Raddish and Rapes. Others use a more naturall help, sowing or planting of Rocket therewith, and especially with Coleworts, for these are most obnoxious to fleas. *Anatolius.*

Against Herbs Caterpillars.

Steep Vine tree Ashes three daies in water, and then besprinkle the Pot Herbs therewith, or smoke them with Bitumen and quick Brimstone. Also there will be no Caterpillars if you steep the seed in a Lee of Fig tree Ashes before you sow it. Caterpillars already bred are to be destroyed with Piss and Lees of Oyl equally mingled, and boyled on the fire, and sufferd to cool again, and so sprinkled on the Pot Herbs. But if you take the Caterpillars of another Garden, and boyl them in water with Dill, and sprinkle that water cold upon Pot Herbs, you shall destroy all Caterpillars that are there. *Anatolius.*

To help Herbs.

All Pot herbs are generally helped if you sow Rocket seed near them. *Fronton.*

To destroy Pot Herbs.

Goose dung dissolved in pickle sprinkled upon Herbs will kill them, for Goose dung is very offensive to them. *The same.*

Of the Secrets of Herbs in Speciall. Chap. 8.

To make broad Lettice.

Lettice will spread it self broad if it be sowd very thin; or when it hath a branch, let that be cut gently, and a Clot of Earth laid upon it, that it may not run to stalk; for it being restrained by that waight, when it cannot run up high, it is forced to spread abroad. *Mizald. Florent. Columel.*

To make Lettice white and fair.

If you would have handsome Lettice, two daies before you take them up, bind their leaves, that is the upper part, that will make them white and fair. Also Sand strewed upon them makes them white. *Florent.*

To make Lettice grow low and like Apples.

You shall make Lettice low, that hath its leaf turned round, and the stalk like an Apple; our Countrey men call it, Apple-wise, or Cabbage-Lettice, if you transplant the root, when it is grown a hands breadth high, taking the Earth from it, and daubing it with Ox dung, and making a heap about it, you water it, and when it groweth bigger, and the plant springs forth, you cut it off with the edg of a Knife, and an Earthen pot not pitched be over it, that it may not grow long but large. *The same.*

To make Lettice sweet.

You shall make Lettice sweeter, if you keep down the sprout, and make it come forth, by refreshing the Earth about it. *The same*

To make Lettice smell sweet.

Lettice will come forth well-sented, if you put Lettice seed into Citron seed, and so sow it in the ground, the same may be done if you steep Lettice seed some daies in sweet water. *Florent. and Mizald.*

That Lettice may have many tasts and formes.

Take Goats or Sheeps dung, and though it be but small, yet make a hole in it, and empty it carefully, and put into the empty place seeds of Lettice, Cresses, Basils, Rocket,

Rocket, Radish, or what you please, close and thick, and set this not above two small hands breadth deep, strewing first some fine tender dung under it, then heaping thin earth about it, water it by degres, and when it is sprung forth besprinkle it with water, daily strewing dung upon it, and when it runs to stalk, use far more diligence and you shall have Lettice grow together with the other seeds were set with it; Others break two or three small Bals of Goat or Sheeps dung, and mingle the seeds with them, and they wrap them all in a small linnen cloath, water them and set them in the Earth, and using such care as is needfull, they produce a Lettice of divers forms and tasts. *Didym.*

To make a Lettice grow from many seeds.

If we pull away the leaves of Lettice that are next the root, and in each space, we hide a seed, as of Basill, Rocket, Cresses, and the like, mingled with dung, there will spring from them all, a crowned Lettice stalk. *Palladius.*

That Beets may be white and larger.

If you would make Beets larger and whiter, cover their roots with Ox dung, and as with the Leek cleave the sprout, and put in a broad stone or Tile-sheard. *Solion.*

To make Cabbage excellent for taste and bigness.

You shall make Coleworts great and of singular taste, if you first of all sow them in a Parsnip, and then if you cut away the small branches that come forth of the Earth, and such as rise up very high, casting fresh Earth upon it, that nothing may stick forth, but the very top; being often dressed and dunged it will thrive the better, and will bring up a branch of greater increase. *Mzild.*

That Smallage may be with very broad leaves and crisped.

Smallage will grow very great, if you bind into an old wollen Cloath as much of the seed of it, as you can take up with three fingers: and then covering it with dung, you presently water it; Likewise Smallage will be very great, if you dig about the roots, and cast straw there, and water it. But it will crisp, if the seed before it be sowed, be gently bruised in a Mortar, and then it be roled with a Roler. *Florent.*

Suddenly to produce Garden Smallage or Parsly.

Let the seeds be of one years standing, and when Summer comes, steep them in Vinegar, let them stand a while in a warm place, then open the earth loose, and put them in, and mingle burnt Bean stalk ashes with them; then sprinkle a little *Aqua vitæ* upon them, and having often watred them thus, cover them with a wollen cloath to keep in the heat; so in a very short time in few houres they will spring out of the ground; remove the Cloath and water them, and the stalk will come forth longer, and will make men wonder at it. *The same.*

That Sparagus may grow in great plenty.

If you would have plenty of Sparagus, fill the furrows with wild Rams horns beaten very small, and water it; Some say contrary to this opinion, if the horns be left whole, not broken in pieces, but bored through and set, they will bring forth Saragus. *Didym.*

To have Sparagus to eat all the year.

If you desire to have Sparagus all the year; when you gather the Sparagus, cut presently the root upon the superficies of it, for the Plant being thus handled will bring forth Sparagus again. *The same.*

That no bind-weed may be in the Vineyard.

That no bind weed may grow in a Vineyard, take Oyl Lees, and purifie them, put two measures into a brass Cauldron, and boyl it at a gentle fire, stir it well with a stick, untill it be as thick as Honey; then take a third part of Bitumen, and a fourth part of Brimstone; beat both of them severally in a Mortar: then strew them very fine into the hot Oyl Lees, and mingle them with a stick, and boyl it again in the open Ayr. For if you boyl it in the house, after you have added the Bitumen and the Brimstone, it will boyl over, when it is as thick as Birdlime; let it cool, annoint the head and body of the Vine with this, and no bind-weed will run about it. *M. Cato.*

That Grass may not grow.

Some report, That if with a Copper fork dipt in Goats bloud, you dig up Grass, it will never grow again. *Cardan.*

Of the Secrets of Flowers in Generall. Chap. 9.

To make Flowers and fruit come forth suddenly.

Chuse what flower you please, it is all one, for it will do the same with all. If you will have a Rose before its time, about *October*, set Quicklime about your Earthen vessels into the Earth, well sifted with a Sive, and mingling dung with it made soft, you shall twice aday cast hot water upon it, and if it be windy or rainy weather, bring the pots into the house, and at night carry them to stand in the open Ayr. When cold frosts and Winter showres are gone, and the Ayr is pleasant, set them in the Sun, if the day be clear. When time requires it, and the Spring begins to come, and the Bud offers to sprout forth, pour on hot water; for it delights in continuall and easie watring; so will that come out first which is the last of the Spring flowers. You must consider that if the Winter be mild, it will bud before the time, and if the South wind blow, and is not cold, and bringing Snow with it; (as *Theophrastus* writes) When the force of growing, and the fertill moysture is affoarded it, sometimes of it self, sometimes from the residue of the humour, whereby fruits spring out. *The same.*

To make Spring or Summer flowers keep untill Winter.

If you bury Plants with their roots, amongst Wine Lees, of which the pils are taken away, or else in Horse dung often renewed, these will bring you most gallant flowers in Winter. *Mizald.*

Of the Secrets of Flowers in Speciall. Chap. 10.

To keep Roses fresh.

Chuse Roses and other flowers, not when they are fully open, but when they begin to open, wrap them in liquid Pitch, and cut a Cane and put them into it, and bury them in the open Ayr, in a place that is steep, least the Rain falling down should hurt them; or cleave a green Cane, and put the Rose or flower into that, and take care to make the cleit unite again, so you shall rejoyce to find that you desire. Or else thus. Make an Oaken vessel, fill it with flowers, and Roses that are not yet open; let it be well covered and Pitched, that no water may enter. Let this down into a Well, or Cistern, or Brook of running waters, for there they will corrupt less, and they will continue long fresh, being shut when all others gape wide, stick the stalk into an Apple, or steep it into Vinegar, setting it in the Sun. *The same.*

To keep Roses fresh a whole Year.

You shall keep Roses fresh thus; Take Wine and Salt what is needfull, and pour them into an Earthen pot, then fill the pot with Roses you would keep, (but you must gather Rose buds not open) put a cover upon the Pot, and set it in a Cellar. When you vvould use them, open the Vessel and take them out, and set them in the Sun, or an Oven, that they may open, and you shall have as fair sweet Roses as if they were new gathered. *Gaspar Schwenckfeld.*

To make a Rose sweeter.

Roses will smell sweeter if you Plant Garlick by them, for such things as languish by cold, are recreated by heat. *Didym.*

To have Roses betimes.

If you will have early Roses, you shall dig about them two hands breadth, and water them with hot water morning and evening. *The same.*

To have Roses every Moneth.

He that desireth to have Roses every Moneth, must plant, dung, and water them every Moneth: but this cannot be had in Northern Climats. *The same.*

An early Rose.

Early Roses are procured otherwise, either planted in Earthen pots or Baskets; and deal with them, as I shall shew you to deal with early Gourds and Cucumbers. *The same.*

To keep Roses fresh and green.

You shall keep Roses fresh and lively, if you put them into Lees of Oyl, that the liquor may swim above them. Others pull up green Barley with the roots and all, and put it into a Vessel not pitched, and they put buds of Roses into that, cover and keep them there. Others cast green Barly upon the pavement, and lay Roses not yet open upon it. *The same.*

That a Rose may spring forth in January.

If a Rose-tree in the middle of Summer be watered twice aday, *Democritus* saith it will bring forth Roses in *January.*

That a Rose may grow when Apples do.

If you Engraff and inoculate a Rose sprig into the Bark of an Apple Tree, *Florentinus* writes, it will bring Roses when Apples are ripe.

To make white Roses.

When Roses begin to open, smoke them with Brimstone, and you shall have them soon. *Didymus.*

That Roses and Jasmin may be yellow.

I shall shew how by Insition Roses and Jasmin may be made yellow : because Broom flowers are the yellowest of flowers; we strive to make Roses and Jasmine as yellow as they; and since Broom is not to be Engraffed by Twigs, or Insoliation, therefore we plant the Rose near to the Broom, and we transplant it with its naturall Earth, for they will grow more willingly in their Parents bosome, than with a step Mother; and we make a hole in the Plant, and when we have cleansed the hole, we scrape it all about and set it in, and fasten in with Clay wrapt about it, and bind it. After this when it is restrained by the growth of the stock, we must separate it from the root, and cut off the stock above the Engraffing; so will the Rose very handsomely grow yellow, and so Jasmin is so comely and shining with yellow colour amongst us, that it will dazel ones eyes. So it pleaseth us on all sides with divers colours that it is joyned to. *The same.*

To make a Rose green, yellow, and blew.

Now let us see if a Rose can be made green, yellow and blew. It may be done thus. On the outside we cleave the stalk near to the roots, as we do Roses, and all the branches of it, and we thrust in plenty of colours, for green, Verdigrease, for blew, Indigo, or a storie so called, for yellow, Saffron, but they must be made into very fine pouder : yet take heed that you put in no Orpiment or any venemous colour, for that will destroy the Plant; after this dung and dawb it in, and it will colour the flower carrying nourishment with it.

To colour Roses or Gelliflowers in a short time with divers colours.

Take the fattest Earth as much as you please; dry it well at the Sun, untill it may be made into very fine pouder, then when it is put into some Vessel, plant some slip of a white flower into it; But take care you wet not the Earth with any other water than with these that follow; wherefore if you would make white flowers red, take Brasil Wood cut very small, as much as you need; and boyl it in water untill a third part be consumed, or a fourth part, and the water will be red; with this twice aday water the Earth Morning and Evening cold : this must be done so long untill the Plant begin to grow; namely, for fifteen or twenty daies. If you desire green ones, take instead of Brasil ripe berries of purging Thorn; if yellow ones, take unripe berries of purging Thorn; if black ones, Gals and Vitriol, and boyl them in water; water the Earth therewith as I said before. But take heed you leave them not abroad in the night, because of the dew that it will easily suck in. But the flowers will not be perfectly died, but partly will have their naturall, partly an artificiall colour, mingled of them both. If you would have them of three colours, in the morning water them with one coloured water, and in the evening with another : and the next day water the Earth died with another coloured water in the morning, and with another sort in the evening, so that morning and evening they may be watered with two different colours, yet so that the sides may vary : which will be done if you do not pour on the water in the evening on the same side of the Earth you poured it on in the morning; and so this Plant with its own naturall colour will have three colours, and of this many more may be produced. *Alexius Pedemontanus.*

That the crown Gelliflower may be made blew.

Cut Succory or Blew-bottles, but the wild Succory is best, that is old, thick above, an Inch broad near the root, and cleave it in the middle, that in the Center of it you may stick a shoot of the flower, pulled from the root; bind it on with a Twig, and heap about it Earth with putrefied rotten dung; so it will bear a flower like the Blew-bottle, which your eyes will be very much pleased with. So if you stick into the root of wild Buglofs any white flowers sprig, you shall have a Purple flower, and tending afterwards into a light red colour. *The same.*

That a Gelliflower may have flowers in Winter.

If about the Calends of *October* you bury the Plants of Gelliflowers, or Violets, or such like, in a heap of Grape stones, the husks being taken from them, or in Horse dung often renewed, you shall have most pleasant flowers in Winter, the same may be done with Strawberries and Melons, but they must be defended from outward cold: but they often dye with their offspring. *Card.*

That Gelliflowers may bring divers flowers upon one branch.

I have seen one sprig bear a Snow white flower, a Purple coloured, and Checkwerd, which is wont to be done either by Art of dressing, or by the fruitfullness of the Earth changed often. Yet I knew many do it, by sticking many severall seeds of Gelliflowers into a Sheep or Goats trundel, or a broken Reed, or a thin rubbed linnen Cloath, Artificially covered with Earth and dung, for these seeds grow all into one root, that sends forth branches with variety of flowers. *Mizald.*

That one Plant of a Violet may bear the colours of all sorts.

If you would have one Plant of a Violet represent flowers of all their colours, put all their seeds into a thin Reed or worn Linnen Cloath, and bury that in earth very well dunged. I have often tried it with great delight, and you will wonder at it as much as I did. *The same.*

To make Lillies Purple coloured.

If you would make Lillies Purple coloured, take ten or twelve of their small stalks and bind them together, and hang them over the smoke: and they will send out of their stalks small roots like little Onyons; When therefore it is time to Plant them, steep these stalks in the dregs of black Wine, untill, when you take them forth they appear like a well died Purple colour. Then Plant them, and pour upon each of them a sufficient quantity of the Wine Lees, and the Lillies that grow of them, will bring Purple coloured flowers. *Anatolius.*

To make red Lillies.

You shall make a red Lilly, if you pour Cinnaber between the rind, taking heed that you hurt not the small round knots: If you will put in any other colour, you may have them of what colour you please. *Florentinus.*

That Lillies may keep fresh a whole year.

Lillies will keep fresh all the year, thus. You must take them branches and all, not yet open but shut, and put them into new earthen vessels, not pitched, then stop the vessels, and lay them up, and so they will keep fresh all the year. If you would in the mean time use any of them, set them in the Sun, that being warm they may open. That Lillies may flower some at one time, some at another, when you plant their roots, set some twelve fingers deep, some eight, some six, and you shall have Lillies a long time; you may do the same with other flowers. *Anatolius.*

Of the Secrets of Fruits in Generall. Chap. 11.

To have early Fruit.

That you may have early Fruit, water them often with hot water, set them in the Sun, and foster them with Pigeons and Horse dung, or with Lime, such as can endure it, as Cherry-Trees, and by degrees cut off all superfluities and unprofitable boughs.

If you would have late Fruit.

On the contrary, if you desire to have late fruit, you must do contrarily; leave them in the shade, and covered over with abundance of leaves; cut off the fruit and boughs that are come forth already, before they be ripe, for they will blossome again and bear new fruit; to ripen these in Winter, inclose them in Earthen pots as they hang upon the Trees. *The same.*

That fruit may be sweeter and smell more pleasant.

You must steep the kernels three daies in Water and Honey, Sheeps milk, or Water and Sugar, as the Antients did, and when they are dried in the Sun, set them, and the fruit will be sweeter. If you vvould have them smell sweeter; vvet the seeds or Kernels in Oyl of Spike, or juyce, or distilled Rose Water, dissolving Musk and Civet in the Water, when you have wet them awhile, dry them, and set them, and the fruit vvill smell very sweet, that you vvill vvonder at it, that the fruit should come so pleasant sented from thee seeds that drank in that sweet sent, but if you break the tops of the seed, let them remain in it but a short time. *Florent.*

To make all fruit greater.

If you would have greater fruit: bury an earthen pot full of vvater about the roots, bend the bough with the blossome upon it, and bring it down into this pot of vvater, fasten it that it may not stir, the pot must stand in the Earth all stopped about the bough, that the spirits may not evaporate: so vvhen the time comes that the fruit is ripe, you shall have huge Apples, and greater than ever grew upon the Tree, the the bark being so thick: for the moysture that the Sun and the Ayr draw from them, is preserved in the pot, and the vapours arising augment and increase the fruit.

That fruit may have what fashion you will.

Frame in Wood the form you vvould have, as great as vvhen the fruit comes to perfection, it vvill be; put Gyp dissolved in vvater about it, near the thicknesse of your little finger, divided two vvaies; Take off this form from the Wood vvhen it is dry, (and it vvill dry suddenly,) you shall do it easily if you first annoint the Wood with Oyl. Bind this form taken off, that is hollow, made of Plaister, and divided in two parts, fast about the fruit that is growing, and is about half the naturall bigness already, leave it so untill the fruit come to its just magnitude. You shall have your fruit the same fashion that the Wood was carved, also you may Write into it it vvhat you pleafe: that you may say truly. Grow, and express my Titles on your skin. *Cardan.*

That fruit may have a purging quality.

If you put about the roots Hellebour, or vvild Cucumber, or Scammony, especially the roots of Plum-Tree or Cherry-Tree, and much more of the Vine, vvhen you take the earth from the roots, their fruit vvill have a purging quality. *Cato.*

How to make fruit, compounded of severall fruit.

In the monstrous compositions and transmutations of nature, there is no better vvay then to do it by Engraffing. I have enough commended it, but I shall hereafter commend it much more: vvhen as by a mutuall complication of divers fruits, and indissoluble convinction is made, and shews the reason of the wonder. And if some Man may think Insirions to be laborious and almost impossible, you shall ease your labour, and help the impossibility by prudent care, and let not ignorant Husbandmen and Gardners dissuade you from that vvhich experience proves to be true: and remember vvhat the Ancients have left behind them: that a Fig may be Engraffed on a Plane Three, or a Mulberry; a Mulberry may be Engraffed on a Chestnut, a Turpentine Tree, and vvhite Poplar, and vvhite Mulberries may grow from thence, Chestnuts upon Nuttrees, and Oakes. The Pomegranate rejoyceth in diversity of Adulteries, and vvill be Engraffed upon all; the Cherry vvill grow upon the Peach and Turpentine Trees; and the Peach and Turpentine upon the Cherry-Tree. The Quince upon the Barbery; the Vine vvill bear fruit upon the Olive Tree, and have Olives that are Olives and Grapes. And *Florentinus* reports that he

saw

saw such with *Manrius Maxieus*, which tasted right like Grapes and Olives together, the Myrtill will grow upon the Willow, and so will the Pomegranate, and others there are, which it is worth considering, far more difficult than these. *Columella* thinks all sorts of sprigs may be Engraffed into any kind. Hence comes the composition of all fruits, and adopting of them all, and hence they produce unusuall fruits. *The same.*

That fruits growing may take all forms and impressions.

If you desire to counterfeit the head of a Man or of any other Creature, you shall make the bigness of the fruit, when it is perfect in Potters Clay, or soft Plaister, that will dry, and carve it with the point of an Instrument, that you may cast out the Pattern, and joyn the frame together again. If the forme be of Wood, make it hollow within, if of Clay, when you have baked it, and the fruit are of good growth, shut in within these Earthen patterns, the fruit, leaving an open place for the stalk, and bind them fast with a strong Twig, that the forms do not open as the Apples increase, and that from the first begining of them, and when you have got them to grow there, and the fruit is come to its full bigness, it will take such figures as you were pleased to carve; and this is especially to be proved upon Gourds, Pears, Quinces, (as *Democritus* saith) Pome-Citrons, Pomegranates, and mad Apples. I find it written by the Quintilii; If you cleave a Cane long-wise, and make hollow joynts within it, and shut into it young Gourds or Cucumbers, they will run all along the Cane, Wantonly, wandring along, and filling up the Cane after the same manner. If you put a Gourd between two Dishes pressed together, you shall have a flat round Gourd, and it will take all figures as you will force it to. If you put it into a case of Earth after the flower is fallen away, it will turn it self into the fashion of a Serpent. *Aphricanus and others.*

How fruit may have no stones nor kernels.

It is an old saying of the Philosophers: and chiefly of those who have set forth choice Principles of Husbandry; if in setting of Twigs, or live roots, you take out the Pith first with an Earpicker or bone-Knife, that the fruit will have no stones nor shels about the kernels, because that which breeds them is of a hard substance; But the *Arcadians* are against this Opinion; Every Tree say they, may live, and have something taken from it; but if the Pith be taken away, it will not only not bring forth fruit without stones, but it will dye and bear no fruit at all; and their reason is, because that is the moystest part and most vitall; for the nutriment, which the Earth affoards, runs through it for the maintaining of every plant: for the pith is as it were the life, and the nourishment runs through it, as through a Conduit pipe; that appears by Twigs that the pith is taken from, they will bend and turn round, untill they be quite dry: and this the Ancients did utterly fear. But we that approve of *Theophrastus* his rules and experience, are of the former opinion, and it is very profitable and usefull. *The same.*

Of the Secrets of smaller Trees or Shrubs in speciall. Chap. 12.

That Apples may continue long in their beauty and force.

Early Pears, Apples, Quinces, that are sweet, are not to be taken, Figs, Tubers, and Junibes with their boughs are to be chosen, but all unripe, but not very raw; those that will fall, must be parted from them; you must search diligently if they be found, and not bruised with your hands. Burn about the branches that are cut off, scalding Pitch, touching them a little; for else they would sooner corrupt, then wrapping them in Hemp or Hurds, cover that round with melted Wax, and being so covered, cut them down into Honey, when they are all let down severally into the Honey, keep them so, that they may not mingle, nor touch one the other: for one will corrupt the other; when they are covered put on the cover of the Vessel, and skin of leather over that, so you may keep them green all the year. So all Apples may be kept in Honey that are laid up for a long time. *The same.*

To keep Apples a long time.

Apples will last a long while that are gathered in their perfection, you must pull them

them with your hand, and that warily, that you bruise them not. Wrap them all severally in Sea weeds or Sea moss, that they may be fully covered, and then put them into raw Earthen pots, put also Sea weeds between, with the stalks of the Apples that they may not touch one the other; put covers upon the pots, and set them in a high cool loft, where they may have neither smoke nor any ill sent. If you have no Sea weeds, put the Apples severally into very small Earthen pots, with covers, and set them up. Some wrap all the Apples single in Potters Earth, and dry it, and set it up. Apples will be kept sound also, laying under them Nut-tree-leaves. But it is better to wrap the Nut-tree-leaves severally about them. You shall keep Apples also, if you put them single into Earthen pots that are Waxed within side, and cover them close. Apples will not corrupt laid in Barley: you may keep them also this way. Take an Earthen vessel not glazed, with a hole in the bottome, and fill that with Apples pulled with your hands, not bruised, nor old, and stop the Vessel close with Butchers Broom, or with some other thing, and hang this upon any Tree, and let it alone all the Winter, and the Apples will remain as they were first put in; which I have also found by experience. Apples are also kept thus. Wrap every Apple severally with dry Fig-leaves, then cover them over with white Potters Clay, and being dry, lay them in the Sun. Wine Lees will also keep them safe, and they will preserve Wine, which all Men may wonder at. For Apples put into a new Earthen pot, and the pot being let down into a Vessel of Wine, that it may swim in it, and the Vessel be well dawbd about, the Apples will be fresh, and the Wine sweet sented. Also they are laid into hollow Coffers with fine flocks, and they are so preserved. But Winter Apples are best kept in Corne. *Apulejus*

How Apples must be kept and laid up.

Apples must be gathered about the Autumnall Equinoctiall, according as the Climat, Ground, and Tree is by nature, and not before the fifteenth day of the Moon; as *Pliny* writes: You must be carefull with your hands in gathering them, that you neither bruise nor hurt them, and you must separate all fallings, corrupt, rotten, worm-eaten Apples, from the sound. They will be best preserved upon boarded flores where no smoke comes, nor ill sent in a cold room, and windows open toward the North: which must lye open in clear daies to let in the light; shutting out the South winds: for the South winds are far more hurtfull to fruit then the North: for those do make the Apples wrinkled and ill favoured. They may be kept also in a cold dry place upon straw, as *Varro* writes. Wherefore they that make Apple-lofts must take great heed that the windows be toward the North, that the Ayr may come to blow upon them. *Mizald.*

That Apples may hang long upon the trees.

Command the boughs to be bended inwards, that the ripening juyce may not fall into them; they will be kept safe against the flattering blandishments of Summers heat. This way chiefly are Pomegranates kept, least they should chap and be spoiled. *The same.*

That Apples may represent any form.

Wrap in Gyp, or figular Clay any Image you please; and cut it into two parts so exactly with a fit Instrument, that the parts may again be well united together: then bake the forme in a Potters Furnace, and when the Apple is come to half its growth, shut it up in these frames, and bind it in fast with strong bands, that the Earthen patterns may not be pulled one from the other, by the Apple that increaseth within them. And when it hath filled up their hollow places, the Apple will represent such figures of living Creatures, whose shape and postures you were pleased to fancy and Carve within. This holds not only for Apples, but also for Pears, Quinces, Peaches, Citrons, Pomegranates, Oranges, and all sorts of Apple fruit. *Mizaldus* from *Aphricanus.*

To make figures upon Apples.

If you cover Apples with boyld Gyp made up with water into a liquid body, and with your Instrument make marks in the Plaister, when the Apples come to their full growth, and you gather them, you shall have those markes apparent in the Apples.

A a

To make Apples sweet.

If you desire sweet Apples, dissolve Goats dung in Mans Piss, and old Wine Lees, and pour that upon the roots. *Mizald.*

That Apples may not corrupt.

To keep Apples from rottenness, smeer the body with the Gall of a green Lizard: and this is a present remedy against Ants. *The same.*

That Apples may not fall.

If Apples fall, cleave the root and drive in a stone that will hold them. *Aphrican.*

To make red Apples.

Water the Tree with Piss, and the fruit will grow red. Some make Apples red upon the Trees, thus. They force Stakes into the ground, and they bend the boughs that have fruit, and bind them to those Stakes, not shaking them, and they fill ditches that are near, or Vessels with water, making their conjecture that the Sun beams at noon shining into the water, may send back a hot vapour, falling by refraction upon the fruit, and may make them red and well coloured. Some set Roses under the Trees, and so make the fruit red. *Berytius.*

Another.

If you Engraff a branch of a Citron or a Pear into a red Mulberry, the Apples that grow from thence will be red, so the Rose Apple that is bloud red was first made. *The same.*

How Pears may be made red and marked.

A Pear Engraffed on a Mulberry will bring red Pears, *Tarentinus*. To mark Pears with what marks you list, you shall learn before concerning Apples.

How Pears must be gathered and kept.

Pears must be gathered as Apples were, and with the same observations, namely, upon a clear day, with a gentle hand, that they receive no hurt, parting the fallings and corrupt Pears from the sound, when the Moon decreaseth, and the Sun shines hot. When you have done this shut them up close in a glazed Vessel, and turn the mouth downwards, and make a short pit to hide it in there, about which water may run continually. Others say they will be excellent well preserved, if you annoint the stalks or boughs with Pitch, and so hang them up. Others keep them in sweet Wine, or boyld Wine, or bastard Wine, that swims above them in the Vessels. Some hide them in Ditches. Many wrap them up in dry Walnut leaves. Others bury them severally in Wine Lees, that they may not one touch another. Countrey Men keep them in Chaff and Corn; some as soon as they are gathered hide them in well glazed Pitchers, and covering the Vessels mouths with Potters Earth, Gyp, or Pith, they bury them in the open Ayr, or cover them with Sand. They are kept best, as all other fruit in Honey, if they do not touch one the other. *Mizaldus. Democritus, Palladius.*

How to mark Quinces.

Quinces will represent any Creatures, if they be put into forms and patterns to grow there. *Democritus.*

How Quinces must be gathered and kept.

You must gather your Quinces very ripe and sound, in a clear day, the Moon decreasing, and being wiped, in a new Vessel with a large mouth, they must be the gentlyer laid at a distance one from another, having first all their hoary down rubbed off. Then when they are laid up almost as far as the brims of the Vessel, they must be so kept close with Hoops or Twigs, that they may be easily pressed down, least when moysture is put to them they should rise up. Then fill the Vessel up to the top with the best and thinnest Honey, that every Quince may lye under it; But you must take heed that you lay no raw Quince into it, for it will grow so hard that it will be good for nothing. I hear that some cut the Quinces first with a bone or wodden Knife (because they fear Iron) in pieces, before they put them into the Honey: also they take out the Kernels which they think hurts the Quince. A thing ridiculous rather than to be believed. Some did put their Quinces gathered and choice into Vessels of sweet Wine, and shut them in, promising that the Wine should be the better sented for it.

Some

Some shut them into a new pot swimming in a Wine Vessel, and they smeer the vessel round. Some keep them wrapt up in Fig leaves. Many lay them in Chests, wrapt up in Hards and Flocks. Many in Saw-dust, Millet, Barley, or Oats, will preserve them safe a long time. But they must not be laid up in a house where Summer fruits and other tender fruits use to be kept: for they will spoil them with their sharp sent, and make them perish. Some keep them in Fig or Walnut tree leaves. Others smeer them over with Potters Earth, and dry them in the Sun, and hang them up, and when they need them they wash off the Earth. Many do severally lay them in wodden Coffers, upon most dry wood, in a most cold place, where no smoke nor ill Ayr comes: that the flowers may be upward, and the stalks downward, and take care one may not corrupt another: then laying between them some Poplar or Firr Tree Saw-dust, they lay on a cover made of Clay and Straw, that the wind may not come in. *Mizaldus, Democritus, Cato, Varro, Collumella, Palladius, Pliny.*

That Plums may grow without stones.

You shall have Plums without stones, if you cut up a small Plum Tree two foot above ground, and cleave it down to the roots, and scraping out with your Knife the pith of both sides, you presently joyn the parts divided, and bind them fast together with a band, and cover the top and sides cleft with dung, Clay, Wax, or defend it with a wet Paper. When one year is over, the scar will be made, and the sides will be grown fast together; Engraff this Tree with Sciences that never bare fruit, and the Plums will have no stones: be they Plums, Cherries, Peaches, Medlars, Dates, or stony Dog tree fruit. *The same.*

How Cherries may be made without stones.

If you would have Cherries without stones, cut the young Tree to two foot, and cleave it down as low as the roots, and scrape out with your Instrument the pith of both parts, presently joyn with a band the parts that are divided, and dawb the top and clefts with dung: after a year the parts separated will joyn: Engraff that Tree with Twigs that never bare fruit before, and so your Cherries will have no stones. *The same.*

To make white Mulberries.

If you will have white Mulberries, Engraff them into the white Poplar tree, and the berries will be white. *Berytius.*

How Mulberries must be laid up and kept.

Mulberries laid up carefully in a Glass vessel, will keep a long time, being soked in their own juyce, or Wine close covered: so they be not over ripe, feeble, and falling away. *The same.*

That Peaches may grow with figures and inscriptions upon them.

You shall make Peaches with inscriptions thus. When you have eaten the Peach steep the stone two or three daies in Water, and open it gently, and take the Kernell out of it, and write something within the shell, with an Iron graver, what you please, yet not too deep, then wrap it in Paper and set it; whatever you write in the shell, you shall find written in the fruit, some do the same in a true Almond with the like success. *Democrit.*

To make Peaches red.

You shall make Peaches red planting Roses under them, you may make the fruit red another way. For if you set the Peach stone in the ground, and take it up after seaven daies, (for in so many daies it will open of it self,) and put Cinnaber within the stone, and setting of it again, you take great care of it, you shall have red Peaches thereby. May be if you will put in any other colour, you shall make the fruit of the same colour. *The same.*

To make Peaches wonderfull big.

That you may make huge great Peaches, Almonds, Nuts, and the like, you shall take three or four Kernels out of them, which you shall joyn so fitly together, that they may seem to be all one body. These being joyn'd, and if need be, tied together, you shall put into some vessel full of earth and dung well mingled, and so plant or set them. But the vessel must have a hole in the cover, through which the sprout may be forced to come forth, so will those Kernels joyn into one Tree, which in its due time will produce exceeding large fruit; some do not put the Kernels into a vessel, but into a Pipe or Cane full of Earth. But if you desire to get such great fruit a far more easie way: You must chuse those Peaches out diligently that appear small and languishing, and that will be a burden to the Tree with too much abundance; that the juyce of the Tree may be disposed to bring up the rest. For so the quantity of juyce being carried to the nutriment of a smaller number, will supply them with plenty of nutriment and make them greater. *Mizald.*

That Peaches may come forth without stones.

We may produce Peaches without stones, by a new way of Engraffing. We set near the Willow a Peach Tree, in a rich moyst ground, otherwise help it by watering of it, that the Tree may swell, and may afford superfluity of juyce to it self and to strong sprigs graffed upon it. If the Willow as big as ones Arm be bored through in the middle, leaving the head of the Peach Tree, we must cut off all the shoots, and we bring this through the hole of the Willow stock; we stop the hole diligently with Lome, and we bind it with a band; a year being over, when they now grow together, that they make of two but one Tree, we cut off as much of it as grows above the hole bored where they unite, that the nutriment may not be carried thither and that the juyce may be called away from the place of Engraffing, and that the other Tree may be bent by the fruit growing upon it, or else bending the head of the Willow like a bow, and setting it into the ground; and when they are united, the Peach Tree being cut off, and the Tree transplanted and covered with Earth about it; so the Peach Tree being married to the Willow, with wonderfull delight will bear Peaches without stones. *The same.*

Another.

You shall bore the Stock of the Tree through beneath, and cut out the pith, and knock in a pin of the Willow or Dog Tree. *Aphrican.*

That a Nut may not bring forth Woddy fruit.

If the Kernell bringeth forth hard woddy fruit, the bark must be cut round, that the noxious fault of the moysture may be drawn away. Some cut off the tops of the roots. Many make a hole in the root, and knock in a Box wedg, or a Copper or Iron nail. *Mizald.*

That Nuts may grow without shels.

You shall have naked Nuts without shels, if you break the Nut shell, and keeping the Kernel unhurt, wrap it in Wooll, or in green Vine or Plum Tree leaves, that the Kernel being covered may not be eaten by Ants, and so it must be planted. *Florentinus* saith the same of an Almond, if Ashes be daily cast about the stock and root, and the same holds in all other fruits, that have a shell above the Kernel, if they be planted the same way. *Aphrican.*

Another.

Dig a pit where you intend to plant a Wallnut Tree, and put into it poudred Earth, and plant there the seed of Fennel Gygant; when it is grown up, open it, and into the pith of it put in the Kernell of a Nut without a shell, and stop it fast with Wax, and so you shall in a long time have the fruit you desire. So we may make a Peach, which they call *Tarentina,* or *Molusca,* when the shell is very brittle and tender, and may be easily broken in ones hands; often water this with Lee for a whole year, and cast Ashes about the roots, as *Damageron* sheweth; and also boring the Tree quite through, you shall make hard stony Nuts very tender. So you may do with a Hazel Nut, and an Almond; before it blossome, scrape the earth from the roots, and for some dayes pour on hot water, and the Nuts will be tender as *Aphricanus* saith: but the former way it will bring a Kernel without a shell and so soft, that it is rather covered with a skin that is tender, then with a shell, that you may eat both together, and this serves for all fruit that are covered with a shell. *The same.*

To make bitter Almonds sweet.

You shall make bitter Almonds sweet, if you bore the stock square, the depth of a small hand breadth, and let the juyce run forth yearly, untill the Almonds be sweet. Some do better digging about it, and casting Hogs dung and Piss to it, and then laying Earth upon it, they water it every year untill the Almonds be sweet: but every Tree that bears Almonds being cut off in the body will never bring fruit; But you shall make a tender and sweet Tree of a hard and bitter, if you lay open the stock as far as the roots that are in the surface of the ground, and water them daily with hot water, before they send forth blossoms. *Aphrican.*

That Almonds may have writings upon them.

Break an Almond shell carefully, that the Almond within may be kept entire, and opening the shell, write what you please upon the shell, and binding it up again, plant it wrapt in paper, and covering it with Lome, lay upon it a heap of Hogs dung. *The same.*

That Pomegranates may not cleave.

When you plant Pomegranates put flint stones first into the pit; but if they be planted already, plant squils near them; for these by a naturall contrariety will not suffer the Pomegranates to chap. Likewise if they be planted with the head upwards they will not cleave. *Aphrican.*

That Pomegranates may be sweet.

Dig about the roots and heap on Hogs dung, and laying Earth upon it, water it with Mans Urine. Or, the Trees will have the sweeter fruit thus: If the roots of the Tree be daily watered with Urine, Goats dung, and old Wine Lees. *Paxamus* and *Anatolius.*

To make Pomegranates grow without Kernels.

If you take from the Tree, as in the Vine, the apparent part of the pith, and cover the Tree that is cleft, and after a certain time you cut away the supereminent part of the Tree, that hath now sent forth a branch, the Pomegranate Tree will bring fruit without Kernels. *Aphrican.*

To make Pomegranates more red.

If you would make your Pomegranates redder, you shall water the Tree with water mingled with Barbers Lee. *The same.*

To know how many kernels a Pomegranate will have.

Open one Pomegranate and count the kernels, and as many as you find there, think that every one hath just as many. *The same.*

To augment the kernels of the Pomegranate.

You may augment the Pomegranate kernels thus, that they may seem to be wonderfull, set a Pomegranate Tree near to a wild Cherry Tree, called the Dog Tree, and bore a hole through the stock of the Dog Tree, and draw the Pomegranate Tree through the hole; when three years are past, you shall separate it from the roots, and shall then cut off the Dog Tree where the joyning is, that it may not draw away the juyce from the strong Plant Engraffed into it, and that it may serve nothing more than the Graff: for thus will it bear fruit, whose stones will be like the stones of the Dog Tree fruit, of excellent taste, and more fair then ordinary. *The same.*

How Pomegranates may grow to a wonderfull greatness.

It is reported that Pomegranates will grow wonderfull great, if an earth Pot be buried about the Tree, or be so fitted that the bough with the flower may be shut into it, bound to a stake that it flye not back again, and the Pot be covered, that no water may come in; for in its time it will seasonably bear Pomegranates of the same bigness, and fashioned after the figure of that Pot or Vessel you bring it into. *Mizaldus*, from *Gargilius Martiall.*

That Pomegranates may be kept green upon the tree.

When Pomegranates are ripe, before they break off, the stalks they hang by are to be twisted, and then they will continue fresh upon the Trees all the year. *Palladius, Pliny.*

How to make abundance of Pomegranates.

You shall have abundance of Pomegranates, if the juyce of Tithymal, and Purslane be equally mingled, and the stock of the Tree be dawbed with it before it bud. *Pallad.*

To make Pomegranate kernels white.

Pomegranate kernels will be white, if you mingle with Potters Earth and Chalk a fourth part of Gyp, and for three years together you strew this kind of Earth about the roots. *Gargilius Martial.*

To keep Pomegranates for uses in Winter.

Pomegranates will be preserved for Winter, if you gather them with a gentle hand, that you hurt them not with hard touching of them, then dipping their stalks into unboyled and liquid Pitch, when they are cold hang them in order. Some dip them all over in the Pitch, and when they are cold they hang them up. Also if you gather them whole and steep them so long in Sea water or scalding brine, that they may drink in the liquor and be wet: and then hang them three daies to dry in the Sun, (but they must not be left abroad in the night) and after that hang them up in some cold place: when need is you may put them into fresh water. Others wrap them in Potters Clay, and when they are dry, they hang them up in a cold place, and at their need, they put them into water, and wash off the Clay. Some wrap them severally in Hay, or stalks, and with Clay and Straw they dawb them thick; and so they bind them to strong great boughs, that the wind may not stir them. Some lay them at a distance one from the other in dry Sand; or hide them in a heap of Corn in the shadow untill they wither. *Mizald. Berytius* and others.

That a Pomecitron may grow with a picture upon it.

You shall make a Pomecitron like an Image, or to a Mans face, or any other living Creature, thus, with Gyp or Clay you cover what you please, and when it is cold you cut it into two parts with some sharp Instrument, that the fore part and the hinder part may fit and joyn again, then when it is dry you bake it in a Potters Oven. And when fruit are come to half their bigness, you must bring those formes round about them, and bind them fast on with bands, least as the fruit grows bigger it do not pull the formes one piece from another, and so the fruit will take the representation of what is carved in the forms. *Aphricanus.*

How Pomecitrons are to be made red, and the middle of them sweet.

If you will have red Citrons, plant a Graff of it upon the Mulberry Tree, and the Citrons will be red. *Palladius* saith, The middle of the Citron will be sweet, if the stock be bored with a slant hole from the bottome, yet so that it come not forth on the other side. So the moysture must be sufferd to run forth untill the Citrons be formed; then the hole must be filled up with Clay. Some affirme that the same thing may be done, if the kernels before they be set, be steeped in Sheeps milk, or in Honey and Water, or Sugar and Water. *Mizald.*

How to preserve Pomecitrons.

If you dawb about well a Citron with Gyp made into a Plaister, you shall keep it sound a whole year; Citrons hid in a heap of Barley will not corrupt. *Sotion.*

To have Citrons all the year.

You shall observe this way to keep Citrons all the year, which is peculiar in *Assyria*, and frequent in many places; When it is time to gather them, cut some part away from the Native branch, checking the luxuriousness with your Knife and leave a part, where you cut it off, by the naturall fertilness of the Tree, it will affoard more Pomegranates, when those are grown great, you may gather the former, and delight your self with a new production of them. *The same.*

That Figs may grow with Inscriptions.

Write what you will upon the Fig tree leaf that you would Infoliate, and the Figs will grow with that Inscription. *Democrit.*

How to make Figs come early.

Figs will be ripe before their time, if you lay near the root Pigeons dung, Pepper and Oyl. *The same.*

To make purging Figs.

When you plant the Fig tree, lay at the roots black Hellebour bruised with Tithymal, and you shall have Figs will loosen the belly. *The same.*

How Figs may be made half white half black.

Take divers branches, and binding the boughs first together, that are of the same age and duration set them in the Pit, dung them, and water them. When they begin to bud, bind again both the buds into one, that they may grow up to one stock, and after two years, if you think fit, transplant it, and you shall have Figs of two colours. Some do the same thing more securely thus: They bind the seeds of two divers Vines in a linnen cloath and plant and transplant the same. *Leons.*

That Figs may last.

Figs will continue good along time, if they be hanged in Baskets in an Oven, whence the bread is taken forth, and then put into a new unglazed earthen pot. But you must gather your Figs with the foundation and stalk they hang by, and sprinkle them in the Sun with pickle and Oyl scalding hot together, then put them into a Vessel, and lute it well, but they must stand one night before open to the dew, and after that you must put them into the Vessel. *Paxim.*

To keep Figs green.

Figs may be kept fresh, if they be so laid in Honey, that they neither touch one the other, nor yet the vessel, which must be carefully covered with a cover, each having its hollow Coffer made, and that gourd-like Coffer being afterwards hanged up, where neither fire nor smoke comes: but they must be gathered with their stalks: for so they will continue sound the longer. *Aphrican. Pallad.*

That Olives may grow sweet.

Take a Sextarius of Oke ashes, of fresh Quicklime a third part, mingle them well, adding a little water that they may mix the better to moysten them into one body; When they have so continued two houres, put this into some wodden vessel with a hole in the bottome, well working it, and pouring upon it three or four Buckets of water, and let the Lee drain through the hole; If the Lee will not make two Buckets full, pour on two Buckets of water more, that you may take two Buckets of the Lee. When you have done this, take green fresh Olives that are not corrupted; then when they have stai'd so long in the Lee, untill they sink to the bottome, or the flesh will come with your teeth from the yellow stones, cast them into cold water, changing the water three or four times; Take great care they do not stand without water: because they will suddenly grow black, and will lose their naturall colour and taste; This seems to be preternaturall, and therefore is very pleasant to behold, that both the leaves and fruit shall retain their Native colour. But they must be left three or four daies in fresh water. Yet if the water be changed four or five times a day, they will be sweet in two dayes, that you may eat them with Salt and Vinegar. This being performed, pour pickle upon them, and so also in two dayes they will be fit to eat. But observe this, that the Olives which did not touch the water, will have a more tender skin, and are more pleasant to eat. But if they did touch it, they must be steeped the longer, and yet they will never be so delicate, because they will have a more sharp skin or cover, although they be green and very fair. Moreover Olives may be otherwise provided. Put dry Olives that never were put into water, into pickle for one Moneth, and then into new pickle for fifteen or twenty dayes, and lastly into one stronger pickle; and they will be sweet. But this way is seldome used. *Alexius.*

Of the Secrets of Shrubs. Chap. 13.

To make Grapes grow in the Spring.

When we see Cherries in the Spring, we wish then for Grapes also; and we may have them, as we collect from the sayings of *Tarentinus* and *Pamphilus.* When their Gum ceaseth to run forth, that the Tree may not grow rotten and Worm-eaten, cause the hoary down that goes about the Tree to be scraped away, for this will much hinder the Graffs. Make an Insition which some call Insoliation; for so it will more easily

sily joyn together. Then open the bark of the Tree, and drive in a thin strong wedg between the bark and the Tree, but gently with a light hand in the levelling of it, that the band of the Bark be not hurt, then taking out the wedg, a sharp sprig of a black and fruitfull Vine must be set into it, and bound fast; so in the Spring at the usuall time when Cherries are ripe it will yield Grapes, when it is forced to draw away the nutriment of the stock it is set into. *The same* from *Tarentinus* and *Pamphilus*.

Grapes without stones.

This is done by dividing the branch that is to be set equally, and putting a stone betwixt to keep them asunder, from the very top; then you must scrape out all the Pith on both parts with an Instrument of Bone, in that part above, or else in that which must be set under ground: or else make it hollow as deep as you can, then bind it close with a strong Twig of Osier, or bind a wet Paper fast about it, and in fat Earth make a hole and set it into it, and bind it fast to a stake knocked down, that it may not be wrested up and down, so will the cleft grow together as before; and it will be better, if as far as the branch is made hollow, you thrust in a Sea Onyon; for this will joyn it like glew, and moysten it with its moysture, and foster it by its heat, like an Engraffing; the same also will fall out, if in setting the branch you take forth all the Pith. *Democrit.*

That the same Vine may bare clusters of white Grapes, and black stones.

That the same branch of a Vine may bear a white and a black Grape, at once, and that in the same Grape some stones may be black and some white and both divided; Take three or four handfuls of divers kinds and colours of Vines or else more, that will easily grow, and bind these equally together very close, and put them into a Pipe or a Rams horn, that they may stick forth at both ends, underneath unbind the branches, and set them in a Pit of well dunged earth, watring them untill they grow and shoot forth; But when two or three years are past, when they are all grown into one stock, break the Pipe, if the horn be already wasted: when they joyn fast, saw it off, and cast Earth poudred fine upon them, and let the fat Earth cover the stock, and when it shoots forth again, leave one shoot, and cut off the rest, least it all be left, the stock cannot nourish them all; then will one Vine rise up by the joyning of all these branches, and will bear Grapes of divers colours. *The same.*

Otherwise.

Let the branches be one black, another white, and when they are pruned off, they must be slit in the middle, taking heed that none of the Pith fall out, and so joyn again the parts divided, that both their buds may fall together equally, as if they were but one: then bind them very close, and with clammy earth dawb them fast, and for three daies water them often, untill from both one Sprig may sprout forth, and bear Grapes, and they will be of sundry colours and kinds. *Didym.*

To keep Grapes upon the Vine untill the Spring.

About the Vine that is full of Grapes, dig a ditch in a shady place three foot deep, and two foot broad, and put in Sand, and stick Rods there, whereby you shall daily help the branches that are full of Grapes, and bind them to them, that you hurt not the Clusters, yet that they may not touch the ground, you shall cover them so, that showrs may penetrate and come at them. *Berytius.*

To make a Grape sweet sented.

If you will have Grapes smell sweet, the branch must be set in the ground, and all sweet smelling things must be cast upon it, or some Unguent or Perfume that we would have the Grape smell of, and it must be steeped awhile in water of the same sent, and drinking in the moysture it will yield a Grape smelling like that. *Paxamus.*

To defend Grapes from Birds and Hens.

That Hens and Birds may let the Grapes alone, give them the berries of the wild Vine to eat; for the like thing almost will befall them that befals Men that eat sour fruits; that set their Teeth on edg. *Cardan.*

That Wasps shall not touch Grapes or other fruits.

Take Oyl into your mouth, and spurt it forth upon the Vines and Grapes. *Democrit.*

Of

Of the Secrets of the fruits of Herbs. Chap. 14.

How Gourds may be made long, great, and thick.

Take the seeds from the Gourds between the top and the middle, and set them upwright, dung and water them. If you desire to have them very great, take the seed from the middle of the Gourd, and turning the top downwards, set them in the ground *Collumella, Palladius, Pliny*.

That Gourds may be broad and large.

Would you have your Gourds broad and great, take the seeds from the bottome of the Gourd, and turn the upper end downwards, and set them in the Earth. *The same*.

That Gourds may grow having no seed.

Gourds will have no seeds in them thus. So soon as a Sprig of the Gourd shoots forth, or of a Cucumber, set that into the Earth, as you set Vine branches, that only the top of the branch may be above the Earth, and when it is increased, set the same again, and so the third time, and cut off what springs from it, about the middle, and above the Earth, and leave only the third sprout, and you shall have Gourds and Cucumbers without seeds. Likewise you may produce the same without seeds, if three daies before you sow them, you steep the seeds in Oyl of Sesama. *Quintil*.

To have early Gourds.

You shall thus make Gourds and Cucumbers grow quickly: put sifted Earth into Baskets, or old Earthen pots, and mingle dung with it, making it moyst. Do this before the usuall time. Plant the seeds when the Spring begins, and when the Sun shines hot, and the showres also are moderate, set your Baskets in the open Ayr, and about Sunset, bring them into the house and cover them. Do this daily, watring them when need is; And when the cold and Ice are perfectly gone, set the Baskets or Vessels in the ground that is well manured and fitted, that the brims may stand equall with the ground, then take all other care about them. If you take away their shoots they will the sooner bear fruit. *Quintil*.

How Gourds and Cucumbers may be made of divers formes, and with Inscriptions upon them.

Gourds will be changed into what form you please, if you make Vessels of Earth, and set them about them when they are yet young, and bind them in, for they will fill up the formes and the Characters. Wherefore also if a Cane be cut long-wayes, and the Pith taken forth, and joyned together again very close, and a Gourd that is small put into it as it grows, it will increase and fill all the length of the Cane. *Quintilius*.

How Gourds are made purgative.

You may make them purgative, as also many other things, if you steep their seed a day and a night before, with Rheubarb, Agarick, Scammony, Coloquintida, or other purgative medicaments, and simples, sowing them afterwards. *The same*.

How to preserve Gourds.

You shall preserve them thus: Cut them when they are tender, then pour scalding water upon them, and all night cool them in the open Ayr, then put them into sharp Brine or Pickle; and let them lye, they will so last long. At this day all the Winter time, they are hanged green upon the Roofs and Planks of houses, and are so kept by our Countrey-Men, and are pleasant to be eaten; and especially those which are called Citruls. *Quintil. Mizald*.

To produce Cucumbers very suddenly.

If in Summer you soke their fresh seeds in Mans bloud, not of a weak, but sound, young, yellow haired Man; for that hath in it a more hot and effectuall virtue; change it often, that it may not consume, but it must remain uncorrupted; let them stay in that for one week, then dry them in the Sun, and making small holes in fruitfull finely poudred Earth, set them in; take heed you turn not the wrong end upwards; It will not be amiss to pour in Quicklime under them: then watring them with hot water or *Aqua vita*, the branch will come forth; cover it with woollen Cloathes, least the heat flye away that riseth; when it seems to creep along, you must set something for it to fasten to, being ready to fall it self, and it will increase to a huge multitude, yet it will in short time leave this life, it hath gaind, and dye; The same may be done with Melons and Pompions. *The same.*

To make Cucumbers and all fruits grow late.

If we would have Cucumbers and all other fruit come late: we know they all fear colds and Ice and cold Rains. Wherefore Plant the seeds in the Summer, heaping dung about them, so they will resist the cold, and not be killed thereby. Also they will continue in force otherwise. Set them in a Pit, and let the Pits be so seasonable, and cover them well on the top, that the Sun and the Winds can do them no hurt; also the vapours arising from the water do help them much to make them continue in good condition. Or set them in a place that is clear and well dunged. If you would have fruit of Blackberry-bush, or of Fennel-Gigant after the Autumnall Equinoctiall, you must cut them up close by the ground, and make them hollow, and with a wodden stick you must thrust in dung between the Pith, and you must put in Cucumber seed; hence will fruit proceed that no cold will kill. *The same.*

How you shall make Melons sweet, and well sented.

You may make Melons smell like Roses, if you set the seed with dried Roses, and plant them one amongst another. But you shall make them sweet, if you steep their seed in Milk and Honey, and when they are cold, you plant them. *Florentinus.*

That a Hartichoke may not be prickly.

Hartichoks will not be prickly, if when you set the seeds you rub the sharp top of them flat with a stone. Or if we cut Lettice into pieces, and set with each seed one piece of Lettice, so will Hartichoks grow very smooth. *Varro.*

How to make Hartichoks sweet sented.

You shall procure sweet sented Hartichoks thus: you must three daies before you set them, steep the seed in some sweet liquor or juyce, and then dry and set them. For they will have the smack of that liquor they take in. They will smell like Bays, if you steep them with Bay leaves, or thrust one seed into a Bay berry, and so plant it. The like experiment serves for other things. *Mizaldus.*

How to make Hartichoks sweet.

Hartichoks will grow up sweet, if the Seeds be steeped in Milk, Honey, or Sugar and Water, or Aromatick Wine, and be dried again and set into the Earth. *The same.*

Of the Secrets of Seeds in Generall. Chap. 15.

How Seeds may be defended against cold, Frosts, and heat.

If there be any fear least the Seed should be scorched with Frosts, cold, or heat; they may be covered with Straw, Rods may be laid overthwart them, and Reeds upon the Rods, or else Vine branches, and Straw uppermost. *The same.*

How to keep Seeds unhurt in the ground.

If Seeds to be set in the Earth, be a little before steeped in the juyce of Howsleek, they will be not only kept safe from Birds, Ants, field-Mice, and other Robbers of them, but also the fruit that springs from them will be much better. *Mizald.*

That Seed sown may be kept safe.

You may preserve all safe that is sowed, if you gather Sout that is in your Chimnies, the day before you sow, and mingle that with your Seed: or sprinkle the Seeds with Purslane-water, that all night they may drink in the moysture. *Mizald.*

That Birds shall not prey upon Seed.

Pliny saith there is Garlick in the fields called *Allium*, which is profitably opposed against the spoil that Birds make, which dig the Seed out of the Earth, if it be boyled, that it may never grow again. All Birds that feed on this will be giddy, that you may catch them with your hands: *Apbricanus* for this purpose boyls a little Wheat or Barly in Wine, or infuseth it mingled with black Hellebour, and he sows this abroad round about the Gardens or Fields: and this will free all Seeds from Birds. But he bids that you should hang them up by the heels upon a Pole, when you

you catch them dead, or drunk. Nor doth he omit the decoction of River Crabs, with which if you sprinkle the Seed, (it is a strange thing) no Birds will touch it; and what springeth from these Seeds will last safe from the injuries of all small Creatures. Some happily do only sprinkle some of this decoction upon the Plants. This I and my friends have tried above a thousand times, but it must be at a set Period of the Moon. *Mizald*.

To free Seed from ever being bitten.

Some bruise the leaves of Cypress and mingle that with the Seeds, and they commit that mixture to a well prepared and dunged ground, and so they free from being bitten whatever grows from thence. Others mingle with the Seed the shavings, scrapings, filings or parings of a dry Elephants or Harts horn, or steep that, and sprinkle the infusion upon the Seed. Some steep the roots of wild Cucumbers a whole day and night in water, and they sprinkle the Seeds therewith, twice and the next day after, they cover the Seeds with Straw, and set them into the ground. Hence they suppose they will prosper better and be more safe from all dangers. *The same*.

That Cattle may not hurt things sowed.

Take no fewer than ten River or Sea Crabs, and put them into a Vessel full of water, and set them in the open Ayr, that they may stand ten daies asunning, after this all Seeds that you would have to remain safe in the ground, sprinkle with this water for eight dayes, and when eight daies are past, repeat it again, untill the Seeds grow up as you desire. You will wonder at the proof of it; for whatsoever springs from those Seeds will not only drive away Cattle from them, but all Beasts in generall. *Mizald. Pallad. Aphrican.*

A prediction of fruitfull time.

What concerns the foreshewing of fruitfullness or barrenness of any Seed, that is sowed or to be sown, you shall proceed thus by the experience of *Zoroaster*, and the old *Ægyptians*; twenty or thirty daies before the rising of the Dog Star, you shall sow a little of each Seed, in some place well fitted for it, the Seed being fresh and good, dividing and setting out their places, only for a tryall of them, and if the weather be very hot, water them seasonably: that which is sowed upon dry ground will spring forth more commodiously, and before the said Star ariseth cosmically, will shew it self very oportunely. This being done, you must carefully observe, when the Dog Star is risen, which of these Seeds sown came forth safe, good, and in a flowrishing condition, and remaind so; and of that you may foretell, that it will be fruitfull and plentifull that year; but that which sprang not forth, or that came forth faint and languishing in the plant, you may believe will be unprofitable and barren. For it is most certain that the mad fiery Dog star doth by its extravagant heat hurt some Seeds, and not others. So that this Star that is hot and dry by nature doth give to us a foresight for the future year, for all sorts of Seed, what will be hurtfull and what beneficiall to us. *Zoroaster*.

A prediction of plenty.

However this be, I will not let pass a most handsome way to presage and foretell, what will be unfruitfull and scant. Which *Virgil* would not conceal from the world from the Nut-Tree: yet some ascribe it to the Almond-Tree.

> *Consider when the Nut-Trees much abound*
> *With blossomes, in the Woods, if fruit is found*
> *To follow in great plenty, Corn will be*
> *With Wheat abundant as Nuts on the Tree.*
> *But if the shady leaves abound much more:*
> *This fils with Straw and Chaff the Threshing-flore.*

Of the Secrets of Seeds in Speciall. Chap. 16.

That Wheat may increase exceedingly.

Wheat will increase out of measure this way: Powder Saltpeter and the froth of Saltpeter, and mingle that with thin Earth, and so cast it into the heaps of Corn. This will also keep Wheat safe and unhurt. *Aphrican.*

To keep Meal safe.

Meal will remain safe for a time, if you bruise fat Pine tree boughs and cast that into it. But some bruising Cummin and Salt equally together, and making dry lumps thereof, put them into the Meal.

How to preserve Barly safe.

The dry leaves of a fruitfull Baytree will keep Barly safe and good, and all Ashes especially of Bay tree wood put to it; Likewise the Herb Howsleek dried, and Calamint mingled together with Gyp, and so mixed with the Barley. Others put a Vessel full of Vinegar and covered with a cover, in the middle of the Barly. *Damag.*

To keep Beans safe.

Beans sprinkled and moystned with Sea water will take no hurt but remaine good. *Didym.*

That Beanes may ripen well.

Beans will ripen well, if you steep them in Niter and water the day before you set them. *The same.*

That Chich Peason may be greater.

Some take a great deal of care more then needs, who desiring to have Chich Peason greater, they steep them with their shels before hand in Water and Niter. *Florent.*

To ripen Peason betimes.

If you will have early Chiches, set them about the time of Barly. *The same.*

That Lentils may grow sooner and better.

Lentils before they be sowed, smeered with Ox dung that is dry, will be better and come forth sooner. *The same.*

That Lentils may grow greater.

Lentils will Wax bigger in their podes, if they be sowed, having bin soked in water with Saltpeter. *The same.*

To make Lupins sweet.

Lupins are made sweet with Sea-water, and River-water, steeped three daies therein : when they begin to be sweet, dry them, and sowe them, and this is given to Cattel with Chaff for good food.

That Pulse may be easily boyled.

When you sow them, mingle Saltpeter with the dung; for so you shall make them fit to boyl. If this succeeds not, and you would have your Pulse boyl suddenly, cast a little Mustard seed into the pot, and presently those that boyl will dissolve, whether you boyl flesh or Pulse. But if you cast in too much Mustard seed, they will all boyl away. *Democrit.*

Of the Secrets of Wood. Chap. 17.

That Wood may not burn with fire.

Wood and Planks smeered with Allum will not burn, nor posts, or dores, or beames, if they be wet with Verdigrease; so that a hard Crust be laid upon them, and Allum, and White Lead Ashes be plentifully mixed with painting. *Archelaus* the Generall under *Mithridates* gave us an example hereof, in a wodden Tower he kept against *Sylla*, which he strove in vain to set on fire, as *Cæsar* did a Castle made about the River Po, of Larch wood. *As Pliny saith.*

Many rare things to paint Wood diversly, which Carpenters make use of, to adorn and make their Tables with Checker-work, and rare Figures.

In the Morning take fresh Horse dung, yet moyst, with straw, as much as is sufficient. Lay upon this, some Wood overthwart, and set some Vessel underneath to receive the moysture that drops from it. If you cannot in one day draw forth as much as you need, you may gather more the next third and fourth day, untill you have enough; then strain it, and add to every measure of that liqour, of Alum, and
Gum-

Gum-Arabick, of each as much as a Bean; Temper in that liquor what colours you please, and make divers Vessels, if you would have many colours. This being provided, put pieces of Wood into the Vessels, and set them by the fire or in the Sun; afterwards when you would use them take forth some pieces, and leave the rest there, for the longer they stay in the Vessels, the stronger colour they will have; so you shall have Wood of divers colours, some clearer then others, some brown, some of a middle nature, and no art can ever wash these colours out. *Alexius.*

A way to make Ebony seem naturall.

All kinds of Wood may be made like to Ebony, especially the harder Wood, which are brighter, as Box, Cedar, Mulberry, both white and black, and these are the best of all Wood for this purpose, but the black Mulberry is best; Take there these kinds of Wood, and for three dayes put them in Allum-water, in the Sun, or near the fire, that it may only heat: then boyl them a while in common Oyl, or Oyl of Sesama, wherein there is of *Roman* Vitriol, and Brimstone, of each the quantity of a small Nut; for the longer they are boyled, they will be the blacker, so they be not boyled too much: for then they will be burnt and brittle. If they be rightly boyled you never saw any thing more handsome. *The same.*

BOOK. X.

Of the Secrets of Mettals.

Metals in — In Generall, of which, Chap. 1.

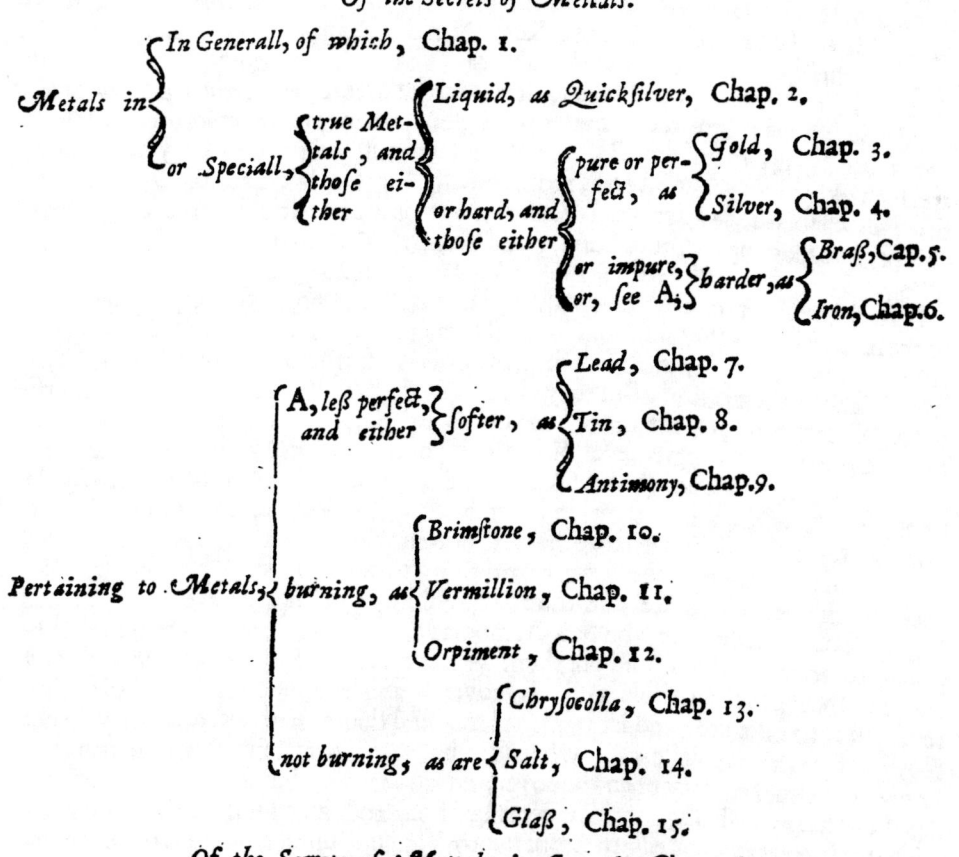

or Speciall — true Mettals, and those either
- Liquid, as Quicksilver, Chap. 2.
- or hard, and those either
  - pure or perfect, as
    - Gold, Chap. 3.
    - Silver, Chap. 4.
  - or impure, or, see A, harder, as
    - Brass, Cap. 5.
    - Iron, Chap. 6.

A, less perfect, and either softer, as
- Lead, Chap. 7.
- Tin, Chap. 8.
- Antimony, Chap. 9.

Pertaining to Metals, burning, as
- Brimstone, Chap. 10.
- Vermillion, Chap. 11.
- Orpiment, Chap. 12.

not burning, as are
- Chrysocolla, Chap. 13.
- Salt, Chap. 14.
- Glass, Chap. 15.

Of the Secrets of Mettals in Generall. Chap. 1.

To transmute Mettals into Calx and water.

Those Mettals that are changed into water must be first calcined, (they are made so in Furnaces, with Salt, or else pouring Vinegar upon them, or Salt joyned with the matter whilst it boyls.) Then by water, the Salt being removed, or else being infused and beaten with the liquid Brass; also Mettals turn into Calx by Salt and fire or by

water

water of separation, or else being attenuated and united to Quicksilver, afterwards beaten with Salt, then the Quicksilver is removed by fire, and the Salt by water. *Cardan*.

How brittleness is taken away from any Metal.

Make it into a Calx, and put it under dung; afterward do thus; when they are red hot at the fire, that they may be quenched, or projected when they are melted, let them be put in *Aqua vitæ* often distilled, or use about them Rosin or Turpentine, or the Oyl of it, or Wax, Suet, Euphorbium, Myrrh, artificiall Borax used by Goldsmiths, to make them melt quickly and to sodder them together. For if a Metal be not malleable, unctuous bodies will ofttimes make them softer, if all these or some of them be made up with some moysture into little Cakes; and when the Metal yields to the fire by blowing with the Bellows, we cast in some of them, or make them thick like Mud, or clear, then set the Metal to the fire, that it may be red hot in burning Coales, take it forth, and quench it in them, and let it so remain half an hour to drink them in. Or annoint the Metal with Dogs grease, and melt it with that, it will take away much of the brittleness of it, and so it may be Hammered, and wrought under it, whereas before, if it were knocked, it would flye into many pieces. *The same*.

To reduce Metals into a body.

But if you would reduce Metals into a body, because being turned into a Calx, they are not easily joynd together again, I thought fit to teach you this, because it is frequent to fall out so in our operations. These things retain that force, Chrysocolla, Argal, Alum, yelks of Eggs, Salt, Alchali, Ammoniacum, Saltpeter, Sope: with all these, or some of them we make Bals, and in a melting pot, where the Calx is melted, they are cast into it at the fire, and the Metals will return to their former condition: when you know that this is done, then take them forth: yet this is worth observing; that if the Calx be of Gold, it must be reduced by yelks of Eggs, and such like things; but Silver is reduced with Argal: but Lees of Oyl is best for this; that when bodies are reduced, they may not want their Lustre, and naturall colour, but may appear more shining and bright. *The same*.

To draw the more noble Metal to the outside.

Now I am about to shew you, how a Man may draw forth the more noble Metal to the superficies, as the ignorant Chymists imagine: for they think the parts that lye in the middle may by their Impostures be drawn forth, and only the worst of the Metall shall be left within. But they are deceived, because in the superficies only the more lose remiss parts come forth, and only a little Quicksilver is called out: for all the things that are the ingredients of the composition are corroding, they leave the harder parts, and only polish and make white: perhaps they are perswaded by the sight of old Meddals, where they find pure Brass withinside, and Silver upon the outside: but these were Soddderd together and beaten with Hammers, and then coyned with Images; but that is now a very hard thing to do, and I think impossible. But these are things that polish: common Salt, Allum, Vitriol, Quick-Brimstone; and for Gold, only Verdigrease, and Salt Armoniac: when the work is to be done, they pouder some part of them, and put them with the Metal into the melting pot, and they lute the Earthen Crucible well, and cover it, and leaving a small vent hole, they set it first at an easie fire, and let it burn there, and that it may not melt, they do not blow the fire with any Bellows: when the burnt pouders sink down, which they know by the smoke, they open the cover and look into it, but the fire is kindled under the Metal more strong, untill it grow red hot, and when it is red hot, they dip it into those pouders: or else they put it into Vinegar, untill it were clean, and having wrapt the work that is smeered, in linnen Cloaths, they hold it in an Earthen pot of Vinegar, and boyl it along time, then they draw it forth, and cast it into Piss, and then they boyl it with Salt and Vinegar untill there remain no foulness, and all the filthy spots are taken away with the medicament: and if you do not thus find it to be grown exceeding white, do the same work once again, untill it be perfect. Or else you may proceed in order thus. Let the work boyl with Salt, Allum, and Argal,

gal, with water in an Earthen pot; when all the outside is white, let it stand a while; then let it boyl with equall quantities of Brimstone, Saltpeter, and Salt, and let it hang three houres in the middle of them, and not touch the sides of the Vessel, then take it forth, and rub it with fine Sand, untill the venome of the Brimstone be gone: then again boyl it as you did before, and it will grow very white, that it will defend it self against the fire, and not be refused for counterfeit; you will find this profitable if you do it well, as it should be, and you will be glad, if you will not abuse it to your own destruction. *The same.*

To guild Mettals.

You shall make Metals and stones look like Gold thus. Take salt Armoniac, white Vitriol, of each a like quantity, Rock Salt, and Verdigrease, three parts of each; make these into very fine pouder, and cover all over with them, any Ring, Stone, or Metal; After that put them so into the fire for an hour, and take them forth and quench them in fresh Piss, wash them, and wipe them. This was an experiment of an ingenious Artificer. *Cardan. Mizald.*

An Elixir, or Cerat to transmute Metals.

Take first of all, of Brimstone extracted from the same species, be it for white or red, and grind that well a whole day or two upon a Glass body, and soke it with the distilled Oyl of the same kind; for white, four days, and five when you dry it; grind and soke it, and rost it between two Vessels, and do it so, so often, untill you have made it like unto Wax; then take it as an Elixir, and pour upon every two parts and half of that, four parts of Quicksilver of the Metal whence you drew your Sulphur, and work every species with its own species, and every kind with its own kind, and do not change them; for if you do, you will erre. Also let your Quicksilver be congealed with the water of the Metal; joyn both these Cerats together, and grind them well with Oyl, grind them a long time, and set them to burn at a stronger fire: for this will harden them: then grind them well, and put salt Armoniac upon them, which was rubified with the fire of the Metal, and afterwards let it drink it in well, and renew it every day, setting it in dung, for this will dissolve it into red water like unto bloud; Let this congeale in a Glass Vessel at a small fire, and when it is coagulated, grind it well, and let it drink in water of Housleek; and dissolve it, and then coagulate it, doing this thrice: for you shall have a Cerat, that if you cast it upon Silver, it will be changed into Gold, or project it upon both kinds of Lead, or upon Iron, and it will transmute them into Gold. And this is the way to colour red; now you know this. But the way to colour white, is quite contrary to this: Which is, That you must take of the Quicksilver of that, or white Sublimate four parts, and of the white Brimstone three parts, grind them well, and cast upon them, of white salt Armoniac extracted out of the stone two parts, and grind that well, and let it drink in sufficiently water of salt Armoniac dissolved, and toste it well gently, and do this three times; but every time bake it more vehemently. After this, grind it well, and let it drink well in water of salt Armoniac, and let it stand with its liquor, and put it into a Glass vessel, and bury it under ground, and change the dung every day, and do so untill it be dissolved. Afterwards grind it, and congeal it, but let the fire be very small untill it be congealed, and it become white or of an Ash colour; and when you find that colour, return to grinding, baking, and congealing, untill it be congealed and grown white: but first dissolve it, that it may run like water, and be not a Lump, or troubled, and you shall have a Cerat very white. Cast one part of this upon 10000 of red Copper, and it will be made Silver. This is the opinion of them, that have worked with Quicksilver and Brimstone: But they that work with Quicksilver alone, proceed thus. Take Quicksilver sublimate fixed, and of Quicksilver dissolved, equall parts, grind the fixed, and let it drink in the dissolved, and grind it well, and bake it a little; do this untill it have drank in all the dissolved; then grind it, and let it drink in the dissolved by grinding it untill it grow like Marrow, and so long let it drink in, untill it hath drank in its own quantity: and bake it between two Vessels, with a strong fire, and if it smoke, return to grinding it again, and sublime it again, untill it will be dissolved in the lower Vessel:

for

for then it will be well done, and send forth no smoke. Project with this, and it will make a good colour : afterwards let it drink in its own vvater, and grind it vvell and diſſolve it. It vvill diſſolve in a ſmall time, afterwards congeal it; and project of it upon vvhat body you pleaſe, and it vvill vvork vvonders, chiefly upon Iron; for it vvill ſoften that, and turn it into good Silver. But ſuch as vvork vvith Brimſtone alone, vvork thus; Take of the whited and ſublimed, four parts, and let it drink in its own vvater : or vvater of Quickſilver. If you deſire to have it only vvith its own vvater : do with it as you did and alter not, and you ſhall make Lead, Tin, and Braſs, good Silver, and ſo ſhall you do Quickſilver in its ſeaſon. But you muſt know that Quickſilver is congealed in both kinds of Lead : alſo prepared Brimſtone is congealed in Iron. You ſhall know how, becauſe it is a great Secret. The vvay of operating is vvith ſalt Armoniac, to take of that diſtilled and the Cerat one part, and let it drink in its own vvater grinding it ſtrongly; diſſolve it, and if it be hard to diſſolve, let it drink in its own vvater and grind it vvell, ſo it vvill diſſolve : and when it is made clear vvater, make it congeal in a Glaſs veſſel by a vveak fire, in the Sun, or upon hot Embers : and this is a huge Secret : and theſe are the four waies of making of white. But to make red, you muſt put for every white thing a red thing, and grind, let it drink in, and bake it, diſſolve, and congeal it; it is in this all one with the former. And if you unite Quickſilver and Brimſtone, and prepare them vvith ſalt Armoniac, it will be excellent : and if you joyn Quickſilver and Brimſtone, and ſalt Armoniac, and prepare them with their vvaters, it vvill be good. Wherefore give God thanks. *Rhaſis in his Book of Experiments.*

To guild all Mettals.

Take liquid Verniſh, one pound, Turpentine, Oyl of Linſeed of each one ounce, mingle them all well, and keep them for uſe. *Alexius.*

To find Treaſures.

Some report that a Candle lighted of Mans fat, and brought to the place where the Treaſures are hid, will diſcover them with the noiſe; and when it is near them it vvill go out. If this be true, it ariſeth from Sympathy : for fat is made of bloud, and bloud is the Seat of the Soul and Spirits, and both theſe are held with a deſire of Silver and Gold, ſo long as a Man lives; and therefore they trouble the bloud; As therefore there is an Antipathy between a Wolf skin and a Sheeps skin, though they be both dead, ſo here is Sympathy. But a *Spaniard* found out Treaſures better vvithout a Candle. Wherefore there is no more certain reaſon of things, than vvhen they are directed by Principles of Prudence; vvhich are next to naturall Principles, fetched from far : but other things that are taken from propriety; are either falſe or very rare. As that is, that a piece of Bread caſt into the Water vvill ſwim directly over the body of a Man that lyeth drowned at the bottome. But to return to my former Hiſtory. I muſt ſearch out the truth by a Generall Method. If therefore this Candle be ſhaken by reaſon of Gold, Silver, or Jewels buryed under ground, it is reaſon it ſhould be moved alſo by Treaſures above ground, and by this vvay ſuch things are enquired into. There is indeed one ſort of Loadſtone that will draw Silver, if then a ſmall piece of Steel vvere touched with that Loadſtone, and were ſet ſo that it might turn about, it vvould turn to Silver, eſpecially a great deal, though buryed under ground. This muſt be an excellent ſtone, but I never ſaw ſuch an one. Another vvay is taken from the ſound; for it ſinks down moſt commonly, and vvhere there is an emptineſs it vvill reſound. And again vvhere a Wall is over thick : that is a token that ſomething is hid there, and this is eaſie for thoſe that take heed to it, which others cannot imagine. Alſo ſome places are tryed with long Steel piercers : ſuch things are done by Candles. *Cardan.*

The way of the true Art of Caſting for Meddals, and all other Formes that are meanly extant, to caſt them of any Metal, Cryſtall, Glaſs, or Marble.

Firſt of all you muſt have Earth ready wherein to imprint your Formes : which ſince it is diverſly made : I ſhall ſet down divers kinds, and of them the beſt : that if all cannot be had, we may uſe them that can be got. But know this firſt, that of

those

those we shall set down here, we may use them severally, or some mingled, or else altogether; for they are all the best. The head of the whole Art is, That the matter we make use of, be very fine, and almost impalpable; because Pictures are more cleanly expressed in it: also it more easily receives all sorts of Metals into it, without corruption, and it is better mingled with the Magistral, and being dryed will grow harder. Lastly, It will serve for many meltings, that you need not break it after the first melting, and so be constrained to make a new Forme. But to express Pictures in Lead, any Earth will suffice, so it be very fine, and well moulded with the Magistral, as I shall shew you.

The first Earth fit to Cast Metals.

Take the stone Emeril, wherewith all kind of Armour is polished, as much as you need, let it be finely beaten, and made red hot in the fire, as I shall teach you underneath, then wet it like paste, make Forms of it to express Figures with; These Forms will remaine good many years, if they be carefully preserved: and if they should be broken they must be poudred again, and mingled with the Magistral; for so they will continually grow better.

The Second.

Take pieces of Pots of Clay of *Valencia*, or of *Trequenda*, in which Pots Glass-makers use to hold their melted Glass in the Furnace. And it will be better to take the bottome of those pots, or else the pots themselves, from the middle to the bottome, casting away the Glass that sticks about them. Or if these cannot be had, take those that can. Take therefore new Chrucibles of the Goldsmiths, as many as may equall the weght of those pots I spake of before: bruise all these to pouder in a Brass Mortar; then grind them with water upon a Porphiry stone, and then by baking it again, make the pouder small, as I shall shew you presently, let it be kept in Leather bags, or in wodden Boxes, that it fly not into the Ayr, being so fine.

The Third.

Take the shels of Limpius, or of Sea Squils, shels of Eggs, of each alike quantity, make them red hot in the fire, and as I said before of Potters Earth, let them be often ground, and kept the same way.

The Fourth.

Set the filings or scales of Iron, or both of them very clean and pure, in an Iron Helmet into the fire, or in some other firm substance, pour strong Vinegar upon them, and let them stand in the fire eight houres; Then pour on more Vinegar, and let it be made red hot in the fire, afterwards grind it, do it again, as I said before, and keep it.

The Fift.

Take a Pumex stone red hot and four times quenched in Vinegar one part, filings of Iron two parts, mingle them, and make them red hot in the fire, as before, then grind them severll times, and lay them up as the former.

The Sixt.

Take the burnt bones of a Weather, especially of the head which are best; then grind and sift them, as much as you need, set them in some Iron vessel so long at the fire, untill they be very red hot, then put as much Suet to them as you can hold in your hand; stir them well with an Iron that the Suet may burn with the pouder, then leave it so at the fire half an hour. This done, take it from the fire, grind it, make it red hot in the fire, moysten it; when you have done this again, it will be very fine and perfect.

The Seaventh.

Take Cuttle bones burnt, poudred and sifted, what is sufficient, and do this as I even now said of the Weathers bones. This Paste is also made of a certain Earth brought from *Tripolis*; also of Vine Ashes, of burnt Paper, of dry Horse dung burnt, of Bricks, Bolearmoniac, red Earth, and such like, which will never melt nor flye in the fire, nor make any scales or crusts, but finely receive any impressions.

The way to reduce the foresaid Earths to such fineness, that they can hardly be felt.

Take the foresaid Earths, or Pouders, which first beat very fine and sift them, and

C c

then

then set them in the fire in some strong Pot, untill they be red hot, and then grind them again with water or Vinegar. When you have done this six times put that into a Glazed Porringer, pouring as much water upon it, that it may swim four fingers breadth above it; mingle them alittle with some stick, that the water may be troubled; then let it stand alittle, and pour off the water by degrees into some clean vessel; when this is done, pour fresh water upon the matter, and mingle them as before untill it grow muddy, then let it rest alittle, and pour it off gently to the first water you poured off. This you must do so long, untill all the fine pouder be carried away with the water. And if any gross pouder be left in the first Porringer, beat it again as before, and add it to the former water set aside. All these things being dispatcht, leave the water so long, untill the pouder be all setled to the bottome; then pouring the water gently off, dry the pouder; then once more beat it finely, and sift it through a fine hair or very thick Silk or Lane Sive, and you shall have a most pure pouder, which you must lay up in some Vessel close stopt, that it flye not away.

The Magistral water, as they call it, to temper the foresaid pouders.

That the foresaid pouders may be temper'd, formed, dryed, and stick together, and not flye, or fall into pouder, such a water, called a Magistral must be provided, which is this. Take common Salt what is sufficient, wrap it in a wet linnen Cloath or put it into a Chrucible, and set it amongst the hot coles, or else in a small pot well Luted, where you can blow the fire with Bellows strongly for an hour; when it is cold grind it, being beaten small, put it into a Glazed Earthen Pot, and pour as much common water upon it, that it may swim above it four or six fingers breadth, and mingle it so long at the fire, untill it be dissolved; and being cold, strain it twice through a fine wollen Cloath, which is called filtring. The use of this water is to moysten, and to make the Earth tough, as I shall tell you underneath. This Magistral water is made also of whites of Eggs, if they be well beaten with a Fig Tree stick, untill they froth; and when they have stood so all night, strain the water that is under the froth, and keep it for the pouders, to make them like paste. This water is better, because the Earth is made more tenacious, and the formes more express and more fine. Wherefore some add to the former water of Salt some of this water; others add Gum water, as their judgment and practise makes them think most convenient.

Of things that must be ready for the Art of Casting.

Since that the work of a good Workman cannot be perfected without the proper Tools, it is necessary to shew you what Instruments are needfull for this Art. First, You must be carefull to have Coles ready of fresh Wood, that is hard and dry, as also Chrucibles without flaws, and cracks, nor white nor black, but Ash coloured; Moreover some thick Paper must not be wanting to ventilate the Chrucibles. Also a hollow Cane to blow out filth out of the Chrucibles. Also a crooked Instrument to take forth Coles from the Chrucibles; also a Press, wherein the Forms which they call Stafetæ may be pressed; that the Metals melted may be more fitly poured in. To these there must be two or more Plates, polished and light, of Nut Tree, Oake, Box, or Brass, between which the Formes may be held fast, and turned. There must be two or more Plagets of Wool ready, by which those empty spaces in pressing of the Forms may be filled up. There needs also a Rule and Compass to measure, and set forth certainly the proportion, of the Forms and Pipes, the Metal must run through. Further there must be an Iron, like a Spade, but with a sharp point, and cutting on both sides, that the wayes of the Forms through which the melted Metals pass, may be made clear. If you want this, do it very carefully with your Knife. You must have also alittle Oyl, and Turpentine, wherewith Paper, or some Cotton Threads must be made wet and set on fire, that the Forms being now dry within, may be very well smoked thereby, to make the Metal run the better. But because sometimes the hollow places are too much filled with smoke, that they are made uneaven, you must have a Hares foot by you, both for other uses, and also to wipe away the Sout; There must be two brushes also, one with thick Bar Wyer strings, another with hayre, such as they make Combs clean withall, wherewith the work before

and

and after casting must be kemmed and cleansed.

The way to melt and Cast Meddals.

First take that Meddal you would Cast, and put it into Vinegar; to which is added some Salt and burnt Straw, then wash it, and rub it well with the foresaid hayre Brushes, then wash it with water, and dry it with some clean Wollen Cloath. This being done, place one part of your Frame, namely the Female, upon a Plate of Oake or Brass as I said: and so that the middle part, namely that which joyned to the other, may lye looking downwards; whatever you mean to cast, be they Meddals or any thing else, you must first cleanse them, and set them in a right passage to that way, through which the melted Mettal must run, especially if it be but one Meddal. But if they be two, let them be placed so in another Forme, that there may be a place left in the middle for the Metals to run in by; But if there be more Meddals than two, each must have a passage made to it, that may carry from the mouth or middle Pipe, the Metal to every Medals impression. This being done, take of the foresaid Earth as much as you please, and being well sifted, put it into a very large Dish, pouring upon it by degrees the Magistral water, untill it be made so moist, that crushed between the hands, it will not stick, but like dry flower, it will stand with a print of the hand closed together; when this is thus moulded, put it upon the Meddals in the Forms, and press it on well with the fleshly part of your fingers, and then with your hands, which will be better done, if you put the other plate above it; after that with some cutting Instrument, and a Rule, let the Earth that sticks about the Forme, and is superfluous, be carefully and equally taken away. This being done, a Wollen Cloath must be laid upon it; then a Plate, and so closely the Forms must be turned with both hands; then taking off the upper Plate, if any thing stick it must be well and lightly taken away with a Hares foot. After this the other part of the Forme must be taken and filled with the same Earth, and it must be pressed well down as before, and made equal with an Iron Instrument; then with the top of the Instrument, the upper part of the Forme must be lifted up a little, and be taken cleanly off with your hands, so that the Meddal may be taken forth; and if it cannot be taken forth easily, it must be lightly lifted up with a thin point of a Pen round about, or else with the point of a Knife, striking it cross wayes, that thereby it may be taken off from the Form against it. But if the Meddal do not appear perfectly Printed, it must again be pressed in a Press between two Plates. All these things being dispatcht, with some crooked Knife that cuts, with Rule and Compass, the Pipes being divided, must be dried at the fire, and by and by with Cotton wet in Oyl and Turpentine, and set on fire, they must be smoked: and if any superfluous fume be left, it must be taken off with a Hares foot. But if you would pour in your Metals, put the Forms between two Plates with a Cloath into a Press, pressing them a little: then pour in your melted Metal, if it be Silver or whited Brass, it will be known by its brightness and clearness; but if it be Tin, it will burn if you cast Hards or Paper upon it; and it will flote excellent well hither and thither, if it be not Tin; for then you must cast in a hundred part of Sublimate, and an eight part of Antimony; for so it will not only run well, but will be a harder Metal. Moreover when the Forms are cold, you must take out your Meddal neatly and keep it; And if you would cast another, you must smoke your Forms again, and then press them under the Press as I said before, and this must be done as often as you would cast more Meddals. But if the Forms seem yet sufficient, and fit to pour in more Metals into them, they must be kept in some dry place; but if they be broken, they must be poudred again, and so the pouder will be made better, as I said before. Again Meddals be they new or old, must both be boyld, and put into the white water, especially if they be not of Tin, as I shall shew underneath.

To make Meddals of liquid Chalk with a Pencill, which is far easier than with the former Forms; but these are not only usefull for one time, nor are there any things made with these much finer, and they cannot again be touched by the Pencill.

Take a fine clean Meddal, well washed and dryed as I said, then annoint it with

C c 2

Oyl,

Oyl, and with the following mixture, which is this: Take the foresaid *Lutum Sapientiæ*, dried in the Sun or at the fire, and made into very thin pouder, and sifted, as much as you need; then make this moyst with common water, annoint the other part of the Meddal: then dry it, and again annoint it with the foresaid Lute, but somewhat thicker, and dry that. When you have done this four times or oftner; the other part likewise that was first annointed with Oyl, must be annointed so that the whole Meddal must be covered over with this Clay, especially if to take forth the Meddal you would not divide the form in the middle. But if otherwise, before the other part of the Meddal be annointed, the Clay that sticks to the Meddal must first be sprinkled over with Cole dust, that the other part being added to it may not stick to it, but may be easily taken away. When you have done this, moysten the other part of the Meddal also with the foresaid Lute, do it on with a Pencill, and that being dried, lay it thicker on, and dry it, and do this four times, or do it as you did, when you made the first. But before the Lute be well dried, you must lightly cut away the superfluous parts with a Knife, that they cleave not together; I mean the parts of that were strewed with Cole dust; But when it is well dried, those joynings must be lightly lifted up with a Knife, that the other part of the Forme may be taken off from the Meddal. When that is taken away, then take away the other which will be done if you strike the Clay lightly with your Knife, the Meddal hanging downwards; All this being ended, take both parts of the Form, and first make a hole on both sides, through which the melted Metals must run; then with some Iron Wyer, bind the parts well together, and bake them in a Furnace, or in burning Coles, untill the Coles be burnt out. And if they should be baked before the parts be joyned, it is no matter, so the parts be afterwards well bound together with a Wyer. But when you would poure in the melted Metals, put them between two Plates, or in a Press, and pour in the Metal, when it is cold take it forth, and you shall find your Meddal gallantly cast. If the work be of Silver, it must be whited as I shall shew hereafter; if of Tin, it needs no whiting; if it be Gold it must be coloured with Verdigrease and Piss, but Meddals neither of Silver or Gold are to be cast in Chalk Forms, but in the former Frames. This Lute being thus prepared, Meddals may be otherwise and more easily Cast, namely thus; Take that which must be formed, and let that be made with Wax and Turpentine mixt, by and by thrust that Wax into this Chalk or Lute, as I said, then make a hole: after that set it at the fire, so that the hole may be in the lowest part, through which all the melted Wax may come forth. This being done, pour in the melted Metals. Alwaies observe this, that the Formes, however they be, must be hot when you pour your Metals in.

A white colour for Meddals, and to white other works, and also to polish old Silver works, and make them as it were new again.

Take Meddals or any ancient work, or new, and lay it upon fire Coles, turning it so often, untill they be of an Ash colour; then with a cleansing brush of Brass Wyer, when it is well cleansed, put it into the following water, which is thus made. Take Sea water or common Water what is sufficient; white Salt one handfull, Argal, Allum, of each a quantity. Mingle them and boyl them in some Glazed Vessel; If the work be Brass to be whited sophistically, take of Silver leaves one penny weight, salt Armoniac one ounce and half, Saltpeter two drams and half. Mingle them and put them upon light fire Coles, in some covered vessel, but with a hole in the middle of the cover, so long, untill all the smoke be vanished, when they are cold beat them very fine into pouder; when you would use them, add one ounce of this pouder to the former water, and boyl it one half quarter of an hour, then put in your Meddals of other works. This being done, pour the water and the works also into clear water, and rub them with Argal and the other Ingredients left in the bottome, very well; lastly, wash them with cold water and dry them.

of

Of the Secrets of Metals in Speciall.
Of the Secrets of Quicksilver. Chap. 2.

The congealing of Quicksilver, with the smell of Metals.

To congeale Quicksilver with the sent of Metals, and chiefly of Lead, is performed thus. Purifie your Lead, and separate it from Dross, when it is melted cast it into a hole, when it begins to be cold, thrust in the sharp point of a stick and pull it forth again, and cast in floting Mercury, and it will congeale. Beat it in a Mortar, and do it often, when you have made it hard, melt it often, and pour it into fair water, doing it over again so often, untill it be hard and will be hammered. This is no unprofitable thing. *The same.*

To congeale Quicksilver in an Iron Helmet or Dish.

There is another way to congeale Quicksilver in an Iron Helmet or Dish, casting water upon it in which Smiths quench their Iron, and add to it twice as much of salt Armoniac, Vitriol, and Verdigrease; and let it boyl at a very strong fire, alwaies stirring it with an Iron Spatula, and if the water be consumed with boyling, pour on more hot water, that it may not boyl over; so in six houres you shall have it congealed, then with a linnen bag, or piece of Leather, press it forth forcibly with your hands, and what you can press forth must be congealed again, untill you have congealed it all, so put it into a Pressers earthen pot with Fountain water, taking from it all dross and filth that is useless, and mingle it so in the same pot, and stir it, untill you have it clear and well washed; Set it three nights abroad in the open Ayr, and it will harden for the Test. *The same.*

A yellow congealing of Mercury, that will be like Rhenish Gold.

Take Verdigrease, common Salt, of each two drams, pouder them, and mingle them well, put them into an Iron Skillet, pour water on them, and let them boyl so long untill the water be purged, and clean, then put into the Skillet Quicksilver one ounce, boyl them again, stirring them still with an Iron Spatula, take them forth, wash and dry them well; After this take Tutie one part, and root of Turmerick one part and half, beat them fine, and make fine pouder of them untill they grow black; This done, lay that black pouder with congealed Mercury one row above another, stopping the vessel, and well Luting of it, then set it six houres at the fire again, alwaies heaping on Coles, untill the Skillet be red hot. At length they will melt, and so shall you have Mercury like to Rhenish Gold. *Out of an old Germane written Book.*

To give the Tincture of Gold to Mercury congealed.

But if you would give the Tincture of Gold to Quicksilver congealed, and to do it handsomely, breaking it into small pieces, you must fill a Crucible with that, and the pouder of Cadmia, one upon another in order, there must be a mixture between them, of Pomegranates, Pils, and Raysins, and Cyperus roots of *India*, called Turmerick, beat these fine and wrap them together, and put them in, Luting the vessel, and drying it in the Sun, or by the fire, then set it on the fire six houres, that it may be red hot, then blow it six houres with Bellows, and force it untill it run, and when it hath run, let it cool all cover'd with Coles, and you shall find most shining coloured Gold. *The same.*

To make Quicksilver fixed with Brass Bals.

There is another way to fix Mercury, and congeale it with Brass bals. Make two round Brass half Sphears, that they may penetrate one into the other, and that there be no vent; put into them Quicksilver with an equall quantity of white Arsenick, and Argal well poudred and sifted: Lute all the joynts without, that they breath not forth, so let them dry, and heap Coles upon them, and cover them six houres. Lastly, Make all red hot, then take them forth, and open the Ball, and you shall find it all congealed in the concavity of the Brass ball; strike it with a Hammer, and it will fall down, melt it, and cast it forth, and it will be of the colour of fine Silver, and will be soft, white, and malleable. Or otherwise. Put a Brass cover upon an earthen pot, and kindling the fire, you shall find the Quicksilver strangely heaped upon the cover,

cover, and it will be congealed more strangly: Others do it with Iron, Steel, Silver, and also Gold, and they use divers wayes; It is good to know some of them, and it will do no hurt to remember it. *The same.*

To congeale Quicksilver with Oyl.

There is yet a way to congeale Quicksilver with Oyl, and I find that many have done it so, yet it retains something, and is a very ingenious way. Make a vessel of Silver, red Arsnick, and Copper, like a Jugg, and cover it well with a cover, that nothing breath forth, fill it with Quicksilver, and Lute the joynts with some Lute, the white of an Egg, or Rosin of the Pine tree, as it is usual, and hang them into an Earthen pot full of Linseed Oyl, and let it boyl twelve houres, take it forth, and strain it through Straw or Leather, and if any be not congealed, renew your work again, and let it congeal; If the vessel should be long in congealing, as much as you find of the weight of the Copper and Arsnick to be lost, you must make good: you may know that by the weight, and so use it. *The same.*

To fix Quicksilver congealed.

Now I come in order to shew you some wayes of fixing; for these alwayes follow congealing, and sometimes retain more or less parts. Wherefore the fixing of coagulated Mercury proceeds thus, and there is reason for it. Provide an Earthen Crucible that will endure the fire, and put into the bottome of it, the scrapings of Elder roots, pressing them in with your hands, and fitting them, then make another lay of Chrystall Glass, beaten in a Mortar, and sifted very fine, then another lay of Pepper, Ginger, and Cinnamon, then put in your congealed Quicksilver, then fill the Vessel with the same pouders in a preposterous order, cover it with a cover and Lute it, and set it awhile in the Sun, that it may grow white: So turn the Vessel, and putting an easie fire of Coles under it, and let it be red hot a top one hour, and underneath afterwards, and it will melt, and you shall find pure silver. If any other thing remain, it will flye away, being not congealed, and of all the wayes that ever I saw, this was the best, and succeeded best; you may try them all, or else it fixeth into that body, that it was congealed into. There is another way of fixing Quicksilver, that is not less profitable, you may use it if you please; pouder Saltpeter and Argal very fine; putting fire to it, it will flame and burn, and what remains turns into water, and the moysture will flye away with an easie fire, and the Salt that remains, must be mingled with three parts of Artificiall Chrysocolla burnt, (for it burns like to Alum) and two parts of salt Alcali, wrap up that which is congealed in a strong vessel, put fire above it, then about it, lastly, beneath it, every six hours, and they will fix some parts of the congealed body. *The same.*

How to congeale Quicksilver.

The fume of Metals, especially Lead, will congeal Mercury. *Cardanus.*

The way to prepare and harden Quicksilver, that it shall be malleable and may be wrought into many Formes. Of which Silver innumerable Statues are made at Vienna *and* Newstade *in* Germany.

Melt Lead and whilst it is hot pour it into a round vessel, and press in a round stone, to make a hole, cover it with a Linnen Rag and put Mercury upon it, and leave it in hot Embers untill it be hard, then breaking the Mercury into small pieces, cast them into sharp Vinegar, and boyl them a quarter of an houre: or let the pieces of Mercury broken boyld with the juyce of Bugloss, a little Vinegar and Oyl as I said before, for this is the way to kill it; Having done thus, add salt Armoniac two drams, Vinegar half a measure: leave the Mercury in a covered pot well Luted, eight or ten dayes, that the Vinegar may take away from the Mercury all the dulness; after this set the Mercury in the fire in a Luted vessel round about, untill it grow red hot by degrees and crack; Lastly, Hang the Mercury in a pot with Brimstone at the bottome to cover it, and Lute it, and set it into the fire, that it may grow hot by degrees, and the Mercury may receive the smoke of the Brimstone, do this for a moneth once a day, and the Mercury will run and be Hammer'd. *Wilhelm and Martine the Chymists of Frederick the Emperour.*

To make Quicksilver of Lead.

To take thin Plates of Lead, put them into a Glass vessel, placing common Salt between them; then cover it very well, and leave it nine daies under ground, and you shall find Quicksilver. *Fallopius.*

The way of Mercury sublimate or Quicksilver that Chymists and Goldsmiths use.

Take Quicksilver one pound, put it into a wodden dish, add alittle Vinegar and Saltpeter; mingle them well, and kill it; then add common Salt beaten half a pound, Saltpeter poudred six drams, Alum burnt and poudred one pound and half; mingle them well, and put them into a Luted Retort, up to the neck; and adding above it a Limbeck, distill it in Ashes, first with an easie fire, untill all the moysture be come forth, which must be kept. For it is usefull for divers things, chiefly to infuse Quicksilver. The moysture being drawn forth, augment the fire continually, untill the Quicksilver seem white, that is, untill it seem to swim above the dregs, like to white Bread. If you would have it ascend higher, as far as the neck, put Paper about that part that appears bare outwardly: then augmenting the fire more, you shall see it ascend by degrees, and the Mercury come up to the very top like a Bell; when they are cooled, and the Limbeck is taken off, take away the Retort, and make it clean on the outside, least being any where broken the Silver should be defaced. Lastly, Break the Retort to come at the Silver; yet so that you be not hurt by the smoke. This way you may provide pieces of two hundred pound weight in one Retort, so you observe the due proportion of things. Moreover pound the matter, that is, the dregs left in the bottome, and dissolve them in scalding water, and strain them; then boyl them, and dry them; There will remain a matter like Salt in the bottome, mingled of Salt and Alum. This Saltpeter is good to sublime new Quicksilver, adding to it Vinegar, or instead of Vinegar, the water distilled by subliming. Moreover the foresaid Quicksilver sublimed with Alum, or Vitriol, may be easily sublimed again, if for every pound of the Silver sublimed, you add Salt or burnt Alum, or Quicklime half a pound, and then put them into a Retort to sublime, as before. The sooner it sublimes the fairer and better it will be, and the oftner it is sublimed, so much the sooner and better it will be done. The Alchymists that follow *Geber* and Dr. *Thomas*, and other Philosophers, take sometimes so much labour in subliming it, that they make it fixed. Some have sublimed it a hundred, some two hundred times: yet lost all their labour; which will certainly fall out, because they ever added the dregs, namely, Salt, Vitriol, or Alum. And since it is the nature of fire, to stay and bind things, that would flye away, it is plain, the oftner they were sublimed, the harder they would be. But that part which by degrees was stopped, being alwaies mingled with the dregs did never appear. Wherefore since they did not consider the causes and wayes as they ought, and they saw the sublimate wanting by little and little, they rather thought it flew away, or wasted in the fire, than that it was mixed with the dregs. When then any Man will procee/ Philosophically to fix sublimate, he must three or four times sublime it with Salt or Alum burnt, or Quicklime, or Vitriol, as I said; for so it will be purged not only from all Earthly matter, but from all superfluous moysture. It is purged from earthly matter, because it remains in the bottome of the Retort, with the other dregs that is with the Salt, Alum, and Vitriol: and from the superfluous moysture, because partly by evaporation, it is resolved with the Vinegar, and partly by often subliming it doth in some wise get the nature of fire; and these are the chief causes to fix it; for those two are the principal, or rather the only parts of fixation. And in this Proposal, I understand nothing by a thing to be fixed, then to be boyled or baked, and to have so great affinity with the fire, that it will flye no more, nor wast in the fire. Wherefore when it is three or four times sublimed as I say, it will sublime by it self without the addition of any other things, so often untill it remain fixed in the bottome, and will not flye nor diminish with any force of the fire. But if you would prepare it sooner and easier, proceed by this most secure and philosophical way: namely, they being sublimed three or four times, as I said, add the fourth part of

most

most pure calcined Silver, as I shall teach you in the proper place, which being excellent well mingled and sublimed, mix altogether, namely that which is sublimed, with that which is left in the bottome, and pouder them, and sublime them again. This must be done so often that it will ascend no more, but stay at the bottome in the most vehement fire. And so it will be perfect, white, clean; will melt, and is penetrable. And if any one would make a greater quantity, and cannot add a fourth part of the best Silver, let him take some part of that which is three or four times sublimed: to which add a fourth part of pure Silver, and sublime it as I said. These things being done, take this fixed Silver, and add to it of Quicksilver, sublimed before, but not fixed, three parts, and mingle them, and sublime them as I said, untill it doth remain fixed. And if yet you would make more quantity, add again three parts of that which is not fixed, and do as before untill it be fixed, and so proceeding continually untill you have quantity enough. This is a better way then to sublime it altogether once. Because ofttimes what is volatil is made fixed, and what is fixed volatil, which Philosophers commend, for it is so made more fit to run, more penetrable, and of greater virtue. And all the secret consists in this way of subliming, as I now said, which way the chief Philosophers, and excellent *Geber*, followed; only they keep it very close, whether it should be sublimed; though he cals it Quicksilver, yet he understands something else, which though it have some similitude with Quicksilver, yet it is apparent, it is brought to some more perfect degree by nature: as for example, Paste is made of meal, not by the first way, but being reduced to more perfection. But this high Science can proceed from none but God, who doth not grant it unto all, but to whom he please, and takes it away also, as all Philosophers grant. *Alexius.*

To call forth Quicksilver from a body.

Oyl of Brimstone, if a body be soked in, it will call forth the Quicksilver forcibly. Annoint your body with it presently after bathing. *Hollerius.*

And it is admirable, that one who is annointed for the Neapolitan disease, if he hold a Gold Ring or Meddal in his mouth, and roul it up and down with his Tongue, the Quicksilver that enters into his body by the Unction, is drawn away by the Gold, and cleaves to the Ring, and it will not be restored to its former brightness, unless it be put into the fire. *Lemnius.*

To extract Quicksilver out of Lead.

You may also draw Quicksilver out of Lead thus: Cast the thinnest filings of Lead into *Aqua vitæ*, that hath no superfluous Fleagme, adding thereto some Argal and Salt, or that may be as much as one half of it, and let the water swim one quarter above the Lead; cover the mouth, and for one moneth bury it under the dung, then take it out, and in a Glass Retort, that it may not ascend with difficulty, putting fire under, distill it, and you shall see the Quicksilver ascend in drops: when you see these marks, increase the fire, and receive it; Or otherwise you may get more Quicksilver an easier way. Let an Earthen pot be full of small holes at the bottome, let it stand in another Earthen pot, and stop the chinks close, set the pot into a low hole in the ground of the same bigness, tread the Earth round about it only with your feet, but fill the upper part half full with Quick-Lime that never felt water, then put in your filings of Lead beat thin, and fill up the total again with Quick-Lime, that the Lead may be placed in the middle, and cast upon it Boys Urine, then set a cover on the top, and stop close all chinks, make a vehement fire above it, and cover it all over, for a whole day, for by the force of this violent fire, the Quicksilver will drop down through the open holes in the bottome, into the vessel underneath, and will be a sixt part of the Lead. *The same.*

To give a Tincture, and to fix Mercury.

Mercury, or if you will Quicksilver, may be fixed, and receive a Tincture the same way, Take Saltpeter, and *Romane* Vitriol, of each three drams, put it into a Chymical vessel, to draw forth the water; cast away the first and keep the last; that is, the water that drops when the Limbeck is red hot; you must keep this diligently without any blowing; The use is this; Take the best Mercury purged as it should be

one

one ounce, Brimstone two ounces, and of the foresaid water three ounces; Let them all stand untill the water grow clear. Distil this again with its sediment, and at the bottome of the Limbeck you shall find Mercury, fixed, red, compleate; I heard of one, to whom I told this Secret, that he without distilling the second time, made Mercury to be as I said now; but that it was too high a red colour, yet the body of it was so hard and fixed, that neither fire nor Hammer could prevaile against it, as he tried. But if that good Man had asked me seriously, he might easily have learned at one boyling to have that colour exact and full; he that hath any ears to hear, let him now prick them up, and only give me thanks for such a Secret for nothing, and let him freely give part of his gains to the Poor. *Mizald*.

The way to make Silver of Quicksilver.

Work and rub very well twice or thrice, purged Quicksilver with salt Armoniac and Piss, and afterwards with Salt, I shall speak of underneath; afterwards rub it again twice or thrice with Piss, every time straining it through a Linnen cloath. This being done, put the Quicksilver into a Crucible, and set it at a temperate fire, and when it is hot, put in burning coles, and when you find that it changeth the colour of the flame of the fire, increase the fire by degrees, untill the flame be blew; then heap on fire apace, and blow well with Bellows, you must be diligent to do it. And if you see it to be fixed, and will not smoke at all, take it from the fire, and you shall have excellent Silver; the Salt is thus made. Take common Salt what is sufficient, dissolve it in Fountain water, then filter it; boyl it again, untill the Salt appear in the bottome, use it as I said. *Fallopius*.

To make Quicksilver into red pouder called precipitate.

Quicksilver purged from filth is put into a Viol, and is dissolved upon Embers with an equal weight of *Aqua fortis*, then by degrees it is distilled off in Sand, untill a red pouder remain in the bottome, that is afterwards put into a dish, and is gently set to heat at the fire; or else in an Earthen Glazed Porrenger; the strongest burnt Wine is sometimes poured and burnt upon it: this being burnt, the pouder is soked in Rosewater, and then dried, after that it is again mingled with Wine, the Wine is burnt upon it, and then it must stand in a hot place to dry. Some dissolve four ounces of Quicksilver in six or eight ounces of *Aqua fortis*, distilled of Saltpeter and Alum of each alike quantity: then they distil off the water untill the pouder be dry, and they burn it gently in a Porrenger; and they keep it in a hot place, least if it take moysture, it should return to its former state. *Andernacus*.

Oyl or Balsam of Quicksilver.

This is done when Quicksilver is purged in the Calx of the Lees of Wine dried: and then is sublimed by Vitriol, Saltpeter, and Alum: after that it is digested in the spirit of Wine rectified, untill it turn to a thick fatness. Hence a Liquor is drawn, and in Sand it is forced with a vehement fire, untill the moysture distils forth like to Milk; it is then poured on again, and the whitest and sweetest Oyl, void of all corroding qualities will come forth; which is the best Oyl of all Metals. If Gold be digested with this, and congealed afterwards, a most excellent Magistral or Elixir may be made, as some say with it. *Paracelsus*.

Of the Secrets of Gold. Chap. 3.

To augment and increase Gold.

If you desire to augment your Gold, if it be made into a vessel or any thing else, and the weight doth not answer the bigness; rub the Gold with Quicksilver with your hands, or fingers, untill it drink it in, and sticking to the superficies, make the weight as you would have it: then prepare a strong Livirium of Quick-Brimstone and Quicklime, and cast it to the Gold into an earthen pot with a large mouth, and putting a few live Coles under it, let it constantly boyl so long, untill you see it hath gain'd its colour, then take it forth and you have it. Or else from yelks of Eggs, and Gold Lytharge distil water at a strong fire, and quench red hot Gold in that; But if you would have every one to increase, here is an excellent Secret; if you do it rightly, you shall make your Gold weighty enough, and it will not hurt the fashion nor inscription, but be diligent. Prepare the most red Salt of old Tiles, that is with us to be sold in most places, and the pouder of Vitriol, and strew this upon your vessel, you shall pouder Silver with *Aqua fortis*, or Lime-water, or some easie way; then again strew the pouder upon the Gold, fill the vessel confusedly, and stop it, set it to the fire eight houres, and do not blow with your Bellows, take it off, and renew your work with the pouders without the Calx of Silver, and fill it up. If the Gold lose its colour, you shall regain it thus. Make a Pap of Saltpeter, salt Armoniac, Vitriol, and pouder of Bricks with Urine, rub your Gold all over with this, and put it into the fire. There is another way to wash it, as some use; Let it boyl in Vinegar, salt Armoniac, Verdigrease, and Argal, that will recover the colour which is lost. If it shines too high, and you wish a colour more moderate, the remedy is, that being wet with Piss it may cool upon a red hot place, so you shall burn Vitriol with it to make it most bright: put it into a vessel covered with Coles, let it boyl untill it change into a most bright shining colour do not turn this Secret, I was unwilling to discover, unto an ill use. You may with the parings of Brass fullfill this work otherwise, this will supply the place of Silver, and make it weigh too heavy. You may do it otherwise; quench old Bricks red hot in Oyl, then beat them to pouder, and mingling them with Quicksilver, grind them upon Marble, and put them in a Glazed vessel upon the fire: draw forth the Oyl, and making your work red hot, and quenching it in this, it will augment the weight of it. But otherwise and more perfectly will Gold be augmented; if you melt two parts of Brass with your Silver, and then beat it into small thin plates. In the mean while prepare a pouder of the dregs of *Aqua fortis*, namely of Saltpeter and Vitriol, and in a strong Chrucible lay a plate and the pouder to augment the Gold confusedly together, untill the Chrucible be full; Lastly, Lute the mouth of it, and let it stand at an easie fire twelve houres, take it away, still renewing the same, untill it come to the perfect weight. *The same.*

To increase the weight of Gold and Silver.

Water distilled in Chymical vessels from Mans dung, will augment the weight of Gold and Silver. *Mizald.*

To draw Gold out of Silver.

Chymists seek to draw Gold out of Silver. It is not a little, but you may pay for your charge and gain by it, yet not much. The way is this. The small filings of Iron must so long stand in a melting pot that will endure the fire, untill they dissolve: then by degrees strew in Artificial Chrysocolla, the Goldsmiths use, and red Arsenick, and after you have strewed them in, cast in an equall weight of Silver, and purge it well, in a strong Test of Ashes, and when all the dregs are taken away, then put it into water of separating Gold, and the Gold will fall down to the bottome of the vessel, take that. I have not found any truer way, of a great many, and more gainfull and laborious; spare no pains, and do it as you ought to do, that you do not spend your time to no purpose. *The same.*

To make Gold.

Take Quickbrimstone, and Saltpeter of each alike quantity, beat them both severally; after that mingle the pouders, and put them into a Glass well Luted Retorts, let it stand in a gentle fire two houres, after that increase the fire, untill the smoke cease; after the smoke, will a flame come forth of the neck of the Glass, and it will ascend by Cubits or Arms two or three, and when the flame ceaseth, the Brimstone will remain at the bottome, as it were white and fixed; then take it forth, and receive the said fixed Brimstone, and as much salt Armoniac, and pouder them all very finely and mingle them; then set them all to sublime, first making an easie fire, and then a stronger, untill it ascend four houres, take forth the sublimate, and incorporate all, both the sublimate and the dregs, and sublime them again as at first, untill six times, and the Brimstone will remain at the bottome of the vessel: take it and pouder it, and lay it upon Glass or Marble in a moyst place, and it will turn to Oyl; pour two or three drops of this upon one duccate melted in a Chrucible, which will be Oyle, lay it on Marble, and it will congeale; of this put one part
upon

upon fifty parts of purged Mercury, and it will be the best Gold. *Carvan a Spaniard.*

An excellent way to multiply Gold.

Let this be handled to the glory and praise of God, which follows concerning the transmuting of some some Metals. And first I say that Silver of it self is true Gold, and it wants nothing but to be concocted perfectly; therefore provide three ounces of fine Silver, and make a Test of two parts of Vine Ashes, or Wood, well burnt and washt, and one part of Hares bones, or Oxe bones well burnt, that they may be white and made into fine pouder, mingle them with the said Ashes, and sprinkle water upon them, afterwards make your Coppel in a strong earthen Dish, or in a hole in the ground, equall to which there must be this heap well polished made smooth, and well dried; Then melt your Silver in the said Coppel, and cleanse it well, and make it refined, that your Silver may be good as any tryed upon the Coppel. Then take your Silver so purged, and beat it into thin Plates, of the thickness of two sheets of Paper or thereabouts: after that you must have common Salt prepared the way that follows. Take an Earthen pot and fill it with Salt, afterwards keep it in a Stove, and make round about it, and over it a strong fire of Coles, for four or five houres. And then let it stand as long as you please to coagulate, and put out your fire; after this take your Salt when it is white enough, and put it into some other vessel, with a great quantity of clean water, and let it all melt a whole day, and move it often to make it melt the sooner. Afterwards take the Tongues to filter with, and distill by degrees the said dissolved Salt into another vessel; then take a Glazed Earthen Dish, and put into it the distilled water aforesaid, and set upon a small fire, and coagulate it by dregrees; afterwards you must have a plain very clean Tin slice to gather your Salt as it congeals, and keep the Salt, for it is prepared; after that take your Silver, prepared and beaten, as I said before, and you must have two Barbers Basons, and in one make a bed of your Salt, and then one of the Plates of Silver, and after that of Salt, and so by turns, untill both your vessels be full, after this joyn one to the other, and Lute well the joynts; then you must have a wind Furnace, made at your discretion, which must have a Grate of Iron, upon which set your vessel covered all within a heap of fire Coles; that it may be alwayes fire-red for five houres, and upon your Furnace there must be a Cap or covering of Iron, which must cover it all over, and at the bottome or somewhat higher it must have a small vent hole. And when the time of your matter is past, take away the vessel, and let it cool; after that take your matter, and set the Salt to drying, and take your Plates and you shall see them grow black from their imperfection. Wherefore rub them as well as you can to hinder their darkness; after that, put them again with new Salt into your vessel, as you did, and set them into your Furnace; do this so often, untill you find your Silver to have no more blackness, and so is your Silver prepared to do your business. Then melt it, and make a long polished Rod and weigh it, to know exactly how much you have, make sixty equal parts of it; then take as much fine Gold as you have Silver, and purge it this following way. Take Baysalt somewhat dry at the fire, but not too much, then take a Brass Mortar or some very smooth thing, and pouder the said Salt in it; then get as many old and red Tiles as you can get, and beat them very fine and sift them very clean; after that take two parts of your Tiles so provided, and one part of your foresaid Salt, and mingle them well; then take the Gold aforesaid, and beat it into thin Plates as you did with your Silver, and take two vessels, as you did for the Silver, and make a bed within of your Cement, and then another of your Plates, &c. untill they be both full, then joyn the Basons together, and Lute them well, and set them in a very hot fiery Furnace for twenty four houres. And the first eight houres let the fire have a cover to moderate the heat of it, and the eight houres following, take off the cover of the vessel; and the last eight houres make the strongest fire you can; and in all the said times you must keep your vessels red hot, as you did with the Silver; then take your Gold, because it is prepared, and weight it, and see you have equall weight with the Silver. Then you must have a vessel made of the best earth well polished; melt your Gold in it, then put into it your piece of Silver aforesaid; and to the first tryal you shall put in a piece of black Smalt, or Enammelers *Ammil*, as broad as your Chrucible, holding down your matter at the bottome, and it will melt, and it will preserve your matter from diminution, after that your vessel must have one cover to cover it; and at the bottome of the said cover, there must be a little hole called (*Bahat*) which shall stand higher than the fire, whereby you may know when your matter is melted, and through which you may continually every four and twenty houres put in a piece of your Silver; after that shut it with a small stopper of earth; and forget not that your matter must be alwayes melted day and night; and be certain that all your prepared Silver will be converted into pure Gold, when it is cast into it. And so you may make your projection infinite. This is *Probatum*; and remember that under the Grate you must put a Platter for your Furnace, or earthen Dish, least if the vessel should break, you should lose too much of your matter. *Raymundus Lullius*.

How to carry away Gold and Silver privately.

Dissolve Gold and Silver in water of separation, or being dissolved, make them black, then melt Gold with Lead, Silver with Pitch or Sand, and so you may safely transport them. *Cardan*.

Water to part Gold from Silver.

Take Saltpeter eight ounces, Vitriol four ounces, Brimstone one ounce, pouder and distill them, and keep the water for use. When you will use them, put in the Gold and Silver, and the Silver will resolve into water, the Gold into Ashes, strain the water from the Ashes. *Fallopius*.

Water to part Gold from Silver another way.

Take Saltpeter one part, Liquid or Rock Alum three parts, half a part of Sand, dry all diligently, and purge them, and distill them at the fire in Glass Limbecks. That which comes forth first is kept by it self, and when the vessel looks red, increase the fire, and another water will come forth, which ofttimes joyns with the former, but it is thus parted. Take a small part of the water drawn off, and put into it of the finest Silver a half penny weight, that is, twelve grains, and then set it so long upon the Embers untill it melt. This Silver will send to the bottome dregs like to Lime, take them out; what remains of pure water, mingle with all the water extracted, and then it will send the same feces to the bottome again as before; take away those, and you shall have all the water most pure, and more fit to dissolve Silver, and all Metals except Gold. *Cardan*.

To separate Gold from Silver.

You shall part Gold from Silver thus; annoint the body of any thing Guilded with Linseed Oyl, and sprinkle upon it the pouder of salt Armoniac and Roch Alum; then when they are all hot, quench them in the water, and the Gold will remain in the water. *From a skilfull Goldsmith. Mizald*.

Liquor or potable Gold.

Plates of Gold purged by the royall Cement, or Stybium, will resolve into pouder by the green Liquor of Salt: then they must be so long washed in distilled Rain water, untill you can perceive no more Salt remaining with it. Or if you desire to do that sooner, the plates of Gold must be covered in Plates of Lead, and must for four and twenty houres be Cemented, (as they call it,) and they are ground fine untill the Calx of the Gold be very pure. Afterwards pour on as much Spirit of Wine upon the washed pouder or purged Calx, that it may swim above it six fingers breadth; and the joynts of the vessel being well stopt, steep them in water temperately hot, or *Balneum Mariæ*, for twenty or thirty daies. Then pour forth a yellow liquor, leaving a white pouder in the bottome, and the Spirit of Wine by a Glass Viol, with a cover, is gently parted from the yellow liquor of Gold, in a Bath; Lastly, The same Liquor of Gold being extracted, it must be elevated to the highest degree, that is, it must be five times forced through a Retort, and this is the absolute preparing of the Quintessence of Gold, which is the chief Secret in Chymistry. *Paracelsus*.

Potable Gold.

Leaves of Gold must be distilled with Spirit of Vinegar, and parted, and then

then digested a Moneth with prepared *Aqua vitæ*, untill a juyce appeare, whereof one Scruple is the Dose, with some other Spirit or Liquor. *Andernacus, Paracelsus.*

Sweating Gold.

Fill a vessel with the best red and black Wine, and set it into the coldest waters; then you must have two small Sawcers of Gold, into one whereof that must receive the other, put in small fine Linnen Rags, and so it is set into the Wine : when these are lighted, the one Sawcer is presently put into the other, and left there untill they are all burnt. When the vessels are cool, and the Ashes removed, the Oyl is collected, and this is repeated so often, untill there be enough gathered. Lastly, All this Liquor is put into a Viol, and is distilled with a cover in hot Ashes. Many use this for Potable Gold, and keep it for a Secret. And this way we may draw Oyls from other Metals, as from Silver, for diseases of the Eyes; from Brass, for diseases of the skin. *Paracelsus.*

Balsam of Gold.

This is the way to make Oyl of Balsam of Gold, which *Paracelsus* cals Butter or fat of Gold; which being taken inwardly, or annointed outwardly, will cure all malignant Ulcers, even an Elephantiasis, and all kinds of Leprosie; and in brief, he sayes it will do more then the mind of Man can conceive. It is thus, A dram of fine Leaf-Gold is to be mingled with half an ounce of Oyl of the Pine tree, and put in a Glass to digest for a Moneth; then the Oyl is washed, and the pouder remaining at the bottome of the vessel is given with Honey. Or better thus, Mingle one dram of fine Leaf-Gold with six drams of distilled Oyl of Mastick, let them ferment thirty daies in Horse dung, then the Oyl is washed with hot water, and the Gold hath Spirit of Wine poured upon it, and stands to digest twelve dayes; afterwards it is distilled in Balneo, untill the Gold stay in the bottome of the vessel like Butter, which is thrice a week annointed upon Ulcers; and also it is good for Limbs that are contracted, and any way weakned. *Andernacus* from *Paracels.*

Aurum vitæ, or precipitate with Gold.

Take two ounces of Quicksilver purged by most sharp Vinegar and Salt, of the best Oriental Gold made into very thin Plates one dram; they must be mingled in a three cornerd Chrucible; some barbarous people call this an *Amalgams*; this is poured into cold water, and if any of the Quicksilver remain, that is pressed forth through a skin, and washed with Salt and Vinegar, untill there appear no dregs, taking care in the mean time that the quantity of the Quicksilver be not diminished. If it should be, it must be so augmented, that for one dram of Gold seaven or eight drams of Quicksilver may be remaining. Then put them into a Luted Retort, and pour on of hot water two ounces, and setting on the cover, bring it forth again by hot Sand; when they are all cold, pour on again the same water, and distill it off as before; do so five times, and then the pouder will be red, which they call *Aurum vitæ*, or Gold precipitate commonly; afterwards the same is put into a Porringer and covered, and is set amongst red hot coles, untill it be red hot; then it is taken forth, and when it is cold, it is moystened with Rose-water, and then dryed again. The Dose to young Children is a half penny weight; but to those that are of years, a penny weight. It cures the Plague, the Pox, Leprosie, Dropsie, and other hard Diseases, it openeth obstructions of the Bowels, cures those who have taken Poyson, it cures malignant Ulcers inwardly taken, or outwardly with Unguents, and Plaisters that cleanse, and is happily applyed to sordid, malignant, hollow Ulcers, but not to such as run over the body. *Andernacus ex Paracelso.*

The way to pouder Gold.

Take Leaves of Gold what you will, put them into a Chrucible or Test at the fire, then take Quicksilver four times as much, and put that likewise in another Test or Chrucible to the fire, but not near, but only that it may heat, but the Leaves of Gold must stand so long at the fire, that they begin to be red hot, but they must not melt; This done take the Chrucible from the fire, and mingle the Quicksilver with the Leaves of Gold, mixing them a while with some stick, then suddenly cast them into

into a dish full of water, and make an *Amalgama*; But if you will do it otherwise, grind the Leaves of Gold with the Quicksilver upon a Porphyr stone, untill they be well mingled, and grinded; then wash them twice or thrice with common water, if you add a little Vinegar or juyce of Lemmons, you will do better, for they will mingle sooner and better; Therefore take this mixture however prepared, and press it through a fine Linnen Cloath, that some part of the Quicksilver may come forth, or press it through a white skin of a Doe or Lamb, which is best, then what sticks in the skin must be ground with live Brimstone first poudred very fine, so much, that it may not exceed half the mixture. Then put all in some Iron Crucible to the fire, the vessel being very close covered, and leave it so untill all the Brimstone be burnt, and what remains be yellow; when it is cold, wash it in a Dish full of water so often untill it look like Gold, and keep it for use. When you would use it, add as much Rosewater to it, or common water, in which Gum Arabick is dissolved, as you need, mingle them, and make a Golden Liquor to write or paint with. And when you have written or painted with it, rub the Letters lightly with some Tooth, which cannot be done with other ground Gold, that all Painters use. *Alexius.*

A way to grind Gold otherwise.

Take Leaves of Gold and grind them in a Glass Dish with Julep of Roses, and stir them with your middle finger, that they may mingle exactly: then put them upon a Porphyr or Marble stone, and grind them well again, pouring water to them by degrees; after that take it away, and put it into a Dish, washing the stone well with water, that you may have it all off; then wash the Gold well with your finger, and when it settles to the bottome, take away the water gently, and pour on more water that is hot, and wash it again, and do this so often, untill the Syrup of Roses be clean washed from it, and the water is no longer sweet; then the Gold must be dried and put into some Glazed vessel upon hot Embers untill it be exceeding hot, and come to its natural colour; when this is done, mingle that with Gum-water, and make a Liquor for use. *The same.*

To repair the Gold colour lost.

If Gold have lost its colour, you shall thus renew it; make a thick substance with salt Armoniac, Vitriol, Saltpeter, pouder of Bricks and Piss, cover the Gold over with this, and set it into an easie fire; It will be done far easier, if the Gold boyle so long in Vinegar with salt Armoniac, Verdigrease, and Argal, until it recover the colour lost. I had not this for nothing, yet I impart it to thee freely, as I do many things besides. *Mizaldus.*

An excellent Cement to purge Gold.

Take poudred Bricks and Saltpeter of each one part, wet with Vinegar what is sufficient: put them into a Crucible, that it may be half full, then Plates of Gold, and so fill it, making one lay above another; yet take care that one do not touch the other. Then stop the Crucible and Lute it well, that no vapour may come forth, place the Crucible upon a stone not above a handfull high, and compass it about with stones that are not very hard, untill the Crucible will receive no more. Then put under a strong fire twenty four houres, and you shall have Gold purified. *Out of a Germane Author.*

Of Secrets concerning Silver. Chap. 4.

An old History of Silver turned into Gold.

A certain *Moor* in the Countrey of the *Moores* came to a Smith, and brought unto him twenty pieces of Silver to put into the fire with a Crucible when they were melted, the Smith that dealt in Brass cast a pouder upon them he had from the *More*; It was a green pouder, making a yellow smoke in the fire, and the Silver was turned into Gold, and the Smith sold that Gold to a Goldsmith at the price of the best Gold. The Smith returned and gave the *Moor* the Money: then the *Moor* taking pitty of the Smith said unto him, I will teach thee to make this pouder; Take calcined or poudred Gold, burnt Brass, *Crocus Martis*, of each one ounce, salt Armoniac rubified, three ounces; elsewhere there is added, Vitriol rubified one ounce; dissolve

the

the salt Armoniac, and with that diffolved in Cerate; that is, with the water of it wet well the faid pouders of Gold, Brafs, Vitriol, and Iron, or *Crocus Martis*, grinding them well upon a Porphyr or Marble ftone, and fo grinding them along time. When the pouders have drank in all that Saltwater, fet them in a Glafs Viol with a long neck in Horfe dung one and twenty daies, changing the hot dung every four dayes. When it is well diffolved and turned into water, congeale it in a Furnace uponhot Embers in fome Glafs Viol, when it is congealed, put one part of that upon ten parts of fine prepared Silver. Note that if any part remain undiffolved, grind it again with the water of falt Armoniac, untill it be all diffolved, do this that you may not loofe your Gold, ever renewing the wetting of it well with the water of falt Armoniac. But if you again diffolve the matter congealed, and do all things in order, as before, one part will give a Tincture to twenty parts, and fo you may multiply it, as oft as you pleafe; for every time you fhall augment ten. I faw that Smith at *Toledo*, and he told me this, and to an old Kinfman of his, and the Smith was an old Man, and I and my Mafter did work as abovefaid; Gold muft be fo poudred with the fume of Lead, or with water, wherein Lead hath been often quenched; or thus; Melt Lead in a Veffel that hath a fmall hole in the top, the bignefs of a Crown, and put the Crown of Gold fo upon it, that the fume of the Lead may come to it upon one fide, then turn it, and when you have done fo, fometimes the Gold will be poudred; But burnt Brafs muft be calcined with live Brimftone; and before it be mingled with them, it muft be wafhed with fair water, or with water and Salt, untill the water come clean away from it. The *Crocus* of Iron muft be made with Vinegar at an eafie fire that it may be red; It is done thus. Put filings of Iron into ftrong Vinegar, let it be clear red Vinegar, fet it in the Sun two or three dayes, then pour off the Vinegar gently, and keep it, and pour on more Vinegar on the filings in the Sun, and do fo untill all the filings be diffolved, or is brought into very fine pouder, and again dry all the Vinegar up in the Sun, falt Armoniac muft be diffolved by cold and moyft, or by hot and moyft. Take two parts of it diffolved, burnt Brafs one part, *Crocus Martis* one part, falt Armoniac the quantity of them all; diffolve the falt Armoniac, and foke the pouders in it, by long grinding of them, then put them in hot Horfe dung fifteen dayes to diffolve, you may diffolve them in a pit; often changing the dung, being hot, then coagulate upon hot Embers gently. One part of this congealed matter will give a Tincture to ten parts of prepared Silver. And if you diffolve them the fecond time, doing all things as was forefaid, one part will Tincture twenty parts, and fo you may increafe it. *This was out of the Practicks of Mafter* Odomar.

That Silver may be fo truly Tinctured into Gold, that you would think it to be true Gold indeed.

Make a mixture at the fire with one part of filings of Silver, and three parts of Quickfilver, let it ftand upon hot Coles in a Glazed veffel, until fo much Quickfilver flyeth away, as exceeds the Silver; then pouder falt Armoniac and live Brimftone, equall for weight with the Silver, and fet this in a Glafs veffel two houres upon hot burning Coles, untill the force of it fublime the falt Armoniac, the live Brimftone, and the Quickfilver, and they ftick to the neck of the veffel: break the veffel, and keep the Silver of a Gold colour, being as much, or more in weight than it was at firft, and prefently provide fuch a water; Take *Roman* Vitriol with twice as much red Cyprus Vitriol diftilled, which they call Coperas, let it be the beft, (for hence depends the whole bufinefs,) fo of Saltpeter three times as much, and a third part of Verdigreafe, a fixt part of Vermilion, and diftill water from thefe in Glafs Stils, two parts of this muft boyl with the Silver you kept at a gentle fire twenty four houres; then increafing the fire of diftilling, make all the moyfture evaporate, and what remains at the bottome, muft be put with the Calx of Chryfocolla, into an earthen Teft, or melting Crucible, with the mouth left open; then Lute it well, and fet it on a melting fire, and you have it; for the Silver looks like Gold, and will never lofe its colour, nor change it, but being expofed to all tryals, will lofe very little of its luftre or none; fo will it reprefent the colour of Gold perfectly and gainfully. Now remember

remember burnt Brass made with Stybium, that being melted with half Silver, will make perfect Gold colour, as you may see. If you mingle it with Gold, it will give a better colour and stand some proofs. Another way to do it excellently; Mingle the congealed with Quicksilver in a Helmet, as I said, with a third part of Silver, you shall find your Silver of a Gold colour : melt it with half Gold, pour it into an Earthen pot and pour Vinegar upon it, and let it boyl six houres, and the colour will rise; but you shall lastly try it like Gold; namely with common Salt, and pouder of Bricks, adding some Vitriol ; and so will your Gold be purged from dross, and will stand all tryals, and will exceed the second, and proceed to the third degree. *The same.*

To colour Silver.

Take good red Wine Vinegar, and put the filings of Iron into an Earthen Crucible of *Raviax*, then take Vinegar wherein the sixt part of it of salt Armoniac is dissolved in it, then put it upon the foresaid filings, that it may swim over them two or three fingers breadth, afterwards stop your vessel, and set it upon small Embers for eight daies, and stir this twice or thrice a day with a stick, and it will be all red or Vermilion, or bloud colour ; after that strain and cleanse it well, and add fresh Vinegar as you did before; and do this so often untill you have enough of this Vinegar, and before you do this, or so soon as it is done, take one pound of Quicksilver sublimed, and one pound of salt Armoniac, and grind it to pouder and mix them together, sublime them thrice together, and every time mingle them; that which ascends with that which remains in the bottome; and your Mecury will remain black at the bottome of the vessel; and the salt Armoniac will ascend high in the vessel; After that mingle the said Mercury with the same weight of the filings of Iron, and set them upon Marble, and they will dissolve into water, when this matter is dissolved, cast it all into red Vinegar, and stop the vessel, and set it three dayes upon a gentle heat, afterwards purifie it by filtring of it, and put it into an Alembick, and separate the moysture from it in Balneo : after that upon Ashes in a Furnace receive in another Glass receiver, as you do *Aqua fortis*, the Oyl that comes from it, or the Vermilion water, and keep it by it self; put fresh Vinegar upon the feces to dissolve them, then filter that, and congeale it in Balneo, afterwards by Embers separate the red Oyl, and so put it to the other, and repeate this so oft untill all be separated, then keep it ; forget not when this is done, to mingle your salt Armoniac with so much Quicklime, or put it upon Marble, and it will dissolve into water, take this and mix it with a third or fourth part of Saltpeter ; So make *Aqua fortis*, and by a Limbeck distill the water upon Ashes in a Furnace : in this *Aqua fortis* dissolve the purest Leaf Gold, as much as you can dissolve ; Then take your red Oyl, and if it be one pound put half a pound of your water with Gold Leaves to it, and put them into a Viol, upon warm Embers, for four and twenty houres, then by a Limbeck, congeal them in Balneo, and after that set it to putryfie in hot Horse dung, in a Viol of Glass, close stopt, for fifteen dayes : after that congeal it like to Honey ; and take fine white Silver Cemented, and annoint it with this Unguent on both sides, and put them into one Crucible, bed upon bed, untill it be full, and to ten ounces let there be one ounce of this Unguent, and shutting and Luting the Crucible, set it in the heat four dayes : after that make a melting fire, to melt it all, and you shall have Gold to twenty four Carats, and if it please you not, beat it again into thin Plates, and annoint it as before, and if the colour be too high, do not put on so much of it, and so your Silver will be perfect. (This Note was in the Margin,) Take one part of filings of Iron, and one part of burnt Brass well washed, salt Armoniac the quantity of them all, let them all boyl well together, then dry them upon hot Coles or Embers, or in the Sun, and make them into pouder, and project one ounce of that pouder upon three ounces of fine melted Silver, and it will appear to be Gold. Also one part of fine Gold, one of fine Silver, and one of melted Brass together, make Gold of eighteen Carats with one of burnt Brass melted. Burnt Brass is made thus; Take filings of Copper one pound, Quickbrimstone a fourth part, mingle them, then put this into a Crucible, and cover it with a Tyle, and Lute it with *Lutum Sapientia, pientiæ*, that no vapour may come forth. Then put the mouth of the Crucible downwards, and cover it with Coles, and let it stand so some houres, then take it from the fire, and you shall see burnt Brass; wash it as you should. *Raymundus Lullius.*

To change Silver into Gold.

Take Quicksilver three ounces, set it into a Glass Retort very well Luted, unto the fire, untill it grow very hot, with which one ounce of Leaf Gold must be first mixed, then take it from the fire; and add to it salt Armoniac one ounce, salt Ellebrot half an ounce, Borax two drams; Quicksilver purged two ounces. This being done, shut the Glass very well with *Hermes* his Signet; that nothing may breath forth, and set it at a Furnace of fire three dayes continually; then take it from the fire; and when it is cold open the Retort, take the matter out, and pouder it very fine; this is called the Philosophers *Elixir*: and when you would make Gold, take the finest Silver five ounces; melt it at the fire, and then put to it of the said *Elixir* one ounce, and it will turn it to Gold. But salt Elebrot is made thus. Take common Salt purged, salt Gemmæ, salt Alkali, of each one ounce, pouder them, and add to them juyce of Mints, juyce of Clove-Gelliflowers, of each two ounces, Spring-water two pounds, mingle all very well; and it is done. But *Lutum Sapientiæ* is made of the best Lute, dry and sifted, and mingled with whites of Eggs. Lastly, Quicksilver is purged with the sharpest Vinegar, wash it three or four times; and then strain it. *Fallop.*

To guild Silver.

Silver vessels cannot be covered with Gold, but by the help of Quicksilver, to whom only it is obedient and tractable: For refusing all other Metals, it will adhere to Gold only as its most familiar friend; and sticks willingly unto it, hardly to Lead, more hardly to Iron, and to Brass but meanly. *Lemnius.*

To turn Silver into a Calx.

Would you turn Silver or any thing else into a Calx, do it thus: make a mixture of the filings of Silver, and three times as much Quicksilver, then with common Salt upon a Porphyr Marble, you must grind them well, when you see they are perfectly united, put them into a Retort that they may ascend the easier, set this to the fire, and by the force of it, drive out the Quicksilver by the Pipe or Neck of it into a receiver; what stayes at the bottome of the vessel, wash well with fresh water, still pouring on more, untill no Salt is perceived, and all bitterness be gon from it; when the water is sweet, it will be turned to Calx. There is another way to do it: dissolve your Silver in *Aqua fortis*, as Goldsmiths use to do, and pour in Spring-water, wherein there is common Salt, so the Silver will fall to the bottome of the Glass; draw forth the water by a Tongue, or Pensils, and set the Calx in a Crucible upon flaming Coles, take it away, and wash off the Salt with fresh water, which you shall do again and again untill all be gone; and the manner of washing must be as I shewed before, so you shall turn Silver into Calx, and soften it like Wax. The filings of it mingled with Mercury sublimate, and put into a fit Glass vessel, and set upon the fire; that the fire may drive forth the Quicksilver, you shall find at the bottome of the vessel fixed Silver like Wax, fit for Jewels, keep it in a little Box. *The same.*

A wonderous way to melt Silver.

That is strang that some say there is a kind of Silver no Bellows will melt; and when Men had done all they could with it, they were taught by the examples of their Pious Predecessours, that those vessels wherein Silver was wont to be melted, had Silver above, and Coles at the bottome, and had holes bored through the bottome, add with Bricks on the tops of Mountains when the winds blew, they melted that Silver; and afterwards with Bellows they purified it again in small vessels. *Cardan.*

To augment Silver, or to make it more weighty.

Some with Salt and old Potsheards, hold Silver beaten into thin Plates in the fire, to draw some moysture from it, and to thicken the parts that make it light. But you shall

shall do it more readily thus: Beat Silver into fine Plates, and strew on by turns Cinnaber and Mercury sublimate, in a vessel will endure the fire, and Lute and bind it fast with bands, that it breath not forth, compass it all over with Coles, and keep it in the fire twelve houres, then take these brittle Plates forth, and put them into an Ash Copel red hot with fire, into melted Lead: and with strong blast of Bellows, force out the Lead into a Receiver, which will draw out with it all the dross, and will leave the Silver pure behind: all Men call this probation by the Copel, because it purgeth away all that is not good Silver. If you find it not weighty, do the same thing often, untill it be as heavy as Gold; we can also otherwise augment Silver, Pour strong distilled Vinegar into a vessel, pouder Stybium and filings of Lead and sift them, what stayes in the Sive must be pounded in a Mortar again, to sift it finer, and then put into the distilled Vinegar, and hid under dung untill all is dissolved, then set the vessel to the fire, and often quench what is within, or else draw forth the water from it, and it will be the same thing. *Geber* saith that made with Brimstone into a Calx, and then reduced to its body, it will get much in weight. *The same.*

To diminish Silver or Gold.

Now remains to shew how Silver and Gold may be diminished not spoiling the fashion or Stamp. Many do it by *Aqua fortis*, but that makes the work full of knots and rugged. But do it thus. Strew pouder of Brimstone upon the work, and set a Candle to it round every way, or burn it under the work, that will burn and consume it by degrees, strike with a Hammer on the contrary side, and the outside will fall off, so much as you please, as you think fit to lay on your Brimstone. *The same.*

To blanch Silver.

You shall white Silver thus: Take salt Armoniac, Roch-Alum, and *Alum Plumosum*, salt Gemmæ, Argal, *Roman* Vitriol, of each alike quantity, pouder and mingle them, and dissolve them in fair water; then let Silver boyl in that, so long as you need, and you shall see your Silver wonderfull white. *Out of the Secrets of a certain lover of those that make Gold.* Mizaldus.

To make vessels as if they were Silver.

Quicksilver mingled with strong Vinegar, will make vessels like Silver, if they be annointed therewith. *Mizald.*

Water that will make Silver of a Gold colour.

Take Saltpeter two pound, Roch-Alum five pound, pouder, mingle, and distill them, keep the water for use. When you would use it, let your Silver melt in the fire, and pour it into the said water, and quench it, and it will be like Gold in colour. *Falopius.*

Water to dissolve Silver.

Take *Roman* Vitriol one pound, salt Armoniac five pound, Saltpeter four ounces, Vermilion three ounces, pouder and distill them according to Art.

Of the Secrets of Brass. Chap. 5.

To guild Brass.

Brass being burnt you shall thus make it look like to Gold, make an *Aqua fortis* of Vitriol, Saltpeter, Alum, Vermilion, and Verdigrease, let the burnt Brass dissolve in it, and bring it to a body again, it will be much of a Gold colour, it is also made blewish, by often strewing into it Silver and setting it to the fire. *The same.*

To turn Brass into Silver.

But if you would turn Brass like to Silver, or else Copper, as Children often use to do and Juglers, that vessels may presently look like Silver; this is the way to do it. Mingle a like quantity of salt Armoniac, Alum and Saltpeter, and with a little filings of Silver, set them unto the fire, that they may be fire hot; and when they leave smoking, strew on this pouder; or else wet with your spittle, and rub them with your fingers, and they will seem like Silver. *The same.*

To white Brass exceedingly.

If you grind salt Armoniac and Egg-shels together, and distil water from them with Chymical vessels, and quench red hot Brass in that, it will be very white. Also Quicksilver drawn from Antimony, doth very well white Copper, if it be projected upon, or else rubbed on, which the Antimony it self in the Mines will not do, called by *Pliny*, *Vomica*, of perpetual Liquor. *Mizald*.

That Brass or Copper may look like Silver.

If salt Armoniac, Alum and Saltpeter, be mingled of each a like quantity, and with a few filings of Silver be set to the fire to be fire hot, when they cease to smoke; the pouder of them but strewed on, or rubbed on with spittle upon Brass or Copper, will make it look like Silver. *The same*.

To dry Brass like to Silver.

Take *Aqua fortis* one ounce, cast into that a penny weight of Silver, first beat thin with the Hammer, and then cut into small pieces, and put it to the fire in a vessel untill the Silver turn to water: Then take it from the fire, and add as much pouder of white Argal, as may drink up all the water, and make a lump of it, and rub any Brass work with it, and it will be white as Silver. *Alexius*.

To melt Copper quickly.

They that will have Copper soon melted and ductile, they add Horse hoofs to it when they melt it. *Mizaldus had this from an Italian, and a certain expert Founder*.

To make Verdigrease.

Take the filings of Copper made into very fine pouder, as much as you please, wet them with old Piss, and salt Armoniac, then dry them in the Sun, then wet them again, as before until it look green, do this so often untill you have Verdigrease enough. *Out of a German Book*.

Otherwise.

Annoint Copper-Plates with Honey and burnt Salt, then leave them to hang in Vinegar two weeks under dung. *Out of a German Book*.

Otherwise.

Or take Copper-Plates fairly polished, then grind Vitriol with Piss upon a Porphyr stone, and with that annoint your Copper all over, and dry it in the Sun, the Plates being dryed and put into a Glazed Pot, must be set upon a strong fire, for two houres, that they may be red hot; In the mean while, take off the cover and see the smoke that comes forth, and when you see it black, take the vessel from the fire, to cool it: Take forth the Copper-Plates, pouder them in your hands, and if there be any you cannot pouder, begin your work again, untill they will pouder. This being done, wash your pouder in hot Water or Urine in a Bason; and when the matter setleth at the bottome, pour off that black stuff swims on the top, and dry the rest in the Sun; Take of this pouder one pound, and of Argal brought to a Calx two ounces, grind them well severally; mingle them, and dry them. Put them at last into the foresaid Earthen Pot and put fire under, and heaping on Coles, untill you see a green smoke; then uncover the Pot, and draw forth the best Verdigrease. *Out of a German Book*.

A way to prepare Copper, so that it may be like to Gold, and may be wrought very well.

Take Copper, *Lapis Calaminaris*, of each half an ounce, Tutty two drams, make the Copper red hot, quench it in Piss, doing it twice: do so with the *Lapis Calaminaris*, and Tutty. Take half an ounce of the dissolved Copper, adding to it Honey one ounce, boyl them untill the Honey look black and be dry, that it may be poudred, afterwards the Honey being beaten with the *Lapis Calaminaris*, and the Tutty, let them boyl again at the fire, untill the Copper be melted, and so it is done. *Out of a Germane Book*.

To give a Tincture to Copper like to Silver.

Take Quicksilver sublimate, salt Armoniac, of each what is sufficient, boyl them in Vinegar, in which quench the Copper first made red hot, and it will be like Silver. *Fallopius.*

To make Copper soft like Silver.

Take burnt Brass, and melt it with Borax in a Crucible, after that extinguish it in Painters Oyl, as the *French* call it, and lay it on an Anvil, and by degrees beat it plain easily, then boyl it again in a Crucible, and quench it in Painters Oyl, and do so five or six times, that it may be soft enough, and that is the fine burnt Brass to unite with Gold, and you may put in half more then you can of other Brass, and the Gold will be fairer than with other Brass. *Raymundus Lullius.*

Of the Secrets of Iron. Chap. 7.

To give a Tincture of Gold to Iron.

You must burn in an Earthen Pot Plates of Iron, putting live Brimstone between them, and Lute the Pot well; then take them forth and they will be brittle; Thirdly, put them into a Pot with a great mouth, and pour in sharp distilled Vinegar, and set them forth in the Dog dayes, if they come not to the redness is required, set them again in the Sun, or in a bath of boyling water, untill they wax red, draw it off with a Tongue, or pour it into some other vessel: Then add Vinegar again, and do the same so often, untill all the Iron be dissolved; Let the moysture evaporate in a Glass still, and the pouder that remains in the bottome, cast upon Silver or any white Metal will make it seem like Gold. *The same.*

To gild Iron.

Take common water three pound, Alum two ounces, *Roman* Vitriol one ounce, flower of Brass one penny weight, salt Gemmæ three ounces, Orpiment one ounce, mingle them and boyl them, but when they begin to boyl, add Argal or the dregs of Wine, common Salt half an ounce, let them boyl alittle while, then take them from the fire, and with that water give a Tincture to the Iron, then put it into the fire, then polish it. *Alexius.*

To make Iron like to Gold.

Take Linseed Oyl three ounces, Argal two ounces, yelks of Eggs boyld hard and pounded two ounces, Aloes half an ounce, Saffron five Grains, Turmerick two Grains; boyl them all sometime in a new Earthen Pot, and make Oyle to Dye Iron. If those Ingredients spoken of be not well covered with Oyl, add more Oyl, and let the Iron be first well polished, and the colour will be Gold. *The same.*

A water to cover Iron with Leaf Gold, or with Gold dissolved with Quicksilver, which Goldsmiths use to gild Silver with.

Take *Roman* Vitriol one ounce, Alum two ounces, salt Armoniac one ounce, bring them into the finest pouder, and boyl them in common water, wherewith when the Iron first made clean and polished is Dyed, add to it the Leaves of Gold, then dry it at the fire, and polish it with a Bloodstone, as the manner is; But if you would gild Iron as Goldsmiths do, with Gold dissolved in Quicksilver, add to the foresaid water, flower of Brass one dram, sublimate half an ounce, mingle them, and when they have boyl'd a while, let the Iron boyl in the same water; If the Iron be so great that the water cannot cover it, let it be well rubbed with the same hot water, and so let it be made hot in the fire, to receive the Gold dissolved with Quicksilver. Now how to do this I taught before in the precedent Book, in the Chapter concerning poudring of Gold. Moreover when the Iron is covered with Gold, it must be smoked at the fire, by a Candle, or with Brimstone, as Goldsmiths do, or with Wax, as they do in *Germany*, which is far better. *The same.*

To make Iron or Silver look of a Brass colour, which is far the best to gild upon, and will longest hold the colour of the Gold.

It is most certain that Gold laid upon white Iron or Silver, will not appear so well as it doth upon Brass, for that so soon as any of the Iron begins to be discovered or the Gold to be worn off, the colours of Iron or Silver shew themselves, but in a red colour it is not so found out: Wherefore some skilful judicious Men cover Wood or any such matter, not with red stone, as most Men do, but with a yellow or Golden,

den colour: For though the Gold in time may vanish away in some part, it is not so easily known as when it is laid upon red or white. This also would be convenient in gilding Iron or Silver. But to pass over this, I shall shew you how to make Iron or Silver seem like Brass. Take flower of Brass, Vitriol, salt Armoniac, of each what is sufficient; bring them into very fine pouder: boyl this pouder half an hour in strong Vinegar, then take them from the fire, and put in Iron or Silver, covering the vessel very close, so long untill it be cold, and so your Iron will be like to Brass, and most fit to be Gilded. *The same.*

How to soften Iron

Iron will be mollified with the juyce of Bean pods, or of Mallows, if you quench it in them, and not in in Water, but to make it malleable, it must lye abroad in the open Ayr upon the ground: Rain will soften it, because it is of an earthly nature, and the Sun melts it, because it is moyst; the fire consumes the sharper part of it, which is as it were venome to it. Wherefore being often fired, it is laid in the open Ayr, and so softned as any thing that is tractable. Also Iron Wyer if it be put into fire, and made red hot, and then suffer'd to cool of it self, it will grow so ductile, that you may use it like a Cord to bind any thing. *Cardan.*

How Iron may be Engraven.

Soft Iron is Engraven thus: You must paint upon the Iron what you desire to carve upon it, and a Pestel of Lead is set against it, then with a Hammer that part is knocked which you would have beaten together, that which must stick forth is received by the Lead and doth not sink down; thus Men make curious Pictures of Animals and Plants, that you would think they were wrought in Wax with sharp Penknives. But if you quench red hot Iron in cold water, it will grow hard and brittle and not ductil at all of necessity, for the cold water compels the fire that is within, and soon consumes the inbred moysture of the Iron, which being taken away that made it ductil and soft, it must needs grow brittle and hard.

To take rust from Iron.

Oyl of Tartar will suddenly take away rust from Iron, and make it bright, and it will also take away spots from the face, and all filthy Pushes that deform the forehead and Chin, by its abstersive quality. *Alexius.*

To cleanse Iron.

Aristotle in his Meteors, teacheth how to cleanse Iron, saying; Iron often put into the fire is cleansed, and the earthly part of it goeth to scales, the nobler part into Steel.

To change Iron into Steel.

The Pomegranate shell will change Iron into Steel.

To make Iron so hard, that other Iron shall not easily cut it.

Distil Earth-Wormes, and apart, distil also Turneps, and roots of Pompions; mingle those waters equally together, and wet your Iron therein, the Iron will grow harder if you put it twice in. *Nostradam.*

Crocus Mortis.

The finest filings of Steel are first washt in Spring water from all foulness, and then dried: afterwards they are steeped in the strongest Vinegar three or four dayes, then they are dried and put into Earthen Dishes, and it is burnt in the Furnace with most vehement flame, untill it grow as fine as pouder of Saffron, in the mean while you must take forth the Dish, and sweep of the finest with a Feather, and then set the Dish into the Furnace again. *Anonymus.*

To harden Iron and to soften it again.

Take Vervin and beat it with stalks and leaves, press the juyce forth through a Linnen Cloath, and keep it in a Glass for use. When you would make your Iron hard, mingle the juyce of Vervin, with an equal part of Mans Urine, who is lusty. You may add also the juyce of that the Latins call *Curculio*, and the Germans *Engerlin*: Make that part of the Iron red hot which you would harden and dip it into these juyces, untill there appear Golden spots, and if it be yet too blew of colour, you shall know by that it is not yet hard enough: or quench Iron in the distilled water.

ter of a Turd. Some diftil water of red Snails, and quench their Iron in that. *Out of a* German *Book.*

To soften Iron.

Receive in some veſſel or Baſon Mans bloud, ſet it aſide untill the thick bloud ſink down, pour off the watry Whey of it, and keep it well for your uſe. Afterwards take a Pencil, and with this Whey ſmeer over weapons made hot, to drink it in, and they will be ſoft. *Out of a* German *Book.*

Another.

Take clarified Honey, freſh Goats Piſs, Alum, *Borra*, Olive Oyl, *Baumal*, and Salt, of each what needs; mingle all theſe together, and dip, and quench your Iron therein. *The ſame.*

Another.

Lay upon Leather ſhavings of Horn and ſalt Armoniac, ſprinkling Piſs upon them, wrap the Iron in the skin, that the Iron may burn the skin, and ſo it will grow ſoft. *The ſame.*

How to harden Steel.

Quench it in cold water, that will harden it; and if the colour of the edg be blew, know the Steel is come to its perfect colour. *The ſame.*

How to ſoften Steel to Grave upon it.

You ſhall make Steel ſoft with a Lixivium of Oke aſhes, and unſlakt Lime, prepare the Lee, and ſtrain it two houres; caſt your Steel into this Lee, and let it ſtay there fourteen dayes, but if you would have it hard as before, quench it in cold water. *The ſame.* — Another.

Take ſalt Armoniac, Quicklime, of each what needs, add a little more of *Venice* Sope, mingle and ſtir them well, leave the Steel in Moſs, that it may be made moyſter, and let it be in the Lee three or at moſt but four hours; then by degrees pour forth the Lee. This way ſerves only for ſmall pieces of Steel, but you may ſoften great pieces if you put them into Cow dung, Alum, and glew moyſtned with Vinegar, as I ſaid. *The ſame.*

To make the edg of Knives hard and firm.

Water of bruiſed Earth-Worms preſſed through a Cloath, and mingled equally with juyce of Raddiſh, will make the edges of Knives and Swords ſo hard, and alſo of other Inſtruments, that are dipt twice or thrice therein, when they are Forged, that they will eaſily cut other Iron like Lead. *Mizaldus had this from a certain Sword Maker at* Paris.

Of the Secrets of Lead. Chap. 7.

To Tincture Lead into Gold.

You may thus eaſily Tincture Lead like Gold; burn Braſs, and beat it ſmall in a ſtone Mortar, and ſift it, alſo Chryſtal Glaſs, and then Leaves of Lead, ſtrew theſe one upon another in order, and fill a Crucible with them, that the burnt Braſs may be at the top and the botrome, put fire gently to it, then melt all with blaſt of Bellows; When it is cold, take all droſs away, and do this work three or four times, and it will be coloured; then take *Terra Cadmia* that is red and finely poudred, and mingling Rayſins, dry Figs, and Dates together, put them into a veſſel, then put Cyperus root, or Turmerick to them; ſtrew in order the half coloured Leaves of Lead, and cover the Pot, yet let there be a ſmall hole through the cover, applying a gentle fire ſo long, untill the moyſture be breathed out, then blow hard with Bellows and melt them, and caſt them into a Rod, there is no Gold like it. But the *Cadmia Terra* will be made Purple colour thus. When the filings of Iron are red hot in the Crucible, ſtrew in ſalt Armoniac, ſtir it, and caſt it into a Mortar and grind it, then put it four times to the fire, and caſt it at laſt into a veſſel, and pour on upon it ſharp diſtilled Vinegar for one Moneth, and let it lye in Horſe dung, take then the Vinegar away, and often with the dregs wet the *Terra Cadmia* and it will be reddiſh, uſe it for other things. There is another way to give it a colour: Take the Crocus of Iron I ſpeak of, and put into a Mortar an equal weight of Vitriol, bloud-
ſtone

stone and Brimstone as much of each, of Orpiment one third part and half, of *Terra Cadmia* rubified a sixt part, cut them all into very small pieces, and set them into the fire in a fit vessel, untill all the moysture flye away, use more fire afterwards, and the force of it will sublime all, one part of this cast upon four of Lead, will make them like Gold. *The same.*

A Secret of the Philosophers to make Gold perfect from Lead.

Take half a pound of Mercury of the Philosophers, and two ounces of their Brimstone; mix them so together, that nothing of either may appear, but a black pouder from them both: put this into a narrow mouthd Glass, and set it into a Furnace in an Earthen Pot between with sifted Ashes, as you know. Let not the Ashes come as high as the matter, and for eight dayes at first make an easie fire, that the Spirits may not ascend, and if any do ascend in these eight dayes, bring them back again to that in the bottome of the vessel, breaking it; and so every eight dayes, after the matter is made, which will be black, and so breaking the Glass, grind your matter and lay it up in another Glass vessel; and do so every eight day, untill you see the matter of an Ash colour: then take away the Ashes one fingers length, so that there may remain but two fingers of the Ashes, and set it in the fire, and let it stand so long there, untill the matter be red; and when you see it red, diminish your Ashes one finger more, and so consequently, untill it be as white as Snow, and which will afterwards return to a red colour. Take one ounce of this Medicine, and project them upon eight ounces of Lead prepared, and the Lead will become black, and hard as Iron; and when it is so hard and black, cast one ounce of it upon three ounces of Lead, and it will turn yellow; and when it is yellow, cast one ounce of it upon eight ounces of Lead prepared, and you shall have perfect Gold, praise God for it, and give something to the Poor. *Mr. Odomar.*

To make Gold of Lead.

Take purged Lead one pound, salt Armoniac in pouder one ounce, salt Elebrot poudred two drams, Saltpeter in pouder half an ounce. Put them all into a Crucible in a vehement fire two dayes, then take it away, and you will find perfect Gold. *Fallopius.*

To make Gold out of Lead.

Mix Cyprus Vitriol one pound, with a pound of Fountain water; first filter it, then distil it in a Limbeck, and keep the water in a Glass for your use. After this put one ounce of Quicksilver into a Crucible in the fire, and when it grows hot, add to it one ounce of the best Leaf Gold, and take it from the fire. Then take one pound of the best cleansed Lead melted, and mingle the said Gold and Quicksilver well with it at the fire, with some Iron Rod, and when they are all well mixed, add one ounce of the foresaid water of Vitriol, and let them cool, and you shall have excellent Gold. But your Lead is cleansed thus; Melt your Lead at the fire, and pour it, and quench it in the sharpest Vinegar, melt it again, and pour it into the juyce of Celandine, then again into salt water; next into Vinegar, mingled with salt Armoniac, and last of all, pour it into Ashes, alwayes melting it first, and it will be excellent well cleansed. *Fallopius.*

Lead and Tin are thus Transmuted.

First melt it in a Crucible, and pour on the weight of it in Quicksilver, and it will be as pouder, then wash it well with Salt and Vinegar, afterwards with water, untill all the blackness be removed, then dry it, and mingle it with common Salt burnt, and calcine it for four dayes and nights at a fire, with a clear flame, afterwards wash it as before with those things, untill all the blackness be gone, then melt it, and bring it into a body by Running of it, so are they purged from dross. After this to a Mare of Lead so purged, you must add five penny weight of fine Gold, and to Tin, two and half of fine Silver, and it is necessary that this Ferment should be mingled with Quicksilver, and made so fine, that it can pass through the middle of a double Cloath. After this put it upon the fire in a Crucible, and make it hot a little, untill it hath taken all in, then put it into one *Thes,* (I think it is a vessel) at a good fire, stirring it with an Iron Rod, untill the Quicksilver flye away, and the Lead remain; calcine it till it be red as Scarlet, or white with red ; then then you must have for one pound of Lead a quarter of Vitriol rubified, and half a quarter of Ocre, (*D'ocre*) one ounce of Tutty of *Alexandria*, and half a pound of Quick-Lime, pouder them all together very finely. After that calcine them seaven dayes in the flame, then reduce them into a body with Saltpeter, Euphorbium, and Rosin, and take what is fine, and you shall have Gold or Silver. And for Tin, take half a pound of Quick-Lime, and one fourth of white Calamine, Allum (*aëriall*) one fourth, do as I said before, and it will be perfect. Observe that Lead may be specially made without the help of the Gold to ferment it, thus : Take Plates of Iron, finely beaten, and make them so often red hot, and quench them in red Wine Vinegar, and in Wine, once in one, and once in the other, that the scales may come off, and they may be purged as Copper and Vermilion. After that make an *Amalgama* of them, with Quicksilver, and do as I said, of Gold and Silver, and you have it perfect. *Raymundus Lullius*.

To turn Lead into Tin.

Lead hath such affinity with Tin, that we may easily turn Lead into Tin, and this is done by only washing of it ; for being often washed, that the earthly parts may be washt away, we see it changed into Tin : for that Quicksilver that reduced it to its purity, and made it clean, is alwayes remaining in the Lead, or part of it, whence it easily makes it sound and turn into Tin. *The same*.

To calcine Lead and Tin.

If we would turn Lead and Tin into a Calx, let the Tin melt in some vessel, and cast it into some very fine Salt, stiring it with small Hazel stick, to separate the parts that cleave to it, and make them turn into Grains like Millet seed, or when it is melted cast it through some narrow passages of a Sive into cold water, and you shall make as it were small Worms, do it again untill you have made them very thin. Then pour the pouders into scalding water, so often changing and straining the water untill it hath conquered the Salt, and is grown sweet. All the Salt being washed away, then put it into an Earthen Pot, and put it into a Brick-Kiln, or Potters Furnace for three dayes, and you shall find it all turn'd to a Calx, or otherwise like small Grains, as *Geber* teacheth. Let it melt in an open vessel, with a large mouth, taking off the top still with a crooked Iron, taking off alwayes the outward skin untill you have it all in Ashes. Then put it in a Crucible, and set it in a Furnace, and opening the stopper, see if it be turned into a white Calx. Or otherwise ; in an Earthen vessel, fenced and well Luted, melt your Lead, stirring it with an Iron Spatula, six houres, that it is turned into pouder, and needs not be done again ; cast this into a Pot, and set it in a strong fire of Reverberation for twenty four houres, and you shall find it white ; sift it through a hair sive and keep it. *The same*.

To handled melted Lead with your hands.

If you annoint your hands with the juyce of Mallows or Mercury, you may handle melted Lead without any harm, so you do it with a quick motion. *Alexius*.

Of the Secrets of Tin. Chap. 8.

To draw a Spirit from Tin.

The filings of Tin must be put into an Earthen Pot, with an equall part of Saltpeter, above this you must place seaven or more earthen pots, with holes through, and stop all the chinks with Clay or good Lute ; you shall set a Glass vessel with the mouth downwards upon the top, or an open Pipe, with a Receiver or Porringer under : then put fire to it, and you shall hear a noise when it grows red hot, the Spirit flyes away in smoke, and you shall find it compacted in the hollow of the pots, and at the bottome of the Glass above : do not spend too much in filing your Tin, but into half so much Quicksilver pour in your melted Tin, then beat it with a Pestle, and you have it presently, and the Spirit will sooner flye, and you have your Quicksilver fixed. If you shall make a hole through the side of your Earthen vessel, you may cast it in by degrees more commodiously, and then stop it. *The same*.

To take away the ringing and softness of Tin.

Tin is like Silver, and they are much of one colour, and stick together. Tin is naturally of that colour, and serves to white other bodies, but it breaks and makes them all brittle, except Lead, and he that knows how to mingle them, hath obtained no small skill. We shall therefore try the best we can to counterfeit Silver, which we shall easily do if we take away the hindrances, namely, the Ringing of it, to wit, the dulness, the Lead colour and the softness: for it is melted before it be red hot, and sticks to the fire, and runs presently. These are the tokens to know it, nor are they joyned in the middle of the substance of it, but we can take these away as being but accidentall. And first, I will shew you how to take away the ringing and softness of the Tin; Some say that will be done with Ashes, Quick-Lime, Oyls, and distilled waters, if it be melted and quenched therein, and also with boyling of it. But you shall do it so more perfectly and commodiously. After that the Tin is melted at the fire, cast in some Quicksilver, remove it from the fire, and put it into a Glass Retort, that hath a great round belly, and a very long neck, and is crooked, let it be red hot in the fire, and by the force of it sublime the Quicksilver, that it may hang in the neck of the vessel, and may descend in drops untill it be all gone; The Tin remaining at the bottome, do this in the same order three or four times, untill like Ice it will not Ring at all; But you shall do it better this way: reduce it into a Calx, as I shew'd you before, that it may blot out that unfixed, and fugitive quality of the Quicksilver, or rather of the Brimstone, which is the cause of it; and if it be not done after the first and second time, do it again the third time, for bringing it into a Body by fit means, you shall have your desire, and it will grow so hard that it will sooner be red hot in the fire, than it will melt; for a vehement fire consumes the moysture of the Quicksilver, which makes it to melt so easily, that it will be more difficult to melt it in the fire, untill it be red hot, but this appears more in Tin than in any other Metals.

To take away the deaf sound from Tin.

If you would take away the deaf noise from Tin, because it is soft of it self; it makes no great noise, for it yields to the stroke, but joyned with other Metals it grows more hard and sounding; but herein consists the business; for it is stubborn and refuseth to joyn with any but only Lead, and it maketh them all brittle. But you shall perfect it thus: Let it dissolve in *Aqua fortis*, so Silver rightly purged is mingled with Lead, or any other thing, only by force of the water, and the vessel must be hot at a gentle fire, and the water by reason of the heat will flye away, then when it is dry take it forth, and put it into some other vessel, pouring on *Aqua fortis* again so long, untill they are totally united and joyned together, or both from the Calx are joyned in water; for there is made (as it is said) a mixture of Spirits and of bodies. If it chance to look dull, melt it, and soke it in the juyce of Sowbreed, so you shall have it sweet, sounding, bright, and excellently white. Also Tin may be mixed with Silver and other Metals, by the means of Quicksilver, which I perceive some have found out and counterfeited very fine Silver. They mingle Silver with Tin melted with Quicksilver, and they continue it long in the fire, and then take it forth, and being brittle, they put it into a Potters Crucible, and hold it in the fire twenty four houres, or under hot Embers.

To turn Tin into Lead.

One may easily turn Tin into Lead, if you often bring it into a Calx, and especially if you put a convenient fire to it in reducing of it: for losing its whissing, it will be easily turned into Lead.

Of the Secrets of *Antimony*. Chap. 9.

To draw a Spirit from Stybium.

You may draw a Spirit from Stybium, (which the Druggists call Antimony) this way; grind it very small with hand Mils, then put into the fire a new Earthen Pot with live Coles about it, and make it red hot all over, and put into it by degrees Antimony, and twice as much Argal, four times as much Saltpeter, finely poudred,

dred, when the smoke ceaseth, set on a cover, that the smoke which riseth may not flye away: take that away at length, and cast in more untill the whole pouder be burnt, then let it stay a while at the fire, draw it away, and let it cool, and take off the dregs a top, and you shall find Quicksilver at the bottome, which the Chymists call the *Regulus*, it is like to Lead, and is easily changed into it, for (saith *Dioscorides*) if you burn it a little more it will turn to Lead. *The same.*

Glass of Antimony.

Take crude Antimony two pound, or three, grind it very fine upon a stone, then put it into an unglazed Dish, and stir it an easie fire; that so it may be purged alwayes working it with an Iron Spatula, or an Iron Ladle, untill it begins to grow as it were into heap, then take it away, and grind it upon a stone as before, then set it to the fire again, and do this ten or twelve times, calcining and grinding of it, untill the pouder grow of a whitish colour; Then put it into a Crucible, with an ounce of salt Armoniac, and put a cover on, and set it into a strong fire, and cover it so with Coles, that the Coles may be three fingers high above the Crucible; so it will melt and be boyl'd sufficiently in half an hour, then take it out, and pour it forth into a Brass Bason, and let it cool, and you shall have transparent Glass of Antimony like to a *Jacinth*: you may give it from three grains to nine, with the same proportion of Gum Dragant, and a sufficient quantity of Sugar, either in Troches, or Electuary, or Pouder. I have used this often with great success for the Colick, and for Feavers.

Oyl of Antimony.

Antimony made into very fine pouder, and put into a Glass Retort, and infused in the sharpest Vinegar, is to be set upon an easie fire, untill the Vinegar is made of a red colour; This coloured Vinegar must be poured off into another Receiver of Glass, and new Vinegar must be poured on untill it hath drawn the same Tincture; now these percolations of the Vinegar, and pouring on of new, must be so often repeated, untill the pouder will yield no more red colour. The Vinegar collected must be distilled at a gentle fire, untill the redness beginning by degrees to condensate, seems to stick to the Limbeck: then cool the vessels, and ferment this red Liquor fourty dayes in hot Horse dung, untill it come to perfect Oyl. *One to Gesner.*

Of the Secrets of Brimstone. Chap. 10.

Brimstone sublimed.

Brimstone purged from all dross, is mingled with calcined Vitriol, and torrefied Salt, and put into a vessel, and is forced with hot Sand, untill yellow flowers appear. If you do this often, the flowers at last will be white, which given alone, or else reduced into Oyl, are a remedy for many diseases. *Anonym.*

Tincture of Brimstone.

Take the Oyl of clear white Turpentine, distilled with Spring water, either in Balneo, or in a Copper, what is sufficient, and as much flower of Brimstone very well ground upon a stone, that the Oyl of Turpentine may swim two fingers above it: mingle them well in a Glass vessel, then set them in the Sun, or in an Oven, or in Balneo for some dayes, untill the Oyl have drawn the Tincture; Then gently pour the Oyl into a Viol; again pour more Oyl of Turpentine upon the Brimstone, and digest it again in Balneo, and pour it off, and do this four or five times, untill Oyl is no more coloured by it; all the Oyl collected must be distilled in Balneo, and there will remain a Tincture at the bottome of the Retort, a remedy for several Maladies.

Oyl of Brimstone.

If you want Oyl of Brimstone, draw it forth thus: You must have a concave Glass, with a wide mouth like to a Bell, when you have Luted it, hang it by the Iron foot with a Thread, and let the large mouth be downwards, that you may receive the Oyl that drops from the brims of the Bell. In the middle of this place a vessel of Brimstone, of Earth or Iron, then set it on fire, and as it burns, put on more

more fresh Brimstone; for while it burns, it will be consumed, and the smoke that riseth from it to the bottome of the Bell, with moyst vapours gathers into a body, and turns to Oyl, and so fals down.

Another that admits and detains fire.

Take live Brimstone that never was tryed at the fire, and mingle it with an equal quantity of Oyl of Juniper, and by the fire in a Glass Retort, draw forth the Oyl, and use it at your need. *The same.*

Of the Secrets of Cinnaber. Chap. 11.

The way to prepare Cinnaber.

All that delight in Secrets of Metals, do confess the Art of making of Cinnaber, but only in small quantity, as two or three pound; but in *France* and *Germany* they make great Lumps which they bring into *Italy*. But since they keep this close, I shall discover it for the publick good. Take Quicksilver nine parts, yellow Brimstone two parts, some take three, others four, some again take as much as of Quicksilver. For to Paint, the plenty of Brimstone doth no hurt, but rather makes the Cinnaber more red, but for other things, three or four ounces of Brimstone are enough for one pound of Quicksilver. The Brimstone must be set in a Dish, or some large Earthen Pot unto the fire to melt; when it is melted, take it a little from the fire: then putting the Quicksilver into some Cloath, it must be by degrees added to the Brimstone, pressing it through the Cloath, and alwayes stirring it untill it be very well mingled, and cold. When they are well mixed and coole, take forth the matter, and pouder it very fine, and sift it to pouder, take as much of this as you please, and put it into a large Glass Retort, covered with *Lutum Sapientia*. But the Retort must be but a quarter full; Then set the Retort into a Furnace upon Ashes, and boyl them three houres at a gentle fire, afterwards increase it. But if you would make a great quantity, add gently some more pouder, alwayes stirring it with some stick, as the Retort stands upon the fire. But that it may be done exactly, you must have a Tunnel stand in the Gourd Glass, through which there must be a Staff put, in the upper part, smeered about with Lute, that when the Staff is put down it may stop the mouth of the Tunnel, with which continually the matter may be stirred and mingled. Then the pouder being first boyled at the fire for five houres, untill all or some part of it be sublimed, put in two spoonfuls of fresh hot pouder, lifting up the Staff that it may be put in, and then letting it down again. The Staff is put into it, to make way to cast in other pouder; and were it not so, the mouth of the Gourd Glass would be so stopt up with pouder, by reason of the subliming of it, that no more could be put in. And in this consists all the Art to make pieces as big as you please. Should the matter be cast in all together, then before it would be sublimed, the very Glass and Furnace would melt, wherefore it must be cast in by parts, that when the first part is baked and sublimed, sticking about the Glass, another part may be added, and baked at the bottome of the Glass, untill it grow red as the first did, and stick to the Glass. Thus continually casting in pouder, a huge mass of Cinnaber may be made, with a hole in the middle, made by the Staff; and if you would stop the hole, draw forth the Staff, and put in more pouder; then stopping the mouth of the Glass, bake it so long, untill the pouder also in the middle be sublimed, stick and fill up the hole. And this is the best way to make Cinnaber, and untill this day unknown in *Italy*. But observe this, That you must sometimes move the Staff, and lift it up, that the pouder stick not to it, and stop the hole of the Tunnel; also if the fire be great and continuall, it will do no hurt. *The same.*

A way to provide Cinnaber to write withall.

When Cinnaber is well ground with water upon a Porphyr stone, and dryed again, it must be put into some vessel of Bone or Glass, and Urine must be poured upon it, and so left for some time, for the matter will fall to the bottome; then by degrees pour off the Urine, and by degrees pour on new Urine, when you have done this eight or ten times, it will be well purged, this being done, take whites of Eggs dissolved in water, first well agitated together, pour that water upon the Cinnaber, that it may swim above it a fingers breadth, and then stir them together; then when it hath settled, take off the whites of Eggs by leasure, and put on fresh, and do this as often as you did it with Piss, this is done onely that the noysome smell of the Piss may be carryed away. When all this is done, add fresh whites of Eggs, mingle them well, and make a Liquor to Write, and Paint. This Liquor must be kept close in some stopt vessel, then when you desire to use it, you must stir it with a stick, and it will be kept and not corrupt. *Alixius.*

Of the Secrets of Orpiment. Chap. 12.

To sublime Orpiment.

First grind your Orpiment as small as you can, and put it into a Glazed earthen Pot, and pour in Oyl, that it may swim above no less then nine Inches, alwayes stirring it with a stick, that it stick not to the bottome; when it is dry pouder it, do the same work with Vinegar and strong Lee, at last put the pouder with Argal, Quick-Lime, and filings of Brass, into a vessel of Glass that is long and vaulted, but you must not fill it to the brim, but as far as the middle of the Glass, Lute the belly well on the outside, and dry it in the Sun, that it may endure the fire: set it in the Furnace, but shut not the mouth that the Spirits be not strangled; and that it may evaporate, let there be a gentle fire at the bottome of the vessel, and so let it be augmented six houres, and by degrees let it be made red hot, and by the force of it, let the volatil part flye to the vaultings of the vessel, and there being turned into white silver, let it remain; break the vessel, take it out, and keep it for your use: The same thing happens in the descent, for it fals down with more ease; but if there be any heavy bodies, mingle them with the lighter, that they may ascend the more easily, this way other Metals also may be sublimed. *The same.*

Oyl of Orpiment or Arsnick.

Orpiment must be ground with a double weight of Saltpeter; then it must be set in a Crucible upon Coles in the open Ayr, and there it must be made red hot; the Chymicks that sit by must put in Orpiment, and let it melt at a gentle fire, untill it will boyl no more; then again he must cast in as much, and let it boyl as the former; he must do this so often, untill he have cast in enough, and now the Saltpeter being consumed, he must for four or five houres make the fire stronger, untill the Orpiment melted at the bottome stands like Butter, and being cooled in the Ayr groweth white; after this it must be bruised, and ground upon a Marble, and in a moyst place, resolved into moysture; and lastly, This Liquor must by Art be distilled in a Limbeck. Thus Oyl of Orpiment annoynted with Honey, extenuates all thickness; and with Turpentine, cures the Leprosie, It is good for Ulcers of the fundament, and those wounds are hard to be cicatrized. *Paracelsus.*

Of the Secrets of Chrysocolla. Chap. 13.

How Chrysocolla called Borax must be purged and increased.

That we now call Borax, the Ancients called Chrysocolla, there were two sorts of it, the Natural and Artificial, as *Dioscorides* and *Pliny* say. They used this in some Medicaments, and to joyn Gold as they do to this day; for there is a vertue in it to melt and consolidate a Metal suddenly; we use it to melt the filing of Gold and Silver, and to bring them to a body, and many Women use it to clear their skin, and to beautifie themselves, because it doth no hurt to the teeth nor skin; The Ancients had a green Chrysocolla, which now can neither be found nor prepared. Some at this day have one that is white, and another black, which perchance comes near the green of the Ancients. The white is in long pieces, and nervous, like to Alum, that many are deceived, or they deceive others; For set upon the fire it boyls, and inflats, and remains afterwards, white, spungy, and brittle like to Alum: but those that are skilfull know the difference between Alum and Borax, three wayes; first by the tast, for Alum tasts sharp, and is astringent, but Chrysocolla hath no such taste, but hath almost no taste at all, that it is a mean, between Oyl and Whey; Wherefore many Impostors to deceive others, put pieces of Alum into Oyl of Almonds, and

and Whey of Milk, some also add Honey or Sugar, to bring down the sharp astringentest taste of the Alum. Others melt the foresaid things at the fire, adding Saltpeter, Soda, of which is made Alum Catinum, or salt Alkaly, and Argal made of Wine Lees : then in a cold place they make little stones, like to Chrysocolla, but they differ a little from them; for the stones of Chrysocolla are long, of Alum square; Secondly when Alum is burnt at the fire, it leaves much burnt matter, so that it is more than it was before, but Chrysocolla leaves very little after it is burnt; The third way to know Chrysocolla from Alum is, that Alum neither melts, nor consolidates Metals so well as Chrysocolla, for though it do in some sort melt them, that happens by the vertue of the Saltpeter, salt Kaly, and Argal, which help in part to make them melt. Moreover it may be known by this, that Saltpeter put into the fire, cracks and sparkles; Some make little stones of the foresaid mixture, dissolved in Whey, and congealed, but they are salt in taste, clear, and too violent in melting. Wherefore when they would consolidate Gold or Silver, they at the same time dissolve them both, that which conteins Sugar in it, makes spots alwayes upon the Silver or Gold. Also some compositions are made, which though they have force to consolidate and melt as Borax hath, yet they differ in forme and taste, I shall tell you some of them a little after. But to proceed to true and perfect Chrysocolla, which is found in our dayes; I say that in former times there were wont to be brought from *Alexandria*, small vessels full of a certain fat, that had small stones in the middle of it, this was called the Paste of Chrysocolla, which the Arabeck writers, and some of the most Ancient called *Nitre* of *Alexandria*. Now it is brought also from the West, I know not why, whether it be made there, or in some other place, namely that it is brought from *India*, because in former dayes there was great want of it here, for at that time one ounce of it was sold for a *French* Crown, and now a Man may have a pound at the same price easily. The way to make it in those places is this; Men find in the Mines of Gold and Silver, and Brass also, a certain water which (as I have seen and tryed, of it self is fit and perfect to consolidate and to melt Gold or Silver, I found the like in upper *Germany*, where there is the like water, which the Inhabitants do not know of; Some take this water with the feces, and boyl it awhile, and being strain'd, in time it will congeale into small stones like to Saltpeter; But because these stones cannot continue so but dissolve, they add to those stones together with the dregs left in the bottome, Hogs grease, or the fat of some other Creature; This being done, they go to the Mines, and there they make a large Ditch, and they lay a foundation at the bottome, and some such matter upon it, and upon that these small stones I speak of, then again they lay a bed of fat, and presently upon that these stones, and so they proceed to what height they please, alwayes laying one upon another, yet so that the last bed be of that fat matter : there they leave it open some Moneths; though most Men do these things at home in the ground, or in large vessels. But when they are minded to sell, or to send their vessels to some other parts, be they great or small as they will, they fill them with that matter together with the stones, and they call this the Paste of Chrysocolla, or Borax; also they send from the foresaid places Chrysocolla, and the stones without the foresaid Paste, but prepared the same way I said; because for these thirty yeares more of that Artificial Borax was brought, than of that fat matter; because in *Italy* they knew not how to use it, nor to repare, and puryfie the small stones : Wherefore they made almost no use of it, but in distillations, for to make Women fair; But of late a certain *Venetian*, and a Woman also that he taught, began to break and make that up again, and they gain'd exceedingly by it, untill by degrees others had got the knowledg of it, though some knew more and some less, and very few knew how to make it as good, which way I shall here lay down exactly. Take therefore this Lump, namely that which contains many small stones in it, and is not at all rancid; for that rankness is a sign it is old, and that the small stones are diminished, and for the most part consumed : then to ten pounds of that Paste, pour in one half Bucket of warm water, and put it into some earthen vessel, and work it well with your hands, and mix it as you do Bread; which when it is done, strain it well, and take

out

out the stones left in the sive, and put them into a Kettle, pouring Oyl of Olives upon them; as you use to do in making of Sallets; then when they are well purged in the Sun, and smeered with your hands, put them into a bag and mingle them well, as they do Sugar-Plums, and keep them in wodden Boxes as the best Chrysocolla. If you desire to multiply them, and to make more, take that strain'd water, and boyl it at a gentle fire, untill it be boyld to a perfect confection, taking off the dregs and some carefully; you shall know three wayes when the confection is boyled, first, if a drop of water put upon the fire do not dilate: secondly as you know Syrups, if it stick in the Paper: and the third is, if a small Cord dipt into it, and drawn through ones fingers, do rub sharply against the fingers. When it is boyled, take the Kettle from the fire, and cover it well with a fit cover, that no filth fall into it, then bury it in the Founders heap, and cover it all over with Bran, and thick Cloaths, a Coverled or Blanket very close pressed upon it; you may also put under hot dung for eight or ten dayes. When that is done take it away, and you shall find a certain fat, or crust in the superficies of it, take that off, and lay it aside, you shall find also some things like to pieces of Ice, which you must take forth also, and put into another vessel, and wash carefully with water, and dry in the shade. This being done, mingle those stones remain'd in the hair-sive with these last, and mix with them, white Alum made of Wine Lees, but not that which is wont to be laid for a Pattern, (for that is nothing worth) but of the best, six pounds, Saltpeter eight ounces, common water three Buckets, and set them at a gentle fire, skimming them well, untill they are pefectly boyled, as before. When that is done take it off from the fire, and set it aside untill it be well setled, then take one Bucket and half of this water, set it at a gentle fire, and when it begins to boyl, add of the foresaid fat, crust or skin, taken away before seaven pound and half, and boyl them, what is needfull, as before; Then take them from the fire, and put them into some wodden vessel, and place cross wayes the vessel close Staves, and at the four corners of the Staves bind a Cord to each, but that the Cords may hang strait down, bind a piece of Lead to each of them, and so let them down into the matter, yet that they hang four fingers above the bottome; this is done to make the matter stick to the Cords. This being performed, you shall lay it up close as you did the other: But this is not put into a Sack, that is a pit, but when that must be taken away that sticks to the Cords, it is smeered with a Feather dipt in Oyl, and the rest that sticks to the Kettle must be sprinkled with Oyl. Moreover the stones to be taken forth must be no smaller then Hazel Nuts; those that are less, must be left in the water, and boyld again, as before: and this must be continued untill all the water be turned to Chrysocolla. But note this, that to the first Mass that is to be dissolved in warm water, you must add the quantity of a Ciche Pease of Hares runnet, that the rest of the parts of the Chrysocolla, may the better coagulate. *Alexius.*

Of the Secrets of Salt. Chap. 14.

Salt Alkali.

Make a Ditch, and lay Wood cross it, and put under them a heap of the Herb Kaly, and kindling the fire, make the herb run in drops by the liquor that comes from it. This Liquor at last congeals and turns to Salt Alkali, that is in colour partly black, partly Ash coloured. It is sharp and salt and corroding. *John Banhinus.*

How to sublime salt Armoniac.

Salt Armoniac is sublimed either with scales of Iron, or cleansed Sand, or by Wine Lees dryed and reduced to Salt, thus: Grind salt Armoniac with an equall quantity of scales of Iron; and put it into a vessel, and first with a gentle fire, and then with a stronger you must follow it, untill it be red hot; and keep that degree of heat twelve houres, then let all cool, and take out what is sublimed, and with as much prepared Salt force it up again, as you did before: do this so often untill the Salt be as white as Snow.

BOOK. XI.

Of the Secrets of Glaß.

The manner of Annealing and Painting upon Glaß.

AS there have been of late years many Arts invented, and others, that in a manner lay rude and unregarded, through the industry of our times are grown to full perfection: So I make no question on the other side, but divers by our Idleness and negligence are utterly lost and forgotten. That I may alledg one instead of the rest, I would know what Lapidary, or any else could shew me the Art of Casting that Marble whereof we see many fair and beautifull Pillars in *Westminster*, *Lincolne*, *Peterborough*, &c. and in many places whole Pavements, as in St. *Albanes* Abby, *Colmanchester*, &c. surely I think not any. And what hath been in greater request then good workmanship in Glass, when scarce now any may be found, (except some new in *London*, and they perhaps *Dutch* men to,) that have but the ordinary skul of Annealing and laying their Colours? Verily I am perswaded if our forefathers had known, how little we regarded either their Devotion or rest in Painting Glass Windows, they would have spared their Money to some better purpose; nay, if we would in many places imitate them so farre, as but to allow our Churches and Chappels Glass, that were well; where many times you shall see whole Panes (whereof some have carried the names of their Devote and Religious Founders; others the Royall Coats either of our Ancient Kings of this Land, their Allies, or of the Benefactors and Lords of the place, Monuments many times of great importance,) for want of Repair, partly been beaten down by the weather, partly by over precise Parsons, and Vicars, (as one in *Northampton-*shiere did in his Chancell, the Arms of King *Edward* the third, and the Dukes of *York* and *Clarence*, taking them for Images,) and the Windows stopt up with Straw and Sedge, or dambd up quite. A regard I confess hath been of these abuses had; but I fear me a great deal too late. The best Workmanship that may be seen in *England* at this day in Glass, is in Kings Colledg Chappel in *Cambridg*, containing as they say, the whole History both of the Old and New Testament. The next to that in *Henry* the seaventh's Chappel at *Westminster*, the one finished, the other wholely built by the said Religious King. There are many good Pieces else in diverse other places, as *Canturbury*, *Lincolne*, &c.

There be six principall Colours in Glass, which are *Or* or *Yellow*, *Argent* or *White*, *Sable*, *Azure*, *Gules* and *Vert*; Black, Blew, Red, and Green.

To make your Or or Yellow upon Glaß.

Your Yellow is made in this manner. Take an old Groat, or other piece of Silver of the purest and best Refined that you can get, then take a good quantity of Brimstone, and melt it, when you have done, put your Silver into the Brimstone melted; and take it forth again with a pair of Pliers or small Tongues, untill it leave burning: then beat your Silver in a Brazen Mortar to dust, which dust take out of the Mortar, and laying it on your Marble stone grind it, (adding unto it a small quantity of Yellow Oker,) with Gum Arabick water, and when you have drawn with your Pencill what you will, let it of it self throughly dry upon the Glass.

Another fair Gold or Yellow upon Glaß.

Take a quantity of good Silver, and cut it in small pieces: Antimonium beaten to pouder, and put them together in a Crucible or melting Cruse, and set them on the fire well covered round about with Coales for the space of an hour: then take it out of the fire, and cast it into the bottome of the Candlestick, after that beat it small into pouder, and so grind it.

Note when as you take your Silver as much as you mean to burn, remember to weigh against it six times as much Yellow Oker as it wayeth, and seaven times as much of the old Earth, that hath been scraped of the Annealed work, as your Silver weighed: which after it is well ground, put altogether into a pot, and stir it well, and so use it, this is the best Yellow.

To lay Gold on Glass.

Grind Chalk and red Lead, of each a like quantity together, temper them with Linseed Oyl, lay that on when it is almost dry, lay your leaf Gold on that, when it is quite dry polish that.

An excellent green upon Glass.

Take a quantity of Vertgrease and grind it very well with Turpentine, when you have done, put it into a Pot, and as often as you it warme it on the fire.

A fair red upon Glass.

Take a quantity of Dragons blood, called in Latine *Sanguis Draconis*, beat it into fine pouder, in a Mortar, and put it in a Linnen Cloath, and put thereto strong *Aqua vitæ*, and strain them together in a Pot, and use them when you need.

To make a fair Carnation on Glass.

Take one ounce of Tin Glass, one quarter of Gum, of Jet three ounces, of red Oker five ounces, and grind them together.

Another Carnation.

Take a quantity of Jet, and half as much Silver scum, or Glass Tin, and half as much of Iron scales, a quarter as much of Gum, and as much red Chalk as these weigh and grind it.

Argent or white.

Argent or Silver is the Glass it self, and needeth no other colour, yet you may diaper upon it with other Glass or Chrystall beaten to pouder, and ground.

Sables or black.

Take Jet, and the scales of Iron, and with a wet feather when the Smith hath taken an heat, take up the scales that flye from the Iron : which you may do by laying the Feather on them, and those scales that come up with the Feather, you shall grind upon your Painters stone, with the Jet and Gum water, so use it as your Gold before.

Another black.

Take a quantity of Iron scales, and so many Copper scales and weigh them one against another, and half as much Jet, and mix them well together. Before you occupy your Iron scales, let them be stamped small, and put them into a clean fire-shovell, and set them upon the fire till they be red hot, and they will be the better.

The manner of Annealling your Glass, after you have laid on the colour.

Take Bricks and therewith make an Oven four square one foot and half high, and when you have done, lay little barres of Iron overthwart it, three or four, or as many as will serve; then raise that above the barres of Iron one foot and half more, then is that high enough. When you purpose to Anneale, Take a Plate of Iron made fit for the aforesaid Oven, or for want thereof take a blew stone, such as they make Haver or Oaten Cakes upon, which being made fit for the aforesaid Oven, lay it upon the cross barres of Iron : that done, take slakt Lime and sift it through a fine Sive, into the Oven, upon the plate of stone, and make a bed of Lime, then lay your Glass which you have wrought and drawn before, upon the said bed of Lime; then sift upon the said Glass another bed of Lime, and upon the bed lay other Glass, and so by beds, you may lay as much Glass as the Oven will contain : providing alwayes that one Glass touch not another. Then make a soft fire under your Glass, and let it burn till it be sufficiently Annealed : it may have (you must note) too much or too little of the fire, but to provide that it shall be well, you shall do as followeth.

To know when your Glass is well Annealed.

Take so many pieces of Glass as you purpose to lay beds of Glass in your Oven, or Furnace, and draw in colours what you will upon the said pieces, or if you wipe them over with some colour, with your finger only it is enough : and lay with every bed of your wrought and drawn Glass one of the said pieces of Glass, which are called Watches, and when you think that they are sufficiently Annealed with a

pair

pair of Plyers or Tongs, take out the first Watch which is lowest, and next to the fire, and lay that upon a board untill it be cold, then scrape it good and hard with a Knife, and if the colour goeth of, it hath not enough of the fire, and if it hold, it is well Annealed.

When you would occupy any Oyled colour in Glass, you shall once grind it with Gum water, and then temper it with *Spanish* Turpentine, and let it dry as near the fire as may be, then is it perfect.

These colours are to be used after one manner, you may buy or speak unto some Merchant you are acquainted withall, to procure you what coloured Beads you will, as for example, the most and perfectest red Beads that can be come by, to make you a fair red, beat them into pouder, in a Brazen Mortar, then buy the Goldsmiths red Ammel, which in any case let it be very transparent, and thorow shining: take of the Beads two parts, and of Ammel one part, and grind them together as you did your Silver, in the like sort may you use all other colours.

The way to work with Glass.

The way to work Glass is this; the boyled pieces of Glass of all colours. (Those that are made at *Venice* is exceeding fair,) are put to a Candle; when you have made them as thin and as soft as you please, presently set them as they should be, and soften them, and break it off, or extend it; for speed this must be done with both hands. The greatest difficulty here is to begin, and when you have learned the begining to attain to the perfection of this Art. *Cardan.*

To make Glass soft.

Glass will be made soft chiefly by Lead, it is made tenacious by long boyling, you must first reduce the Lead and Metals into a Calx; for the more impure part is consumed, and the dark part, and the force of it remains in the Glass. *Cardan.*

To divide Glass.

To divide Glass, wet a Thred with Oyl and Brimstone, compass the place about with it, light it, and do it again untill the place be very hot, then presently tye the Glass about with another thred wet in cold water: and it will break in that place as if it were cut with a Diamond; but this takes up much time, also it is done with a Wheel of Brass, and by the Emeril. *Cardan.*

How to soften Glass perfectly.

If Goats bloud, and Ashes of Glass be in equall quantities put into Vinegar; and then distilled by a Chymical vessel, and the Glass be steeped in the distilled water, it will become pliable and draw out like Wax. But it will grow hard again, and turn to its former nature, if you put it into cold water, or it be washed in it. *Out of the Secrets of an Ingenious Artificer. Mizald.*

Another way yet.

If you boyl Glass in Goats bloud and juyce of groundsel, or steep it therein, it will be as soft as Wax or Clay, that you may frame what you please with it, but if you dip it into cold water, it will be as hard as before. *Geber* and *Albertus.*

To make Glass green.

Green Glass is made of Fern Ashes, for it contains some Salt in it, as Kaly doth; and thence it is better made. *Cardan.*

To make Chrystall run.

Pouder and sift Chrystal through a very fine Sive, with half as much Salt of Argal, and make little Bals of this, and let them stand in an unbaked Earthen Pot, in a red hot Furnace, all night, and not melt; it will fitly melt afterwards in a vessel, when all the dross is purged from it; if perhaps it be dreggy it is discovered to be false; for it must be transparent and clear, and if you add more Salt to it, it will melt the sooner; some are wont to prepare Chrystal otherwise, that it may melt the sooner, and so it will be more fit for service. A great Iron Spoon is to be well Luted, and the broken pieces of the Chrystal, are put into it and set into the fire, untill they grow red hot, then they are to be quenched in Oyl of Argal, and this is to be done so often, and then they are to be poudred in a Mortar, that the pouder may melt the better. This is used to counterfeit Jewels. *The same.*

To joyn Glass.

The white of an Egg beaten and mingled with Quick-Lime will joyn the broken pieces of Glass, and all earthen Pots, that they cannot be broken there, by reason of the clammy tenaciousness thereof. *Mizald.*

To joyn pieces of Glass.

Take Liquid thick old Vernish, and joyn the pieces of Glass therewith, joyn them well, and bind them together, that they may not dissolve. Then set them into the Sun or an Oven for many dayes, untill the Vernish be very well dryed; scrape away finely with a Knife what sticks without, and they will be excellent well glewed, so that no moysture nor any thing else will ever unglew them; but there must be care taken, that no liquor that is over hot be poured into the Glasses. *Alexius.*

How to glew Glass together.

Take Verdigrease what is sufficient, and incorporate it with liquid Vernice, and use it. *Roscellus.*

Glew for vessels of stone.

Take red Lead, white Lead, Quick-Lime, writing Vernish, of each half an ounce, all must be finely poudred, and incorporated with four whites of Egges. *Roscellus.*

Another.

Take liquid Vernish, white Lead, Balearmoniac of each what is sufficient.

Another.

Take whites of Eggs what is sufficient, a little Verdigrease, mingle them for the same use.

Another.

Take Verdigrease, red Lead, liquid Vernish, of each what is sufficient, mingle them.

Glew for Glasses.

Take common Salt dissolved in common water, sifted Ashes of each one ounce, Meal of the best Wheat two drams, mix them for use. *Roscellus.*

Another.

Take Harts Horn, beaten Bricks, Greek Pitch, scales of Iron, whites of Eggs, of each what you need, mingle them. *The same.*

Another for Glasses and Earthen Vessels.

Take Quick-lime, Bones of Animals, white Lead, of each one ounce, red Lead two ounces, Verdigrease, Argal, of each two ounces, beat all these into most fine pouder, and mix them with liquid Vernish. *The same.*

Another.

Take Lime, white Lead, whites of Eggs what may suffice, mingle them. *The same.*

Another for Glasses and Stone Pots.

Take Glass beaten, Quick-Lime, Milk of Figs, of each what needs, mingle them. *Roscellus.*

Another.

Take new Wax, Greek Pitch, Mastick, Frankincense, pouder of Brick, of each one part, grind what must be ground, and mingle them at the fire. *The same.*

Another.

Take Quick-Lime poudred, liquid Vernish, whites of Eggs, of each what is sufficient: grind them together upon a Porphyr stone, and make Glew for stones.

Another.

Take Mastick half an ounce, beaten Glass, white Wax, pouder of Brick, of each half an ounce, mingle them all well at the fire, and make Glew for stones. *Roscellus.*

The Composition for Looking-Glasses.

Those that are called Steel Glasses are made of three parts of Brass, and of Tin and Silver one part, with eighteen parts of Antimony. Some and very many leave out the Silver to save charges; Those make Plates of Tin one pound, Brass a third part,

part, and when they are melted, they add Argal one ounce, white Orpiment half an ounce, and boyl them on the fire so long as they smoke; Then they make the Metal melted twice, into long Tables, and when they are hot, and plained with the grounds of the Gum of the Larch Tree, and Vine Ashes, they strain them into Looking-Glasses: after this they work the Glass fastned to a Table with Glew, very smooth with Water and Sand; and after that with Emeril, or pouder of Pumex stone, and a fourth part of the Calx of Tin. But Silver Glasses are mingled with less labour, because Silver alone, as fit to performe what we desire of Glasses is more splendid, and there is less fear of breaking it. *Cardan.*

Glasses that Men make in these dayes make Men seem young.

Glasses that make Men look young, are such as shew no rinkles, and have some red mingled with them; Moreover those Glasses shew no rinkles that are not exquisite, and yet are clear, and such they seem to be, and are found out by chance, and by Art, that some will make Men appear ten years younger than they are. *The same.*

How a thing may seem to be multiplyed.

Amongst those sports that are carried about, that Glass is no small pleasure, that set to the eye, makes us see more commodiously. For of these things that deceive our sight, a more convenient way cannot be found, than in the Medium, (for that being changed all are changed) wherefore that must be prepared of more solid Glass, and that is very thick, that it may more fitly be brought to the plains and corners, whereby we would increase the number of any thing; but in the middle of them the Angles must have a mark fit for the eye, to disperse the sight that it may not behold the true Object; when therefore these severall plains are prepared, if you hold them to your eye, and desire to see a face or Eye, you shall see it all Eye; if a Nose, all Nose; so it is with the Hands, Fingers, Armes, that you shall not see a Man but *Briareus*, that the Poets speak off, who had a hundred hands, if you look on a piece of Money, you shall see many pieces, that you cannot touch the true Money, but you will be deceived, and it is better to give it than receive it : If you see a Galley a far off, it will seem to be a whole Navy. If you look upon a Souldier in Armes, you think you see an Army Marching, and every thing seems double, Men seem to have two faces, and two bodies, and so are made divers wayes of sight, that one thing may seem to be another, all these things are apparent to those that seek for them, and make tryall of them. *The same.*

In plain Glasses how the feet may seem upwards, and the head downwards.

If any one desire with plain Glasses to seem with his feet upwards, and his head downwards, (although that way of representation be proper to concave Glasses) yet I shall indeavour to do it with plain Glasses : you must place two good plain Glasses long wayes, that they may stick together, that they may not nimbly remove here and there, and may make a right Angel; when it is well prepared, hold it against your face long wayes, as it is made to cleave together; that in one Glass half, and in the other the other half face may be seen, then you shall turn the Glass on the left or right side, looking directly upon it, and your head will seem to be turned, and when according to their breadth they shall divide your face, you shall see your Figure so, that your head will appear beneath, and your feet above : If the Glass be large, the whole body will seem to be turned upside down, this comes by a mutuall and manifold reflection, for it flyes from one to another, that it will seem to be turned. *The same.*

A Glass to discover Secrets.

The Composition of a Glass to see hidden things in, is made thus. Joyn two plain equall Glasses of Chrystal made by Art, (such as are made at *Venice*, that will not be fouled so much as Steel Glasses will,) exactly, that they may to a hayr stick fast long wayes, and that it may turn about an Axeltree like a covering, so that the superficies of the one, may with the superficies of the other sometimes make one plain Glass, and sometimes a solid, right, obtuse, acute or what you will; then hang up this Glass aloft, directly against the place where any thing lyeth hid; that the face of the Glass may be perpendicular from above the plain; but the moveable face of

Gg 2 the

the Glass, must be placed opposite against the length of the place desired: then whatever shall be done in that Chamber, if there be light, when you turn about the moveable Glass, that it makes an equall Angle, which you may judg by your eye, whilst you find what you seek for, for you shall see all things; If the place you desire to see be above the place you are; you must hang the Glass in a higher place. *Cardan.*

A Glass to see things done afar off in other places.

By the same reason, if you would see what is done afar or five miles off, where there are wals between, as where a City is besieged; hang the Glass in a high place, perpendicularly, or equidistant to the horizon, it must be very large, and you must have another Glass in your hand, that the face of it may respect the other (not lying quite with the face upward, nor yet raised perpendicularly) which hangs above; then by degrees go farther from the first Glass, strait forward against it, and by little and little, sometimes bend to the left or right hand, untill you see the place plainly in your Glass, then scarce stirring it from its Situation, you shall see all things that are done there; and there is no other hindrance of this, as I said, than fire Engins of the Enemy. *The same.*

A plain Glass made of many, wherein the Image of one thing shall appeare to be many.

Prudent Antiquity invented a Glass made of many plain Glasses, to which if one thing were opposed, you might see many Figures of the same thing, as we find by *Ptolomy* his Writings, and the making of it is this. Upon a plain Table or place where you desire to set up such a Glass, place a half Circle, and divide this equally with paints according to the number of the figures, stretch forth strings to them, and cut off the ends; then raise up Parallelogram plain Glasses, of the same breadth and height, glew them fast together, and set them that they may not be pulled asunder, as they are joyned long wayes, and raised upon a plain superficies; lastly the Spectators eye must be placed upon the center of the Circle, that he may have his sight uniforme to them all, and in each Glass you shall see a severall Image, and placed round about, as you often see in dancing or upon a Theatre; Therefore they called this a Theatricall Glass; for all the Lines from the center fall perpendicular upon the superficies of them, wherefore they reflect upon themselves, and so they bring the Images to the eye, each Glass sending forth its own, so by turning it, and placing it diversly, you shall see divers Images in divers Posturs. *The same.*

To make a multiplying Glass.

A Glass is made to see many things with: for by opening and shuting it, one finger shall shew to be above twenty, you shall make it thus. Raise two Brass or Chrystal right Angled Glasses upon the same Basis, and let them be in one and half proportion, called *Serquialtera*, or in some other proportion: and according to the outside of multitude they must be fastned together, that like to a Book they may be shut and opened very fitly, and the Angles may be varied, as they use to make them at *Venice*; for if you look with one face, you shall see many more faces in them both, and this the closer you shut them, and make the Angle less, but opening them wider the faces will seem less, and as the Angle is more obtuse the fewer faces shall you see. So pointing with your finger you shall see more fingers, and the right side shews the right side, and the left the left, which is contrary to Looking-Glasses, and this fals out by mutual reflection, and reverberation, whence ariseth a change of the Images. *The same.*

A Glass wherein you may see your back.

If you would see your back, you shall do that with two plain Glasses, which the greater they are it is so much the better. You shall place the first behind you, between lying flat, and standing upright, in a middle posture, and the other in a higher place than you stand, between lying flat and standing upright, before your face, and you may very well see your back parts. Remember also, for example, if you place a Ring on the Glass that is opposite to you, and that the Ring it self be a Glass, as if a Saphyr be set in it, you shall see in the Glass the Picture of the Ring, and your Image will seem like the Jewel in it: this fals out by reason of manifold reflection; the same is done by two Glasses, and far more wonderfully by three. *Cardan.*

A Glass to see your Belly and Throate.

But if you would see things that lye deep, and obscure, as your Belly and Throat, or a dark Chamber, place a great Glass vessel full of water direct against the place, and the light behind the vessel, that the vessel may stand in the middle, in a right Line, between the light and the place, which you desire to see; then taking away all other light, place your eye where you may not hinder the light of the vessel, but yet may look into the place, and you shall see all as if it were a clear light. *The same.*

A Glass that represents many Figures of the same thing.

There are Glasses that shew many faces, as consisting of many plain Glasses. But these are very well known, that is worth admiration, which with one superficies will represent many Figures. I had a plain square Looking-Glass, that shewed both my ears doubled, as if the second were the Image of the first; also it was farther off; that made me believe that there was a plain Glass in *Spain*, that would shew the Image double, one of the face, and that the nearest, like the true face, and the other as of a dead Man; the same reason serves for both, I will demonstrate the reason of it, that we may know the thing, and know how to make it. For they that see such things are terrified, not only with the strangness of the thing, but also with the Image it self. For those hinder ears seemed very pale, now because these fingers were paler, and not so lively, and conspicuous, and like to the former Images, it is manifest, as in a double Rainbow, the latter is the representation of the former. But how comes the reflection? for we do not alwayes see two Rainbows, and but in few Looking-Glasses two Images. Wherefore let the eye be *A*. that which is seen, *B*. the Glass, *C*. the meeting at equal Angles in the point *C*. let the concurs be with the right Line, and *B*. perpendicular in *D*. where also *B*. will be seen; since therefore *B*. and *A*. are very much inclined, because *A. B. C.* differ but little from the superficies of the Glass, the refraction is in *C*. because the Glass is not exactly plain in *E*. wherefore *E*. is higher than *C*. wherefore *F*. will be seen higher above *D*. But what shews higher and under an equal Angle, is thought also to be farther off, wherefore *F*. will appear also after *D*. *Cardan.*

To see in plain Glasses things that are afar off, and in other places.

Thus a Man may see safe and secretly not suspected, those things that are done afar off, and in other places: which could not be done otherwise; but be diligent in the situation of your Glasses; Let there be a place set in the house, or elsewhere, whence you desire to behold something, and at the Window or over against a hole, place a Looking-Glass, very upright, just against your face, or if need be, fasten it to the Wall, moving and inclining it every way, untill it will represent the place sought for, which looking upon it, and coming near to it, you shall obtain: and if it difficult, with a quadrant or some such Instrument, you shall not be deceived: and raise it perpendicularly upon a Line, cutting the Angle both of reflection, and meeting of the Lines, and you shall clearly see what is done in that place. So it will fall out in diverse places. Hence it is, that if it cannot be conveniently done with one Glass, you may see the same thing in many Glasses, or if the Object visible be lost by reason of too great distance, or be hindred by Mountains and Wals between, you shall set another Glass above, overagainst the other upright upon a Line, which may divide a right Angle, if you do otherwise, it will never come to pass; thus you shall see the place desired: for one sending the Image back to the other, the Image that is ten miles off, and often reflected, will flye into the eye, and you shall see what comes next: while the Image is produced in right Lines, the turning of places and wals cannot hinder the visible Object; the making of it is easie; Thus it is usuall to convey Images; But if you desire otherwise to see any thing that stands high and upright, which you cannot see, set two Looking-Glasses fast together long wayes, as I said, upon a pole; or top of a Wall, fast, that one may stand higher, and may receive the Object, and the other fastned to a Rope that it may be fitly moved when you please, and when at first it makes sometimes an obtuse, sometimes an acute Angle, as there shall be need, whilst by the Line of the thing seen, by meanes of the second Glass the sight is refracted, and the Angles of incidence and reflection are equall; and if you seek to behold high things, raise it higher, if low things, set it lower, untill it makes refraction to your sight, then shall you see it : if you have one Glass in your hands, and look into that, it will happen the more easily. *The same.*

A Looking Glass to shew the houres.

There are some have made Glasses that shew as many faces as there are houres in the day, *Ptolomy* is my witnes. Also part of the Image declared part of the houre. Let then there be a square right Angled, a third part longer than it is broad, and it must be divided into twelve equall squares, A. B. C. D. E. F. G. H. K. L. M. N. by the same reason make a Glass divided, by so many spaces, and upon them the highest vaile in A. B. and in B. than in C. and in C. than in D. so that it may touch the Glass. Let there be the same proportion between E. F. K. and L. that A. hath to B. and F. and G. and L. to M. as B. hath to C. and G. to H. and M. to N. as C. hath to D. but let the parts of the vail be so distinguished, that the higher may by degrees be removed upon the lower, as first from A. to B. then both parts of the vail, from B. to C. lastly all the parts into D. Whence it comes, that as the weight is heavier, it will be carried about in a shorter time, that in the time of removing, they may be equall; add therefore Clock-Wheels to all the three squares, that there may be three Wheels, and in each of them the differences of equation, as it is in the Planets, that the motion may be the swifter for the shorter Wheel, whereby the weight is more increased : so it will fall out that after the first square, the second will be uncovered, and after that the third, and in each severall faces, that for the number of houres and parts, so many faces and parts of faces will be seen in the Glass. But all these things are easie to be seen in Clocks unequall houres used by the *Romans* : for the Wheel that turns having an Axeltree upon which it moves out of the center of it, it will move so much the swifter in that part next to the Axeltree, by how much the Axeltree from the same part, is removed from the center of the Wheel. *Cardan.*

To make a Glass shall shew nothing but what you please

Also a Glass may be made, that one may look into it and not see his own face, but some other Image he cannot tell how; you shall fasten a plain Glass upon a Wall, upon a plain erected perpendicularly, and at a known portion of the Angle, let the head of it be inclined, over against ; cut the Wall at a certain quantity of some Picture or Image, and oppose it against it, according to the quantity of the portion, and cover it that the beholder may be ignorant of it, and it will seem the stranger, nor can he understand it. The Glass in a place appointed will refract the Image, that between the sight and the Object by the Glass, there shall be a reciprocall stroke, there place the eye, and you shall find the place as I taught you before; wherefore he that looks into the Glass coming to it, he shall see neither his own Image, nor any thing else, but when he is right against it, and comes to the place appointed, he shall see the Image of the Picture or some other thing, which he cannot see elsewhere. *The same.*

That one looking into a convex Cylinder Glass, may see the Image of something hanging in the Ayr.

Also a round Pillar like convex Glass or half a cylinder of it, (which I think makes little difference) may be so placed in a house, or some place appointed, that it shall represent clearly the Image of something hanging in the Ayr, which is very strange If you desire to see it, make it thus. Make fast a segment of a Cylinder in the middle of the house, right up upon a Table or Tripode, that it may stand perpendicular to the ground, then place your eye at some hole or chink somewhat distant from the Glass, and let it be fastned that it may not remove here and there ; then break the wall overagainst the Glass, and make it like to a Window. Let it be made
like

made like a *Pyramis*, and let the cone of it be within, the Basis without, as it is wont to be done there, place the Picture or Image, that you may see it with your eye, but not be reflected by the superficies of the Pillar Glass; that the picture placed without it cannot be seen through the hole by the eye, may seem to hang in the Ayr, which is strange to the Spectator. Also a Pyramidal convex Glass will do the same : if you set it so that it may represent the same Image : it will be done also another way As I shall shew underneath. *The same.*

That by a sphericall concave Glass an Image also may seem to hang in the Ayr.

Also the same Image may be more easily seen to hang in the Ayre by reflection, than in a convex Cylinder, by a concave sphericall Glass, but more strangly in a segment of it; for it will seem far from the Glass, whereas it appears in the center of the Sphere. You shall place that in some obscure place, and when you are a little removed from it, you shall see your head turned downward, but do you with fixed untwinkling eyes look upon the center, untill you see without the Glass a reflexed Image hanging in the Ayr, parted quite from it, so long as the beames of your sight pass through the center of the Glass, you shall see an Image and apparition in the Glass also, the nearer you come to it, the greater it will be that you will think you touch it with your hands. If the segment of the Glass be great, no Man can choose but wonder : for if he comes nearer, he will be frighted by the Image, and nose will seem to come and hit against nose : but if any one draw a Sword against it, he will think another comes against him, and thrusts him through the hand that he will pull his hand back, and if when one bends, another holds up his fist behind him, he that looks into it will seem to take a box on the ear, will be afraid, and turn aside his face. That you may more easily find the center, use this Rule, that you may not divert to Mathematicks. With a piece of Paper, or Wax, take the compass of the segment, that you may bring a string from both sides, and cut it in two parts perpendicularly, and in the Lines that meet or semidiameters, you must necessarily find the center; which may be known in all concaves. There are also many experiments of concave Glasses which I shall set down in that which follows. *The same.*

The representations and operations of concave Glasses.

The center of a concave semicircle being now found, it will be easie to know all the differences, because by that all the rest are regulated and known. If then you will see your head downwards, without the center of the Glass, look into it, it must have a head, and your head will seem downwards, and your heels upward presently. if it be not a perfect half circle, but only a segment of it, you may the more easily set it into a head, and you shall see the huge faces of great Bacchus, and your fingers as thick as your arm; *Ausfius* (as *Seneca* sayes) made such concave Glasses to represent his Image greater, than it was, who was a great example of lust, and so disposed his Glasses, that when he was buggered he might observe all the motions of the buggerer, and by a false resemblance of a great Prick, he might please himself. But letting pass this, that which is the right side seems on the left, and the left on the right; and holding the Glass a little from you, your face will seem greater then nearer to the center : you shall see two faces and four eyes, if you move a large Glass, or your head, but in a small Glass you cannot see them together. When the eye is in the center, it will see nothing but it self, when you are past that you shall see two faces, and two heads turned upside down, so long as the Line passing through the center may strike upon the distance between the eyes : but all things will seem to move the contrary way : the Spectator without may see by two Axeltrees of his eyes, that all things shall appear double, as oftimes it happens many wayes for a thing to be doubled in appearance. So also let the Glass lye upon the ground, or upon some Table, and let the distance be moderate, and let them look one upon another : the Mans face will seem long and narrow, crushed together, and very ill favoured. But such a Glass hath this excellence above others, that it will burn a great way, and that very strongly. But he that desireth to try it, must hold the Glass against the Sun beams when they shine, and he must place Tinder, or some thing that will take fire in the place of the center; which is found out by removing it further and nearer it, and the conus of the light shews it self, add sets the fuel on fire. If it continue long, it may melt Lead or Tin, yet I remember that I have read that the beams have melted Silver and Gold. The greater segment it is of a greater circle, the further it will burn. *The same.*

The wonderfull faculty of a Chrystaline Prisma.

A segment of Chrystal hath the forces of many Glasses, that it will represent many formes, and those turned upside down, as concave Glasses, also Men with but one eye, and others with four eyes. Also in it appear many beautifull colours worthy imitation if it were possible, especially whilst it is held long-wayes against the Sun; but held to the eyes, then especially where Trees and Fields are, it shews the beauty of the Heavens, Crowns, Rain-bows, Tapistry spread every where, most orient colours, Red, White, Green, Blew, Golden colours and all mingled and most delightfull colours. It shews another shape of things against it above, as if there plains upon the tops of Hils. Also it represents the horizon, and the Countries with a vast distance and pleasant beholding of them, for it doth not hurt but refresh the sight, but it must be a great segment and most pure Chrystal.

BOOK. XII.

Of the Secrets of Stones and Jewels.

Stones both { precious, in { In Generall, of which, Chap. 1. / In Speciall, and they are distinguished either { by sight, or colour, { extreame, so some are { White, Chap. 2. / Black, Chap. 3. } / mean, so some are { Red, Chap. 4. / Green, Chap. 5. / Blew, Chap. 6. } } / or touch, and some are for sculpture, { Fit, Chap. 7. / Unfit, Chap. 8. } } / lesse precious, of them. Chap. 9. }

Of the Secrets of precious Stones in General. Chap. 1.

Deceits in Jewels.

Jewels are counterfeited many wayes, but those are all reduced to three wayes: The first of these is common, to put the colour between two plain pieces of Chrystal, with transparent Glew, when these are Glewed, the Jewel is set into a Ring, that the place where they joyn may be hid; this is a base vulgar way. But the greatest fraud is, and it is not common, but the Author whereof was *Zecolinus Medulanensis*, who took a small shiver of a true stone, as for a Carbuncle of a Carbuncle, of an Emrald for an Emrald, and it was little worth by reason of its weak colour, whereof there was great plenty and ever will be, as there will be of such Impostors; under this he set an equall thick Chrystall stone, and he joyned them fast as he could with Glew very finely, putting between them the proper colour, as bright red for a Carbuncle, green for an Emrald, blew for a Saphyr; and to hide the joynt, he set it into Gold, whereby also all suspition of fraud was taken off. For it is forbidden in the more noble Cities to set a counterfeit Jewell in Gold. In this way of cheating there wants nothing but the authority of him that sels it. The joyning lyeth hid within the Gold, and by reason of the thinness, the colour makes it beautifull; the uppermost superficies being of the true stone represents the lustre of a true Jewel. This wonderfull Impostor cousned Jewellers themselves, untill his fraud was found out, and then

then he fled for it, and was condemned to banishment by all the more noble Cities, and thus by too great a quantity of Gold, he proftituted our City to shame in all parts; yet this was no contemptible Villany, for a Jewel worth three Crowns of Gold, was ofttimes sold for three hundred Crowns, and many times for more. The third way to counterfeit Jewels is far more nobler, and not so much condemned, Art and Nature only contending together. A Jewel is changed in a Jewel by help of the fire. A clear Saphyr, but yet of a weak colour, is set to Gold, and put into the fire by degrees untill it grow soft, the Gold is red hot for two or three houres, then the Jewel is taken off, and suffered to cool by degrees, and it will be a Diamond: for the stone remaines, and no File will touch it: all the blew colour of it also vanisheth. Wherefore we seek for Saphyrs of the faintest colours: for they are the basest, and they sooner turn into Diamonds and more perfectly. He that first found this out grew very rich in a short time; but when it was discovered, there is yet gain to be got by it; for it shines very much by reason of the hardness of the Saphyr. Some with Sea water make a baser and softer stone a fair Diamond. Some do not bake the Saphyr in Gold, but only in the fire, wrapt in Clay, and so it succeds well enough; But note that fire must be put by degrees about a cold stone, and again when you have done your work, you must let it cool by degrees, for to take it suddenly forth of the fire is not safe. The fault is, if there remain any print of the blew colour upon the stone. *Cardan.*

To make precious Stones.

You shall thus prepare matter to counterfeit precious Stones. Fill a bladder with many whites of Eggs, mingled and shaked together: then put it into boyling water to boyl a long time; and when you take it forth, lay it up to dry in a place where no dust comes, untill it be grown as hard as Glass; After this divide it into pieces, and presently after that, cast them into what waters you please to Dye them of full perfect colours, that they may seeth there, and drink in the colours you desire for a yellow. If you would have a Topas, dissolve Saffron in water; for a Carbuncle, the scrapings and dust of Brasil; and so for the rest; A very gallant Invention, and easie to be made, that I gain'd of an experienced Artist, and thought fit to communicate to thee, but not with that mind that thou shouldst deceive any one. *Mizald.*

To counterfeit precious Stones.

You shall thus make precious stones of all colours: Bake in a Potter or Glaziers Oven the hardest whitest Flints you can get, untill they will be finely poudred. One part whereof being sifted through a Hair-sive from the Chalk, or otherwise, must be mingled with three parts of red Lead, and Lead purged from the dross, and put so into a Goldsmiths Crucible, but not to fill it up. A little of the filings or Leaves of fine Gold must be added to it, if you would conterfeit a Topaz or a Jacinth; or a little of the filings of Steel for an Emrald, or some *Lapis Lazuly*, for a Saphyr or Amethyst: and so for other colours; then mingling all together well, they must be set into a very strong fire of reverberation as they call it, so long untill they melt, and are as thick as Honey. Let it stand in the same fire untill it cool of it self, then break the Chrucible, and you shall find a very gallant matter, to make stones off to be cut by a skillfull Lapidary into what formes you please, and polished, and lastly by a cunning Artist to be set in Rings. Some burn Flints and beat them to pouder with an Iron Pestle and Mortar to make an Emrald, in Copper for a Topaz, without mingling any other colour. If for the pouder of Flint you would use calcined Crystal poudred, you shall have all things more fine, perfect, and harder, as I have proved a hundred times. *Mizald.*

To make double Stones, such as they make at Millan.

Take Gum of Mastick, and beat it with some colour and Oyl, and a little Wax, and water also is need be to colour it. This being done, take two pieces that are equall, of Chrystal polished by the Wheel, of what forme and bigness you please, yet so that the upper piece be thinner then the neather piece, and let them be glewed as close together as the Nail is to the Finger on all sides. Put the lowermost of these upon burning coles with a fire Pan, untill it be very hot, then stick the foresaid coloured

loured Gum upon the point of a Bodkin, and lay it upon this lowermost stone that it may melt and run, and so Tincture it as well as you can untill it be sufficient, then presently put the upper part that is the thinner very hot upon the other, and so it will joyn perfectly, without any thickness, and will be all transparent. Then set these Jewels in Rings with a Leaf of Gold under them for Rubies, green for Emrals; but I shall shew in its proper place, how to make Leaves of all colours. *Alexim.*

To make Jewels shine.

If you would have a Jewel for to shine,
Seek for a polish'd piece of Marble fine,
Under the Stone, the Jewel must be got;
With little water-file you hurt it not;
The harder t'is, the more t'wil shine I wot.
      Arnoldus de villa nova.

The way to cut Jewels by the same Author.

If you with Iron hard stones would divide:
Or he that would use Iron Tools are tri'd,
To cut those Stones which Kings love above Gold,
Who held Romes government in times of old,
Let them bear what I have found out by care,
That is of great price, singular and rare.
I sought a large Goats Piss, and eke his Blood
That fed sometime on Herbs, for that was good;
I warm'd the Blood, which helpt to cut the stones,
As Pliny shews, amongst the Roman ones.
He writ of Arts, the people did approve,
And by his skill in Jewels gain'd their love.
Who knows stones virtue, he will love them more,
By knowing them, than ere he did before.

Engraving of Jewels.

Thus for to cut your stones, make Iron hard,
For he that will divide stones, is debard,
If that he knows not how the time to find,
The point to temper, when Goats seek their kind.
That is the season, for only the fat,
Of a Goat is thought best, and good for that.
For if hot Iron, quenched be therein,
It presently to harden doth begin.   The same.

What Images and Inscriptions ought to be Carved upon Stone.

What Inscriptions and Figures should be made upon stones to procure the happy influence of the Heavens upon us, remains now to be spoken of; and how they must be fitted to them, and a Rule for to take and chuse them in season. Upon an Amethyst there is ofttimes Engraven a young Man carrying a white Rod in his hand, with a Hat on his head, and wings on his feet, and sometimes holding a Cock in his left hand, whom all know to be Mercury; nor doth it differ from the virtue of that stone: from hence it promiseth wisdome and understanding to them that carry it with them, since the nature of it is very subtile. Upon Agats we find Engraven Scorpions, Spiders, Serpents, and other venemous Creatures, sometimes a Man pursuing Serpents; and Men know that to be *Æsculapius,* the Celestial Serpent catcher; wherefore it cures venome, and the biting of Scorpions: it is found in the River *Achates* in *Sicily,* where the greatest Scorpions are bred, and by those stones are the Serpents of that Province destroyed, and nature repairs this defect by their virtue. Also upon a Bloudstone, there is inscribed one carrying a Snake: I have read that the Magicians
amongst

amongst the *Persians* gave counsel to their King, that he should carry this stone with him, and they hold it good against poyson, as *Haly* writes. Upon the Jasper they Carve ofttimes, Lions, Cocks, Eagles, Victories, Trophies, Brigandines, sometimes *Mars*, sometimes an armed Souldier treading upon Serpents, and having a Buckler about his neck; a Man suitable to the virtue and hardness of that stone; Sometimes they make a Man a Warrier, a Conqueror and invincible. King *Nechepsos*, for the pain of his stomach was refreshed by the virtue of this; he commanded a Dragon to be the Inscription, putting forth his Sting; upon a Loadstone is often seen the Figure of the Bear called *Ursa Minor*, because it seems most to be in love with the Pole-Starr: for Iron touched with this, turneth toward the North Starr, and it makes it capable of its forces, as being Saturnine. In the stone Selenites, the Picture of the Moon is alwayes found, and he that carryeth it about him bound with a Silver string, and is ruled by the Moon; Upon the Saphyr many Figures of living Creatures are Engraven, that it may cure the diseases of them; upon the Jacinth are Lightnings and Thunder, that it may preserve those that wear it from them: Upon a Cornelian are sundry Figures very diverse, by reason of the diverse virtue and operation of it, that stone is easily found, and easie to be Engraved. Whence we have a report that the Children of *Israel* in the Desart Carved multitudes of them. I have now given you examples how upon severall stones that are set, fit Inscriptions may be made of Heavenly configurations for their virtues. Some also make Rings of Metals to set the stones in, addicted to that Planet, that they may contract an easier faculty of operation: as of *Saturne* from Lead, Sun from Gold, Moon of Silver, that *Saturne* may become *Solar* or *Lunar*, which I suppose must needs profit much.

Elections necessary in carving of Stones.

But some say they receive greater virtue from Heaven, to communicate it, if they be Engraven at set and convenient times; for so they are animated, and configurations do more flow from the constellation or Star into them: and this lay for the ground and root of all these things: for if you would procure love, you must Engrave in fit and friendly Aspects: if you would increase hatred, use ill destroying Aspects for your season, and when you know the affection, so chuse your time: For if Men will make the Image of *Saturn* or *Venus*, they expect untill *Saturn* be under *Aquarius* or *Capricorn*, but *Venus* must be under *Taurus* or *Libra*, and the truth will appear. In the Engraving of them we find the Sun in *Leo*, the Moon in *Gancer*, and *Mercury* in *Gemini*, and *Virgo*; So they do inscribe the figure of a Lion or a Crab, when they see the Sun and Moon in *Leo* or *Cancer*, and they do it presently. But they take the chiefest care that the Moon be free and far from all Impediment, as from *Mars* and *Saturn*, and from the Suns combustion. Moreover they consider, not to do it when her course is void, but when shee increaseth and moves swiftly, and hath not too great a heel, (for these are ofttimes the terms of misfortunes) they will seek her in a happy scituation, in a fortunate Trigonal or Hexagonal Aspect, ascending in the Eastern point, or in the Meridian, not in the descending part, she must not decline, for then the Planet mourns and is stupid; the Diurnall signs must ascend in the day, the Nocturnal in the night, that she may the more easily recover them, and may bring no Impediment; On the contrary you proceed preposterously, if you intend to breed hatred or weakness; when they seek to Inscribe the figures or the signs, you shall find that they do it as much by the following Triplicities. For the first Triplicity consists of *Aries*, *Leo*, and *Sagitarius*, whereof in the day the Sun is Lord, and in the night *Jupiter*, but in the twilights the cold Planet of *Saturn*; and by such signs and cold Inscriptions they cured cold diseases, as Dropsies and Palsies: so according to the other Triplicities they Inscribe the other signs to cure other Infirmities. But I will not omit that which Men of all ages testifie, that the virtue of them will fail and be lost, wherefore those that our Forefathers made are now worth nothing, as we shall find. *The same.*

Of the Secrets of Jewels in Special, and first of white Jewels. Chap. 2.

To try a Diamond.

A Diamond doth differ so much with a Loadstone, especially an *Indian* Loadstone that laid by it, or as *Albertus* hath it, under it or above it, by the opinion of some Men, it will not suffer the Loadstone to draw Iron; and if it take hold the Diamond will put it off again. By this means you may know true Diamonds from false, which are many now adayes. But we can find no such experience in our dayes, unless it be so that all Diamonds be false. *Mizald.*

How to counterfeit a Diamond.

First provide Crystal, and set it in a Crucible in a Potters or Glaziers Furnace all night, quench it in water, then pouder it very fine and grind it, and mingle it with salt of Argal, and with water make Pellets, let them digest all night, remaining in a most vehement fire red hot, but yet not melt, then take them forth, and put them into another vessel, which will better endure the fire, let them stand in that two daies, and you shall have an excellent Diamond. *The same.*

A colour to be put under true as well as false Diamonds.

Take the smoke of a Candle covered with a Bason, and mingle that with Oyl of Mastick, which in the hollow of the Ring must be set under the Diamond. *Alex.*

How to polish a Diamond.

It cannot almost be worn by any other thing than the pouder of it self, nor polished it is so hard. *Cardan.*

To counterfeit Pearls.

You shall counterfeit Pearls thus: Take the white stones out of the heads or eyes of Fishes, cleanse, dry, and pouder them, and with whites of Eggs well beaten, and the froth taken away, mingle them, and stir them so long, untill they come to a Paste, or thick lump; make small Pearls with this, whilst the matter is soft and tractable, and with a Hogs bristle make a hole through them; then dry them, and boyl them in Cows Milk, and in a private place farre from the Sun and dust, dry them again, untill they be perfectly hard. This you shall see will please you. *Mizald.*

A way to make Pearls joyn to naturall Pearls.

Take clean Eearth, such as Potters make Pots of, make round Pearls, with a hole in them, of what bigness you please. Then dry them in the Sun or which is better in some Furnace; for so they will be harder. When this is done, wet them with Bolearmoniac lightly with the white of an Egg, then cover them with Leaves of Silver, being first wet with water, when they are dry, polish them with a Tooth, and they will be Orientall. Then take some bits of white Parchment, and wash them in warm water, untill the water grows something thick, then strain it finely, and when you would use it, remember it must be hot. When this is done, fasten each Pearl through the hole of it, with a Needle or Bodkin, yet so, that you stop not the hole, then plunge it into that water where the Parchment was dissolved, and draw it forth presently again, and turn it to all parts of it, that the Glewey Liquor may run equally about the Pearl; If it seem not great enough, dip in the Pearl again, so will the Silver whiteness shine better, through this thin Liquor, that the Pearl will seem to be natural. And if you compare them with the naturall Pearls, they are fairer, as being more round and clear. *Alexius.*

How to dissolve Pearls.

To dissolve Pearls, wash them being whole, and strain the juyce of Lemmons twice or thrice, then put them into it, and set them in the Sun, in five or six dayes they will be dissolved, that their substance will be as thick as Honey. They may also be dissolved in distilled Vinegar. *Cardan.*

How to make a Calcedon.

When you put Crystal into the fire to melt, mingle a little of calcined Silver therewith, let it stay in a Furnace twenty four hours, so one part will shine between, and another will be cloudy and dull. *The same.*

Of the Secrets of black Jewels. Chap. 3.

To counterfeit Amber.

You shall counterfeit Amber thus. Take Chrystal beaten into very fine pouder, and whites of Eggs, excluding the Cock-Treads, and beat them, and take off the froth so long, untill they be resolved to water; mingle the foresaid pouder with them and work them together, adding a little Saffron finely poudred, if you desire to make yellow Amber; then cast all these into a hollow Reed, or some Gut, or some Glass Viol, and put them so long in scalding water, untill you find they have got a solid hard consistence, take them out, and grind them upon a Marble, and make them of what Form you please, if you will make little Beads for *Ave Maries*, or Hilts of Swords, make the holes before you let it dry, after that set them in the Sun; you may also mingle what colours you will, and counterfeit such precious stones as you desire very handsomely. But then the matter must be strain'd before it be boyled, that the body of the Jewel may be transparent and clear. *A Secret of an Ingenious Artificer, a friend of mine.* Mizaldus.

To make Amber otherwise.

So shall you imitate Amber, if you melt Mastick in a Pot and strain it, to cleanse it from filth, that it may shine the clearer, then mingle a little Turmerick root with it, and make forms; So if you put into melted Crystal, Argal crude, made of white Wine, and put all into a vessel with the mouth Luted, and keep it twenty four houres in the fire. *The same.*

How to melt Amber.

Amber may be handled with your hands like Wax, and made into what formes you please, if it be cast into melted Wax skimmed. For so it will become so soft and tractable, that you may conveniently use it for Seals, or other things which you desire to make. *Mizaldus had this of an Ingenious Lapidary, and Caster.*

Of the Secrets of red Jewels. Chap. 4.

To make a false Ruby.

Some make a Ruby after this manner; They take Salt called *Alkaly* four ounces, pouder of Crystal three ounces, and of the beatings of scales of Brass, (as they call it in the Shops of *Italy*,) half an ounce, and of Leaf Gold six grains, all must be mingled and melted in a Goldsmiths melting Pot in a Reverberatory. When the Crucible is cold and the fire abated, it is broken, and the matter must be taken forth, and given to a Lapidary to forme and polish, and then delivered to a Jeweller to set it in Gold, you may try the same with any other colour of a stone, untill you shall receive a various Method and a multitude of wayes from us concerning these things *Mizaldus.*

The way to make Rubies.

If you would make counterfeit Rubies; Take Gum Arabick, Alum Succharinum, Roch Alum, of each one part, mingle them and boyl them, in common water, adding a little Verzinum cut in small pieces, *Alumen Catinum* what is sufficient, (for the more you put in, the darker will the colour be, let drops of Mastick be Tinctured herewith. After this take two pieces of Crystal that are equall, and totally polished, in what forme and magnitude you please, yet so, that the upper piece be the bounds of the under piece; Glew them, and joyn them together in each part, as the Nail to the Finger; Put the undermost of these upon an Iron Shovel, and set it into the fire untill it be hot, then take the foresaid Tinctured Mastick, and put it upon the point of a Bodkin, and lay it upon the hot Crystal, that it may run so much as you think fit; by and by lay the other piece, namely the thinner, being hot upon the other, and it will Glew fast to it without any thickness, and it will be a transparent Jewel all over. *Alexius.*

How a Carbuncle may be counterfeited.

But to make a Carbuncle the Greeks call a Pyropus, we a Rubine, and others that are more brown called Garnats, you must do thus, to make it also send forth a Purple

ple Splendor, or seem with a more lively Skarlet red within the whole body, and if you make it clear, it will be very well pleasing and perspicuous. Put Chrystal into a strong Crucible to melt in a Furnace, add to this a little red Lead, and let it stay there twenty four houres; the next day take it forth, and let it cool, then pouder it in a Mortar and sift it, and add thereto a very little calcined Brass, set it again into the fire, and when it is melted, add to it a little of this pouder; keep Tin melted three dayes in the fire, and mingle the yellow of it that will fall to the bottome, that that filth may never swim above it any more, and stir it with an Iron twenty four houres; never cease but stir it, untill it grow cold, so will all these stones look red; more weakly and wanly, as you please. *The same.*

To counterfeit an Amethyst.

If you would counterfeit an Amethy, take Salt called *Alkali* three ounces pouder of Crystal four ounces, filings of Brass half an ounce; let them all melt in a strong fire in a Goldsmiths Crucible, and when the matter is cold take it forth, breaking first the Crucible. *Mizald.*

How to make an Artificiall Jacinth.

Put Lead into a strong Earthen Crucible, and set it in a Glassmakers Furnace, let it stay there six weeks, and it will be like Glass, and of the colour of a Jacinth that is naturall, and you will be very glad that it cannot be discerned from a true Jacinth, this is accounted the chief amongst these things. *The same.*

How to counterfeit a Chrysolite.

A Chrysolite shall be made thus; mingle with melted Crystal a sixt part of scales of Iron, and let the Crucible that is strong to endure the fire, stand in a vehement fire for three dayes. *The same.*

To thicken thin Balagii.

Balagii as thin as Paper may be made thick after this manner; Take the best Chrystal Tinctured of the colour of Balagii, and one grain of Mastick, and upon the point of a Knife or stick hold it to the fire, untill it yield a drop like to a Pearl, with this joyn the Chrystal with the Balagium, for that drop joyns without a body, nor doth it change the colour; deliver this to be polished, beautified, and last of all, to be set into a Ring; and it will be very fair, as if it were all Balagium. *Alexius.*

To counterfeit Coral.

You shall counterfeit Corall by this ingenious way; Take the scrapings of Goats Horns, and beat them together, and infuse them in a strong Lixivium made of Ash wood for five dayes. After that take it forth, and mingle it with Cinnaber dissolved in water, and set it to a gentle fire, that it may grow thick. If it be of the true colour of naturall Corall, you may make it of what forme you list, dry it, and polish it according to Art. *Mizald.*

How to melt Corall.

Corall will dissolve in juyce of Barberries as Pearls in Vinegar, of which Liquor one spoonfull exhibited cures the dysentery. They both are astringent and cooling, and stayes excretions of bloud, strengthening a loose and decay'd stomach, as *Dioscorides* and *Galen*, and all Physicians say.

Of the Secrets of green Jewels. Chap. 5.

How to make an Emrald.

You may make an Emrald thus. Burn the best Brass three dayes in a Furnace, take it forth and beat in a Mortar and sift it, the vessel must be again set with Oyl into the Furnace: and stay there four dayes at a weaker fire, with twice as much Sand, that Glass is made of, when it is hard in the vessel, keep it at a more gentle fire twelve houres, and you shall find it thick and green, most pleasing to the sight, that it will allure your eyes to behold it. *The same.*

How Emralds and other precious Stones are to be made.

Take Salt *Alkali* what is sufficient, and dissolve it in common water, then strain it through a Cloath of Wollen, and dry it, and then again dissolve it in water as at first, and dry it. When you have done it the third time, pouder it, add to it Chrystal

ſtal beat into fine pouder, and ſifted by the Apothecary, two ounces and half, Salt *Alkali* two ounces, flower of Braſs infuſed in Vinegar and ſtrained one ounce, put them into ſome new well Glazed veſſel, well Luted about and cloſe that no vent come forth, when it hath ſtood in a Potters or Glaſsmakers Funace twenty four hours, take them out, and make Artificial Jewels of them like to the moſt precious. *Alexius*.

To counterfeit a Topaz.

Whites of Eggs mingled with unſlakt Lime, and long beaten with pouder of Saffron, in a Moneths time will grow ſo hard that they may counterfeit a Topaz, if they be put into a round frame to dry, and then taken forth to poliſh, and Artificially ſet into a Ring. Mizald. *had this from an* Italian.

How to counterfeit a green ſtone.

A green ſtone is counterfeited thus : Melt a Cryſtal, and add a tenth part of Iron to it, and one part of Braſs twice calcined for twelve houres, mingle them, at the fire with an Iron Ladle, without intermiſſion, and it will be like an Emrald. If you deſire it of a clearer colour, mingle a ſixt part of calcined Lead and Tin ; after ſtir it, and leave it in the fire twenty four houres, when the veſſel is removed from the fire, when it grows cold it will a be green. *The ſame*.

How a blew is counterfeited.

If you would make a blew ſtone, put into melted Cryſtal, a little of that Earth which I ſhall tell you of for the Saphyr, mingle it well, ſtirring it with a Rod, whilſt it drink it in, leave it ſo for twenty four houres, then mingle it wit an equall quantity of calcined Silver, keep it in the fire as long as you did before. *The ſame*.

Of the Secrets of blew Stones. Chap. 6.

A Turky Stone.

Some ſay that Turky ſtones ſet into Rings, if a Man fall from his Horſe, will receive all the hurt and be broken into pieces, and ſave the Maſter : but they add, it muſt be given to you for a gift. This ſtone is clear as the blew Sky. The proof of it is, that it will ſeem greeniſh in the night, that the part from you and that in the bottome is black, that it hath veins in the lower part, that it is light, and not very cold ; laſtly, that Lime diſſolved and laid upon it, will appear blew, and receive the colour of the Jewel. And when it is ſo, it will not be tranſparent nor a Jewel, for the file will touch it ; alſo ſet near to the fire the colour is increaſed, but it faints and decayes by the moyſture of your hands. *Cardan*.

To counterfeit a Saphyr.

The Tincture for a Saphyr is eaſie, thus : Put into a Furnace poudred Glaſs, with that blew Earth which Potters call Zaphyron, half as much mingled with it, let it ſtay ſo in a ſtrong Crucible three dayes, and it is done. *The ſame*.

To change a Saphyr into a Diamond.

This Secret of Stones ſeems to be common, becauſe all uſe the ſame way almoſt, and I diſlike it not : but when I have ſet down the way they uſe, I ſhall ſhew you one far better. Firſt of all they take the filings of Iron or of Gold : but the moſt uſe filings of Gold, for they think it more fit for this purpoſe, becauſe it is dearer ; but they are deceived, for filings of Iron are far more fit for it : They put theſe filings in a Crucible into the fire, untill it doth not melt, but only is grown red hot, then they bury in it Saphyrs that are of a faint colour and white, and they leave them not there very long, then they take them forth (and if they are not come to the true colour of Diamonds yet) they put them in again, and this they do ſo often, untill they come to the perfect and true colour. This done, they ſet them in Rings, having firſt annointed the beaſil of Rings with the foreſaid Tincture. *Alexius*.

Another way for that much more perfect.

Take white Emmil, commonly called Smalt, finely poudred, filings of Gold or Iron, of each one part, mingle them ; then take a Saphyr, and wrap it in fine Emmil made with Spittle into Paſte, and dry it well at the fire ; After this bind the Saphyr with a thin Iron Wyer laid into the fire to make it pliable, that you may taking

ing the Wyer in your hand draw the stone out of the fire; thus being bound about you must lay it into the said Iron filings and red hot Emmel, and let it remain there a while as I said before, then take it forth, and if the colour be not yet perfect, put it put it in again, untill it be perfect as it should be. *The same.*

To turn a Saphyr into a Diamond.

If you please to change a Saphyr into a Diamond: find out a Saphyr of a weak colour, that it may be almost white, cover it over in filings of Iron in a Crucible, and when it is red hot at a most vehement fire, but yet it must not melt, spare not to look to it, least you hold it in the fire longer than you should, when it comes to a perfect colour like to a Diamond take it forth and use it. *The same.*

How to soften a Diamond.

A Diamond, that (as *Pliny* saith) will not break upon an Anvil, will grow soft, and almost melt in hot Goats blood, so the Goat sometime before drank Wine, fed on Parsely, or Siler Montanum. *Albertus.*

Of the Secrets of Jewels fit to Engrave. Chap. 7.

How to make a Sardonyx white.

The white Sardonyx which others call *Cameum*, if you like it, and desire to imitate it, do thus. Beat small a great deal many of those Fish shels, that are small, and Women use to adorne their faces with the colour of them, for Ornament sake; put them into purified juyce of Lemmons, and for ten daies cover them in dung, and grind the washed mixture with the white of an Egg upon a Porphyr stone, and make it of what fashion you please, dry it, and set it into a Ring you like. *The same.*

To make Cameum Stones or the Sardonyx.

Take white Sea Cockles finely poudred, as much as you please, put them into juyce of Lemmons, and filter them five or six times through a Wollen Cloath called a Filter, strain it that the Liquor may swim three or four fingers above it, and leave it so ten dayes in a vessel well covered. Then pour forth the juyce gently, and wash what is left in the bottome with Fountain water; then grind it excellently well upon a Porphyr stone, with whites of Eggs first diligently beaten: But when the matter is Liquid as you would have it, and fit to receive impressions, take hollow frames and smeer the inside of them with sweet Oyl of Almonds, and in those patterns forme the matter, as if it were Wax. But before you take it out of the formes, the forms must be carefully clapt together, especially on that part where the figure must be made upon the plain side: Wherefore when the Impression is made, it must be taken forth with the point of a Knife, and laid upon a Paper in the Sun untill it be dryed; But when you would joyn it with a black Crystal, or to a Cornelian, or to some other stone, take a grain of Mastick, fasten the grain upon a Knife or Wodden Pin, and put it to the fire: and when you see the Gum begin to drop, you must have the small Picture and the little stone hot on that side they are to be joyned, by that Mastick now melting, for being cold, they can never be rightly joyned. And if you would have the said matter Dyed with any colour, when you have taken it forth of the juyce of Lemmons, you may mingle any colour with it tempered and ground with the white of an Egge, but the colour must be very fine, otherwise the matter will neither be solid nor fit to recceive an impression, but he that knows well how to do this by practice, may counterfeit very rare things, not only in Carmenian and other small Stones for Rings, but also in all other kind of Imagry, as well convex as concave. *Alexius.*

By what Art Jewels are Engraven.

Jewels are Engraven and pierced through by a wonderfull Art. The Art is this: A great Wodden Wheel is compassed about with a Cord, and with the same Cord again about a little Wheel, which is above the great Wheel, as you see

see them here described upon one side. Wherefore so great a part of *A. B. C.* which is *A. B.* as great as *D. E. F.* is wholy carryed about, the small Wheel *G.* is turned. Wherefore as often as *A. B.* is contained in *A. B. C.* so often in one turning of the greater Wheel, which you may call *H.* the small Wheel *D. E. F.* will be turned about. Wherefore what proportion of magnitude there is wherein *H.* is wheel'd about, or of the Axeltree to the circuit of *G*, such will be the proportion of the number of revolutions of *G.* to the revolutions of *H.* Therefore *G.* will be turned about with most violent force, because it turns in a very short time: Wherefore the Axeltree *G. K.* will penetrate, and break, and diminish Jewels; For that purpose Teeth being made upon *G.* which shall carry about the Axis of the other Wheel taking hold of the Teeth of it: and the greater the Wheel is, the swifter it will be turned about. *Cardan.*

Of the Secrets of Jewels unfit for to be Engraved. Chap. 8.

To make a Diamond of a Saphyr.

You may convert a Saphyr of a feeble colour into a Diamond, if you cover it in a heap of filings of Iron, and set it in a Crucible so long in the fire, untill it be red hot; when it is come to perfection, and very much like a Diamond, then take it forth, polish it, and set it handsomely into a Ring. *I had this of a Goldsmith.* Miz.

Of the Secrets of Stones less precious. Chap. 9.

How to break hard Stones with your fist.

We break a stone as thick as ones hand only with the fist, which we cannot break with the Hammer. You must do it thus: The stone is laid out upon a plain Board, but better upon a plain Stone, one end must stand alone, that it may lye alone without any force used to it, then it is stricken with ones fist lifted up high, with that stroke it strikes upon the plain board, and breaks into many pieces. But if your fist strike sooner or later, then you touch the extreame Table of the stone, your blow is lost, and the stone breaks not. So I have broken Tiles with an easie blow, for when the end hits upon the Table, by the force of the blow, the weight joyn: with the stroke, and it is all one as if it were hit with the vehement force of a Hammer. Let the plain be *A. B.* the stone raised upon it *C. D.* and let this be forced so violently upon *A. B.* that the Ayr which is in the middle right under *E.* cannot slip away: for all motion needs time, since therefore it slips not away it must needs break the stone; because two bodies cannot one penetrate the other, but that which is solid must be divided. Wherefore this is manifest, that the broader the stone is, and the more equall their plain superficies is, and the higher we raise the stone, and the sharper we strike, the easier will the stone break; I have seen some set it upon a Rope and break it. *Cardan.*

To soften all stones.

All stones will be easily made soft, if you let them lye all night in the hot bloud of an Ox, and Weathers fat, and strong Vinegar. *Mizald.*

To break stones.

Olaus Mognus reports, that nothing will sooner break stones than Hogs grease set on fire; which is very likely, because it is moist fat mingled with Salt, and therefore the flame lasts long and sharp.

A way to make a stone that being wet with spittle shall flame.

Take Quicklime, purest Saltpeter, Tutie of *Alexandria* unprepared, Calamita, of each one part, live Brimstone, Camphir of each two parts; reduce them all into the finest pouder, and sift them; then bind up this pouder well in a new linnen Cloath, and put it into a Crucible, then set another Crucible upon it, and with Wyer of Iron and *Lutum Sapientia* fasten it well, that it may have no vent, so set it in the Sun to dry. Then set the Crucibles in a Brick-Kiln, or Potters Furnace, untill the matter be burnt, then take it out, and you shall find your matter like the colour of Brick and as it should be; This made wet with a drop of water or Spittle, and Brimstone presently put to it, will flame, and you may blow it out again. *Albert.*

A stone that is fired with Spittle.

It consists of Quicklime three pound, Greek Pitch, three ounces, an ounce of Loadstone: pouder them, and bake them in an Earthen Crucible in a Brick-Kiln; then bury it in Oyl of Bayes fifteen dayes, and after that keep it dry. *Cardan.*

Otherwise.

Take Quick-Brimstone, Saltpeter purged, of each a like quantity, Camphyr twice as much, add them to new Lime, and pouder them all in a Mortar, so fine that they flye into the Ayr, bind them all close in a Linnen Cloath, and put them into an Earthen Crucible, well Luted with Clay; dry it in the hot Sun, set it into a Potters Furnace, and when the Earthen vessel is baked, wherein the greatest care is to be had, they grow as hard together as a stone. Take it forth for your use. *The same.*

To take forth a Toadstone.

Some take a stone out of a Toad, which the *French* Men call *Crapandina*, after this manner: A Toad is forced into any hole with a red Cloath, and exposed against the heat of the Sun, when it is most violent hot, and there he is burnt so long, and tormented with thirst, untill he be constrained to vomit up the burden of his head at his mouth; and this must be received by a vessel underneath at a middle hole of the Cave, or taken away otherwise, and that quickly, that he suck it not in again; some obtain their purpose something a safer way and more easily: by putting a Toad into an Earthen Pot that hath many holes bored in it, and setting that Pot in an Ant-Hill, for the Ants to eat him up; for when they have eaten his flesh, the stone with the bones is left behind, as I and many others have often tryed. *Mizald.*

To try a true Toadstone.

The *Crapandine* or Toadstone, we speak of before, you shall prove to be a true one, if the Toad lift himself so up against it, when it is shew'd or held to him, as if he would come at it, and leap to catch it away: he doth so much envy that Man should have that stone. *Mizaldus* had this from the report of one of the Kings Physicians, who affirmed to him that he saw it.

How to make divers Marble Formes.

You shall thus make Images and Statues of Marble: boyl the tops and the bark of the Elm and Poplar tree, and whilst it is scalding hot, put in pure Quicklime, untill it be like to Curds of Milk; then add the whitest Marble poudred and sifted, and cast this into Forms, and dry them in the fire: thus you may make very rare vessels with small cost. *Cardan.*

To cut Crystal.

Hard Crystal by this Art may parted be,
Get a fit Plate of Lead, and I tell thee,
Two Pins to this on both sides must be fast,
Which are wont commonly the Lead to wast,
Ith' middle, for the Lead doth cut alone,
And to cut besides the Plate there is none
These are the outward keepers of the Lead,
For to direct it right the course to tread.
Nor can soft Lead cut that which is so hard
Unless some things be added ne'r debard,
As pieces of the Furnace, that may grate
And stick close to the Leaden tender Plate.
And pieces of Bricks likewise can do it,
If whilst you work you cast water to it:
And if Goats Bloud the Crystal hard doth first
Temper, it works a Diamond, to cut the worst.

Arnoldus de villa nova.

How the River Pebbles are made.

Stones are worn by the running of the water, and so become round. *Scaliger.*

Glew for to joyn Stones.

Take Vitriol half a pound, Gals beaten two ounces, sharpest Vinegar one measure, put them to the fire, untill the Vitriol be dissolved, then add filings of Iron one measure, Writers Sand a third part : mingle them well, and with this joyn the chinks of Stones; when this is done, take liquid Vernish, Linseed Oyl, of each one part, mingle them at the fire, and dawb that outwardly on the joyning. *Out of a written Book.*

A way to hide things in solid bodies.

Of the Fragments of the Onyx, white Lead, Egg-shels, and Wax, a Glew is made, which will hide all cracks and chinks in Marble Wals, two whites of Eggs, and other white things may be added, Gyp, and changed according to the Subject, because of these some are whiter, and some not so white; the same reason serves for Flint-stones, Woods, and Metals. *Cardan.*

BOOK. XIII.

The efficient causes of diverse works are, God, Nature, Art; concerning Divine and Naturall Operations, I have Treated in the Precedent Books: Now I proceed to things Artificial, which by the diligent dexterity of the hand, and cunning Industry of Men, are brought to pass; as Houses, Fountains, Cloath, and divers kinds of Vestments, and other things, the Secrets whereof I thought to defer untill now.

Of the Secrets of Houses. Chap. 1.

Buildings that may heat the Ayr much.

IT is manifest that Houses may be built, which even in Winter time will not a little heat the Ayr: but these Houses must not be Erected upright toward the center of the Earth, but that they may perpendicularly receive the Winter Sun; To give you an example, Let the House be in *A.* upon the plain *A. F.* the perpendicular from our zenith to the center of the Earth *A. B.* which differs from the Equinoctiall circle XLIV. parts and a half; Wherefore it will be from the Winter Equinoctial LXVIIX. parts, wherefore let *B. C. F.* be a quadrant, and let *B. C.* be XXII. parts, of which *B. F.* is LXXXX. parts, wherefore the point *C.* will be distant LXXXX. parts from the Winter Tropick; therefore when the Sun is there, a plain or hollow Cylinder superficies being raised *A. C.* will receive the Sun Beams at Noon, perpendicular, make the Arc *C. E.* of XLVII. parts, and according to the declination of the Sun every day describe the parts, and let the pile *A. C.* be turned backwards, and so it shall all the year receive the Sun Beams perpendicular, that Pot-hearbs and fruits may be had before their time, and the House be made a pleasant place to dwell in. *Cardan.*

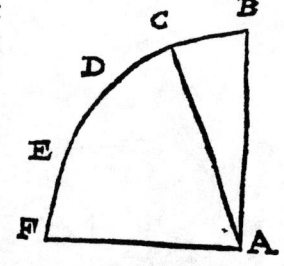

How Chambers may be made very rare

After the custome of the *Carthagenians*, let the Wals be dawbed with Pitch, against the injuries of the Sea, Winds, and Weather; It is good counsel not to be neglected, though it be *Pliny's*. But there are better Pargettings which may be numbred amongst the delights of Chambers. And with small cost they are made most pleasant, being of long continuance, and like Marble it self; thus: Work the whitest Lime slakt in water; but beat the froth of it, which is fittest to make the Pargetting, in a Marble Mortar a long time, temper and work it, that no Wheyish water be left, then is it most fit; make a Ruff-Cast, whilst it is fresh, and with Plaining-Tools strike it over and beat it, untill it lye thick; if it chap, amend it with handfuls of Broom, or Marsh-Mallows, for so it is well known that the chaps will be mended;

that

that no crack shall remain at all, when the crust is dry and thickned, melt Wax and Mastick of each a like quantity, adding a little Oyl thereto, and with that, and live coles in a Chafing dish, heat it and spread it, untill the Wall drink in all the Unguent, and it will shine like a Glass; and be whiter than Marble, and if it chance by heat of the Dog dayes to lay on this Plaister, then cut old Ropes very small, and mingle with the Lime, for that will free it from cracks; and if you please to have any Images or Carvings, either falling in or sticking forth, made upon the Wall, you shall suddenly performe that with Seals and Prints of Gyp; indeed the matter made with Wax, thickned with white Lead, or Quicklime, dawbed on with the foresaid Unguent, will keep the Wall comely and entire for some ages. *The same.*

To plaister your Habitations.

If you would Plaister your House, take the most Chalky Earth, or red Earth, and pour into it Oyl Lees, put in straw, let it stand four dayes to settle, when it is well purified, cut it with a Spade, and dawb it on, so will it not rub off upon your Cloaths, nor will Mice make holes in it, nor any Grass grow upon it, nor will the Plaistring crack. *M. Cato.*

How to make Floors.

When you make a Floor, lay the ground not by a Rule, but lightly beaten, and pare it, after that sprinkle it well with Lees of Oyl, and let it drink them in, then break the clods well, and level it with a Roler, or a Platter, and beat it; then again sprinkle on Lees of Oyl; when they are dry, neither Mouse nor Ant will breed there, nor will it grow dirty, nor will Grass spring upon it: Chalk will make it very solid. *Cardan.* from *Cato.*

Another.

Make a Corn Floor thus: beat the Earth small, sprinkle on Lees of Oyl well, that it may drink in very much, break the Earth and level it with a Roler, or a Rammer: when it is levelled, neither Pismires will trouble you, and when it Rains, it will not be dirty. *Cato.*

A Chimney that will never smoke.

The winds beat back the smoke, and the narrowness of the Chimney will not let it come forth, or if it be narrow at the bottom it will not receive it, the winds are the chief cause. For the smoke alwayes riseth higher within, because it is light, when it riseth against the wind, and chiefly when there is any quantity of green Wood in the Chimney, the smoke being driven back; that Chimney that hath holes of four sides, is freed from all winds: for there is help every way as I found out by reason. On the four parts, East, West, North, and South, place two hollow earthen Pipes, one opposite to the other, that one may carry upwards, and the other downwards; for it is impossible that eight winds, whereof four should blow upwards, and four downwards, can blow from the four principal quarters of the Heavens. And therefore the smoke cannot be forced back; and that also is found perfect by experiment. But the widness at the bottome is no small help; sometimes the Pipes that are sloping are safest, but the safest of all is that, which is compassed with a Case, and beneath is not fastned to the House. *Cardan.*

To make a Chamber seem green.

Take a green Glass, transparent Lamp, that the beams passing through it, may receive the colour of the Medium; and (that which is of much concernment herein) mingle Verdigrease with the Oyl, or with any liquid matter you burn in the Lamp, grind them well, that the Oyl may be green, and make your Wicks of Linnen, of the

the same colour, or of Cotton smeered with the same, and burn this in that Lamp the light will make all seem green that it fals upon, even the faces of the beholders. *The same.*

To make the Chamber and all other things there to seem black.

Mingle Ink or Sout with the Oyl, or some such thing, but cuttle Ink is best, for put into a Lamp, when it burns it makes a black light. So *Anaxilaus* made those that stood by like black *Moors* with it. See more of this before, Book the third.

Of the Secrets of Gardens. Chap. 2.

That a Garden may be green and flourishing.

A Garden will flourish, if you beat claver Grass and cast it into the water and sprinkle it therewith, or water the Furrows with Fenegric bruised in water, or lay an Asses scul in the middle of the Garden. *Vindanionius.*

To make a quick-Hedg.

At a fit time gather the ripe Seeds of the greater Bramble called *Cuminum*, and of the white Thorn, add to these the Seeds of brank Ursine, and with Teare Meal with water infuse them all, untill they be thick as Honey : and with that mixture wet old worn Bucket Cords, or Sea Ropes, or any others that are decayed and worn, and rotten, and lay them so, that between their threads and hayres, the Seed received may be preserved, unto the beginning of the Spring. At that time, where you will make your Hedg, make two Furrows, two or three foot one from the other, about a foot and half deep : and lay in the foresaid Ropes with the Seeds thrust into them, and cast light Earth upon them, and if there be need, water them now and then; thus within one Moneth or thereabouts, the tender Thorn will spring forth and grow; you must help it : and in the void spaces of the Furrows you must plant together Thorn Bushes, that will be a most strong Fence for a Garden or Field, and a most safe Fence against outward injuries. Others teach us to raise up an Osier Hedg in the space between the Trenches, upon which the Thorns in the Trenches growing up, may rest themselves to strengthen them before they have any strength. Others raise a Quickset Hedg thus. They cut Thorn Bushes that are of some thickness into pieces, and they carefully lay them into the Pits digged about a hand breadth in height, and they daily nourish and refresh them, with digging about them and watring them, if the time require it, untill they bud forth, and they begin to have Leaves, and thus they make a strong, safe, and long lasting Hedg. *Democritus, Columella,* and *Diophanes.*

To make wonderfull Hedges.

If you inclose many seeds of divers kinds in Wax, or any tenacious matter, and draw it forth at length, and lay it in ground that is well dunged and manured, a wonderfull Hedg will spring forth of that heap. *This was the experiment of a Kings Gardner.* Mizaldus.

A water-Pot to water Gardens.

Amongst Vessels none is more admirable, and common than a water-Pot, as big as an Amphora, like to a Wine Flagon; It is with a small neck, and with holes at the bottome, like a Sive, the uppermost part hath only a small mouth. It is made of Clay by the Potters; you may make it also of any other matter; when it is empty, the mouth above being open, it is dipt into the water, and it is filled to a certain proportion; then stopping it with your Thumb, you draw it from it, and hold it on again; and so water the Garden with it, and when you will stay it from running, stop it with your Thumb. *Cardan.*

A Secret for Gardens that want Rain.

If a Garden want a water Pit, or Fountain, or Fish-Pond, dig your Garden three or four foot deep, like a place to set something in; for so will the manuring not care for drought. Wherein observe this also, that what Plant is not helped by the moysture, you must divide that : and in Winter you must set it in ground manured toward the South, but in Summer toward the North. *Mizald.*

To try Land for a Garden.

You shall find what Land is good for a Garden, if it be washed in water and dissolved and leaves much Mud therein. If a watry matter hath the upper hand, you may be sure it is unfit and unfruitfull. If you take it into your hand between your fingers, and find it to be very clammy and tenacious like to Wax, be certain it is of no worth; but before you must pick the Stones out of your Garden ground; also it must not be full of chaps, least the Sun penetrating, burn the roots of your Plants. But that Earth is temperately fruitfull, which is neither too wet nor too dry: Add to these things e That ground which being newly Dug, Birds come unto, especially Crows, following the Digger; If the ground be bad, some say it may be helped, if upon barren ground fat Soyl is spread, or upon lean dry Earth, moyst and fruitfull Earth.

What things are to be observed in Dunging of a Garden.

At what time soever you please to dung your Garden or Field, you must take great care that the Wind may blow from the Western Equinoctial, and the Moon must be decreasing and dry. For by this observation the increase is wonderfully augmented. *Pliny.*

When your Garden is to be Sowed.

I am not ignorant that some say a Garden or Fields is not to be Sowed but when the Rain is faln upon it to water it. And if Rain fals seasonably I deny it not. But as it ofttimes happens, the Rain fals late, though the Garden or Field be dry, the Seed may alwayes be sown, as *Columella* saith. And in some Provinces where the temper of the Climate is so, they observe this Rule. For what is cast into dry ground lyeth uncorrupt as if it were in the house: And when Rain fals, what was sown many dayes comes forth in one day; but it is in the mean time in danger of Birds and Pismires, unless before it be sown care be taken by such helps as I shall shew hereafter. However it be, be sure that the Garden or Field that must be Sowed in the Spring, be digged about the end of Autumne, before the Frost comes. And the ground that must be sowed with Pot-Herbs in Autumne, or with Plants, must be turned up at the begining of Summer; that either by the Winter colds, or Summer Suns (I speak of great Gardens,) the Clods may be dissolved. Also to kill the roots of Weeds and ill Herbs; And when the time of Sowing comes, which is proper to every Countrey, the Garden must be Weeded, and all such things puld up by the roots, and then it must be Dunged; When this is done, it must be made into severall Banks and Beds, which must be so ordered, that the Weeders hands may reach half over the breadth of them easily, least whilst the Gardner goes to pull up unprofitable Weeds, he tread in the mean while upon the Seeds: But the greatest care is when you Sow your Seeds, that the season be calm, and clear weather. For when the Heavens are propitious, in moyst places the Seeds do suddenly spring forth where the Sun shines: and Age doth somewhat help them; And therefore heed must be taken that the Seeds be not old, burnt, mingled, lean, decayed, or adulterated; And when you cast them forth, avoid very cold Northern weather. For at such times it is apparent that the Earth is shut up and child, and will not willingly receive the Seed and foster it, but in clear and temperate hot weather it is otherwise; But if there be any fear that they should be burnt by heat or cold, or Frosts, the Seeds must be covered with Straw; and Rods must be laid across, and over the Rods, Reeds, or Vine branches. There are Greeks that write of Husbandry, who give counsel to sow when the Moon increaseth, that is from the first quarter untill the full, whilst the Moon is under the earth. Others thinking of a more safe way, do not approve of Sowing so soon; wherefore they divide the Moon into two, or three, or four times; labouring by this means to avoid the uncertainty of the future time: and remembring the rustick saying of *Columella, Do not fear to sow*; Wherefore he that would sow at a certain time, must take care to see that the Seeds be good, and fit for the ground, the dung good, and water near; For good Seeds will bring forth good planters, good Earth, in which they are sowed, will fost them well, and make them fruitfull, the dung will make the Earth more full of Juyce, and more loose, that the

Rain

Rain may enter and disperse it self to the roots, and the water as it were from a brest, will nourish and foster all. *Mizald.*

A rare Secret to keep Seed in the ground without any hurt.

If Seeds that are to be Sowed be moystned a little before, in the Juyce of Housleek, they shall not only be preserved safe from Birds, Ants, field-Mice, and other Thieves in Gardens; but what springs from them shall be much better. *Aphricanus.*

A Remedy against all mischiefs and hurtfull things in Gardens.

The Greeks report that Seeds will be preserved from all evils and Garden Monsters, if you lay in the Garden, the Skull of an Ass, but it must not be of a young one that never knew Venery, or if you set it up upon a Pole in the middle of the Garden: For whatever is in view of it, it preserves and makes it fruitfull.

To preserve Gardens.

If a Vine be twisted and set over against Pompions, it will not only hinder Thieves from coming in, but keeps all mischief from Gardens. *Dioscorides.*

A fit time to water the Garden, and what water it must be.

Watring which is done in Summer, and chiefly about the rising of the Dog Star, is wont to profit and to be much approved, morning and evening, least the water should grow too hot by the Sun, and burn the roots. But the watring then also must not be too much, because the roots will be over soked and drink too much: and you must not draw forth your water from wels that are too deep, least the cold water that is too raw, hurt the roots. But if you can get no other water, you must dr. v it up some houres before, and set it in the Ayr that it may be warm. You shall know how to water them by the Age of the Plants. For young Plants are not so thirsty, and old Plants desire much watring: but it must be done gently by a water-Pot, that the roots may drink in equally and not be drowned with it: for so they preserve their vegetative life which would vanish by exhalations of the Earth. Wherefore Plants must not generally be glutted, but as they are thirsty, so must water be showred on them, as nourishing them from a brest, and not drowning them. *Mizaldus.*

Against Thunder, Lightning, and Hail.

The tinkling and ringing of Bels, (be it far from superstition) or the loud sounds of Canon, that make a huge noise far and wide, are a most present remedy for noise in the Clouds, against Thunder, Lightning, and cruel Hail, that is threatned by them. For by the force of the sound moving the Ayr, the exhalations are driven upwards, and of all sides to the third Region. Also whosoever are defended by a skin of a River Horse called *Hippotamus*, are never touched by the Thunder. Also no Tempests can hurt them; as *Archibius* writ unto *Antiochus* King of *Syria*, if a Hedg-Toad be shut up close in a new Earthen Pot, and set under ground in the middle of a Garden or Field; also many Plant about the circumference of it the Bay trees very thick. Others hang up Eagles Feathers, or the skin of a Sea Calf in the middle of the Garden, or else at the four corners; An Onyon doth not by its small body escape the force of Thunder, but hath by nature a force against the stroke of it. *Mizald.*

Another.

Some say that a Thunder-Bolt hung at the Door, will keep the house safe from Thunder. *Guliel. Gratar.*

Against Frosts, and Mildews, and Smoot.

If you would prevent Blastings and Mildews, burn much Straw if you have it, or else Herbs pluckt up in Gardens, Shrubs and Brambles in many places; especially on that side the wind blows; for *Diophanes* saith, that the mischief that is near is so turned away. Moreover the smoke of three burnt Crabs, with Ox or Goats dung, or Chaff, is a most sudden Remedy, as *Apulejus* writes. See more Book the Ninth.

A Prognostick of all Seeds, whether they will be fruitfull or barren.

What concerns the fruitfullness or barrenness of all Seeds, either sowed or to be sowed,

sowed, the way to know is this. Twenty or thirty dayes before the rising of the Dog-star, you shall carefully sow in some place well manured of every true Seed that is fresh, for to make a proof, a little in spaces well divided and marked: and if the Ayr be very hot, you shall water it in time, that what is cast into dry ground may spring the better, and before the cosmical rising of the said Star, it may come forth seasonably; when this is done, you shall observe diligently the Dog dayes being over, which of the said Seeds came forth safe, lively, and without hurt, and so continued: and you may say certainly that the same Seed will grow fruitfully and plentifully that year: but the other that came not forth, or else sent out a faint languishing and decaying Plant, you may perswade your self that it will be of no use, and barren for that year. For it is as certain as can be, that the mad and burning Dog-star, by his extreame heat doth hurt some Seeds, and others not at all; From this you may fetch the Judgment of hurt or benefit for the future year for all kind of Seed, for the Star that is dry and hot by nature, will foreshew and declare what is for your use safe and good, and what shall be of no profit but hurtfull to you. *Mizalds*, from *Zoroaster*. And this is true by the experience of the *Ægyptians*.

Against Garden Caterpillars.

If you smoke your Gardens with Bats dung, and stalks of Garlick, taking off the heads, that the smoke may flye all over the ground, it will kill the Caterpillars. *Anatolius*.

For Moths in Gardens.

Bury under ground a Sheeps Paunch, that is fresh and full of dung, and unwasht, but not very deep, only in the superficies, you shall find it full of these Herb-eaters, and having taken them there, destroy them. *Diophanes*.

Against Garden Fleas.

Fleas will not hurt Plants, if for a natural meanes you sowe Rocket Seed amongst the rest in many places.

Against Hail that is coming.

If you would hinder Hail that is ready to fall down, carry about the Garden or Field a Sea Calfs skin, or of an Hyena, or Crocodile, and in the middle hang it up as is written by *Philostratus*.

Otherwise.

Some who observe Hail coming on, bring a huge Looking-Glass and observe the largness of the Cloud, and by that Remedy, whether objected against, or despised by it, or it is displeaseased with it; or whether being doubled it gives way to the other, they suddenly turn it off, and remove it. Many more are affected with this superstition, that they compass round all the Garden with Keys of many Doors hanging upon a Cord, and they suppose the Hail will pass away with the Cloud to some other place, and do no harm there. Some there are that walk through a Field or Garden with a Marsh Snaile in their hands: and returning as they came in, they set the Snail in the same posture upon the ground, and they cast clods upon his crooked back, that he cannot turn, but may lye on his back, and lye with his face upwards toward the Cloud swelling with Hail. Some command this to be done at six a Clock morning and evening. There were some of the Ancients, who for that purpose composed about the Garden or Field, with a white Vine, or else they stuck up an Owle with his wings spread abroad in the middle of the Field. *Mizald. from Columella, Philostrates, and many more of the Ancients.*

Of the Secrets of Garments. Chap. 3.

To take away all sorts of spots out of Garments and Cloath.

Take common Salt very well beaten, black Sope of each what is sufficient; mingle them well, and smeer over the spots therewith; then when they are dry; first wash them with a Lixivium, and after that with warm water, and they will be gone. *Alexius*.

To take off spots from Silks and other Garments.

Burn the fore feet of a Weather to ashes, and make pouder of them, and strew it upon the

the clothes, first wet in water; after that when they are dried in the Sun, wet them again with water, and strew pouder upon them as before; Having done this over again oft times, wash off the pouder very well with water, and doubtless the spots will be gone. *The same.*

A Sope to take all sorts of Spots out of Clothes.

Take half a Buls Gall, one or two whites of Eggs, and mingle them well, adding burnt Allum one pound, pouder of Orris six ounces, a little beaten Salt, and mix them, this being done, add as much white Sope, cut or scraped in, so much as may serve to make Balls, dry them in the shade, for the Sun hurts them; If you will sell them, make them of the same weight; when you would take out spots, first moysten the Cloath with cold water, and then rub it well with the foresaid Sope, then wash it off with cold water; If the spots yet appear, dry the Cloath, and then wash them as you did before, and it takes them clean away. *The same.*

Another.

Take white *Venice* Sope one pound, yelks of Eggs six; beaten Salt half a spoonfull, juyce of Beets what is needfull; Mingle them and make a Mass for Balls, and dry them in the shade. When you will use them, first wet the Cloath with water, then rub it with the said Sope, wash it again off with water, and it is done. *The same.*

Another.

Take white Sope rasped one pound, Goats Gall, or Ox Gall, *Alum Catinum*, of each one ounce, yelks of Eggs three, a few Ashes, mingle them all well in a Mortar, make Balls, use them as before. *The same.*

Another.

Take the Gall of an old Ox, what is sufficient, Fenegrick finely poudred one pound, white Sope one pound and half, strong Lee three measures, mix and boyl them at the fire untill half be consumed, and keep it to take forth spots. *The same.*

Another.

Take Roch Alum, Quick-lime of each one pound, Argal six ounces, white Sope scraped three pound, Spring water four pound; mingle them, and boyl them awhile at the fire, then strain it and keep it for your use. When you will use it, wash the fat spots on both sides, with this liquor being hot, then wash it out with fair water; Then wash the spots twice or thrice with Sope and Water, and they must vanish. *The same.*

Another.

Take River Water two measures, one Ox Gall, burnt Alum four ounces, Argal burnt three ounces, Camphyr two scruples, mix and boyl them untill half be consumed, then strain it, and wash the spots twice or thrice therewith and it takes them away. *The same.*

To take Spots from Purple colour be it in Wool or Silk, without hurting the colour.

Take juyce of Saponaria as much as you please, and put it upon the spots, and let it lye so two or three houres, then wash it carefully out with hot water. If the spot be not gone, do it again; If the Cloath be not Dyed in Grain, add a little Sope to the said juyce, and mix it well, and wash it again, and it will take out the spots. *The same.*

To take Spots from white Silks and Scarlets.

First wet the spots with three times distilled *Aqua vitæ*, then lay on the white of an Egg, and dry it at the Sun, wash it off well with cold water. ~~It takes the spots away at~~ twice doing. *The same.*

Another.

Take Alum-water what is needfull, and wash out the spots with it very well, rubing the Cloath, then wash it with cold water, and it takes them off, and chiefly if you do it twice. *The same.*

Another.

Take Lee what you think fit, put it into some clean Earthen Pot to the fire, untill they begin to boyl, then add Alum beaten, Argal in pouder, white Sope rasped, of each

each three ounces, Ox Gall two, mix and boyl them to the consumption of a third or fourth part, and make water, wherewith spots washed twice or thrice and dryed again, and lastly washed with cold water will be taken off. *The same.*

For spots of Cloath.

Take Beech Ashes what is need, with cold water make a Lee, add thereto a few Lees of Wine, and a little burnt Lome out of the Furnace, make a Lee to wash spots out of Cloaths. *Out of a Germane Book.*

A way to make a water that shall restore colour to a spotted Linnen Cloath.

You may prepare it thus. Take Argal four ounces, little Basons of water two, let them boyl untill a fourth part be consumed, then add white Sope rasped, and Alum each one ounce, leave it so two dayes, then use it as you were taught before. *Out of a Germane Book.*

To take Wine out of any Cloath.

Take Lee made of Beech Ashes, and white Argal of each what is sufficient, steep the Cloath in that all night; lastly wash it out and leave it in the Sun to dry. *The same.*

The way to take all spots out of Crimson Silk.

Make a Lee of Vine Ashes, into two small Basons of this Lee cast in Argal half an ounce, and leave it awhile, afterward strain it through a Cloath, and add Alum and hard Sope of each two drams, soft Sope half a dram, of common Salt a quarter of an ounce, as much of salt Armoniac, juyce of Celendine half as much, Calves fat a quarter of an ounce: mix all these and strain them through a Linnen Cloath. And if need be you must take the sheerings of Skarlet Cloath; and add Brasil Wood cut small to it; boyl them a little at the fire, and strain them again through a Linnin Cloath, so you have a red water will take forth all the spots.

For spots in Plush.

Take as much Vine Ashes as you please, Argal half an ounce, Roch Alum one dram, *Venice* Sope one dram, soft Sope half a dram, common Salt two drams, salt Armoniac two drams, juyce of Celendine one dram, Calfs Gall two drams, mix and strain them all through a Linnen Cloath; when you use it, take shorn Wool of the same colour with the Velvet, and dip it in the former liquor and rub the spots with it. *Out of a Germane Book.*

How to take Ink spots out of Cloath.

First wash the Cloath in the sharpest Vinegar, pressing and rubbing it forth well with your hands, and then with water and Sope, and it takes them out. *Isabella Cortese.*

For spots of Cloath.

Take Roch Alum three drams, Argal one pound, white Sope one ounce, Fountain water, pouder them, and boyl them gently at the fire in a Glazed vessel, then filter them, and wash Cloaths therein. *Roscellus.*

That Cloath may recover its former colour.

Take Quick-lime two ounces, Vine Ashes one ounce, Fountain water two ounces, mix them. *Roscellus.*

To blot out spots of Ink or Wine from Linnen or Wollen.

Take juyce of Lemmons, or of Oranges or Citrons what you please, wet the spots therewith, and dry them often, then wash them with cold water, and it blots them out; If the spots be from Ink, wash them forth with white Sope and Vinegar. *Alexius.*

To restore Cloath to its former colour that is decayed by Spots.

Take Argal calcined one ounce, strong white Wine Vinegar one measure, mingle them and set them so long to the fire, untill they begin to boyl, then take it from the fire, and in that water wet the Cloath often by degrees, and it will gain its former colour. *The same.*

A water to tak spots from any Cloath what colour soever they be Dyed.

Take Ox Gals two. Alum, red Argal of each two scruples, white Tartar four ounces, Camphyr one scruple, common water two measures, pouder what is to be poudered,

poudered, mix and boyl them untill they cease to froth, then add *Aqua vitæ thrice distilled* four ounces, keep it for use. If the Cloath be Purple, take a piece of Cloath like that Cloath, and wet it in the water aforesaid, and rub the spots with it very well twice or thrice, then wash them forth with cold water. But if the Cloath be any other colour, take always a piece of the same colour, and do as I said. *The same.*

To take Oyl or any fat from Cloath without washing.

Take forefoot bones of the feet of a Weather, as many as you will; burn them well in a Potter or Brickmakers Furnace, and beat them into very fine pouder, and first heating it, strew it upon the spots in the Sun untill it grow black, and when you see that, take that away presently, and strew on more, do this so oft untill the pouder will grow black no more; and so the spots will come forth not hurting the colour. *The same.*

To restore lost colour to any Cloath.

Take Oke Ashes one pound, pour on four measures of water, and let it stand so all night, when you have drawn forth the Lee, put into it two Buls Gals, and one handfull of Beet Leaves dryed, let them boyl together half an hour, untill the Leaves sink to the bottome, let them cool; after that boyl the Wool of the same colour you would Dye your Cloath, in the Lee only till it begin to boyl, and let it stand aside fourteen dayes; so will the Lee draw out the colour of the sheerings of Wool. Then crush forth the Wool, and Dye your Cloath in the Lee, and it will regain its former colour. *Out of a* Germane *Book.*

How to blot out spots from Woollen Cloath.

Take a Lee made of Beech Ashes, add to it Wine Lees, and burnt Lome of a Bakers Oven, of each a little; Dip the Cloath in these as far as it is spotted, and it will take forth all the spots. Lastly wash it in fair water, and leave it in the Sun to dry. *The same.*

Another.

Take *Alum Fecum* six ounces, crude Argal four ounces, Alum two ounces, Camphyr, Dragons bloud, of each half a dram ; pouder these, and mingle them well in poudring them, add to these Buls Gals six, and small Basons of Fountain water as many, mingle them together with the foresaid matter in the Skillet, and set them to the fire untill a third part be boyled away, strain and press them through a Cloath. But if you have no Gall nor Camphyr, it is no matter, for water will suffice; But you shall fit it for use thus. With a new Linnen Cloath dipt in this water, rub the spots, and do this so often untill they be out. When the spots are gone, wash the Cloath where the spots were in hot water; But if you would blot out spots in white Cloath, take the foresaid water, adding a little Sope, distill this, and do with the rest as with the former. *The same.*

That Moths may not touch Garments.

That Moths may not touch Garments, boyl Oyl Lees to half; annoint the bottome of the Chest with this, and outwardly, also the feet and corners, when it is dry, put in your Cloaths, doing this, no Moths will hurt you. *M. Cato.*

To make black spots upon white skins, that they may be like Leopards, or Panthers skins.

Take Lytharge one ounce, Quick-lime two ounces, Water three measures; mingle them, and set them upon a genle fire, untill they only heat, and boyl not, then take them from the fire and stir them, and make a mixture, and make spots with this Tincture, with a Pencil made of Hogs Bristles. Then dry them in the Sun and beat them afterward with a Wand, and it is done. If the spots appear not right, do it again as before, and you shall obtain it. This colour is firme, and colours the skins: if you Dye your Hayr or Beard therewith, they will be comely. *Alexius.*

Shooes will never wear out.

Albertus saith, That to be at small charges for Shooes, you may have the best, and almost everlasting, made of the back part of an Ass, where he useth to carry burdens upon: these Shooes will never wear out, for if a Man alwayes walk amongst

Stones

258　　　　　　　　*Secrets of Fountains.*　　　　Book XIII.

Stones or Thornies they decay not. But with too much age they will grow so hard that it is impossible to pull them on. *Cardan.*

Of the Secrets of Fountains. Chap. 4.

That Pits in Marshy places may have fresh water.

The sides of the Wels or Pits must be fenced with everlasting work, as when we make an Arch to build Bridges over Rivers. For fastning in Piles, we stop matter about them, beyond the place we draw forth water; So Masons may fasten and lay stones and cement in a dry place, when the waters run all about them. The way to do it is this. First make a very large Pit, suppose the Diameter to be a hundred foot, first having knockt in very long Poles, all the Mud that is in the circumference of the Pit, is to be drawn forth with Shovels, or Vessels, and cast on the other side the Piles. So will the Sea be kept of, and the Pit will be defended from the violence of it; when that place, the water being drawn forth is either dry, or almost so, again within this Fort drive in another rowe of Poles exceeding long, which rank of Piles shall be ten foot distance from the former, which must be filled up with the Mud digged forth: the same must be done there, or four times, untill you can draw forth fresh water. *Scaliger.*

The Clesibick Engine.

The way to make this Engine is this, as *Janelius Turrianus* of *Cremona*, a man of great wit in all things that belong to Engines hath expressed it in the work it self. There must be had a Brass Pot, the upper mouth whereof, out of which the water must be cast is B, at the bottome thereof, there must be two holes C.D, upon which little Boards or Leather must be fastned, as in Bellows, which from the lower part must be lifted up toward A. but if they be pressed together, they shut those mouths, and there must be fastned to the Pot by the mouths, C. and D. two Pipes, on the right and left side, and draw forth to E. and F, and set into the vessels in G. and H. The Vessels or Buckets must be empty, and let down into the water, having holes at the bottome K. and M, in the middle over which there must be Boards or Leather fastned as before in the Pot, that may be lifted upwards, when the holes are pressed upon, and shut them also exactly. But in the Buckets there must two great Pins or Plates be set M. and N. polished by the Turner, and well Oyld, to fill the Buckets to a hairs breadth, then with Bars and Rules they must be so fitted, that going up and down, that when M. ascends and the Bucket under it is left empty, N. in its turn may descend, and fill up the Bucket with its Pin, and force out the water contained in it. It being thus prepared, when out of E. the great Pin M. is drawn forth, the place E. is left empty in the Bucket, wherefore the Board or Leather over K. riseth up, and the water runs forth to E. untill the Bucket be full by reason of the first motion: In the mean while N. is pressed down, it begins to draw from the bottome by alternat motions by turns, and the Pin M. descends and when the water contained in the space E. cannot run forth again, M. shutting to a hayr the upper capacity of the Bucket, nor descend back by K. because the Board presseth upon the hole, and the more it is forced by the weight and violence from above by the water, the closer it lyeth upon the hole, wherefore the water must needs flye forth at G. for there only is passage for it, and runing up by the Pipe E. the measure of water enters, lifting up the cover into the Pot by the hole C. untill the Pot be full, afterwards when the force ceaseth from E. the Leather fals down, and the Board over C. and the Vessel A. remains full. But in the mean while, that M. descends to K. N. riseth to the top of the other Bucket, and the Bucket is filled with water by the same reason, and when it descends again, it forceth out the water by H. to D. into the Pot, which being already full of water, and cannot run back at C. the Board and Leather sticking more close to the hole, the

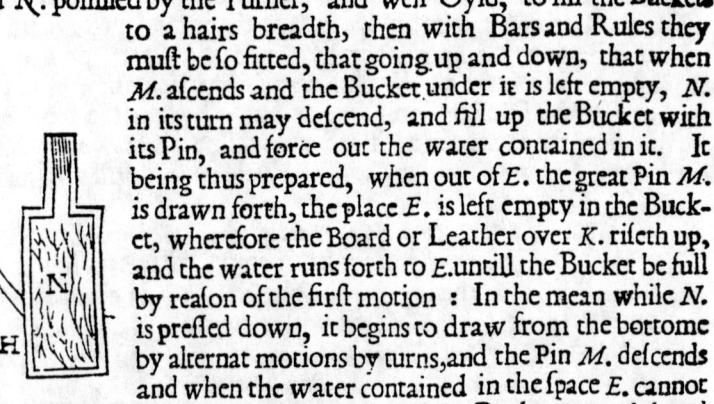

more

Book XIII.   *Secrets of Fountains.*   259

more the water from above presseth upon it by a second reason of naturall motion, whereby also heavy things move upwards; the water ascending by *A*. runs forth at *B*. and thus by alternat motion, and the Pot being alwayes full, from the holes in the bottome, *K*. and *I*. as much water will ascend to *B*. as you please. *Cardanus de Subtilitate.*

The Brambilick Engine.

Of the same kind is the Pump of Ships, whereby they Pump out water when the Ship is in danger, by example whereof *Bartholomeus Bambillus* made an Instrument, which I saw at *Millan*, no way inferiour to the Ancients for the Workmanship, *B. A.* is the Pipe that is hollow within, being made of Wood turned round, fastned in with Bars and Rules, it is larger upon the upper part, than all *D. M.* and narrower beneath, where it is received in the Vessel *C.* full of water, that is bored full of holes on the sides, that the water may come in, but no small stones nor Sand, the bottom of the Vessel *C.* being firme, thus the Pipe may when need is, draw forth pure water out of the Vessel, and draw no stones nor Gravel, which might stop the Pipe. In the place *M.* where the narrower part is joyned to the broader part, there is a Leather made fast above on the part *M.* and a thin Plate of Lead goes over that; that when it is elevated on the part *Q.* by its weight it may fall down again, and cover the Pipe *L.* exactly, but the Pin to stop it must be *A. E.* less than the breadth of the Pipe, put in the upper part where *D.* is, it stops the hole of the Pipe to a hair, but *O. P.* must be empty, at the bottome of the Pin three Iron feet must come forth to the sides of the Pipe fastned within, which you must cover about with Leather, least they should grate upon the Pipe to wear it away, these are like to a three legd Stool: beneath they stand farther off, where *F.* is than where *E.* is above. It is plain therefore, that all the space by *N.* is empty; and besides those Rods, there is nothing in it, wherefore the way is open from *O.* and *P.* to *N.* and again from *N.* to *O.* and *P.* for all the space above *F.* is empty, and there is nothing there contained but the Pin, and the Rods *H.* At the bottome of these Rods is the circle *F.* fastned to the ends of them, nor is it all empty, but only in the middle, and where the hole is left, with a Leather upon it, and over that a thin Plate of Lead, to cover it, as I said of *M.* so that being covered no Ayr can enter, and yet the Leather with the Lead may be lifted up toward *N.* and uncover the hole. This must be done thus: fasten the Leather about half of it to the circle that contains the Rods, the other half must not fasten to it, and only must exactly cover the other hole when it lyeth close to it. Again from the heads of the Rods three other Rods must proceed right forth, sticking within side to the sides of the Pipe. These a Leather must cover round, to *F.* the upper part, sticking to it as far as *G.* exactly to the sides of the Pipe within, that not so much as any Ayr can pass from *K.* to *N.* so it will be that *H.* will seem to be a Bucket turned downwards, for *F.* is the bottome, and covered all over with Leather, round in form, and it is open and wide at *G.* This done, so fit *A.* the Pin, that it may pass up and down, sometimes descending as far as *M.* on that side *G.* of the Bucket turned downwards, and sometimes drawn up again to the place where it is now described to be. All these things being so orderd, let *G.* lye above *M. Q.* and begin to be raised, then the Ayr containd in the space *H.* being rarified, draws up and elevates *Q.* by this meanes the Ayr ascends from *L.* into the space *K.* and thereupon the water riseth from *B.* to *L.* but when the Pin fals down, by pressing the Ayr and heaviness of the Lead *Q.* descends presently: Wherefore the water in *L.* must needs stay there, for opening the covering *M. Q.* if the Ayr should descend, that little quantity of Ayr that is in *L.* above the water, would be troubled, because it can draw no other Ayr from *K.* by reason of the covering *M. Q.* but the Ayr that was contained in *K.* whilst it ascends by *G.* lifting up the

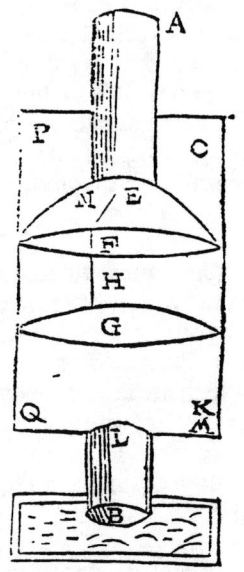

cover

cover *F*. it flyes into the space *O*. and by the hole *P*. it gets forth, thus by often ascending and descending by *G*. and the Pin, the place *L*. is filled with water; After that *G*. being elevated; and by reason of the first motion that the Ayr in *K*. may not be disturbed too much; the covering *Q*. being elevated, the water enters into the space *K*. untill it be filled, and with that the space *H*. also, which as I said is common with *K*. because *G*. is the mouth of the Bucket, that is open, and shut no where; wherefore let it be now full, and the Pin descends again, the water that is in *H*. will lift up the cover, and fill the spaces *N*. and *O*. and when the Pin is drawn up again, least the water which ascended to *O*. should fall back to the cover *F*. hinders it. Which by its own weight and the weight of the water upon it, stops the hole as fals-down. Therefore it is manifest that by this Engine the water will always ascend, and never descend, wherefore when it comes to *P*. it runs forth at *P*. the mouth of the Pipe into what place you will, and then with small labour you may draw as much water from *B*. as you please; for the Pipe being full, the Pin moves the easier. *Cardanus de Subtilitate*.

Pipes to draw forth water.

But Pumps whereby Ships are kept dry, and also Wels, and Water Trenches are made with more single fashion, the reason *B*. and *C*. continuing, that Stones may not hinder the Engine, the Pin hath four pieces of Leather at the bottome, and as many near about, but about two Cubits or something more distant from them, which are fastned above, their length is the breadth of a hand: and as they are drawn up, the water enters to avoid vacuity: when they are descended, they are dilated by reason of the forcing of the Ayr, but by reason of the quickness, some water passeth again from above, wherefore not only by drawing, but also by pressing down the water ascends. *Card. de Subtilitate*.

That water may draw forth it self.

How water may ascend as much as it descended, whilst it is helped by motion of rarefaction, I shall shew by example. Let a vessel be full of water, let the top be *E*. the bottome *F*. in which must be a Pipe, *A. B. C*. but *C. D*. must be a streight Line perpendicular to the Horizon, as raised by a Level: Fill the Pipe *A. B. C*. with water, and let the water come forth by *C*. I say it will draw forth all the water above the Line *C. D*. but nothing of that which is beneath the Line *C. D*. but the Pipe will hang full, and the vessel will be full of water as far as *C. D*. this example shews the truth of it. May be some will say this must be only to draw water, but it is not so, for be it Wine, Oyl, or Milk, the Vessel is filled with it is all one. Wherefore I must give you a reason of this experiment. Since then the water which is above *C. D*. is to a hair as much that ascends, as that is that is poured forth by *C*. whether the Pipe be larger in *C*. then in *A*. or narrower; because alwayes the Pipe is exactly full, the water that ascends runs forth by *C*. but because the water is lighter in the part above *C. D*. than it is in *C*. it comes to pass because the water above *C. D*. desires to descend, that it may be lower than that which is in *C*. wherefore it presseth the water and forceth it into the Pipe. But that which is beneath *C. D*. desireth not to be in *C*. because *C*. is higher than the place of it, wherefore it will not ascend, but the water that runs forth by *C*. makes no stay, being yet lower than the water contained in the Vessel; because that attraction is made only by reason of continuity, and the continuity depends upon rarefaction, which can be none with the water that goeth forth at the mouth of the Pipe *C*.

Lastly, All this speculation is ended by this Argument, that all water that must draw other water after it, must be contained in a Vessel, otherwise it can make no attraction, but it is helped by the Ayr that comes to it, and that like a continued body, it may come to be equally ballanced, since there the mouth *C*. is lower it will come to that, but when it is higher it will not fall down, because that which is right against the lower part as in *A*. will be forced to ascend to *C*. which is right against *D*.

But

Book XIII.   *Secrets of Fountains.*

But if the water first descend, and then ascend, as in the following Figure from *A.* to *B.* and so to *E.* after that it may come to *C.* and to *D.* if *D.* is not so much distant from the Line *B.* as *C.* from *A.* the place is descended from. But there must be a certain difference of height in the severall places, of *A.* and *D.* for the longer the way is, the greater must be the difference, of *A.* and *D.* according to the measure of the height. Hence grew the errors of some, who endeavouring to draw waters by a Level, made great loss and expence. In therefore every Mile, it must be a hand breadth higher than *D.* as in ten Miles ten hands breadth. The evident cause of this is the roundness of the water, which also may be seen in the superficies of Cups. Wherefore though *A.* be higher than *D.* by level, yet sometimes it may not be higher than the middle place between *A.* and *D.* also it was some force. But these things are almost besides my intention, yet because of the great danger, and frequent errors, I would set it down. *Cardan. de Subtilitate.*

Herons *Engine.*

Now I must speak of motion, compound of levity and gravity; for example, take the wonderfull Engine of *Heron*, which I have often handled; It is thus, *A.* is a Laver full of water, under that is a Vessel *B.* and that is also full of water joyned to *A.* that from one to the other the water cannot pass; under the Vessel *B.* must another Vessel stand, called *C.* and it is empty : the Pipe *D.* must come from *B.* to *C.* and the top of it must come almost to the uppermost Laver; there must be another Pipe *F.* that must ascend above the highest Laver a pretty deal, and set into the highest Laver must pass through the middle of it, unto the bottome of the middle Vessel, yet it must not be joyned to the bottome at *F.* whose top is set into the lower Orifice of the Laver, it must end beneath in the very division between the two Vessels, yet so that water may be carried out of the Laver by the mouth above into the Vessel *C.* then shall we see the water that is in the vessel *B.* sent forth by the Pipe *E.* and so continue untill all the water be forth of the Laver, that must be demonstrated how it is done by two compound motions. The water that descends by the Pipe *F.* into the middle Vessel *B.* but that place being full of water, the water is forst to ascend by *E.* the other Pipe, as it is preserved by the Ayr, and so it runs forth. *Cardanus de Subtilitate.*

Archimedes's *Engine to draw water.*

There is an Invention of *Archimedes* called a Screw, which *Diodorus Siculus* speaks of twice in his Ancient History, saying that *Ægypt* was drawn dry by help of *Archimedes* his Engine, which if it be so, seeing that *Archimedes* lived in the times of the second Punick Warr, I know not how he could of old live in *Ægypt.* Yet howeit is, the Instrument is very noble, and not unworthy such an Author. *Vitruvius* speaks of it at the end of his Book. But *Geleaz de Rubius* a Citizen and Smith of our City, of whom I shall speak underneath. When he thought he had been the first Inventer of what was found out long before, he ran stark mad. I saw him turning about a winding Engine, and afterwards very shortly he run out of his Wits. The Engine was thus. A piece of Wood *A. H.* that was solid and strait, and equall, and long, and inclined to the superficies of the water, and fastned

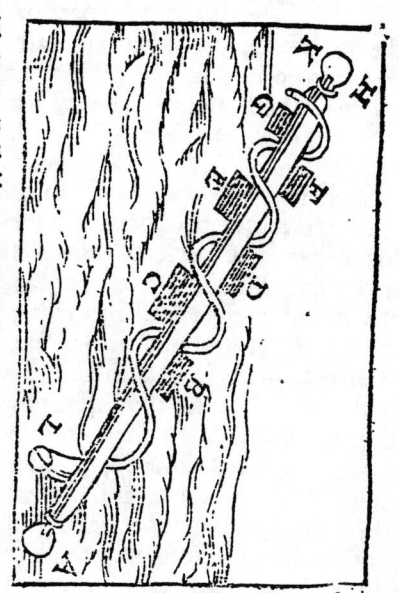

into

into the Channel of the River as much as need is, must hang above the water, with a single Pipe of Metal as you see, like a Screw that must be wound about it: some use very many of them, but I think three is enough, and it must ascend so by degrees, that it may fill up all the spaces, the Pipe hath two Orifices; the lowermost widest, and the uppermost narrower. Let this be called *K.* wherefore it must be demonstrated, that when the beam is bounded by the ends *A.* and *H.* it may be so turnd about, that the motion of the water may turn it. Secondly, When it is turned about, the water will ascend and run forth by *K.* for the wings that are added to it *B. C. D. E. F. G.* with spaces between, here one and there another, on severall sides, or where the Pipe and the Beam are joyned; meeting the water-course must needs turn the Engine, for you may make them longer and broader; but the weight *A. H.* is but small, and is made also far less, by reason of the inclination, and of the little Boards, set into the Sockets, so that it may be turned about; Also this may be seen by Mils in Rivers, where though the water run very gently, as in the River *Poe,* and *Ticinus* by this cunning are Milstones driven about, whereby the Corn is ground; And it is clear that the water ascends from *L.* to *K.* for when *E.* is lifted up, the succeeding part is made the lower; wherefore the water will descend, and when that ascends, the part that succeeds descends; and the same reason shews that the water alwayes tends towards *K.* and this doth excellent well agree with the experiment, and I have tryed it more than once; when therefore the Axis or Beam is turned about by the received ends where it is thrust in *A.* and *H.* untill the Pipe be filled with water, it will run forth at *K.* upon the bank of the River. *Card. de Subtil.*

BOOK. XIV.

Of the Secrets of Meteors.

Signs before hand of fair Weather. Chap. I.

THe Moon appearing sharp on the third and fourth day, and clear, signifies fair weather. Also when she is in the full, if she be clear it is a sign of calme weather, also if she be half full, and clear, it signifies the same: but if she be somewhat red, it imports Winds; if any part be dark it shews Rain. So the Sun rising clear portends a fair day, and a small cloud appearing before he rise, it will be fair, but when he sets, if clouds gather about him confusedly, we must fear Rain: But if he set fair without any clouds, he promiseth a fair day. But if the Sun come forth without a cloud, and clouds afterwards that are somewhat red draw about him, it will not Rain that night, nor the next day. Clouds that are very red, and divided about the Sun setting, bid us fear no Rain. The Owl singing all night, and the Chough making a noise mildly all day, and many Crows coming together as it were rejoycing and cawing, signifie fair weather. *Aratus.*

Tokens before hand of tempestuous Weather, and what signs there are that foreshew Rain. Chap. 2.

The Moon on the third and fourth day having obscure and dark Horns, signifies Rain. But the circle about being red or fiery colourd, shews a Tempest. A full Moon with some black about foreshews Rainy weather. But when about a full Moon two or three borders of black appear, that is a sign of great Tempests, especially the blacker they are. A red Sun rising with some black, is a token of Rain. When the Sun riseth, if about the Beams of it a dark cloud be seen, it signifies Rain. If when the Sun sets it hath a black cloud near on the left side, you must expect Rain suddenly. Thunder and Lightning, on what side they are, they signifie where Tempests will fall. If the Wind proceeds sometimes on the South quarter, and sometimes from the North; And moreover if Birds of the Marshes, and Sea Birds are still washing themselves in the water, it foreshews a Tempest. A double Rainbow is with Rain. Sparkles flying out of Pots or Brass Kettles shew Rain. A Crow washing his head upon the Shore, or entring into the water, or crying much in the night, signifies Rain. Hens basking often in the dust, and craking, and Crows

and

and Choughs coming in flocks, and cawing, and Swallows flying about Lakes or Fish-Ponds, or Rivers, and making a noise, shew Rain. Also Flyes biting hard, and Gees crying for meating, and Spiders without any wind falling down, and the flame of Candles appearing black, and flocks of Sheep jumping and sporting, signifie a Tempest; Oxen looking toward the South, or licking their hoofs, and mowing and going into their Stals, shew Rain. Likewise when the Wolf is so bold as to come near the Houses, and Dogs scrape up the ground, and the Howlet hoops in the morning, and small Birds flye toward the Sea, they signifie Tempests. When Cranes come sooner than ordinary, and make hast, that shews a sudden Tempest. Mice piping signifie showrs. Moreover where many signs come together, there is more certainty. But especially observe, the quarters of the Moon both increasing and decreasing, For these change the motion of the Ayr. *The same.*

The signs of Tempests by the boyling of Sea-water; also what Winter-Thunder shews. Chap. 3.

I have often observed when I passed in a Ship-Boat to some farther part of the Sea, putting my hand into the Salt-water, that the Sea water was luke warm, and that is a sign that there will be a Tempest within three dayes, and the Winds and Floods very violent. For when there hath been a Tempest in the deep Seas that are remote, from whence it cometh to us, the Sea-water moved and troubled grows hot, as our hands are heated clapt together, and these Tempests roule to us, and the Waves rise to a great height. So at the beginning of the Spring, Southern Tempests force out the Grass, that are heated by the beating of the Ayre. Likewise if it Thunder in Winter, and Lighten much, this shews that Tempests will follow, and Whirlwinds, and great inundations. For since that distemper happens contrary to the course of Nature, and the Ayr is thereby troubled, there must needs be some violent cause for it, to move those Tempests; For I never observed any such thing, but the day following horrid Tempests rose, and mighty Rains fell. Thunder and Lightning are usuall in Summer, as also burning Feavers, and if these invade in Winter, and are raised up, it must proceed from some violent cause, which the contrariety of the season could not suppress and hinder. To which that of *Hippocrates* may be referred; Those are sick with less danger, to whom the Disease is more naturall according to their age, custome, or season of the year, than to those, with whom these considerations agree not. *Lemnius.*

Signs that shew that the Winter will last longer. Chap. 4.

The Scarlet Oke or common Oke bearing much fruit, shew that the Winter will continue the longer. And Sheep and Goats being leaped, and desiring to be leapt again, signifie the longer Winter; If flocks of Cattle dig into the Earth, and hold their heads toward the North, they foreshew a fierce Winter. *The same.*

Predictions whether it shall be a forward or backward year. Chap. 5.

It is good to know whether it will be a forward or backward Spring; For it is best to sowe more plentifully with your Seed, where the year will be backward, because some of the Seed will be corrupted in the mean time. If therefore it Rain after the Vintage, before the Pleiades set, it will be a forward year: but if it Rain about the time of their setting, it will be moderate: But if it Rain after they are set, it will be a backward year. *Democritus* and *Apulejus* say, That you must expect such a season, as you find upon St *Brunias* day in the *Roman* Calender, that is upon the twenty fourth day of *November*, which some of the Greeks call *Dios*. Others affirme from a certain Observation, that according to the twenty fourth of *November*, from whence Winter begins, such a season will continue in the following Moneth of *December*, and according as the twenty sixt day of *November* happeneth, so will the season be in *February*. But this happeneth so sometimes, and sometimes not at all. Moreover from observation they say, that from the seaventh day of *March*, untill the fourteenth day of the same Moneth, the Ayr is wont to grow colder: for in those dayes the fourty Martyrs were delivered into the hands of the *Pagans*, and tormented by them, to give testimony to the Christian Faith. *Didymus.*

Ll The

The signs of events from the first Thunder every year after the rising of the Dog-Starr. Chap. 6.

The first Thunder every year that happeneth after the rising of the Dog Starr is to be observed: and you must take notice in what sign of the Zodiac the Moon is then. For if it Thunder when the Moon is in *Aries*, it is a sign that Men shall be frighted and doubtfull, and be much troubled, and flye away, but after that all shall be quiet. If it Thunder, the Moon being in *Taurus*, it signifies corruption of Corn, Wheat and Barley, and abundance of Locusts coming, but joy at the Kings Court: but to those that live Eastward, famine, and penury. If it Thunder in *Gemini*, it shews troubles and diseases, corruption of grain, and of Trees: In *Cancer*, corruption of Barley, and drought, and death of Oxen, but plenty of Rain about *March* and *April*. In *Leo* destruction of Wheat and Barley in Mountain Countries, and Itch and Scabs. In *Virgo* the Kings death, and a stranger to come to Rule, danger to Marriners, and smoot of Corn. In *Libra*, Wars and Plagues, and corruption of fruit. In *Scorpio* hunger, but Birds shall increase. In *Sagittarius* it signifies rising in that Countrey, in Hill Countreys plenty of Corn, but scarsity upon plain Land. In *Capricorn*, it signifies Rain for fifty dayes, and the Kings disgrace and treason, and ill words not fit to be spoken, and the appearing of another King from the East, who shall rule over all the world, there shall be plenty of fruit, and great Men shall dye, but Sheep shall increase. In *Aquarius*, great Wars near the Sea, fruitfullness of other fruits, but Pulse to be scarce. In *Pisces*, some corruption of Corn, and the death of some great Man. *Zoroaster*.

Signs of Rain. Chap. 7.

That indeed is strange to those that know not the cause, that if Rain be not near, the Moths will dance; but if it be near, they are only turned round, for they are not so much affected with the moyst Ayr, and therefore they do not leap forth so much; and for the most part when Rain is at hand, the Ayr is moyst. *Card*.

What foreshews Winds. Chap. 8.

The Sea swelling foreshews Winds, and when it roares much about the Shore, so do the tops of Mountains being clean, also Thorns and dry leaves turned round the contrary way by the Winds. In Summer, which way soever Thunder and Lightning are carryed, from thence you must look for Winds. Which way soever Stars that fall bend, they foreshew Winds to be expected from that quarter. *Zoroaster*.

How to drive away Hail. Chap. 9.

Some say that if you hold a Looking-Glass against the Cloud that hangs over you, the Hayl will pass away: also if you compass the place with the skin of an Hyæna, Crocodile, or Sea Calf, and hang the same up before the Doors of your house, for then the Hail will not fall. Moreover, if you hang the Keys of divers Houses upon a string round that Countrey, the Hail will be gone. Also if you set Woodden Buls in the Houses, it will help much. Also if you hold a lake Snail in your right hand, lying upon his back, with a little earth about him, that he cannot turn himself, and creep away, which he cannot do if the Earth be made hollow under his feet, for when he can find nothing to fasten his feet upon, he must stay where he is, and having done this, no Hail will fall in the Field nor any other place there. Some say that the Snail must be laid so at six a clock in the morning, or six at night. *Apulejus* saith, That at *Rome* a Grape was Painted upon a small Table, and was consecrated in the Vineyard, when *Lyra* set, and so the Grapes were preserved; now *Lyra* begins to set about the tenth of the Calends of *December*, it sets perfectly on the first day of the Nones in *February*, that is on that very day, and this is the tradition from the Ancients. But I think many traditions are very unseemly and to be rejected, and I warn every Man to give no heed to such fopperies: also the pieces of a water Horse skin laid at the severall corners of the Field, hinder and keep off the Hail that threatneth us. *Philostratus*.

Against Thunder. Chap. 10.

Bury a Sea Horse skin in the ground, in that Countrey, and no Thunder will fall there.

Another

Another.

The Bay tree is a remedy against Thunder, as *Pliny* writes. Wherefore the Ancients fearing Thunder, wore a Crown of Bays upon their heads. The same is reported of the Figtree. *Guil. Gratorol.*

Against Tempests. Chap. 11.

In *Apeninus* of *Italy*, between *Bononia* and *Pisa*, when a Tempest riseth the Women run about, and they charm it with a Chees pressed on the day of our Lords Ascention, lifting up their hands, and they make a cross over the Chees, like to a Chrifts-Cross, that is pressed into it, and so they suppose they shall be free from the Tempest; In the same *Apeninus* they keep an Egg shell, out of which a Chicken was hatcht on the Ascention day, and they bind this on the top of the house, and they think that will preserve those Houses from Tempests. Others spreading a Table in the middle of a Chamber, they lay between two burning Wax-Candles a Thunder-Bolt stone, and it will sweat, which seems strange to them; yet it is as naturall as the sweating of Glass Windows at that time, or in Winter, when the Stove is hot. Moreover Tempests will not hurt fields, if beaten Coral be strewed at the four corners of the Field. *Wierus* and *Fallop*.

How a Rainbow may be seen. Chap. 12.

A Rainbow may be seen divers wayes, but the most commodious way is to prepare it of Crystal, or of a stone called Iris, with six Angles like unto Crystal, which the Ancients ever called by that name: which being opposed to the Sun Beams, will make a shadow like to the Rainbow, trembling upon the roof of the Chamber, and upon the floor underneath. For so a Hexagon is made of it; else if you make a Trigonal by Art nine Inches long, and two fingers broad, and then polish and make it all convenient. When therefore you desire to see a Rainbow, take a Crystal or Glass Prisma in your hands, and hold it longwayes to your eyes, if you look upon the inferior superficies, you shall see severall colours, as Purple, Green, Yellow, and Blew: and if you turn your eyes to the uppermost superficies, the situation of the colours is changed, the perpendiculars being changed; and this is seen more clearly in the Sun, and it is no contemptible Observation. If you look upon Gardens you shall see them all distinguished with Tapistry, adorned with Flowers and Crowns, and Men walking like to Angels, and the very hems of their Garments garnished with the same colours: if you hold it the broad way toward your eyes, you shall see the colours the broad way; if you hold it above or under your eyes, you shall see all turned, or upright without any colours, and he that looks upon it will appeare with four eyes, but all bending inward, by reason of the convexity of the eyes, but covering one superficies with Wax, and often turning it before your eyes, you shall see such things that will make you disdaine rather than take pleasure in it. Also we may see the sme thing thus. If the Glass be dipt into a Bason full of water, the diligent looker into it shall see upon the wals, the colours of the Rainbow, and more apparent; Otherwise hold a Glass or some round transparent body against the Sun, sprinkling water on the outside, this being beaten upon by the Sun-Beams, and being reverberated by the clear Ayr upon some plain Subject, will represent a Rainbow by the various reflections of the Sun. So casting water before the Sun by drops, a black superficies being over against it, upon which it may reflect, will make a Rainbow, as it fals ofttimes out with Marriners, by reason of the motion of the water. The same we see frequently about Candles when the South wind blows, and especially those see it that have moyst eyes. *The same.*

To make a flying Dragon. Chap. 13.

There is also an Artificial Invention, which some call a flying Dragon, or a Comet; the way to make it is this. Make a square of the thinnest Reeds, or let the length to the breadth be one and half in proportion, and let there be two Diameters, and let them be set at the opposite parts of Angles, and bind a Cord where they cut one the other, and the like Cord must be tyed with two others proceeding from the ends of the Engine: and so cover this over with Paper, or fine Linnen cloath, that there may be nothing heavy in it, then it must be entrusted to the Wind from high

Towers, Mountains, or tops of high places, when the Winds are equall and uniforme, not too strong least the Engine break; nor too weak, least the Ayr be too calme; for that will not bear it up, and the winds being still, will but make you loose your labour. It must not flye right forward, but obliquely, which is performed by a Cord drawn from one end, and at the other end a long tail, which you shall make of Withs set at equall distance, and Papers every where tied to them, so it must be let go, gently pulling it, by the Artists hands that holds it, who must not be idle and carelels in casting it forth, but he must do it forcibly; and so will this bottome mount up into the Ayr, when it is once a little raised, (for here the wind is broken by reason of the turning of the houses,) that you cannot easily governe it with your hands. Some place a Lanthorn above it, to make it shew like a Comet. Others place a Squib wrapt up with Gunpouder, and when it rests in the Ayr, by the string a burning Match is sent up, by a Ring or some slippery thing, and this presently runing up to the Sail, gives fire to the mouth of it, and with a great Thunder, the Engine breaks into many parts, and fals down upon the ground. Some bind a Cat or Puppy to it, and they hear them cry in the Ayr. Hence an Ingenious Man may begin some Principles, how a Man may learn to flye, with huge wings bound to his Arms and Brest, but he must learn from his Childhood to move them by degrees, alwayes from some higher place. If any one think this to be strange, let him consider what *Archytas* the Pythagorist invented, as the tradition is, for many of the noble Greeks, and *Favorinus* the Phylosopher, the most exquisite for ancient memorable things, have written affirmatively, that *Archytas* made the forme of a Pigeon of Wood, by his Art and Mechanical Industry, that flew up and down, for it was so balanced with weights, and moved with wind that was secretly shut up within it. *The same.*

BOOK. XV.

Of Organick Secrets.

Of the Secrets of Letters, namely how a man may speak secretly. Chap. 1.

How to hide speaking.

VOices may be concealed six wayes: First by absence, and this is the safest way, and if it be not discovered, it cannot be suspected. Then follows mumbling or low speaking, which is unseemly and full of suspition, and ofttimes is the cause of great mischiefs. The third is to speak in a forrain Tongue, as *Greek, Latin, Germane, Italian*; this also breeds suspition and is unseemly. The fourth is by nodding, as Men playing, but this is most ridiculous and unhandsome. The fift is by words that signifie other things, which is most common with Juglers: The *Italians* call this speaking after *Calman*, and this wants long observation: yet if one can do it handsomely there can be no suspition; It is profitable to instruct Children that serve in the house. The sixt is when we speak by cutting off some words, or pieces, this is not rediculous, and becomes a grave Man, because it makes a doubtfull sense, and it is so lawfull that it is familiar in the Writings of great Men. *Card.*

Speaking by Whispering.

Speaking by whispering fals out two wayes, the one is in the Pipes which we both pipe and speak; the voice is made matriculate by the Tongue, it is concealed to those that observe it not, a small is hid under a great, and a shadow under a sound. Those Pipes are made of single Reeds of Wood, with one board hole, set under it, through which we blow: but that is covered all over with a thin membrane, so both the voice and speech resounds. But the other way consists in raysing of voices by equall spaces, whereby severall Letters are signified, and by Letters words, and the whole speech wants only use, but it is no hard matter for those that are accustomed to it. *The same.*

How

Book XV.   *Secrets of VVriting and Coyning.*   267

How when a City is Besieged, one may speak afar off by Torches.

There is another remedy to comunicate your mind when Cities are besieged which is safe and alwayes in a readiness; and they that come to relieve the place or shall come, may understand as much as they that are in the City, and it differs little from a Letter. If therefore the City desires to signifie to him that is sent to enquire, what relief there needs, or to the General that comes to bring help, they must place upon five Towers far distant one from the other that they may be distinguished, five single burning Torches, and all those severall persons that hold them, must have the words in writing before them, which they would have signified, and that it may succeed by Letters which belong to his Torch severally, or two or three holding up that one Torch or more, or holding it down, or bending it to the right hand or to the left, to emply the signification thereof. By the same reason the counsell of the Generall that comes to affoard relief, though there be an Army between, may be understood from a very high Tower, by joyning the Letters together, which the enemies cannot take notice of, though they knew it, because the Torches are held low of those that come to bring help. *Cardan.*

A way how any affairs may be signified to Friends from a besieged City.

Its now time that we give you to understand how that any business may be signified from afar off without a Letter; and that that may be easily performed with a Torch we shall shew. Some will think, as indeed there are, two wayes; the first of which we found described in an old fragment, written by *Polibius*; and a second invented by us, which although they shall seem obscure and lame; yet we shall not think from our business to explain it, and to give so full and compleat instruction of it, that it may appear serviceable. He (I mean *Polibius,*) commanded severall Brass Vessels to be brought, and these long on both sides, and narrow, and deep, either three or four square, and in these as it is wont to be in Lamps, a piece of wood which was put upon the wood of the Torch laid in the vessel, just under this at the bottome of the Vessel the principall matter was to be writ in, *viz. We want Corne; a great Plague in the City; a sedition among the Citizens; the Castle is taken; tomorrow we break forth,* or the like. When this is done, fill the Vessel on both sides with water, and light the Torch, and suffer it to remain lighted a convenient time, at the end of which ye take away the Wood that covered the Torch, which presently sinks to the bottome, and then the water being let out, there remains at the bottome what was writ before, which the other reads. But this way I dare not approve of, because it is very uncertain, hardly shewing what we desire. But besides this he mentions another which is not unconformable to what we mean, which is almost after the same manner. According to his appointment both sides of the said Vessel were to have five little Tables, in each of which so much of the Alphabet as you have here described, and the like Figures so placed as you see underneath. But they that would signifie what they would have, must provide ten Torches lighted, and place five at the right hand, and five at the left. And first of all wave your Torches so long till the others to whom you will signifie, wave again in token of answer, least the beginning should be uncertain; use this Method, first wave with your right according as the number of the Table is, in which the Letter stands, and then with the Torch at your left hand according to the number at which the

Letter

Letter stands in your Table. As for example, I would signifie *Veniemus, viz.* (*we will come*) wherefore for *V.* the first Letter I find in the fourth Table, and the fourth Letter, for which I lift up four Torches at the left hand; and finding it the fourth Letter in that Table, I lift up four Torches on the right hand, which is easie to be understood. Then for *E.* I move one of them at my left hand, and five at the right; for *N.* three at the left, and two at the right : next for *I.* two at the left and four at the right. Again for *E.* one at the left and five at the right : proceeding to *M.* the Table gives me direction to lift three at the left and one at the right : for *V.* four at the left and as many at the right : and less for *S.* four at the left and two at the right. But we from this and the other have drawn another way which is only performed with two Torches to avoid confusion, and trouble. Therefore having appointed two Torches very long ones, that they may be able to declare the whole sentence of the figures, and placed at such a distance according to the distance of them, to which this sign is proposed; as it may be to the distance of four cubits. The sign being given and received on both parties; and the Torches being lighted, or hidden, that the begining may be understood, the left being lifted up signifies one, but it must be lifted up ten cubits, being held so low first before that it may not appear : one inclining to the left, and the other to the right, and you may according to your pleasure order the Letters, as for *A.* you may make *N.* or any other Letter as you shall think fit. You have therefore eight Letters, but you have but four if you move both the Torches together. As for example, lift up *I.* and it is the other hidden signifies *L.* which same Torch being inclined to the left makes *M*, and to the right *N*. Again the left being lift up, and the right kept down makes *O.* which being enclined to the left makes *P.* and to the right *Q.* The left hand being deprest, the right hand will make three other notes, and the left three more, insomuch that the may make up a compleat Alphabet : There remain yet besides these three other differences which are made by the left Torch inclined towards the right, when the right is likewise moved either upwards or downward, or to the left hand. To these we determine 0.1.2. and so it may be repeated 3. 6. 7. that at the second turne it may be constituted from one even to one, and the second constitution will make 9. 18. 27. and so you have it from one to 38. but if you will repeat four signes, the first sign will make 27. the second 54. the third will signifie 81. which will arrive in all to 119. so to the fift place 81. 162. 343. and the whole 462. And thus you see how with only two Torches the whole may be signified in a far more compendious way then the former, and this way you will find ever true, and hardly erronious. But as I told you, in the use of this you must evermore observe to do it in a clear night (I mean without mist) and likewise without Moonshine, a little use will make it every way perfect.

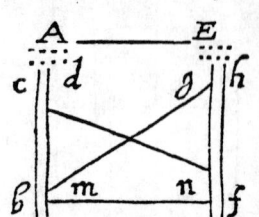

How Letters that cannot be defaced may be written upon Mens bodies.

If you please at any time to write new Figures upon a Man, you may easily do it in a hot house, dividing the uttermost skin with a Razor, or a Lancet, first marking the Letter with Inke upon the skin; then fill up the cuts with red Lead, or blew, or with some Earth of the same colour which you would have it ; and presently the colour being contracted by heat, the skin will grow into that forme. Another was as I learned by experiment without a Stove. Let Cantharides be infused twenty four houres in water that parts Gold, then with a fine Pen make Letters or any forme you please, upon the skin, that you leave some prints of the water, and presently white blisters will arise in those places where the water came : when these are broken and grown whole again in one day, a white mark for ever will be there; and it will not be taken off, unless by force, and it will exactly represent what was written there. *Cardan.*

That Letters may be white where the pattern is black.

If we would have white Letters in a black Pattern, there is a more secret way to express our minds. Beat the yelk and white of an Egge well, that it may be like to writing Inke; make Letters or descriptions with it, when they are dryed, rub over

the

the Paper with a black colour, and stain it therewith; but when the Letters are covered with these shadowes, if you gently scrape them with a broad Iron or a Knife, they will break through their dark vail as through clouds, and will be exceeding white. *The same.*

The way to write in an Egge.

Grind Alum very fine a long time with Vinegar, and draw what forme you will upon the Egg-shell, drying it in the hot Sun, put it three or four dayes in Brine or sharp Vinegar, when it is dryed, rost it, when it is rosted take off the shell, and you shall find the Letters written upon the hard white. Hence ariseth another, you must wrap the Egge in Wax, and with a Pin make Letters upon the Wax, where the Letters are, fill it up with moysture, and let it steep in Vinegar twenty four houres, take off the Wax, and the shell after that, and you shall read the Letters upon the Egge. *Aphrican.*

How to make Letters that lye hid appear, and to hide those that are visible.

If you desire that Letters that lye hid may be seen, and those that are seen may be hid, you may do it by the distilled liquor of Vitriol, or *Aqua fortis* poured on, untill it be dissolved; and therewith make Letters upon the Paper, for when they are dry they are Engraven: Moreover you shall grind burnt Straw with Vinegar, and what you will write, let it be written between the former Verses writing at large; then boyl sour Gals in white Wine, and rub the Letters gently with a Spunge wet in this liquor, when it is boyld as it ought to be, the naturall black colour will lye hid, and be extinguished, but the former colour that was invisible being rubbed up, will be very apparent. *The same.*

How to conceal writings.

Dissolve so much Copperas in water, that scarce any print of black may appear in writing; when this is dryed, write upon the same words and the same dashes, other words with Rain-water, and coles of Willow made thick; which will be like to true Ink. When it is dryed, and soked in, and you desire to read it, boyl Gals in water, and dipping a Sponge therein and pressing it forth again, rub over the Epistle newly written, that neither the cole nor any drop nor Gals may stick to it, the former writing will shew it self with the colour of the Gall, and will stick fast to the Paper, and be apparent. *Cardan.*

Letters rising suddenly in any place.

You shall make black Letters, and coloured that shall immediately come forth, upon any place, if you write upon your hands or elsewhere secretly with Vinegar or Piss, for when they are dry, there is nothing to be seen; and if you would have them to be read, rub them over with Soot, or some colour that is sold abundantly in Painters Shops, and the Letters will be exceeding black; if you would have them to be white upon Paper, write them with Figs milk, and when they are dry strew cole dust upon them, and rub them. *The same.*

Letters that will be made visible by fire or water.

You may thus make Letters visible by fire or water, writing Letters between the Verses, and the severall distances of Lines. Let your Letter contain what you please, that he that sees it may think it was written at randome, and if it be intercepted, he shall understand nothing or very hardly any thing of it. If you write with the juyce of a Lemmon, Orange, Onyon, or any sharp thing almost, if you heat it at the fire, their sharpness will presently discover them; It is some thing more curious to write with Alum dissolved in water; and when it is to be read, it must be dipt in water, and the Letters will be very visible and curious, but if you would have them white as milk do thus: first grind Lytharge and put it into an Earthen vessel with water and Vinegar, boyl it and strain it, keep this, then with juyce of *Lemmons* of the Citron kind, write Letters, and when they are dry they will be hid, if you dip them in the liquor you kept, you shall see them white as milk: If Womens Brests or hands be wet therewith, and the foresaid liquor be sprinkled upon it, they will be white as milk, use this if at any time you have need of it. So Letters written with Goats Suet, upon a stone, that they are scarce to be seen, if you dip the stone in Vinegar

negar will appear presently, as if they were Engraven. But if you write with water only, and would have the Letters appear, that we may more readily provide for a Journey, pouder Gals and Copras very fine, and strew the pouder upon Paper, rub it with a Cloath, and polish it well, and it will be like the Paper, and stick fast; bruise Juniper Gum, the Painters call Vernish, and add that to the other. When you would use it, write upon it with Water or Spittle, and the Letters will be black. *The same.*

Letters not to be read but in the night.

Letters that are not to be read but in the night, must be written with the Gall of a Tortois, or Fig milk, if you put it to dry at the fire, or else write Water of Glow-Wormes. *Albertus.*

The way to read Letters that are concealed upon the Paper.

There being three sorts of things wherewith Letters may be written and lye hid, and imperfect; either because something is wanting, as for want of Sope, Ashes, or Coles : or else it is written with Water, Gum Arabick, Coperas, or by something perspicuous, as Alum, (for in Water it will appear white,) or from density; as things written with salt Armoniac, for the fire condenseth them : It is necessary that he who would make tryal of it, must look through a Paper annointed with Oyl, against the Sun, or dip it into the water, or hold it against the fire, and strew Coperas beaten upon it. *Cardan.*

That Letters at set times shall decay and vanish away.

How doth it exceed the wit of Man to open the Secrets of nature? Infuse Steel pouder in water of separation, three parts, and add to it the Soot of melted Pitch, or of Turpentine, that it may be more black, and cover the vessel, grind it well on a Marble, write, and when the Letters are old they will vanish. I thought not fit to conceal this, and the chief of the business is to make tryall of it often : for if it stay long on the Paper, you must add some more *Aqua fortis* to it, and if you be carefull, no prints of any yellow will remain, let this be your rule. There is another way like to this, if it be better to counterfeit so : Take Chrysocolla, salt Armoniac, and Alum equall parts, pouder them all, and put them into an Earthen Pot, and make a strong Lee with Lime, and lay a Linnen Cloath over the mouth of the vessel and strain it in ; so let it boyl a while, mingle it with Ink, and when you write Letters, they will last a certain time, but after that they will vanish away, keep this for your use. *The same.*

A way to take off Letters.

Mingle white Lead in Summer with Fig milk, and make little Cakes of it; dry them in the shade, and grind them, do this four times, and then keep it; when you have need wet the Letters gently, and strew on that pouder that it may stick every where, let it lye on twelve houres, rub it with a thin somewhat rugged Cloath, wherein you must wind up some Cotton. *Cardan.*

How to blot out Letters.

Take common Salt, Rock Salt, Roch Alum, of each two ounces, salt Armoniac four ounces, mingle and distill them according to Art. Letters moystned with this water will vanish. *Fallopius.*

To blot Letters quite out.

But if you seek how to take Letters quite away, or blots or spots; write with water of Coperas, and Saltpeter with a Pen upon the Letters, or rub them with Salt Alkali, and Brimstone made into small Pellets, and this will eat them quite out. *The same.*

How to write Letters upon Stones.

If you would with ease write upon a Flint; rub it all over with Wax, and then Engrave upon it what you please, but the Wax must be perfectly scraped away to the Flint, that the Flint may be seen : then steep the stone seven houres in the sharpest Vinegar, and take it out again, and if it stay longer in, the crust will sooner fall off; For it fals out almost as in Mens bodies, when Causticks are applyed; for the long stay in Vinegar supplies the place of a stronger Medicament, and the quantity of of Vinegar it is steeped in. For it dryeth and penetrateth; whence the stone must needs yield; and it is evident that this will serve for other stones that are not much harder. *Cardan.*

To blot out Letters.

You shall easily take off Letters thus: Take the flesh of a Hare, dry it, and pouder it, and mix it with Quick-lime, and lay it upon the Letters, and rub it on, and in three dayes no Letter will be seen. *Out of a very old Book.* Mizaldus.

How to make up Letters, that they cannot be privately opened.

The way to make up Letters well and seal them, is both usefull and necessary. If then you have a Seal, before you lay on Wax, cut the place under it into many small pieces, if you then drop on Wax, it cannot be taken off by any Art, but the Paper must be broken: therefore the fraud will be discovered on the contrary side when the Letter is opened. If there be no Seal, on the other side the part *A. D.* must be divided with a Rule and a Point; when therefore it is folded, the part *A. D.* will stick to the Letter, (which must be long and right Angled) by two incisions, one that toucheth *A.* and the other must be brought very near to it, to the other side of the Epistle by *B.* then it must be brought back again by *C.* and lastly the part being cut, and made sharp, the part with a point *E.* must be reduced again, under *B. C.* from *B.* to *C.* so that the part that covers *B. C.* must be square, and not sharp: then on the contrary side the part that is equall and like to the leaves, must be cut off exactly, which is *A. D.* so will the parts be like on both sides, and no man can easily find how it is made up; also the Inscription must be made on both sides upon the place that is fastned. *Cardan.*

How a Letter is to be opened secretly.

Some use to open Letters Sealed with a hair of a Horse tail, but they first warme the Wax a little, this business requires skill, and agility of the hands and judgment: you must restore it just against the former place, least by often Sealing, the situation being changed should discover the fraud. Otherwise annoint the place of the Seal, and then pour upon it very fine Gyp with water, and a little Fish Glew, or Gum Arabick; let it harden and so you shall have a false Seal. *The same.*

That Letters may not be burnt.

That Letters may not be burnt, take the sharpest Vinegar, and whites of Eggs, and mingle and beat Quicksilver therewith, wet the Paper thrice with this mixture, and dry it as often; Then write upon it what you please, and cast it into the fire, and it will leap forth and never burn. *Out of an old Book.*

To defend Letters from Mice.

Temper your writing Ink with Wormwood water infused, and this will keep your Letters from Mice, as the herb will keep off Moths from your Cloathes. *Dioscorides.*

That white Letters may be read.

Salt Armoniac poudred and mingled with water, will make white Letters no what different from the Paper; but hold them to the fire, and they will be black. Thus things written with pouder of Alum, will not appear, unless when you will read them, you dip the Paper into water. *Mizald.*

A Lacedemonian Writing-Staff.

They had two round Staves, that were well polished and equall exactly, and in Paper they wrapt up one as in a Screw, and equally from top to the bottome, so that none of the Wood might be seen, then at both ends they cut off the heads that were not covered after that fashion you see here on the side; The Generall took one of these Staves, and the other was left in the City, when there was need to write a Letter, they wrapt the Paper about the Staff, as I said, fastning it at both ends, and also in the middle in certain places with Wax; then they writ what they pleased: and then pulling the Paper off from the Staff, they sent it for a Letter. *Cardan.*

To make Letters visible in water.

Write with Water wherein Alum is dissolved, and when you would read it, dip the Letter into the water, and the writing will be very legible. *Alexius.*

That white Letters may grow black suddenly.

Write upon your hands secretly with Vinegar or Piss, or upon some other part; when the Writing is dryed and nothing to be seen, rub it over with Soot or colouring which is sold plentifully in the Painters Shops, and it will be very black; if you would have the Letters white, write upon the Paper with Figtree milk, dry it, and rub it over with Charcole pouder, and make it smooth. *The same.*

The best way to make Ink.

Take the best Galls cut into three or four pieces or gently bruised, as much as you please, and when they are fryed awhile in a little Oyl, put them into a glazed Pot, pouring upon them so much white Wine that it may swim above them three or four fingers breadth; Then add Gum Arabick beaten half a pound, Coperas beaten eight ounces, mingle them and set them in the Sun for some dayes, stirring them daily. After this when they are a little boyld, as much as is needfull, strain it, and it will be perfect. But to the dregs that are left, you may pour on fresh Wine, boyl and strain it, and this may be done so often, untill the Wine takes no more Tincture from the dregs. These Wines being mingled, add Galls thereto, Gum and fresh Coperas, as before; then setting them in the Sun, and boyling them again, it will be much better than before. For the oftner you do these things, the Ink is made better; and if the Ink should be too thick, add a little of the Lixivium to it, and it will be thinner. But if it be too thin, add a little Gum Arabick. The Galls must be small, curled, and hard, as the Coperas must be blew, and the Gum must be clear and brittle. *Alexius.*

Powder of Ink that one may carry in a Journey: so it be mingled with Wine or Water; also this pouder makes Ink the better.

Take Peach Kernels, or of Apricots, or of Almonds, and make them red fire hot, take them away and keep them; This being done, take Rosin of the Pitch Tree what is sufficient, put it into some Vessel or Pot over the fire, and with a Candle or Cole fire make it hot, then cover it with some cover, that the smoke may breath forth, and not be put out, but be very well received: when the Rosin is quite consumed, and the Vessel cold, wipe off the smoke that sticks upon the cover, and keep it. If any one would not wast so much time to provide this smoke, let him buy it of them that make Printers Ink. Take of this smoke one part, and of the pouder of the burnt Kernels two parts, Coperas one part, firyed Galls, as I said before, one part, Gum Arabick four parts. Pounder and sift them, and mingle them, and keep this Pouder in Leather. When you would use it, take a little of this pouder, and put a little Water to it, or Wine, or Vineger, mingle them well and use it. And thus you have Ink presently, that every one may carry about him, and not fear spilling of it; and if you put this pouder to bad Ink, it will make it most perfect. *The same.*

Ink easie to provide, and at no great charge, and it is not only fit to write with, but also for Printing of Books.

Take of that colour they dye Hides with, as much as you please, Gall of a Cuttle what is sufficient, mingle them for Writing Ink. But if you would make it better, add the foresaid pouder of those Coles, Vitriol, Galls and Gum: you may add a little Vernish or Oyl of Linseed to it, to make it hold together the better, and be more moyst. Moreover Ink to Print Books with, is made only of the smoke of Rosin, as I said before, adding liquid Vernish what is sufficient, and boyling it a little, and so make your Ink thicker or thinner as you will; for in Winter it must be moyster, and in Summer faster. If you would make it thinner, add more of Oyl of Linseed, but if thicker, less Oyl and more Soot, and boyl it better. But the harder Ink makes the finer Letters. If you will make red Ink, for smoke, take Cinnaber finely poudred; if green, take flower of Brass called Verdigrease; if blew, as they did a few years since, take *Germane* blew, or Glass Emmil, to be had at *Venice.*

Do the rest as I said for common Ink. *The same.*

Perpetuall Ink.

Artists call that perpetual colour *Stuchum*, with which chiefly Letters are written upon Sepulchres, the Letters being first Carved in the Marble. It is made of the smoke of Oyl of Linseed, and Ship Pitch mingled. For the blackness of that smoke never changeth, nor is the Pitch corrupted by Water or Wind. *Cardan.*

Red Writing Ink.

Take Brasil Wood cut small one ounce, white Lead, Alum, of each two drams, grind and mingle them; pour on Piss as much as will cover them, let them stand so three dayes, stirring them three or four times a day: then strain it through a linnen Cloath, and put it into some Glazed Vessel, or a Mortar, and dry it in some place out of the Sun and Wind, and keep it. When you would write with it, temper it with Gum water. *The same.*

A water that rubs out the Letters or blots upon Paper.

Take white Lead the best, finely poudred, Fig-Tree Milk, of each what is sufficient. Mingle them into a lump, when it is dryed, wet it again in Milk, do so six times, and pouder it; when you would take off Ink or Letters from the Paper, take a Linnen Cloath wet in water, and crush it forth again, and touch the Ink or Letters with it untill they be wet: and that being done, strew on the foresaid pouder, and let it lye so for one night, in the morning, rub it gently with some dry Cloath of Linnen, and the Paper will be very white, and fit to write upon. If the Ink be not out, do it again, and then it will be gone. If the Paper grow too thin by rubbing, it must be made thicker with Glew, that Joyners use to joyn Wood, being a little melted, and some white Lead, or Wheat flower must be mingled therewith. *The same.*

For Golden Letters.

To write with Golden Letters, take Saffron and Orpiment of each a like quantity, make them wet with Goats Gall, and leave it buried under Horse dung so long that it be grown thick, Write or Paint with this; you may do the same with two drams of Aloes, and as much Saffron, and those being finely poudred, mix them with the white of an Egg, and beat them very well. *Out of certain Painters experience.* Mizald.

Othermise for Golden Letters.

Take Orpiment, Cryftall, of each one ounce, make them severally into pouder, mingle them with the white of an Egg, and make a liquor to write. *Alexius.*

For Silver Letters.

You shall without Silver make Silver Letters thus; Take the best Tin one ounce, Quickfilver two ounces, mingle them and melt them, then grind them with Gum water, and make your Letters with that. *Mizald.*

A green colour to write.

Take Verdigrease, Litharg, Quickfilver, of each what is sufficient, grind them, and mingle them together with a young Boys Piss, and you shall have a most beautifull colour like to an Emrald, not only to Paint but also to Write. *Alexius.*

For green Letters.

You shall make green Letters thus: Take Rue leaves, press forth the juyce, add a little Verdigrease and Saffron, grind them, and when you will use them, mix them with Gum water, and Write. *Mizald. Alexius.*

A green liquor to Write and to Paint.

Take Verdigrease, as much as is needfull, put it into Vinegar to dissolve: then strain it through a fine Cloath; when you have done that, grind it on a Porphyr stone, very well with common water, adding a little Honey; when it is well dryed, grind it again upon a Porphyr stone, with Gum water, and you have done. *The same.*

To prepare blew Ink.

Blew must be ground with Honey as Verdigrease was, but it must not be strained; but it must be tempred with the white of an Egg beaten, or Gum water, and this

Gum is made of Isinglass, melted and strained as you do with Gums.

To prepare Cinnaber.

When Cinnaber is well ground with common water upon a Porphyr stone, and then dryed, you must put it into some bone or Glass Vessel, and pour Piss upon it, and let it stand awhile for the matter will fall to the bottome; after this pour off the Piss gently, and pour on fresh, when you have done this eight or ten times, it will be very well purged: Then take the whites of Eggs very well beaten, and it will dissolve into clear water: pour this water upon the Vermilion, that it may swim a fingers breadth above it, and beat them again well together; when it setleth after this, pour off the whites of Eggs gently, and pour on fresh, and do as you did with the Urine, and this done only that the stinking smell of the Piss may be taken from it: Then add whites of Eggs a fresh, mingle them well, keep the Liquor in some close Vessel: when you will use this, stir it with a stick and it will keep very long uncorrupted. *The same.*

A Liquor to Write that shall be whiter than the Paper, and shall be very legible.

Take whites of Eggs very well washed, and grind them well upon a Porphyr Marble stone with water: then put them into a Dish, and let them stand untill the matter sink to the bottome; then take away the water gently, and let the matter dry of it self or in the Sun, and keep it; when you will use it, take Ammoniacum, paring away the yellow skin, as much as is needfull, lay it into distilled Vinegar one night untill it be dissolved: then strain it, and add to it some of the foresaid pouder, and you have the whitest liquor that is to Write and to Paint with; A chief Woman of *Italy* useth this liquor to beautifie her face, because it hurteth neither skin nor Teeth, and makes the face so white that you would think it not Painted but naturall. But if you will use it for your face, the liquor must be more clear and thin, that it may penetrate and hold on the better. But if for this purpose you add a little burnt Lime it will be the better. *The same.*

The way to prepare Vernish, to make Paper or Parchment smooth, that we Write upon, which is better and fairer then we use commonly, nor doth it smell so ill as the common vernish doth.

The Vernish Writers use for Books, is Gum of Juniper beaten to pouder; Also of this Gum boyld with Linseed Oyl, is made liquid Vernish. Scriveners use the foresaid Vernish poudred, that the Paper may receive the Ink better, and it may not spread. But if you would provide better and far less cost, take Egg shels cleansed and finely bruised, and set them in a Crucible well stopt, into a Potters or Glassmaker Furnace, so long untill they be well calcined to Ashes, then sift them, and make a most white pouder. When you will use it, put a little of it upon Paper, and with a Hares foot spread it here and there, and wipe away what is superfluous, and it will be excellent to write withall. But if when you have written and dryed it, you desire to take away the pouder, rub it with a little crums of Bread, and it will fetch it all off. *The same.*

The way to make white Table-Books, to blot out, and to Write upon with a Brass Pin, such as are made in Germany.

Take clean sifted Gyp, what will serve your turn, and dissolve it with Harts Glew or with some other Glew; When it is dry, and polished, and scraped, it will be clear, then dissolve it again, and scrape it as you did at first; then take Cerus, poudred very fine and sifted, what may suffice; mingle it with Linseed Oyl boyled, and make an Unguent to annoint your Tables: When they are well smeered, dry them in the shade five or six dayes, then with some Cloath dipt in water, and pressed forth again: polish your Tables, and let them remain so fifteen or twenty dayes, untill they be well dryed, and then use them to write upon, and to wipe out again what you have Written. *The same.*

How Books may be Guilded.

Take Bole Armoniac as big as a Nut, Sugar Candy as big as a Pease: grind them together

together into most fine pouder : then add whites of Eggs, and mingle them well and beat them; Then take a Book well bound, and under the press smeered with whites of Eggs, when this is dry, smeer it with the foresaid composition, let it be well dryed, and rub it to polish it, and to make it smooth : when you would lay on the Gold, first moysten them with common Water : then suddenly laying on the Gold, press it gently with Silk, when they are dryed, polish it well with a Tooth, and with a cold Iron make impressions. *The same.*

BOOK. XVI.

Of the Secrets of Sciences.

have finished the Secrets of Arts in the precedent Book, which we make use of as Instruments to learn divers Arts and Sciences; Now it remains, that having finished the Instruments, we fall to the Sciences and Arts themselves, and Expound those things which we suppose to be Secrets in them. Now Sciences are either Physical, Metaphysical, Mathematical, or Moral; I have before in many places spoken concerning Physical Science, concerning the rest we shall prosecute some things in this Book. Wherefore Metaphysical Science comprehends under it what may be said concerning God, and concerning the Angels both good and bad. I have done something concerning God and the Angels before in the first and second Book. But here I shall handle this Subject by a high Metaphysical way. For before I only propounded the bare knowledge of God and the Angels, not as it was to be referred to any operation or effect that proceeds therefrom, which I shall now dispatch in a few words, that here I may seem to deliver the forme, and before nothing but the matter. For I shall not here expound what God is, or how many Persons there are in the divine Nature, or what the Angles are; but how God being known to us is to be applyed by us, and the good Angels are to be gaind to favour us, the evill are to be driven away far from us, for by this meanes we shall obtain all good things, that this deservedly ought to be accounted the principle part of Secrets.

How we may bind evill Spirits. Chap. 1.

Since therefore there is no reason why we should make the good Angels subject to our wils, we must Covenant with the evill Spirits, and because we cannot move those above, we will move those that are beneath. The Magick Art is easily learned, for if the Devil find you love him, and desire it, he will soon teach you it. But there are divers Instruments in the Magick Art which the Devil applies himself unto; as a Circle, divers Characters, Names, Plants, Roots, Unguents, Glasses, Rings: but to let pass the rest. The ignorant people are deceived hereby, that they suppose some divine virtue to be in these things, when as there is nothing less. For the Devil as *Wierus* well maintains, is not so much delighted with any Signs, Characters, Words, or Creatures, as if he could be enticed like a Dog with a piece of Bread; nor can any thing offend him so much as to make him flye. But this virtue is in these Characters, Signs and Letters, Names, Imprications, Herbs, Roots, and the like, only by accident, that the Spirits may be called forth and commanded, that is, they will be bound this way, that they may bind many souls, and lead them away captive.

The preparation to the Magick Art is sevenfold. Chap. 2.

The first is, That a Man meditate day and nigh, how he may arise to the true knowledg of God : both by the revealed Word from the first beginning of the Creation, and also to ascend by the scale of the Creation and Creatures, and by the admirable effects done by the Creatures visible and invisible which God hath made. Secondly, It is requisite that a Man should descend into himself, and study to know himself exactly, what he hath mortal in him, and what immortal, and what is proper to every part, and what differs from it. Thirdly, To learn by his immortal part, to worship, love, and fear God, and to adore him in spirit and truth : and to

do

do that with his mortal part, which he knows to be pleasing to God, and profitable for his Neighbour. These are the three highest and first principles of Magick, by which whoever provides himself to attain and long after true and divine Wisdome, thereby he may be accounted worthy for Angels to do him service, not only secretly but openly and face to face. Fourthly, Since from his Mothers Womb every one is destinated to some course of life he shall follow and labour in, every man must first know whether he be fit to learn Magick, and what kind of Magick: which every Man will perceive that reads these things of ours, and understand them easily, and he shall find the successes of it, if he make tryal. For only to Babes and humble minds doth God give such great gifts of this kind. Fiftly, A Man must marke whether he manifestly perceive the Spirits assisting him, when he undertakes great businesses. If he find this, it is plain that by Gods Ordinance he was ordained for a Magician, that is, to be such a Person whom God employes by the Ministration of the Spirits, to performe such things. Here, for the most part Men sin either by negligence or ignorance, or contempt, or too much superstition. Also Men sin by Ingratitude against God, whereby many famous Men have afterwards ruind themselves. Men sin also by rashness and frowardness; and sometimes when the gifts of God are not had in so great esteem, as is required, nor are preferred before things less necessary. Sixtly, He that will be a Magician must have belief and silence, especially that he reveal no secret, that the Spirit forbids him, as it was with *Daniel*. This must be concealed, and not blabd about: So St. *Paul* had no liberty to reveal what he saw in a Revelation. No Man would imagine how much is contain'd in this one Precept. Seventhly, He that will be a Magician must be exceeding just; that is, he must undertake nothing that is wicked, unjust, or unlawfull, no not so much as to think of it, and so he shall be protected from above from all evill. Moreover when he perceives any Spirit working about him, either by his outward or inward senses, he must afterwards govern himself according to these seven following Rules, that he may obtain his Magicall end. The first Rule is, That he must know how that God hath appointed him such a Spirit, and let him think that he hath one that is a supervisor of all his actions, and imaginations; wherefore let him lead his whole life according to the Rule prescribed in the Word of God. Secondly, Let him alwayes pray with *David*; *Take not thy holy Spirit from me, and strengthen me with thy free Spirit; And lead us not into temptation, but deliver us from evill. O Heavenly Father, give no power to a lying Spirit, as thou didst over Abab, that he might perish, but preserve me in thy truth.* Amen. Thirdly, Let a Man exercise himself to try the Spirits, as the Scripture admonisheth us: for Grapes are not gathered from Thorns; Let us try all and hold what is good, flying from what resists the Will of God. The fourth is, That we be very far removed from superstition. Now it is superstition here, to ascribe Divinity to things wherein there is nothing that is Divine: or else to go about to worship God with a worship of our own fancying, without a command from God; Such are all the Magical Ceremonies of Satan, who will impudently be adored as God. Fiftly, We must flye from Idolatry, which of its own disposition ascribes Divine power to Idols, or other things, which were not so ordered by the Creator or the Law of Nature, as your wicked Conjurers fain many such things. Sixtly, We must flye from the cunning fraudulent wicked imitation of God in the work of the Creation, and of his Power, to do as he did, and to produce things by words, which are no causes of them, for that is proper only to God the Creator who is Omnipotent, and is not communicated to any Creature. Seventhly, We must rest upon the gifts of God, and of the holy Ghost, that we may be diligent to know them, and adorne them with all our power and with all our strength. *Out of the Magick of the Ancients.*

Of Magick in Generall. Chap. 2.

There are many wayes wherewith Magicians allure the Devils; how to contract them into a few, I think fit to refer to this place, what *Cornelius Agrippa* hath written concerning severall kinds of Magick, in his declamation concerning the vanity of Sciences, and excellency of Gods Word; saith he, here it is requisite to speak of Magick;

Magick, for it is joyned and Cousin-german to Astrology; for he that professeth Magick without Astronomy, he doth nothing but run into errors. *Suidas* thinks that Magick had its name and original from the Magusæi, the common opinion is, that it is a *Persian* word, and *Porphyrius* and *Apuleius* confirme it, and that it signifies in that Tongue a Priest, a Wiseman, or a Philosopher. Magick then comprehends all Phylosophy, Physick, Mathematicks, and the force of Religion is to be annexed unto them. It contains *Goetia* and *Theurgia*, which are severall sorts of divination; Wherefore many divide Magick two wayes, namely into naturall and ceremoniall Magick. *Agrippa*.

Of natural Magick. Chap. 4.

Some say that naturall Magick is nothing else but a high power of Naturall Sciences, which therefore they call the top point of naturall Phylosophy, and the compleat accomplishment of it, and which is the active part of naturall Science, which by the help of naturall virtues, and by a mutuall and convenient application of them performes things beyond admiration. The *Ægyptian* and *Indians* did chiefly use this Magick, where there was a faculty of Herbs and stones and other things that was proper for this use. They say that *Hierom ad Paulinum*, makes mention of it, where he saith that *Appolonius Tyanæus* was a Magician, or a Philosopher, as the *Pythagoreans* were. And of that sort were the Wisemen that came with gifts to adore our Saviour Christ, which the *Chaldæe* Interpreters of the Gospel expound Philosophers of the *Chaldeans*. Such was *Hiarchas* amongst the *Brachmanæ*, *Thespion* amongst the *Gymnosophists*, *Budda* with the *Babylonians*, *Numa Pompilius* with the *Romans*, *Zamolxides* with the *Thracians*, *Abbaris* with the *Hyperborei*, *Hermes* with the *Ægyptians*, *Zoroastes* son of *Oromasus* with the *Persians*. For the *Indians*, *Æthiopians*, *Chaldeans* and *Persians* most excelled in this Art of Magick: and therefore (as *Plato* hath it in his *Alcibiades*,) Kings Sons were bred up in it, that according to the pattern of the worlds government, they also might learn to governe their Kingdoms. And *Tully* saith in his Books of Divination, that no man comes to be King amongst the *Persians* before he have learned the Art Magick. Wherefore naturall Magick is that which contemplates the forces of all naturall and celestiall things, and searcheth out by curious enquiry the sympathy of them, and so brings to light the secret powers of nature: so coupling the Inferiours with the forces of the Superiours, as by certain charms, by the mutuall application of them one to another, that from thence there arise wonderfull miracles, not so much from Art as from Nature, and Art only ministers to Nature performing these things. For Magicians are most accurate searchers of Nature, conducting those things that are prepared by nature, applying Actives to Passives, and so ofttimes produce the effects before it is determined by Nature, which Vulgar people think to be Miracles, when they are but naturall operations, only the time is prevented: as if one should produce Roses in *March*, and ripe Grapes, or Beans, or make Parsly grow to perfection in a few houres, and greater things than these; as Clouds, Rain, Thunder, and Creatures of severall kinds, and many transmutations of things, which *Roger Bacon* boasts he made many by pure and naturall Magick. These have written of the operations of it, *Zoroastes*, *Hermes*, *Evanthes* King of the *Arabians*, *Zacharias*, *Babylonius*, *Joseph* an *Hebrew*, *Borus*, *Aron*, *Zenotenus*, *Kirannides*, *Almadal*, *Thetel*, *Alcindus*, *Abel*, *Ptolomæus*, *Geber*, *Zahel*, *Naxabarub*, *Tebith*, *Berith*, *Salomon*, *Astaphon*, *Hipparcus*, *Alcmæon*, *Apollonius*, *Triphon*, and many more, of whom some of their Writings are yet entire, and there are fragments of the other which sometimes came to my hands. Few of the later times have Written of naturall Magick, and they but a few things, as *Albertus*, *Arnoldus de villa nova*, *Raymundus Lullius*, *Bachon*, *Apponus*, and the Author of the Book to *Alphonsus*, set forth under the name of *Peccatrix*, who notwithstanding together with naturall Magick mingleth much superstition, as also the rest have done. *The same*.

Of Mathematicall Magick. Chap. 5.

There are also other very wise Imitators of Nature, and bold Inquisitors, who without naturall virtues, only by Mathematical Arts, do promise to call in the influences

ences of the Heavens, and thereby to produce works like unto nature, as bodies going or speaking that have no naturall virtues. Such was *Architas* his wodden Pigeon, which flew, and *Mercuries* statue that spake, and the Brass head made by *Albertus Magnus*, which is reported to have spoken. *Boetius* a Man of excellent judgment was surpassing in these things, a very learned Man to whom *Cassiadorus* writes thus about it. Thou saist he hast a design to know high matters, and to work miracles. Metals roar by the skill of thy Art, and make a greater noise then in *Diomedes* Tower, a Brazen Serpent hisseth: Birds are counterfeited, and those that have no voice of their own, sing sweetly: I can say little of him who imitated Heaven, I think that is spoken of these Artificiall things which we read in *Plato, Lib. 11. de Legibus*. Art is given to mortall Men, that they should produce some things afterwards, not that are partakers of truth, and of Divinity as it were, but some Images like to them, and Magicians, bold Fellows have proceeded so far as to attempt upon any thing, that old and strong Serpent being their greatest helper who promiseth knowledg, that they like Apes strive to imitate God and Nature. *The same.*

Of Inchanting Magick. Chap. 6.

There is also another sort of naturall Magick which Men call Witchcraft; which is performed by Cups, love Potions, and many Bewitching Medicaments, such as *Democritus* is said to have made, that Sons good and succesfull might be begotten: and another how to understand rightly the voices of Birds, as *Philostratus* and *Porphyrius* say of *Apolonius*. Also *Virgil* speaks thus of some of *Pontus*:

> *With these I saw Maris a Wolf be made*
> *And souls from Graves to rise, and to invade,*
> *Corn that was sown, and carry it from thence*
> *Unto some other place.* ———

And *Pliny* reports that one *Demarchus* a Parasite, in sacrifice which the *Arcadians* made to *Jupiter Lycaus*, of Men, eat the guts of a Child, and turned himself into a Wolf: for which cause St. *Augustine* thinks, that from the changing of Men to Wolves, *Pan Lycaus* and *Juniper Lycaus* had their names given them. The same St. *Augustine* relates, That whilst he was in *Italy* some Women-Witches, like to *Circes*, giving an Inchanting Medicament to strangers in Cheese, did convert them to Horses, and when they had carried such burdens for them as they pleased, then would they convert them into Men again, and that this thing befell at that time one Father *Praestantius*: But that no Man may think these things to be madness and impossible, let them remember what the Scripture saith of King *Nabuchadonozer*, changed into an Ox, and to have fed upon Grass seven years, and at last by Gods mercy to have been made a Man again: whose body after his death his Son *Evilmerodat* gave to Vulturs to be devoured by them, least he should rise again from death, who so lately had from a Beast become a Man again. *Exodus* speaks many more such things of the Magicians of *Paraoh*, but of those, whether they were Magicians or Enchanters the Wiseman speaks thus, *Thou O Lord didst abhor them, because they did by their sorceries work terrible things in thy sight.* Moreover I would have you to know this, that these Magicians did not only search out things naturall, but also such things as accompany Nature, and do after a sort forsake it, as motion, numbers, figures, sounds, voices, consents, lights, and the affections of the soul, and words. So the *Psylli*, and the *Marsi*, called Serpents, and others by other means treading them down, did drive them away: So *Orpheus* by Musick allaid a Tempest for the *Argonants*: and *Homer* saith that *Ulisses* had his bloud stopt by words; and in the Laws of the twelve Tables there was a punishment inflicted upon them who had used any Enchantment upon Corn in the Fields; that there is no question but Magicians by words only, and affections, and such means, did produce some wonderfull effect, not only in themselves, but upon other things: All which things they supposed did not otherwise infuse an imbred force into other matters, and draw them unto them, or drive them from them, than the Loadstone doth Iron, and Amber Chaff, or as the Diamond and Garlick hinder the Loadstones operations, and so by this graduary concatenation and

Sympathy

Sympathy of things. *Jamblichus, Proclus,* and *Synesius* confirme from the opinion of Magicians, that not only naturall and celestiall gifts, but, also intellectuall and divine gifts may be acquired; which *Proclus* in his Book of Sacrifices, and Magicians confesseth, namely, that the Sympathy of these things, the Magicians were wont to call forth Spirits. For some of them proceeded so far in this madness, as to suppose that by divers constellations of Stars, and intervals of times, and some rules of proportion being observed as they should be an Image framed by the influence of the Heavens, should receive both life and understanding, whereby they that came to ask counsel of it, should have an answer given them, concerning Secrets of hidden truths. Whence it appears, that this naturall Magick sometimes was converted into *Goetia* and *Theurgia,* and oftimes by the fraud of Divels Men were ensnared in errors. *The same.*

Of Necromantick Goetia. Chap. 7.

The Ceremoniall kinds of Magick, are *Goetia,* and *Theurgia. Goetia* was begun by holding commerce with unclean Spirits, in rites of wicked curiosity, unlawfull Charmes, fitted for execrations, and it was forbidden and banished by all Laws. Of this sort are those whom we call at this day Necromancers and Witches.

> *Such Men whom God doth hate, Heavens defame*
> *Born to do mischief, who the great Worlds frame,*
> *And Laws of the fixt Stars pervert, they know*
> *To turn things topsie turvy, where they grow,*
> *Rivers and Heavens course to stop devise,*
> *Mountains they turn, raise Earth above the Skies.*

These are they that call up the Ghosts of dead Men, and such as the Ancients called *Æpodor,* which bewitch Children, and make them speak like Oracles, and carry Devils with them to consult with, as we read some such thing concerning *Socrates;* and such as it is reported that feed Spirits in Glasses, by whom they falsly say they do Prophesie. And all these proceed two wayes, for some of them study to call up and to command evill Spirits by some virtue, chiefly of divine names whereby they Conjure them: for since every Creature feareth and reverenceth the Name of him that made them. It is no wonder if these Charmers, and *Infidels, Pagans, Jewes, Saracens,* and all prophane Persons, or Sects, do bind the Devils by invoking the Name of God. But others most wicked, who are most to be abhor'd, and no punishment is bad enough for them, submitting themselves to the Devils, do Sacrifice to them and adore them, and are guilty of Idolatry and most base dejection. Which faults though the former are not guilty of, yet do they expose themselves to manifest dangers; for the Devils being commanded by them, do obey, that they may deceive those that are in errors. And from this stinking Art of Charmers, that makes a fair shew, all those Books of darkness came, which *Ulpian* the Lawyer condemns as not fit to be read, and saith they ought presently to be burnt. Of which sort one *Zabulus* who was given to unlawfull Arts, writ the first as it is reported, after him one *Barnabas* of *Cyprus*: and to this day there are Books carryed about with false Titles, under the names of *Adam, Abel, Enoch, Abraham, Solomon;* also of *Paul, Honorius, Cyprian, Albertus, Thomas, Hieronymus,* and of one *Eboracensis,* whose Trifles were followed foolishly by *Alphonsus* King of *Castile, Robertus, Anglicus, Bachon,* and *Apponus,* and other Men very many of corrupt wit. Moreover they have made not only Men, Saints, Patriarchs, and Angels of God to be Authors of such wicked Opinions, but they brag of Books written by *Raziel, Raphael,* Angels of *Adam* and *Tobias.* Which Books, who ever shall look acurately into them, and consider their Rules and Precepts, their Ceremonies, Customes, the Words and Characters, the order of making them, the absurd Phrase, will plainly discern that they are only meer toyes and Jugglings, that are contained in them, and were invented in these later times by Men who were totally ignorant of ancient Magick, and by such who were the Artists of most desperate devices, borrowed from some prophane observations, mingling some Ceremonies of our Religion therewith, and inserting some unknown names and signs to terrifie ignorant and rude Men, and to amaze the Vulgar, and such who understand not sound Learning. Yet for all this, these Arts are no Fables; for if they were not reall, and that many hurtfull and strange things were done by them, Divine and Humane Laws had not so severely forbad them, banishing them from the Earth. But the reason why Charmers use only those evill Spirits is this, because good Angels will hardly appear, for they wait for Gods command, and they hold no commerce with any Men, but those that are pure in heart, and holy Men: but the wicked Angels are easily called forth, being fraudulently favourable, and faining themselves to be Gods, being alwayes ready at hand to deceive Men, that they may worship and adore them. And because Women are more greedy of Secrets, and not so cautelous and more subject to superstition, and are more easily deceived, therefore they shew themselves more ready to wait upon them, and they do strange things, as Poets write of *Circe, Medea*, and others, and *Pliny, Tully, Seneca, Augustine*, and many other, as well Philosophers as Catholick Doctors and Historians testifie the same, and so do the Scriptures also. For in the Books of the Kings we read, that a Woman Witch of *Endor*, called forth the Ghost of *Samuel* the Prophet, or some evill spirit that appeared in his likeness. Yet the Hebrew Doctors say, which also *Augustine* to *Simplicianus* doth not deny, but that it may be possible, that it was the true Spirit of *Samuel*, who might easily be called back again, within a full year after his souls departing from his body, as Inchanters teach. Also Magicians and Necromancers suppose that it may be done by some naturall faeces, and sympatheticall bands, as we handle it in our Books of occult Philosophy. Therefore the Ancient Fathers who were skilled in spirituall matters, ordained not without cause, that the bodies of the dead should be buryed in some Sacred place with Candles burning about them, water sprinkled on them, and to cense them with Frankinsence and sweet sents, and should be purged with Prayers, so long as they stood above ground. For as the Hebrew Masters say, our whole body and carnal part, and whatsoever that is ill disposed in us that rests upon the fleshly matter, is left behind for the Serpent to feed upon, and as they call him, for *Azazel*, who is Lord of the flesh and blood, and is Prince of this world: and in *Leviticus* is called Prince of the Wilderness, to whom God saith in *Genesis*, *Dust shalt thou eat all the dayes of thy life*; And *Isaiah*, *Dust is thy bread*, that is our created body of the dust of the Earth, so long as it is not sanctified and changed into a better state, that it belongs no more to the Serpent but unto God, and is made spirituall of carnall: as St. *Paul* saith, *It is sown a naturall body, it shall rise a spirituall body*. And elsewhere, *We shall all be changed*, because many shall be left behind to be the perpetuall food of the Serpent. Wherefore by death we lay down this filthy and loathsome burden of the flesh, which is the Serpents meat, to receive it again hereafter in a better condition, changed into spirituall, which shall be when the dead rise. And it is already accomplished in those who have tasted of the first fruits of the Resurrection, and some have obtained this during this life, by virtue of the Spirit of God, as *Enoch*, *Helias*, and *Moses*, whose bodies were changed into a spirituall Nature, that they should not see corruption, and were not left as other Carcases are, to be the Serpents food. And this is that Dispute that *Michael* had with the Devil about the body of *Moses*, that *Jude* speaks of in his Epistle: but this shall suffice concerning *Goetia* and Necromany.

Of Theurgia. Chap. 8.

But for *Theurgia* many think it not to be unlawfull, as if this were governd by God and good Angels; when as often times under the Names of God and of good Angels, it depends upon the frauds of wicked Devils: for not only by naturall forces, but also by certain Rites, and Ceremonies, we procure and draw to us those Celestial and Divine virtues, whereof the old Magicians have written great Volumes, and given many Rules. But the greatest part of all the Ceremonies consists in a double cleanliness; first of the Soul, next of the body, and of such things that are about the body, as the skin, clothes, houses, vessels, utensils, oblations, offerings, sacrifices, the cleanness whereof disposeth Men to the society and view of Divine matters, and is chiefly ly required in sacred things, as *Isaiah* speaks, *Wash you make you clean, take away the evill of your doings*. But filthiness which ofttimes infects the Ayr, and Men, troubles that most pure influence of Heavenly and Divine things, and drives away the clean Spirits of God. But sometimes unclean Spirits and powers that deceive, that they may be worshipped and adored for Gods, require his cleanliness also: Wherefore here we have reason to be very cautious, whereof I have discoursed at large in my Books of occult Philosophy. But *Porphyrius* disputing much of this *Theurgia*, or Magick from Divine causes, concludes at length, that by divine consecrations, a Mans mind may be made fit, to receive good Angels and Spirits, and to see the Gods. But he denyeth absolutely that by this Art, a Man can returne to God; Wherefore of this rank are the Art, *Armadel*, the Art notary, *Pauls* Art, the Art of Revelations, and many such superstitions, which are so much the more dangerous, as the ignorant hold them to be more Divine.

A most safe counsel against the Machinations of the Devils. Chap. 9.

A most safe counsell against the plots of the Divels, may be seen in this Written Law of preservation; I shall add the words of *Chrysostome* in setting it down; As, saith he, none of you will go into the Market without your shooes and garments, so never go abroad untill you have consulted with Gods Word; when you are passing over the Threshold of your dore, repeat these words, *Satan I defie thee, and O Christ I am united to thee*. Never go forth without saying these words, this will be a staff for you, and your Armour, and impregnable Tower, commending your self to God with this saying, you may go abroad, for so no Man that meets thee, nor yet the Devill can hurt thee, when he discerns thee alwayes thus armed. And here teach your self these things, that when you hear the Trumpet sound, you must be ready in arms, and raising a Trophy against the Devill, you may receive a Crown of righteousness, which we must purchase and gain by the favour and bounty of our Lord Jesus Christ, by whom and with whom, be glory to the Father, and also power and honour to the holy Ghost with them, for ever and ever.

What must be done when Men are hindered that they cannot lye with their Wives. Chap. 10.

Igmarus Archbishop of *Remes*, writes thus concerning copulation hindred by the works of the Devill. If by sorcery and Witchcraft, and such damnable Arts the Secret but never unjust judgment of God permitting it, and the Devill preparing it, a man cannot render due benevolence; such Persons are to be exhorted, who are fallen into such mischiefs, that with a contrite heart, and humble spirit, they should confess themselves to God, and to the Priest sincerely, &c. In a Controversie, where the Husband is accused to be unfit for copulation by reason of Witchcraft. *Ulricus Molitor* writes, That in the counsel of *Constance* it was decreed, that first he should be enquired into by the Physicians, whom the Laws determine to be bewitched, or over cool'd, whether there be not some other cause of his weakness: and then that for three years the Wife should after this live with her Husband, and in the mean time he should make tryall of his abilities; and that they should freely give almes, and fast often, that God the Author of Matrimony might take that mischief from them; A decree worthy to be recal'd for our imitation. *Wierus*.

Another remedy of the same evill, from the same Author.

There is one reports that a Noble Man of his Countrey swore that he enchanted a Man that he should never lye with his Wife, and that he was restored by a certain dexterity, whereby he confirmed the perswasion of another, bringing to him the Book of *Cleopatra*, which he had written concerning the ugliness of Women, and he read the place where it was prescribed that one that was so charmed should have his whole body annointed with the gall of a Crow, mingled with Oyl of Sesamam, and that the remedy was certain. When he heard this, he believed the words of the Book, and did so, and he was presently cured. For as one is hurt by wicked credulity, so it is credible he may be restored by the same.

Exorcisms when, and how and by whom they must be performed. Chap. 11.

Moreover if this calamity doth not pass away by the foresaid meanes, and the work of the Devill remaines, one may rebuke him by the Doctrine of Christ *Mark* the 16. that those who *believe in his name shall cast out Devils*: Wherefore by the example of the Apostles of the more pure Christian Church, one may cast this Divell out in the name of Christ. But the Minister being zealous, and relying upon the testimony of a good Conscience, having that peculiar gift of the holy Ghost, namely of casting forth Divels, and being armed with the sword of the Spirit, and on all sides fenced with the divine Panoply, and taking with him above all the buckler of Faith, whereby he may extinguish all the fiery darts of the Devill, that he may not hear from Christ with Christs Disciples who could not cast out a Divell, *O perverse and incredulous generation, how long shall I be with you? how long shall I suffer you? let him firmely adhere to this promise: Amen I say unto you, he that believes in me, he shall do the works that I do, and greater than these, because I go to the Father, and whatsoever you shall ask the Father in my name, I will do this, that the Father may be glorified in the Son; If you ask any thing in my name I will do it.* Luke also writes that seaventy Disciples returned with joy to Christ, saying; *O Lord the Devils are also subject to us in thy name; but he said unto them, I saw Satan falling from Heaven like unto Lightning; behold I give you power to tread upon Serpents, and Scorpions, and upon all power of the enemy, and nothing shall hurt you.* So at the name of Christ all things in Heaven, in Earth, and Hell bow the knee; and there is no other name given to Men under Heaven, whereby they may be saved. By this only word of the eternall Father, all things were created, Heaven and Earth and all things therein contained. At his pleasure all the Angels come to nothing; At the coming of Christ they all trembled and fled, and in respect to his command, as many Devils that held miserable Martals in close custody were affrighted. The Disciples that believed in this Name cast out Devils. The evill Spirit in *Macedonia*, St. *Paul* cast forth out of a Maid that was possessed with a Devill, by these words: *I command thee in the name of Jesus Christ to go out from her, and he went out the same instant.* So St. *Peter* commanded the Spirits to come forth, who only desired one dayes respite to stay in the bodies they possessed; as *Clement* testifies. I read in the Presbyter *Hieronymus*, in the life of *Hilarion* an Hermite of *Palestina*, of one who was a great Man about *Constantinus*, who was born in *Germany* of *French* Parentage, and from his tender years was possessed with a Devill: whereupon he was brought to *Gaza* to *Hilarion*, and he expounded both in the Syrian and the Greek Tongue (which he had never learned) the manifold causes of the being possessed; to whom the holy Man answered; I care not how thou didst enter, but I command thee to go forth in the name of our Lord Jesus Christ. In this name *Simon* the Apostle broke the Image of the Sun, and *Jude* of the Moon, the Devils being driven forth in the forms of Blackmores. St. *Thomas* drove forth a Devill out of the Idol of the Sun, and St. *Philip* drove forth a Dragon in *Scythia* under the statue of *Mars*; and St. *Andrew* drove out seven Devils in the shape of Dogs that lay under the Monuments by the way side, and that did much hurt to Passengers; so we read that *Sylvester* shut up a Dragon in the Capitoll, and St. *Philip* drove away the Leviathan: *John* the *Evangelist* conquering the malignity, drove forth a Devill, who had remain in the Temple of *Diana* two hundred and fourty years, with these words; *I forbid thee in the name of Jesus Christ of Nazareth, that thou stay here no longer, and presently he went from Ephesus.* Wherefore by the command of *Domitian*, the holy Man was banished into the Island of *Pathmos*; when therefore *Cynops* who was the chief Magician there, in the Town of *Paza*, raged against the Doctrine of *John*, and the miracles he did in the Name of Christ, and by the false accusations laid against *John* by the Priests of *Apollo*, made the People mad, and by his own Conjurations called them off from *John*, bragging that he also could raise the dead, and Divels also came out of the Sea in the shape of dead Men; At length *Cynops* said to *John*, come if thou darest to *Pathmos*, and see what power I have, and you will admire more; where-

whereupon *John* returned with all the company, commanding those three Devils who newly arose in the shape of dead Men, that they should not depart: Wherefore *Cynops* clapping his hands, and a terrible noise being heard at Sea, leapt into the Sea again, and vanished, the Devils crying in the mean while, *Great art thou O Cynops, and no man beside thee.* But *John* in the mean while prayd unto the Lord, that this Magician might live no longer, and presently a vehement murmuring was heard at Sea, and great storms coming on upon that place where *Cynops* leapt in, he was never seen more; and the Devils who stood in the formes of Men, as if they had been but now raised from the dead, were Conjured by an Apostle of God, saying; *I command you in the name of Jesus Christ crucified, that you forsake this Island, and never come hither again,* and they presently vanished from them all, expecting *Cynops* in vain whether he would rise out of the Sea any more. Thus it appears how much the name of Christ hath profited true Christians, and imitation hath helped them. This Conjuration, this is a most vehement and strong exorcisme, this is a certain way to drive Devils from us. This is a short forme: these are the Characters by which we call upon Omnipotence, to do things above the common way; this is true Doctrine, and a solid foundation; this is the Philosopoers stone, and far more excellent than that, concerning which Chymists deceived contend so much; this is the corner stone, by which all the building is firmely knit together. These are divine Testaments and Monuments of sacred things; these are the vestments of a true Priest; these are the pure Ensignes; these are our Ceremonies in casting out of Devils, content with a few things, of easie use, and with mean apparel. This Art is higher than Heaven, deeper than Hell, free from danger, an enemy to shadows, a contemner of Apparitions, a hater of Idolatry, that wants neither Frankinsence nor Wine, that bears rule over all Ghosts, Hobgoblins and Specters, that despiseth all Sepulchres, and Apparitions of the Dead, and vain fears, and occurrences of the night, and meetings of infernal Spirits, (as *Capnion* saith, driving them away with boldness, conquering fate and nature, and whatsoever we rightly can desire, if we observe the forme given to us by our Master, and performe it without ceasing, and be not wearyed in fullfilling of it. Christ by his word cured all maladies, and cast out Devils; If therefore you would work securely, you must needs set before you that counsel of St. *Paul, Whatever you speak or do, do it all in the name of our Lord Jesus Christ.* This is a safe Medicament, and it is the very panacæa, or rather health, and the very soveraign remedy of all infirmities. Therefore *Nazianzen* in his defence saith thus rightly, that the Divels tremble when the Name of Christ is called upon. Against this no delusions of making Men impotent, no charmes of Witches, nor any works of the Devill can hold out a moment, but they vanish in a trice. Wherefore *Lactantius* speaks most true, that the Devils fear just Men, that is, those that truely fear God; that being adjured in his name, they go out of bodies, and being forced by their words, they not only confess themselves to be Devils, but also tell their names, because they cannot lye to God by whom they are Conjured, nor to just Men, by whose voices they are frighted. Wherefore oftimes making great houlings and cryes, they cry out that they are buffeted, that they burn and are ready to depart. We may see more clearly than at noon day, that in this Method of curing, that is founded upon the holy Scripture, there is no opinion of blasphemy fomented. *The same.*

Of those that are possessed by Devils. Chap. 12.

Although sometimes there are Physicall causes of their frensie or madness, yet it is certain, that the Devils do enter into some Mens hearts and make them mad, and do torment them; because it is a truth that some men are ofttimes cured without Physicall remedies. And many times these diabolicall spectacles are prodigies, and significations of future events. Above twelve years since there was a Woman in *Saxony,* which had never learned any Letters, yet when she was hurried by the Devill, after her torments she spake in Greek and Latin concerning the future War in *Saxony.* The meaning of her words was this; *There shall be great famine upon the Earth, and anger upon this People.* Above sixteen years since there was a young Maid

Maid in *Marckia*, who snatched hairs from her Cloaths, and those hairs were turned into Money of that place, and the Maid devoured them with a great crashing under her Teeth, for a long time : and those appearances of Money were sometimes suddenly snatcht out of her hands, and they were Money indeed, which some Men keep to this day : and now and than the Maid was cruelly tormented, but after some Moneths she was freed from that disease totally, and she lives yet in good health; There are frequent Prayers of good Men for her, and of purpose all other Ceremonies were admitted. I heard that there was a Woman in *Italy*, which also never learned to read, who when she was tormented by the Devil, being asked which was the best Verse in *Virgil*, answered :

Discire justitiam moniti & non temnere Divos.
Admonish'd justice learn, not to contemn the Gods.

Concerning those miserable Maids that I hear to be tormented at *Rome*, I think they were tormented by the Devill, and they signifie the punishments of *Italy* in respect of other Nations : and I doubt not but by sincere Prayer of Pious Men that mischief may be removed, and the Devils may be cast out. They also shall do well, that are not Epicures, but who rightly call upon the Son of God our Lord Jesus Christ, that they seriously command those Devils to depart from those miserable Maids, and to Preach to the Catholick Church concerning the future judgement of the Son of God, when the malice of the Devils shall be made manifest, and concerning the punishment of the Devils. But this must be done in earnest, and all Ceremonies laid aside, of Bread worship, and holy Water, and false invocations used by *Cornelius Agrippa*, or *Petrus Aponensis*, and such companions. I know many examples wherein it is most certain that holy Prayers have done good. *Philip Melanchon.*

If Cattle suffer any preternaturall disease, what must be done. Chap. 13.

But if Cattle be supposed to suffer any preternatural malady (which yet is most hard to know, because oftimes in pasture grounds they lick up venome, or draw it in with their breath.) First of all you may give them a Medicament against Poyson, or other like diseases, and do all things else, which from natural conjecture and Art, (whereof *Vegetius* concerning the Ferriours Art, and Physick for Cattle hath written most learnedly and largely in four Books, and so have *Columella*, *Cæsar*, *Constantinus*, and many more modern Authors) we think to be good, and then wait with patience for the event. But if those things help not, but that the herd of Cattle dye: we must set *Jobs* patience before us as a Glass to look into : and what calamity or loss we sustain, we must acknowledg it proceeds from God, who giveth and taketh at his pleasure, nor must we wickedly run to Southsayers, or Diviners, or Witches, which is contrary to the express Word of God, which things by a Sacrilegious imitation seem to confirme and approve the Idolatry of *M. Cato*, by Ceremonious purging of the fields, by solemne Sacrifice, with words and vows dedicated to the Earth, that she may nourish the Trees that are newly set : intreating the Trees also that they will be transplanted and grow in some other place; begging also of Rapes when they sow them, that they will be good to him, and his Family, and his Neighbours : pouring out Prayers to *Mars* to keep the Field and Cattle. Also we read in *Vegetius* of an excellent perfume for the Diseases of Cattle, which though he writes that this will purge Creatures by Ceremony, as he was ill perswaded by other Men, to take away the Witchcraft, and drive away Devils, and stop Hail; yet he adds, that by its smell, namely a natural cause, it hath force to resist the diseases of Men and Beasts, and to purge the Ayr. It is this, Take Quickbrimstone two pounds, Bitumen of *Indea* one pound, Opopanax, of the prickly Herb Panax, Galbanum, Castoreum, fresh Orris, of each six ounces, salt Armoniac two ounces, Salt of *Cappadocea*, Harts Horn, male Jet stone, and female, of each three ounces, Bloodstone, Loadstone, Litharge, of each one ounce, Sea Horse stones, Tails, and Hoofs, of each in number seven : Sea Grape three ounces, Harts Marrow, Cædar Oyl, liquid Pitch, of each three pound, Cuttle bones seven, Gold half an ounce, Gold Ore

Ore one Carrat; mingle all these, and with fire make a smoke. But if you cannot find the stones mentioned, or cannot buy them being too dear, the rest will serve turn. Yet in the mean time we must enquire carefully, whether there be not some strange thing bred there, or some Wasps nests; as I remember one *Latamus* did in *Holland*, who coming into the Stable, laid secretly in the Manger the dung of a Wolf, by the smell whereof, as by the presence of the devouring Enemy, by reason of antipathy, the Cattle were frighted as if it had been Witchcraft, and ran up and down here and there, and seemed to be hurried with unusuall fury, whereupon the Countrey People being amazed, supposed it was some Witchcraft, whereupon they all ran to him that acted this part, who stood and observed it as out of a Watch-Tower, and was famous for curing those that were bewitched, who concealing the matter of the Inchantment, namely the Wolfs dung, being secretly taken away, he soon cured the Cattle. For he did it by taking away the cause, and the effect ceased; and thus he did all he did in his Art: but good Men admonished him, that he should renounce this fraud, least he should deservedly suffer for a cheat. *John Wierus*.

Of naturall sleeping Medicaments, wherewith sometimes Witches are deluded, with their Unguents and some Soporiferans Plants, that exceedingly trouble the mind. Chap. 14.

Sometimes to set forth Witchcraft, some naturall Medicaments are applyed, wherewith when they have annointed themselves, and rubbed it in, as the false Devill instructs them, the Witches sitting by the fire side, believe that they shall presently flye abroad, and wander far and wide into the Ayr to Dance, and enjoy most pleasant Banquets, Copulation, and most curious sights: whereas that great deluder makes them to Dreame so, when as these ignorant People by reason of the drowzy Unguent only, are fallen into a deep sleep, and a Lethargy. That these things may not be taken for lies, I think fit to alleadg here, what that most ingenious searcher into naturall causes that are hid, *John Baptist Porta* of *Naples*, writes in his second Book of Naturall Magick. Such a cursed desire, saith he hath invaded the minds of Men, that they abuse those things which nature hath freely given them for their good, that with many of these heaped together, they compound the Witches Oyntments, which though they mix a great deal of superstition therewith, proceeds from natual causes, as one shall find that looks into it; and I will relate what I had from them. They take male Childrens fat, boyling them in a Brass Kettle with water, making thick that which last of all sinks down, this they lay up for use continually, with this they mingle Smallage, Wolfs-bane, Poplar buds and Soot; or otherwise thus: They mingle together water Parsly, common Acorns, Cinquefoyle, bloud of a Bat, sleepy Nightshade and Oyl, (for though they mingle divers things, yet they differ little from them) then they first rub well all their parts, untill they be very red, and the heat called back, and rarified, which was cold, and afterwards annoint them with that Oyntment; They add the fat to relax the flesh, and to open the Pores, or else they put in Oyl instead thereof, that the force of the juyces may penetrate into the parts, and that the Unguent may be better and more usefull; I doubt not but this is the cause. So in a clear Moon shine night they seem to be carryed through the Ayr, to Banquets, Musick, Dancing, and to lye with fair young Men, which they most long for: Such is the force of Imagination, and the custome of impressions, that almost all that part of the Brain which serves for memory is filled therewith: and as they are very credulous by nature, they take impressions that change their Spirits, because they think of nothing else almost night and day: and they are helpt forward also, by feeding upon nothing but Beets, Roots, Chestnuts, Pulse. Also *Cardan* tels us of an Unguent of Witches, almost like to this, and after they are annointed with it, they seem to see wonders, for he speaks there of things that are not, and yet seem to be. It consists of Boys fat as they say, juyce of Smallage, Wolfs-bane, Cinquefoyl, Nightshade, and Soot; but they are supposed to sleep when they see these things. But they hope for to go into Theaters, Orchards,

Orchards, Feasts, and to hold commerce with fair young Men, Kings, Magistrates in brave Apparel, and to see all things they delight in, and they suppose that they enjoy it. They see also Devils, Crows, Prisons, Desarts, and Torments; these are then the causes of violent Dreames: hence it is also that he saith they live upon Smallage, Chestnuts, Beans, Onyons, Coleworts, and Pulse, all things that provoke turbulent Dreames. So Magicians when they Dreame, suppose they are carried into divers Countries, and therefore to be affected diversly, each according to his temper, the unguent helping it forward. And I will here add an Oyl that is not unlike to the former, to cause a long and deep sleep. Take seeds of Darnel, Henbane, Hemlock, red and black Poppy, Lettice, Purslane, of each four parts, berries of sleepy Henbane one part, make an Oyl of all these according to Art, and for every ounce of this Oyl, mingle one scruple of Opium of Thebes: Then take one scruple or one and an half, and it will make a Man sleep two dayes: I would willingly add here a Liquor, that one drop of it doth wonderfully provoke sleep, or two drops being given inwardly; or else so many drops of the Liquor, as you would have a party to sleep howers; but it is best not to repeat. Some of the simples of it are Darnel, Moonwort, Opium, Henbane, Hemlock, kinds of Poppy, furious and sleeping Nightshade, Mandragora, water Lillies, and such things, which are found and are not unknown to those that are skilled in naturall things, whereby the understanding is either taken away or else troubled: that he who useth them, both in his speaking, hearing, and answering will appear to be mad, or he will sleep deeply for some dayes: but I had rather conceal here the use of them, and the Waters, Wines, Powders, Troches, Oyls, and other things, I think not fit now to teach you how to make them, least I should seem to some to give Men occasion of doing mischief. *Wierus.*

That the Devil may seem to answer. Chap. 15.

The Devill will give answers thus; A Statue is made of Copper, like a Man with a Crown, and Cloaths of Gold, with horns upon his head, face, feet, and hands being cole black, and with Talons upon his hands and feet like to a Griffin; Put into the right hand of this Image an Iron Scepter well Guilded, and Touched with a Loadstone, let this Image sit upon a Throne of shining Brass or of blew colour, place about the whole Fabrick some Pillars of Glass, as I have had such a one in my hands that was solid, or if you please let it be hollow Glass fastned to the Throne. Then hang this Engine by a small Thread perpendicularly, that you may turne it about as you will; Then at the top of a fine Wand set in a piece of a good Loadstone secretly, and then putting the Wand to the parts question the Image; unknown Characters, and marks, and figures, are set upon the Wand; Also a Loadstone may be hid in a Gold Ring; By the same way we place a statue upon the Altar, made of very light matter, and in it an Iron touched with a Loadstone. But the Loadstone must be placed on that side of the Wall, that when the Iron bends that way, the face of the Image may respect the sacrifice: and it is very probable, that by such Arts the wily Priests of old did often delude the People that were very ignorant and not acquainted with such Jugglings. *Cardan.*

A Statute that may seem to be carryed which way it please. Chap. 16.

To these so many famous operations, add this, that a Loadstone put under the Table, will carry about nimbly an Iron laid above the Table equally ballanced, with no little wonder to the standers by. A Bason of Wood is set upon the Table full of Water, and a small Ship swimming in it, made of very fine Boards, without Nails, but it is only glewed together, at the head of the Vessel sits a fair Woman Rowing the Boat with bending the Oare, so that the Oare moves with the motion of this Boat, and with that the Womans body: under the lowest part of the Womans foot, there must be a Nail with a broad head stick forth of the Plank, and that broader part is called the Cap, it must be so fastned that it may lye hid under the fore-Castle and yet not touch the water; then take a piece of an excellent Loadstone, and set it into the head of a Wand of Firr, or Horn, that the stone may not be seen when it is put under the Plank, and so the Loadstone being put under the Nails head, the Boat will

will be carryed whither you will as you move the stone, and they that cannot see the Wand will think that the Image is alive, and Roweth the Ship whether she pleaseth, and seems to hear and to Row up and down; the matter doth not pass to it, but something like to a spirituall substance, for the Table would hinder the motion of it, because two bodies cannot penetrate one the other. *Cardan.*

A statute that killed those that touched it. Chap. 17.

It is wonderfull that *Boetius* relates, for he saith that when King *Chennetus* had killed *Cruthlintus* Son of *Fenella,* and also King *Malcolm Duffus* and Kinsman to *Fenella*; he commanded to make a statue by wonderfull Art, in whose hand there was a Golden Apple full of the most Noble Jewels, which when any man touched, he that touched it was presently stricken through with many Darts, and was accessary to his own death. Wherefore by that deceit he killed the King who thought nothing of it, when he had invited him unto the Town of *Fetircarium*: and having Horses provided, he presently got to the Sea, and escaped into *Ireland.* I understand that lately a Thief was so taken, who went to pick a Mans Pockets, for the Engine was fastned very strongly to his Pockets. *Cardan.*

A statue that alwayes looks toward the Sun. Chap. 18.

I remember that I read how that in the house of *Apis,* there was an Image of the Devill, that would turn the face of it toward the Sun in what part soever the Sun moved: It will not be difficult for us to imitate that in any statue, if you look to the reason of a Clock with the Ropes and weights unseen, and it is more pleasant to see that sight, than to read of it the reason how to make it. *Card.*

Stones that will make one know future things.

It is evident that there are some stones, that held under ones Tongue, or tyed about the neck, or set in a Ring, will lead a Man rightly to divine and to foreshew future things. But five things are necessary for this; First, That that Man be a naturall, for such will speak truth, are moderate, and born under *Venus* Planet. Secondly, That at that time that Star bare rule: that also will be known by cogitations whether they are true or false, and also by Dreames. Thirdly, That that stone move enthusiasmes, that is, Religion in the soul. Fourthly, That it agree in kind with that Star signifying Truth. Fiftly, That the stone be properly effectuall for it. And if when that Star rules, you have it about you, may be it will profit the more. *Cardanus.*

To divine.

So we read that the Ancients by certain naturall things were wont to divine concerning future events. So a stone that breeds in the sight of the eye of an Hyæna, held under ones Tongue, is reported to foreshew things to come. The Moon-stone called *Selenites* doth the same. So it is said of *Anchitis* that it will call forth the Apparitions of the Spirits above, and *Synochitis* will call up the shades beneath. Likewise the Herb called *Aglaoptis,* and *Marmoritides,* that grows upon the Marble stones, in *Arabia* on the *Persian* side, as *Pliny* saith, doth as much, and that Magicians use it, when they would call up Spirits, and there is another Plant called *Theangelida,* which Magicians drink to divine with. *Aggrippa.*

Another.

He that will foretell things was wont to have a fume applyed to stir up his phantasie, which fumes being agreeable to certain Spirits, fit us to receive divine inspirations: So some say that a fume of Linseed and Fleaseed, with the roots of Smallage and of Violets, will make Men see future things, and is good for divination.

Of Geometricall Secrets. Chap. 19.

To find the circumference of the Earth.

Thus Men found out the compass and diameter of the Earth; For either by Eclipses of the Moon they learned the distance of houres under the same equinoctial Circle, being equidistant: and when they had this, they got the knowledge of the distance of places by a Land Journey. For multiplying by twenty four the parts of one day, and divining by the houres of distance of the Moons Eclips, they

O o found

found out the circumference of that Circle : then by a Geometricall demonstration, they attained to know the circumference of the Equinoctiall Circle which is the greatest, and of the whole earth; which multiplying by 7, and deviding by 22. they found out the earths Diameter exactly as needfull is. Or proceeding from the South full North, they augmented the height of the Pole one degree. And measuring the way, they found 1587. *Italian* paces : and by these now we measure the distances of places, and not by the paces of *Ptolomey* : Wherefore multiplying 1587. by the degrees of Heaven 360. for it is divided into so many, we shall shave 31500. Miles. If we multiply this circumference of the whole Earth by 7. and divide it by 22. the Diameter of the Earth will be 10022. Miles, but it is folly to take this quantity so exactly; wherefore casting away 22. say that the Earths Diameter is 10000. Miles; but those that Sail are driven with many errors, Sailing of their own mind, not a direct, but a crooked voyage, and also being deceived by the uncertain and various force of the Winds, wherefore they have written that the compass of the Earth is far more. But this reason as it is most true, so it depends upon most certain experience, and it hath much helped the *Spaniards*, who understanding that so long and continued a Voyage was repugnant to the magnitude of the earth, they diligently found out their error, and they contracted it to a third part of the time and distance almost. *Card.*

How to find out the hour of the day when the Sun shines.

You shall find out the hour of the day at any time when the Sun shines by this rule. Turn your back to the Sun, and thrust forth your arm, and with your left hand placing your Thumb upon your fore finger, that the small shadow of the body of it may fall upon the palm of your hand, then place a Style or Gnomon under your Thumbs joynt, and consider the shadow that fals perpendicular to the superficies of the palme of your hand, for if it fals where the fore-finger joyns to the hand, it is either 24. or 8. if upon the top of it, 23. or 9. if on the top of the middle finger, it is 22. or 10. if on the top of the Ring finger, 21. or 11. if on the the top of the little finger, it is 20. or 12. if on the last joynt 19. or 13. if on the second joynt of the same 18. or 14. if on the root where it joyns to the hand, 17. or 15. In the beginning of the Table Line 16. but it is certain that this observation is not exact. *The same.*

A solid Geographical Sphere.

If any one desire to describe the world upon a Sphere, he may do it easily and finely in five dayes by the words of *Ptolomey*. First make a Brass Sphere exactly round, thus : make a Brass Semicircle according to the quantity of the Diameter, and apply it to the Sphere on all parts; if it fit right every where, it is exactly round, where it exceeds, so much must be taken away, and where it is wanting, you must add to it; and when it is perfectly round, joyn it on both parts, and set it in round Rings, that it may not turn about too loosely, nor yet too harshly; after this describe the Equinoctial Circle with Gold very thin, equally distant from the Poles, with great care, and divide it into 360. equall parts, and to every part make a distinction, and to every five parts set the number increasing by 5. and so fasten an immoveable Semicircle, that is equally joyned to the Sphere, to the place it relies upon, that when the Globe moves, that may stand immoveable : and divide it so, that where it cuts the Equinoctial Perpendicular, from that point, let there be 90. equall parts distinguished between both the Poles, that the whole Semicircle may be divided into 180. parts, with their severall divisions, and numbers set down at every 5t. division : so that the numbers begining from the Equinoctial, may terminate on both sides to 90. divisions toward the Poles. When therefore you will write the places upon it, seek for the number of longitude in the Equinoctial, and turning the Globe, set that number under the Meridian, and finding the latitude of the place in the Meridian, of one side or other, by degrees and the parts thereof, just against that make a prick for that place, as it is in magnitude, and do so for all places. But through all the five degrees of the Equinoctial, you shall draw by the immoveable Miridian, Meridian Lines from Pole to Pole, which will be 36. Circles : but you shall mark them with a sharp point

point of a Bodkin, and also the parallels, and the beginings and ends of the Climats, upon each half of the Globe that is made fast to a degree of the Meridian, and turning the Sphere about, untill it come again to the first point, you shall marke them well with a sharp Instrument. After this, you shall make all the Circles of Gold very small, except those of the Climats, which shall not be so small, and distinguish Seas and Rivers by a blew colour, Cities and Towns by red, Mountains by Silver colour, Hils and Wood by green, the Earth by gray, and set the names of them all over them in black. But you must observe one thing, that the forms of places must be distinguished in a threefold magnitude, The chief City in the biggest, common Cities in the mean, Towns in the smallest; and if you will distinguish Princes Dominions, compass them about with a green Circle; but that must chiefly be remembred, that you make use of the latest and the most correct Commentaries, and to use a decent magnitude, which is, that the greatest Circle may be as long as a Man. *Cardanus.*

To poyse all things by four Weights.

If one desire with four weights to weigh all things, which are from 1. to 40. so that no other weights shall be wanting; you shall do it, if the first weight weigh one pound, the second three pound, the third nine pound, the fourth twenty seven pound; with these you may weigh all weights from one to fourty pound; as if you would weigh twenty one pounds, put in one scale twenty seven, and three in the other nine pounds; If you desire twenty pounds, put in one scale twenty seven pounds, and 3. and 9. and 1. in another; by the same reason you may weigh with five weights all weights from 1. to 121. namely by 1. 3. 9. 27. 81. Also by 6. to 364. namely 1. 3. 9. 27. 81. 243. *Gemma Frisius.*

Of Secrets in Arithmetick. Chap. 20.

To tell any number that any Man thinks.

A Man hath thought of a number which to find out do thus; bid him to treble the number he hath conceived, to take half from the treble number, then again to treble the quotient, and again to take but half of this. But if in the first halfing of it the treble number was odd, (for you must ask him that) bid him make it equall by adding one to it, and then take half of it, for this addition keep 1, and for the second 2: when you bid him do so again: then bid him cast away 9. as oft as he can from your last number, and do you as often count 4, and then cast away what is more. Suppose one think 7. treble that, it will be 21. make it 22. half is 11. but do you keep 1. bid him again treble 11. and that will be 33. and again because you cannot take half but by adding 1. make it 34. half thereof is 17. keep you 2. for that, then bid him cast away 4. as oft as he can, and because it can be done but once, keep 4. for that: enquire no farther; if you kept 3. as you ought, add that to 4. and it makes 7. *Gemma Frisius.*

To discover to one a thing that is hid.

If three diverse things be hid by three severall Persons, and you by Arithmetick as a Prophet, would tell every one what thing he hid, do thus. Let there be three things *a. b. c.* concealed in your mind, and keep them there in order, as first, second, and third; before they hide the things, cast before them 24. Dice, and give to the first Man 1. into his hand, to the second 2. to the third 3. then place the three things in order, and say there when I go away, let one of you severally hide any of these things, which they please, but upon this condition, that he who hides *a.* the 1. shall take off the Dice remaining, which are 18. as many Dice as he hath already in his hand, but he that hides *b.* the 2. must take double as many, and he that hides *c.* the 3. must take four times as many, and let them leave all the remaining Dice upon the Table, or in some open place. Then the three things and Persons being fixed in order in the memory, let him go away untill they hide the things and consult together. Then come back again and see what Dice are left upon the Table, which are alwayes 1. or 5. or 3. or 6. or 7. If then there remain but 1. the 1.

hid *a.* the 2. *b.* the 3. *c.* If 2. then the first hid *b.* the second *a.* the third *c.* You shall understand the rest by the Table here joyned. *The same.*

The remainder.

The Dice.	The Persons.	The Things.
1.	1.	*a.*
	2.	*b.*
	3.	*c.*
2.	1.	*b.*
	2.	*a.*
	3.	*c.*
3.	1.	*a.*
	2.	*c.*
	3.	*b.*
5.	1.	*b.*
	2.	*c.*
	3.	*a.*
6.	1.	*c.*
	2.	*a.*
	3.	*b.*
7.	1.	*c.*
	2.	*b.*
	3.	*a.*

To find out the scituation of the World, and to conduct a Ship to any part of the world by a Star seen, and also to find out the distance of places by a Geometrical way.

It is very easie to shew both on the foreside and backside of the Astrolabe the place you would go unto; that it will perhaps be needless to use many words about it. Far on the backside of the Astrolabe, looking to the ends of both places from whence you come, and whether you go, observe the difference of longitude, and count this on the degrees of the frame toward either East or West, according to the scituation of either Countrey, and at the end apply the Geometrical quadrant, and then account upon that the distance from the Equinoctial toward the Pole, and there you shall find the end of the latitude required, placing the quadrant over the place that you seek for. That therefore I may be something more sure of the Voyage I undertake, especially wanting a good Wind, and favourable Gale; do thus, knowing the hour of your place, apply the place of the Sun to it, and bring the Geometrical quadrant over it, and the Rete so standing, that Line brought back to the point of the Countrey you Sail unto, which was marked before, will presently shew whether any Star of that place come up to the Meridian Circle, or else come directly over your head: then keep this Star alwayes in your sight as the guide of your Voyage, and set the Sayls and Steer that way. For if perhaps any noted Star be in their Zenith, you have as it were *Mercuries* Image to paint with his finger the way you must Sail. But if it come to the Meridian of that place, and varieth something from the Zenith in latitude, you must search out the difference of altitude, both of the Star and of the Zenith of the place. If therefore you do conceive as it were in your mind, and with your eyes a huge great Circle, runing through the Poles, and the Star you see, and in that, (though it be difficult) you imagine the portion of this difference, you shall find the place of the Heaven, though perhaps there be no noted Star in it. Which notwithstanding must be referred in a right Line between the Star formerly found, and the Pole; And so you have the place of the Countrey under

Book XVI.   *Secrets in Arithmetick.*   291

der the Star, by your eye as it were, and that for that time. But though you have not so exact a compendium of your way, you have that which is remarkable, for the artifice of Steering a Ships way consisteth not in a Line; but every hour we must bethinke our selves of one or another point of the Heavens, and that it is just over the head of that Countrey; and therefore continually according to the number of houres passed, it must be turned right with the Zodiack. This is for Sailing in the Night. But in the Day when the Sun hides the Starres with its Beames, the Sun must guide you: by the height of the Sun seek out the latitude of the place; that will direct us by the parallel of the Equator, whilst perfecting the difference of longitude, the miles at Sea answer thereto according to reason: and when you have brought it to that difference as the place you Sail to requires, know that you are now in the Meridian of it. And now the Ship must be guided by it directly upwards or downwards, untill the latitude of the place taken by your Instrument, agree with the latitude found before.

Such is the fear to Sail when winds are ill.

And that you may know by the way how much compass you take by this right Angle, you shall find it out of the last proposition but one, of the first Book of *Euclide*, for if you multiply the Ark of the difference of the longitude and latitude of them both square wayes, and the products be joyned together by addition; and the square root of the whole be sought for, that shews the longitude of the Voyage to be made by equall degrees twice, which are next in a parallel. For that reason of Miles which is commonly taught, to the degrees of the Equator, is held only true and exact about the Circle of the Equator; namely that for *Italian* Miles the distance be multiplied by sixty, for *Germane* Miles by fifteen, for *Swedes* Miles by twelve, for this learning would serve but for eighteen degrees; but I shall give a more exact reason of this in its proper place. *Gemma Frisius.*

How knowing the distance of the way, you may find the latitude and longitude of the places.

Properly, as when by an Astrolabe knowing the distance of the place, we know the longitude and latitude; or knowing the distance and latitude we know the longitude. Let therefore the Meridian Circle be *A. E. B. F.* fastned upon the foot *A. M.* imagine the Poles of it to be *K. F.* and your Zenith to be *E.* another immoveable Circle must be the Equinoctial *A. B. C. D.* fastned upon the foot *A. M.* cutting the former Circle at right Angles, and to be turned about in the Poles *F.* and *K.* by Pins that old it on. There must be also another turning Pin in the Zenith, *C. E. D. L.* Let therefore the distance be *E. N.* that is known and right; number therefore, all of these Circles being divided into 3600. parts severally, those parts in *. E. D.* by *E. N.* and place *C. N. D.* upon a right way from your City, to the place *N.* and where the point *N.* falls, draw *G. K. H. E.* the moveable Circle of the Meridian, you shall find then by the Arch *K. N.* the latitude of the place, or elevation of the Pole, and by *G. C.* the difference of longitude of the place *N.* from your City: and the longitude of your City being now known, so will also the longitude of *N.* and if the altitude of *N.* be known, and the right way *E. N.* turning therefore about the Circles *C. E. D.* and *N. H.* untill the ends of the Arches *E. N.* of the right distance, and *K. N.* of the known altitude of the place *N.* meet together, there will then be made an Arch *G. C.* that is known, namely the difference of the longitude of the place *N.* from your County. But it is manifest, that by a contrary reason, having the longitude and latitude of the places, the distance also will be known. And if you would have the Instrument to serve for all Countries,

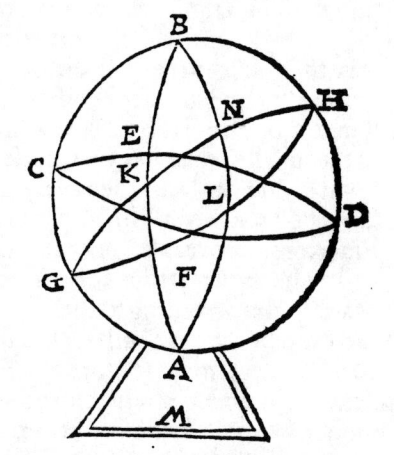

tries, make the Pins *E. L.* moveable upon the Meridian Circle, *A. K. B. F.* that under any altitude the Zenith may be placed. Moreover make the severall divisions very visible at every tenth division, and less apparent at every fifth division, and at every fifth division with a Golden colour, that they may be carefully distinguished, as in Goldsmiths ballances. But the number is not necessary, because you must every where make a beginning. *The same.*

To find how many Miles a Ship hath Sailed, or a Cart hath gone.

When we will make a Cart or Ship, that may shew unto us how many Miles they have passed: Let there be a Wheel twelve foot and half in compass, and a Wheel about an Axeltree with a small Tooth, which as the Wheel turns about, meeting with the Wheel of C. C. C. C. Teeth, may carry off one of them; so C. C. C. C. revolutions being performed by the first Wheel, of V. M. feet, there will be a thousand paces gone. But when this Wheel is turned about, with another small Tooth, it must uncover a Bushel, out of which a stone must fall into a Brazen Vessel under it, that by the noise and number of the small stones, it may discover how many Miles you go, or it being turned will shew in the other Wheel a thousand paces; Thus in Artificiall Engines, (as *Vitruvius* teacheth) it is easie to come to an exact knowledg of things. But for contemplation, that which was named before shall be an example. *Cardan.*

An Instrument of perpetual Motion.

Antonius de Fautis Tarvisinus, a Man of our times very learned and ingenious, supposed that an Instrument of perpetuall motion, might be made after this manner, as I shall describe immediately. But to make this clear, he sets down three experiments which he had proved: First, That if a Loadstone be made round, it hath two opposite points exactly; whereof one alwayes tends to the North, and the other to the South, if it hang at liberty and equally ballanced, and likewise if it be put into a Wodden Box, and that be so often turned in the water, untill those points which he calls the Poles, respect those parts of Heaven they are bent unto. I have shew'd this thing in another place. His second supposition is, which he assumes from an experiment, that the North Pole draws the South Pole of the other, and the South the North; if the two Loadstones be round, which depends almost upon the first supposition: for if the North Pole respect the North opposite to it, therefore the other Pole must be placed South, because they are in opposite parts as you shall see in the Figure. For if the North Pole be applyed toward the North, or the South Pole toward the South, the stronger will drive the weaker away from it, and makes it returne back, where the Wheel can but lightly move. His third supposition is: That an Agent acts more than it resists; and he saith he had found this also by experience. These suppositions being laid, he took a round Frame of Silver very thin, like to the frame of a round Looking-Glass, and divided the circumference of it, and to each division he applyed an Iron Needle, and he made the distance of one from the other about the bigness of a Pease, then he placed a Loadstone in the middle, that was very perfect, and of an Oval Figure, and at the ends of the Oval Figure he placed the Poles, and he set a Wheel upon the Axeltree, and in the Center of it a Silver Pin, as it were the Diameter of the Wheel, the Axeltree and Pin were immoveable, but the Wheel moveable. Now that it must move perpetually, he proves it thus: For since the ends of the Stone attract those parts that are nearest, and according to their scituation, and one directs the Needle to the North, and the other to the South; *O.* must needs descend to *P.* and *P.* to *Q.* and likewise *A.* to *B.* and *B.* to *C.* for thus the Eastern part is carryed to the North, and the Western to the South: wherefore they will help one the other, and it will be but one motion from the first supposition. And because by the third supposition every part attracts more then it resists. The parts *F.* and *T. G.* and *V.* resist less than the parts *N. R. O. A.* are attracted; and especially because the former stand equally ballanced, and perpendicular, and therefore in their own nature immoveable, but the parts toward the East and West are shelving and moveable. And if any one say that the West part rests by ascending, if the East part must descend, he saith, that as to motion

Book XVI.   *Secrets in Arithmetick.*   293

tion of gavity, they are equally ballanced, as the upper and the lower: therefore they hinder not by reafon of gravity, but only as much as is the gravity of the Wheel which is very fmall. Therefore fince the motions of the Stone do mutually help one the other, and the gravities do not hinder, the Wheel will always be carried about, which he faith he hath tryed, there will therefore never want a caufe of fuch motion, and fo it will be perpetual. For the Needles turn the Wheel about; Again he placeth another Stone which muft ftand perpendicular with the former, and he ufeth the fame reafon and demonftration to prove this motion to be perpetuall: And this invention hath that difficulty in it, that the Iron is moft fuddenly carryed to the Stone, whence the Wheel being moved turns about with force; but they feem to want a perpetual inequality, becaufe that interrupts the motion; now no man can doubt but that all motion muft be remifs, that muft be perpetual, as that of the Heavens, and if they fhould be remifs, it would be flow alfo: becaufe it is obnoxious to all impediments. *Cardanus Lib.* 9. *de varietate rerum.*

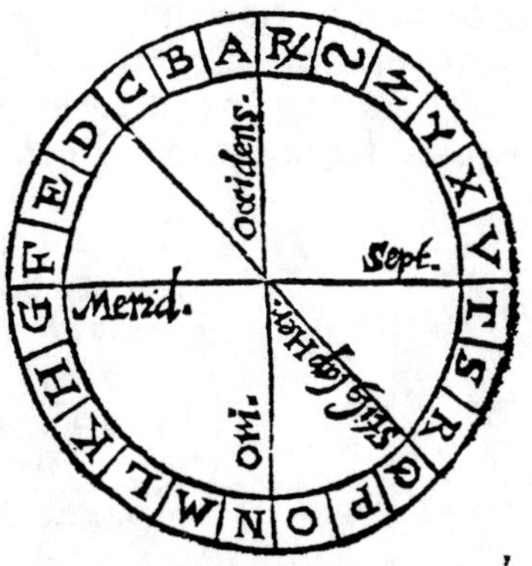

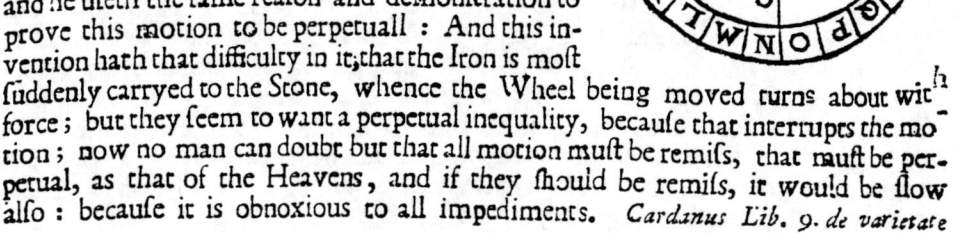

Fraud in Ballances where things heavier fhall feem to be lighter.

We can make a Ballance, that being without Weights fhall feem to be equall, and when juft and known Weights are put into the Scales, the weight of things fhall feem more then they are. For thus, as *Ariftotle* faith, they who fold Purple deceived their Cuftomers. The reafon is this. If you would have a Scale that for eleaven ounces fhall weigh twelve, Take the Beam *A. B.* of fome Mettal, and divide that into twenty three equall parts, for eleven and twelve joyned make fo many: at the end of eleven, and beginning of the twelf part, faften the tongue and the hole wherein the toung of the Ballance turneth, wherefore it is plain that *D. C.* is an eleventh part longer than *A D.* and fince *D. C.* is fomewhat longer than *A. D.* and heavier, you muft file it lighter, or make a hole in it, or put a lighter Scale to *C.* than to *A.* fo then whilft the Scales are empty, the Beam *A. C.* turns neither way, but ftands even, for the Scales are made even by the thinnefs, to make good that which is under the hole of the Ballance; but when on the part *C.* you fhall put in a Weight of eleaven ounces, and another of twelve ounces in the Scale *A*, the Scale will be equall; fince therefore the Weights are known and good, and when the Scales are empty, there is no fault that appears, this fraud in buying of commodities, may be perceived, if you change the Scales, putting the weights into *C.* and the commodities into *A*. For the fide *C.* will hang under for two reafons, both becaufe the greater weight is in that Scale, and becaufe *C. D.* it is longer than *D. A.*

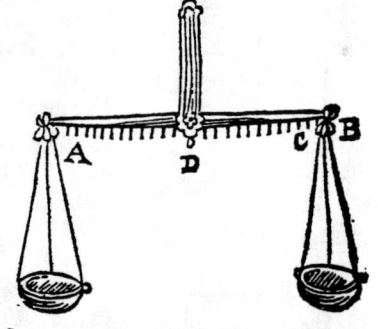

How Weights may be twice as foon drawn up, and with half a Cord.

There is an Inftrument to be admired, which yet is made with fmall labour. *Gabriel Arator* obferves that it may be made, that Weights may be drawn upward twice fooner than they ufe to be the ordinary way. Let the height be *A. B.* the middle of it *D.* and a weight hanged at a Cord, *D. C.* at *C.* In *D.* muft be a Pulley, wherein runs the Rope in *A.* when therefore it is drawn, the Pulley as far as *E. D. C.* will be made twice fhorter in quantity, when therefore *D.* fhall be in *A.* alfo *E.* fhall be in *A.* now this happeneth becaufe *D. C.* is doubled, both afcending
ing

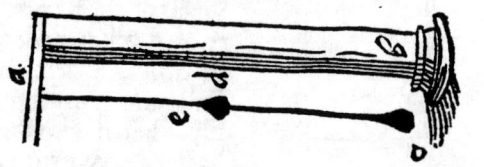

294 *Secrets in Arithmetick.* Book XVI.

ing and descending, therefore it will not fit, but when *D.* is in the middle of *A. B.* or below it. Now this Instrument wants greater force, than if the Weight were simply drawn. Yet because this attraction may be eased by the reasons aforesaid, it may be so made as to draw up with the same force, and in half the time: so much can Art and Ingenuity do. *The same.*

An Instrument whereby he that draweth is drawn.

There is an Instrument made by Art, but not by one Art only, and if you hang by your hands upon it, whilst you draw the more forcibly are you drawn. It is this, *A. B.* is the Pavement above, of him that suddenly pulls the Cord, and *C. D. E.* is a piece of Wood or Iron bent down with great force, unto which the Cord *C. D.* is fastned, but *D. F.* is a piece of Wood under the roof, and hinders *E. D.* to return; but to *F. D.* you must hang on the Weight *E. G.* so that *F. D.* may be brought about every way, when *F. D.* is not pressed by *E. D.* for *F. D.* is fastned into a Pully: when therefore *C. D.* is drawn, *F. D.* slips back towards *E.* but yet upon one side by reason of the Weight *G.* therefore the Iron *E. D.* that was held back by *F. D.* will fall back to the roof *H. E.* drawing *D. C.* upwards. *Cardan.*

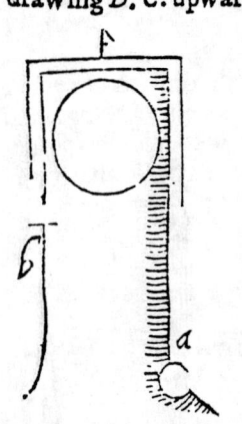

An Instrument whereby any one may draw himself upward.

An Instrument that will easily draw a Man upward, There must be a Wheel with an Iron hook, and in that a small Pulley as the fashion is, about which runs the Rope, at the Rope must be the Weight *A.* somewhat lighter than your body, on the other side must be a Staff overthwart *B.* wherefore hanging a Weight at the hook, you shall draw below *B.* that the Weight *A.* may ascend upwards, and *B.* may come downwards. Therefore one sitting upon *B.* and on the otherside taking hold of *A. C.* with his hands, because the Weight *A.* is but little less in weight than your body is, that descending, you shall ascend easily: when you would come down, you shall do that at pleasure, because your body is heavier than *A.* let go the Rope, and you come down suddenly. *The same.*

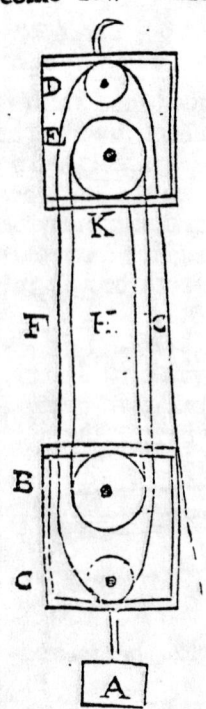

An easie way to lift up Weights.

There is also another Instrument in Pulleys, and it is thus made: The Weight *A.* is fastned to the lowest Pulley, wherein are two small round Pulleys *B.* and *C.* that turne about; In the upper Wheel there are two more Pulleys, *D.* and *E.* the Cord is brought about *D.* and it descends by *F.* to *C.* and it ascends by *G.* and it is turned about by *E.* descending by *H.* it is turned about by *B.* and ascending, it is fastned to the Wheel in *K.* wherefore the weight is drawn from *L.* and because it is supported by *F. G. H. K.* there will be no more than a fourth part of the weight *A.* that is sustain'd by the severall Cords, wherefore it may be drawn up with a quarter of the strength. And if in the severall Wheels there were three Pulleys, it might be done with a sixt part of the strength: and thus a Boy may draw up a huge Weight, unless the heaviness of the Ropes, unevenness of the Pulleys, and difficulty of motion hinder him: but because there is a proportion of times, as being more powerfull, he shall draw with two Pulleys four times more easily, with three six times more easily. than it with the same strength, and somewhat greater, he stood above to draw with one Cord, and far more easily by six or four fold, the more the length of the Cord addeth to the weight, whence it will fall out that the same Boy shall

scarce

Book XVI.   *Secrets of Musick.*   295

scarse in an houres time draw up the same weight with those Pulleys, that a Man who is six times as strong may do presently with one Cord, standing above it. Therefore there is Art and Ingenuity that every one may raise any weight: But that the Cord may be drawn by many, it is drawn under the Pulley, as it is equidistant from the Earth. But to draw things more easily, we use a Crane, which Instrument is in use every where: for this by turning about the Axeltrees, the Cord being turned about, draws up any Weights. But here also the labour may be eased by length of the Axeltrees: for the longer they are, the easier they draw. *The same.*

Wheels to draw up much water.

Munster relates, That at *Aisua*, with two Wheels, and Carts made of Ox hides, water is drawn so suddenly out of the deepest pits with such mighty force, that though the Wheels be made of Wood, and kept moyst, yet they will strike fire; consider that that Instrument hath three notable properties, height, capacity, and celerity.

Of Secrets of Musick. Chap. 21.

A Harp that shall make one to sleep.

Prepare the matter of the more gentle Wood, that it may make the sweeter Musick, and not so high, as of Firr, and Ivy, of one make the upper part, and the under of another; Fiddle strings must be made of Adders and Serpents, but of their guts, or membrane that joynes to the backbone, which you must take forth of a running River, and hanging it up by the head, the rest must corrupt; fit these strings to a Fiddle or Cythern, and playing on it with your fingers, it will make a pleasing soft, gentle, sound, and will make those that hear it sleep soundly, that they will shut their eyes whether they will or no, and sleep will be propounded. This must not seem strange, if the *Pythagorians* used this also, who when they would discuss diversity of cares by sleep, they used certain Songs that made them sleep soundly and gently: and when they awaked, when they arose they had other Musick to drive away sleep and stupidity, and to make them fit for business. Great Winds will make Men sleep soundly, and appease the troubles of the mind. Also that is very strange, that the noise thereof hinders conception; for whilst it enters into the mind by the ears, how that noise can hurt conception, I leave it to mens arbitration who are credulous: but that this offend no man, it were better to let it pass. *The same.*

A Harp that being plaid on shall play on another that lyeth by.

Tune the Strings alike, and fit them both for perfect Musick, if you strike one of the great Strings with your fingers, the other will answer, and sound deeper, so will the sharp Strings, but they must be at an even distance. If it be not very evident, lay Straw over it, and you shall see it move. *Sueton Tranquillus* in his Book of History of pasttimes, saith, that the Strings of Instruments in Winter being moved with your fingers, when one is touched another will sound, thus any Man that hath no skill in Musick, may Tune an Instrument, if one be well Tuned and lye by, and he take the other in his hands and turn the Pins up and down, and strike them, untill the String of that Instrument which lyeth by move, which is a sign of the same Tune: So in the rest. *The same.*

To make a deaf Man hear the sound of an Harp.

If you will have a deaf Man hear the sound of an Harp, or else stop your ears well with your hands that you may not hear it, then take the head of the Harp or Cythern fast by your Teeth, and let another Play upon it, and you shall hear a sweet sound in your brain, and may be a sweeter sound: and not only taking hold of the head with your Teeth, but only a very long Spear that shall touch the Harp, and by that the sound is clearly heard, and you may say it was not the sense of hearing, but tasting whereby it was perceived. *The same.*

That Harps, Cytherns, and other Instruments, may be Played upon by the Wind.

This remains that I think no wayes unpleasant, that Harps, Cytherns, and other Instrumets should be Plaid upon by the Wind. You shall do it thus. When there is a great Wind, set your Instruments over against the Wind, as Cytherns, Pipes, Flutes, Dulcimers; for the Wind coming runs forcibly into them, makes them sound gently, and runs through the gaping Pipes, and so by the sounding of them all, those that stand near will perceive a most pleasing Musick, and delightfull. *The same.*

A continuall sound of a Trumpet.

Some say that in the Countrey *Obdora*, beyond the River *Obium*, there are Instruments that like Trumpets sound of themselves: and although all that History of the River *Obium*, and a Golden Statue be false, yet the thing it self is not only possible but very easie to be done; as both in *Holland*, and *France*, Mils are moved by Wheels, so may Drums beat, and Trumpets sound, and not only with rude noise, but most harmoniously, and that continually, as Organs are blowed by Bellows. Need I not describe the manner, when it is easie to say and understand it, but it is hard to do it? for in place of Bellows and fingers, multitude of Bellows alone will suffice, but the Pipes must be made Musically and the elevations by turns. In *France* they may be made upon a plain, because the Winds are so frequent; but not in *Italy*: unless upon the tops of Mountains, or amongst Rocks; But Trumpets want not much art, when as the Ayr collected in the large hollow Pipe, is forced to enter in by a small Pipe into the Brazen Pipes: and they may be made Musicall, but it is still equall. *Cardan.*

Harmony of Bells.

The former History calls to my mind the memory of that I saw at *Brussels* in *Flanders*. Many Bels were set round about in a circle upon a Tower, as it is usuall, and they had Musicall proportion in their sounds: some that are skillfull Play upon them according to the Notes some pleasant Tune, and they would make you admire at the Musick, for the Bels do not hold the sound, but it ceaseth presently with the stroke. The same is done at *Lovans*, and at *Antwerp*, and this may be imitated by Pitchers and other Vessels. *The same.*

Of Astrological Secrets. Chap. 22.

Of the rising of the Dog-star, and the foreknowledge of those things which fall out thereby.

The Dog-star riseth upon the twentieth day of the Moneth of *July*. But you must observe in what house the Moon is when the Dog-star riseth; For if she be in *Leo* when the Dog-star riseth there will be great plenty of Grain, Oyl and Wine, and the price of all other things will be very low. There will arise many tumults and slaughters, there will be contentions, and abundance of plenty: one Nation shall invade another, and there shall be Earthquakes and Inundations. But if the Moon be in *Virgo*, there shall fall much Rain, and great abundance of things, Women will miscarry, Servants and Cattle will be cheap. If she be in *Libra*, the King will be moved, and there will be meat convenient for four footed Beasts, there will be tumults amongst the people, scarsity of Oyl, corruption of Grain, but there will be abundance of Wine and Fruits of Trees, that have a hard shell. If the Moon be in *Scorpio*, there will be tumults amongst Priests, destruction of Bees, and a pestilential season. When she is in *Sagittarius* it will be a fruitfull year, and Rainy, with abundance of Grain: there will be joy amongst Men, but great death of Cattle, and great plenty of Birds. But if the Moon were in *Capricorn*, when the Dog-star riseth, there will be marchings of Armies, and great store of Rain and Corn, and abundance of Wine and Oyl, and all things cheap. If she be in *Aquarius*, the King shall dye, Corn shall corrupt, Locusts will abound, there will be seldome any Rain, and the Plague shall spread. When the Moon is in *Pisces*, if the Dog-star arise, there will be much Rain, Birds will dye, Wine and Corn will be abundant, Mens bodies will be overrun with Diseases. But if when the Moon is in

Aries,

Aries, the Dog-starr rise, there will be great death of Cattle that feed in herds and flocks, plenty of Rain, little Corn, plenty of Oyl. But if it be in *Taurus*, there will be plenty of Showres, Hail, Mildews and Plagues. But if she be in *Gemini*, there will be much Corn and Wine, and of all Fruit, the King shall fail. Men shall dye, Armies shall march. If she be in *Cancer*, there will be drought and famines. *Diophanes.*

The rising and setting of the apparent Stars.

Since it is necessary for Countrey-Men to know the rising and setting of apparent Stars, I have written so concerning them, that such Men as know no Letters, only by hearsay may easily understand the times both of the rising and setting of Stars. The *Dolphin* riseth in the Calends of the Moneth of *January*. On the twenty sixt of *February Arcturus* riseth in the evening. On the Calends of *April*, the *Pleiades* set at midnight, and on the twenty third of *April*, they rise with the Sun. On the twenty ninth of *April*, *Orion* sets in the evening. On the thirtieth day of *April*, *Succula* rise with the Sun. On the seaventh day of *May* the seaven-Stars rise in the morning. On the nineteenth of *May*, *Succula* rise in the morning. On the seventh of *June*, *Arcturus* sets in the morning. On the twenty third of *June*, *Orion* begins to rise. On the tenth of *July*, *Orion* riseth in the morning. On the thirteenth of *July*, the Dog-star riseth in the morning. On the twenty fourth of *July*, the little Dog-star riseth in the morning. On the twenty sixt of *July* the Eastern Winds begin to blow. On the thirtieth of *July* the clear Star in the Lions brest riseth. On the twenty fifth of *August*, the *Arrow* sets. On the fifteenth of *September*, *Arcturus* riseth. On the fifth of *October* the Crown riseth in the morning. On the twenty fourth of *October* the seaven-Stars set when the Sun riseth. On the Calends of *November* the seaven-Stars set in the morning, and *Orion* begins to set. On the two and twentieth of *November*, the Dog sets in the morning. *Diophanes.*

The twelfth revolution of Jupiter, and what that Star effects by runing through the twelve houses of the Zodiack.

The Zodiack is divided into twelve houses. Three for the Spring, *Aries*, *Taurus*, *Gemini*; Three for Summer, *Cancer*, *Leo*, *Virgo*; Three for Autumn, *Libra*, *Scorpio*, *Saggitarius*; Three for Winter, *Capricornus*, *Aquarius*, *Pisces*. But *Jupiter* being in any house of the twelve, will produce such effects. When *Jupiter* is in *Aries*, which is the house of *Mars*, the whole year shall be Northerly, participating also with the East Wind, the Winter shall be cold and full of Snow. Also the showres will be continuall, and great floods. After the vernal Equinoctial, the water is changed into soft and condensed water. But the Summer will be regular and wholesome. The Autumne will be hot, and diseases will raign, especially by distillations from the head, and Coughs. Champion grounds will be most fruitfull, and we ought to pray that no Wars arise. *Democritus* saith, that Wine will be good and lasting, and the year will be seasonable only for planting of Vines. But Corn must be well fenced in Granaries because of Rain. Birds will be scarse, and it will be fit to dress Gardens. But when it shall be in *Taurus*, the house of *Venus*, the begining of Winter will be temperate and Rainy; but the middle will be much troubled with Snow, and the end will be cold. And the greatest cold will be from the middle of the Winter untill the vernal Equinoctial. The Spring will be temperate and moyst untill the Dog-starr arise. The Summer will be hot, the Autumne cold and full of diseases. But young people shall most be troubled with blear eyes. The Caterpillars shall abound most in Mountain places. Wine shall suffer detriment. Wherefore it is necessary to gather Grapes late. Trees will be very fruitfull, and small Birds scarce. The year will be improper for Saylers, and in this year some noble Man shall dye. But *Democritus* saith, That in this year there shall be much Hail, and Snow: and that the Easterne Winds shall not blow equally; and we ought to pray against Earthquakes and Wars. But when *Jupiter* is in *Gemini* the house of *Mercury*, the whole year shall find a South and South-West Wind. The beginning of the Winter indeed shall be windy, the middle temperate, and the end cold and windy. The Spring shall be temperate, and not much Rain, Corn shall

shall be much, and the Winds fair. Corn shall corrupt upon the floor, especially in *Syria*. Diseases shall arise about Autumne, in young Men especially, and of those of middle years, and Women. Also there will be blear eyes when the Summer is hot, and Women will dye. Trees will be fruitfull; and Fountains shall fail. It will be best to lay up Corn, by reason of the next years barrenness. *Democritus* saith, That Hail will be very hurtfull, and we must pray against the Plague. But if *Jupiter* be in *Cancer* the Moons house, the Winter commonly will be cold from the East, and dark, and there will be many inundations. About the Winter solstice there will be no great overflowings of water; and there will be great Hail after the Spring Equinoctial; craggy places will bring most Corn. The year will be wholesome except Autumne. *Democritus* saith, That in Autumne hot pushes will break forth about the Mouth. Wherefore in the Spring we must eat Potherbs, and purge, especially young Men, and drink Wine; Olives will be plenty. But when *Jupiter* is in *Leo* the Suns house, the begining of the Winter will be cold, and watry with great winds, that Trees will fall, the middle will be temperate, and the end cold. The Spring will be wet, and the Summer the same, and Springs will fail, and Pasture for Cattle. A dry Winter, and sickly, by reason of distillations and Coughs. Wherefore Men must eat bread sparingly, and drink much Wine. Corn will be indifferent. Wine and Oyl will be in abundance. The year will be good to Inocculate, but not to Plant. Tame Creatures that are great will dye exceedingly, but wild Creatures will increase more. A Man of note shall dye, and we must pray against Earthquakes. When *Jupiter* is in *Virgo*, the house of *Mercury*, the begining of the Winter shall be cold, the middle temperate, and the end very full of Ice, Showres, and great Inundation, that many places will be drownd with Rain; The Spring will be Rainy and hurtfull to Trees. When the Spring ends there will be Haile. The Summer will be Rainy and dark; and Corn must be suddenly brought in, that the Rain hinder not. The Autumne will be Windy and healthfull; The Vine will be fruitfull; and it will be a fit year to Plant Vines. Corn will easily corrupt. The year will be safe and subject to no disease. But we must pray for Fruits. When *Jupiter* is in *Libra*, the house of *Venus*, the begining of the Winter will be wet, the middle temperate, and Windy, the end moyst and cold. The Spring will be temperate with diseases from the head. The begining of Summer will be like to the Winter, and a dangerous year for Teeming Women. *Democritus* saith, That in this year there will never be great Rains, nor much Haile, but the Winter will be wet. When *Jupiter* is in *Scorpio*, the house of *Mars*, the Winter at first shall be cold, the middle hot with Hail, and the end moderate. The Spring will be cold untill the Summer solstice, and there will be Rain and Thunder, Springs shall fail, and Corn will be indifferent in price. Wine and Oyl shall abound, and Oxen shall dye. *Democritus* saith, That there will be great Rain, and diseases in Autumne. Wherefore we must pray against the Plague; and we must as he saith eat little, and drink freely. When *Jupiter* is in *Sagittarius* his proper house, the Winter will be temperate, and wet, yet neither hot nor cold. There will be great Floods, and when the Winter ends, there will be Winds and cold. The Spring will be Southerly and Rainy: the Summer will be temperate and more cold. The Floors must be fenced because of Rain; Autumn will be safe because the East Winds blow. The former and later Fruit will be good, but what comes out about the middle of it will be nought; Corn will abound both in Champion and Mountain grounds. Wine will last that is latest gathered from Grapes. All Trees will be fruitfull; The year will be fit for Planting and all other things. A great multitude of larger Creatures, and especially of Dogs shall dye. The Sea will be tempestuous, and evening Winds shall be great. Some principall Man shall dye. If *Jupiter* be in *Capricorn*, the house of *Saturn*, the begining of the Winter shall be temperate, the middle moyst and cold, the end Windy : but the waters overflowing will be hurtfull to Grain and other things. But water, cold and Snow will increase by heaps. The Summer before the Dog-star rise will be equall and moderate, but afterwards it will be hot and sickly. The East winds will blow clear, and there will
be

be Earthquakes. Champion grounds will bring most fruit. Mildew will destroy Vines. Trees will abound with fruit, and the year will be fit for small Creatures; but hurtfull for great ones, and chiefly Oxen. In Autumne will be many diseases, especially Headach, Bleareyes, &c. We must pray that Fruit be not hurt by Wind and Frost. When *Jupiter* is [in *Aquarius* in *Saturnes* house, the Winds will be very good for Corn, and fruits of Trees especially, the begining of the Winter will be cold, and the end windy. The Spring will be wet and winterly with Frosts. The Summer will be without Winds, by reason of the vehemence of Eastern Winds. There will be Rain also in Summer, that Corn shall be drown'd in part. In Autumne watry Winds that hurt fruit shall blow. Also there will be hot diseases, that fall upon young Men from a moyst cause, and upon middle aged Men. There will be Frost that will spoil most Grapes, yet all Corn both sooner and later will prosper. Birds both tame and wild will dye. There will be many Shipwracks, and a noted Man shall dye. Prayers must be made against pestilential diseases, Earthquakes and Thunder. Lastly, When *Jupiter* is in *Pisces*, his proper house, the Winter begins with Rain, the middle will be Windy, the end will be Snow and Hail. In the Spring fair Western Winds blow; the Summer will be hot, the Autumne fiery, especially for Women and young Maids. Also ill Winds will blow that blast Trees; Corn will be good: but the Floors must be fenced against Rain: it is a dangerous year for Childbearing Women. *Democritus* saith, That both Wine and Oyl shall abound, but we must pray against Earthquakes. *Zoroaster*.

Of Secrets belonging to Peace. Chap. 23.

That nothing but peacefull matters may befall a Man.

If a Plant of Turnsail called the Suns Bride be gathered when the Sun is in *Virgo*, about the begining of *September*, and wrapt up in the leaves of Bayes, with a Wolfs Tooth, no Man can speak against him that carryeth it but peacefull words; *Albertus* is the Author of this, who writ this and innumerable more Secrets out of a Book of Secrets of *John* King of *Arragon*, and I have by me the Coppy of it, written in a very old Manuscript, which was never yet Printed, and it is full of Secrets unspeakable. *Mizaldus*.

Of Secrets of War. Chap. 24.

A Warlike Stratagem.

An Elephant seeing a Ram grows mild and very gentle, and by this devise the *Romans* put to flight the Elephant of King *Pyrrhus* of the *Epirots*, and won a great victory from him.

That one may not be hurt by his enemies.

If a Man put on the skin of an Hyæna, and rush into the midst of his enemies, none can hurt him, and he may pass without fear; as *Orus Apollo* saith in his Hyroglyphicks.

The reason of scaling Ladders.

The reason of scaling Ladders which are necessary in Besieging of Cities, is thus described by *Polybius*. Let the Wall be *A. B.* that is X. foot high, the Ladder *A. C.* that is XII. foot long; for being set to the Wall, it will be so far remote *C. A. B.* that is XLIV. foot, for X. multiplyed into it self make a C. and XII. into it self make CXLIV. Wherefore being a square and equall to *A. B.* and *B. C.* then *B. C.* will be the side of the square XLIV. wherefore *B. C.* will be VI. foot and three quarters; and so three quarters of *A. B.* and so it will not be hard to clamber up, nor yet dangerous, that it may be easily driven back; which things will fall out where *B. C.* is very short, nor will it easily break, which would be where *B. C.* is very long, for they are harder to deal withall when they are so ex-

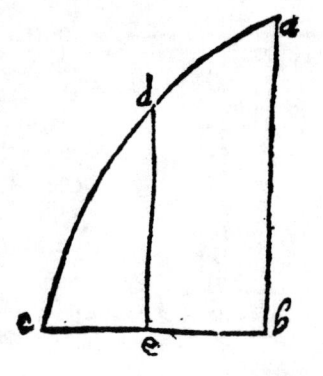

300 Secrets of Peace and War. Book XVI.

ceedingly long. Also a Prop D. E. must be just in the middle of A. C. for it will fall out to be in the middle proportion, and of A. B. as Euclide demonstrates it: therefore he saith, that a Captain Generall of an Army must be skilfull in Astrology and Geometry, and he shews why D. E. must be in the middle, for if D. be next to A. the Ladder will be the weaker, and if it stand lower it will be too upright; also the joynts and ends must be fenced with Iron, and there must be a sharp point below that it may stick fast to the ground, and there must be a Spear point perpendicularly made above, that it may stick fast to the Wall. *Cardan.*

Slings for War to cast forth great Weights.

Whatsoever is moved by violence, is moved the swifter, the more suddenly it is moved and at a greater distance, for if the space be very long and it moves very slowly, or very swiftly in a very short space it will not be cast far off. It will flye a great way the farther it is distant from that which is laid under it, and the greater the Angle is. Let A. B. A. C. A. G. be double to A. D. A. E. A. F. and let B. C. be treble to B. G. and D. E. treble to E. F. let E. and B. be the Weights to be moved, and to flye with equall swiftness: and E. must come to D. and B. to C. B. will be cast twice as far and more than E. and if E. come to F. and B. to C. then E. is sixfold more than E. yet it is not necessary to keep this proportion exactly. But that a great weight may be cast forth, there must be so much the more violence used, and the Engine must be the more solid. These things being laid down, a Sling Engine may be made three wayes, and each of them may be varied many wayes: But I shall only divide them single, and one of these into two. The first is performed by force of Men, (whilst they with one voice and strength, (for that is most considerable, that they joyn their strength, that it is almost incredible) pull a Rope about fastned to a Beam, or Staff, that casts forth one or more stones. The second is, that the beam A.B. may be bent backwards by force, in the end whereof there must be a Bulwark C. and when it returns it comes with a mighty force, for whatever is bended by violence returns to its own place, and sometimes farther at the same time, unless the force of it be hindred. But how it may be drawn back by a Capstand suddenly and easily, I have often shewed. But there must be an Iron in the Beam, according to its length: yet this way is subject to many dangers, least the Beam break, or the force fail, because it hath only a naturall force. But the third way is the best of all; there must be four Ropes before, twisted from a perpendicular one fourth part of a right line, and four Inces thick, a Beam must be set perpendicularly into them, fastned to the superficies, and in this there must be another strong Beam, fenced about with Iron, and for the distance of the cast, there must be a fortress at the end; It must be drawn by Capstands and Screws, untill it be equidistant from the plain, and so by the right perpendicular with a fourth part. This Sling when it is let flye, hath a mighty force: yet it differs much from the Sling of the Ancients, whose Operation was equidistant to the plain, and by a right Line. It is of this sort, if G. the other side of the Beam stick fast to the plain; For then it will cast more strongly, yet not farther, for it will bear more force. This way hath that convenience, that A. B. D. D. the Ropes may be led slack, and so the Sling may be as suddenly bent. Because being let slack, and drawn farther and twisted, they will be more effectuall to cast forth. Also four Ropes have

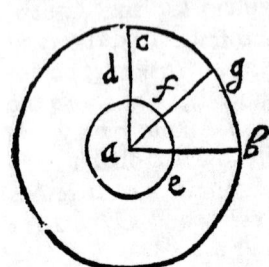

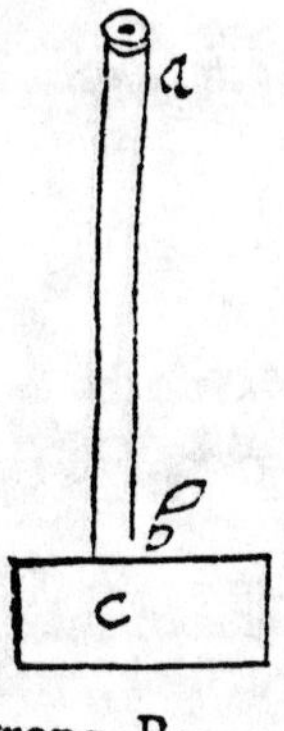

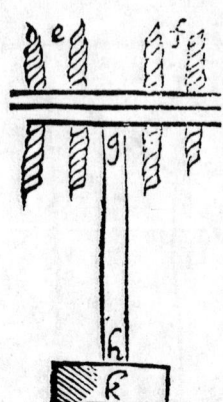

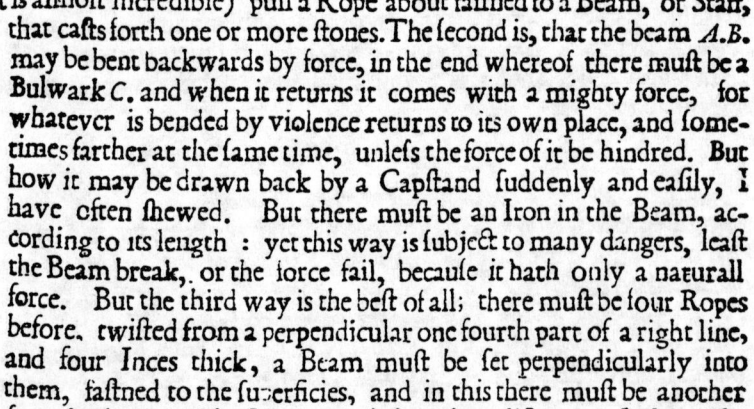

far

Book XVI. *Secrets of Peace and War.* 301

far more force to cast forth than one Beam; nor will they so easily break or grow weak. *The same.*   *The Engine called Poliorchetes, and a Ram.*

Poliorchetes was an Engine so called from destroying of Cities: There was one made against Rhodes, that was 125. foot in height, in breadth 60. and weighing 360000. pounds weight, and it was so well joyned, that it was safe against fires, and it would contain a stone of 360 pound weight, to cast it forth. Whereby it may be easily known what force there is in one to contain, and in another to sling forth. It consists of a Roof, covered with raw Hides and Twigs, that are hid with earth upon them to keep away fire, and this was to defend it: there were Wheels and Cords to draw it near to the Walls; And a Ram, that will as easily beat down Walls as our fire Engines, but it is hard to bring it to the place. It consists of two Beams, both standing forth right at length, and one placed upon the other; and that which is the lowest hung by the upper Beam with Cords and Iron Hoops; here and there were Pins, to which other Cords were fastned, and they drew the lower Beam, which the more forcibly it was drawn back, with the greater strength it came forward again. There was a frontispiece of Iron to defend it, that fire might not consume it, and that it might dig through Walls. It had two Hooks to make it like a Rams head: for it was not sharp at the end that it might break the more. Nor was it equall that it might beat down the sides of the Walls. The Horns of it were not straight, that when it was drawn back it might with main force draw the stones with it which it wrapt it self into, and so should suddenly cast down the Walls. That Ram that is set into Engines with roofs, hath three points, least in returning, if it had Horns, it might be wrapt within the Bricks, and so draw up the Basis of the Engine. It was wont to be in danger of fire-Darts; now these fire-Darts were like to Arrowes with a sharp Iron head; betwixt the Pipe and the Shaft there was a matter contain'd made with Bitumen, Rosin, Brimstone, Hurds, and burning Oyl, which being kindled was to be extinguished: when it stuck fast the Iron being shot in, the fire would not be quenched with water, but only by Earth. Some with *Sagapenum* added the Marrow of an Ass, which were not fit to cast forth, because, as I said, they would not send forth directly forward: And also with such force, that they made a noise like Thunder. Moreover those roof Engines, stood upon eight Wheels, and the greater of them had more, and they were made to turn every way. That will be done if one Axeltree be contain'd in another, as if the Wheels *A. B.* be turned upon the Axis *C. D.* and the Axis being made, a Beam be fastned into it by *E. F,* but the Screw must be in *F,* upon which it must turn, as oft as need is to turn about the Engine: for thus the Wheels and Beam of the Engine being directed another way, that lyes upon the Axeltree perpendicularly, the Engine may be turned which way you will. *The same.*

The reason of fiery holes under ground, which they call Mines.

Moreover the same way is to make Mines as to make Engines, but the Mines are more wonderfull. *Franciscus Georgius Senensis*, was the Inventor of this formidable work. He taught the *Spaniards* to overthrow the *Lucullian* Fort, near to *Naples*, which the *French* kept, it is now called *Ovum*, carrying the Temple with the *French* that were within it, off from the Mountain into the Sea; Wherefore when a Tower is not upon a Mountain at all, and it seems impregnable by reason of the scituation, they dig a Mine obliquely, four cubits high, and two in breadth; and the obliquity is of no great concernment when you are far from it: but when you come to the place you design to overthrow, the Hole must be oblique, as near to *A*. also there must be some solid Mountainy substance, least the force of the fire shut in, should vanish by the

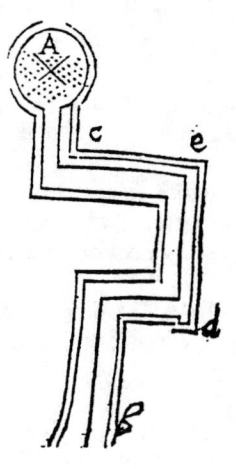

rarity

rarity of the place. Then almost all that place is filled with Gunpouder, that is very fine: and a Cord is drawn from *A.* unto the Mine *B.* here next to *A,* where the Pouder is, let it be thick and broad like to Flocks of Wool, and the whole Cord is boyld in Brimstone, and Vinegar, and Saltpeter, and then covered with Pouder it is dryed in the Sun; Then being dryed again very fine pouder is strewed upon it, and it is put in the Cane from *A.* to *B,* then with Wedges and Stones as far as the Dore *C.* and as far as *D.* it is fast shut up, so diligently that only the hollow of the Cane is left open. Wherefore *B* the begining of the Rope being kindled, the fire runs presently to *A.* by reason of the Pouder, and sets all the pouder on fire, and the place being stopped with Wedges and Stones; and if they should be driven forth no place would be open, because *E.* is not right against *A,* nor is *D.* right against *C,* nor is *B.* right against *E. D*; it is necessary that the Mountain break, and turn over all that is above it, shaking the whole Mountain. Wherefore the way *E. A.* must not be short, nor the place *A,* be any thin part of the Mountain, least where the obstacle is small the fire should break out, and leave the upper part untouched; Wherefore obliquity is the cause of so great a miracle, that even the Mountains will break asunder. *The same.*

Pouder that burns suddenly and vehemently.

But Pouder that burns easily, and whose flame scorcheth vehemently, is made of Gunpouder, Brimstone, and Greek Pitch, a third part. *The same.*

Gunpouder that will shoot away Bullets and make no noise.

Wherefore that which burns must be exceeding thin and dry, as Straw, distilled Wine, Gunpouder. But in this there is some earthy substance, and for this is the Saltpeter, and so it makes a crack. Wherefore some have endeavoured to make Pouder without Saltpeter, that might shoot a Bullet and make no noise; And this may be done gently without any great force. And *Brassivolus* reports, that the Duke of *Ferrara* found this out, and it was only shooting without any force about twelve paces: But as I said it is impossible to do it with great force. The Saltpeter being taken away, Gunpouder may be so made that it may shoot a Bullet and make no noise. But alwayes the more of the noise you take away, so much you take away from the force of it.

Another.

That Gunpouder makes a noise, the cause is the earthyness of it, for the bigger and harder the Corns are, the greater noise they will make. Wherefore that Gunpouder may drive forth the Bullet without noise, the Pouder must be ground very fine. *Felix Platerus.* D.

Gunpouder that works wonders in Warlike Engines.

If any one bruise and mingle with common Gunpouder a twelfth part of Quicksilver, so much Marchazite, and Colophonia as it ought to be done: and if he fill warlike Engines with this Pouder, when fire comes to it, the Engine will break with a huge noise, that it will kill many standers by. Contrarily if you mingle burnt Paper with this Pouder. or what will do the same, common Hayseeds two parts, very finely poudred and mixed, it hath a most violent force, and yet neither flames, nor makes so great a noise, by such a Pouder an ingenious Man will invent strange Experiments. *The same.*

The Gunpouder.

Take Saltpeter one pound, Coles of Teil tree, or Juniper, of each three ounces, Brimstone two ounces, and two drams: grind them very finely, moysten them, and by a Sive make it into Corns. *Lucas Rhor.*

Gunpouder without noise.

Take common Gunpouder, Borax, of each half an ounce, Fennelseed two drams, the Borax and Seed must be very finely poudred and mingled with Gunpouder. *Anonymus.*

A way to defend Cities.

But to pass over these things, I shall proceed to Arguments of divers Arts of Ingenuity. I will take five from Architecture. First to fortifie Cities. This

consists

consists of a threefold Art. By hindring, repelling, and security of the defenders: and besides this we need not find out any thing. We hinder three wayes; by Water, Ditches, Walls. A Ditch makes the approach difficult, no small defence by reason of the descent, but much more by reason of the ascent. Therefore both banks must be steep, but chiefly that next the Town or City, fourty paces broad, and very deep: For if you make it threefold, you shall not make it only impregnable, but it makes your enemies despair of taking it. This must have seven stops of runing water, for that which springs up cannot be intercepted nor taken away by any Art, but when it asists it drowns those that enter, making their feet slippery, and when they are heavy and wet, they can hardly ascend, and hinders digging of Mines, that they can be hardly sprung, whereby Wals are subverted. Moreover it dissipates and dissolves what is cast in, and it hinders fire that is thrown to destroy the Wals passing farther. The Wall must be thirty paces thick with a thin cement, and made of Brick, outwardly it must be of hard Flint, and bunching forth a little to a round Figure. For single Walls upon each shoulder (for this kind of measure is explained) must contain twenty of our Bricks, but twenty two smaller Bricks, as the Crassily: The height of it must be a hundred paces, for there must be ten under the Ditch, sixty unto the top of the Ditch, and thirty above, and it must be fortified with a very thick Rampire within. These do something in Towns, and less in Cities, where the main strength lyeth in the Souldiery: but if this be present, the City is totally impregnable thereby. Repelling consists in Rampires, and Towers, every two hundred feet, with a right Wall in the middle, but above inclining to a Circle. For so it will not hinder the shootings of the Towers, and the Enemies fire-Balls are made ineffectual. The uppermost part of the Wall must be round, least pieces be broken off by the Engines and kill the Defenders. Within the place there must be Trenches the Defendants can safely pass through. The Earth also must be made hollow at the bottome, that the sound may be heard of those that dig the Mines, and the Souldiers may walk about securely. The reason of Arching is this, The rounder it is the firmer it is, unto a perfect Circle: thicker at the bottome, and as they ascend higher, thinner, unto the very top point; the sides both wayes, where they begin to compass, are made of the broader thiner Tiles, that by the multitudes of them the cementing of them may hold the faster. The foundation sticks forth, and if it stand upon a Wall, the Wall is cut away, that like a Pit it may receive and retain the Foundation of the Arching. The thickness of it in comparison to the Wall must be one and half; but that which is laid for the Foundation must be thicker and firmer. Within every hundred paces, there must be a Privy-house and a Well, for want of water makes the Souldiers depart, besides the profit and advantage of it against fire, also it may be boyld and cast upon the Enemies heads, and a thousand other conveniences arise from it. Dung corrupts the Ayr; but many secret wayes through the Wals into the heart of the City, drive away many inconveniences, and are an infinite convenience to the Defenders, and they leave no cause of Retreat to them. But four or five secret wayes besides must be made into thick Woods that have not been cut down many years, and none must know these wayes, which must be made for five Miles or farther, besides the Prince himself. For this is gallant to send forth Messengers, to bring in Provision, and more assistance. The Walls of the City houses, as I said must be surrounded with another Wall, and fortified that no house may stand without it. Lately, When *Bura* was taken, a Cottage fell with the shot of a great Gun, for it stood somewhat without, and the chief of the City that went in there to consult were destroyed. And when the *French* besieged our City, *M. Antonius Columna*, and *Camillus Trivultius*, were slain by the same accident: and thereby their Forces were somewhat cut short at first, and after that broken, and lastly their power was totally defeated in Lombardy. But the use of private wayes that go secretly beyond the City to send forth Spies is necessary almost; and we must not forthwith flye to this remedy, nor yet stay so long untill all remedy be too late, but when the Siege is fierce, we must do it when Men dream not of it. *Cardanus.*

To make Bridges over Rivers.

But now I pass onto another example, and it is no less usefull. *C. Cæsar* was the Author of it, as he relates in his fourth Book *de Bello Gallico*. He made a Birdg over the Rhyne in ten daies by this invention, which because few understand it well, I am resolved to explain it. Fasten on both sides two Posts, signified by the Letter C, that are a foot and half thick, and so long, that being droven into the bottometome of the River, their tops may reach the superficies of the water, and let them stand two foot asunder. Then you shall fasten upon one side sharp Posts driven into the bottome with Engines, and fastned with Pipes, lying upon one side according to the course of the Rive, so that one of the Posts be near the Bank. Strike down as many that are equall to them, and so joyned as they are, fourty foot asunder, in the lower part of the River lying bending against the force of it, and them be called F, the highest Junctures C. and F. must be joyned with a Beam two foot broad, namely for the magnitude of the joynting, with two Braces or Pins or Cramps on both sides, from the inward part of the Post to the outward, that the severall Braces may embrace the severall Posts, and bind them fast. Equall unto these, and just over against them, on the other side of the River, must be driven in the like, that one Beam may be right opposite to another.

A Scheme of a half Bridg upon one side.

A. are the superiour Piles, against the River B. B. the inferiour Piles fastned to the Bridg are C. the two upper Posts D. A Beam two foot broad, E. E. E. E. are the Pins that fasten the Beam O, with the upper and lower Piles, F. are the two lower Posts joyned in like manner. Joyn these Beams placed according to the the course of the River I. with many other cross Posts laid upon them and fastned together also, and laying long Poles and Hurdles upon these a Bridg is made. To secure these many Posts must be driven in at the upper part of the River, bending upon one side to break the force of it; but far more bending than the Piles, and let them be beaten in fast, and joynd to the wole work. So the upper Piles will receive the force of the River, and the Beams that lye along, and the whole frame the more the water presseth it, by mutual embracing stands the faster. But this Bridg is strong enough and sufficient for all service, and cannot be carryed away. For sudden passage, Ropes only are extended, or Capstands are used or skins blown up, or Post fastned together. *The same.*

Præsages of victory.

Foresigns of victory are taken from four Observations. From Heaven, as when some firm sign is seen in Heaven that is proper to one side : as a Cross for Christians, the Moon for the *Mahometans* : and by such things as fall from Heaven, as Thunder and fire. Fire falling signifies Ruine, but if Spears seem to burn it signifies Victory. But the Generals Dreams are to be regarded, if he be a just Man, for such Dreams will shew the event, if he be wicked, he may see it clearly, as by Victory or fortune that chearfully moves him to sight; For the joyfull Dream that *Pompey* had when he lost the *Pharsalian* Battle, was not only false but destructive. But it is more certain and frequent from living Creatures : Crows and Vultures, what side they respect, they foreshew ruine, because these animals feed on Carcasses. Bees are worse, sitting upon the Standards, or upon the Generals Tent : for this Creature without revenge, when he hath made his Honey, is wont to be driven forth of the Hive with fire and smoke. Also a certain *Helvetian* General, who was famous for nine Victories, did foretell the tenth by the Enemies Dogs coming into his Camp from the Enemies Tents, for they forsake ill luck. Also Horses that neigh

and

and rejoyce shew Victory, and sad dull Horses shew loss and danger; Also some things use to happen to Conquerours that give them clear admotion, and they that shall be conquerd are not so plainly admonished. *Cardan.*

Signs of destruction of Cities.

Armed Men seen in the Clouds, are signs of the ruine of a City; such appeared in the dayes of the *Machabees*, when the War was most miserable, and after that when *Vespasian* Besieged the place, destinated for that War. Also some say there were some seen in *Germany*, but not constantly for many dayes. *The same.*

BOOK. XVII.

Of the Secrets of Mechanical Arts.

In the two precedent Books, I have finished the Secrets of Arts and Sciences, which they call Liberall; but to perfect this Learning concerning Secrets, I shall speake something of Mechanical Arts in this Book. Mechanical Arts are so called, that by use of Hands and Instruments performe their work, as is the Millers and Smiths Art, and such like, and the Secrets of them I shall here touch upon very briefly.

Of the Secrets of Millers. Chap. 1.

A wonderfull Instrument to boult Wheat.

Though these things may seem to be spoken by the way, yet that it may shew the Artificial Invention of Men, that took its begining from the nature of the Ayr, there was a most gallant Engine found out to boult Meal, and it was above three years since that I resolved to disclose it, that Men may also understand, with what small matters so they be Ingenious, wealth may be gained. For now that all Bakers find the profit, and the Emperour hath granted the Man a priviledg, that no Man shall have it without his consent, he lives by this Industry, and in a short time he hath built him a House. For not only Bakers, but Colledges of Priests, and Sacred Virgins that are Nuns, and all Nobles that keep great Families, and have great profit. I may say also necessity of it, and many more, whom not so much the profit, as the wonder of it hath moved, have caused it to be made. The making of it is this. There is a small Wheel B. and at the end of that is a handle A. to turn it about; these two are set beyond the Engine. When the Wheel is turned about to which there are set opposite two little Wodden Teeth C, and two more next unto it, and they are set opposite also, but as it were in the middle place between the former, that when the Wheel is once turned about, it may touch the broad Board four times, and the plain square $D. E.$ that is hanged on both sides to the Capsula, that as the Wheel turns, the Board with a trembling motion being touched with the small Teeth may alwayes shake. Moreover the Wodden Tooth C. and a small part of the Board are compassed about by the Capsula, upon the Wood or Board $D. E.$ stands a Meal boulter $F. G.$ hanging obliquely, and from $G.$ fastned in $H.$ that it fall not out. This consists of very thin, and exceeding light Boards on all sides, except in the middle where the Meal is shaked forth of the Sieve: for as it is usuall that part is made of Linnen. All these are included on all sides in a Coffer, on the top whereof there lyeth the small Capsula K. and in that being square as in a very light Wodden Dish lyeth the Meal, and this is so hanged up, that it may easily be shaken, but it is shaken by a small Cord fastned to it by the other part of the Wheel, namely, on the right and by B. you must observe also that the Boulter $F. G.$ is open at both ends, on the upper end to receive the Meal from the Dish, at the lower end, that it may cast forth the Bran by G. And the whole Case is divided into three parts, $L. M. N.$ raising up partitions of thin strong Boards that stand immoveable: It may if you please be divided into four parts. This being done; When the Wheel $B.$ is turned about, the Cord shakes the Dish, and the Teeth the Board, the Dish shakes forth the Meal into the Boulter $F. G.$ the Board shakes the Sieve, and thence it comes

306   *Secrets Mechanicall.*   Book XVII.

to pass that the finest Flowre is first sifted out, and falls into *N. M.* part of the Capsula, but descending and being more violently shaken, the lower part is sifted forth not so fine, into *L. M.* And lastly there descends by the lower Mouth of the Sieve, *G.* the Bran of the whole into *L. O.* and thus are three parts severally taken, the heart of the Meal in *N. M.* courser Meal in *L. M.* and the Bran in *L. O.* But all the Meal that flyeth about, must necessarily return to its place, so that nothing will be lost, because the Capsula hath no vent; But it is needfull (which you may easily perceive by reason) that the Boulter *F. G.* must not be so sloping, for the Meal would come as far as *G.* and be cast forth with the Bran. Wherefore if you bring the partition *L.* as far as the mouth of the Sieve, or any other partition, as of the Dish, you shall, as you see, with that bend back the upper mouth *C*, that you shall not lose a half penny worth of Meal. Now conceive what great commodity ariseth by this one Instrument. First, With one Mans labour who turns the Wheel and puts Meal into the Dish, and when all places are full, gathers up the Flowre and Bran that is Boulted, he doth the work of three Men that Boult. Secondly, For this work, that is neither laborious nor hurtfull, any Man may do it, and ordinary people may be had farre cheaper than Boulters are. Thirdly, That all the Meal is collected, and nothing lost, whenas such as Boult by shaking their hands and Arms are in pain, and can do no more than they can do with their Arms, and therefore no small part of the Meal is lost. Add to this, that a Linnen Boulter that only trembles is not so much worn, but far less than when Men sift Meal, for they must of necessity oftimes shake the Sieve violently. Also it is a shorter work, because the Meal is sifted exactly, that the Bran is clear Bran. All these things are done without fouling the house, or hurt, or discommodity to any; Moreover the nature of the Instrument is to make two or three sorts of Flowre, which cannot be done by Men-Boulters, first uncertainly, secondly unconstantly. *Card.*

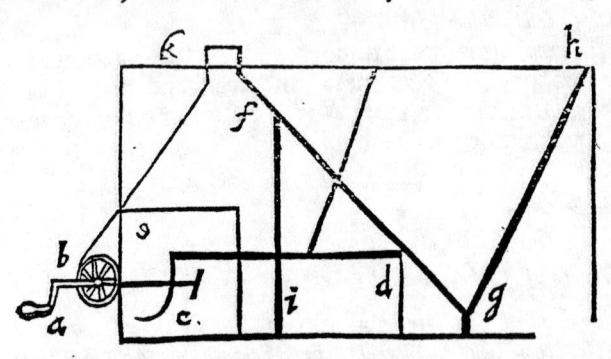

To make a Wind-Mill.

I will not pass over what is so admirable, and I could not believe it before I saw it, nor can I relate it without suspition of levity it is so common. But desires of knowledg overcome modesty. In *Italy* therefore in not a few places, and in many places in *France*, there are Mills made to turn about with the wind; and with such mighty force, that they are able to carry about three Horsemen with their Horses; and they are for so present profit, that they will grind eight *Mellan* Bushels every hour, that is, about 3000. pounds of Corn; And this work is made with such Industry, that when the wind ceaseth, it will even turn about of it self. When I had seen many, I observed one more diligently about St *Maturinus*, when I take that long and continual Journey. For example, It shall suffice to relate the manner of the Engine. Let the Tennon be set upright and propt up with many posts *A. B.* upon this the whole Engine must be held up. There must be a post on the Door-side, *C. D.* to turn the whole Frame about at pleasure; And it is so fitted, that the wind may come to the Sails obliquely, not just in the face, nor yet sideways, which are fastned and thrust into the round Beam *E. F.* that stands right forth over against the door,

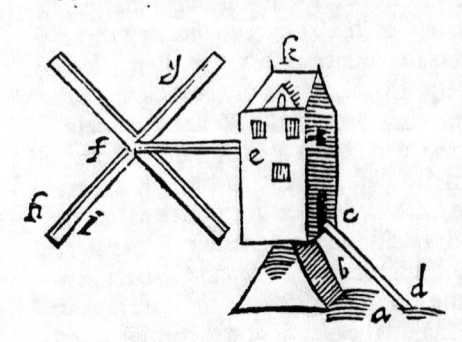

door, and turns about: Wherefore two and two Sails are oppositely joyned together, and they are not far distant one from another, yet they are not faftned into the same place of the Beam, and they reach forth almost as far as the ground, such is the length of them; each of them consists of two superficies, and each of them hath four or five hands broad, and the Sails are stretched forth to cover them, but the upper superficies G. H. looks a little backwards, as the former K. L. is equidistant from the superficies of the last Engine. As therefore the Ayr presseth down the uppermost superficies of the Sails, which is equall to the lower, the whole Wheel, and with that the rest that are containd in the Engine are carried about. For if the Sails were raised perpendicularly upon the superficies of the Engine, and according to the length of E. F that they might receive the wind, as Wheels and Sails of Water-works do, the Wheel would be hindred as much by the upper Sail, as it is forced by the lower; Wherefore for this reason it is made, that when the Ayr presseth down the superficies G. H. directly, the Wheel G. L. should be turned about. But why also without wind it should be almost turned about, the cause is the motion now began, and the force acquired, whereby the Engine equally ballanced is moved, as I speak elsewhere of a Ring. Also the wind though it seem to cease below, yet it beats upon the upper Sail. Wherefore I would have this explained more diligently. *The same.*

Of the Bakers Art. Chap. 2.

A way to make Bread that shall keep long uncorrupted.

But to return to my principall purpose, the generall cause of keeping it is drying of it; For things dryed keep very long; so that Bisquet may be kept a whole year good. For (as I have proved elsewhere) all things that corrupt, corrupt by reason of sound moysture; and therefore the watry moysture being taken away it will keep long. But it being difficult to take away the watry moysture, but some of the radical moysture that is fat must be consumed also: hence it is that this doth not nourish so much as common Bread: but also in Ships by the moysture of the water, it will all grow mouldy, and for the most part it will corrupt also, wherefore they are forced to bake it twice or thrice, or to eat it corrupted: But Men say that in the Island *Sava*, which is two hundred miles from the *Moluccos*, Bread is made will last three years; we know not how they make it, but if it be reduced to our principles, the generall rule must be urged. Wherefore it must be thick and fat, and baked at an easie fire, mingling something therewith that naturally resist putrefaction. But perhaps we cannot attain to it, because our Ayr is thiner or moyster than the *Indian* Ayr, or from some other cause more fit to breed corruption. *The same.*

An Oven that will save charges.

An Oven to bake many things, that is also usefull, and is now used at *Millan*, sparing two parts of wood of three, because the fire shut in hath three times more force. Make a square Oven about two cubits broad, and one cubit high, and a half, with Lime and Bricks. Above let there be four large holes, round, as big as your pots and dishes, cover the upper superficies within all with Brass, but where the holes are, cut away the Brass, and let the pieces serve for covers. When therefore you use it, set your dishes and pots in their places; when you need no vessel, put on the coverings that the Oven may have no vent; under the upper place there is a cavity, and a square little door, by which you put in Wood and Coles: but on the side there is a much larger but lower door, and in the lowest part of it, in the middle place there is a single Iron Grate, through which the Ashes fall down; wherefore it is plain that the door you put the wood in by is in the upper part, and the other in the lower part. Also flesh is Roasted upon a Spit, setting Hinges on the sides of that door by which the Ashes are drawn forth: for there the coles will roast flesh, and the flame in the upper place will turn the Spits, if a Wheel be set as it should be; but then since it hath a vent you cannot save so much Wood. *Card:*

Of

Of the Art of Cookery. Chap. 3.

To keep flesh long uncorrupted.

It is reported that in the Mountains of *West-India*, flesh is kept so long uncorrupted that is beyond belief, for near the City *Cuzcum*, Horses having been killed above four Moneths, will be as fresh and without any ill sent, as if they were but newly killed. I suppose the cause to be not only the cold, which though it be exceeding great here, yet in greater cold flesh will not be preserved so long. Wherefore I conceive that the Ayr is thin and brackish, may be the flesh of it self conduceth something thereto. For flesh corrupts sooner in Water than in the Ayr, because the Ayr is thiner, if all other things be alike. And again by the same reason flesh will keep longer if you fasten a brass Nail into it, because the force of the Brimstone dryeth it. *The same.*

That boyl'd flesh may seem raw.

If you dry Lambs blood and strew it on flesh that is boyld it will seem raw, for it dissolves and changes the colour of the flesh.

That flesh may soon grow tender.

The flesh of Cattle that are slain will soon grow tender and soft, that are hung in a Figtree. *Plutarch* in his Symposiacks demands the reason of it. For saith he, when a Cook had amongst the Meats of *Ariston*, had offered a dunghill Cock in sacrifice to *Hercules*, that was, fresh, tender, and would even break in pieces, *Ariston* said, the Figtree made it tender so soon, affirming that all Birds be they never so tough will grow tender by hanging in a Figtree. The reason he gives is this, That the Figtree sends forth a vapour that is strong and digesting, and thereby flesh is digested and concocted. The same is done by laying them into an heap of Wheat, and cover them all over with it. *Mizald.*

To keep flesh from corrupting.

If a Nail of Brass be stuck into Hogs or Crows flesh, *Plutarch* saith, That by its astringent faculty and drying, it will keep their flesh long uncorrupted. Those that dig forth Mettals know this by certain experience by abiding in the Mines; and *Langius* saith, That he that shall enquire after it may here be satisfied of it. *The same.*

That flesh cut in pieces may grow together again.

The roots of Comphrey that are black without and white within, and glewy, if they be boyld with chopt Meat, will soon make them grow together again, as if they had never been cut. *Alexius.*

To make flesh be quickly boyld.

Some say it is certain that a piece of a Melon put into the pot will make the flesh boyl suddenly, and others say that Nettle seed or Mustard seed will do the like, or stalks of the Figtree. *Mizald.*

That old flesh may sooner be boyld and wax tender.

Monks Rheubarb, some call it patience, (it is a plant with a great top, and large long leaves, and the stalk is red when it is ripe, and the root yellow,) boyl this with flesh, and it makes them tender and more fit to be eaten. *Alexius.*

That a roasted Peacock may seem as if he were alive.

Kill the Peacock, either thrusting a Feather from above into his brain, or cut his throat as you do a young Kids, and let the blood run forth of his throat; then divide his skin gently as far as his tail, and being divided pull it off from his head all over his body Feathers and all; keep this with the skin cut off, and hang the Peacock by the heels upon a Spit, having stuffed him with sweet Herbs and Spices, and roast him, first sticking Cloves all along his brest, and wrapping his neck in a white Linnen Cloath, alwayes wetting it, that it dry not. When the Peacock is rosted, take him off from the Spit, and put his own skin upon him, and that he may seem to stand upon his feet, make some Rods of Iron fastned into a Board, made with leggs, that it may not be discerned, and drive these through his body as far as his head. Some to make sport and laughter, put Wool with Camphir into his mouth, and they cast in fire when he comes to the Table. Also you may gild a rosted Peacock, strewed with

with Spices, and covered with leaves of Gold for your recreation, and for magnificence; The same may be done with Pheasants, Crains, Geese, Capons, and other Birds. *The same.*

That a Wren may rost himself upon the Spit.

It is most wonderfull that a Wren a small Bird put upon a woodden Spit that is very thin, should turn about and rost himself; But that must be a fresh Nuttree stick, which *Cardan.* did not observe. *Mizald.*

That a Chicken may be soon rosted.

Also I thought fit to let you know, that a Wallnut put into a Chickens belly will make him rost quickly. *Mizald.*

To rost a Goose alive.

Let it be a Duck or Goose, or some such lively Creature, but a Goose is best of all for this purpose, leaving his neck, pull of all the Feather from his body, then make a fire round about him, not too wide, for that will not rost him : within the place set here and there small pots full of water, with Salt and Honey mixed therewith, and let there be dishes set full of rosted Apples, and cut in pieces in the dish, and let the Goose be basted with Butter all over, and Larded to make him better meat, and he may rost the better, put fire to it; do not make too much haste, when he begins to rost, walking about, and striving to flye away, the fire stops him in, and he will fall to drink water to quench his thirst; this will cool his heart and the other parts of his body, and by this medicament he loosneth his belly, and grows empty. And when he rosteth and consumes inwardly, alwayes wet his head and heart with a wet Sponge : but when you see him run madding and stumble, his heart wants moysture, take him away, set him before your Guests, and he will cry as you cut off any part from him, and will be almost eaten up before he be dead, it is very pleasant to behold. *The same.*

A Lamprey fryed, boyld, and rosted, at the same time.

First torturing the Lamprey with rubbing him with a sharp Cloath, thrust a Spit through him; and wrap all the parts boyld and fryed, three or four times in Linnen Rags, strewing Pepper with Wine, and upon the boyled Lamprey, Parsley, Saffron, Mints, Fennel, bruised with sweet Wine, and make them wet with water and Salt, or Broth, command the fryed parts to be wrapt in Oyl at the fire, alwayes moystning it, with a bunch of Origanum sprinkling it, when part is torrefied, take it up it will be excellent meat, set it before your company. *The same.*

To rost Fish upon a Paper.

Make a Vessel to fry them in of single Paper, put in Oyl and Fish into the Paper, upon the red Coles without any flame, and it will do it sooner and better than any other way. Let it not vex you to alow more Oyl, for perhaps it will not be hurtfull to know it : So

You may take all the bones out of some Fish called Piones.

If you take out his guts and wash him, and let him stand twenty four houres in sharp Vinegar, and stuff him with Spices, you may boyl or rost him, and his bones will not hinder you to eat him. *The same.*

Another.

And for that cause the invention was found out how to fry Fish upon a Paper, as well as with a Frying-Pan. Take a single Paper, and raising up the sides like to a Lamp, pour in Oyl, and before it soke through, set it upon the clear coles without any flame, for the Oyl will not pass through, avoiding the fire, nor will the Paper burn, because it cannot dry, the Oyl preserving it. But fire cannot be without extream drynefs, nor can flame or motion so attenuate as to make it burn, but it will grow hot by degrees putting under fresh Coles, and so it will boyl, which is very strange, for the Fishes will be well fryed in it. *Cardan.*

Excellent seasoning of Fish.

You shall excellent well preserve Fish thus : Fry them meanly with Oyl, but not perfectly : then strew Salt upon them, that they may not be salt or fresh, and laying

ing Bay leaves and Myrtle leaves between, when they are alittle dryed, lay them up in a Pannier. *The same.*

To provide good Mustard.

Sudden and excellent Mustard for Sawce, wheresoever you are, may be thus provided, Take two ounces of Mustard seed, with half an ounce of common Cinnamon, which you find in the Shops. Both must be finely ground and mixed with sufficient quantity of Vinegar and Honey, and make a Paste of it, and make Cakes or Balls thereof, and dry them in the Sun or in a hot Oven, when you please dissolve one Ball in Wine or Vinegar, or some other moysture, and you have Mustard easie to provide, very pleasant to the pallate, and good for the Stomach. *Miz.*

That Coleworts may not boyl.

Paxamus one of the Greek Husbandmen seems to me to have written well, that if one pour in a little Wine into the boyling Coleworts, they will boyl no more, but losing its force, it will change colour and dye. *The same.*

That a Pot may never boyl.

The shell of a female Tortois laid over a Pot, will cause that the Pot shall never boyl. *The same.*

Of the Confectioners Art. Chap. 4.

That Olives may be soon seasoned.

If you will soon Pickle green Olives, cut them, and for twenty four houres let them lye warme in water and Lime, and twice as much Ashes, then being taken forth, wash them five times in warm water, and after that in salt-water. *Cardan.*

Myrtle berries, and Boughs of a Figtree, how they may be kept green.

Myrtle berries with the Stalks, and Figtree Boughs with their Leaves bound into small handfuls and laid into Oyl Lees, may be kept green, but the vessel must be luted with Gyp; and thus they are seasoned, but it is better to see them than to eat of them. *The same.*

To keep Rheubarb long.

Wax if any thing will preserve the forces of it, for it keeps out the Ayr, it keeps it moderately moyst; Rheubarb can be preserved for twenty years no better way than this. *The same.*

To make red Wax.

Take Wax one pound, Turpentine three ounces in winter, Vermilion well ground upon a Painters Stone, common Oyl, of each one ounce, melt the Wax and Turpentine at the fire, then take them off, and after they are alittle cole, add the Oyl and the Vermilion, mingle them well and keep it; some for Cinnaber put in red Lead three ounces for every pound of Wax. *The same.*

To make green Wax.

Take Wax one pound, Verdigrease ground, common Oyl of each one ounce; Melt the Wax at the fire, and when it is almost cold, add the Verdigrease, and Oyl, mix it well, it will be green. If you would make this Wax hold fast, add the quantity of Turpentine spoken of for red Wax. *The same.*

To make black Wax.

Take one pound of Wax, melt it at the fire, add unto it black Earth, and common Oyl of each one ounce, mix them well, untill the Wax be cold, if you will have it stick fast, add Turpentine as I said before. *The same.*

To make white Wax.

Take Wax as much as you please, and of Fountain water twice as much, mingle them, and set them over the fire untill the Wax be melted, then let them stand awhile, untill all the Wax swim on the top of the water. Then take some Glass vessel, whose outside is smooth, and wet it in cold water, then dip it almost up to the middle of it in the melted Wax, and take it forth with the Wax that sticks unto it, let the Wax cool, and then take it off from the vessel: do this so often untill all the Wax be taken up from the water: then set that Wax thus ordered in the Sun, and
dew

dew in *May* : and turn it often, and leave it there so long untill it be as white as white Lead. Some do whiten it three dayes, observing the foresaid manner when the Sun shineth hottest. And because all that Wax is fine, and will easily melt in the Sun, you must twice in the day sprinkle cold water upon it.

Another.

Lay any Wax in the Sun, wet it twice a day with Fountain water, and you must often wash it in clear water, and make it into Cakes that the Sun may have more operation upon it; and you shall have most white Wax for any purpose. *Ludolphus Rolevincus.*

Of the Smiths Art. Chap. 5.

Clocks without a Cord.

The Wheels serve for a Cord; in some Mils are set upon them in the forme of a Snail, with twenty six Teeth and some have more; by these Teeth the Axeltree that drives the whole Engine, is carried about; In another there is a Wheel with fourty eight small Teeth, placed at the bottome, and that fastens in the other Wheel; that when is turned about with the force of the other Wheel that is in the bottome, the other that layeth hold of it with as many Teeth being turned also, the whole Engine is carried about. *Cardan.*

Vessels that will not break.

He also taught how to make Vessels to melt Mettals with; for they are made chiefly of the tops of Rams horns, and of bones calcined to ashes, and poudred with a Pestle. But if you add to this Emeril, or the tops of Bucks horns, or the Jaw bones of Pikes calcined and quenched twice or thrice in Vinegar, the Vessels will not break, nor the the Mettal wast away: these things are added and put in especially at the bottome, that it may not drink in the Mettal. *The same.*

A Lock that may be shut with any name.

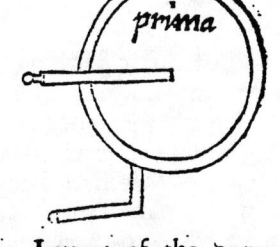

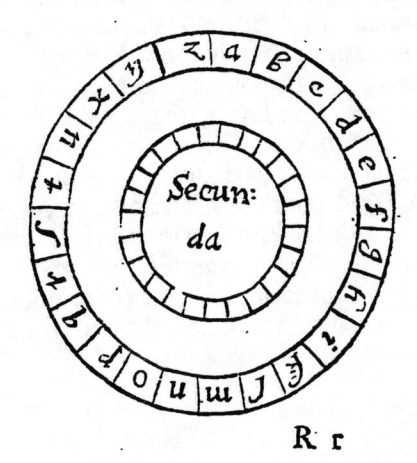

Janellus made this, it consisted of only seaven Letters, and it could be opened by no other name than the same it was locked by. There was first a solid Rundle smooth on the outside; on the forepart there was a Pipe that stuck forth straight from the Center, at the end whereof there was a short Screw that went into it, on the brim of this Rundle there was another empty Pipe, that was round, equall in magnitude and equidistant and over against it two small Lines distinguished the brim, on these Lines the seaven Letters of the name must be placed right one against the other, as you turn about, or fit the Rundles in such order, as you are minded to keep. As for example, let the name you will keep be *Serpens*, all the Rundles must be set directly between the two Lines, with the Letters one against another, that you may either open or shut the Lock. For there will be seaven Rundles in the Margin that have the Alphabet upon them, whereof I have described one upon the Margin for an example, or as many in number, as the number of the Letters are by which it must be shut. In the middle must be a large Circle distinguished with so many spaces, as there are Letters in the Margin, and as many toothed Rundles, as there be orders of the Alphabet. These I have described in the third Figure, adding the small Tooth, as in the fourth the hinder part of the Rundles of the second Figure, with the space in the middle Rundle, into which the small Tooth of the small Rundle is fastned. Whence it is manifest that when the second Rundle is turned about, it will draw the third along with it, and yet unless the Letter be fastned in its proper place, one cannot be joyned to the other nor taken from it. When the Lock is shut, the rounds will turn about easily, that so the reason of the name may be confounded. *The same.*

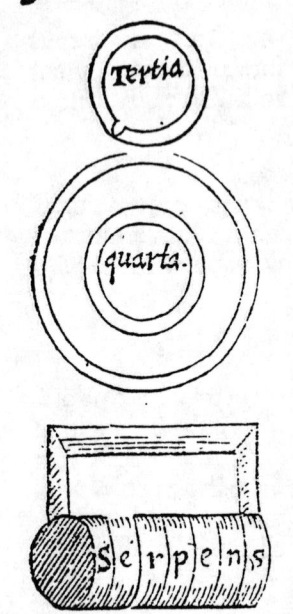

A Chest to hide Muney in and it cannot be discovered.

No Man is ignorant that the matter must be Iron, and the Plates must be thick. Also the usuall way is to have a double bottome in the Chest, or little concavities on the sides, and secret small Cabinets and by places, but all these can hardly deceive a cunning Man, when he compares together the thickness of the parts and sides, wherefore on the sides or corners on the more sloping places, make a little hole, and let the cavity within inside be as much as you will, and many hollow places if you think fit, shut money in, and stop up the cavity with Cotten, and then with thin Saw dust, and the white of an Egg fill up the hole. that he which shut it up shall hardly find it. *Cardan.*

Another.

A Board is so laid over the hole that no chink may appear. Into the piece that is to be removed, a small Mettal Screw is fastned that must receive it, and a Pin is put into it, other Pins or Nails like to that are disposed of in the Chest after a certain order, when the place is to be opened, take away the Nail, and thrust in another Screw into that in the Board and pull up the Board. Alwayes remember that the empty place must make no noise when you put any thing into it, wherefore stop it up with Cotton, or some such thing, and thus you may contrive many secret wayes. *The same.*

Another excellent one and there is no better.

You shall fasten to a Board with Screw-Pins a Lock or Iron Plates to which the covering of the Chest is made fast: under the Lock or Plate let there be little dores of hollow places, when you would open it, you must have an Iron Instrument, as you see here represented, at the end thereof there must be a concavity, which may take fast hold of the head of the Screw-Pins, so that they may be turned back and unscrewed, to take off the Lock or Plate from the Chest. But that the work may be firme, there must be under the Screw-Pins Screw-receivers, to receive them firmely in, and these must be placed on the side of the Chest under the said thin Plates. In Trunks also that are coverd with Cloath within side, many other wayes are thought upon. But chiefly care must be had that the hole may be totally concealed, as I taught in the former example, or that it be firmely garded with a Plate, and so it will lye hid the more, and the concavities may be covered with the heads of the Pins that run into the Chest that is to be parted from them. *The same.*

A

A strong Lock.

It was a matter of no less Industry, that was lately brought to me, an unusuall kind of Lock, whereby perhaps it may be thought not to be so commodious as the rest, but it was not unpleasant to behold for the ingenious contrivances in it. There was an Iron Pipe *A.* six fingers in length or more, upon which there was placed a covering *B.* and it was made turning like to a Sithe, and so fast to it, that there was a hole cut on the side of the Pipe, that it might be set into it on the one side, and again if the Lock were to be opened it might be drawn forth again. But that it might be opened by no Man without the help of the Key, a Wedg *D.* as thick as the Pipe would bear it, was put into the Pipe, *G.* with two points into two holes *E. F.* made like handles, or bolts: but the points on both sides were armed with fins, which when they were passed the holes did extend themselves, and so neither could the Wedg be taken forth, nor the Bolt removed, unless the fins were contracted by help of a Key, whereby they hindred the Wedg to be drawn forth. But that Key *F.* was not made after the ordinary manner, for being long like a little Staff, it was thrust into the Pipe *H.* at one end, and by the two distances in the head of it *I. I.* it pressed the fins of the Wedg, and so the Bolt, the Wedg being taken out was easily drawn forth.

That doores may be opened by none but some of the houshold.

But I return to Mechanical matters. I shall describe two wayes how to make Locks for Doores, that only those of the house can open them, and no other Men, and by these you may invent infinite more. Let *A.* be the Ring of *G.* joyned with a solid Iron stick *B. C.* Another Ring is *C. D.* in the middle whereof *B. C.* is carryed about (because it is round and not joyning to the Ring) it is within the Posts, and *A.* stands looking forth beyond them. The Staff is answerable to *C. D.* but *D. E.* is a plate of Iron, joyned with the Ring *C. D.* that the Ring being brought about it may be lifted up, but of it self it fals down of its proper motion; *F.* expresseth a hook of Iron fastned in the other Post, *G. H.* is part of the door, in which are the Rings. Wherefore when *A.* is carryed about, it doth not move *C. D.* both because of the weight *D. E.* and also because the Staff is not fastned to *C. D.* But when *G. H.* is stirred, *E.* sticks fast to *F*; therefore *D. E.* cannot be elevated, but because *B.* sticks moderately to *C. D.* the *C. D.* fastned to it is elevated, and *D. E.* the Plate, and the Door is opened, wherefore pulling vehemently, or not moving of it, *D. E.* holds fast; But it is moved moderately, and so between to immoveables that are contraries, the mean is moveable. *Card.*

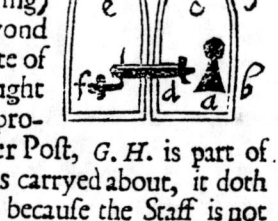

Another way more acute than this.

A. is a Ring that sticks forth beyond the Door, and joynd to a Staff that within the Door is fastned to the Ring *B.* To *B.* there is joyned above another Staff *C.* so that *A.* being carryed about, *C.* is also turned about with it; now *C.* sticks forth somewhat beyond the Post on the inside, so that if it be turned about, it may not fall upon *D. E.* Now *D. E.* is a Plate fastned into a Post *G. H.* with a Pin, that it may both fall down and be raised up. Where the hole is larger, by which the Pin *D.* is thrust in; It fals upon the hook *P.* as before, that is fastned into the other Post. All this Artifice is covered with a hollow Woodden Board, fastned to the Post *G. H.* that it may not hinder the moving of the Bolt, as in other things that we would keep secret, because all things are not to be communicated to the wicked World. He therefore that knows it not, is three wayes deceived in going about to open it; First, Because in other works *D. E.* is fastned to *B.* and the Door opens from the left hand to the right; but here it is clean contrary, for the foldings of the Door are here opened, because *C.* presseth down *D*, and so by reason of the under lifter, *E*, is raised up. Secondly, Because *C.* sticks forth farther from the Gate than *D. E.* unless *A.* be drawn back, *C.* will not fall upon *D*, and therefore it will not open. Thirdly, Because if the Door be not immediately opened, *C.* will fall below *D.* and *E.* will fall again, because the length *C.* is scarse extended beyond *D.* Whence followes the fourth mistake, That unlesse a man make two contrary operations, the Gate cannot be opened. For one must pull to shorten C. and thrust from him, that it may open; which two contrary motions for them that are not used to it, to performe is not very easie. *The same.*

An Instrument that turns Spits about with the least fire.

A Plate of Iron is fastned upon the sides of the Chimney wals on both sides, in this there is a hole into which the point of of an Iron Rod is thrust, to be turned about; There is a thin Fann, and at the bottome it hath a Wheel with Teeth, whose other point alittle more blunt is fastned into the upper hole of the Pin, and it is to be turned also to that. In the same Pin, near to the upper hole there is another hole on the side, into which is thrust the point of another Iron Rod, by which, near the point that is in the Pin, an Iron Wheel with small Teeth is carryed about, so that the Teeth lay hold of the Tympanum, and the turning point, as it doth on the adverse part which is inclosed in a Rundle: about the middle of it a Wooddden Wheel is carryed about, and is made hollow with many circles, in the hollow cavities whereof an Iron Chain is made to compass it, and it goes again about the round handle of the Spit, and as many hollow circles as be in the Wooddden Tympanum, so many Chains there may be and so many Spits. Wherefore it comes to pass that the Iron Rod that is made unequall as it were with Wings, and as it were inclining, is turned about by the smoke, whereby the Tympanum turns about the Wheel, which carrying the Chain about with it by reason of inequality, turns the Wheel handle of the Spit. And it turns with such ease the Fann blowing equally ballanced, and perpendicularly, that without any fire, so there be no Spit, the Tympanum will turn the Wheel set into it, and the reason of it is not difficult. For the Ayr that under the Chimney being straitned is forcible, as I shewd elsewhere concerning secret places under ground: And this is an Argument that the Ayr flyeth upwards. And this fals out the more when the Engine is light and well polished, and the space of the Chimney about the Fann kept close on all sides, that little Ayr may get forth. That I may be more clearly understood what I mean by the name of a Chimney, as I use the name also elsewhere largly according to the liberty I have; knowing that it should more properly be called a fire or smoking cover: for it is driven about rather by a flame than smoke, by reason of the vehement motion, but not at all by live glowing Coales. Also the Spits must be round on that part that they are leane upon, the Engine that turns them at a distance, for those that are square are not easily turnd. *The same.*

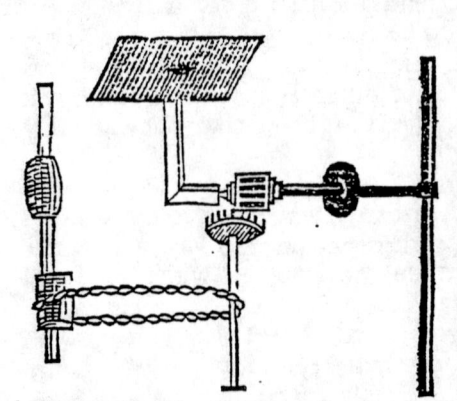

Folding Tables.

It is no contemptible way of a Table that I saw often, especially in *Gaunt* in *Flanders*; Take a square Margent, as it were four cubits long, and as many cubits broad, or not much less *A. B.* In the middle of this let *C. D.* lye overthwart, a Board nine Inches broad fastned to the Margent with Nails, and in it there must be two holes, into which Pins may be thrust low to hold it fast. There must be four Pillars at the ends of the ledges, and four holes next to them, the severall holes must not be set opposite one to the other in the sides of the longitude, but at such a distance that the bolts may not hinder one the other. But the holes must come as far as the superficies of the Ledges, being square, deep, and broad,

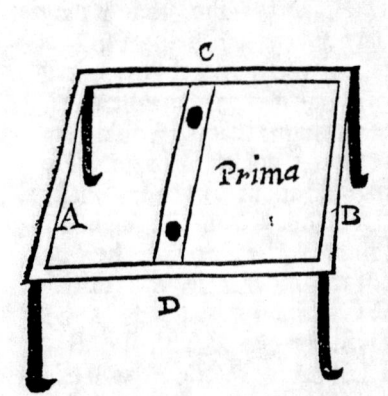

broad, according to the ends of the bars that must fit them and go into them, for they must all be so deep, as is the least height of the bars, or that the ends of the Posts that go into them may fit them exactly in all respects. Under the Boord *C. D.* a post must be set, wherein there must be four great deep incisions according to the magnitude of the barrs, on that part they are at the broadest, and as broad to receive them when they are thrust in; There is also a long board *E.* and as broad exactly as the Margent *A. B.* and it hath two pins that are thrust into *C. D.* with holes that it may be lifted up, and fall down again, it cannot stir from its place, and it alwayes stands by the Margent, unless some Man will for some other cause take it away lifting up the Pins; Moreover the board *C. D.* is scituate upon the ledg, and it elevates for its thicknesse *E.* the board from the Margent, when the bars are extended. Lastly, Make two Boards *F.* and *G.* exactly equal in height to the Table *C. D.* and such a proportion both in their length and breadth, that they may to a hair fill up the spaces about *C. D.* of the Margent, so that *C. D.* and *F.* and *G.* being joyned together, may equall *E.* these must have two bars and two Keys, and they must be firmly glewed underneath, but the length of the bars must be equall, to the length of *A. B.* and the latitude as great as is the latitude of the cavities in the Margent that receive them, the depth also in the ends must be perfectly equall to the cavities of the Margent, but it is augmented by degrees from both ends toward the middle, so that the middle be to a hair higher then the ends, as much as is the thicknesse of the Boards *C.D.F.G.* which I supposed to be equall. Also in the middle of the greatest depth two bunches stick forth of the sides, which being expounded, I shew the matter to be perfect. For when you thrust in the ends of the bars into the Margent that is opposite, the middle of them will lye upon the cavity of the Beam underneath it; and since *F.* and *G.* fit the places about *C. D.* they will neither exceed the Margent nor fall short. And because the height *F.* and *G.* is as much as *C. D.* there will be one Table as it were made of three *C. D. F. G.* of one height, upon which *E.* being laid will represent a square Table, and that is solid. But when you pull forth the bars which are broader in the middle, they will exceed the cavities, and they will by degrees lift up the Table *E,* which by reason of the Pins will be lifted up, untill the outward skirts *F.* and *G.* fall beyond *E.* for then will *E.* fall upon *C. D.* and *F.* and they will agree with it, and fit it: but the bunches they have will keep them in, that they be not drawn forth more, and leave the chink wider with *E.* nor can they fall out, because the ends of the bars are contained by the Table *C. D.* because they come exactly to the middle of it, as I proved, nor can they be higher or lower than *E.* because the difference of the middle of the bars from the ends, is supposed to be equall to the depth *C. D.* Wherefore the bars will lift up the Tables, to which they are fastned above the Margent to the quantity of the depth *G. D.* since therefore *E.* is above *C. D.* it is for the counter-ballancing of *E. F.* and *G.* which was to be proved. But it is manifest that when you would again reduce *F.* and *G.* under *E.* that you must lift up the ends of *E.* at both ends.

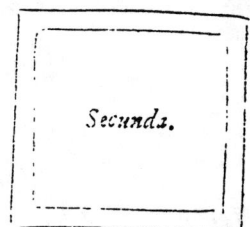

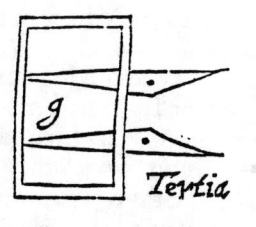

That Chests may have a pleasant colour.

All Woodden houshold stuff that is rubbed with Lees of Oyl, and polished, will be wonderfull pleasant to behold. *Mizald.*

That smoke shall not deface Chests.

All Wood steept in Lees of Oyl or wet therein, will burn with no smoke, that shall offend. *The same.*

Iron Hoops that will fit all Vessels.

It is a great profit in house-keeping it with Iron bands, all Vessels be hooped about, for every year the charge is almost an eight part saved. True it is that Iron Hoops are sometimes broken, but Woodden Hoops often when new Wine works. The remedy is, Iron Hoops that fit all Vessels, which I saw brought to *Millan* out of *Germany*, near to the Church of St. *Ambrose*. The making of them is this; parts of Iron Hoops for very great Vessels are a very little crooked and joyned together, with flexible fibras as it were knots; wherefore by the help of these clasps they are made so crooked, that you may make them fit for the smallest Vessels, in some of these there are Nails sticking forth on the outside upon each other half, and on the other half there must be holes which receive the Nails of the other part, so it comes to pass that sometimes produced they make a long circle, and sometimes taken in they make a small compass, but with many folds, the ends are joyned with a Screw that goes into them, which being included in a single hole of the adverse part, as in a Ring, and sticking forth, is set in with that part that is prominent into the small receiving Screw, the parts of the Hoops being joyned together; but being turned about with a Spar of Iron, it fastneth the Hoop, that all that was too loose is made fast and puld in, that no Wine can run forth. *Cardan*.

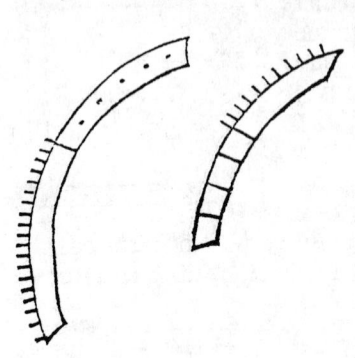

The way to Engrave Coats of Armes.

It is a wonderfull Ingenuity to Engrave Armes, of which I shall speak partly here and partly elsewhere, I have said already. Wherefore here is another way. They boyl Pitch, Oyl of Linseed, and some Frankinsence, and they make it thick; this they smeer on, which they call Vernish; They frame upon it with the point of a Bodkin or Graver what they please; then they fill up the place the Vernish was scraped out of with *Aqua Regia*, to which they add *Mercury* sublimate and Verdigrease, and in twenty four houres they Engrave any Figure upon Iron Armes, as fair, that Seals cannot be made better in Wax. *The same*.

To harden the edg of Knives.

Water pressed through a Cloath from Wormes beaten, and mixed with juyce of Radish in equall portions, makes the edges of Knives so hard and tuff, and of Swords also and of other Instruments, that are quenched twice or thrice in them when they are Forged, that they will easily cut other Iron like to Lead. *This Secret came from a Sword-maker of Paris*.

Otherwise.

You shall thus make the edge of your Knife, Sword, or other Instrument excellent. Put into one pound of young Mens Piss as much Soot as you can hold in your hand, adding four ounces of Linseed Oyl, mix them all and boyl them together, and when your Knife or Sword is red hot in Forging or any other thing made to cut, dip it in this decoction, and temper it well according to Art. *From a famous Cutler. Mizald*.

That all Instruments of Iron or Steel may be preserved safe from rust and cankering, and be alwayes very bright.

Annoint them with Vinegar mixed with Allum, or with white Lead or Stags Marrow, for these are held to be better than Oyl; but the best and most profitable of all is, to grind the filings of Lead very finely in a Mortar, adding a little Oyl of Spike thereto : (which besides the other thing, will make them smell well) and with this as with an Oyntment you must rub over your Iron or Steel. Thus may you carry any Arms through the water or foggy Ayr, and they shall never rust nor canker. *From a cunning Armour-Smith*.

Book XVII. *Secrets Mechanicall.* 317

A little Ship that shall Sail of it self, and be the Authour of its own motion; the same reason serves to make a Bird that shall flye.

The matter must be made of the pith of Bul-Rushes with bladders or skins, such as are used by Gold and Silver Leaf beaters; bound about with Sinews; When a semicircle forceth one circle, it will compell the others to move, whereby the wings will be wasted. *Scaliger.*

A wonderfull Candle or Lamp.

By this way was a wonderfull Candle invented, made on all sides like to a Tower, having but on hole in it D. whereby the Oyl is poured into it, untill it be full. It is solid Tin, and when it is turned and lyeth downwards, the Oyl cannot run forth at D. For should it run out, that which is in C. should descend by it gravity, and to fill up the vacuity, and what is in B. to C. and what is in A. to B. Wherefore that which is in A. must needs be empty, therefore there will remain Oyl in B. C. and D. and nothing will run forth. But how then can it come forth when the Lamp is lighted the Oyl being consumed in F? for it must come through the Pipe E. from D: for thus of necessity we must fall to the former reason of avoiding vacuity. For whether the Oyl be drawn forth by force of the heat, or fall down of its own accord, it is all one as to the consideration of vacuum, as one would suppose. But experience teacheth, that when the Lamp burneth it grows empty by degrees, but the Oyl will not descend of it self. The cause thereof is, that the fire when it burns rarefies and attenuates the Oyl, that being rarefied swels, and swels forth at the hole D. and the lighter part of it in the mean time ascends to the top of the Lamp, where A. is written; which being filled with much Ayr, fils it up more and more, increasing by degrees, untill all the Oyl be spent. Wherefore it is necessary to take great care for this, that the Pipe D. E. F. be not too short, or the Wick too great in F. for both wayes the Oyl will too soon swell and run forth. Thus the *Athenians* found out a Lamp, which they placed before the Image of *Minerva*, which would burn all the year. For A. B. C. D. the space was augmented according to the dayes of the year; it may be perhaps more convenient if Grates of Iron were born up with a Corke. Wherefore Oyl being poured into a great Vessel, the flame of the Wick remaing, might endure a whole year, but it must be such a Wick that will not burn and yet continue the flame. This may be made of Carpasium Linnen, or of the Threads of hard stones that have a crust on the outside. *Cardan. de Subtilitate.*

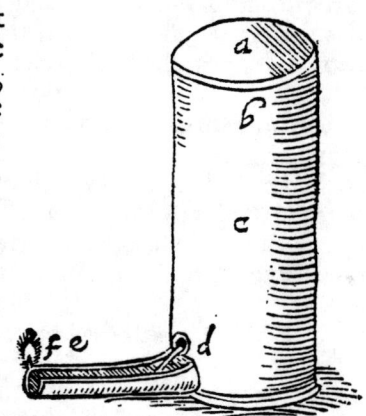

A Candle or Lamp to last all the year.

Because we speak now of a Lamp that had its mouth beneath, whereby the Wick is supplyed, I shall shew, not that it is indifferent but necessary that it must be so, if the Lamp be to burn constantly. For if the mouth of the Lamp should be in the upper part, that the Oyl may be consumed, the fire will still be farther removed from the Oyl, wherefore it will not burn well, nor will it last long. But if with a Corke and an Iron it descend into the Lamp, it will indeed last the longer; but if it be a long Lamp the fire will lye hid under the Lamp, nor will it burn above it, and the light will be dull; if it be a broad Lamp, it will darken the light, yet it may last long; wherefore this way you shall make a Candle to continue a whole year. Let the Lamp A. contain as much Oyl as will serve for one day, make B. sixtimes bigger, and joyn that to A. above it, then make C. six times as big as B. and joyn it above to B. strongly. Then make D. six times as big as C. with one sixt part, and joyn it after

the

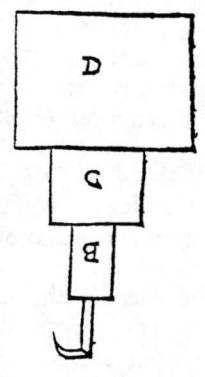

the same manner to C. and let the whole Lamp be well and close Sodderd, and will hold Oyl for a whole year, and the Wick alwayes burning and giving light. *Cardan. de varietate.*

Of the Secrets of Painting. Chap. 6.

To make Ultramarine blew without Lapis Lazuli.

Take Silver calcined with *Aqua fortis* one ounce, salt Armoniac two drams and half, Vinegar what is sufficient: mingle them, and leave them awhile, untill the matter settle at the bottome, then when the Vinegar swims on the top, take it off gently: but the rest of the matter left at the bottome, must be put into a Glass Retort, well stopt for twenty five dayes, and you shall have most pure *Indian* or *Ultramarine* blew. *The same.*

A colour of the same to Write and to Paint.

Take Verdigrease, Litharg, Quicksilver, of each what is sufficient: grind them and mix them well with a Boys Urine, and you shall have a most beautifull colour like to an Emrald, either to write or Paint with.

A green colour.

Take Verdigrease well ground, what is sufficient, Saffron four hairs, put them into the strongest Vinegar, adding as much juyce of Rue; then when Cloathes are first wet in Urine and dryed again in the shade, and dryed twice or thrice in the juyce, and again dryed in the shade, they will be perfect. *Alex.*

A green colour like an Emrald.

Take common Oyl or Oyl of Linseed very clear one pound, Allum bruised half a pound, mingle them and put them over the fire in a Pot, untill the Allum be dissolved, then add as much Verdigrease ground into very fine pouder, that it may be covered in the Pot by the foresaid Oyl; then laying on the cover, take it from the fire, and let it stand so eight or ten dayes, then grind it well again, adding a little Rosin water to it, and the colour will be very fair, and like to a natural Emrald. *The same.*

The way to make all sorts of green Leaves, that they shall appeare to be naturall.

Take green Leaves, and bruise the great Veins on the backside with some Wooden Pestle, then colour them with this following colour: Take common Oyl, or Linseed Oyl, or of any other thing that will make a smoake, what you need, burn this in a Lamp setting an Earthen Pot over it, that it may receive all the smoake. Then collect diligently all the smoake that sticks upon it, and mix it with Oyl of liquid Vernish, and make a Tincture, and Dye the bruised side of the Leaf therewith, with a Linnen Cloath or Cotton, then lay the side that is coloured upon a double Paper, pressing it lightly down with your hand, or some Cloath, that the Paper may be Dyed. Then taking away the Leaf neatly, you shall find the Paper curiously Dyed, to every small Vein, that it will seem to be naturall; If you would have them look green, take the sharpest Vinegar, Verdigrease, Urine, of each what may suffice, boyl them, and make a green colour, and with this Dye the Paper that is formed, and this way you may many make gallant things, to adorne your Chamber within side. *The same.*

To colour Ivory and bones with a green colour.

Take *Aqua fortis*, and let it devour as much Brass as it can, lay bones into that of what fashion you please to make them, for one night, and they will seem to be true Emralds for colour. *Mizald.*

To dye things red.

Madder Dyeth the bones red, and the feet of Sheep, if they feed on it some dayes, though they touch not the root that is red. The same thing may be seen in the flesh of this Creature boyld and rosted, for they have a skin as red by this means, as if they had been Dyed with Brasil or roots of wild Bugloss. *The same.*

A way to provide colours of all sorts of Mettals.

Take a Touchstone very well ground with the white of an Egg, and make a liquor

quor and write therewith, and rub upon the Letters, Gold or any other Mettal, and it will receive the colour of it. *Alexius.*

A golden Liquor to write withall, and to cover Iron, Wood, Glasses, Bones, and other things with Gold.

Take a new Egg, break a hole at one end and take forth the white, and fill it with Quicksilver, and salt Armoniac finely poudred, that there may be two parts of Quicksilver, and one of salt Armoniac; when the Egg is filled, and the matter well mixed with a stick, put a cover over the hole, and then Wax, then putting half an Egg shell over this, lay it in Horse dung twenty five dayes; Then take it out, and you shall have a most fine coloured Liquor for Gold, to Write or to Paint any thing; if the matter be too hard and thick, mingle some Gum water with it, and it will be better. *The same.*

A golden Liquor without Gold.

Take the juyce of fresh Saffron flowers, or if you want that, take Saffron ground, and the best Orpiment, and clear, of each one part; mingle and grind them with Goats Gall, or Gall of a Pike, which is better; then when it hath stood in some Vessel some while under the dung, take it away, and keep the Liquor to write withall, and Paint, and you shall have a most pure Gold colour. *The same.*

A Violet colour to Write or Paint with.

Take dwarf Elder berries that are ripe, what is sufficient, bruise them, and lay them in a hot place sometime to ferment: then bruise them again, and press forth the juyce in a Press; then take Quicklime half a Dishfull, put it into some Porner, pouring water upon it, untill the water swim above it, two or three Sawcers full, then pour off the water, straining it gently; and wet fine old Linnen Cloathes in it, and dry them in the shade; Then boyl some Allum in water, and after that cast in the foresaid Cloaths, and let them boyl a while; when they are well dryed in the Sun, dip them twice or thrice into the foresaid juyce, and dry them in the shade, placing them equally upon some Net, that the colour may not run off from any part, and so you shall have coloured Clouts, that must be kept in some place from the Ayr and dust. And this is the true way to Tincture Cloathes, with any colour to Paint or Write, which was alwayes observed by a Noble Painter whose name was *Evangelista*, and he much approved it. *The same.*

Solid and fair Images.

Lantern Horns with clear Fish Glew are with water made into Formes and Figures, and chiefly naked Girls are made therewith: for it easily takes a Rose colour upon the Transparent white, nor will that Union be dissolved by repercussion of the fire. You may have lively Images made thereof, and divers Flowers and Herbs of sundry colours, that many live by this Art only. *Cardan.*

Indian blew or perfect Ultramarine.

Take the best *Lapis Lazuli*, that is Marble, and of a blew colour, and that is well Dyed with some Golden and green Veines (such a stone being long burnt red hot in the fire, then laid to cool will not break, but remains hard and blew as before) one pound, break it into small pieces, and put them into burning Coles, untill they be very red hot; then quench them in distilled Vinegar and dry them, and with the following water, grind them like to Vermilion upon a Porphyr stone. Take Spring water one measure, Crude white Honey two ounces, mix, and boyl them, skiming them well; then when it is taken from the fire and grown cold, add by degrees not too fast, the bigness of a Nut, well ground of Dragons blood, then strain it through a Cloath. But observe that the water be not too red nor too clear, but between both namely it must be a clear Violet colour, that the blew colour may take a Violet colour. Then grind the foresaid stone thus prepared very fine with this water like to Vermilion, for one hour or longer; then set it aside in a larg open mouthed Glass, and dry it in the shade. After this bring it into very fine pouder, and keep it in Linnen Cloathes thick Woven, and fast bound up; when this is done make a Cake. Take Rosin, Colophonia, Mastick, Linseed Oyl, Turpentine, new Wax, of each two ounces, bruise what will be bruised into very fine pouder, mix and boyl them;

untill

untill it be finished, stirring it continually. It is enough, if a drop of it be dropt into cold water, and it will not stick to your hands being moyst, when it is hot strain it through a thin Cloath into cold water a Bason full, (for when it is cold it will not run) let it lye so long in the water untill it be grown hard, then take it forth, dry it, and mingle it with the foresaid pouder this way. This Paste when it is broken into small pieces, must be put into a Brass Vessel, tind within, and fire must be set under; when it begins to be hot, presently pour in one ounce of bitter Oyl of Almonds, and let them boyl a little while together, but not long; Then you must have the pouder of *Lapis Lazuli*, ready in another Vessel, and let some body help you to stir it continually with a stick, whilst you pour forth of the other Vessel the matter gently into the pouder: and this must be done untill they are excellent well mingled: when they are cold, you must work them with your hands, first wet with Oyl, and knead them well and make Paste like to Bread, and keep it in some Glass Vessel at least ten dayes. When you will extract your blew; take a Lee made of Vine Ashes, and let it be so hot that you may endure your hands in it: than take the Paste, and put it into a Glazed Vessel, and pour as much Lee to it as you think fit, handle the Paste gently and work it, untill you see the *Ultramarine* appear and come forth; When you see that, pour off the Lee with the blew into some Glass Vessel, then with other fresh hot Lee in another Vessel, work it again, and handle it as before, and alwayes so proceeding and repeating of it, untill all the blew be come forth. But observe that from every pound of *Lapis Lazuli* you shall lose but one ounce, and there remain eleaven; namely, of that which is perfect five ounces, of the middle sort three ounces, and three ounces of the last sort; one ounce of the pure and best is worth at least two Crowns and half, the middle sort is worth one Crown, and the worst a third part of a Crown; when you have extracted all the blew, observe well the similitude of it, that you may joyn like to like in three divisions, then in clear Lee, wash every part by it self, changing the Vessels, untill they be pure and well cleansed from the filth of the Paste, then dry it in the shade in a close Chamber. Then take *Aqua vita* one cup, and steep in that a little of the best *Verzium*, and with that water besprinkle your blew, then dry it; do this for three dayes, that all the blew may participate of the water, and so it will be a pure colour and excellent. They must be severally laid up in bags of Leather. *Alexius*.

The way to provide red Lake.

Take Purple Flocks one pound, boyl them in Lee untill the colour come forth, then strain the Lee and presse forth well all the substance; If there be any more colour in the Flocks, boyl it again in fresh Lee as before; then set all the Lee thus coloured at the fire, and let it not boyl; add bruised Allum to it, dissolved in hot water five ounces, strain it into some Glass Vessel, pouring on hot water, and do that so long, untill it be no more coloured, but clear without any colour at all; when this is done, take forth the colour that remains in the Strainer, dry it in the Sun and keep it. *The same*.

To Dye Bones green.

Put a great piece of Quicklime into Fountain water one day, the next day stir it with some stick, and at Noon again, and in the Evening, then strain it and keep it. In the mean time take the bones to be Dyed, and boyl them in common water, wherein as much Allum is dissolved as can be; when they are well boyled in the foresaid water, take them out and dry them, and scrape them a little on the outside, then put them into the foresaid water of Quicklime, adding Verdigrease what is sufficient; boyl them all well together, then take them forth and dry them, and make what works you will of them: if you want Lime water, take Piss, which is held to be as good. *The same*.

Another to Dye Bones or Ivory green, like Emralds.

Take *Aqua fortis* and let it consume as much Brass or Copper as it can, put your bones into that, first wrought into divers Formes, and let them lye there all night, and they will be of true Emrald colour, if in the former water you put Silver instead of Brass it will be better. *The same*.

To Dye Bones red or blew or other colours.

First, The Bones must be boyld in Allum water, as I said: then Lime water or Piss must be ready, into that *Verzinum* must be put, or marking stone, or blew, or some other colour, together with the bones, and they must be well boyld, and so bones may be Dyed of any colour. *The same.*

A rare Secret to Dye Wood severally, which Carpenters use to make Tables with, with Checker work and Figures.

In the morning take fresh Horse dung, and get wet straw and all what is sufficient, lay some Wood across over this, and a Vessel underneath to receive the Liquor; If in one day you cannot have enough for your use, gather as much the next; the third and fourth day as may serve your turn: Then strain it, and add to every measure of that Liquor, Allum and Gum Arabick, of each the quantity of a Bean; In that Liquor temper what colours you please, and make divers Vessels, if you will have diverse colours; When this is done, lay your pieces of Wood in the Vessels as you think fit; and set them in the Sun, or by the fire: when you will use them take forth some pieces, and leave the rest within, for the longer they lye in the Vessels, the better will the colour be, so shall you have Wood of sundry colours, some clearer, some darker, and no Art can wash them out. *The same.*

A way to make Ebony that it shall seem to be natural.

All sorts of Wood may be made like to Ebony, but especially those that are the hardest and the clearest, as Box, Cedar, the Mulberry both white and black, these Woods are the chief of all for this work, yet the black Mulberry is the best; Take therefore some Wood of these kinds, and lay it in Allum water three dayes, either in the Sun, or by the fire, that it may only be hot, then boyl it in common Oyl or Oyl of Sesama, wherein there is as much Brimstone and *Roman* Vitriol, of each the quantity of a Hazel Nut, for a little time; the more you boyl them, the blacker they will be, so you boyl them not too much. For that will burn them and make them brittle. If they be boyld as they should be, nothing can be desired more handsome.

To Dye Skins blew.

Take dwarf Elder Berries, or common Elder Tree Berries, as much as you think fit, first boyl them, and smeer the Skins therewith, and wash them very well, and then wring them forth: Then take the Berries as before, and boyl them in water where Allum hath been melted; again wet the Skins in the same water once, and dry them, and Dye them again, and wash them in Fountain water, and with a Knife on the other side scrape off the water, this being done, Dye them again, with some of the former colour, dry them and they will be very blew. *The same.*

To Dye Skins red.

The Skins must be first wet, washed, pressed forth, and stretched out as before; then put them into water wherein Tartar hath been boyled, and Salt, then being wrung forth, add to the former water, Ashes of burnt River Crabs what is sufficient, and rub the Skins very well therewith, then wash them with common water and press them forth; After this take madder root what may suffice, mix it with water of Tartar, and rub the Skins well therewith, then again add the Ashes of burnt Crabs, rub them and wash them, and wring them forth, then Dye them with Brasil Wood, especially if they do not yet seem red enough; Madder roots must be temper'd with hot water wherein Tartar hath been boyled, and they must stand all night, then there must be added some Allum made of Wine Lees, or Allum *Catinum* dissolved in water; Also the Skins may be Dyed with the shearings of Purple, boyled in hot Lee; and with a colour drawn from thence they will be very fair. *The same.*

To Dye Skins green.

Take purging Thorn, Allum, of each what may suffice, Fountain water as much as will swim one fingers breadth above them, mix them and give them one boyl: then when this is strained, the Skins first wet, washed, and dryed must be well rubbed, with the said Berries boyld; then rub them again, with pouder of

Allum, and next with Sheeps dung burnt, and put into the foresaid water; then again with the berries; and when they are again washed in the water and dryed, let them be twice Dyed with the colour, and they will be perfect. *The same.*

Otherwise.

Take the ripe Berries of purging Thorn, then boyl them as much as you please in water of Allum, with this twice Dye the Skins, being smeered with it, washt, and wrung forth: when they are dry, let them be Dyed yellow with Privet Berries boyld in Allum water, and a little Saffron, and they will be fair. *The same.*

To Dye Skins blew another way.

Rub the Skins only with the Husks of black Grapes, untill they be Violet colour, then with pouder of *Indico*, rub them well, wash them and dry them. Also *Indico* pouder may be temper'd with red Wine, that the Skins washt therewith may be Dyed. *The same.*

To Dye Skins red.

Let the Skins be well washt, then laid in Galls for two houres, and wrung forth, they must be Dyed once with a dark colour, with Alum water boyld with Verdigrease; Then smeer the Skins twice with *Verzinum* boyld with Lee. But if you would Dye the Skins like Does Skins, the dark colour must be boyld in Lee. *The same.*

Another to Dye Skins green.

Take Berries of the Elder Tree bruised, and of dwarf Elder Berries and purging Thorn bruised, what is sufficient, Allum as much as you please, mix them, and first let Privet Berries boyl once in the Lee, then add the Berries of both Elders, and when they have once boyled also, take them off the fire, when they are cold, first rub the Skins with the Berries, then with Sheeps dung burnt, after that wash them with the water of the former Berries, and scrape off the water from one side, and dry the Skins. If they be not Dyed enough, with a Pencill Dye them again, adding some powder of *Indico* to make them more perfect. *The same.*

To Dye Goats Skins green.

Take Goats Skins Male or Female, polished with a Pumex stone, then annointed with Oyl, and last of all washt; after this rub them well with strained hot water, wherein there are one ounce or two of beaten Galls, leave them so one hour, then take them forth, wring them out, and stretch them abroad. Then take the Berries of purging Thorn collected in *July*, when they are green, dry them and pouder them finely, mix with the pouder of the said Berries two ounces of poudred Allum for every Skin, pouring in hot water upon them: when it is cold pour it forth upon the Skins, pressing the colour in with your hands; After this add a little Goats dung burnt, and bruise and rub them again, then wash them, and scrape off the water with a Knife as before, and stretch them forth. Then take the Privet Berries well ripe, and boyl them whole in Allum water a while, with this and the Berries being cold, rub the Skins with your hands, and strew the said Ashes upon them, wash them with the water of the Berries being hot, and scrape it off with a Knife; then when they are once with the Pencill Dyed with the green water, dry them and they will be perfect; If you would have the colour darker, when you boyl your Berries and Allum, add a little fine pouder of *Indico*.

The Dying of Skins with the Flowers of Lillies

Take fresh blew Lilly flowers, dry Berries of purging Thorn, Allum, bruise them all, and mix them with a little Spring Water, and keep them in some clean Vessel; Then when the Skins are first annointed and washt, Dye them with the Berries and Ashes as I said, then wash them, scrape off the water with a Knife, and dry them; After this Dye the Skins, with the foresaid colour kept in a Vessel, then rub them, wrinkle them, smooth them according to Art. *The same.*

To Dye Bones blew and red.

Since all white Bones, especially Harts horn may be Dyed, take what Bones you please; which being first prepared and fitted for your use, boyl them a while in Allum

lum water, then take them forth and dry them; After this take Verdigrease, Goats Whey, of each what is sufficient, mix them, and together with the Bones set them in some Brass Vessel fifteen dayes in Horsedung; then take them forth and they will be compleat; If you take for Whey, Piss, you shall do excellent well; would you make them red add Vermilion, or Lac, put them into some Woodden or Glass Vessel, and not into Brass. *The same.*

To Dye Hogs Bristles or what Brushes are made of to Brush Cloathes.

Take the Bristles well washt, then put them so long into water where Allum is boyld, untill they look somewhat yellow, then take Madder in pouder, what is sufficient, and lay it in Ginegar, and after that pour all into boyling water standing over the fire, and when they have boyld a while, take them from the fire, and let them stand untill they be cold, and they will be compleat. *The same.*

To Dye Bristles yellow, green, blew, or any other colour.

The Bristles being first washt, and boyld in Allum water, must be Dyed with a dark colour, and Saffron, if you would have them yellow, or with the juyce of either Elder, or Lilly Flowers for blew, or Verdigrease for green; so doing this, and making experiment, you may Dye Bristles of many other colours. *The same.*

To make Purple, and a Golden colour, to Write and Paint.

Take Pewter melted in the fire one pound, and add to that when it is removed from the fire, Quicksilver eight or ten ounces, stirring it continually, pouder of Brimstone and salt Armoniac poudred, of each one pound. Mingle them all very well, and grind them in a Mortar, of Stone, Glass, or Brass, then put them into a great Woodden Retort, Luting the Vessel two fingers higher then the matter, and boyl them in a Furnace, first with a very gentle fire, then augmenting it, and still stirring with a stick, untill they turn yellow. then take them from the fire, and let them cool, and so shall you have a most gallant Purple Tinctured with a Golden colour; which must be after this ground with Lee and Piss, or with Lee, adding a little Saffron thereto, it must be diluted, and tempered with Gum Water, as I shall speak more plainly underneath. *The same.*

The way to make Lac of Verzinium.

Take any Flocks one pound, boyl them in two Sextarii of Lee, untill the Flocks dissolve in the water. Then put it into some Stone or Wodden Vessel, casting in by degrees Allum powdred one pound, alwayes stirring with a Woodden Spatula, then again two Sextarii of cold water being poured in, by degrees, you must strain all in a Bag, and keep what stayes behind in the Bag, in a Glass Vessel. Then take raspt Brasil Wood one pound, and boyl it in a Sextarius of Lee, or one pint and half, untill it be boyld away a fingers breadth; strain it, and add Gum Arabick poudred one ounce, boyl it again untill half a finger be wasted, then add thereto the matter kept in a Glass Vessel, mix them well, then strain it and take it forth, and make Pils of what is left in the Strayner, and dry them in the shade, and they will be perfect. *The same.*

The way to make white Table Books to Write in and rub forth again, with a Brass Pen, such as are made in Germany.

Take clean sifted Gyp what is sufficient, and dissolve it with some sort of Glew, when it is dry scrape it and polish it to make it clear. Then dissolve it, and scrape it as before. After this take white Ceruse poudred and sifted what is sufficient, mix it with Linseed Oyl boyled, and make an Unguent to smeer over the Tables, and when they are well annointed, let them dry in the shade five or six dayes, then polish the Tables with some Cloath dipt in water and wrung forth again, and let them stand so fifteen or twenty dayes, untill they be well dryed, and use them to Write with, and to rub out what is written. *The same.*

A way to make red Ink.

Take Rasped Brasil Wood one ounce, Ceruse and Allum of each two ounces, grind and mingle them, and pour as much Piss upon them as may cover them, let them abide so three dayes, stirring them three or four times a day, then strain it through Linnen, and put it into some Glazed Pot, from the Sun and Ayr; and when you

You would Write with it, temper it with Gum water. *The same.*

To Gild Skins, wherewith Hangings and Tapistry is made

Take Linseed Oyl three pound, Vernish, Colophonia, of each one pound, Saffron bruised half an ounce, mix and boyl them so long at the fire, untill a Hens Feather put into them and pull'd forth again, seem to be burnt: then take them suddenly from the fire, and cast in by little and little Aloes, Hepatica poudred one pound, stirring it still well with a stick, least with too great heat they should boyl over; for when they rise, you must take them suddenly from the fire, untill they sink down again; then set them on the fire again, and boyl them so long, untill they are well mixed; then take them from the fire, and when they settle, strain it and keep it in some Vessel: And if for Saffron you take the yellow flowers of white Lillies you shall do well; But if you would Gild your Skins, first lay on Silver Leaf, or Tin, with whites of Eggs or Gum Arabick, then annoint them with the foresaid Unguent, and they will suddenly receive a Gold colour: after that dry them in the Sun, Printing on the Formes, or Painting them, and they will be most beautifull. *The same.*

To Dye Silks Scarlet colour, which they call Chermesin.

Take hard Sope scraped what may suffice, dissolve it in common water, then lay in the Silks wrapt in some fine Linnen Cloath, and boyl them at the fire half an hour, stirring them some time that they stick not to the Vessel: Then take them forth, and wash them, first with Salt water, then with fresh, and for every pound of Silk take one pound or more of Allum dissolved in a sufficient quantity of cold water, and lay your Silks without the foresaid Cloath into that for eight houres. Then take them forth and wash them, first in fresh water, next in salt, and last in fresh, suddenly casting them into a Kettle, with Cochyneal thus prepared. Take for every pound of Silk, Cochyneal poudred three or four ounces, boyl them in so much common water as will cover the Silk four or six fingers, adding to every pound of Silk, Galls beaten to pouder three ounces, if you want Galls, take instead thereof white Arsenick half an ounce, for a pound of Silk, which will make the colour better, but that the water and the steam thereof is very dangerous. When it begins to boyl cast in the Silk prepared as I said, and boyl it four houres, then take it forth and dry it in the shade, and it will be perfect. *The same.*

The way to prepare Verzinum for four colours.

Take Verzinum what is sufficient, and boyl it in a sufficient quantity of water, untill a third part be consumed, or untill it be four coloured; then take it from the fire, and divide it into four parts, keep one by it self, and that will be Rose colour, add to the other a little Lime water and it will be red, to another a little Lee, and it will be Violet colour, to the last a little Allum and Argal, and it will be a dark blew, but when you add these, the Verzinum must be warm. *The same.*

Red Verzinum another way.

Take a measure of common water, and add as much Lime to it, as the quantity of a Nut; then let them stand so all night, and take Verzinum scraped what is sufficient to fill the Vessel half full, and pour upon it Lime water strain'd, let them stand four houres, then boyl them, untill half be boyld away: Then take them off the fire, and pour them genly into some other Vessel; and add to it a little poudred Allum, about the bignesse of a Pease, and keep it. If you would write with it, add some Gum water to it, but if you had rather have it red, add Lee four ounces more or lesse, and it will be perfect.

How to provide a Purple colour.

Take black Myrtle Berries two pound, Allum one ounce, burnt Brass half an ounce, water half a measure, mix these in a Brass Kettle, and boyl them untill two fingers be wasted, strain it when it is cold, and put it into a clear Vessel, and leave it untill it be thick enough.

The way to provide a Rose colour.

Take Wine or Vinegar as much as you please, put fine pouder of Allum into it, when that is dissolved, make a strong Lee of Lime, then take Brasil Wood and
Allum

Allum what is sufficient, and wrapping them in Linnen, hang them in the Lee, and leave them there one day, then press forth the Liquor, and hang them in again; do this over three or four times, when you have pressed forth the colour the fourth time, leave it to dry. *The same.*

Another.

Take red Lead two parts, white Lead one part, pouder them and mix them well; or take Orpiment and red Lead of each one part, and mingle them well. *The same.*

How to make a bright Bay.

Take Brasil Wood ground, and white Vitriol, mix them and boyl them at the fire, or mix red Lead and Gums with a black colour what is sufficient. *The same.*

A yellow.

Take Berries of purging Thorn about St. *Lawrence* day gathered, bruise these, and add a little poudred Allum and keep it in a Brass Vessel.

Otherwise.

Take Pomegranate Pills, take away the ruff outward skin, cast it aside, and cut the rest into pieces, pouring on water, boyl them twice or thrice at the fire, add poudred Allum, and let them boyl once more. *The same.*

Another.

You shall make an excellent yellow colour, if you mix the yelk of an Egg with Saffron: Or take Saffron and pouderd Allum, and put them into a Linnen Cloath, pour on Vinegar and press it forth; also you may mingle Saffron, the yelk of an Egg, Gum Arabick and Allum, and keep it for use. *The same.*

To make a green.

Take Berries of purging Thorn, gathered after the feast of St. *Michael*, bruise them and pour on water, and add a little Allum, mix them well, and leave them so two dayes. *The same.*

Another.

Take Honey what is sufficient, add some Vinegar to it, more then the Honey a little, mix them well in a Glass or Copper Vessel, which is better, stop it, and set it twelve dayes in Horse dung; Also take distilled Vinegar, pour it into Copper, put in filings of Copper, and let them stand in a hot place; when the Vinegar looks green, pour it off into some other Glass Vessel, pour on more Vinegar, and set it aside as I said; do this repeating it so often, untill you have colour enough, strain it and leave it to thicken. *The same.*

To grind Gold to write and to Paint.

Take as many Leaves of Gold as you please, Honey three or four drops, mix and grind these, and keep it in some Bone Vessel; if you will Write with it, add some Gum water to it and it will be excellent.

Another.

Take as many Leaves of Gold or Silver as you please, put them into a clean Glass Vessel, and steep them with water a finger deep only, untill they be well steeped: then fill it with common water, and mingle them, and let it stand half an hour; This being done, pour off the water gently, that the Gold may remain in the bottome, which must be dryed and kept close covered in a Vessel, when you will Write with it, add some water to it. *The same.*

Otherwise with Purple.

Take Purpurine as much as you please, put it into a Vessel with Piss, or Lee, mingling it with your finger, and stirring it well; when that is done, fill it up with Piss or Lee; and leave it so to settle: then steep it again, changing the Urine or Lee so often, untill the last Water or Piss remain clear, then strain the Water gently, and to the rest of the matter add a little Saffron and Gum water, and make a Liquor to Write or to Paint. *The same.*

A Composition called Sisa, commonly in which Leaves of Gold are polished and set.

Take the best Gyp, Bolearmoniac, Aloes Hepatica, Sugarcandy, of each half a dram,

dram, grind them all severally, and placing one upon another, add a little Civet or Honey.

To set Gold, a simple Composition.

Take the best Gyp, Aloes Hepatica, Bolearmoniac, of each one part, pouder them all, and beat them with whites of Eggs, and strain them; if it be too strong, add common water unto it.

Otherwise.

Take Gum water what is sufficient, and stick Gold in that alone, upon Paper, Parchment or Skins, and it will be good, also whites of Eggs, and Fig Tree milk are commended.

To set Gold upon a black matter.

Take the smoke of Lamps that dyeth them black, and set Gold upon that with Gum water.

How Marble or Wood may be Guilded.

Take Bolearmoniac, Oyl of Nuts of each what is sufficient, pound them and grind them together: when you will lay on Gold, see that this Liquor be not moyst, not too dry. *The same.*

To make Gold Letters without Gold.

Take Orpiment, Cryftall, of each one ounce, pouder them all, mix them with the white of an Egg, and make a Liquor to write with. *The same.*

To make Silver Letters without Silver.

Take Pewter one ounce, Quicksilver two ounces, mix and melt them together, then beat them with Gum water and write. *The same.*

That Letters may be green.

Take Leaves of Rue, and press forth the juyce, add Verdigrease and Saffron, of each alike, grind them, when you will write therewith, mix them with Gum water.

To write white Letters.

Take Fig milk what is sufficient, and set it in the Sun in a Glass Vessel for half an hour; when you will use it, take Gum water, mix and write with it. When you have written, all the Paper must be Tinctured with Ink, and when it is dry, it must be well rubbed with a Linnen Cloath, that the Letters written with Fig milk may be taken off, and those spaces may remain white; For that milk hinders the Ink to enter there. Yelks of Eggs also are held to be good, if a Liquor be made with the water beaten and one write with it: then the whole Paper must be dipt in Ink, and dryed, the Letters must be rubd off with a Knife or some Cloath, and the Letters will remain white. *The same.*

A green Liquor to Write and to Paint

Take Verdigrease what is sufficient, put it into Vinegar untill it melt, then strain it through a fine Cloath, and grind it finely upon a Porphyr stone with commin water, adding a little Honey. When it is well dryed, grind it again upon a Pophyr stone with Gum water, and it will be perfect.

To make blew another way.

Grind *Indico* as Verdigrease, with Honey, but it must not be cleansed; It must be tempered with the white of an Egg beaten, or with Glew water, and not Gum water. Glew water is made of clear Isinglass, melted and strained as they do Gum water.

The way to make Vermilion to write.

Vermilion very well ground upon a Porphyr stone with common water, must be dryed afterwards and put into some Vessel made of Bone or Glass, and Piss must be poured on, and so left to settle, for the matter will fall to the bottome, then pour gently the Piss off, and pour on fresh. When you have done this eight or ten times, it will be well cleansed. Then take whites of Eggs well stirred, and let them dissolve into pure water; pour that water upon the Cinnaber, that it may swim above it a fingers breadth, and stir them together: then when it settles, take away the whites of Eggs gently, and pour on fresh, do this as often as you did it with Piss. This is done

done for no other cause, but to take off the stink of the Piss; When all this is done add fresh whites of Eggs, and mix them well, and make a Liquor to write or to Paint. But this Liquor must be kept stopt up in some close Vessel. When you will use it, you must mix it with some Liquor: It will keep uncurrupted very long.

Aqua fortis for Silks, Marbles, and Linnen Cloaths to Gild them.

Take Parchment Glew, and gently smeer over Linnen Cloathes therewith, that the water may soake in. This done, take Ceruse, Bolearmoniac, Verdigrease, of each one part; mix and grind them upon a Porphyr stone to pouder, put that into some Glazed Vessel, adding as much liquid Vernish as is sufficient, and set it at a gentle fire that it boyl not. But upon Marble you must not lay Glew but *Aqua fortis*. *The same.*

How Books may be Gilded.

Take Bolearmoniac as big as a Nut, Sugarcandy as big as a Pease, they must be poudred finely together; then add whites of Eggs and mix them well, grinding them; Then take a Book well Bound, and being smeered under the Press with whites of Eggs, and let dry, it must be smeered with the former Composition and suffered to dry, then rub it well and polish it smooth. When you will Gild them, first wet them with common water, then suddenly laying on the Gold and pressing it down with Cotton gently, when it is dry polish it with a Tooth, and with a cold Iron Print Formes upon it. *The same.*

To preserve whites of Eggs uncorrupt, to prepare Vermilion, and other colours without Arsenick, a thing that few know.

Take fresh whites of Eggs entire, and pour upon a hundred Eggs a third part of Vinegar, and leave them so twenty four houres; Then strain it through a fine Linnen Cloath gently, that the whites of Eggs may not break; let them stand so eight dayes; when they are strained again, keep them for use in some Vessel covered.

Aqua fortis for Painting.

Take Gum, Armoniac, three parts, Arabick one part, Sagapenum four parts, mix them and put them into Vinegar, untill they grow soft, then beat them, strain them, and keep them for use. *The same.*

Another for the same.

Take Gum, Armoniac one ounce, Arabick three ounces, let them stand twenty four houres in Vinegar, untill they grow soft, then add yellow Honey the quantity of a Nut, one head of Garlick cleansed and bruised, a little Aloes Hepatica, mix them and boyl them awhile in Vinegar, strain them, and press forth all the substance. If it be too moyst, boyl it again to a fit consistence, and keep it in some Glass Vessel; when you will use it, Tincture that with it which you would Gild, when it is dryed, and made moyst with your hot breath, presently clap on your Gold leaves, and with a Pencil or Cotton keep them on.

A way hitherto not known, but easie, to grind Gold or Silver of a pure colour, which may be polished and illustrated with Gums.

Take as many Leaves of Gold as you please, set them to the fire in a Crucible, then take four times as much Quicksilver, and set it likewise to the fire in another Crucible, but not near that it may only heat; But the Gold Leaves must be so long left at the fire, untill they begin to wax red, but do not melt, then take the Crucible from the fire, and mingle the Quicksilver with the Leaves of Gold, stirring them a while with some stick, then suddenly cast them into a Dish full of water, and make an *Amalgama*. If you desire it otherwise, grind your Leaves of Gold with Quicksilver upon a Porphyr stone, untill they be very well mixed, then wash them twice or thrice with common water; If you add a little Vinegar or juyce of Lemmons, you shall do best, for they will mingle better and sooner; Take this mixture prepared either way, and press it through a fine Linnen Cloath, that some part of the Quicksilver may come forth, or press it through some white Does or Lambs skin which is better: what sticks in the skin must be ground well with live Brimstone, so that it may not exceed half the quantity of it. Then set it in a Vessel of Iron to the fire, being very well stopt, let it stand there untill all the Brimstone be burnt, and what remains is yellow, when it is cold it must be so often washed in a Bason of water, untill it be like Gold, and so kept for use. When you will use it, add as much Rose water or common water wherein Gum Arabick is dissolved, as shall serve turn, mix these, and make a Golden Liquor to Write and to Paint with; and when you have Written or Painted therewith, rub the Letters gently with some Tooth, which cannot be done with other ground Gold, which almost all Painters use. Some of the Ancients used this Secret as I read in old Books: But when you polish it, you must lay a Paper upon it, and then again without a Paper, especially where the Letters do not shine well, *The same.*

To make Gum called Vernish, that is gallant to illustrate Gold, as all other works coloured or not coloured.

Take Benzoin well poudred between two leaves of Paper, put it into a Glass, and pour on so much *Aqua vitæ*, that it may swim above it three or four fingers, and put in five or six leaves of Saffron grosly bruised, or entire; let it stand one or two dayes, then strain it; when you would illustrate Gilded workes herewith, smeer this on with a Pencil, and they will be fair and bright. This matter will soon dry and last many Ages. If you would grind leaves of Silver, do as before, but for Brimstone take Salt. If you would illustrate Gum works, Take the best of Benzoin, namely the white parts of it that are in the middle, what shall suffice, adding as much *Aqua vitæ* as I said before, but add no Saffron; with this Gum many things may be smeered, be they Painted or not, as Tables, Chests, especially of Ebony or Nut Tree: Also Skins whether Gilded or not, for it not only makes them bright, but preserves the colours; Moreover being it dryeth suddenly, and admits neither dust nor filth, but may be brusht off with a Fox tail or Cloath.

The easie way to grind Gold or Silver that skillfull Artists use.

Take leaves of Gold, and in some Glass Vessel mix it with Julep of Roses, do it with your finger to mix them well, then grind them upon a Porphyr Marble pouring water gently to them: Then take it away wiping it off into a Dish, and washing the stone well with water. Then stir the Gold well with your finger to wash it, and when it settleth in the bottome, pour off the water by degrees; and pour on fresh water hot, and wash it again, do this so often, untill the Julep be well washt away, and the water tast no longer sweet. After this the Gold must be dryed and set in a Glass Vessel over hot Embers, when it is very hot and hath regaind its natural colour, temper it with Gum water, and make a Liquor for your use. *The same.*

A Golden Liquor that is easie and of no great price.

Take yellow Orange Pils, with the inward pith scraped well away, fine yellow pouder of Brimstone, what is sufficient, mix and grind them well together, and put them into a Glass Viol in a moyst place for eight or ten dayes, then take away, and heat it at the fire, to Write or to Paint with. *The same.*

Another to Gild any Metals.

Take liquid Vernish one pound, Turpentine, Linseed Oyl, of each one ounce, mix them all well, and keep them for use.

The best way to make Ink.

Take the best Galls cut into three or four parts, or gently bruised, as much as you please, and when they are fryed awhile with a little Oyl, they must be put into a Glazed Vessel, pouring on as much white Wine, that it may swim three or four fingers over it: then add Gum Arabick poudred half a pound, Vitriol bruised eight ounces, mix them and set them in the Sun some dayes, stirring them continually. After this when they are sufficiently boyl'd, it must be straind and that is all, yet to the dregs remaining new Wine, may be added as often untill the Wine is no more Tinctured by the feces. Mingling these Wines together, you must add fresh Gums, Galls, and Vitriol, as before, and when they are set again in the Sun, and boyld again, the Ink will be better than it was, and so it will be the oftner you repeat this. If the Ink be too thick, add a little of the Lixivium, and it will be thin enough, if it be

too

too thin, add some Gum Arabick. But your Galls must be small, hard, crisped, your Vitriol blew, and your Gum clear and crumbling. *The same.*

Pouder for Ink that any man may carry with him on his Journey, to temper with Wine or Water, and this Pouder makes Ink better.

Take Peach or Apricock, or Almond stones sweet or bitter, put them in the fire untill they burn red hot, then take them out and keep them. After this take Pitch Tree Rosin what is sufficient, put it into some Pot to the fire, and when it is kindled with some Cole or Candle, put on the cover, that it may smoke and not go out, and the smoke be well received; when the Rosin is all consumed and the Vessels are all cold, wipe away the moysture that sticks upon the cover and keep it. If one will not spend so much labour to make it, he may buy it of those that make Printers Ink. Take one part of this smoke, pouder of the burnt Kernels two parts, Vitriol one part, fryed Galls, as I said before, one part, Gum Arabick four parts; pouder them, sift them, and mix them for a pouder to be kept in Leather. When you will use it, take a little of this pouder, add a little water to it, Wine or Vinegar, mix them, and Write therewith. Thus you have Ink suddenly, that any one may carry with him, without danger to spill it; If you add this Pouder to ill Ink, it will be perfect. *The same.*

Ink easie to prepare of no great price, not only fit to Write, but also to Print Books.

Take of the Tincture Hides are Dyed with, as much as you please, Cuttle Gall what is sufficient, mix them for Ink. But if you will make it better, add the foresaid pouder of Coales, Vitriol, Galls and Gum. Books may be also Printed with this Ink, especially if a little Vernish and Linseed Oyl be added, that it may be more liquid and hold faster. But Ink to Print Books is made only of the smoke of Rosin, as I said, adding liquid Vernish what may suffice, and boyling of it a little, make thick or thin Ink which you will. In Winter it must be more liquid, in Summer more firme; if you will make it more liquid, add more Linseed Oyl, if thicker less, and more of the smoake, and boyl it better, but thick Ink makes the neater Letters. If you will make red Ink, instead of smoake take Vermilion finely ground, as much as you please; for green, take Verdigrease; for blew, as they used some few years past, take *Germane* blew, or Glass Ammil, which comes from *Venice.* The rest are performed as we speak of common Ink. *The same.*

A Liquor to Write with shall be whiter than the Paper, and you may read it when it is Written.

Take Egg shels very well washt, and grind them upon a Porphyr Marble stone with Water, and let them stand in a Dish untill the matter settle to the bottome, then pour off the Water gently, and dry the matter either by it self, or in the Sun; When you will use it, take Ammoniacum, taking away the yellow outside, what is sufficient; put it into distilled Vinegar, for one hour, untill it be dissolved, then strain it, and add some of the foresaid pouder to it, and you have the whitest Liquor that is to Write or Paint with. A chief Dame of *Italy* useth this Liquor to Paint her face, because it hurts not the skin, nor Teeth, but whites the face as if it were natural. But if you will use it for your face, the Liquor must be very thin, that it may last the longer, and penetrate the deeper; but if to this you add some little of burnt Lime, as I shall shew in the Book following, you shall make it excellent. *The same.*

Pouder that rubs away blots of Ink, or Letters Written upon the Paper, a thing most commodious and worth knowing.

Take Ceruse well ground, Fig-tree Milk, of each what is sufficient, mingle them and make a Lump, when it is dry, wet it again with the Milk, and doing this six times, pouder it and keep it; When you would take blots of Ink or Letters from Paper, take a wet Linnen Cloath, wring it forth, and wet the Letters or blots with the Cloath, when this is done, strew on the foresaid pouder, and leave it so one night, then in the morning rub it gently with a dry Linnen Cloath, and you shall see the Paper very white, and fit to Write upon. If it hath not taken off all the Ink, do it again and it cannot fail. If the Paper be worn too thin with rubbing, it may be thickned with Glew, Wood is joyned with, eafily melted, and mixed with a little Ceruse or Wheat Meal to rub it with. *The same.*

A way to prepare Vernish for Parchment, or to smooth Paper we use to Write with, which is better and fairer than that we commonly use, nor doth it smell ill, as the ordinary Vernish doth.

Vernish that Scriveners use for their Books, is Juniper, Gum poudred; of this Gum also boyld with Linseed Oyl, liquid Vernish is made; Scriveners use the foresaid Vernish ground, that the Paper may take Ink better, and that it may not run through; But if you would provide better at less cost, take Egg shels cleansed and gently poudred, and in a Pot of Earth well covered with Water, let them stand in a Potters or Glass-makers Furnace, so long untill they are calcined to Ashes, sift them and make a very white pouder. When you use it, put a little upon the Paper, and disperse it here and there with a Hares foot, and what is over, wipe it off, and it will be excellent to Write with. But if after you have Written with this, and dryed it, you desire to take off the pouder, rub it a little with Crums of Bread, and it will wipe off all the pouder. *The same.*

A Liquor to make Lines, which when you have Written upon them may be taken away, that they shall appear no more.

Take as much calcined white Argal as a small Nut, dissolve it in a Bason full of water, then strain it, and add as much pouder of Touchstone to it, as may suffice, mix it, and make a Liquor to draw Lines; when you would take them off, rub the Paper with crums of stale white Bread, and it will take them off that nothing shall be seen: This is a Secret worth knowing, and very profitable. *The same.*

A reason to Paint solid things upon a plain.

But what is Painted upon a plain Table seems to be solid: and chiefly for two reasons, one is the shadow, whence the eye judgeth so. If there be a shadow it seems a dark and solid body. I think the sense judgeth thus from a continued custome, as they relate, that in the Islands newly found out, that were not before inhabited, Birds will not flye away, but be taken with Mens hands. The other is to consider what part of the body is to be seen, as in a Cube, the upper part the forepart, left or right, the other superficies lyeth hid, therefore you shall place the shade to the light, that you describe before you half the height of the house, but the body for the Lines that are extended from the eye to the Cube above the plain, is to be set at one corner, and the light must stand on one side. Again there is one reason for a Table that hangs on a Wall, and another for that which lyeth under our eyes and hands equidistant to the Horizon. But in all this is general, that you must set the Table in the same place, and express the Angles and Points in the same plain, both to your eyes and the light, as the bounds of the thing seen. For when the Angles are equall, and are helped by colours and shadowes, they must needs represent the same bodies. For like represents the like, and the same the same. Yet remember to observe the place of equal sight, that is, the head of the Figure of a Man when a man is Painted on a Table, for all beneath that will shew low, and what is above it high, as if they truely were in such a posture, the eye will judg so. Therefore to make solid representations, observe these four Rule: the forme of the thing, taken by the beams of the eyes; the shadow, by the beames of the Sun; the colour, which must be no other than of that body under that light, and under that posture; and lastly, the situation upon the Table, as the Mans posture requires that is Painted, whose Crown must be right against your eyes. *Cardan.*

To make Figures bossing forth upon Wood.

But I shall add the Invention of *George Joachimus* an Ingenious Man, who taught us how to make Figures upon Wood; you must take hard, round, polished Wood,

not

not green, nor too dry, as thick as your fist or more, and lay it some dayes in Water, untill it swell, work that with a punchion of Iron, and a Woodden Hammer by degrees, it must be a Wedg with a Margent as you see in this Figure; that it may not go in deep; when you have done what you desire, with a Turners Art, plain the Wood exactly, as far as the Chizel went in, then let it dry in the shade, for the parts of the Wood forced in will thrust themselves forth again, and represent the forme you made: the Chizel must be somewhat blunt. *The same.*

A Golden Liquor to Gild Skins, Silver, and Glass.

Take Linseed Oyl three pound, boyl it in a Glazed Vessel at a gentle fire, untill it seem to be enough, into which a Hens Feather cast and presently taken forth, may easily acquaint you with it, for if when you take it forth it be bare, it is boyld enough, but if the Feathers stay on, it must be more boyld. But the safer way to boyl it without any danger, is to make a Furnace that the Pot may be set upon it, where no flame can come to the Oyl to set it on fire. When the Oyl is boyled enough, take Pitch, Rosin, dry Vernish, of each eight ounces, Aloes Hepatica four ounces, pouder them all, and put them into the Oyl, and stir them still with a stick, especially now the fire being augmented; and boyl them to the consistence of a Julep. If the Liquor seem clearer and brighter than it should do, add of Aloes Succotrine one ounce and half, or two ounces; adding less of Vernish, and so the Liquor will be somewhat darker and more like to Gold. When it is boyld take it strait from the fire, that it flame not, (for it would consume all) then you must have the sharp pointed bags, and one of the ends must go into the other, pour the Liquor suddenly into this, that it may run out thin before it be cold, and so all unprpfitable matter will stay in the bottome. This will keep long, and the older the better, it is Aloes makes that Golden colour, the rest make the body and thicken it. If you would have it thicker, when the Oyl is sufficiently boyled, take forth what you please of it, and then follow the order prescribed; when it is done it will not be above three or four pounds, and it cannot be made of less weight. Artificers make forty or sixty pound together, and keep it well from dust. If you would Gild Glass or Pewter, touch them with a Pencil, and the Vessels will be of a Golden colour. *Alexius.*

To make Marble or Alabaster of a blew or Violet colour.

Take the juyce of red Carrots, blew Lillies, white Vinegar, of each what may suffice. If the said juyces are not at hand, provide them at such a time as the flowers and roots may be had and keep them for your use; or if one be wanting use the other alone: mingle them and boyl them a while, adding to each pound of the juyce and Vinegar pouder of Allum one ounce; Then lay your Marble or Alabaster in the said Liquor, and boyl them so long untill they be well Tinctur'd; If the Marble be too big to put in, let them only be made very hot in the place where they lye, and then Tinctur'd with the scalding juyce, and they will be curious. *The same.*

How Roses or Clove-Gelliflowers may be beautified.

Take salt Armoniac what is sufficient, grind it on a Marble with Vinegar, and a little Sugar-candy, and keep it for your use; When you will use it, take Roses or Violets, and with Wax stick them on, that they may lye plain, then Paint upon them what you please, with the said Liquor, and let them remain one hour, to dry; then lay on Leaves of Gold or Silver, and with Cotton press them gently down; what is not fast on, must be wiped away; and what you have Painted on will appear beautifully. *The same.*

To illustrate Pictures.

Take hard white Rosin one pound, Gum two ounces, *Venice* Turpentine one ounce, Linseed Oyl two ounces; First melt the Rosin at the fire, and strain it, then let the Gum stand in common Oyl, untill it be soft; When it is strain'd mingle all well, and boyl them at a gentle fire, stirring them continually, untill they be well mixed, then keep them for your use. If any clean Picture be annointed with

this

this mixture it will shew very clear and bright. *Alexius.*

Another of the same that will dry suddenly.

Take male Frankinsence, Juniper, Gum, what is sufficient, mix them and make a very fine pouder, add *Venice* Turpentine what may be needfull, and mingle them well at the fire, strain it and keep it. When you use it, first heat it, and gently smeer the Picture over with it, and it will soon dry and be handsome.

Another of the same.

Take Linseed Oyl what you please, distill it in a Glass Retort, untill all the Oyl be come forth, take of it one ounce, Vernish and Amber three ounces, mix them well at a gentle fire, and make a mixture, which being hot, may be used for all sorts of Pictures upon Wood or Cloath; But you must be industrious and skilfull to use it.

That any one that is ignorant of Painting may with a Pencil draw the likeness of any Man, so he learn only to liken the colours.

This is done by the shadow reflected upon a Table underneath, or upon some strong Paper, (It is easie for one that hath skill.) If the Sun shine not, you must do it by Candle light: There are many other accidents, and you shall know them better than I can declare them, if you be diligent in your work. He that knows this may learn the principles how to deliver a message secretly or what he please, to one that is far off, and shut up in Prison, and no small Inventions depend upon it, you shall help the distance by the magnitude of your Glass, you have enough: They that boast they have done this, have told us nothing but trifles, and I think that no Man hath yet found it out. *The same.*

Verses for colours or flowers to Write and to Paint.

He that will flourish Books with colours gay
Must wander in Corn fields betimes it'h day,
And sundry sorts of flowers he shall find,
Those he must take of each in every kind,
And bring them home, not mixt, and one by one,
Bruise them upon a polisht Marble stone.
And grind them well with Gyp that's boyld, and save
Them for his use, he shall dry colours have;
Into fresh green if you will change the hew,
Do as I say you'l have them alwayes new.

Marcellus Palingenius.

A way to Paint Vessels and Glasses, of the same Author.

You Artists that would fain learn to Engrave
Glasses, this is the way that you must have.
Pick up fat Wormes the Plough turns out of th' ground
And let a Goat unto a post stand bound,
And fed sometime with Ivy, his hot bloud,
Mingled with Wormes and Vinegar is good,
To smeer the Glass all over; this alone
Serves to Engrave the Glass with Emril stone.

To Paint Glazed Vessels.

If any Man will Glazed Vessels Paint,
Let him on Marble grind your Roman Glass,
Into fine pouder, as I you aequaint,
With Gum and Fountain water, at this pass
Paint Potters Vessels, and when they are dry
Put them into the Furnace, they must be
Of Earth, that strength of flames and fire try,

And

And from the Furnace Vessels you shall see
Fit for great Kings, but know that you must grind
Your Glass full fine, between two Marbles red,
And mix it well with fat Gum to your mind,
Fast Pots with this must Painted be and spread,
Then dryed, and in a Potters Furnace well
Baked, for this is right as I you tell.

How to Paint with green Glass.

Take you burnt Brimstone and calcined Brass,
And mingle them with powder of fine Glass,
Thrice mix them all with liquid Gum, and let
Your Pots be Painted and ith' Oven set
When they are burnt the colour will be green,
Thus is the worth of Glass for to be seen.
　　　　　　　　　Marcellus Palingenius.

Of white Glass to Paint Potters Pots.

White Glass for Pictures thus must be prepar'd
Mix burning Glass with Brimstone, and them beat
To powder, for this pains must not be spar'd,
Then Paint your Pots, and do it very neat,
And set them in the Furnace, let them burn,
Well as they must, and this will serve your turn. The same.

A black Glass to Paint those Vessels.

To Paint them balck you must grind Lazurestone
With Gum, and mix fine pouderd Glass in one,
Grind it full well, the colour will look blew
But being bak't it taks a blacker hew: The same.

To make very green Glass.

Take of the finest powder of burnt Brass,
Mix it with Verdigreese to make green Glass,
And poudred Glass must also added be
Paint Pots herewith that shall ith' Furnace hold
To make them green this Art I do unfold.

To Paint Ivory, the same Author.

To Paint your Ivory you must Engrave,
Upon the Bone such Pictures you would have,
And lay them in with Gold; a bladder of a Fish
Call'd Husa must be had, and put into a Dish,
With Fountain water, if you boyl't 'twill melt,
This is the Secret, see you no Man tel't The same.

BOOK. XVIII.

Of the Secrets of Sports.

THere are made Artificial Lights, by Lamps, Candles and the like, of some certain things and Liquors, chosen at convenient times according to the Stars, and composed in congruity with them, which when they are lighted and burn alone, are wont to produce some wonderfull things and celestiall effects, which Men oft admire, as *Pliny* speaks from *Anaxilaus,* that the sperm of Mares when they take Horse being burnt in a Lamp, will make the standers by seem to have heads like to
Horses,

Horses, the like is done by Asses, and Muscitiones mixed with Wax and lighted will make Flyes appear, and a Serpents skin lighted in a Lamp will make an apparition of Serpents. And some say that when Grapes are in the bud, if one bind about them a Viol full of Oyl, and let it remain untill the Grapes be ripe, that Oyl being afterwards burnt into a Lamp; will make Grapes be seen; the like is done with other fruits. If Centory be mixed with Honey and the bloud of a Houp, and put into a Lamp, all the standers by will seem greater than they are, and if it be lighted in a clear night, you will think the Stars fight one with another. Also the Cuttle fish Ink burnt will make Men like Blackmores. Also Men say that a Candle made of some things under the dominion of *Saturn*, if it be lighted and extinguished in the mouth of a Man newly dead, as often as it is lighted again it will make Men very sad and fearfull. *Corn. Agrippa.*

That the standers by may seem to want heads.

Let Orpiment finely poudred boyl in a new Pot with Oyl, it will not be amiss to put in some Brimstone to, set on the cover of the Pot, and let not the yellow smoke flye away; burn this in a new Lamp, and all the standers by will seem to want their heads, and hands, pressing their eyes with their fingers, untill it be lighted, and then you shall see it by degrees how it may be done. *Alexius.*

A sport of Dogs.

The Herb Hounds-tongue bound to the Matrix of a Bitch, will call all the Dogs of the Town or City to the place where it is hid or buried, and if it be hanged about the Dogs neck that he cannot get it off, he will turn up and down untill he be half dead. If you wear it under the bottome of your foot no Dog will barke at you. *Albert.*

A sport with Bread.

If you put with Bread into the Oven a Nut shell filled with Quick-brimstone, Salt peter, and Quicksilver, when it waxeth hot the Bread will so leap up and down, that it will make all the Spectators laugh. *Mizald.*

How you may see all things in the dark with their colours, which the Sun shines upon without.

If any Man desireth to see this he must shut all the Windows, and it will be good to stop all places of vent, that no light may come in to spoil all: only make one hole quite through, and let the hole be fashioned like a round Pyramis, let the base of it be toward the Sun, and the Conas toward the Chamber, over against it let the Wals be white, or covered with white Linnen or Paper; so all things being enlightned by the Sun, you shall see Men walking in the streets with their heads downwards, and what is on the right hand will appear on the left, and all contrary, and the farther off they are from the hole, the greater will their shape be, and if you bring the Table or Paper nearer they will shew less; But you must stay a while, for the Images will not appear presently: because sometimes the like makes a great sensation with the sense, and carryeth in such an affection, that only when the senses act, it remains in the things sensible, and hinders them, but when they have done acting, they stay long upon it, which is easie to perceive. For those that walk in the Sun, if they come to a dark place, that affection goes with them, that they can see nothing or very hardly, because the affect made by the light is yet in their eyes, and when that is by degrees vanished we see all clearly in a darker place. But now I shall declare what I ever concealed and resolved to do so still: that if you desire to see all things, with their colours. Place a Glass opposite that may not dissipate and disgregate, but may collect and unite: then coming to it and moving it, untill you find the proportion of a true Image, by a due appropinquation of the Center, and if you look intently into it, that you can discern the countenance, gestures, motions, and habits of Men, and Clouds in the Sky, with a blew colour, and Birds flying; If you can do this rightly, you will be very glad and wonder at it, all topsie turvey, because they are near the Center of the Glass; but if you shall set them farther from the Center, you shall see them greater and in their right posture. That it may be more clear let the Sun shine upon it; if not, by directing the Glass, by reflection of the Sun it shall shoot forth, that it shall be illustrated with great brightness, yet at a due distance, so oft changing the situation, untill you know you have attained it: Hence Philosophers and Physicians may see in what part of the eyes sight is placed, and the question of seeing by intromission is answered, which is so much disputed; nor is there any better way to demonstrate it: for the Species enters the sight of the eye as by a Window, and is like a Glass, a small portion of a great Sphere, being placed behind in the eye; If any one measure the distance, sight is in the center of the eye, which I know will much delight ingenious Men. *The same.*

The way to Dance upon the Ropes.

The way is this; A bold Man and experienced walks with naked feet upon a Rope very hard stretcht, and in his right and left hand he holds a Weight of Lead, of ten, fifteen, or twenty pound; when he swarves to the right hand; (being carefull of his business, and also very bold) he stretcheth forth his left hand, and puts it forth, and draws it in, so before the right hand can over-weigh the left he ballanceth them, and brings his body to an equall poys, and so by degrees he brings his weights and arms to the former posture: this is necessary, for before he fall, one Weight must be heavier than the other. This poys is acquired by degrees, wherefore before he fals he stretcheth forth and puls in his arm, and so bends on the other side, that he will not fall. He may fall if the Rope be not exactly extended, if his Limbs be astonished in the mean while; If he do not carry his body well; or if he be weary, or want art or use, that he extend his hand too late untill he sinks, or extends it too much as to the contrary side. I pass by that the weights must have a certain proportion or very near thereto, according to the weight, magnitude, and strength of every Man. If these six circumstances be, he is in no danger. Therefore a certain Boy with balls under his feet, and sometimes shut into a Sack all but his arms, walked upon a Rope extended between the tops of Towers, we being much afraid of his life. Another ascended from the ground to the top of a Tower, which is harder, because his loins are much strain'd in this exercise. Also he let himself fall by the Rope down flat from the Tower without Weights to the ground, only stretching forth his hands; for he had such force in his hands and arms, that he used them for Weights; The same Man, which is most strange, hung by his foot by a very small Cord from the Rope, from the very top almost of the Tower, a horrible sight. Then by the strength of his loins and back, he laid hold of the Cord with his hands, and returned back to the Rope. They both made us believe they would fall headlong, but the top of their foot held by the Rope, with their heads downwards, you may understand what force there was in the top of the foot, for they hung only by the bending of their Toes, and that backward. The Boy also with the balls cast himself headlong, and one of them sticking between the sole of his foot and the Rope, he hung fast I know not how, that he should not fall by the roundness of it. But the Art and boldness of *Turks* exceeded all credit and expectation. I say what I saw and all our Countrey also. They were two young Men with no great bodies, but well set, each of them at first taking a Man upon his shoulders, ascended by the steep Rope, to half a right Angle, and that without any help of Weights: then adding Daggers about three hands breadth in length that were very sharp pointed, and had edges like to Razors, fastned to their Ankles, they mounted again the same way, with a Man on their shoulder, and so stretching forth the legs, that it is not easie to walk so upon plain ground, then laying a Plank upon the Rope, and having under his feet Stilts, which our Citizens call *Scantia*, he walked upon this Board thus laid, whenas the Plank by it self could not lye there one moment, then he put under his feet five round pieces of Wood, on both sides, that you might see them all, but they were pierced through with an Iron Wyer, to make them hold fast together, and with these he walked upon the Rope, no Man can go so upon plain ground, nor yet stand therewith, the round pieces of Wood, that were no thicker than a Mans arm, falling here and there. After this laying under his feet round Brass Dishes, not bound, which he was forced to keep on with his feet by extending them, he walked upon the Rope. After this he stood sitting in a Kettle, and the Kettle stood tottering upon the Rope, O horrible spectacle. But that which was next to a miracle, he withdrew his Pole and Weights from the Vessel, that the Kettle seemed almost to hang pendulous in the Ayr. For he brought his Spear that was behind between the Vessel and the Rope before him; he Danced by measure upon the Rope, the Drum beating, and sometimes he cast himself headlong out of it, hanging only by the heel, (this I saw with my eyes) and sometimes by the Tarsus and boat of the foot. It would amaze a Man to see the other to stand upon the lesser Rope extended, which was not above an inch thick, and holding all his upper part unmoved, to move the lower part with the Rope so violently; that here and there above twelve hands breadth he moved so swift as an Arrow from a Bow. But what was not so strange yet was above credit for humane power to do, that when he had ascended out of the field to the top of the Tower of Joves Fort, which is wonderfull high, with his Weights; then from the top of the Tower he ascended to the beam by the Rope, which stood so upright from the plain, that it was above three parts or four of a right Angle, and he came down more strang ly then he went up, namely headlon g as if he would have fallen upon his head. We observed that with his great Toes of both feet, he held the Rope against his other Toes to sustain so great force. And it could not otherwise be, that he should ascend a Rope that was so upright, or descending not fall upon his head. He would when he did this for a good reward, take up a Man upon his shoulders, but no Man would undertake it, it was so rash. No wonder that the greatest Princes are delighted with this sport it is so rare. The people supposed it was done by the Devil, and was no Mans work. *Cardan.*

A flying Dragon.

There is an Artifice some call a flying Dragon, some a Comet, it is made thus. Make a square of thin pieces of Reed, the length to the breadth must be in proportion one and half, there must be two diameters at opposite parts, or Angles, and where they cut one, the other a string must be fastned, and being of the same quantity, must be tied with two others that come from the ends of the Engine, it must then be covered with Paper or fine Linnen that it may be equally poysed, then it must be let flye from the top of some Tower or Hill, or high place. When the winds are equall, not too strong least they break the Engine, nor too weak : for they will not raise it, and you will lose your labour : It must not flye right forward, but obliquely, which is effected by a long tail, that proceeds from one end to the other, which you shall make of Withs set at equall distance, and Papers bound here and there: thus being set out, drawing it gently, it must be guided by the Artists hands, who must not force it off drowsily and idly, but forcibly, so will this Ship flye into the Ayr, and when it is once raised a little (for here the houses hinder the wind) you can scarce rule it with your hands. Some place a Lanthorn above it to make it seem a Comet; Others a Squib wrapt up in Paper with Gunpouder, and when it is setled in the Ayr to hover, a lighted Match is sent up by the Cord by some Ring or thing that will slip, and presently it gives fire to the open mouth of it, and with a great crack the Engine is rent in pieces, and fals down to the ground. Some bind a a Cat or Whelp to it, to hear them cry in the Ayr. Thus an ingenious Man may invent principles how a Man may learn to flye, with huge wings tied to his arms and brest, but he must use himself to it by degrees from his youth, ever choosing some higher place. If any one wonder at it, let him think what the Pythagorist *Archytas* did, for many noble Greeks, and *Favorinus* the Philosopher, most exquisite for old Monuments, have written affirmatively, that *Archytas* made by Art a Pigeon of Wood, so poysed with Weights, and the Ayr included, that it flew by them. *The same.*

To make Men seem to be dead.

Boyl Wine with Salt untill a third part be consumed, then kindle and burn the Wine, removing all other light, and they standing still will seem to be dead. *Cardan.*

A

A double Glass.

It is pleasant to make a double Glass as you see here; In the middle a Candle burns, between the superficies of the Glass some divers kind of moysture or water is placed, so you shall have a double light, and variety of wonder. Some put small Fishes between the Glasses, and a little Bird sometimes wondred at the Fish, and sometimes peckt at them. You may joyn many Candles, Lights, Vessels and Liquors to make it more strange. *The same.*

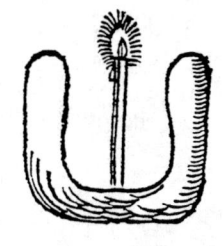

To make Women hold their water.

There is a certain prickle in the tail of a Ray Fish, and Authors write that there is nothing in the Sea more execrable, for it will performe many wonders: amongst the rest, if you give your mind to it, where the ground is soft or in a Garden, and an old Wife pisseth, stick down presently the prickle there, that it may all lye hid, and she shall never make water untill you pull it up again; stay but a few daies, and she will piss presently, thus young Lads will make old Women often hold their water, if they forbid them the use of any. *The same.*

That Women shall eat nothing at the Table.

Women will eat nothing at the Table, if you put under the Dish of meat Basil roots and all, and they not know of it. *Florentin. Geoponicus.*

That Guests shall not eat when they sit down.

That Guests may not eat at Table, do this. Though it seem not very probable, I will not leave it out. You must have a Needle that dead people are often sewed up in their winding sheet, and at begining of Supper secretly stick this under the Table, this will hinder the Guests from eating, that they will rather be weary to sit than desirous to eat; take it away when you have laughed at them awhile. *The same.*

That a Baker cannot put his bread into the Oven.

Take the Halter a Thief was hanged with, and when you have it, tye it about the mouth of the Oven: if the Baker would set in his Bread he will run here and there, and never find the right way, and if he do put it in, the peel will be cast forth again, which is very stange, and much less true. *The same.*

That one may speak in his sleep.

A Frog and an Owl will make a Man prate, and of these especially the tongue and the heart, so the tongue of a Water-Frog put under ones head will make him talk in his sleep, and the heart of an Owl put upon a Womans left brest when she sleeps, will make her, as some say, reveal all her secrets. Some report that a Screech Owls heart will do the same, and the fat of a Hare put upon the brest of one that sleeps. *Agrippa.*

That one cannot sleep.

The eye of a Swallow laid in the bed, will not let one sleep till it be taken away. *Albert. Magnus.*

That a Woman in her sleep may confess her wicked deds.

But if you will hear what is more admirable, of her own accord, against your will, that your Wife shall relate in her sleep the wickedness she hath committed, which I see *Democritus* knew, and it is more prevalent for Women than for Men, because they are more given to prate. In a stormy night when a Woman is fast asleep, lay upon her brest where her heart beats some tongues of lake Frogs: (you may do the like with wild-Ducks and Owls tongues, because they cry in the night) and let them lye there, and ask her what you can, and be not weary to ask again if she answer not presently; for at last she wil speak and reveal all from her heart, and speak all truth to every question. Some say this may be done by some counterfeit charms where there is no superstition. O strange, how should this be that a Woman should reveal in her sleep freely that which men labour in vain to find out when they are awake? who can beleive it! but come gently to her, and she will speak flatteringly, use this at your need. *The same.*

Playes against Jests.

If the Napkins and Tablecloaths be strewd on with pouder of Vitriol, where they wipe when they are washt, they shall be all black though the Linnen be very clean; if you rub the Knives with juyce of Coloquintida, all will tast bitter, if with Assa, they will all stink. *Cardan.*

The first Pastime.

Take two narrow Boards not long, in which there must be holes, *A. B.* and *C. D.* near the ends of the Boards, but there must be a Thong cut at *E.* and *F.* long wayes; put *E.* upon *A.* and by the lower part *G.* let it be drawn through both holes, after that through *B. C. D.* by turns upwards and downwards, then again through *C.* let it be drawn downwards, that it may ascend upwards, and so by the same manner untill the Table *A. B.* may be drawn forth by *F.* the hole of the Thong, and so the Thong will be fastned in both the Boards; Wherefore it must be drawn forth the contrary way. So we sport as I did with my mouth when I was but young. *The same.*

The second Pastime.

The same is done if two thin Boards as long as ones little finger and equall one to the other be taken, and three holes made in each of them, at even distance as you see here, the Thong also overthwart by the ends, must be divided in *G.* and downwards, wherefore bring the head of the Thong *K.* upwards by *B.* but *L.* by *C.* over against it, that the ends may stick forth on the same part. After that bring *L.* through *G.* then through *A.* upwards, that *L.* may tend downwards; then bring *L.* downwards again by *D.* and upward by *F.* and down again and upward by *E.* then again by *D.* after through *H.* the division, you shall thrust the Board *A. B. C.* then bringing *L.* back the contrary way by *D.* it will rest in *E.* as *K.* doth in *B*. *The same.*

The third Pastime.

Another: You must have two Points and fold them as you see here, and tye them together with a Thread of the same colour, and pull three little Buttons over them, such as are the *Pater Noster* Beads: they are *A. B. G.* but they are not set in the middle, that you may know where the Thread lyeth: then reduce the ends *D.* towards *C.* and *E.* towards *D.* making a knot upon the Beads; then deliver this into any Mans hands, and with a Pen-Knife cut off the Thread *B.* beneath *D.* and *E.* and the Points will remain whole, the Buttons falling off. *The same.*

The fourth Pastime.

The like almost is done by a doubled Thread as *A. B. C.* bring the end *D.* by *A.* that *A.* may lye hid under one finger, and *C.* under another finger, and the part *C. D.* may be doubled; then cut *C. D.* with your Knife, and there will seem to be four ends and beginnings, let therefore *C. D.* fall away secretly, and there will appear but two ends, though the Thread seemd to be cut into four parts. I add this, that every man may understand the art of Jugling to be all of this kind, that before you know how it is done, you will wonder at it, but when you do know you will see they are Childrens sport. *The same.*

To find out Theft.

If you will find out theft, you may thus recover things that are stolen away. There is a stone called an Eagle-stone, and it is as if it were with Child. For shake the stone and it ratleth in the belly, if therefore you pouder that stone and bake it with Bread, and give it unknewn to a Thief, when he cheweth it he cannot swallow it down, but he will choke or be discovered for a Thief, for he can never swallow it. *The same.*

To see strange things in a Urinal Glass.

Take Saffron bound up in a Linnen Cloath, a little, put it into Spring water untill it be well colourd by it, then take whites of Eggs, and shake them seaven or eight times with the said water: after that, put this water into a Urinal Glass full of clear water, and you shall see strange things in it. *Fallop.*

To make Bread Dance upon the Table.

Put Quicksilver into a Quill, stop it, and put it into hot Bread, and it will Dance. *The same.*

An Artificiall Vision.

The night seems to be the mother of these devices; yet though these deceits be fooleries, they are sometimes causes of very great things. As it fell out with *Cenethus* the second King of the *Scots*, who when the Picts had taken his Father *Alpinas* and killed him, and had frighted the King himself, and his Subjects, that he could not perswade them to take revenge; for great part of the Nobility and Souldiers of the Kingdome were slain in the Battle with his Father; he therefore called the chief Men together, and Treated them courteously, and invited them to his Court, and Feasted them. The night following, when all was quiet, he sent a Man severally into all their Chambers, with a Staff in his right hand of rotten Wood, that shines like a Torch in the dark, (I have spoken of this elsewhere,) with a Garment made of a Fish skin with the scales on, which also shines wonderfully in the night, especially by the help of the rotten stick; now there is a huge company of these great Fishes in *Scotland*,) In the left hand which they put to their mouth, there was a great Ox horn, for in that Island there are such Ox hornes; All these blew terribly through their horns, saying, that they must asist the King; that the Picts should suffer for their wickedness, that the *Scots* should have a great Victory, and that they came from God to declare as much. It was easie to delude Men that were sleepy, who could see no man going in nor coming out: for when they went away they had turnd in their Coats, and hid their sticks; when in the morning they came to Councel, every one told what he had seen and heard; But the King fearing lest this trick should be discovered openly, to conceal it, first shews that he had also seen the same, and therefore wished them not to speak of what they were admonished by God, for so they might anger him that was now their friend. They all upon this, no Man knowing the business agree to a Warre, and the event proved no less than an answer to a Divine Oracle. For the Picts were conquerd, once, twice, and thrice, at last the *Scots* conquerd them, that they left not one alive. *Card.*

The second Vision.

Another that many have used. They scatter Beetles, or Snails, or Crawfish in Church-yards with small Candles; Others more cunningly hide Candles in dead Mens Skuls, and make them look terrible. But if small Candles be placed upon Locusts backs, they will fright Men exceedingly, for the Candles will seem to leap. *The same.*

The third Vision.

Another that deceives Chyrurgions also, and they think the part is certainly wounded: the hand being so smeered with a Salve, that it is but reasonable, as many other things are known by use and experience. A *Grecian* taught many such Secrets, who came to us, but they are only for sport and for no profit. By reason, because in Wounds there is a cavity, blood, and sometimes sinews to be seen, but almost alwayes the lips of the Wound; the cavity is counterfeited by the sticking forth of the sides, the blood by red Lead, Lac, Vermilion, and best of all, Dragons blood; the sinews by Threads, the lips of the skin and flesh by white Lead, Rosin, Tallow, or white Wax; This is the experiment, but use makes the fraud perfect. *The same.*

The fourth Vision.

Another, Whereby all things in the house seem to move as in an Earthquake, but the sight only is here deluded. First, The Roof and Walls must be over the Wood or Cement streaked with streaks like to Serpents obliquely, and so Gilded, that

that they may shine: then will the flame of a Candle, as I have shewed elsewhere, tremble, and to give it no other name, all things will quake and tremble in appearance. For because the part *A. B.* (but the winding cannot be well expressed in Plano) is seen near to the Line *A. C.* but the light is carryed by *A. D.* of necessity *A. B.* must seem to move, for the right motion of the light is carryed obliquely; then both by reason of the proper quavering of the light, and for the obliquity of the motion, it will seem to tremble. A dark fire with smoke do much further this business; for a weak action is more easily vitiated than a strong, but when smoke is with the flame, and the flame is weak, that which proceeds from a small substance makes but a weak sight. Wherefore such a fire with such a flame and a light smoke will cause this apparition. *The same.*

The fift Vision.

I cannot pass by what I learned in my sleep this night, which is the twenty eight day of *January* 1554. precedent. When I last transcribed this Book, I saw a Wall whereon were Painted very many Images, whereof some walked, others seemed to talk, some stood, others sate, and some walked up and down. Then said I it is strange. But one that was present said, this is no wonder, but you were the Inventor of this reason; I truly remember it; then he replyed, This Wall is in the secret walk over against the high way, which you know to be much frequented, and now by accident the Souldiers pass by it. Let the Sun shine in the way, and you have shewed how Images may be seen by shadows in the opposite Wall; But these many in the outsides of the Wall that are so confused, and some in the middle, and those you see siting, are all Pictures made by the similitude of shadows, that when the shadows depart from the Wall, some of the Pictures seem to move. Then said I, you can scarce distinguish the Pictures from the shadows. But saith he, this was the work of an excellent Art, for by a reason taken out of your Book, the Master of the house invented this, they are the representations of Men talking and no Pictures, but shadowes. For these two stand in the way, and they presently departed; but I recollecting my self, understood that the same might be done on a Table, that might be copied out. *Cardan.*

How Visions may be made in the Clouds.

Nicolaus Siccus chief-Justice, a famous Man, whom I name for his honour, saith that he had tryed it when the wind blew, that if Pictures be carryed on Horseback, that are light, as made with Feathers, or printed upon Paper, and tyed with a Thread to the Horse Saddle Bow, will flye up into the Ayr, that if the Thread be small, the matter seems wonderfull, and there is reason for it: for when the Wind comes against it, and the Picture is broad and light, it cannot fall right down, nor yet stand against the force of the Wind as other things that use to fall down, because it is held by the Thread; It must therefore needs flye upward and be the cause that Men shall think it an apparition: but I doubt much whether it will reach so far as the Clouds or not; For either the string will break, or the force of the Wind doth not reach so far, or such a length of Thread cannot retain such a force. But let others try it: a more compendious way is described in *Æsops* Fables; for an Eagle bred up, which was wont to flye aloft, and an Image fastned to her feet, and then let flye, will cause the sight of an apparition. We use these Arts to put courage into the Souldiers, when Enemies are ready to fight them, and it is not amiss. *The same.*

A Necromantick Sport.

That is also a very pleasant spectacle, as it was to me, wherewith *Andreas Albinus*, a most learned Physician of *Bononina* frighted a certain credulous Lover: He set a dead Mans head upon a Table, and he promised unto us that the head should reveal which of us was deeply in love with a certain Citizens Daughter. We that understood not that Pastime were troubled at it, as if that Oracle should be pronounced by help of the Devil, but they that observed the Jest, laughed at it. The business was thus: The Table stood upon four Pillars, like to feet, and one foot was hollow

low set under the Table that was perforated quite through that hole, and all the Table was covered with fine Tapistry, that the hole of the Table should not be seen: upon that place stood the dead Mans head : the Pavement also in that part had a hole made through, where the hollow Pillar held up the Table, that from the lower Room to the upper, and from the upper Room to the lower a voice might proceed. Whereupon he that was in the lower Room putting a Pipe into the hollow Pillar of the Table, and setting the other part of the Pipe to his ear, heard with ease what the other in the upper Room asked, and he answered according to his questions. This succeeded the better, because they knew the secrets of both these Lovers, and so knew how to delude them : for so they handsomely acted their parts, having conferred together before. And to make this Oracle the more to be believed, he set lighted Wax Candles about the skull of the dead Man, and he repeated some strange words. *Andreas Albius.*

Another Jest of Stage-Players.

This also seemed strange to many, but when I shall shew you the way to do the like, you will think it a silly thing. A certain Man brought a Glass to us, we looking into it, he put in a Ring, which as oft as we desired, it would leap in the Glass. This Trick was performed thus. There was a fine hair of a Womans head made fast to the Ring, and to the fingers of the Man that made the sport : when therefore the Ring must Dance, the Stage-Player moved his fingers, and the Ring moved therewith, and we saw not the hair. The Fellow concealed this Jugling by a cunning device; saith he, this Ring will not Dance like fair Maids, unless I Pipe and Taber with my fingers to it. *A Venetian Jugler.*

To make one fart.

If you take an Asses hairs that grow near to his Pisle, and cutting them small, you give them to any one to drink with Wine, he will presently begin to fart. *Albert.*

Otherwise.

Also take Emmet Eggs, and bruise them, and put them into water, and let any one drink thereof, he will presently not cease farting. You may do the same with Wine. *The same.*

What things cause farting.

Some things are esteemed Witchcraft rather than Medicament : it sufficeth to rehearse the most easie; Emmets Eggs, or Chestnut flowers, will make one fart. *Cardan.*

That he who hath a Rupture shall have his Testicles to crack and make a noise.

That the Testicles of one that hath a Rupture may make a noise, do this; When you see him come to the fire to warm himself, put either Elder or Figtree green Wood to burn upon the fire : for so they will so crack, that he will be forced to be gone. Whether that proceeds from the vapour that he sends forth, like to that Wind, which is also wont to do hurt. *The same.*

A wonder of a Drum Wheel.

Some things are also made, which although they be no apparitions, yet they make people admire. A Wheel of Parchment is painted with divers figures, that the fashion of the Picture may descend by degrees; and again those that descend may be received by others that ascend : for their situation bends obliquely : and as it were by equidistant Lines; A light is placed in the middle, which like to the flame that turns the Spits about, turns the Wheel, and because alwayes Figures different in situation are seen to come on, they all seem to ascend or descend which is admirable. *Cardan.*

A Pastime to boyl Pease in a Pot.

He that would make Men laugh to see Pease leap forth of a boyling Pot, let him put in some Quicksilver, and he shall see a pretty Jest, unless the brims of the Pot be too high, or the fire too small. I have tryed it. *Mizald.*

That an Egg may ascend into the Ayr.

You may make an Egg to ascend into the Ayr thus. Fill the empty Egg shell with Dew, taken in *May*: (for at other times as in Summer and Autumn, it is no true Dew, as we prove by Physicall reasons) set this against the Sun at noon day, and the Sun will draw it up, and if sometime it rise hardly, when it begins to rise, it will rise best by help of a Staff or Board. *The same.*

Chess Play.

This puts me in mind how with two colours, or with one only, a Man may shew many differences, as in Chess Play, with Chess Men, which is Printed. They that set forth the *Spanish* Book have confounded all. Wherefore the black places must be distinguished by black Lines, as in Checker work, and the white must be left pure and clear, but the Chess Men that must be black all over, must be blackt with Ink, the white Men must have only some black streeks round about, and all that is within must remain white. *Cardan.*

That three scroles untouched shall change their places.

There is yet one Pastime that three scroles untouched shall change their places. He that knoweth it not will admire it; There are three long scroles made of Paper or Linnen, and they all severally exceed one the other in length equally: for being all made equall with one head, they equally being turned about, are out of their places, and they are in a different situation, for the longer will be in the middle or first place; but if the same that is the longer be in the last place, it is immoveable, scarce any man can think but that this is done by the Devil; yet this proceeds from nothing else, but because at the end of the resolution, the longer remains, and the last in its revolution remains where it began. Some were in an error to think this was done by force of words, and they gave answers as from an Oracle to all questions: for if the scroles changed their places, then it was good to begin, and the effects would be good, otherwise all would prove infortunate, and they would not change their belief for reason and experience, when they had got a custome to believe. *The same.*

A Sport concerning flesh.

Lute strings cut small, and strewed upon flesh new drest, (be it rost or boyld) will make the Ghests think that the flesh is rotten, worm eaten, and naught; He that knoweth this Trick may when he please beguile the rest, and eat all himself. *Mizald.*

That a Wman may tell all that ever she did.

When you will have a Woman or Maid to tell you all that ever she did, take the heart of a Pigeon, the head of a Frog, and dry them both, and pouder them, strew the pouder upon the brest of her that is asleep, and she will discover all. *Alb.*

Wonders of a Woodden Statue.

It is very strange what I saw done by two small Images of Wood, playing together, by the means of two Sicilians: They were both run through with one Thread here and there, and being fastned, one of the Statues would stand still, and the other Danced all sorts of Dances, whilst the Artist plaid upon the Pipe, the Thread being extended both wayes: so they Danced wonderfully with their heads, legs, feet, arms, and moving them so many wayes, that I confess ingeniously I cannot understand the reason of so great curiosity in work. For there were not many Threads nor yet sometimes slack sometimes strait, but there was but one Thread in each Statue, and alwayes extended. For I have seen many others that went with many Threads, and those sometimes strait sometimes loose, and that I did not wonder at. But this was rare, wherein all the Postures and Dancings were answerable to the Tunes were plaid. *Cardan.*

Hairs that turn to Serpents.

These are wonderfull things: That the hairs of a menstruous Woman will turn into Serpents and Wormes if they be buried in Horse dung a short time. So may the putrefied menstruous blood as well breed Toads and Frogs: for it is easily corrupted and changed; and oftimes Women generate forth with the Child, Toads, Lizards, and such

such like things. And we read that the Women of *Salerna*, when they first conceive when the Child should come to take life; they kill such a Creature with the juyce of Smallage and Leeks. When a certain Woman besides her expectation was supposed to be with Child, instead of a Child she was delivered of four Creatures like to Frogs, and she ofttimes miscarryed upon some such cause; I believe there is no other cause to be given of this monstrous conception; For by the corruption of Mans seed, as it were Wormes will breed in the intestins. *Alcippe* was delivered of an Elephant, and a Maid at the beginning of the *Marsian* War, generated a Serpent. So hairs taken forth of Horses tails and cast into the waters will receive life. Basil bruised between two Tiles, and laid in a moyst place where the Sun shines much will breed Scorpions : yet *Galen* denieth it. The dust of a burnt Duck, if it be kept covered between two Dishes in a moyst place, will strangely bring forth a huge Toad. But a Frog may more easily be produced suddenly, if you consider their original; I do not speak of them that by a legitimate order of nature, that is by coupling in the water, have their beginning, but such as breed of themselves and are called temporary, and are only bred by Summer showrs upon the shores and dusty Sands by the way sides, and they are commonly short lived; or ofttimes the blasts of Wind, raging upon the tops of high Mountains, raise the dust, which being mingled with water, nor only is converted into Frogs, but into stones also. *Philarchus*, and *Heraclides Lemnus*, are my Authours, that it hath sometimes rained Frogs; and one of them saith, that about *Dardania* and *Paonia* the same accident hapned in such abundance, that their houses and high wayes were full of them. And *Ælianus* when out of *Italy* he came from *Naples* and went to *Puteoli*, saw Frogs, part whereof, namely the head crept, with two feet, the other parts being not yet formed, was drawn like to slimy mud grown together; so of the same body, one part was alive, and the other part was Earth. *Macrobius* saith, that in *Ægypt* Mice breed of showrs and Earth, and in other places Frogs, Serpents and the like, so that their production is easie. For if a Man but spit, presently a Frog was bred of his spittle; and *Daumatus* a *Spaniard*, as oft as he pleased, would presently produce a great multitude of Frogs, likewise of Wormes, with the filth that comes from young Sows when they go to Bore, and the blood, after the manner aforesaid, when the Sun enters the first degreee of *Capricorn*, that they may Farrow at the end of *Pisces*, being fed well with Milk, and Crums of Bread. And the filth of a Boar called *Apria*, which is the same which in Horses is called *Hippomanes*, being taken, and hid in a Glass well covered under Horse dung, that the heat rising may not flye away, and so left for some dayes, and what comes of it kept in a Leaden Box, will serve for use. He that knows how to compound that rightly, shall see no common experiment. But if any Man desires to know this more curiously than is needfull, the reason whereof we know by experiment with Horse dung, a strange way to produce a Mandrake. If any Man will make a monster to breed out of an Egg; (I hear now they begin to call it by a borrowed name,) he must instead of the cock-tred put in humane vitall virus, and cover it well that the vivifical heat flye not forth, they say this will hatch a monster, part a Chick and partly a Myrmidon. *Avicenna* doth not deny it; If cause be I shall speak elsewhere more at large, it is enough to shew you the way : I omit many and greater matters which ignorant people will not believe. These shall serve to be spoken of menstruous Births; and the force of dung in production. *The same*.

To see Castles and Towers in the waters.

Put Water into a Glass Vessel like to a Chamber-Pot, and taking a little Saffron bound in a Linnen Cloath and putting of it into a little of that Water, untill it be Dyed, rubbing of it; then put the white of an Egg well broken with your fingers, seaven or eight times to it, and cast all that into the Water, you shall see as it were Towers, and Towns, and Castles in the Water. *Cardan*.

That in a Mans Bed Lice may seem to crawle, so that a Man cannot sleep.

If you would have Lice seem to crawle in a Mans bed, so that he cannot sleep, cast into his bed one ounce, or half an ounce of Alkakengi, and if you take the Feathers

thers of a Buzzard and make a light therewith, they that see it, will appear all to be infirme and consumed. Take a yellow Locust, and dry it, and pouder it, and put it into a Funeral Cloath, and light it with Oyl of Elders, and in what place soever you are, that shall befall you as I said, and you will admire it. *Albert.*

How a Bucket of Water may be held up.

I have spoken of those things that support more than reason seems to allow, and of those things that mutually support one the other; now I must demonstrate how any thing may seem to support it self. Let there be a plain Table *A. B.* and a Staff *C. E.* let the external part of it be under the handle *D.* of the Bucket full of Water, *G. F. H.* and between the Staff *C. E.* and *F.* the bottome of the Bucket, place a stick *E. F.* that is streight, and right that it cannot fall, I say the Bucket will hang and cannot fall. For it is plain that *F.* being the bottome of the Bucket, the Staff *E. F.* and *F.* the Center of gravity, and Center of the Earth that is *K.* and the Center of the Bucket that is *L.* are in one right Line, which is *K. F. L. E.* If then the Bucket fall, it must either fall by the right Line *F. K.* or else some side as *G.* or *H.* must incline; should it then incline toward *H.* to *M.* I draw *K. M.* because therefore two Lines are drawn from *K. K. E.* and *K. M.* to a circle, and *K. E.* passeth through the Center of the Circle; that is, of the Bucket. It follows by *Euclides* demonstrations (*Elementorum tertio*) that *K. F.* is lesser than *K. M.* therefore the Center of gravity *F.* is removed far from the Center of the Earth *K.* wherefore what is contrary to reason, what is heavy should ascend moving naturally which is impossible. Therefore the Bucket will not fall, inclining it self to either side; nor yet by the right Line *K. F.* because the Angle *F. E. C.* is a right Angle, and it is plain that *D.* descending to *L.* you may draw *L. B.* which shall be equall to *E. B.* Wherefore since *L. B.* is opposed to a right Angle (*per quintam primi*) the Triangle *L. E. B.* shall have two right Angles, or else the greater side is not opposed to the greater Angle, both which are contrary to what *Euclides* writes, *Elementorum primo.* Whence follows a greater wonder, that a thing that would fall of itself, putting more weight to it, it will not fall. For placing the part of the Staff *B. D.* greater than *D. C.* the Staff will fall, because the end of it by falling, comes nearer to the Center of the Earth *K.* and so *C.* may rise, and so it will fall; yet adding weight to the Bucket it will not fall. But you must (least the standers by laugh at you when you should fail in your experiment, for ignorant people where the business succeeds not, blame not the Man but the Art) be very diligent to see that the upper superficies of the Table be set exactly level, and the stick be perfectly streight and doth not bend; also the stick *E. F.* must be right, and close set to the bottome of the Bucket, and *C. E.* so that it make the Staff *C. E.* stand firm to the handle *D.* and that the point *F.* be the Center of gravity, and the Bucket round. Many will read this, but few will understand it; For you must understand more then is Written, yet you want nothing to the perfection of it. *Cardan.*

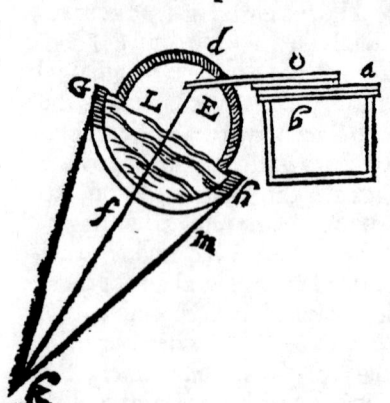

Whether a Woman be an Adulteress.

They say that if any one lay a Diamond upon a Womans head, she will shew whether she be an Adulteress; for if she be so, she will be frighted and leap out of her Bed, if not, she will embrace her Husband with delight. *Albertus.*

Sticks

Book XVIII.   *Secrets of Sports.*   345

Sticks that mutually support one the other.

Some seem to be supported of themselves, and support others, and yet fastned no where. As I take the stick *A. B,* I lay *C. D.* upon that, and upon *C. D. E. F.* and let it fall under *A. B.* I say then, that unless they be taken asunder they cannot fall, for *A. B.* is supported by *E. F.* and *E. F.* by *C. D.* and *C. D.* by *A. B.* therefore neither of them will fall, but the place *D. B. F.* supporteth and is supported; this is clear by experiment, therefore it is sustained by something: wherefore by all, because the same reason serves for all, and so it is most firme, and the more it is pressed, the firmer it is; and it will not fail unless one of them break. *Cardan.*

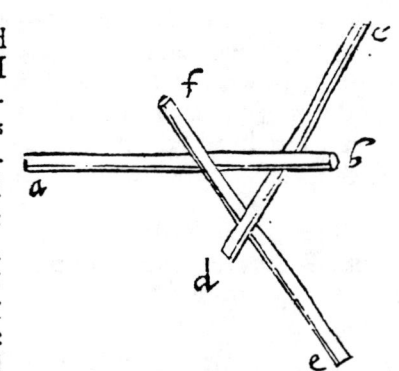

That a Woman may confess her doings.

Take a live water Frog, and take out his tongue, and turn the Frog into the water, and put that tongue upon that part of the heart of a Woman that beats when she sleeps, and ask her any thing; she will tell you true. *Albertus.*

A Weapon that hangs by no bands.

Likewise I read in Books, that in the Temple of *Diana* of the *Ephesians,* the Weapon of *Cupid* hang, being tied by nothing to hold it up. If any one desire to do the like, he may easily attain to it: take a light Sword, and let the haft be a Cane, and set a Loadstone as big as the bone of your Arm into the roof of the Temple, that is made hollow, and of excellent virtue; put your Weapon to it, and it will seem for many ages to hang of it self, and it is no great wonder. *Cardan.*

A Jugling Ring.

A Girdle or Jugling Ring is made thus: There must be three Circles made, or more if you please, so Woven with one Line that shall stir about only, and that neither of them may touch the other in any part; so two of them will seem to hang pendulous in the Ayr, by a wonderfull Art and crafty Invention: but it is far more easie to do it than to describe it: although as I could, I have drawn the forme of it. The reason is this, if we will make a threefold Ring, we must describe two Circles, then we must take what number we please, which being divided by three, the number of the Circles of the Ring, will leave a unite over and above: as for example, sixteen, which being divided by three will leave one, and five are the quotient; wherefore divide the outward Circle into sixteen equall parts, and describing them, make as many divisions in the lesser Circle, yet so that the lower points may cut the upper points in the middle; then drawing portions of Circles from the lower point to the upper, and from that to the lower, ever intermitting two, it will at last returne when three Circles are finished to the same point, and so one circle is made three; But I have let go those outward Circles, or those that are first described, that the reason of the description may be better understood: Moreover it is best to blot them out, that the work may seem more absolute and compleat. But the bodies of the Rings must not touch one the other, by the Insections that are made upon the solid body; for so they will seem to hang by themselves, when it is not so. *Cardan.*

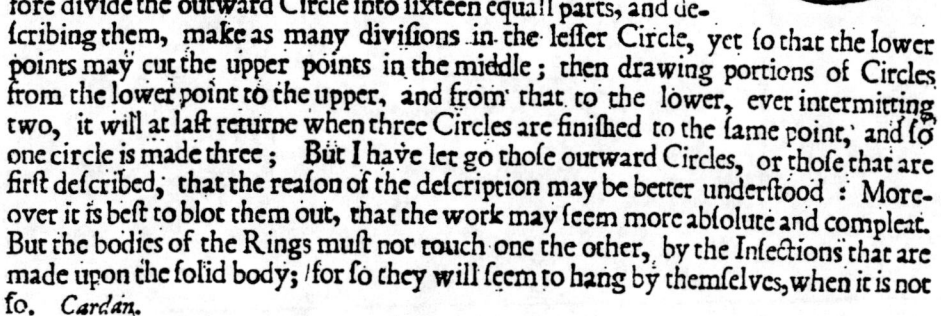

To find a Thief.

If any one bake the pouder of an Eagle-stone with brown Bread, and give one that he suspects, a piece of it to eat, he can never swallow the Bread he hath chewed. *Mizald.*

Whether a Woman be deflowred.

The smoke of the seeds of Purcelane, or of the leaves of Burdock, let into the se-

X x 2   crets

crets of a Woman by a Tunnel or otherwise, will make a Woman that is corrupted Urine presently, but if she be honest it will not. *The same.*

How to keep Wine fresh in the heat of Summer, and the coldest of Winter.

Put your Wine in a Glass Viol, and inclose it in a Box made of Wood, Leather, or any such like; between the Case and the Viol put Saltpeter, and it will keep it fresh both against violent heat, Frost and Snow. *Approved out of a Manuscript.*

Iron and Steel to make very hard.

Quench your blade of either mettal seaven times in the blood of a male Hog mixt with Goose grease, at each time dry it at the fire before you wet it, this makes it exceeding hard and not brittle. *From an experienced Armourer.*

A sure way to play at Nine-Pins so as to strike all down.

The Nine-Pins standing in an equall square, a good Player striking the first Pin somewhat low, shall strike down the second and fift; these in their violence may strike down three, six, and nine; the Boule being in motion, may strike down four and seaven, which four may strike down the eighth, and so all nine may be struck down. *Often tryed.*

To Rost a Capon at a Souldiers back whilst he March five or six Miles.

Take a Capon truss it up as usuall, Lard it very well, stuff it well with Butter, provide a piece of Steel the length of the Capon, and big enough to fill the belly of it, heat it, and stop it with Butter, wrap it up close that no Ayr comes at it; its said the King of *Sweden* eat them no otherwise drest while he was in the field.

How to make Coffe.

Take the Berry, put it in a Tin Pudding-pan, and when the Bread hath been in the Oven about half an hour, put in your Coffe, there let it stand till you Draw your Bread; then beat it and sift it; mix it thus, first boyl your Water about half an hour, to every quart of Water put in a spoonfull of the pouder of Coffe, then let it boyl one third away, clear it off from the setlings, and the next day put fresh Water, and so add every day fresh water, so long as any setlings remain. *Often tryed.*

FINIS.

A Catalogue

Courteous Reader, These Books following, are Printed for Simon Miller, *or Sold by him at the Starre in* St. Pauls Church-yard.

Small Folio.

Doctor *Lightfoot* his Harmony on the New Testament, which will shortly be re-printed with large Additions.

The Civil Warres of *Spain* in the Reign of *Charles* the fifth, Emperour of *Germany*, and King of that Nation, wherein our late unhappy differences are paralleled in many particulars.

A general History of *Scotland*, from the year 767. to the death of King *James*, containing the principal Revolutions and Transmutations of Church and State, with Political Observations, and reflections upon the same : by *David Hume* of *Godscroft*.

The History of this Iron Age, wherein is set down the original and causes of all the Warres and Commotions that have happened in *Europe*, from the year 1600. to this present year 1659.

Mr. *Paul Baine* on the *Ephesians*.

Eighteen Books of the Secrets of Art and Nature ; Being the summe and substance of Naturall Philosophy, Methodically Digested. First designed by *John Wecker* Dr. in Physick, and now much augmented and enlarged : By Dr. *R. Read.* A like work never before in the English Tongue.

The Queen of *Arragon*, a Play.

In Quarto large.

Jo. Barklay his *Argenis*, Translated by Sir *Robert le Grise* Knight, by his Late Majesties special Command.

Quarto small.

An Experimental Treatise of Surgery, by *Felix Wortz.*

Abraham's Faith, or the good Old Religion, proving the Doctrine of the Church of *England* to be the only true Faith of Gods Elect : By *John Nicholson* Minister of the Gospel.

The Anatomy of Mortality : By *George Strood.*

Three Treatises : 1. The Conversion of *Nineveh* touching Prayer and Fasting. 2. Gods Trumpet sounding to Repentance. 3. Sovereign preservatives against distrustfull Thoughts and Cares : By *Wil. Attersoll* Minister of Gods Word at *Isfield* in *Sussex.*

Aynsworth on the *Canticles.*

Paul Baine, his Diocesans Trial.

Gralle against *Appolonius.*

A Treatise of Civil policy, being a clear Decision of 43. Queries, concerning prerogative, right and priviledge, in reference to the supream Prince and People: By *Samuel Rutherford* Professor of Divinity of St. *Andrews* in *Scotland.*

Politick and Military Observations of Civil and Military Governement; containing the Birth, Encrease, Decay of Monarchies, the carriage of Princes and Magistrates.

Mr. *Pinchin* his Meritorious price of Mans Redemption, cleared.

Astrology Theologized, shewing what nature and influence the Stars and Planets have over Men, and how the same may be diverted and avoided.

Wells his Souls progress.

Christ tempted, the Devils conquered; Being a plain Exposition on the fourth Chapter of St. *Matthews* Gospel : By *John Gumbleden* Minister of the Gospel.

The Saints Society.

Dr. *Stoughtons* thirteen choice Sermons, with his body of Divinity.

The Reasons of the dissenting Brethren concerning the Presbyterian Government, together with the Answer of the Assembly of Divines.

Camdens Remains.

The Harmonious Consent and Confession of Faith, of all the Protestant Reformed Churches in Christendome.

The Argument and Confession of Faith, of all the Congregational Churches of *England* agreed upon at the Savoy. 1659.

The description of the Universall Quadrant, by which is perform'd with great Expedition the whole Doctrine of Triangles, both plain and Sphericall: Also the Resolution of such Propositions as are most usefull in *Astronomy, Navigation*, and *Dialling*: By which is performed the proportioning of Lines for measuring of all manner of Land, Board, Glass, Timber, Stone, &c. by *Tho. Stirrup* Mathemat.

Large Octavo.

A Treatise of the Divine Promises: By *Edw. Leigh* Esq; Master of Arts of both Universities.

Florus Anglicus, with the Lively Effigies of all the Kings and Queens since the Conquest, cut in Brass.

The Reconciler of the Bible, wherein above two thousand seeming Contradictions are fully and plainly Reconciled.

Evidences for Heaven, containing infallible Signs and real demonstrations for assurance of Salvation: published by *Edw. Calamy* Minister of *Aldermanbury, Lond.*

The Life and Reign of King *Charles* from his Birth to his Death, By *Lambert Wood.*

The Night-Search, the second part: By *H. Mill.*

A view of the Jewish Religion, with their Rites, Customes and Ceremonies.

Usefull Instructions for these Evill times; held forth in 22. Sermons, by *Nicholas Lockyer*, Provost of *Eaton* Colledg.

The Nullity of Church-Censures, or Excommunication, not of Divine Instion, but a meer humane Invention: Written by the famous *Tho. Erastus*, and never before Englished.

Small Octavo.

Ed. Waterhouse Esq; His Discourse of Piety and Charity.

Panacea, or the Universall Medicine; being a Discourse of the Admirable Nature and Virtues of Tobacco: By Dr. *Everard* and Others.

A view and Defence of the Reformation of the Church of *England*, very usefull in these times.

Mr. *Pet. de Moulin*, his Antidote against Popery; published on purpose to prevent the Delusions of the Priests and Jesuites who are now very busie amongst us.

Herberts Devotions, or a Companion for a Christian, containing Meditations and Prayers usefull upon all occasions.

Extraneus Vapulans, or the Observator rescued from the violent but vain assault of *Haman Lestrange* Esq; and the backblows of Dr. *Barnard* an *Irish* Dean: by P. *Heylin* D.D.

Ovid de Ponto, in English.

The Loves of *Clivio* and *Lezio* a Romance.

Mr. *Knowles*, his Rudiment of the Hebrew Tongue.

A Book of Scheams or Figures of Heaven, ready set for every four Minutes of times, and very usefull for all Astrologers.

Florus Anglicus, or an exact History of *England*, from the Reign of *William* the Conquerour, to the death of the late King.

Lingua, or the Combate of the Tongue, and five Senses for Speriority: a serious Comedy.

The Spirits Touchstone; being a clear discovery how a Man may certainly know whether he be truly taught by the Spirit of God, or not.

The poor mans Physician and Chyrurgion.

Physicall Rarities, containing the most choice Receipts in Physick and Chyrurgery, for the cure of all Diseases incident to Mans body: By *R. Williams*. To which is added the Physical Mathematicks: by *Hermes, Tres. Magistus.*

The Idol of Clowns, or the Relation of *Wat Tiler*'s Rebellion.

The Christian Moderator, in 3. parts.

The Golden Fleece, or a Discourse of the Cloathing of *England.*

Dr. *Sibbs* his Divine Meditations.

Vigerius Preceptes of *Idiotismes.*

Grotij Poemata.

Three Books of Mr. *Mathews* Minister at *Swansey* in *South-Wales.*

1. The Messia Magnified by the mouths of Babes in *America*; or *Gaius* and *Gamaliel*, a helpfull Father and his hopefull Son; discoursing of the three most considerable points: 1. The great want of Christ. 2. The great worth that is in Christ. 3. The good way that is chalkt out by Christ.

2. The new Congregationall Church prov'd to be the old Christian Church, by Scripture, Reason, and History.

3. The Rending Church-member Regularly

Star in St. Pauls Church-yard.

gularly cal'd back to Christ and his Church.

A Physical Dictionary.

Duodecim.

Doctor Smith's practice of Physick.
The Grammer War.
Possellius Apothegmes.
Fasciculus Florum.
Crashaw's Visions.
The Juniper Lecture.
Helvicus Colloquies.

The Christian Souldier, his Combate with the three arch-enemies of mankind, the world, the flesh, and the Devil.

Seasonable advice to the Aprentices of the Honourable City of *London*, touching their duty to God and their Masters.

Hensius de Crepundiis.

The History of *Russia*, or the Government of the Emperour of *Moscovia*, with the manner and fashions of the people of that Countrey.

Drexelius's School of Patience.
Drexelius his right Intention of every ones Action.

A School or Nurture for Children, or the Duty of Children to Parents, very usefull for all that intend to bring up their Children in the fear of God.

Viginti Quat.

The New Testament.
The third part of the Bible.
Sir *Richard Baker's* Meditations and Prayers for every day of the Week.

Playes.

The Ball.
Chawbut.
Conspiracy.
Obstinate Lady.
The *London* Chanticleers; a Comedy full of various and delightfull Mirth, never before published.